Johnson examines in this volume. Although it came much sooner than expected, armistice found many plans ready, but it found the Cabinet quite unready, precipitating three months of improvisation which augured badly for Britain's plans. Recovering admirably, the Government moved toward the fulfillment of long-range plans in 1919, producing landmark reforms in welfare and housing. As Johnson explains, "the denouement was a product of zeal, vigor, over-optimism, blunders in finance and decontrol, overtures to co-operation across class lines, hindrances from Labour, and the sheer disruptive effect of four and one half years of war." Johnson concludes that Britain made a sustained and thoughtful attempt at reform which prevailed against the chaos of armistice to create changes marking 1919 as a major period of reform.

LAND
FIT FOR
HEROES

*The Planning of
British Reconstruction
1916–1919*

LAND
FIT FOR
HEROES

PAUL BARTON JOHNSON

THE UNIVERSITY OF CHICAGO PRESS   CHICAGO & LONDON

Library of Congress Catalog Number: 68–27444

The University of Chicago Press, Chicago 60637
The University of Chicago Press, Ltd., London W.C.1

ACKNOWLEDGMENTS

Winston Churchill dedicated his work, *The Aftermath*, "To All Who Hope." He had the right. He knew that generation and its sufferings; he had served it greatly by labors varied and substantial, in war and in the first travail of peace. But the claim to speak to and for a generation rests on birth: it is not a reward earned by calculable service alone but a privilege, a gift of History accorded only to those singled out by time and joined by a shared experience. Churchill was of that generation and its passions. His patent to address it as an equal was not the sort that passes by inheritance. With that generation, it passed away.

To one not of that heritage there remain the pleasures of other dedications. All who study Britain's reconstruction owe a debt to H. N. Blakiston, who aids users of the Public Record Office with wisdom and generosity, though they voyage from places—Vermont or Chicago—as improbable as Xanadu. I owe a debt also to his colleagues past and present, from William Winder and Jeffrey Ede to Alexander Wardle. No less substantial are the claims of J. U. Reid and his Treasury staff, of William Hogsdon of the Ministry of Agriculture, and Sir Thomas Sheepshanks. As these men helped with government files, so for private archives did A. R. Kerrell-Vaughan of the National Housing and Town Planning Council, Sir Frederick Osborn and Miss Evans of the Town and Country Planning Association, and Miss Bach of the Liberal Party headquarters, along with the staff of the Royal Institute of British Architects, the Labour Party headquarters and library, the Institute for Public Administration, and the Town Planning Institute.

My brevity, I know, will be excused by the librarians at the Universities of Chicago and Edinburgh, the National Library of Scotland, the Registry Office in Edinburgh, the Institute for Historical Research, and the British Museum, whose kindnesses would make a list as long as this Acknowledgment.

Interviews full of insight and fact were accorded by many participants: Arthur Greenwood, Sir Arthur Salter, Lord Inverforth, Professor W. G. S. Adams, Sir Thomas Gardiner, Thomas Jones, Professor R. H. Tawney, H. E. Dale, E. H. E. Havelock, B. Seebohm Rowntree, Sir Richard Redmayne, Sir Rhys Rhys-Williams, and J. J. Mallon—for World War I—and Lord Reith, Lord Layton, Sir Norman Brooke (the late Lord Normanbrooke), Sir William Holford, Margaret Cole, Sir John Wrigley, and R. S. W. Pollard—for World War II—and G. D. H. Cole and Major Lionel Ellis for both periods. R. L. Reiss and his effervescent colleague, William Wallace, gave help beyond reckoning.

My debt is cheerfully acknowledged to Hutchinson and Company, Ltd., for permission to quote excerpts from Christopher Addison, *Four and a Half Years*, Vols. I and II; to Viscount Addison and to A. P. Watt and Son for permission to quote excerpts from Christopher Addison, *Politics from Within*, Vols. I and II; to Charles Scribner's Sons and to Odhams Press, Ltd., for permission to quote excerpts from Winston Churchill, *The World Crisis*, Vols. IV and V; to the Passfield Trust for permission to quote excerpts from *Beatrice Webb's Diaries* (ed. Margaret I. Cole); to Viscount Addison for permission to reproduce the photograph of his father; and to the Keeper of Public Records and the Controller of H. M. Stationery Office for permission to quote from files at the Public Record Office, and from British Government Publications.

To all of my colleagues at Roosevelt University, but especially to Richard Hooker, Walter Arnstein, and Otto Wirth, as to Professors George Shepperson and John Brown of the University of Edinburgh, go inadequate thanks. I am, with legions of others, happy to be the debtor of Professor Charles Loch Mowat of the University of North Wales, whose wit and endless encouragement are matched by the inspiration of his splendid example. The friendship and efforts of Kate Larimore Turabian, Beatrice Barton, Viscount Addison, Edna Coulson, Lilian Robertson, Helen Bailey, Harriet Fisher, and Mildred Brody Greene are reflected in all of the following pages.

But most of all, this book is dedicated to Dorothy, who had the whole idea.

PAUL BARTON JOHNSON

CONTENTS

vii

Contents

1

The Peace Book

"We all know," wrote Sir Daniel Hall, "that a great effort at Reconstruction lies before us." For many Britons these words of 1917, from a renowned agriculturist and civil servant, rang true. He put in words their inward thought—part faith, part resolution—that reform would brighten Britain infinitely and permanently in the aftermath of Armageddon. Even now, when prophecy sounds hollow and men's past convictions seem as unreal as they are remote, the vision has power to move the blood. It was indeed a great prospect.

This very grandeur, however, was bound to move some to sarcasm. "It is the greatest office ever created in the world," scoffed one member of Parliament when the Ministry of Reconstruction was proposed.

> It would be perfectly right to magnify this office; it is the greatest office ever created in the world, because it is to consider and give advice on the Reconstruction of this great Empire in the situation in which it finds itself after the war.

The hope and effort stirred others to unwonted rhetoric. For once, even a civil servant's prose took wings, in the unlikely context of an official committee report:

> Few can fail to feel the force of inspiration and experience which is being born of the war, or to recognise the strength of the new hope with which the people are looking forward to the future. The nation ardently desires to order its life in accordance with those principles of freedom and justice, which led so many of its best sons to the field of battle.
>
> . . . no one can doubt that we are at a turning point in our national history. A new era has come upon us. We cannot stand still. We cannot return to the old ways, the old abuses, the old stupidities.

1

As with our international relations so with the relations of classes and individuals inside our own nation, if they do not henceforth get better they must needs get worse, and that means moving towards an abyss. It is in our power to make the new era one of such progress as to repay us even for the immeasurable cost, the price in lives lost, in manhood crippled and in homes desolated. . . . We stand at the bar of history for judgment, and we shall be judged by the use we make of this unique opportunity. It is unique in many ways, most of all in the fact that the public not only has its conscience aroused and its heart stirred, but also has its mind open and receptive of new ideas to an unprecedented degree.[1]

Toward this vision the state sustained for three years a continuous and ever-widening effort to plan for recovery, reconversion, and a whole new era of reform. Three successive governments supported the work. Three distinct but continuous agencies of reconstruction, aided by departments hard at work on the same tasks, carried the cause from modest beginnings in 1916 to a climax in 1919, when an imposing record of administrative and legislative change proved the strength of those hopes.

Government and Parliament did not work alone. At first, it is true, war had stunned the nation's great reform organizations and had reduced men to dismay. Thus in August 1914 the leader of the Garden Cities and Town Planning Association automatically assumed the worst consequences for reform; he wrote to his cohorts that of course they must suspend work. In the House of Commons, some men reacted in the same way. A keen new member of Parliament, fresh from a hard and successful fight for Lloyd George's insurance plans, was aghast: "When one thinks of all our schemes of social reform just set a-going and of those for which plans had been made in this year's Budget, we could weep." But this man, Christopher Addison, would become Minister of Munitions and would use his position there to establish lasting precedents in workers' welfare; this same man, as Minister of Reconstruction from 1917 to 1919, would do more than any other minister to make 1919 a great year of fulfillment.[2]

1. Alfred D. Hall, *Agriculture after the War* (London, 1916), p. 130; Great Britain, *Parliamentary Debates* (Commons), 5th Ser., 96 (2 August 1917), c. 2444, 2479. Hereafter, references to the *Parliamentary Debates* are abbreviated *P.D.(C.)* and *P.D.(L.)*, respectively, for statements in the House of Commons and the House of Lords. All references are to the 5th Series. See also Great Britain, *Parliamentary Papers*, vol. 9, "Interim Report of the Adult Education Committee," Cd. 9107 (1918), pp. 28–29.

2. Garden Cities and Town Planning Association, Minute Book 2, folio 158 (27 August 1914); Maurice Bruce, *The Coming of the Welfare State* (London: B. T. Batsford, 1966), p. 189, citing Christopher Addison, *Four and a Half Years* (London: Hutchinson, 1934), 1:35. Hereafter, this work by Addison will be cited as Addison, *Diary*.

Unofficial groups and individual men and women had many roles to play. But the special function of the departments and the cabinets was to prepare a "Peace Book" on all the plans and necessities of the transition and reconstruction, as complete and ready as the famed "War Book" itself. They achieved—not, it is true, a single handy volume (records of the Ministry of Reconstruction alone constitute ninety volumes), but something better—the true "Book of Reconstruction" as planned, debated, and carried out, a living segment of history written in deeds, conferences, laws, reports, inquiries, speeches, and sheer work. That was the real book, of which the present work is but a poor and belated summary. Its authors were more numerous and varied than the hundreds whose names appear in official files, for much of a whole nation was inscribed there.

From oblivion to . . . ? When 1922 blighted government plans and buried successes beneath the rubble of a panic retrenchment, the campaign was almost forgotten. The interwar years either consigned the faith and the works to oblivion or preserved denatured vestiges as proof of deliberate partisan electioneering, instinctive tribal self-delusion, or simple bad faith. The fiasco of "homes fit for heroes" became a staple of politics.

It may seem incredible that three years of hard work, backed by more than a hundred volumes of archives, debated by a nation for a period longer than the war itself, could so long and so unanimously be treated with partisanship or neglect. The very names of key participants— Haldane, Montagu, W. H. Beveridge, Arthur Greenwood, J. J. Mallon, J. L. Hammond, B. S. Rowntree, Ernest Bevin, John Whitley, Christopher Addison, Beatrice Webb, Sir Robert Morant, Lord Rhondda, Sir Bertram Dawson, Susan Lawrence, Lord Selborne, Winston Churchill, Sir Auckland Geddes, Lord Ernle, Sir Hubert Llewellyn Smith, Raymond Unwin, and Lloyd George—should have prevented this neglect. But such was the fact. The causes for this treatment—worth a study in themselves —were many, but it is not unfair to say that they were symbolized in a phrase. The House of Commons in 1919, Keynes alleged at second hand, were "a little group of hard-faced men who looked as if they had done well out of the war"; and most of a generation accepted the verdict.

The Ministry of Reconstruction itself, where mentioned at all, was labeled "ephemeral." The motives for the three-year effort were conveniently simplified:

> The original inspiration and the continuing stimulus for reconstruction came from the need to urge the people on. . . . Government

3

emphasis on reconstruction grew out of the sufferings and the low spirit of the citizens during the three bitter years beginning in 1916. Housing policy . . . graduated into the world of party politics. With the slogan "Homes fit for Heroes," it started its career as a pawn in the political game of bribing the electorate with vague promises of social reform. . . . Responsibility for the post-war housing had become a government matter, and "Homes fit for Heroes" was to be a popular election cry.

The whole was held up in cruel contrast to the bitter recollections of armistice hopes:

> We were wrought up with ideas inexpressible and vapourous. . . . Yet when we achieved and the new world dawned, the old men came out again and took from us our victory and re-made it in the likeness of the former world they knew. . . . We stammered that we had worked for a new heaven and a new earth, they thanked us kindly.

Reform had lapsed, in this view, as 1919 began; little was being done to fulfill pledges made; and as early as spring of 1919 opinion had already hardened against serious reforms. Simultaneously a tempestuous and unanimous cry for return to 1914 raised the fateful issue of decontrol, and a government incapable of resistance or independent thought ran before the storm. The dominant forces of the day all pushed in one direction, and the result was both a blow to reform and a decontrol ramp.[3]

Now the thinking has changed—is changing still, perhaps too much. Monographic studies, one of the prime agencies in the new appraisal, reveal the work of Rowntree and Bevin for reconstruction—or flatly hail the 1919 Housing Act as a triumph alike for war and for Liberal reform. Reviving the whole controversy about reconstruction and 1919, but raising

3. See below, p. 18, for the "Peace Book" concept. For views on reconstruction, see H. F. Heath, in *Viscount Haldane of Cloan, O.M.: The Man and His Work*, ed. Lord Grey of Fallodon (London: Oxford University Press, 1928), pp. 27–28; Margaret I. Cole, ed., *Beatrice Webb's Diaries, 1912–1924*, with an introduction by Lord Beveridge (London: Longmans, Green, 1952), p. ix (hereafter cited as Webb, *Diaries*); Samuel J. Hurwitz, *State Intervention in Great Britain: A Study of Economic Control and Social Response, 1914–1919* (New York: Columbia University Press, 1949), pp. 291, 287; Marian Bowley, *Housing and the State, 1919–1944* (London: Allen & Unwin, 1945), pp. 3, 4; *New Statesman*, 12 (14 September 1918): 463; G. D. H. Cole, "The Government's Industrial Failure," ibid., 15 (21 August 1920): 542–43; R. H. Tawney, "Abolition of Economic Controls, 1918–1921," *Economic History Review*, 13 (1943): 1–30; and John Ehrman, *Cabinet Government and War, 1890–1940* (Cambridge: Cambridge University Press, 1958), p. vii.

the debate to high level, the remarkable studies by Richard Titmuss and Stanislaw Andrzejewski reveal as much by their assumptions as by their conclusions: they take for granted that war's benefit to social reform is proved, and move from there to cite reasons. The direct and positive relation of war to reform, of Mars to the Millennium, is in danger of becoming a cliché. Luckily, a group of impressive new works, restating old versions or progressing to new and subtler conclusions, saves us from concord. Perhaps now, thanks to this rich harvest of study and judgment,[4] we stand nearer to two great truths: the truth about reconstruction, a time-bound episode in the history of one island; and the truth about "war and reform," a timeless topic on which Britain's experiences may throw light. We are nearer, at any rate, to the narrative of State action. That story—the primary aim of these pages, and task enough—is no negligible part of the larger, living "Book of Reconstruction."

The four books. Those who wrote the actual Book of Reconstruction out of their deeds between 1916 and 1921 were distinctive men and women, with long careers stretching before and after. The authors of that volume were neither that phantom disembodiment called History, nor characterless extras hired but for the moment, but particular—and, let it be confessed, often peculiar—men and women of flesh and blood. I have not wished to forget that fact nor what it means.

Each man writes many books: not only the book of public life, to which he may contribute but a line, but also the book of himself. Each person, adding to the public "Book of Reconstruction," simultaneously wrote a chapter of autobiography. This chapter, once set in the context of a whole life, takes on new significance: the public events throw light on the man and the pattern of the man implies a judgment on reconstruction. Thus the careers of Morant, Beveridge, Llewellyn Smith, and Addison make manifest the continuity with renascent reform before 1914. The careers of some who stayed in the civil service (Heseltine, John Anderson) and of others who found their way into the Labour Party (Haldane, Addison, Greenwood) tell of other continuities, personal and

---

4. Asa Briggs, *Social Thought and Social Action: A Study of the Work of Seebohm Rowntree, 1871–1954* (London, 1961), chap. 5; Alan Bullock, *The Life and Times of Ernest Bevin* (London, 1960), 1: 71–72; Stanislaw Andrzejewski, *Military Organisation and Society* (London: Routledge & Kegan Paul, 1954), pp. 27–29, 74–75, 101–6, 115; Richard Titmuss, *Problems of Social Policy* (*History of the Second World War; United Kingdom; Civil Series*, ed. W. K. Hancock, vol. 20) (London, 1950), pp. 500–505; R. B. McCallum, in *Law and Opinion in England in the Twentieth Century*, ed. Morris Ginsberg (London: Stevens & Sons, 1959), p. 75; Philip Abrams, "The Failure of Reform, 1918–1920," *Past and Present*, no. 24 (April 1963), pp. 43–64.

national. A composite of aims and activities—industrial democracy, housing reform, efficiency in management, rural betterment—among Quakers like Malcolm Sparkes and Rowntree and in the unquenchable colleague of Rowntree, William Wallace, tells much about the staying power of British reformism before, during, and after the war.

Other men's lives, and the place of reconstruction in their lives, reveal the opposite lesson: war could call men to public life, just for once, or war alone could give them a role in reform. Such is the case with Professor Garrod, who later shook the dust of London and the red tape of Whitehall from him forever to return to Merton; such is the career of Sir Ernest Benn, whose wartime fling at state activity made him a lifelong advocate of individualism and author of *The State the Enemy*; and such was the case for Sir Thomas Gardiner, sent to the Ministry of Reconstruction from the Treasury (sent, in truth, as a sort of spy), who performed zealously and then rejoined the silent but lynx-eyed guardsmen of the public purse.

In or out of character, their reconstruction interlude was but part of a career that richly deserves fitter tribute than I have provided. What a goodly company to work with—and, even vicariously, to live with! And how hopeless the task of portrayal, given their rainbow variety! First, the long-lived Addison, who declaimed from his father's farmhouse table in the 1880's, and lived on to render judgment on a second reconstruction from the House of Lords: a friend of state initiative who yet insisted on defending profit as the reward for efficiency; a physician who championed Lloyd George's health insurance in defiance of medical opposition; a protégé of the Welsh wizard who wrangled with him from their very first meeting to the bitter estrangement of 1921; a convert to Labour who saw his housing campaign fatally compromised by workers' conservatism. Addison was a walking compendium of those judgments, pragmatic, humdrum, and near-Utopian, that ran through men's minds in those years.

> Some people think my job is to build fairy castles for some dim and distant future. Let us hope that people will be free to do so when this beastly business is over. . . . My first job is to try to arrange that the first six or twelve months of peace, when war-making . . . has suddenly ceased, do not land us in a mess at home.

But if he wrote this, and snorted "if *memoranda* could get us anywhere," he could become almost poetic over the great "lessons of the war" and predict that Whitley Councils "would transform the outlook in British industry in the course of a few years." [5] His emphasis on efficiency and heightened output sounded like the ultraconventional publicity of business centralization and trade war; his memoranda on finance matched anything from the labor press; and his outbursts of idealism and hope reflected a Britain that thought itself in the "antechamber to the millennium."

It is indeed becoming more and more apparent that reconstruction is not . . . a question of rebuilding society as it was before the war, but of moulding a better world out of the social and economic conditions which have come into being during the war.

The War has thrown all preconceived ideas as to trade organisation into the melting pot, and every thinking man . . . agrees that if we are to regain and to hold our position in the markets of the world there must be a new outlook on the part of both employers and employed; the old jealousies between firms must be abandoned once for all, and what is equally important, the "Ca' canny" methods . . . must be discontinued. The war . . . has proved that in the face of national necessity we can rise to heights of industrial organisation and cohesion such as would have been deemed impossible.

Arthur Greenwood also was part of that nation, breathing "the larger air of common sacrifice" [6]—and he mirrored its traditional practicality, its yearning for high achievement.

Greenwood could state the circumstantial case for placating labor, run a thread of analysis through the fearful intricacies of unemployment insurance, and pour out his heart in rhetoric, all with equal ease. He needs —they all need—fit memorial: these, and their kindred spirits of generosity and hope, and all the others, even the prickly ones: Ernest Bevin, hurling scorn at ministers from the conference floor; taciturn, skeptical Bonar Law; the furious Francis Acland, always in the right; Mrs. Webb, chainsmoking her way disdainfully through committee sessions—awaiting the night, and her diary. All left their mark, and a goodly one. They need no other memorial. Seebohm Rowntree lives in the past work and present zestfulness of Wallace; Morant lives in an army of awestruck disciples; Vaughan Nash lives in the softspoken praise of E. H. E. Havelock.

5. Addison, *Diary*, 2: 312, 416, 580, 582.
6. Vice-Chancellor of Sheffield University, quoted in File 7716, Box 71, Part 1, of Ministry of Reconstruction Records. Hereafter, all references to Files or Boxes refer to Ministry of Reconstruction Archives, unless otherwise specified; "F." means "File." See also Great Britain, *Parliamentary Papers*, vol. 14, "Report of the War Cabinet for the Year 1917," Cd. 9005 (1918), pp. xix, 100–101.

For my part, I have done one thing that I think they might deem best: I have told the story not simply as it culminated in results but as it unrolled in plan and first efforts—as it slowly developed from the merger or the battle of rival schemes and jostling men. I have recorded the appearances—history as actually seen—as well as the truer but lesser history of things substantiated, and thereby have included the false starts, the early and continuous initiatives that came to nought or got short shrift in cabinet, the campaigns that proved off target and the ones that the armistice caught undone, and—absolutely above all—the talk. A world of committee sessions, arguments voiced and echoed, memoranda and countermemoranda, is the result; but the topic, after all, is the *planning* of reconstruction.

Maxims for statesmen? Each man, indeed each episode, may figure in many books, some far from the shelf of reconstruction. The whole story of 1916–19 amounts to a footnote, at least, in the literature of planning. Further, and indeed very seriously (inasmuch as many participants or later scholars studied the record for lessons), the story of reconstruction figures in the literature of political science. First, because it confronts us— in the "Ministry of Reconstruction"—with that nice problem, whether to rely on the tried departments that have the experience and power but may not use it, or to set up a gadfly and a rival; second, because it reveals the interplay of structure and policy, of impersonal form and very personal —even covert—preferences; third, and above all, because it tells a grim story of the terrible importance of cabinet organization. Professor Hans Daalder's splendid study[7] makes it needless to expatiate, but later pages will reveal that problem pointedly enough.

As foreword, it must be stated that reconstruction worked through at least four structural systems that were markedly different. First, a top-level informal group of powerful heads of departments, working with the Prime Minister himself but with little staff (1916); second, a group whose ties with the cabinet were slender and with departments nil, which consisted of brainy amateurs almost willfully selected for their prideful pugnacity (1917); third, a full-fledged but small ministry whose head (Addison) held cabinet rank and was close to Lloyd George, and whose jurisdiction seemed to girdle the globe; lastly, a medley of improvisations in 1919, some parts being cabinet committees, ostensibly with full powers, and others being crash programs of inquiry—plus the cabinet itself, reverting to the Asquith model.

7. Hans Daalder, *Cabinet Reform in Britain, 1914–1963* (Stanford, Calif.: Stanford University Press, 1964).

The importance that these structural changes implied is shown by the simple fact that, in World War II, the government chose *not* to follow the example of World War I. Therefore there was, from 1939 to 1945, no separate Ministry of Reconstruction; there was no distinct reconstruction staff (or such, at any rate, was the intent). There was no hive of brilliant gadflies.

In this striking contrast between government methods, and in many others, lies rich material for a comparison of planning in two world wars. Indeed the effort of 1916–19 was part of many stories, not one alone. A treasury of political lessons; a book of contrasts between the first and the second British reconstruction; a volume of collective biography; a treatise on war and reform—all these were implicit in the "Peace Book."

2

The Asquith Reconstruction Committee

"In accordance with the decision of the Cabinet," Asquith minuted, "I propose to set up, on the analogy of the Committee of Imperial Defence, a Committee over which I shall preside, to consider and advise with the aid of sub-committees upon the problems that will arise on the conclusion of Peace, and to co-ordinate work which has already been done by the Departments in this direction." With this announcement on 18 March 1916 by the Prime Minister, official British organization for reconstruction began.[1]

By 2 December 1916 the "Reconstruction Committee," thus announced, had held six meetings, launched nine subcommittees, and received five reports.[2] It had a permanent secretarial staff and had compiled probably the best estimate of housing needs thus far this century. It had worked out complete programs in agriculture and in forestry, and it had probed commercial and industrial policy. It had foreseen nearly every problem that reconstruction would raise between 1917 and 1919. But the first steps toward these substantial achievements were modest indeed. The first meeting of the Reconstruction Committee gave slight hint of the scope, or the accelerating pace, that official planning would soon show.

For the committee's first meeting, on 24 March 1916, Asquith convened seven colleagues: Andrew Bonar Law, Colonial Secretary; Arthur

1. F. 241, Box 40, in Ministry of Reconstruction Records. See also Cabinet 37/144/44. All citations beginning with the abbreviation "Cab." in notes hereafter refer to cabinet and War Cabinet files at the Public Record Office, London. The first number identifies the class list, the second number the volume; the third number, if given, indicates the page.
2. The name "Reconstruction Committee" first appeared as the heading to minutes of the first meeting, on 24 March 1916. Vaughan Nash, its Secretary, was borrowed from the Development Commission, in whose offices at 6A Dean's Yard, Westminster, the Reconstruction Committee continued to meet and work under both Asquith and Lloyd George.

Henderson, President of the Board of Education; Austen Chamberlain, Secretary for India; Lord Crewe, Lord President of the Council; Edwin Montagu, Chancellor of the Duchy of Lancaster; Lord Selborne, President of the Board of Agriculture; and Walter Runciman, President of the Board of Trade.[3] Asquith began by asking Runciman to explain the work under way in his department. A number of committees, Runciman replied, were in existence.

The form of this beginning had treble significance. Asquith would base his policy on work already begun; he would base it on the departments; and he would stress problems of trade. More than a list, Runciman's reply was a revelation of the impact of war. One committee dealt with trade relations, another with demobilization, a third with the shipbuilding industry, and a fourth with commercial intelligence. Three other committees were to consider Britain's industries in the light of postwar world competition.

War was shaping the content of reconstruction. The topics that men discussed were precisely those that war was forcing on their attention. "The country would be very nearly stripped of timber in a short time," warned Lord Selborne; he urged the promptest action on both afforestation and food supply. Here was testimony to heightened needs for construction and to a new wartime level of food consumption; here too was testimonial to the power of the submarine. War, furthermore, which had cost Britain some of her peacetime markets, stirred fears for postwar recovery; hence the Committee on Commercial Intelligence, and hence the explicit references to preventing "resumption of Germany's . . . peaceful promotion" and commercial penetration. War helped explain Austen Chamberlain's stress on "the vital industries which we cannot afford to have under foreign control."[4]

If war was giving positive content to reconstruction, was it not limiting reconstruction at the same time? Agenda limited to the postwar recovery of trade and to obvious and specific tasks of demobilization and resettlement would never encompass the nation's hopes for reform. The link between war and reconstruction seemed to imply a minimal, blinkered

3. Asquith, Runciman, Crewe, and Montagu were Liberals; Bonar Law, Chamberlain, and Selborne were Conservatives; Henderson belonged to the Labour Party. Maurice Hankey, the cabinet Secretary, was also present. Minutes are in F. 2, Box 40.

F. 241, Box 40, lists later members of Asquith's Reconstruction Committee: Walter Long, President of the Local Government Board; Lord Crawford; Herbert Samuel, Home Secretary; Thomas Mackinnon Wood; H. R. Duke; and H. J. Tennant.

4. F. 2, Box 40. Moreover, a memo of 1 March 1916 from Runciman to the cabinet (Cab. 37/144/Doc. 2) stressed the fear of foreigners' economic power; ten of the twenty-four topics cited for inquiry involved neutrals or enemy nationals.

postwar effort. Instead, could not war bring a new vision of reconstruction? Was no force at work to give reconstruction fuller scope from the very start?

Three topics large with significance were indeed mentioned that day: the use of munitions factories for civilian purposes, continued central control of railways after the war, and representation for labor on the committees of inquiry. Potentially, these were great themes, and it is arguable that broader vistas opened then and there. Labor representation was endorsed; inquiry into central control of railways was approved; but 1916 was to produce no important sequel to these decisions. The tone and context of the meeting were cautious and commercial. When Montagu insisted that "the enquiries to be set on foot must cover the whole life of the nation after the war," Bonar Law countered that "at the moment they were only considering the appointment of the industrial and commercial committees proposed by the Minister"! Bonar Law's retort was just. In fact, the appointment of the Balfour of Burleigh Committee on Commercial and Industrial Policy was the chief outcome of the meeting.[5]

Conceivably, a reconstruction effort might have begun with a comprehensive program of national reform—perhaps even explicitly deduced from preconceived visions of the national welfare. As the organizational counterpart for so ambitious an attempt, one can imagine a well-staffed independent ministry or committee of specialists, freed from departmental limitations. Asquith's conception of reconstruction and of the Reconstruction Committee, however, was anything but that.

Reconstruction had been given a direction, form, and content. The impress of March 1916 might have proved permanent. But later material abundantly proves that the content and direction of reconstruction *significantly grew and changed*. Originally, few humanitarian objectives had been mentioned and only a single welfare measure was proposed.[6] Thinking had centered on making existing economic institutions stronger: ideas had moved down the worn grooves of imperial preference or national self-sufficiency. Fundamental change had been mentioned only for railways. Of law reform, education, local government, housing, finance, and health, nothing had been said.

But by the end of the year so much had been added that one must speak of a whole new agenda. Housing was by far the most important

5. Minutes, F. 2, Box 40; "Conclusions," Box 40. For the immediate sequel, see "Reconstruction Committee, Conclusions," 24 March 1916, Cab. 37/145/13.

6. The proposal of soldiers' and sailors' resettlement on the land was the lone instance.

addition—no mere item but a program conceived on a scale without precedent. Housing, moreover, had been recognized as central; its intrinsic worth made it so. But it was central, even more, in the functional sense: on it many another program—farming, relief to unemployment, industrial reconversion—would depend. New and major proposals also were made for health and education, forming—with housing—a new core of reconstruction tasks. Other topics, of lesser importance only by comparison, were under study: labor-management relations, women's employment, land reform, coal conservation, and industrial controls. Horizons had widened. In two cases—forestry and agriculture—the horizons had virtually been reached; Parliament would soon adopt the Agriculture Committee's plan in the Corn Production Act.

How and why had this evolution, just short of a complete change in kind, occurred? The influence of Vaughan Nash, the Secretary of the Reconstruction Committee, goes far to explain it. His influence pervaded the whole. Others played their part. Some of the ministers on the committee were keen on a broader conception of the task and had already pressed for action. Thus Runciman had outlined for Asquith in late 1915 a series of issues requiring prompt study lest "we be unprepared at the time of peace." In March 1916 Selborne was strongly pressing the cabinet to authorize resettlement colonies for veterans; and his energy helped produce the Reconstruction Committee as well as the colonies he wanted. Mentioning Selborne's project in the weekly summary for the King, Lord Crewe threw light on the origins and hinted at limitless scope for the work.

> This subject is in reality part of the great problem of reorganisation and of restoration after the war, bound up with all the social and commercial activities of the country. It is now some time since this proposal has been before your Majesty's Government . . . progress in carrying it into effect should no longer be delayed.[7]

But for the next four months the initiative lay with the departments; their role was the greatest.

New Tasks Are Proposed

"To co-ordinate work . . . by the Departments" was a goal that Asquith had proposed. Accordingly, in a letter of 28 March 1916 each government department was asked for details of its work. Replies to this letter helped

7. Cab. 37/144/2; Cab. 37/144/35. See Cab. 37/144/39, Lord Crewe's weekly summary on behalf of Asquith to King George V, dated 16 March 1916.

13

transform reconstruction.[8] One report alone[9]—from the Board of Trade —listed no fewer than seven new and major problems that it planned to tackle:

1. *Forecasts of the postwar industrial situation.* Completed questionnaires (forms "Z 8"), already coming in from more than 50,000 employers, would furnish such data as the number of government contracts and of newly recruited laborers. Consultation with trade committees already appointed by the Board of Trade would keep the survey up to date, and more systematic surveys would be launched.

2. *Return of soldiers and sailors to civil employment.* The Board of Trade and the War Office had already consulted; their plan was based on "systematic registration . . . through the Labour Exchange organisation." Interestingly, it provided "a free policy against unemployment, valid for one year."

3. *Transferring labor and industrial plants from munitions work to peace work.* The need for joint consultation by the Board of Trade and the Ministry of Munitions was made clear. Here, too, unemployment insurance had to be considered; and a temporary extension to all munitions workers was under consideration.

4. *Restoration of prewar conditions of employment.* Full data must be collected on all agreements that suspended old trade-union rules.

5. *Relations of capital and labor.* One department within the Board, seeking industrial harmony and efficiency after the war, was probing such questions as compulsory arbitration, profit sharing, and the continuance of the "truce" between labor and management.

6. *Provision of employment.* A committee should be formed of the various departments that might in any way control public employment so that schemes for such employment might be prepared, to be put into force as required.

7. *Assisting emigration.*

In this list, women's employment figured only as a subsidiary topic, but the question merited study in its own right in the eyes of the National

8. In notes to and including note 31, each letter or memorandum is identified by a Roman numeral and a page number, which indicate its place in a printed collection of documents entitled "Correspondence with Departments concerning Problems which will Arise at the End of the War" (in Box 40). Document 1, p. 1, is the circular letter Nash sent to all departments for the Reconstruction Committee on 28 March 1916.

9. Memorandum No. 1, enclosure to Letter XII, 3 June 1916, pp. 18–20. See Cab. 37/144/2 for Crewe's summary of questions under inquiry on 1 March 1916.

Health Insurance Commission of England and the Home Office. Wartime work, and its effect on health, needed investigation; [10] and thought must be given to the reinstatement of men and the displacement of women when peace came. [11] For good measure, the Home Office added that the time was ripe to study factory legislation:

> The emergency employment of women on a large scale has given a great impetus to welfare work, which we should certainly try to maintain in full vigour after the war. Some things cannot, of course, be secured by legislation—some can. We had already noted before the war, for consideration . . . such matters as first-aid arrangements, messing arrangements, etc. There is also the very important question of female supervision.

As for the mines, the Home Office pointed out:

> (a) The Coal Mining Organisation Committee has proved invaluable as a means of securing joint consideration of questions affecting the coal industry by representatives of the three parties concerned—the Government, the owners and the miners. There no doubt will be difficult questions when the war terminates (e.g. in connection with the return of enlisted miners), and it would be desirable to keep the Committee in being.
>
> (b) It may well prove desirable that the development of the home resources of pit timber should not stop with the war, and that systematic steps should be taken to organise a supply permanently. If so, the question of continuing the present emergency machinery on a permanent footing should be considered.
>
> (c) The large question of the development and utilisation to the greatest advantage of our coal resources, and of economy in the use of fuel, is coming up for consideration, and Government action will almost certainly be necessary.

Most of these new problems—or at least an awareness of them— could have originated from the war. [12] Three other problems, however,

10. Letter XV, 10 June 1916, pp. 37–38.
11. Letter III, 28 April 1916, p. 304.
12. In Letter XV, p. 38, the National Health Insurance Commission (England) urged a campaign against infant mortality. The proposal bears comparison with Lord Rhondda's motives for recommending a Ministry of Health in early 1917.

had been on the minds of various departments for years, the first of which was tuberculosis. The National Health Insurance Commission defended an inquiry into the problem not by pointing to "war lessons" or "defence needs" but by noting that a systematic campaign against tuberculosis had been under way since 1911.[13] In a second case, having dismissed as "minor" some issues arising from abnormal school conditions in wartime, the Scottish Education Department turned to "more important questions" that "were under consideration before the war": revising the system of grants, pooling education funds, raising the school-leaving age, and so on.[14]

"Before the outbreak of war," the third reply of this type began, "the Board of Education had formulated proposals for the development of a National System of Education which had been adopted by the Government, and for which provision was made . . . in the Budget . . . introduced on the 4th May 1914."[15] The scope of these "proposals" is breathtaking: an extended scholarship system, a complete revision of the Regulations for Technical Education, reform of the Examination in Secondary Schools, and a new pension system were only the beginning. Others may have gained impetus from the war (such as the promotion of scientific and technical education), and still others definitely stemmed from wartime conditions (for example, the study of children's employment). In a 6,000-word memorandum on "Recent Proposals for a National System of Education," the Board of Education gave even stronger proofs that prewar reform was fusing with the new reconstruction effort. But something exceedingly current also was revealed: an angry debate had erupted in the London *Times* that spring, alleging near-disaster through official ignorance and inattention to German monopolies in chemical processes. The debate had broadened swiftly. It became an onslaught on educational bias in the civil service; it led Lord Haldane to make a notable speech to the Lords on scientific education. The culmination was a "Memorial on the Neglect of Science," signed by many of Britain's foremost physicians and scientists. Exposure, one of war's first and most authentic services to reform,

13. Letter XV, p. 38.

14. The Scottish Education Department, unlike most departments, invited the Reconstruction Committee to assume primary responsibility in probing these topics. See Letter VI, 16 May 1916, p. 6. A confidential letter of 20 April 1916 to Nash indicated that "these reforms were desirable before the war almost as much as they are now, but it was impossible in the then state of affairs to secure any consideration . . . from any individual Minister. Even now, purely departmental action—or even joint action by the two departments of education—might prove inadequate; what was needed was a strong *ad hoc* committee." See F. 27, Box 14.

15. Letter VII, 18 May 1916, pp. 7–9.

was here plainly manifested; and the Board of Education obviously had been stirred.[16]

Although some of the other departments' replies to Nash were brief, the Local Government Board report took in a veritable panorama. Its President called for sweeping reform in child welfare work,[17] and pointed out changes overdue throughout the entire range of the Board's duties: provision of work, women's employment, housing, health, and relief of distress caused by the war.[18]

The departments had picked up the ball and were running with it. Their dynamic initiative was in no way surprising. They were remaking the agenda of reconstruction now; they had set the context in which it was born. Their anxious debates lay back of Asquith's statement of December 1915 that "not even our preoccupation in the endeavour to secure victory ought to prevent us from taking measures to secure that the problem shall be carefully explored by expert investigation"—perhaps the first of his indications that reconstruction was under study. At the very start, early in 1916, it was from a department—Runciman's Board of Trade—that strong pressure for reconstruction plans had come. From Selborne and the Board of Agriculture had come the final shove, for the first time bringing the cabinet to the point of decision on postwar problems.[19]

Meanwhile the staff of the committee had grown. Alfred Zimmern, J. L. Hammond, H. E. Dale, and Arthur Greenwood—names famous then or later—had joined it by midyear.[20] Staff work emerged as an independent theme. In May, inquiries began on employers' associations,

16. Letter XIV, pp. 23–35. See the London *Times* for 7, 10, 14, 17, and 26 January 1916 and for 2 and 21 February 1916. For Haldane's speech, see H. A. L. Fisher, *An Unfinished Autobiography* (London: Oxford University Press, 1940), p. 95, and *P.D.(L.)*, vol. 22, c. 655–83 (12 July 1916). See also Marwick, *The Deluge*, pp. 228–31, and Sidney Pollard, *The Development of the British Economy, 1914–1950* (London: Edward Arnold, 1962), pp. 93–94.

17. Walter Long to Cabinet, "Maternity and Child Welfare Work," 21 June 1916, in Cab. 37/150/9.

18. Walter Long to Cabinet, "Reconstruction Committee," 8 June 1916, in Cab. 37/149/14. For reference to another Local Government Board document, see Recon. A/43, Box 90, Part 1.

19. See note 7 above. Asquith's statement is mentioned in the *Journal of the Royal Institute of British Architects*, 23: 155–56. Documents 61 and 76, Cab. 37/144, deal with the action on Selborne's land-settlement proposals.

20. Greenwood was added at Zimmern's suggestion. Nash brought in, as his private secretary, the young E. H. E. Havelock, who worked through the war years with Nash on reconstruction. In February 1919 he went with Nash to the Development Commission, and he succeeded Nash as its Permanent Secretary in 1936.

which culminated two years later in the Report on Trusts.[21] In early June, impressed by all the action, Montagu spoke expansively:

> I gather that in the course of time we shall collect in one volume a series of reports and of memoranda, of draft statutes and of Orders in Council which together will make what used to be called a Peace Book. The whole of what is regarded as advantageous peace policy will be found in one volume.[22]

Gaining momentum, the Reconstruction Committee set up three new groups: one to review education as a whole, one to study women's employment, and one on the topic that would become the acknowledged pivot of all reconstruction—the wartime pledges to the trade unions to restore prewar conditions and restrictions on work. At the same time, the committee placed on the agenda, firmly and irrevocably, the problem of housing. It voted that memoranda on "housing and public works at the end of the war should be supplied by the Departments."[23] If there was one moment when official planning turned the corner from minimal to maximal goals, this was it. Henceforth no mere restoration, no efficient but conventional process of demobilization, would pass for true fulfillment. The slogan "Homes Fit for Heroes" was still to be invented; but after June 1916 housing and reconstruction were linked.

Housing and Rural Reform

The first reply to Nash's housing inquiry was a warning that normal methods would not work. The Office of Works and Public Buildings acknowledged that it was pondering an unusually large number of building schemes, of the sort that would provide employment, but it stressed that these were nowhere near enough. Drastic mass unemployment must be expected—3,300,000 men and women, not counting the armed services. An "enormous amount of work" would have to be provided. Some good would result from conventional schemes for re-siting vital

21. Perhaps originating with Asquith, the inquiry enlisted efforts of H. E. Dale, Professor Geldart (Vinerian Professor at Oxford), and William Beveridge, then at the Board of Trade. Memoranda on foreign antitrust legislation and on industrial combinations resulted, in November 1916 and July 1917. See F. 30, Box 71, Part 2, and Files 539 and 939, *ibid.*; see also below.

22. "Memorandum on Publications and Purposes," 6 June 1916, in F. 81, Box 40, and Cab. 37/149/6.

23. "Reconstruction Committee—Conclusions, June 23, 1916," in Box 41; Cab. 37/150/14 is the same document. The "Proposed Agenda" by Nash (Cab. 37/149/8 of 6 June 1916) lists housing as a topic for action. See also "Actions Taken or Proposed " 6 June 1916, in Cab. 37/149/9.

industries or replacing temporary buildings with permanent structures, but housing schemes must be the main reliance. Quoting an impressive array of arguments, beginning with prewar Land Enquiry reports and ending with the 1916 Congress on Home Problems after the War, the Office of Works hammered home two main points: "The question of housing accommodation will inevitably have to be taken up as soon as the war is over" and "the execution of housing schemes would . . . meet a very pressing need, and would provide a very large amount of labour, whilst all the material . . . could be produced in this country." They appended the estimate from Henry Aldridge, the famous Secretary of the National Housing and Town Planning Council, that 400,000 new urban and rural cottages were needed, but the office warned that time and Treasury approval were essential if schemes were to be ready.[24]

Hardly less sweeping were the Development Commission's ideas.[25] Its 12,000-word reply again and again drove home three key concepts. (1) State aid was indispensable ("It is useless to expect either local authorities or private persons to put effort and capital into reclamation. . . . If anything worth mentioning is to be done it must be done by the State"). (2) Considered in the larger context of postwar reconstruction problems, the reforms *gained* rather than *lost* importance ("If the War should be . . . followed by unemployment on any large scale, the case for the immediate inception of many of these schemes will become overwhelming"). (3) The law on land acquisition must be reformed, or many programs would be blocked.

Of the many, many suggestions, only seven can be listed: (1) the establishment of model farms and (2) the extension of agricultural credit where this might encourage better farming techniques; (3) reclamation of wasteland and (4) arterial drainage of various districts; (5) leasing of land by the state for afforestation, perhaps on a basis of profit sharing with the owner; (6) promotion of rural industries, especially sugar beet production; and (7) aid to rural transport, especially by the construction of canals and light railways.

It was an integrated program. Earnings in rural industries could supplement the rather low incomes from marginal reclaimed land; better transport, bringing farmer and market closer, would further encourage the

24. Letter XVIII, 11 July 1916, pp. 44–49. Schemes that were ready or being prepared were listed, to a total of about £1,000,000. The criteria suggested for postwar projects were the same as those that were applied in early 1919.
25. Letter XIX, 21 July 1916.

drive for greater production. And the program was thoroughly infused with a different and special spirit on finance. "Economic considerations" (the Commission bowed to the tribal god) had always guided it, but now it was guided "in the wide sense of those words."

> They have not felt it necessary in all cases to insist that money spent from the Fund on schemes other than those of an educational or experimental nature should return directly to the Fund a commercial rate of interest: they have often been satisfied with a scheme if convinced that its indirect results would compensate the State for the pecuniary loss involved in a free grant or a loan at interest below the market rate. Similarly, in the following survey the Commissioners have recognised that the general welfare of the State may require the country to face a pecuniary loss for the sake of gains which cannot readily be reckoned in money, e.g. to spend freely, and without direct returns, for such objects as the greater production of food-stuffs at home, and the greater employment of men upon the land.

In another reply, "Housing and the War," the Local Government Board described a thoroughly alarming situation. Private building had almost ceased; a promising increase in local authorities' accomplishments had been abruptly halted by wartime restrictions on loans; and, worst of all, after the war the costs of labor, building materials, and capital would be high—and such capital as came forth might have to be utilized "for other purposes even more directly concerned with the prosperity of the country and the promotion of its trade." Granting that "housing of the working classes can scarcely be looked upon as a financially economic proposition at the close of the war," the Board nevertheless noted that "all parties seem to be agreed that . . . it must be tackled." Convinced that "there is little hope of private enterprise meeting the building needs," the Board also dismissed direct state action as "not likely to prove economical, though it may set a high ideal in this as in other matters." "Few will . . . suggest that further State assistance should be given to private individuals," and little could be expected from Public Utility Societies. Nor could local authorities be expected to leap to the task: "There is at present no duty imposed generally on Local Authorities to provide housing for the working classes." State aid to local authorities—the one remaining hope—might follow the lines of the 1914 Act (grant of a percentage plus a loan at minimal rates), or an annual efficiency grant, or an annual grant of four-fifths of the annual deficiency,[26] or "the capital grant pure and simple."

The Treasury usually objected to outright grants, but "the abnormal circumstance that . . . cottages must cost far more than they can produce in rent" justified the grant, and ensured that it would continue only while circumstances remained abnormal. The Local Government Board was speaking from experience (wartime experience, we should note). Here and there the Board, the Treasury, and the Ministry of Munitions had partially housed munitions workers, so to speak, by giving local authorities "a capital grant representing a proportion of the increased cost due to the war," varying between 20 and 35 per cent. The procedure was most cautious: the standard cost was set in prewar prices but the aim was to "give the smallest grant which would induce action" and never to pay the extra wartime cost in full. "On the whole"—in the view of a smug, old, and sluggish department—"this arrangement has worked well."

Three departments had replied. It was Vaughan Nash who gave the next impetus. Having urged Asquith to ask for exact data on "indispensable additions to housing accommodation," he gave the inquiry a sharp turn by stressing the insufficiency of private effort. Nash's questionnaire, sent in late July to all departments, went beyond the conventional encouragement of "private enterprise." It asked, pointedly: "Assuming that private enterprise will be *unable* to meet within any reasonable period the deficiency of housing . . . at the end of the war, what action, if any, should be taken by the State . . . (in addition to the action proposed in the . . . Board memorandum)?"[27] Nash inserted the thought that the government's conception was not enough; he selected quantity as a crucial consideration. We have every right to consider his move a landmark.

The Secretary, Vaughan Nash

To those who knew Nash his contribution came as no surprise. As Secretary of the Reconstruction Committee he was in a good position to propose new lines of endeavor. As the former Private Secretary to Asquith, Nash was likely to get the Prime Minister's support. And three things we know about his previous career suggest that he preferred a liberal and humanitarian, even radical, reconstruction. In the war years

26. The third alternative (embodied in the Griffith-Boscawen Housing Bill of 1912), like the first, involved too much machinery and labor in checking details and in working out the scheme of payment, the Board said. Still, such plans had the merit of not "openly lending money at the rate which involved a loss." See p. 3 of "Local Government Board Memorandum on Housing and the War," 29 June 1916, marked "R.C. 27," in Box 40. We should note that all but the Griffith-Boscawen plan had actually been tried.

27. F. 167, Box 30, Part 1.

he was one of a small, informal group of civil servants, journalists, and public men who met weekly to chat at the Garton Foundation in Dean's Yard, where the ideas of labor intellectuals and advanced liberals were shared. In his earlier years Nash had been a journalist, and his highly favorable accounts of the dockers' strike of 1889 stand out conspicuously.[28] Still earlier, he had submitted an essay on the cooperative movement in a nationwide contest that had been sponsored by the Co-operative Union of Manchester.[29] The essay reveals the real man. Breathing indignation at the prevailing stress on organization and size, which he felt was destroying the spirit of the movement, Nash had appealed for reaffirmation of the movement's transcendent ideals. Those who have read it will not wonder at Nash's later proposal that local reconstruction committees be "trained on" with wartime control agencies for their postwar duties: the ideal of a living, self-governing cooperative community was the same in both cases.

Nash had already played a part in bringing housing to the fore; now the departments gave him a second opportunity, and he seized it. Up from the Local Government Board came Walter Long's memorandum, "Maternity and Infant Welfare Work."[30] Nash, broadening the matter into a general inquiry on the nation's health, asked eight departments for ideas. The Home Office declared it was awaiting the first opportunity for "general revision of the Factory Acts, which was in contemplation when the war broke out." From the Local Government Board, Walter Long criticized "the disintegration which has taken place in recent years"; in England alone there were "no less than six Departments . . . dealing with different aspects of the Public Health question." To reduce waste, overlapping, and friction, Long's department proposed not a Ministry of Health but that "responsibility for the main lines of policy" be put in the hands of one cabinet minister, the President of the Local Government Board.[31]

Nash had meanwhile received the answers on housing. From Noel Kershaw, of the Local Government Board, came an eleven-page memorandum and twenty-three pages of tables. Kershaw estimated that 150,000

28. See Hubert L. Smith and Vaughan Nash, *The Story of the Dockers' Strike* (London, 1889).

29. Vaughan Nash, *The Relation of Co-operative to Competitive Trading* (Manchester: The Cooperative Union, 1887).

30. Cab. 37/150/9, 21 June 1916.

31. Together with enclosures, Long's reply, dated 19 October 1916, forms Letter IV in a printed collection entitled "Correspondence on the Question of the Conservation and Health of the Population," in Box 40. The Home Office replied on 30 August (Letter III), the Privy Council on 23 August (Letter II).

houses were needed in England and Wales. To Nash, who knew Aldridge's estimate of almost half a million, the low figure may have come as a shock. Kershaw added that the many prewar factors that impeded the building of workers' homes could not "be seriously mitigated, much less removed." Pervasive pessimism led him to extreme caution. "It would seem reason-able . . . to aim generally at restricting permanent housing by Local Authorities to the making good of any proved deficiency at the beginning of the war. On these lines probably few mistakes would be made."[32] This when men were not thinking at all of *restricting* and when the mood favored anything but timorous hesitation to avoid making "mistakes"! Nash took the matter a long step further. Summing up all the memoranda, he circulated an estimate of the British housing deficit: "200,000 at least" by the end of 1917. Perhaps through tact, Nash used Kershaw's estimate, and he cited no solution other than the Local Government Board's scheme, but he warned that some of the estimates were twice as high as Kershaw's. The £2,000,000 Kershaw contemplated would provide only 33,000 houses. Something nearer £12,000,000 would be needed to make good the deficiency in England and Wales, with a further £4,200,000 per year for normal population growth.[33]

Initiatives confined to Whitehall, Nash concluded, might come to nothing, and he took the extraordinary step of inviting a stimulus from nongovernmental housing reformers. Early in December he asked for reports from the Garden Cities and Town Planning Association, and he made it clear that he wanted the reports immediately. The nation's most advanced housing organization busied itself to reply.[34]

"What the files will not tell you," Sir Alfred Zimmern wrote in 1953, "is what a grand person Vaughan Nash was."

> It was he who made the whole thing. . . . We were a small friendly team with Nash as the presiding genius. . . . My mind goes back to Nash as an embodiment of post-laissez-faire Liberalism at its best. He had the devotion to principle of the Liberals of the

32. Kershaw's memorandum of 23 August 1916 for the Local Government Board is in F. H. 213, Box 33. It is one of two replies remaining, of twelve received.

33. Nash's memorandum, "The Housing Question," is in Box 41; letters and minutes in F. 30 show that the Reconstruction Committee discussed the Local Government Board memorandum on 13 October. On 1 December the topic was adjourned; see Cab. 37/161/1.

34. Garden Cities and Town Planning Association, "Minute Book Three," p. 23 (entry for 8 December 1916).

Gladstonian period together with a rich humanity derived from a clear knowledge of social problems and the life of the poor.[35]

Nash excelled in tact, and years of acquaintance with departmental sensitivities helped him smooth the path of reconstruction. Letters on housing were sent first to the departments; and when the explosive topic of land acquisition arose he quietly referred it to interested colleagues in a semiofficial way.[36] But Nash could be diligent as well as diplomatic— where he cared strongly. As a result, over the whole contentious area of the state's economic role after the war his initiative shows through. He backed the first studies for a central power authority.[37] Outspoken in advocating the use of war property for peace purposes, he asked the War Office and Munitions for their full inventories. ("Your letters are not easy!" groaned General Brade, but he set to work.)[38] In the crucial area of controls, Nash knew that J. L. Hammond was probing everywhere for "war experience of industrial and commercial control which may be useful for dealing with after-war problems." Hammond had accumulated fascinating case studies, and Nash perhaps sympathized with Hammond's assessment.

> It is not suggested that after-war conditions will . . . admit of the retention of all that has been gained . . . either in respect of increased economy or efficiency. . . . Much of these gains are due to the fact that with a single guaranteed market, manufacturers are spared the cost and labour involved in finding their own markets and are thus enabled to concentrate on production. But . . . after allowing for the disappearance of this factor, the experience of associated work which manufacturers will have had may make them reluctant to abandon it and willing to consider the substitution of some system of common control . . . carried out on the basis of the trade, for the system of Government control now in force.

In any case, Nash wanted more; and he helped Hammond get shipping data. The Reconstruction Committee, Nash explained, was "securing a record of measures adopted by the Government to assume control of

35. Zimmern to the author, February 1953. The view is shared by E. H. E. Havelock, and Greenwood partially concurred. G. C. Upcott and Ernest Benn, however, deemed Nash weak and inactive.

36. Letter of 26 October 1916, F. 401, Box 1, Binder 1.

37. F. 452, Box 1, Binder 1. By 1919, four reports covered this ground (see below).

38. Files 24 and 29, Box 2, Part 1.

industry during the war" because of their "important bearing on transition problems and more permanent problems."[39] But cooperation and the desire for consensus always prevailed. "What weighs with me," went a characteristic note, "is that . . . as so many public Departments . . . are interested . . . it would be a great public benefit to secure a water-tight agreed scheme."[40]

First Fruits

As testimony to other energies the Reconstruction Committee had released, five comprehensive reports stood virtually completed in December. Unquestionably, the foremost project was that of Lord Selborne's Agricultural Policy Sub-Committee. So united that it adopted its basic policy in its first three sessions, Selborne's committee met twenty-three times in three months, and by mid-December it was revising proof on its first report. A monument to the galvanizing effect of war as well as a landmark in British farm policy, the huge and closely reasoned document rested on three major premises.

1. A great increase in cereal production was possible without a decrease in meat or milk.
2. Prerequisites for this gain were the cultivation of more land (especially grassland) and better cultivation of all land.
3. More scientific grassland management and meat and milk production were possible and necessary.

Proposals for implementation—the heart of the report—jolted complacency and conventional thinking. (*a*) Drainage systems, the lack of which was causing a deterioration in fertility, must be restored. (*b*) A standard minimum wage must be guaranteed for all agricultural laborers, enabling them to pay an economic rent for cottages and gardens. (*c*) The State itself must ensure that a new and adequate housing supply would be built. (*d*) "Stability must be assured to . . . agriculture by securing it against . . . a disastrous fall of the price of its staple products. Assistance given by the State to achieve this end should . . . give the greatest stimulus possible to better farming." (*e*) The state must forcefully instruct farmers and landowners alike on their duties, "in the interests of national security" and must set up industrially managed farms as models. Small holdings

39. Files 191, 324, and 704, in Box 71, Part 1, Binder 113(1), and F. 190, Box 9.
40. F. 445, Box 6, Part 1, contains Nash's letter of 27 November 1916. Evidence of his work with departments, and of their response, also is contained in F. 190, Box 9; minutes of testimony on emigration are in Box 90; and Letter XXIII is in Box 40.

should be encouraged. (*f*) The State must subsidize and expand education in forestry and farming.[41]

This was a clean break with laissez-faire. It was, in fact, economic nationalism—but humanitarian and near-socialist with its price supports, minimum wage, and state-run model farms. Again and again, war produced similar new formulations, as pragmatically open and unorthodox as they were vast in scope.

The best example of what could be accomplished by giving a department its head, Selborne's report also illustrates how war could stimulate thought. War had exposed forty years of erroneous farming policy in an instant. Revealing a perilous dependence on food imports, the war had condemned the dogmas that bred such dangers; overnight it converted men into protectionists and interventionists.

A twenty-year program of forestry and a detailed scheme for army demobilization also were practically finished. The latter contained important precedents for unemployment insurance and donations; the former brought forward Sir Francis Acland, as dynamic a figure as Selborne (who had nominated him) and a good deal more pugnacious. In 1919 Acland would inflict a tongue-lashing on the House of Commons. In 1916 he had whipped his Forestry Sub-Committee through its assigned work, producing a full-fledged proposal for the next two decades, and then he whisked it abruptly into a major inquiry on Lands Clauses Acts. If he succeeded, the whole process of acquisition of land for public purposes would be so speeded that housing, farming, and a dozen other causes beyond the narrow range of forestry would benefit.[42]

By December the oldest subcommittee had two reports to present. On imports and exports, Lord Balfour of Burleigh's committee had attained a consensus as remarkable as Lord Selborne's, and as unorthodox. At the start, its worried chairman had exhorted members to "cast aside any

---

41. F. SG 90/1921 of the Ministry of Agriculture and Fisheries contains these resolutions, all minutes for October 1917, and numerous erudite monographs of the Selborne committee. See also *Parliamentary Papers* (1917–18), vol. 18, Cd. 8506, "Report of the Agricultural Policy Subcommittee of the Reconstruction Committee," Part 1, which was printed in March 1917. In Box 8, F. 1500, is Heseltine's statement that the Corn Production Act of 1917 was based on this "interim report." For the debt of the Selborne committee to Milner's earlier committee, see Lord Ernle (Rowland Prothero), *Whippingham to Westminster* (London: John Murray, 1938), pp. 279–85, 290–91.

42. See Cab. 37/161/1 of 1 December 1916 and a memorandum on "Existing Sub-Committees of the Reconstruction Committee" (from early 1917) in F. 491, Box 40, for mention of the demobilization report. For Acland, see Files 66, 445, and 497 in Box 6, Part 1.

abstract fiscal dogmas." The outcome was a curious blend of nationalistic protectionism and liberal hostility to government control. Definitely, Britain must be protected from dumping; enemy domination must be blocked; and key or pivotal industries must have protection. But the bans on enemy imports, and on some British exports, were recommended with obvious reluctance; they involved, it was carefully noted, no pledge to any special line of policy beyond the immediate period. A general tariff was mentioned, but merely as one of several possible methods. All this still looked, verbiage apart, like an unsavory combination of narrow nationalism and special privilege, but the remainder offset the favoritism. In exchange for being protected, industry must accept the state's conditions, which Balfour of Burleigh spelled out: Cooperation of employer and employee might be fitted into the plan; provision for profit sharing might be included; and safeguards for the consumer and state control of industrial combinations could be established.[43] Like the Selborne committee, the Balfour of Burleigh committee had thought through the implications of policy.

Varied and Growing

But reconstruction, as a whole, was more and less than these reports suggested. It was less in that most of the work was unfinished. But it was far more in that at least twenty-five single- and multipurpose projects were underway, pursued by six Board of Trade committees, by eight sub-committees of the Reconstruction Committee, by staff work in the committee or for it, and by five other departments. It had grown up every kind of way. An agglomeration of committees purely departmental, of other committees born in or run by departments but nominally under

43. See especially Minutes of First Meeting, 25 July 1916, in Binder "C.I.P. 1," Box 8 (Commercial and Industrial Policy, 1916–1917), Board of Trade Committee Papers. The binder includes many other background papers, Board of Trade reports, and communications from other ministers and from the trade. In Reconstruction Files, see Papers 5 and 6, Box 41. Reports appeared in May and April 1918; see *Parliamentary Papers*, 1918, vol. 12, for Cd. 9033, "Interim Report on the Importation of Goods from the Present Enemy Countries after the War," and for Cd. 9034, "Interim Report on the Treatment of Exports from the United Kingdom and British Overseas Possessions and the Conservation of the Resources of the Empire during the Transitional Period after the War." The surprising delay in publication caused Sir Edward Carson to complain in 1918; see Cab. 21/108 for the file "Trade War," containing his memorandum, G. 190, as well as a letter of 31 July 1918 that registered the same complaint. For a note on the composition of the committee, see Cab. 37/149/Doc. 4.

Asquith and Nash, of staff studies in or outside Nash's office, and of authentic subcommittees of the parent committee, it was an administrative perfectionist's nightmare.

Nash liked it that way. What did it matter if, instead of being under his thumb, a committee was controlled by a separate department? All was under his eye; moreover, all must ultimately be put into effect by the departments. Besides, the departments were eager for work, and often were already at work. And as for coordination and overview, he, as Secretary for the Prime Minister's Committee, could guarantee these.

If questions of authority, power, and organizational tidiness did not trouble the men of 1916, such questions arose later. Mrs. Webb would see reconstruction as a savage struggle between the Reconstruction Committee and the departments, and Addison's ministry suffered some conflicts with departments. In any case the very creation of his ministry implies that the system of 1916 was defective; hence an appraisal of the 1916 system is obligatory.

The reality was neither departmental dominance nor jangling rivalry but a kind of symbiosis and interlocking membership. No major department was unrepresented on the Reconstruction Committee and, conversely, no departmental committee lacked its contact with Nash's office. Asquith and Nash kept lines blurred and tension minimized, and nothing in the record of 1916 shows them wrong.

As there was little conflict between committee and departments, there was little conflict, as yet, between reconversion and reform. The agenda of the Reconstruction Committee, embracing what men sought as desirable as well as what they accepted as necessary for the transition, showed no imbalance; and work that fell to the departments shows that neither type of project, reconversion or reform, was being sacrificed to the other. The Board of Trade had a solid group of six committees that worked on tasks of the transition period; but the Local Government Board had health and housing reforms in its charge. True, a few reconversion projects were finished, but the housing study was far advanced. Early in 1917 proposals for the important Whitley Council reform would come from the committee on relations between employers and employed. Toward the end of the year, several reform studies were launched. If trend lines meant anything, it was the reform sector of the agenda that was gaining.

Sharp distinctions, however, do not ring true. Slighting neither the reforms that men had long sought nor the tasks of transition that men now realized they must perform, official planning tended to fuse the two.

Reform was used as an aid to reconversion and reconversion was shaped into a vehicle for reform.

By the end of its first year, reconstruction combined the standard agenda of British reform with the special agenda necessitated by war. None of the work was perfectly completed; all of it was under way. Official reconstruction had become a rich, varied, and growing enterprise.

A Grand Design?

Of overall patterns and strategies no record remains; the Reconstruction Committee and its staff never made explicit the grand design they envisioned. But reconstruction was not formless; its aims were obvious, its premises were nearing definition, and its sequence was roughly identifiable. The aims, shaped more by fears than by hopes, reflected three awesome problems: tremendous unemployment (as high as 3,300,000, according to the Office of Works), general and extreme dislocations in enterprise, and fierce foreign competition. To fend off such disasters was the first task of official planners. But other aims had their place, beyond short-term imperatives of survival. The documents drove home the message that Britain suffered terribly from underuse of its resources; hence the planned revival of farming, the educational reform to make the most of precious talent, and the program to safeguard key industries— hence too the work on forestry and on coal. A broad attack on ill health and child labor and improvements in maternity care and housing (a whole agenda in itself) rounded out the long-term program.

Much was embryonic or totally lacking. There were no cost estimates (save for housing), no specific plan to raise the money, and no choice as yet—although one was vital—between the priority for reform and the priority for the war debt. There was no command structure to solve the final problems of coordination and crisis administration. Public support was not being enlisted, and even the need to inform the public was poorly grasped. Only Milner, at grips with the problem of food supply, had clearly seen the need for maximum publicity. Nothing like an exact timetable of action, moreover, had been sketched.

Still, eight governing concepts had somehow emerged.

(1) *The state must help.* More often reluctantly than with enthusiasm, state aid was accepted as inevitable. The insufficiency of private capital and the proved disinclination of private enterprisers in housing was common ground. (2) *The abnormal would prevail.* The premises of prewar economics would be irrelevant for the transition period—"business as

usual" was suspended beyond the duration. Planners worked on assumptions of abnormality.

(3) *Controls would persist.* The retention of controls was presumed, with significant demurrers by the few who predicted there would be no serious postwar shortages. The distinction between the control of prices and the control of materials had not been widely discussed, but neither kind was ruled out. (4) *Labor support must be sought.* Toward labor as toward controls, the attitude was similar: no approach, and no degree of cooperation, was barred in principle. Labor, already offered a part in planning reconstruction, soon would be offered a role in the decisions of industry. Concern for the workingman's reaction also was evident in the appointment of a committee on pledges. It helps explain the concept of balancing one kind of protection with another in both the Selborne and Balfour of Burleigh reports.

(5) *Demobilization would be gradual, on the assumption that reemployment would be slow.* Plans were for release not by length of service but by availability of jobs, with early discharge for those who were usable in running the demobilization. The decision to augment the Labour Exchange staff bespoke the overshadowing fear that the key problem would be joblessness. (6) *Preparations must be completed in wartime.* Readiness was all. The documents stressed what genuine preparedness entailed: not simply early decisions on principle but adoption of a complete and workable scheme, the placing of specific contracts, Treasury approval of costs, and—prerequisite to all this—a complete inventory of needed data. The Board of Trade, the Local Government Board, the Ministry of Munitions, and the War Office were all, Nash was assured, collecting data for forecasts. In turn, the concept of readiness led directly to two others.

(7) *No available instrument should be neglected.* Thus a heavy reliance on the departments was implied, if only because of their availability. But thanks to war, whole new instrumentalities had now proved themselves. Clearly, Nash and Hammond hoped for their use. (8) *Preconditions and implications must be thought through.* Examination had shown that no program was simple. Adequate housing could not result from a fiat on house-building alone; land law also must be changed. Industrial postwar policy could not consist of a single protectionist plank; good politics and the national interest, even apart from fairness, required parallel safeguards for other interests. Balfour of Burleigh's committee report had proved as much. And the Selborne committee had preached the same lesson of interdependence by an impressive display of proliferating but united measures:

farm price supports, minimum-wage guarantees, major housing efforts for the countryside, state controls on methods—all to the simple end of boosting farm output.

Functionally, these comprehensions and goals were nowhere near enough. Officials were quite unready for the coming of peace, but the outlines of what was needed were now in sight. Working with the grain of Whitehall's methods, planners envisioned an adaptation of existing institutions rather than the remaking of all things, but its conception of the specific tasks ahead was large indeed. Gradualist and ameliorative from one view, the government's scheme envisioned an effort that would be anything but gradualistic in the first crisis months, when swift and ready programs could make all the difference. Administratively, the structure (eclectic and loose-jointed) and the men within it had proved themselves adaptable. Like the substance of the agenda, they had shown themselves able to grow.

The December Crisis

Nash continued to forward these efforts; but he could not ignore signs that the whole of the work was in peril. Political crisis, which threatened Asquith's position, menaced all the achievements made thus far. In the second week of December 1916, Asquith resigned. Lloyd George became Prime Minister. Asquith's fall brought the organization in its old form to an end.

How important was the Asquith committee? In some ways it outranked and outperformed both of its successors. It launched reconstruction; it gave the task a breadth of conception which it never lost. The committee's claim to fame can be put even more strongly: the only reforms that were achieved in wartime were due to it. No measures that were recommended by the later committee or ministry became law until 1919. By contrast, the Corn Production Act, the forestry program, and the Whitley Council program were adopted or passed in 1917. This is the test of solid results, and the Asquith committee does not lose by it. But there is another test.

Reconstruction was a task in search of a form. The structure of committees and ministries could be all-important because success or failure in the substance of planning could depend on the nature of the planning vehicle. We will see the Minister of Reconstruction striving in 1918 to gain cabinet action because, to him, nothing was more urgent than the creation of a Home Affairs Committee to supervise reconstruction. Delays in forming such a committee led him to threaten resignation. We will see that the House of Commons in 1917 questioned the need for a ministry, and we will notice that in World War II the cabinet—consulting what it thought was past experience—chose *not* to set one up. These were all questions of form and structure, and rightly they were deemed vital.

Asquith chose the best form. He did not, like Lloyd George, set up a brilliant group of amateur reformers to coruscate in limbo; nor did he bother with a full-fledged ministry that might clash seriously with other departments. His Reconstruction Committee derived from and rested squarely on the departments; in fact, it consisted of ministers. This in itself was a cardinal virtue. Nothing could be done against the departments; nothing indeed could be done, save at huge cost, without their active help. In the end, they would have to carry out reconstruction, and it made sense to prepare them by involvement in the planning. To all these dicta of realism the Asquith committee conformed, without incurring the implied defects. Departments might take segmental views, stressing customary work and shunning the novelty of reconstruction; but the very form of the Asquith committee was a safeguard. Because it included the Prime Minister, it was at all times backed by the indispensable and sufficient authority; this was its second virtue, the complement to the first. Asquith could ensure coordination; he could spur laggards; when the time came, he could decide.

The case for such authoritative support and sanction—that is, for a close link to the cabinet and the Prime Minister—is eloquently put by the whole history of reconstruction from 1917 through 1919. But the merits of a departmental basis are less obvious. It is arguable that, by determining to work through and with the departments, Asquith settled for what they would willingly propose; thus a departmental consensus might tacitly set limits to reconstruction. It is not self-evident that this was for the best; indeed, Lloyd George struck out along other paths, apparently to avoid the risk of compromise and stagnation.

I conclude that Asquith's committee implied a conscious acceptance of the risk, together with an equally strong determination to offset it. Rather than settle for a minimum, his committee encouraged the departments to voice the whole range of their proposals. From what was offered, the secretariat emphasized the most forward plans and the Secretary challenged departments to aim at new goals. Of course it was vital that several departments had been keen on improving the national life. Except for this, and for Nash's diplomatic skill in drawing the departments out, the results might have been bad. In 1916, however, the caliber of the

Secretary, the ideas of the departments, and the very form of the Committee created a combination of factors that made for success.

Lloyd George's later record shows there were alternatives. The second Reconstruction Committee, conceived in irritated repudiation of the Asquith legacy, made few concessions to the departments; it seemed designed to bypass, encroach, or ignore. The Ministry of Reconstruction, which Lloyd George also set up, hints at the same. And there was still another way, nominally departmental, to escape from departmental conservatism: to remake the departments. Lloyd George tried to do just this with the Local Government Board; in 1919 he put Addison, Morant, and their men in charge, ousting entrenched rivals and renaming the whole the Ministry of Health. The record does not demonstrate the superiority of these stratagems.

Intrinsically superior in several ways and vindicated by results, the form of the Asquith committee should have been preserved. Instead, the structure was changed, and not for the better. The years 1917 and 1918 show that reconstruction suffered not simply from interruption of work but from the change in form. The changes, of course, were not pure loss. Fated to be a gadfly, the Lloyd George committee played its role well. The Ministry of Reconstruction, simply as a ministry, kept a valuable corps of troubleshooters ready for action; it gave Addison influence by giving him status. But, under these later forms, the work met obstacles—lack of cabinet attention, inability to speed departmental response, and intolerable delays in final decision—which under the Asquith committee could almost automatically have been surmounted. Months were lost and, ultimately, substance was sacrificed as a result.

The Reconstruction Committee of 1916 made important contributions to its successors. The training of its staff was directly carried over. Eight active subcommittees worked on into 1917, helping preserve continuity; and subcommittee reports left their mark on the final results. In the intangibles of lessons learned and comprehensions gained, however, continuity was partly lost. Men had learned in 1916 that demobilization might require drastic rethinking on insurance and they had seen multiple proofs of the interdependence of government policies. In late 1918 these understandings had to be revived. "Persistence of learning" was far from perfect.

What, finally, was the importance of the Asquith committee? All other considerations apart, what counted most was the simple fact that Asquith had taken action. He had set up a committee—at the highest level—and had modeled it on the Committee of Imperial Defence. The parallel was significant. No less a task than national survival had been entrusted to the Defence Committee. By analogy, the tasks set for the Reconstruction Committee ranked high indeed. Asquith had given the plainest proofs that reconstruction was too important to be left either to uncoordinated piece-meal efforts or to chance.

Nash looked at things differently. Responsibility left him no time or room for reflection or complacency. Late in December he warned Hankey, the Secretary of the War Cabinet, that questions were accumulating that called for decision. Although four major reports were in, the education review was hardly under way, the housing question had simply been held over at the latest meeting, and all the efforts of staff work and committees needed continuity and support.

Nash could hardly have known it, but in fact changes were being made that would greatly benefit reform both in and after the war. Lloyd George was proving a master at recruitment. From the quiet of Sheffield University, H. A. L. Fisher was summoned to public affairs overnight by a telephone call from Downing Street—characteristically asking his presence for breakfast with the Prime Minister! He was astounded next day by the offer of the Presidency of the Board of Education. Totally inexperienced in governmental work, but sensing that the war was his opportunity, Fisher launched at once into a program of major change. Through a two-year campaign he saw a new Education Act put onto the statute books, and he also carried to success a program of pensions and salary revisions. By these measures—raising the school-leaving age to fourteen, and making the teaching profession far more attractive—he strove to keep more children in the classroom, and to insure that better qualified teachers would be there to teach them.

Another December recruit, Rowland Prothero, became President of the Board of Agriculture. Unlike Fisher, Prothero (later Lord Ernle) had been in the House of Commons since 1914; and he was much better informed on current policy toward farming. Service on Milner's committee on food supply in 1915 had alerted him to the dangers of Britain's situation. He had deplored the complacency with which Parliament refused in 1915 to follow the Milner committee's recommendations; he was all the more delighted when the Selborne committee in 1916 took over those proposals bodily. By Prothero's appointment, wartime causes gained a popular and powerful leader. Prothero put the case unceasingly to farmer audiences for recruiting women laborers, induced farmers to undertake the high risks and costs of converting pasture to wheat acreage, persuaded even the War Office to abate draft calls of farm laborers, and mightily increased food output. Postwar plans for land-settlement and for aid to farm workers would find in him an indispensable and untiring advocate. In these two men, and in Rhondda and Addison who took over the Local Government Board and the Ministry of Reconstruction, Lloyd George would make a world of difference for many a reform.

But Nash of course could not foresee this. On 8 February 1917 he reported to Hankey that on such "really urgent questions" as housing, civilian demobilization, control of exports, and materials supply "we are being held up here pending the decision of the War Cabinet concerning the authority to be put in charge of Reconstruction matters."[44] Despite the urgency of this appeal, reconstruction marked time until Lloyd George revived it under a new committee.

44. F. 241, Box 40, contains Nash's appeals to Hankey of the War Cabinet secretariat. Cab. 37/161/1 has the minutes of the 1 December 1916 meeting of the Reconstruction Committee, doubtless its last; F. 491, Box 40, contains a list of subcommittees of the Reconstruction Committee.

For H. A. L. Fisher and the Education Act of 1918 as well as the Superannuation Act, see Fisher, *An Unfinished Autobiography*, pp. 91–92, 94–95, 103–8; Marwick, *The Deluge*, pp. 243–45; Mowat, *Britain between the Wars*, p. 208; Taylor, *English History, 1914–1945*, p. 184. For Prothero and farming, see Lord Ernle (Rowland Prothero), *Whippingham to Westminster*, pp. 279–85, 290–91; Mowat, *Britain between the Wars*, p. 251; Marwick, *The Deluge*, pp. 90–91, 171–72; Mancur Olson, *Economics of the Wartime Shortage* (Durham, N.C.: Duke University Press, 1963), pp. 23, 73–116.

The swift and early progress of Fisher's plans for education, through the War Cabinet, is reflected in WC 75, 20 February 1917, Cab. 23/1, and WC 217, 17 August 1917, Cab. 23/3. Positive decisions—but lengthier discussions—on farming measures are reflected in WC 66, 14 February 1917, and other sessions of February 1917, in Cab. 23/1, and in WC 112, 3 April 1917, in Cab. 23/2. Hereafter the letters "WC" before a number will be used to identify the particular session of the War Cabinet, using the style on the documents themselves.

3
The Second Reconstruction Committee

The new Prime Minister began to assemble his own Reconstruction Committee in mid-February 1917. Dissatisfied with the previous membership —"a mere shadow of Asquith"—he called upon representatives of more advanced thinking. Mrs. Sidney Webb, Dr. Marion Phillips, Leslie Scott, and B. Seebohm Rowntree led the list; Thomas Jones, Professor W. G. S. Adams, and Philip Kerr came from his new "kindergarten cabinet" on Downing Street. Only the Secretaries, Montagu and Hammond, had served on the old committee.[1]

Lloyd George had brusquely vetoed the idea of deputizing Edwin Montagu to work with Vaughan Nash and Maurice Bonham-Carter in a reexamination of the 1916 work. "Bring me a list of persons with ideas," he ordered, and—according to his Puckish and dark-eyed assistant, Tom Jones—he spent a spare ten minutes considering the list. H. G. Wells and George Bernard Shaw were struck out, Seebohm Rowntree was added, and the list was trimmed—with the caution that it must have "one of the Webbs." Then the invitations went out.[2]

1. See War Cabinet 67, 15 February 1917, in F. 573, Box 40, in which Lloyd George told the War Cabinet he was about to appoint a new Reconstruction Committee that would replace the old Reconstruction Committee. By its terms of reference it was "to consider (1) the Terms of Reference and composition of the existing Sub-Committees of the Reconstruction Committee; (2) what further enquiries should be made in connection with Reconstruction; (3) Reports made to the Prime Minister from the Sub-Committees; and (4) Recommendations to the War Cabinet as to what immediate action should be taken in connection with the Reports of the Sub-Committee."

2. See Beatrice Webb, *Diaries*, p. 82, for the account given by her "fellow Fabian" on the committee, Tom Jones. The improvisation did not end there but included a last-minute drafting of Dr. Marion Phillips, who formed part of a Labour Party deputation to Lloyd George and thus came to his attention. The letter of Thomas Jones to "E. T. J." (Mrs. Jones), 6 March 1917, is in the private diary of Thomas Jones, from which he supplied this excerpt to me (henceforth, it will be cited as Jones Diary).

Not until 16 March did the committee meet. Until then, one member of the new committee struggled with her mixed feelings. To Beatrice Webb, Lloyd George's administration had from the first represented "the supremacy of all I think evil and the suppression of all I think good." But curiosity began to overcome these misgivings. "Full of interest in Reconstruction and eager to begin devouring Reports," Mrs. Webb worried lest they "waste a good deal of time in disjointed effort." Seebohm Rowntree had already suggested that "the keen members of the Committee might meet together and allocate work to be undertaken by particular members." Mrs. Webb pondered the possibilities and disadvantages of "internal groups," took note of "a feeling among . . . the old Committees that we are going to try to 'boss' them," and drafted agenda and organizational forms for the work to come. The whole prospect looked vastly encouraging: the task was "an attractive one," with the committee made up, she noted, "of young and vigorous persons with . . . the youngest and ablest of the ex-Cabinet Ministers as Vice-Chairman."

> Out of the fifteen members there are three Fabians, as well as two Labour men, and one of the two Assistant Secretaries—Arthur Greenwood—is a Fabian. The Conservative M.P.'s are progressives (Hills and Leslie Scott), and there is the attractive young leader of the *Round Table* group—Philip Kerr—one of the Prime Minister's secretaries.[3]

At the first meeting Lloyd George spoke "for about half an hour in the most impressive and inspiring way about the great task confronting the Committee, his high hopes for it and the need of painting a new picture of Britain with fewer grey colours in it."[4]

> The task before them was gigantic. Much work had already been done: but a great deal remained to be accomplished. . . . There were two main kinds of questions—first, those which would arise

---

Seemingly, neither Montagu nor Nash was consulted. Invitations went to E. S. Montagu, the Marquess of Salisbury, Professor W. G. S. Adams, Sir Arthur Duckham of the Ministry of Munitions, Major J. W. Hills, M.P., Thomas Jones and Philip Kerr of the cabinet secretariat, Leslie Scott, K.C., M.P., J. H. Thomas, M.P., Sir J. Stevenson of the Ministry of Munitions, Mrs. Sidney Webb, Mrs. H. J. Tennant, and B. Seebohm Rowntree.

3. See Mrs. Sidney Webb to T. J., 19 February, 9 March, and 15 March 1917 in Jones Diary. Jones chatted with the Webbs and the Tawneys on 25 February at Mrs. Webb's invitation. See Beatrice Webb, *Diaries*, pp. 71, 80, 81. Mrs. Webb's view on Montagu quickly became hostile.

4. T. J. to E. T. J., 17 March 1917, in Jones Diary. See also Thomas Jones, *Lloyd George* (Cambridge, Mass.: Harvard University Press, 1951), pp. 124–25.

immediately at the end of the War and would require settlement without delay. Secondly, those which looked to laying the foundations of a new order.

Under the first division fell the demobilisation of the Army. . . . Similar was the problem of the millions of men engaged on war work, . . . steps should be taken . . . by way of public maintenance, public works, unemployment insurance, or other means. He could not say when the War was coming to an end; but the Committee must proceed on the hypothesis that it might be soon.

But the Committee's work did not come to an end there: they had power to assist in painting a new picture of Britain. It was common ground to everyone that conditions before the War were often impossible and stupid. The Committee must advise the Government what steps could be taken to make a repetition impossible. The counsel which it must give must be sound and, above all, fearless. There were questions such as land, labour, wages, and Local Government—to which last he attached great importance. . . .

No such opportunity had ever been given to any nation before— not even by the French Revolution. The nation now was in a molten condition: it was malleable now and would continue to be so for a short time after the War, but not for long. It was for the Committee to advise the Government on the way to give to the nation a shape which would endure to the advantage both of the nation itself and of the whole Empire.[5]

The new committee faced serious internal problems before it began to rise to the challenge of Lloyd George's address. Should it content itself with studying the Asquith committee's reports, or should it strike out on new lines? Should the whole committee, or only the vice-chairman, provide direction? Looking back from 3 June, Beatrice Webb complained that "for the first two months Montagu and Vaughan Nash succeeded in holding up the Reconstruction Committee—their intention being to use it as a mere panel from which they might select advisers on this or that question." "But after the Easter recess," she noted, "there was a concerted revolt among the members . . . for the carrying on . . . as a self-governing body."[6]

5. Vaughan Nash's minutes, in Box 40, show that the Prime Minister accepted the suggestions in the Ministry of Munition's committee report to the Reconstruction Committee and that the latter was free to call for reports or other help from the government departments.
6. Beatrice Webb, *Diaries*, p. 86.

Although Mrs. Webb was strongly biased and prone to overstatement,[7] there was a real struggle. Montagu sought to give a strong lead; he went beyond the routine function of summarizing the past situation and supplied the second meeting of the committee with a major policy paper on future work. The document was one of the most coherent and broadly conceived statements that wartime was to produce, but its merits were given scant consideration,[8] once Montagu opened the meeting. He spoke in favor of formulating policy from available data; he opposed new investigations, reinvestigations, or even the review of particular reports. A chorus of dissent arose from Major Hills and Leslie Scott, from Sir James Stevenson and Mrs. Webb, all insisting the committee should not tie its hands. No clear plan for organization emerged. Between meetings Montagu sought to build his own role. His memorandum on procedure was only partly reassuring to his testy new colleagues.

> In deciding what subjects we should submit to the Prime Minister ... I shall always be anxious to look for advice ... in due course I should hope to cover the whole field of our investigations by various forms of enquiries, after considering the recommendations of my colleagues ... with the Prime Minister and the Government Departments.

"He wants to give the go-by to the Reconstruction Committee as a whole," Mrs. Webb protested; "the Committee should disclaim all responsibility." But letters from colleagues heartened her ("We have a clear majority")

7. For her, the legacy from 1916 already was a "litter" of subcommittees; see *ibid.*, p. 82.

8. Montagu made a conventional but useful distinction between (1) items that "must be put into operation immediately peace is declared" or sooner, and (2) items it was not absolutely necessary to put into immediate operation. The first category included (*a*) demobilization of munitions workers, (*b*) housing of the working classes, (*c*) obtaining and distributing supplies and providing for shipping, (*d*) useful public work, (*e*) use of factories and land then in government hands, and (*f*) reconversion of private factories to peacetime work.

Along with public health services and education, Montagu put into the second category the improvement of subsidiary communications, encouragement of inventions, control of merchant shipping, local government and the Poor Law, liquor traffic, emigration, central departmental machinery, standardization of statistics, and extension or permanent enactment of war legislation. On finance, he noted that the Treasury had begun to consider control of capital issues, but the Board of Inland Revenue could not proceed with the review of income tax that had been promised before the war. As for railway control, the Board of Trade had received a scheme from part of the Railway Executive Committee. The memorandum is in F. 491, Box 40.

and soon the committee was, in fact, self-governing.[9] It divided into panels, each with considerable autonomy, for which the whole committee set the agenda. In April the panels—its new investigative teams—set to work.[10]

Three Months' Work

The committee had said it wanted work and it was as good as its word. By 5 July 1917, when a detailed progress report appeared, the main committee had met eight times and had put its panels through twenty-four sessions. Subcommittees, some dating from 1916, were maintaining the pace. One dealt with trade, the other with power.

Commercial and industrial policy. Far from slackening, the Balfour of Burleigh committee had produced a report on shipping that had gone through the Reconstruction Committee to the cabinet[11] and had recommended policy on "essential industries." The latter was a striking case of just those features for which the 1916 reports had been notable: strong protectionism, balanced by state scrutiny, not excluding the possibility of state enterprise itself. A Special Industries Board should be created to prepare schemes for aiding essential industries—like those producing magnetos or synthetic dyes, "absolutely indispensable" commodities that had been under enemy control. But aid would be contingent on efficient production at reasonable prices; failing that, said this conservative group of businessmen, the state should undertake the work.[12]

9. See "Proceedings, Second Meeting, Reconstruction Committee," 22 March 1917, in Box 41, and "Conclusions," *ibid.* The "Memorandum on Procedure" is R.C. Paper No. 52, in Box 40. Letters from Mrs. Webb to Thomas Jones are cited from Jones Diary. See R.C. "Conclusions—29 March 1917," in Box 40, and Beatrice Webb, *Diaries*, p. 80.

10. See R.C. "Conclusions—19 April 1917," in Box 40.

11. See "Reconstruction Committee—Progress Report," 5 July 1917, in Box 40. (Hereafter the Reconstruction Committee meetings will be identified by initial and number: thus "RC 3" means the third meeting of the full committee. Summaries of conclusions are in Box 40. If no authority is cited hereafter in this chapter for subcommittee or panel work, the "Progress Report" is the source.)

12. Submitted on 16 March 1917 but printed only in March 1918, this "Interim Report on Certain Essential Industries" is in *Parliamentary Papers* (1917–18), vol. 13, Cd. 9032; see WC 67, 15 February 1917, Cab. 23/1, for cabinet action. For a postwar parallel, if not a result, see the files of the Key Industries Committee, 1921–35, in the Board of Trade committee papers. RC 8 and memorandum "R.C. No. 46" in Box 40 show endorsement of the recommendations on shipping, and deal with other communications between Balfour of Burleigh's committee and the Reconstruction Committee. Mrs. Webb's view that the Reconstruction Committee had been "warned off" the Balfour of Burleigh subcommittee reports is shown in Thomas Jones' diary for 16 July 1917.

Electric power. Haldane's Coal Conservation Committee had gone far into the much disputed question of electricity supply. It was a whole cluster of problems, on which no less than four clashing reports were to appear in wartime. Haldane's group reported resoundingly in favor of a thoroughgoing reorganization on *national* lines, ending once and for all the prevalent localism and inefficiency. "Super-power" generating plants must be set up; large distribution areas must be established, with only one supervisory authority per area. A single national Board of Electricity Commissioners should control. The committee's proposal stopped short of nationalization, but was bold nonetheless. England's system—local, private, and weak—might have been transformed by this, the first to give "authoritative acceptance to the principle of reconstructing electricity supply on a national scale."[13]

Other "Asquith" subcommittees. Reports on agriculture, demobilization, and mining were almost completed. Recent changes in labor policy, however, had held up the War Pledges Subcommittee. Thus began delays that overshadowed that topic and lasted to the end of 1918. Other committees were probing women's employment and acquisition of powers.

The Reconstruction Committee approved some of these reports, scrutinized nearly all, sniffed a bit disdainfully, and set up committees of its own.

Proliferation. One such new creation filled a major gap: it dealt with civilian war workers' demobilization, overlooked in Asquith's time. Another committee was formed to study land acquisition, a root problem whose solution was a prerequisite to the solution of many others. Leslie Scott, heading this committee with the same spirit Acland had shown in 1916 on the same topic, would eventually produce major legislation with its aid. There was more: a conference on a Ministry of Supply, on a committee on road transport, and another on shipping.[14]

Amid all this bustle—necessary and not at all surprising—something

---

13. For comparison with other proposals on electricity, see below, pp. 426–28. On publication of the report, see F. 1500, Box 8, and Addison's memorandum of 25 October 1917 to the War Cabinet. See Great Britain, *Parliamentary Papers* (1918), vol. 7, "Interim Report of the Coal Conservation Sub-committee of the Reconstruction Committee on Electric Power Supply in Great Britain," Cd. 8880. Submitted on 17 April 1917, the report bears a preface by Addison dated 7 December 1917. This report reappears as Appendix I to the Coal Conservation Committee's final report, Cmd. 93. See the comment by W. Hardy Wickwar, *The Public Services: A Historical Survey* (London: Cobden-Sanderson, 1938), p. 174.

14. F. 886, Box 40, shows further subcommittee activity. See RC 2, 4, 6, and 8. The Civil War Workers' Demobilisation Committee is henceforth designated as the C.W.W.C.; see Cd. 9231, pp. 20–22.

new and remarkable appeared: a major policy statement on industrial controls. Altogether unexpectedly, the committee had stumbled on this huge question while probing shipping. It threshed out its detailed recommendations, which were sufficiently strong: the state must control food and shipping and imports and exports after the war; the needs of home industries must come first; and so on. But it is the rationale that holds the eye.

> The case for control is that the transition period is bound to present conditions which it would be impossible for private trade to contend with without grave danger to the interests of the community.
>
> If the various systems of control . . . were suddenly abolished, merchants, manufacturers and financiers might indeed rejoice, but we should have . . . intolerable confusion, with freights and prices soaring up. . . . The only safe forecast is . . . of insufficient food, materials, and above all of shipping, and this means that the stampede would, if it were unregulated, be tremendous; that articles of necessity would be elbowed out by luxuries; . . . bricks and timber and girders needed for building workmen's houses might be used up in building great houses or theatres. . . . Control is not advocated because a crippled community will require crutches, but because with the depletion of necessary stocks and the deterioration of works and services of all kinds . . . and the limited supply . . . some temporary system of State guidance, information and direction is indispensable before free methods of trade can be relied upon again.[15]

Many times, warnings against swift decontrol were to be voiced. This exposition, by Montagu, was second to none.

Meant as a warning of things to avoid, it looks today more like a prophecy of things to come. Much of the forecast ultimately came true, as licensing requirements and permit systems went into discard and prices began to soar. But this would not be evident until early 1919. By that time new conditions obtained, and new factors were at work: an unexpectedly good supply of raw materials, a dire need to create jobs, a slump in business initiative, and a logjam in Whitehall's administrative machinery. These factors, working over the three months after the armistice, sufficed to move a wavering government by spring of 1919 away from the presumption that controls must stay on. But, up to the armistice, the

15. See RC 5 and R.C. Documents 68 and 82, Box 40.

presumption *for* controls seemed strong and agreed upon. The rationale for it was typified in Montagu's words. Control, in that formulation, was not a matter of intrinsic merits or of underlying theory. Instead, the case for control rested on predicted conditions of fact; it rested, first of all, on shortages of shipping and supplies. Hence it was a persuasive argument. Hence, too, it was vulnerable.

The Machinery of Government Committee. Of all the new creations launched by Lloyd George's Reconstruction Committee, none was as completely fitting and fated as the committee that bears forever Lord Haldane's name. It was as inevitable that Lord Haldane should be drawn further and further into reconstruction work as it was natural that he and the Webbs should have found each other by mutual magnetism of intellect. High-minded, proudly independent of party, steeped in German philosophy and literature, living for the state but destined never to be truly welcomed by it, these three—the Webbs and the man who had transformed Britain's fighting forces while at the War Office—had often met: the Webbs sometimes at his table, he at those exercises in austerity that passed for meals at theirs. There in 1917 they no doubt discussed the disgraceful jingoism that had driven Haldane from office on the absurd charge of pro-German sympathies; for it is clear, from the Haldane archives for that period, that this misadventure in mid-career brought Haldane such encomiums, from distinguished figures throughout the land, as most men receive too late to hear.

Morant, greatest of civil servants but with blood that boiled most unbureaucratically, wrote of his "rage and grief" at the ouster; and the King sufficiently indicated his respect by a tactful request for Haldane's opinion on a nice point of royal prerogative.

In this context it is safe conjecture that this topic drew the three together in 1917.

But it is not conjectural that the Webbs gossiped with Haldane about reconstruction. Doubtless they knew that the Prime Minister had invited Haldane to "talk reconstruction," and they kept him informed of their exploits with—and against—the Reconstruction Committee. In July 1917 Haldane agreed to head an inquiry in which the Webbs were enormously interested: the machinery of government.

The "Haldane committee," as history knows the Machinery of Government Committee, had a breathtaking mandate, a splendid career, and a ludicrous afterlife. It carried a letter of marque to examine any and all phases of central government. Called before its row of glittering eyes—in what psychological state it is better not to think!—the nation's highest civil servants chose the better part of valor and testified so fully that, to this day, the records of the committee constitute a treasury of wise and candid comment.

As Professor Daalder has ably shown, the members had the widest latitude, ranging from a study of the cabinet itself and its improved functioning to questions purely interdepartmental or even departmental. In fact, they dealt with all, preparing a magnificently consistent and rigorously thoughtful (i.e., doomed) set of principles for a true functional system of departments, and also a plan for a small cabinet armed with an independent secretariat. Where testimony fell short, they were not shy. From Beatrice Webb alone came everything from total systems to the sharp verdict that a Permanent Secretary should never lift a pencil from his desk. On into December 1918 they voyaged, to put in at last with muffled oars—for Sir George Murray, the cautious traditionalist, vowed to counter every drastic recommendation by Morant with his personal dissent. This insured a weak report.

Its work done, the committee and its document waited. The document, and the great cause of central reorganization, still wait. The report was, to quote Sir Arthur Salter, a "treasury of good counsel"; and it was intended by Morant, Haldane, and Mrs. Webb to be "a revolutionary document." Into the 1930's, however, it almost wholly lacked influence. Indeed two of its rather easily adoptable proposals—for a Ministry of Supply, and for a Ministry of Justice—were turned down. The former was in reality rejected by the coalition cabinet of 1919–21, when departmental jealousies prevailed. The latter was rejected in 1924 at the moment of seemingly greatest opportunity. Lord Haldane, Lord Chancellor in that year, refused to use his position to adopt the very idea that had come from his own hand.

The outcome was a defeat not only for the zealots of 1917 and 1918 but also for that most traditional department, the Treasury. For the Treasury had had a part (perhaps unsuspected by the Webbs) in the whole inquiry. In 1916 the Treasury officials had supplied Montagu, then Financial Secretary, with details on waste that was caused by a bad division of functions among departments. It was from this basis, departmental and Asquithian, that Montagu launched the idea of a complete study next year. The hopes of all—cautious departmental civil servants, and enthusiasts for drastic change—were disappointed in the end. But in 1917 the auguries were excellent.

Toward a Ministry of Health. One of the Reconstruction Committee's most promising ventures, a new initiative in favor of a Ministry of Health, was wholly *ultra vires*, as Mrs. Webb saw. The story began and ended outside Dean's Yard, with the man who was soon to be Minister of Reconstruction: Dr. Christopher Addison, then Minister of Munitions. Almost alone in the medical profession, Addison had fought like a tiger on behalf of the national health-insurance plan advocated by Lloyd George. His interest in a broader structure, the Ministry of Health, grew during his service (to 1916) for the Board of Education, which also had important health duties. He was an heir to the half-century of campaigning for the true integration of positive state aid. In 1917 Addison called together Lord Rhondda, head of the Local Government Board, and Sir George Newman, then the principal medical officer ("P.M.O.") of the Board of Education.

> I have been urging Rhondda to go the whole hog at the L.G.B., and arrange for . . . a big Public Health Department, making Newman P.M.O., bringing in Infant Nurseries, Schools for Mothers and Health Insurance, and leaving the medical service of school children . . . still under the B. of E. I sent him a memo which Morant, Newman and I had prepared in the summer of 1914.

Rhondda, enthusiastic, told the cabinet a Ministry of Health was urgent. He, Addison, Milner, and Henderson conferred with the redoubtable Sir Edwin Cornwall, head of the National Health Insurance Commission. Instead, Sir Edwin championed the interests of the voluntary groups, the Industrial Approved Societies;[16] but Addison won Milner and Henderson with his case for unifying the "medley of health services." "There is no hope of running Health Services efficiently, unless the whole group is worked with a united purpose under the direction of a Central Authority. . . . If we left it until after the War, we might be too late."[17] Past and future came into view in these hurried talks: the past when Morant and Addison helped carry health insurance in 1911, the future when Addison would take Morant with him into the very ministry they were planning. There Addison would lose his reputation, and Morant his life.

Rhondda fretted in the present: "Already my proposals for Health reform are held up." He thought his plans for infant welfare might save 1,000 lives a week; hence a subcommittee of the main committee was improvised. Luckily, Michael Heseltine became its secretary: "*the* man

16. Addison, *Diary*, 2: 317, 321, 355; Christopher Addison, *Politics from Within, 1911–1918* (London: Herbert Jenkins, n.d.), 2: 222; and George Newman, *The Building of a Nation's Health* (London: Macmillan, 1939), pp. 118–25.

17. Addison, *Diary*, 2: 355, and *Politics*, 2: 221. See also Margaret H. T. Rhondda, *D. A. Thomas, Viscount Rhondda* (London: Longmans, Green, 1921), pp. 263–68, and Marwick, *The Deluge*, pp. 240–42.

for the job," said Rhondda; a "brilliant young civil servant," Mrs. Webb felt. Thus Heseltine, a "Morant man" and already experienced in the Home Office and the Insurance Commission, took the stage for reconstruction. Then Addison's secretary at Munitions, he followed him first into the Ministry of Reconstruction and then into the Ministry of Health. He and Rhondda, a terror to sluggards, whisked the subcommittee through its paces; Milner, of the cabinet, had its report by May. "The Reconstruction Committee," Mrs. Webb jotted, "was somewhat surprised that the job had been done without its knowledge between two of its meetings."[18]

The grand strategy of the report was to unite *and* divide: to unite, within a new ministry and on the basis of the old Local Government Board, all health functions from all other departments; and then to divide the new ministry in two. One of its divisions would handle health; the other would absorb all remaining duties of the Local Government Board. The new minister would be able to extend new medical services, to be administered through local authorities and through insurance committees, which the ministry would coordinate better. For the moment, health functions in other departments would remain there. A short bill should at once be introduced: "Any further delay progressively increases the difficulty of setting up such a Department, owing to the multiplication of authorities and the creation of vested interests, which proceed almost unchecked in the absence of a Ministry of Health."[19]

"If the Insurance Companies don't defeat it," Mrs. Webb predicted, "we shall have a Ministry of Health in a few weeks." Newman, Morant, Montagu, and Addison watched with delight as the proposal withstood the first onslaught from the industrial insurance societies. On 5 June it reached Lloyd George. But there immediate hopes were checked. Until he could hear the views of these "approved societies," Lloyd George decided he would go no farther. Determinedly, Morant began to take the case to the societies themselves. Enactment, expected that summer, did not come for two more years.[20]

But, in the summer of 1917, if one attack on health problems had been halted, another had begun. Its focus was not on a *central* structure but on

18. Beatrice Webb, *Diaries*, p. 87; Addison, *Diary*, 2: 358–60, 365, 379, and *Politics*, 2: 222. See also F. 676, Box 30, Part 1, and Doc. 51, Box 40, for Rhondda's and Montagu's roles.

19. R.C. Doc. No. 81, May 1917, in Box 41.

20. Webb, *Diaries*, p. 87; memorandum by Montagu, F. 676, Box 30, Part 1; Addison, *Politics*, 2: 222–23, and *Diary*, 2: 379, 390–91, 397. Early discussion by the War Cabinet, and its eventual decision to defer, are shown in WC 115, 6 April 1917, Cab. 23/2, and WC 156, 6 June 1917, Cab. 23/3.

substantive questions and *local* responsibilities. To Mrs. Webb it was an attack on the Poor Law.

This new effort, however, was the work of one of the "panels." It is time to look at them.

Health, Housing, Labor: Tasks of the Panels

The specialized "panels" of the committee were the children of the "members' revolt" that had so satisfied Mrs. Webb. If the revolt had any meaning, the panels were free to do almost anything, and should—in the event—do much.

The Education Panel proved inconsequential, although it labored mightily in the cause of adult education. Its final report is probably the most eloquent piece in all the sonorous and touching literature of reconstruction, but at no time did the panel back a major proposal, and it lost its one battle: with the government itself over the Education Bill.[21] Nor did Panel 5 (Control of Industry) achieve results. Mrs. Webb resigned herself to enjoying the spectacle presented by the panel's celebrities, Sir James Stevenson and Sir Arthur Duckham—two "capitalists turned bureaucrats."[22]

Panel 4 and Panel 3, however, embraced mighty themes. The former concentrated on housing. Montagu and Rowntree were at work at once; and the panel rolled up its sleeves to draft a complete scheme. Thus, by a fusion of the best in the Asquith and the Lloyd George groups, the momentum Nash had imparted was saved. From March 1917 on, the panel labored prodigiously. The result, by midyear, was a full housing program, bold and distinctive, that the reconstruction team battled for even beyond the armistice.

Housing did not exhaust the panel's energies: Poor Law reform was added, and again it was Montagu who gave the lead. He asked Mrs. Webb to draft a memorandum. But she saw, and seized, the opportunity to "get on with the Minority Report." In her words, "Instead of preparing a memorandum I offered to get some sort of agreement between the Majority and Minority of the late Poor Law Committee and the Local Government Board." Once, such a task would have seemed impossible. But, where the rival schools of Poor Law reformers had formerly seemed unappeasably estranged, now the gap was far narrower; and Mrs. Webb made much of the point. Changes since 1909, she told the panel, made

21. Webb, *Diaries*, pp. 86–87.
22. *Ibid.*

agreement very likely. This approach brought results. By July 1917, the new atmosphere led to the appointment of a "Local Government Committee" under Sir Donald Maclean, M.P. Off to a flying (and apparently unanimous) start, the committee at once passed the key resolution: "that the Boards of Guardians should be abolished and that the [Poor Law] Union area should be superseded by that of the County and County Borough."[23]

Neither of these labors ended in 1917; neither housing policy nor Poor Law reform became settled before the armistice. But two of the great continuing themes of effort, for the duration of the war, had made their appearance.

Panel 3 (Wages, Employment, etc.) launched a study of unemployment, reviewed actions of the War Pledges and Women's Employment subcommittees, and analyzed for Lloyd George the Labour Party's new program.[24] But this was minor; "Whitleyism" was the important new sphere it entered.

Joint Industrial Councils of employers and employed, or Whitley Councils (as everyone came to call them, after the Speaker of the House, John Whitley), provoked the stormiest debate in the short but gusty life of the Lloyd George committee. The essence of Whitleyism was that the path to industrial reform must be a path of consultation and that both sides must be equal. On every question of social and economic change the Whitleyite answer was the same—an answer not of substance but of method: Joint Industrial Councils, some at the workshop level, some for an entire industry, must be set up to thresh out the answer. Perhaps the Whitley idea became popular almost as soon as it was announced because it offered a third choice in place either of laissez faire chaos or of governmental control. Whatever the reason, Whitleyism gained immense favor. And Speaker Whitley's committee report, bouncing through the Reconstruction Committee very early, was soon before the cabinet, where opinion was strong for adoption.

Brief and ominous as a lightning storm, a struggle within the Reconstruction Committee interrupted this easy progress. Just when her

23. "Changes . . . since the report of the Poor Law Commission," she told the panel, made agreement likely. See record of the first meeting, 19 April 1917, Box 40, and Webb, *Diaries*, p. 87. For the final work of the Maclean committee, see Great Britain, *Parliamentary Papers* (1917–18), vol. 18, "Ministry of Reconstruction. Local Government Committee. Report on Transfer of Functions of Poor Law Authorities in England and Wales," Cd. 8917. F. 1633, Box 7, summarizes the Maclean committee's first meeting; see also Docs. 1 and 4, Box 88.

24. F. 617, Box 40; Webb, *Diaries*, p. 87.

colleagues were about to relax, after having voted approval, Mrs. Webb flared into criticism. Her own term for the result—"an animated debate, I being in a minority of one in opposing it"—is gross understatement. A blizzard of documents descended; the Speaker of the House was called in; Panel 3 added Lord Salisbury for its extra sessions; and the air crackled with argument. Whether Mrs. Webb simply disliked the first report (on national councils) for its scope, or was angry at a plan that she disliked in principle, or was horrified that a good idea would fail through bad presentation, she wrote as if reconstruction itself was at stake.

Perhaps it was. In form a debate on Whitley Councils, it was at bottom a debate on the political prerequisites of reconstruction, and it brought out choices with utter clarity—the most fateful choice, perhaps, the government was ever to make. After the choice had been made, Mrs. Webb's effort to dissuade the government failed. The Whitley Report became a command paper and was on its way to becoming a national cliché.

The government's response and Mrs. Webb's warnings are equally important: the one measured the enthusiasm, the other the hostility, that Whitleyism evoked. Not one for halfway measures, Mrs. Webb began by sending her colleagues a sixteen-page memorandum of dissent. The "dangers and difficulties which may be caused by the immediate publication" of the Whitley Report as a government program, she wrote, were seven.[25]

> (1) Whatever is left out will be believed to have been negatived. (2) Labour would infer that the most urgent of all questions—the Government pledge that "Trade Union Conditions" are to be restored—should be thrown into debate, industry by industry, in these Industrial Parliaments. The Trade Unions of the skilled crafts will fear that they will be outvoted on this issue by the representatives of the employers, in conjunction with those of the women and the labourers. The cry will be raised that this is how the Government intends to evade its responsibility (which is a separate responsibility to each Union, irrespective of any mass vote).

This specific danger related to the scope of this first report rather than to Whitleyism as an idea. The first report, perhaps unwisely, started with the highest possible level at which Whitleyism could be instituted, an industry

25. "Report of Sub-Committee on Relations between Employers and Employed— Memorandum by Mrs. Sidney Webb," Box 40.

as a whole, for each of which a National Joint Industrial Council was recommended.

(3) The report sinned further by a favorable mention of profit sharing. This was unthinkable, Mrs. Webb warned, in view of the "fanatical hatred" for that idea in some quarters. (4) Further, it was unclear if the councils were to be merely old joint bodies under a new name or, instead, were to be "a leap into the dark." The existing "tried and true machinery" of joint committees or conferences would be superseded, and strong protest would be certain.

(5) Constitutions proposed for these councils overlooked a plain lesson of experience:

> All the existing machinery which has proved successful is based on the meeting of the employers either with the representatives of a single Trade Union or with those of a small group of allied Trade Unions. . . . But the proposal . . . is absolutely the opposite. . . . The National Industrial Council is to be "representative of employers and workmen"—not representative of Employers' Associations and Trade Unions. . . . It may be safely predicted that no Trade Union would dream of accepting it. . . . If the scheme is to have any chance of acceptance . . . the workmen's representatives on the National Council, equally with those on the District Councils, must be appointed by the Trade Unions as corporate bodies and by them alone.

Which trade unions would be represented? To represent a whole industry would mean forming a council that would be impossibly large, or omitting some unions, or ignoring proportion. The new circumstances born of war would treble the complexities that "during a whole century or more . . . prevented the formation of any Trade Union exactly coincident with an industry, . . . [would] interpose obstacles to schemes of federation of the different Unions belonging to one industry, let alone their amalgamation," and would surely "prevent the coming into being of the National Industrial Councils now proposed." Variety among unions themselves, plus each union's knowledge that it would be in a minority, would stir enough fears to doom the experiment. On the hardest question of all— the government's pledge to restore prewar trade-union conditions—Mrs. Webb stressed that the pledge was made *to each trade union.*

> The several Trade Unions in each industry may have . . . hopelessly divergent views, impossible of settlement by mere majority vote. The Trade Union will feel that, in view of the inevitable

divisions in their own ranks, to entrust this subject to the Councils would be to give the decision to the representatives of the Employers' Association.

(6) The proposed functions were hopelessly wide. Each existing joint council was strictly limited to subjects on which all of the included trade unions had identical common interests. To fix rates for a whole industry by *majority* vote was nonsense inasmuch as trade unions "invariably" insisted that their spokesmen be limited to precise, specific subjects on which they had instructions. (7) The mere idea of binding decisions doomed it all. "Active hostility," class bitterness, and suspicion of governmental intent would be the result, not industrial councils.

The urgency of Mrs. Webb's words took the debate far beyond any routine context. Planners were being challenged to look at the very rock of reconstruction: that peril whose depths reached down into decades of distrust, whose jagged visible edge was the warborn issue of pledges. Misguided, reconstruction could be dashed to pieces on it, shattered by the unappeased hostility of the very workers whom reconstruction was meant to help. Wisely directed, its course charted by this fearsome landmark, reconstruction might find safety and success. The worst danger, that the rock might simply be ignored, had prompted Mrs. Webb to write.

Impressed, other members replied reassuringly, through Montagu: the government would hold small conferences with unions and employers for the industries in which several competing unions then covered the ground. Mrs. Webb was right: negotiations of the councils should result in recommendations only, particularly on the fulfillment of pledges.[26] The panel construed the report so as to meet Mrs. Webb's charges: the councils were to consist entirely of representatives from employers' associations and trade unions, rather than be of some new composition, and their decisions would be binding only if they were signed by the bodies concerned.[27]

The Reconstruction Committee may have shared some of Mrs. Webb's premises but it had not followed her to the point of rejecting the report. Why? An eight-page, unsigned and undated document, "Memorandum on Mrs. Sidney Webb's Statement," may throw some light.[28] It amounts to a rejoinder that Mrs. Webb's gloomy interpretations and predictions were not necessary. To her prediction that "whatever is left out will be believed

26. "Memorandum on Procedure" by Montagu, R.C. Doc. No. 53, Box 40.
27. F. 617 and Documents 64, 65, 66, in Box 40.
28. R.C. Doc. 58, Box 40.

to have been negatived," the memorandum replied: "There are . . . no grounds for assuming that this will be so"—especially if the Prime Minister supplied an explanation. Again, Mrs. Webb's pessimism was countered by the cheerful thought that "if the Trade Unions adopted the principle of Industrial Councils, it is not too much to suppose that they would realise the difficulties of representation and endeavour to find ways of meeting them." The document presumed that the Whitley idea would get logical, fair, and disinterested consideration; it presumed that the manifest good intent behind official reconstruction in general, and behind Whitleyism in particular, would be recognized and would dispel doubts. The Reconstruction Committee had approached Whitleyism in this spirit, detached and not distrustful; thus it had given its endorsement and had assumed that others would do the same.

In short, the committee had not accepted Mrs. Webb's warning that, in labor circles, the presumptions were strongly against all government proposals and would be overwhelmingly against any proposal that, even by far-fetched reasoning, could seem to menace labor's precarious share of power. It was not axiomatic to the committee that the government's good faith was everywhere suspect among workingmen and that, therefore, the government must go to the limits of the possible and the imaginable in order to dispel this skepticism.

But what if such views, however unfair or groundless, prevailed? Mrs. Webb was not alone in declaring that labor would judge official plans in no normal or friendly spirit. "Labour stands apart, intractable," H. G. Wells had proclaimed,[29] and Zimmern sought to warn his colleagues time and again. During this very debate Arthur Greenwood tried to show the committee why the pledges question would supply, for all of labor, the acid test of government intent. Trade unions, he reiterated, were defensive by their very origin; it was their business to be suspicious; and in this spirit they had not only perfected trade-union rules over the years but had cherished these prewar rules and conditions as their one means of industrial control. War had led them, for patriotism's sake, to suspend the rules in return for government pledges of restoration. But war had deepened anticapitalist feeling and had created a feeling that

> Government promises have repeatedly been broken, . . . Government intervention in industry has worked against . . . labour, and . . . brought labour into greater subjugation. . . . A false step by the

29. H. G. Wells, *What Is Coming?* (London, 1916), p. 117.

Government would, in the absence of a restraint such as the war has imposed, result in upheaval. . . .

If a literal restoration be regarded as impossible or undesirable, alternative arrangements must be made in accordance with the purposes of the surrendered regulations and practices and with the desires and aspirations of the Trade Union movement. It would not be in keeping with the pledges which have been given to substitute new arrangements . . . for other ends than those which Trade Union practices and rules had in view, e.g. industrial peace or increased productivity.

This was the very center of the dilemma: restrictive practices versus productivity.

Greenwood did not have to be told that the world outside labor was clear on the priorities; it must be productivity and output first, to obtain competitive advantage in the post-armistice trade war both as a good and as a means toward survival and reform. He felt sure, however, that reconstruction planners had to be told that labor exactly reversed these priorities. Labor would be in no mood to abandon prewar restrictive practices simply because they were restrictive. And Greenwood said the unwelcome words that Whitehall needed to hear: A general restoration of the framework of old rules was possible and the government's responsibility could not be evaded. "In the main the pledges have been given by the Government and employers have been required to adopt them. The Unions are therefore entitled to hold the Government primarily responsible for their fulfilment."[30] Government must take the first step.

But the interlude passed. The War Cabinet approved the Whitley committee's first report on 7 June 1917 and directed the Minister of Labour to circulate it to unions and to employers' associations. It was

> sent out by the Ministry to 146 Trade Unions, 37 Trade Union Federations and 107 Employers' Associations and Federations; also to the Parliamentary Committee of the Trades Union Congress, the General Federation of Trade Unions and the Federation of British Industries. Of the replies received, none directly opposed the Whitley Scheme; 86 stated conditions which they considered essential . . . and 5 expressed opinions that the Scheme was not applicable to their respective industries.

30. "Restoration of Trade Union Rules," F. 617, Box 40.

In October the government adopted the policy and entrusted to the Ministry of Labour the establishment of such councils in the industries of Britain.[31] From that moment, the official version of Reconstruction was identified fatefully with the cause of Whitleyism.

Fresh Starts and New Plans

"We shall be marooned . . . by an enraged Whitehall," Mrs. Webb forecast; but the committee careened on. In the last fortnight of its organized life, new committees and completed reports heaped up. Under Lord Haldane a new "Machinery of Government Committee" braced itself to consider the whole structure of central administration.[32] Montagu called for an American-Allied conference on economic policy, adding the disconcerting thought that the dawning prospect of total Allied triumph rendered obsolete the assumptions that underlay all extant studies of trade.[33] Further statistics came in, underlining an urgent shipping problem.[34] Plans for housing and for local-government reforms took clearer shape.

A vast new memorandum on unemployment, by Rowntree and C. Delisle Burns, added new points to the growing consensus on the topic. Going beyond the usual warnings about dislocations and shortages, it forecast for the first time that immediate postwar enterprise might indeed be artificially and dangerously stimulated, rather than the reverse, by the very fact of shortages. It stressed the need for a "watchdog committee" to gather data and to keep absorption of labor steadily before the government as a major goal of policy. Schemes of work, it emphasized, must be fully prepared in advance, so that they might be utilized at once; but a survey of present plans and data revealed inadequacies and unreadiness throughout.

> No time should be lost in preparing plans for the 300,000 workmen's cottages which are immediately required. These plans should be brought to such a state of completion that work upon them could be commenced the first day that labour is available.[35]

31. John Barton Seymour, *The Whitley Council Scheme* (London: P. S. King, 1932), pp. 16–17. For cabinet discussion see WC 157, 7 June 1917, and WC 165, 19 June 1917, in Cab. 23/3, and WC 247, 9 October 1917, Cab. 23/4.
32. Webb, *Diaries*, p. 91.
33. "Post-War Commercial Policy," Doc. 121, Box 40, identified as Montagu's by a 16 July 1917 letter from Beatrice Webb to Thomas Jones (in Jones Diary).
34. Letter from Alfred Booth to Lord Balfour of Burleigh, 6 July 1917, Doc. 120 in Box 40.
35. F. 11498, Box 39.

Convinced that the Reconstruction Committee—far from "a satisfactory creation"—would not survive the summer, Mrs. Webb nevertheless began outlining a program of work for the autumn. She confided to Thomas Jones the tasks that weighed on her: a commercial policy that would be an alternative to the "litter of reactionary reports" from the Balfour of Burleigh committee; decisions on emergency powers to be retained; problems of finance and taxation.

> We are deciding on great expansions in housing, education, health. How is this expenditure, this huge war debt, to be met? If we leave it to the Treasury no expenditure will be provided for except the interest on the War Debt.[36]

Abruptly, on 18 July, the end came—"the last meeting of the autonomous Reconstruction Committee with Montagu in the Chair."

Mrs. Webb summarized the morning's newspapers:

> Montagu has been appointed Secretary for India; Winston Churchill, Minister of Munitions, and Addison (who failed at Munitions) Minister of Reconstruction. . . . A Minister of Reconstruction clearly means that the Reconstruction Committee either ceases to exist or becomes a mere advisory Committee or panel of advisers to the Minister.

Her comments ascribed the change to defects of the committee as a structure ("As I predicted, the machine was too rickety to survive") and, implicitly, to faults of its staff. She judged Montagu "without capacity for work . . . wholly inexperienced in committee work." She declared Nash "woolly-headed, easily frightened off any decisive step . . . suspicious and secretive"; the members of the secretariat were "preachers of ideals rather than practical administrators." Weeks before she had concluded that

> what is needed is a powerful brain as Minister of Reconstruction with a first-rate staff of civil servants and an advisory committee of picked amateurs to start ideas and represent the ministers on Sub-Committees. . . . The essential requirement is one big brain at the top. Sidney and I think the best man available is Winston Churchill.[37]

36. Webb, *Diaries*, pp. 84, 88, 91; letters of 1 July and 16 July 1917 to Thomas Jones, in Jones Diary.

37. Webb, *Diaries*, pp. 59, 84–91, and letters of Beatrice Webb to Thomas Jones, March through July 1917, in Jones Diary. Her comment of 3 June—"The office-holders have a contempt for the Committee and the Committee have a contempt for the officers" —mirrors her attitude from the time of the first meeting, if not earlier.

Valuable as commentary, her remarks fail to explain the events adequately. They fit too well with original bias; they sort too ill with the committee's record of sustained and energetic work; they tell nothing about the creation of a ministry. This question, which requires a larger context, will be approached in chapter 5.

The contentious and combative tone of Mrs. Webb's remarks aside, they are nevertheless an authentic element in any final assessment of the Lloyd George Reconstruction Committee. The members were an aggressive lot, proud of their talents, sure that they were distinctive. The potentially worst results of their arrogance, fortunately, did not occur. They did not bring reconstruction to shipwreck upon the shoals of Whitehall rivalries; they did not sacrifice the momentum and insights gained under Asquith. It was their style, of course, to disparage what had gone before, but in reality they built upon the housing studies that Nash had promoted. They took over, directly, the project of land-acquisition reform from Acland's committee; they gave their full endorsement on Whitleyism, shipping, and coal—where the Asquith committees had set the line. They carried forward the work of their predecessors—a service to reconstruction—but in a much humbler role than the pathfinding role they coveted.

Was another and greater historic function designed for this committee? Was it not this group, and it alone in the whole series from Asquith through Addison, that might have challenged official reconstruction to transcend its own limits? Specifically, was it not this committee, with its Beatrice Webb and its Fabians, that might have effected the changed attitude in labor and the *modus vivendi* with the unions that could have saved reconstruction? The most that Asquithian or conventional Liberalism might attain through its own forces and dreams was hinted by the trend line of 1916, but that trend line would never have satisfied labor. Nothing, perhaps, could have induced labor to cast its lot with the government. But was not every effort at accommodation and understanding justified, to maximize the chance that labor would at least have given official reconstruction an unimpeded try? Might not an honest effort, coupled with such measures from the labor program as patently demonstrated government faith, have at least headed off the militant strike activity that would deny reconstruction the means of success? The burden of Mrs. Webb's and Arthur Greenwood's plea was that, when the suspicions were so great and the risks of social upheaval so high, nothing conceivable should be neglected that might build a bridge of understanding and cooperation to the house of labor.

It will always be possible to say that they were right—and impossible to prove it. We can know with certainty only that numerous thinkers alleged the need for such a gesture toward labor; that in early 1917, more than before or afterwards, something was attempted; nevertheless, the committee did not fulfill that role or effect that result.

Despite all modifications, the feeling lingers that a unique chapter was being closed. The Reconstruction Committee, for all its conflicts and diversities, with Mrs. Webb ever critical and despondent, had nevertheless set to work with a will. No other papers and memoranda pulse with such dogmatic conviction. Never thereafter did talent and zeal combine to produce such scintillation. The main lines may have been laid down earlier; the most important collective research came later; but Lloyd George's Reconstruction Committee displayed the greatest creative activity and individual genius. Was it Lloyd George who called forth this spirit? After thirty-five years, his opening address lives on. Old men forget; but Seebohm Rowntree and Tom Jones and their colleagues quoted it superbly to me, unasked, when they remembered little else. It may also be that early 1917 was a moment like no other, and that the moment called the spirit forth. It seems especially fitting to insert at this point the most extraordinary document—a remarkable essay in which J. L Hammond compared the situations in Great Britain after two great wars.

> The Peace of 1815 was followed by one of the darkest chapters in British history. . . . During the present war we have escaped some of the worst evils of the great war with France; for the power of Trade Unionism has prevented a corresponding fall in the workmen's standard of life. . . . On the other hand, many of the problems that arose with the return to peace a century ago present themselves in greater or lesser degree to our Government. . . .
>
> . . . The Reconstruction Committee aims at something much more ambitious than the mere smoothing of the path of transition. The war has thrown all the belligerent people on to their resources and every nation has to consider its future in a new and more serious spirit. The war has put a new value on life and given a new clue to the sources of power. To the Reconstruction Committee is assigned the duty of finding what measures promise to develop the strength and vitality of the nation and to arrest the waste of our strength. Education is obviously of vital significance in this connection. We have learnt in the most terrible of schools that it is a crime to let our youth grow up in relative ignorance and neglect, when

time, trouble and money would give us a well-educated and healthy nation. And this subject is closely related to such topics as housing, public health and Local Government. We have learnt again that Trade Unions, supposed by the men who made peace in 1815, to be a curse of workmen and mischief in the State are in truth an indispensable source and guarantee of strength. It is no exaggeration to say that the country should not have carried on this war if the Trade Unions had had less power or if they had withheld their active co-operation. Industry which seemed to our ancestors to be essentially suitable to irresponsible autocracy seems to our generation to be the joint interest of all who are employed in it. No question is more important than that of the future relations of Capital and Labour; for unless this new sense of a common responsibility can be given expression, a very vigorous part of the population lives under a constant feeling of restraint and repression, and industry itself is at less than half power. The Committee on Capital and Labour is therefore engaged in exploring the whole subject of the form and medium in which Capital and Labour can live and work together on terms of mutual respect and confidence. Agriculture, again, is engaging the attention of a Committee which recognises that the problem is much more than a question of prices and wages and that the task before the country is nothing less than the reconstruction of village society as a free and living community.

There is one important element of hope in the prospect. We have spoken of the revolution in the outlook of the age. The generation of 1815 lived under the shadow of the iron laws by which economists sought to explain the phenomena of their changing world. It was believed that industry followed its own laws and that men and women had to conform to them. This war has taught us that there is no such word as impossible and that resolution and imagination can surmount difficulties that were thought insuperable. The note of 1815 was a note of despair; the note of 1917 is a note of hope.[38]

---

38. "Reconstruction," unnumbered, undated, unsigned document in Box 40. For the same idea, and for citation of English works expressing it, see Charlotte Leubuscher, *Liberalismus und Protektionismus in der englischen Wirtschaftspolitik seit dem Kriege* (Jena: Gustav Fischer, 1927), pp. 1–2.

4

A New Impulse to Housing Plans

From its beginning to its dissolution, the second Reconstruction Committee set its heart on devising a huge housing program for the working classes. Before the first panel had even been appointed, a housing scheme was being prepared—Montagu, not wasting a moment, had set Rowntree to work. Plans for housing called forth the committee's best energies. Every month—sometimes every week—a new proposal or working paper appeared, and each was discussed with quarrelsome candor.

It was all typical of this most busy and disputatious committee, and what happened at the first meeting was "most typical" of all. Glancing over official estimates of housing needs, the committee promptly found them all "far too low." This was exactly what the nation's most advanced housing reformers were saying, and the panel took their side. Also, the major housing societies were warning of serious discontent if the existing court powers for rent control were allowed to lapse. The panel again concurred. For them, as for the reformers and crusaders outside Whitehall, it followed that

> a maximum effort must therefore be put into building which in the circumstances . . . private enterprise cannot be expected to supply. . . . Communal action will be required. . . . The question of standard cannot be neglected. The lowest standard which decency requires is three bedrooms and two living rooms for an average family. . . . It is the duty of the State, in the emergency which will arise at the end of the War, to make adequate provision to supply the deficiency of houses of a decent standard.

The panel called for further studies of land acquisition and building materials and the effect of local bylaws, an adumbration of the reports of the Leslie Scott, Carmichael, and Tudor Walters committees at the end of the war.[1]

It was neither accidental nor irrelevant that Lord Salisbury, past president of the Garden Cities and Town Planning Association, was a panel member. His group met repeatedly in early 1917 to draft housing proposals specifically for the Reconstruction Committee. Vaughan Nash's invitation was beginning to produce results.[2]

The panel's estimate of total needs far exceeded the Local Government Board's view; most important, it declared that the state should "supply the deficiency of houses." Compare this with the Board's quavering hope that "a proportion at all events of the necessary houses" be built—or that "the position . . . not go from bad to worse"! In the second Reconstruction Committee, discussions began on a higher plane.

There is no substitute for detailed appreciation of the documents, but a glance ahead is useful to show the larger outline of events. From the first panel meeting, Panel 4 studied data and chose questions for study. Rowntree's huge and detailed memorandum came before the panel on 8 May. Lord Salisbury circulated a favorable analysis, and this "Salisbury commentary" was adopted by the panel on 15 May. At once the full Reconstruction Committee voted to consider the matter, but new items interposed. Leslie Scott criticized both of the foregoing memoranda, and Lord Rhondda sent the cabinet a memorandum from the Local Government Board. Discussion continued within the panel, to and beyond the official dissolution of the Reconstruction Committee. Meanwhile, a recommendation in the name of the panel had gone to the Local Government Board.

Estimates and Solutions: The Rowntree Memorandum

Rowntree began with the statistics of housing needs.[3] He was right; quantity was of the first importance. As men grasped this fact they would see the urgency of new methods and of state action. Official statements far underestimated the housing shortage, said Rowntree, who spoke of the wartime shortage alone, not the larger and older problem of slums. The number of houses needed for the working class within twelve months after the war, just in England and Wales, was not 120,000, as the Local Government Board said, but 300,000. And even this quantity would

1. "Record of First Meeting," Panel 4, 19 April 1917, Box 40.
2. Garden Cities and Town Planning Association, "Minute Book Three," pp. 46, 48, 54, 63, 81. Identical proposals were being shaped for presentation to the Local Government Board; see especially *ibid.*, p. 93.
3. Doc. No. 89, Box 40.

merely make up for average deterioration and wartime interruptions. "A building programme, unprecedented in scale, must be carried out within the first year or two after the close of the War, before we can even restore the status quo *ante bellum.*"[4]

Rowntree also appealed to the new interest in better farming. "The exigencies of war have reminded us how grievously we have neglected the development of the country-side, and it is of the utmost importance to atone for our neglect. . . . The great increase in . . . land under the plough will necessarily involve . . . material increase in the agricultural population." Referring to the deep fears of unemployment, Rowntree said that "industrial dislocation . . . must inevitably follow the cessation of war. . . . With some forethought it will be perfectly possible so to organise the building of workmen's cottages that work can be begun the moment the workers are available." Shrewdly, he added that a large saving in unemployed benefits would be realized, tending to offset the cost (probably £26,000,000) of housing subsidies.

State aid must be invoked. "The Government must ease the financial situation [because] the cost of building at present is abnormally high, and . . . will still be high at the end of the War. Until it becomes normal . . . no appreciable number . . . will be built unless action is taken by the Government." But the form of aid was not easy to determine. Rowntree decided against state lending at a loss (i.e., below the market rate); the aid must take a form that would cease when the abnormally high building costs ceased. The best form would be "a loan at the market rate plus a capital grant." Conceivably, there were three recipients: the local authorities, the Public Utility Societies (private collective ventures that were statutorily limited in profits), and the private builders. Rowntree ruled out the last, on technical and political grounds,[5] thus putting an even greater burden on government to fill the need; and discounted the role of the Public Utility Societies.

It followed that housing must be provided "by local authorities or by the State direct."

4. Rowntree cited the 1912 Land Enquiry Committee estimate that 3,139,472 persons in England and Wales were living in overcrowded conditions. To reach the total of 300,000 houses, he allowed 175,000 to make up for interruptions to normal annual building as a result of the war, 75,000 more for houses that would normally be built in the first postwar year, and 50,000 houses for land settlement for soldiers.

5. Safeguarding the Exchequer would be difficult, for one thing. For another, a government loan would be impracticable. And the lack of a loan would prove a crucial deterrent because the private builder, working on a very narrow margin of capital, must sell his houses immediately.

But by which? Ideologists here chose sides, and passionately. But Rowntree's choice was not perfectly clear. There was "a good deal to be said for direct State action in securing the erection of houses," and ultimately his memorandum did not exclude this possibility, but he distinguished "the erection of the houses" from "their ultimate ownership." The latter involved supervision and management, for which local authorities could hire experts within their areas without the "costly and complicated machinery" the central government would need. Therefore, "whatever action may be taken in regard to the building of the houses, it is not desirable that the State should continue to own them if such a course can be avoided." The state would aid; the local authority would own.

Such a partnership in responsibility would pose knotty problems, the most difficult being the problem of incentive: the state would be asking local authorities "to undertake work which in the past they have been very reluctant to do." Could financial assistance be devised that would offer adequate inducements? Under existing law, local authorities could "obtain the whole of the capital required . . . from the Public Works Loan Commissioners at the lowest rate sanctioned by the Treasury Minute in force at the period," to be repaid in sixty years for houses and in eighty years for land. As far as the "loan of capital" was concerned, this would have to suffice. There remained the grant-in-aid. On it depended the active cooperation of the local authorities—and thus the success of the emergency housing program itself. The grant-in-aid, the critical element, must provide the inducement by safeguarding local authorities against loss caused by building when costs were abnormally high. Rowntree put the definition of such loss into a formula: "The difference between the cost of building during the period under consideration, *and its future normal cost.*"

But all this involved a leap into the dark. The future normal cost, and thus the loss, could not be forecast precisely; hence state aid could not be set at a precise figure in advance. Hence "block" grants were out of the question; they would inevitably appear insufficient to timid local authorities and unsafe to the Treasury.[6] Nor was this all. It was certain that, eventually, building costs would fall below the immediate postwar level of costs, bringing down—along with the burden of expense—the revenue from rents for houses of every type, the old and the new, the cheap and the dear. Certainty and uncertainty, combined, would deter

6. Partly sharing Treasury views in this matter, Rowntree warned that "too liberal a grant"—more than covering the temporary inflation of building costs—would make local authorities reluctant to do without a permanent state subsidy.

local authorities from building, until this normal level had been reached.

The "Rowntree solution" for all this was a threefold plan: (1) the government should arrange with local authorities for the houses to be built *immediately* at the close of the war, by those local authorities; (2) houses would be valued by an impartial valuer in three years' time, when presumably prices would have reached their normal postwar level; (3) then the government would undertake to refund to the local authorities, as a grant-in-aid, the difference between the actual cost of the houses and the estimated cost at the time that the valuation was made. As safeguards, Rowntree spelled out two provisos, one mandatory and the other permissive. First, where local authorities constructed the houses, the government must approve the plans and specifications as well as the contract prices; second, either the state itself might do the actual work of construction, or alternatively the local authorities themselves could build the houses. In the latter case, an immediate partial grant might be wise.[7]

The basic outline of a complete proposal was ready. But over one question—the *basis* for eventual valuation, three years after construction —Rowntree paused. The choice was between "estimated cost of building" at valuation time and "rents receivable." Technical but not at all trivial, the choice concerned that future moment toward which all eyes would in fact be turning after the dawn of peace: the critical moment when reciprocal obligations of the Treasury and a local authority would be totted up. Only then would it become perfectly clear whether a local authority had broken even or incurred a heavy loss. Anticipations of this result would be the decisive factor in determining whether housing was undertaken at all. Rowntree chose "estimated cost." His logic suggests a Liberal's reluctance to disturb normal economic patterns. Only through this choice could a precedent be avoided for the permanent subsidy of uneconomical housing.[8]

7. If the state built, the local authority would simply take over the houses three years later at the determined value; this would be speedier. If local authorities built, borrowing all the capital from the state, at "valuation time," three years later, they would get the difference between (*a*) the valuation of comparable houses at that moment on a cost basis and (*b*) the actual cost of the houses they had built—along with the interest and sinking fund they had paid on that difference.

8. Typically, rents rose slowly, Rowntree noted: by valuation time they probably would not have reached a level at which they represented a commercial or economic return on the value of the postwar houses. But the existing principle was the principle of the "commercial return." Unless the principle of state subsidy were adopted, it was "essential" that rents receivable represent a commercial return on the cost. If, in the nature of the case, rents could not represent such a return, the "rents" basis for valuation was not appropriate. Rowntree forecast that "if . . . the grant in aid were such as to enable houses to be let without loss to the local authorities at a figure lower than was

Rowntree had devised his proposals with many goals and values in mind, which one can see between the lines: the humanitarianism that dictated that housing should begin at once; the concern for economy that controlled his choice of the valuation basis; and the lingering respect for localism. Together, they made a plan that was both new and controversial. Less debatable were four other points. (1) Probable and serious shortages of timber, bricks, and cement showed that "the control of the building trade . . . must be continued after the War" lest materials be used for nonessential building. (2) Demobilization of building-trade workers must be rapid. (3) Tight control of some building materials by manufacturers' combinations would cause real difficulties. (4) For prompt building it was "absolutely essential that the necessary land should be secured in advance" and prompt possession arranged (the Local Government Board should aid here by surveying local needs and readiness, and Parliament might have to help by facilitating the prompt acquisition of land).

Rowntree could not have known it, but he was sketching the agenda for the Ministry of Health of 1919. Anticipating what Addison would later do as Minister of Health, Rowntree urged that the Local Government Board work with a committee of building experts to devise economies. Rowntree reckoned that, at £300 per house (40 per cent above prewar levels), 300,000 cottages would cost £90,000,000. The state would probably pay £26,000,000 in grants.

The Board should use questionnaires (Rowntree supplied an elaborate one) to find the areas of greatest need. It should see that "all preliminary steps . . . were taken with the least possible delay." And

> if any local authorities declared themselves unwilling . . . to build
> . . . or to take over on an agreed date houses to be erected by the
> Government, then it would probably be necessary for the Government to build and continue to own the houses; but . . . such a step
> is to be deprecated if it can possibly be avoided.

As late as the armistice, the imperatives Rowntree had identified so masterfully had not been fulfilled. Not until December 1918 were the

---

justified by the cost of building at the time" (as would be true if the "current rents" basis were allowed), "then local authorities would quite reasonably refuse to continue building unless they received a subsidy. This . . . would establish an entirely new principle, namely, that if local authorities built, even at times when building costs were normal, they could look to the State to make good any loss which such building might involve."

basic financial terms decided. But no blame for this appalling delay attached to the second Reconstruction Committee. It had leaped to perform its duty.

Lord Salisbury Endorses

Lord Salisbury backed Rowntree with vigor.[9] The goal was 300,000 houses, and, even at a loss, houses *must* be built; yes, local authorities must be used. The government, however, should "retain requisite powers to deal with recalcitrant authorities and undertake the building of houses." This went beyond Rowntree; and Salisbury demanded immediate action on the questionnaire, on the purchase of land options, on new land laws, the investigation of timber supplies, and extension of rent control.

The Rowntree and Salisbury papers were basic; the contributions of the committee to housing progress stem chiefly from them. Provisionally, they were adopted in mid-May. Briefly, however, Leslie Scott challenged them in June. With the enthusiasm for village revival that marked him through the interwar years he called for much more rural housing.[10] Lord Salisbury, who jumped into this debate with a new memorandum, once again championed compulsion of local authorities, which Rowntree had shunned. But all three men were of one mind on fundamentals.[11]

Lord Rhondda also agreed, and this fact was most encouraging to the Reconstruction Committee. Rhondda and four other men from the Board met with Salisbury, Montagu, Rowntree, and Nash in May. Rhondda pronounced Rowntree's idea of state building and financing a "very bold suggestion" and agreed that "after all this was the day for bold steps." The goal of 300,000 houses seems to have been accepted by the

9. R.C. Doc. 83, Box 40.

10. For years Scott (later Lord Scott) headed the Council for the Preservation of Rural England. His ardor, fertility with new schemes, and sense of a new opportunity combined with a new duty pervade his memorandum of 19 June 1917 (in Box 40). Although in principle favorable to an "economic rent" basis, Scott argued that, with prewar rural cottages letting for one or two shillings a week, the transition to economic rents must be slow.

Like current authorities, Scott recommended a wholly new and democratic kind of Public Utility Society that would be broadly responsible for local building. Such societies, with tenant representation, would revitalize the countryside, he thought. He cited Cd. 8277, "The Minority Report of the Departmental Committee on the Employment of Soldiers and Sailors on the Land"—as elaborated by Ernest Betham, Secretary for the Housing Organisation Society, in the *Contemporary Review* (June 1917).

11. Salisbury counseled against Scott's "Public Utility Societies"; now was no time for experimental innovations. See memorandum of 26 June 1917 by Lord Salisbury, in Box 40.

Board. This looked very much like a victory; unquestionably, it was a splendid augury.[12]

Thanks to the second Reconstruction Committee, the momentum that had been gained in 1916 was not lost. Thanks also to the committee, the level of debate was no longer the same. Rowntree and his colleagues had brought about not simply a rescue but a transformation. The Rowntree memorandum left nothing out; henceforth discussion on housing would revolve around a *complete* proposal. Furthermore, the plane of effort had been lifted: the target of 300,000 houses, now formally endorsed, meant that old goals had been disapproved. It meant, significantly, that the voice of unofficial campaigners had now become a voice *within* the circles of government.

A basic service of careful thinking had been completed. By his example Rowntree had shown that sound housing policies must take account of much more than housing alone. Questions of cost led to questions of rent, which in turn led to such topics as wage policy and the revival of agriculture. Questions of supply, licensing, and controls could not be escaped, and they in turn raised questions of governmental structure and operation.

Rowntree and his colleagues, moreover, had helped rout the last spokesmen for "normalcy." Whatever their other differences, the members of his panel concurred in rejecting any hopes or plans based on "business as usual."

The Housing Panel, born within the second Reconstruction Committee, was to live on after its parent had died. Panel members would meet again to battle, and sometimes to plead, with the Local Government Board, even into 1918. Meanwhile, the Reconstruction Committee, officially superseded by the Ministry of Reconstruction in July 1917 and gradually merged with the Ministry thereafter as far as personnel was concerned, ceased to function as a unit.

The committee had shown both the faults and the virtues that went with its form. It was admirably suited to play the gadfly, to roam free (as a group of departmental representatives could not do), to challenge fixed ways and to propose new goals (as befits an assemblage of amateurs). The new targets for housing were a measure of its success on these lines. It

12. See minutes of "Conference on Housing at the L.G.B., May 16th, 1917," in Box 37. For the Local Government Board, Hayes Fisher, H. Munro, A. V. Symonds, and J. A. E. Dickinson accompanied Lord Rhondda. Transmittal of other Reconstruction Committee papers is mentioned in a letter by Hayes Fisher (successor to Rhondda at the Local Government Board) to Christopher Addison on 13 October 1917 (F. 1980, Box 30, Part 1).

lacked two virtues of the Asquith committee: direct rapport with the departments and the full authority or backing of the Prime Minister. As items on the reconstruction agenda multiplied, and as each project moved from its first draft to complete formulation, the need for these cardinal and complementary virtues would become overwhelming. It would be one of the first tasks of the incoming Ministry to meet this need.

5

Enter the Minister of Reconstruction:
July–December 1917

The Ministry of Reconstruction, with Christopher Addison at its head, was established only after many days of hot debate. In Parliament, the New Ministries Bill was at once challenged by members who disliked government interference in any form.

> What the people of this country want is not a Ministry of Reconstruction, but a Ministry of Resurrection. The people of this country want the chance to live again after being buried beneath the mass of Regulations that have been imposed upon them since this War broke out.[1]

Others denounced the broad mandate which the bill would give the minister. Such a "roving commission" was an impossibility, said a few; and many critics declared it undesirable.

Lord Salisbury tried to bar the new minister from "going into vast after-war problems which do not arise immediately out of the war." W. A. S. Hewins almost succeeded in passing a resolution that would have confined the ministry sharply.[2] A new *ministry* was indefensible, many argued; the Prime Minister should handle these tasks directly. This would simply prove to be a "Ministry for overlapping."[3] Economy was being ignored. The integrity of Parliament was more and more threatened. Rare indeed was the member who objected that the ministry

---

1. *P.D.(C.)*, vol. 96, c. 2465; see also *ibid.*, c. 1617–19, 1636–38, 1664, and 2339–40.
2. For Hewin's action, partly based on his protectionist views, see *ibid.*, c. 1655–58, 1667–70, and 2367–2414, and his *Apologia of an Imperialist* (London: Constable, 1929), 2: 152–58. For Lord Salisbury's action, see *P.D.(L.)*, vol. 26, c. 244–53 and 356–58. For general criticism, see *ibid.*, c. 475–80, and *P.D.(C.)*, vol. 96, c. 2354–57, 2365–66, 2392, 2395, and 2407–8.
3. *P.D.(C.)*, vol. 96, c. 1613, 1640, 2229–31, 2347, 2374–75, 2378, and 2438–39.

would not prove strong enough; instead, the popular cry was that the country was "crawling with Government officials."[4]

All these were, in one form or another, generalities; but the most frequent objections were soundly circumstantial and painfully to the point.

> This office would not have been established at the present time but for . . . political expediency. It became necessary to effect certain changes in the Ministry of Munitions and also to increase the debating power of the front Ministerial Bench. . . . The Prime Minister therefore resolved to call in the imaginative and brilliant . . . Mr. Churchill . . . to repair the broken fortunes of the Ministry . . . The question arose as to what should be done with . . . the Member for Hoxton (Dr. Addison) . . . As Minister of Munitions, he had been well-intentioned but rather weak. He did not understand the labour question. . . . The mishandling of labour policy on the part of the Ministry of Munitions was the primary cause of a good deal of labour unrest. . . . The Prime Minister was determined not to drop his Hoxton pilot. He owed many obligations to the right hon. Gentleman, who had been faithful among the faithless and who, in the far-off pre-war days of the Insurance Act, was almost the only doctor in the country who had a good word to say for that measure. How then to scrap him and reward him at the same time ? . . . Since the Prime Minister had already created every possible Ministry that could by any stretch of imagination be supposed to be associated with the . . . War, the one thing to do was to create a further Ministry to deal with problems that would arise when the War was over.[5]

Addison, "a very amiable Minister of very average ability," was being accommodated; it was all "a Bill for the reconstruction of the Ministry."[6]

4. W. C. Anderson, a Labour Party spokesman, was alone in taking the view that "gigantic changes must now come in any case. . . . What is wanted least of all . . . is superficial window-dressing, or lulling the mind of the country into a sense of false security by persuading it that something is being done, whereas the Ministry set up under this Bill may really mean little and accomplish less." See *ibid.*, c. 1645–46. For more typical views, see *ibid.*, c. 1613–17, 1622, 1637, 1641, 1651–56, 1659–63, 1677, 2162–70, 2173–74, 2361–65, 2395–98, 2418–20, 2424, and 2445–59, and *P.D.(L.)*, vol. 26, c. 242–46, 247–48, 253–55, and 476–77.

5. *Ibid.*, c. 1641–42, speech of W. C. Anderson; see also c. 1682 for Addison's being "utterly out of touch with labour." See *P.D.(C.)*, vol. 97, c. 1442: "This Bill was brought in in order that one Member might get a post in the new Government."

6. The quotation is from W. C. Anderson; see *P.D.(C.)*, vol. 96, c. 1641–42. See also *ibid.*, c. 1645, 1649–50, 1666, 1668, 1682, 2341, 2393, and 2402; *ibid.*, vol. 97, c. 1442; and *P.D.(L.)*, vol. 26, c. 248.

The government's defense of the bill was partly conciliatory. The Ministry would not be large, and would have only advisory, not executive, powers, but it would make an important contribution by coordinating work now scattered among the different departments.[7] This was the great need, and spokesmen for the bill lauded Addison as a man with special fitness for the task.[8] A ministry, they added, would have the stature commensurate with the tremendous field of reconstruction; and it would be responsible to Parliament, as a committee would not.[9]

The debate was bitter. Opposition votes actually defeated the government at one point. Concessions had to be made, limiting the duration of the new office.[10] It was an inauspicious beginning. "The debates in the House," wrote Michael Heseltine months later, "impressed me . . . with the desirability of publishing Reports wherever possible."[11] Later, and more than once, the Minister seemed impelled to caution by memories of that hypercritical House of Commons.

Was a ministry necessary? Why not carry on reconstruction through committee work? And why appoint Addison? Was the new ministry, in fact, a by-product or an afterthought in a change dictated by concern for the situation at Munitions? Up and down Whitehall, men echoed the charges of members of Parliament.

The new ministry, said one school of thought, was window-dressing; the new minister, Christopher Addison, was being saved from disgrace and rewarded for faithfulness. Thus, often explicitly, runs the answer given me by Sir Horace Wilson, E. H. E. Havelock, Sir George Upcott, Sir Percy Barter, and Sir Thomas Gardiner; thus said Seebohm Rowntree. The memoirs of Beatrice Webb, like the contemporary articles in the *New Statesman*, are in keeping with this view. In detail, this answer implies that (*a*) a ministry was not needed or desirable and committees were quite adequate; (*b*) neither zeal for reconstruction nor concern for efficiency dictated the choice of minister; and (*c*) Addison was not a good administrator. Sir Percy Barter, Addison's Private Secretary in three ministries, so declared; Sir Thomas Gardiner remembered that, to some of the staff,

7. *P.D.(C.)*, vol. 96, c. 1608–9, 1648, 1673–75, 2357–58, 2366–67, 2385–90, and 2423; *P.D.(L.)*, vol. 26, c. 257–58, 477–80.

8. *P.D.(C.)*, vol. 96, c. 1766.

9. *Ibid.*, c. 1607–9, 1623–26, 1628–29, 1647–48, 1658, 1671, 2176, and 2386–87; and *P.D.(L.)*, vol. 26, c. 249, 251, and 257. See also F. 1127, Box 40.

10. See Hewins, *Apologia*, 2: 157–59; *P.D.(C.)*, vol. 96, c. 2413–14, 2428–29, 2483–86, 2513, and *P.D.(L.)*, vol. 26, c. 363–64 and 476.

11. F. 1500, Box 40.

Addison was "the Moke" (from the Spanish for "donkey"); Morant wrote critically of Addison's methods.[12] For E. H. E. Havelock and Sir George Upcott the judgment on Addison broadened into a judgment on the unorthodox techniques of Lloyd George, which they compared very unfavorably with those of Asquith and Vaughan Nash. Inclined to consider the ministry a failure, Havelock and Upcott ascribed the failure partly to methods that were "typically L.G.," as well as to Addison's clumsy relations with other departments. Rowntree recalled unhappy experiences at the Ministry of Munitions when Addison had been in charge. His successor, Winston Churchill, reported spending his first weeks at Munitions in revising the central administration so that he was freed from petty detail.[13]

The most circumstantial charge, however, is that Addison had come to disgrace when the Amalgamated Society of Engineers struck on 5 May 1917 against the management of Munitions, and that only Lloyd George's intervention saved the day. The causes and course of this strike are not wholly clear and remain in debate.[14] Labor unrest, already high, increased when the Munitions of War Act was amended to allow non-union personnel to go into ordinary commercial work, allegedly in conflict with pledges made to the trade unions. Exemptions from military service, hitherto based on an agreed "Trade Card" scheme, had been greatly narrowed without the support of the A.S.E. Their delegates, meeting in London on 5 May, voted to strike. The strike, which lasted from 5 May to 19 May, did enormous damage to the reputation of Addison and his ministry. True, he had been in continuous negotiations from 2 May, and the delegates had telegraphed their members by the end of 5 May that "there should be no stoppage of work" in view of the adequate arrangements, which had been agreed upon. The A.S.E. executive committee repudiated the strike; Addison offered to negotiate, and did so until full agreement was reached.[15] It was the arrest of some strikers, however, and the searing attacks on Addison and the government in the House of Commons that caught the public eye. And the press, blaming the strike on Addison, in effect credited the Prime Minister with bringing about the

12. These interviews occurred in 1953. For a negative comment on Addison by Lord Curzon, see Lord Beaverbrook, *Men and Power 1917–1918* (London: Hutchinson, 1956), p. 131. For Sir Robert Morant's critical view, see note 32 to chapter 15 below.

13. Winston Churchill, *The World Crisis, 1916–1918* (New York: Scribner's, 1927), 2: 6–7.

14. *History of the Ministry of Munitions* (London: H. M. Stationery Office, 1922), 6, Part 1: 64–120.

15. See Addison, *Diary*, 2: 368–75, 378–83, and *P.D.(C.)*, vol. 98, c. 1068–69.

settlement. It is small wonder that Mrs. Webb spoke of "Addison, who failed at Munitions."[16]

But was Addison at fault in the A.S.E. strike? Other data and statements suggest he was not. Within a week of the settlement Lloyd George, reporting personally to the House of Commons, gave Addison full credit for initiating the negotiations and carrying them to a successful conclusion. It is a story full of ironies (the original communiqué, hinting at failure by Addison, apparently had come from Downing Street), but the exoneration was complete.[17] Nevertheless, the refutation did not catch up with the charges. It therefore is extremely probable that Addison was transferred not for failure but for the reputation of failure. Nor does the exoneration refute the general charges of mismanagement; but against them there is other evidence. Addison's policy on the trade-card scheme—a carefully reasoned policy, backed by the cabinet—was not abandoned by Churchill. And Churchill was to be castigated by the *New Statesman*, just as Addison had been.[18]

To refute part of a hypothesis, however, or to expose it as unproved is not to establish the truth of the official rationale, nor of the one that Addison implicitly offers: He and the ministry were chosen on merit, and the Prime Minister was chiefly concerned with making real progress on reconstruction policy. The "true explanation," admittedly resting on inconclusive proof, must begin with the Ministry of Munitions, not with the Ministry of Reconstruction.

Lloyd George was utterly occupied with the present. The war effort came before all else, and the output of munitions was at the heart of this effort. Addison had to be eased out of the Ministry of Munitions once the strike erupted. Public opinion and bad relations with labor were reasons

16. See *ibid.*, c. 1390–98, 1771–73, and 1876–1920. For a biographical statement on this critic, W. C. Anderson, see *New Statesman*, 12 (1 March 1919): 459. See Webb, *Diaries*, pp. 89, 91, and Addison, *Diary*, 2: 376–84. For details of the A.S.E. strike, see G. D. H. Cole, *Trade Unionism and Munitions* (Oxford: Clarendon Press, 1923), pp. 144–51.

17. *P.D.(C.)*, vol. 93, c. 2025–26, quoted also in Addison, *Politics*, 1: 150. The entire story is told by Addison in *ibid.* (2: 127–59) and in *Diary* (2: 350–88). Addison thought that someone close to Lloyd George had altered the correct notice on the strike settlement to bolster Lloyd George's prestige, regardless of the harm done Addison. "Sardonyx" expressed exactly the same view in the *New Statesman* (10 [13 October 1917]: 34–35): Lloyd George's complete and thorough clarification, vindicating his Minister of Munitions, was forced from him by a question in the House. Of course, Lloyd George turned on Addison in just the same way in 1921 and made him the scapegoat for housing failures. See also *History of the Ministry of Munitions*, vol. 6, Part 1.

18. Addison, *Politics*, 2: 114–44; Addison, *Diary*, 2: 342–47, 403. *The Nation* (21 [30 June 1917]: 311) praised Addison's work. For the criticisms of Churchill, see *New Statesman*, 10 (March 1918): 562–63, and 11 (April 1918): 30, 107–8, and 324–26.

enough, and only a superlative record as administrator would have out-weighed such calculations. Moreover, although Lloyd George knew the truth behind the A.S.E. strike, he had much to gain by replacing Addison. Churchill's administrative skill would be a great asset, as would his presence on the front bench. The clue to the change is that the real priorities concerned the immediate conduct of the war, not the distant prospects of postwar.

There were nevertheless positive reasons—at least of the sort that might have moved Lloyd George—for creating a ministry, and especially for choosing Addison as minister. Addison was well known to the House, and particularly well known to Lloyd George. For, at their very first meeting in 1910 after Addison entered Parliament, the latter had tartly commented to Lloyd George on a flaw in the health insurance plan; and Addison had thereupon campaigned personally to amend one feature of that plan, carrying his initiative to victory in a free vote, apparently by sheer force of professional argument. This done, he worked for the measure with all his strength; and friends of health insurance credited him with winning support of many professional physicians to the new system. He thought of himself—and of Lloyd George—as a "left-wing Radical" in those days, and his name became linked with educational reform, with the drive for a Ministry of Health, and with two significant innovations at the Ministry of Munitions: the establishment of joint committees with workers' representation, and the establishment of health reforms in factories. It was he who formed a "Reconstruction Committee" at the Ministry of Munitions in April 1917—a vital step for future planning, as will be seen. Addison had piloted a land-acquisition bill through Commons.[19] He was utterly loyal to Lloyd George. And, although to others the case for a ministry was unconvincing, to Lloyd George it may have made sense; creating new ministries was his style.

19. Addison, *Diary*, vol. 1, *passim*, and 2: 347, give some indication of Addison's involvement in prewar and wartime reforms. See also R. J. Minney, *Viscount Addison, Leader of the Lords* (London: Odhams Press, 1958), pp. 118–35, and Bentley Gilbert, *The Evolution of National Insurance in Great Britain: The Origins of the Welfare State* (London: Joseph, 1966), pp. 366, 369, 403, 430, 436. A note by either Nash or Haldane in F. 168, Box 14, regarding the chairmanship for a committee on the Ministry of Health in 1917, states that "the name on which important opinion converges is that of Dr. Addison. . . . He was a great success when Parliamentary Secretary to the Board of Education." Bonar Law spoke highly of him to W. A. S. Hewins (see Hewins, *Apologia*, 2: 153 and 156). See the favorable comment in A. J. P. Taylor, *English History, 1914–1945*, p. 148. For the Reconstruction Committee set up by Dr. Addison at Munitions, see *History of the Ministry of Munitions*, 6, Part 2: 80, 82, as well as G.T. 6041, Appendix, p. 4, in Cab. 24/67.

The personal style of the new Minister of Reconstruction—material, staid, workmanlike—showed in his choice of priorities. "The first thing to tackle at Reconstruction," Addison wrote in July, "is to secure that some provision is made for the millions of demobilised soldiers, munition workers and other war workers . . . on the Declaration of peace."[20] He had no patience with those who overlooked such obvious duties.

> Some of these people haven't begun to comprehend the things for which we must get ready in advance of demobilisation. . . . They seem to think that my job is to build fairy castles for some dim and distant future. Let us hope that people will be free to do so when this beastly business is over. On the assumption, however, that we win the war, my first job is to try to arrange that the first six or twelve months of peace, when war-making in all its branches has suddenly ceased, do not land us in a mess at home.[21]

When, therefore, he called his first committee meeting, the topic was the demobilization of civilian workers. Other minds were converging on the same topic. The idea of a single Demobilisation Committee reached the War Cabinet; Addison concurred, and the proposal was endorsed. Responsibility was fixed in the Ministry of Labour. It was on such "urgent industrial requirements" that the new minister concentrated his first efforts.[22]

But tasks, even so defined, were enormous; and other tasks would crowd in. Within a fortnight Addison was grappling with the housing question as well, although it had not figured at all among his most urgent priorities. He was fast discovering, moreover, that even within his preferred list each item had ramifications that grew and grew. "My present job . . . with every day seems to loom up as more intricate and prodigious," he confessed.

The "raw materials" question was a case in point. To make even a beginning on it, four lines of approach were called for.

1. Available stocks and future demand must be estimated. Addison bethought himself of many former colleagues at the Ministry of Munitions

---

20. Addison (*Diary*, 2: 414) records a discussion with Vaughan Nash on 20 July 1917.

21. *Ibid.*, p. 416.

22. *Ibid.*, pp. 415, 417, 424, 425. Addison accepted his appointment on 17 July, and Lloyd George sent a circular letter to the departments on 22 July that described the Minister of Reconstruction's powers and position. Utterly fatigued, Addison in effect took a vacation from 25 July through 24 August 1917 (see *ibid.*, pp. 422–23). For endorsement of the Demobilisation Committee proposal, see WC 216, 15 August 1917, Cab. 23/3.

who might help on this,[23] and on 4 September he "got together . . . the people who are concerned with the Executive control of Materials representing the War Office, the Board of Trade, War Trade Department, Ministries of Munitions and Food." Balfour of Burleigh pledged that his committee would "concentrate *pro tem* on the . . . supply of materials for home requirements." On 1 October the Central Committee on Materials Supply was established, with Clarendon Hyde as its chairman. Addison expected much from the committee and from the experts who would help it.

> Each member stands for intimate knowledge and high repute in his special branch. . . .
>
> When I was at Munitions I had a view of how the war has altered the channels of supply as well as the proportions of different supplies in our requirements, but the survey of the past weeks has shown that, between ourselves and the Allies, the dislocation of peace-time arrangements is almost universal. For all we know it may be a long time after peace is declared before control can be unloosed, and unless reasonably sufficient arrangements are made beforehand there will be ructions and complaints all over the place and much more prolonged unemployment than need be the case. We mean, if we can, to make our British arrangements for the turn-over as good as anybody's. I hope the best.[24]

2. An international, or at least inter-Ally, side must be tended to. Addison saw the need for more definite arrangements with the Allies: "The whole machine ought to be ready to work on the cessation of war."[25]

3. Planners dared not overlook "priorities"; no forecast was so optimistic as to eliminate this topic. The machinery for setting and supervising priorities already existed. Addison's colleague John Wormald, who had been apportioning materials to civilian industries through a standing Priority Committee at the Ministry of Munitions since February, now offered his help. By 10 November Wormald's group had agreed to help collect orders for postwar work, and the Ministry of Munitions' Reconstruction Committee agreed to consider adapting their system to reconstruction tasks.[26]

23. *Ibid.*, pp. 413 and 417–26. See Addison to Stanley, 6 September and 14 September 1917, in F. 1405, Box 15, Part 1.

24. *Ibid.* For the composition of the committee, see F. 5705, Box 15, Part 1.

25. Addison, *Diary*, 2: 425–28 and 455. The cabinet also asked Addison to study the economic questions related to the peace negotiations.

26. *Ibid.*, pp. 425, 429, 442–44.

4. The state, as producer and buyer on a gigantic scale, was accumulating huge war stores. Lord Salisbury agreed to tackle the topic; his Surplus Government Property Advisory Committee was formed by 13 November.[27]

All these dimensions of the "raw materials" problem—supply and demand, world organization, priorities and their administration, governmental property including both war stores and national factories—thus had been foreseen. Their interrelation was grasped. Basic work of study and organization had begun. Addison's farsighted planning reflected experience at the Ministry of Munitions, which prepared him to cope with a problem central both to short-term reconversion and to long-term economic recovery.

To find the unidentified problem and set a new committee to work on it was Addison's first technique. War factories were to come in for the same kind of study.[28] A Financial Facilities Committee was formed in December: "The control of Finance is as tight as that of materials and we must be equally ready with the ways and means of sufficient release of finance."[29] Soon another group convened: the Engineering (New Industries) Committee; and Addison chose to preside over its first meeting. The gesture was appropriate: he was convinced that, to fight unemployment, new kinds of firms must be developed. In general, Addison was a friend to innovations. He became enthusiastic over the new techniques of cost accounting that had helped rationalize production: "We shall be fools if we fail to make use of these striking lessons after the war." He gained a name for being "keen on development."[30]

And Whitleyism, in many men's minds the clue to the success of reconstruction, would gain his emphatic support.

> If we are going to make any use at all . . . of the lessons of the war we must promote as quickly as we can a better system of Organisation in Industry and, by common effort, not only avoid rows but promote development whenever possible, and this is where Whitley's Report may be so important.

Addison and the Minister of Labour urged acceptance of the Whitley Report, which the cabinet voted on 9 October 1917. Arthur Greenwood

---

27. *Ibid.*, pp. 431, 435, 438, 440, 444.
28. *Ibid.*, p. 444.
29. *Ibid.*, pp. 426, 442, 446–47, and 456. Sir R. Vassar-Smith, chairman of Lloyds, presided; Sir John Bradbury represented the Treasury.
30. *Ibid.*, pp. 414, 419.

and Ernest Benn (from Addison's staff) set to work to promote councils in the various trades.[31]

Thus one phase of demobilization had led to another. Housing also came up; and Addison saw its multiple meanings. But it had its perils—especially, he feared, on the material side. He therefore was delighted by a talk with Sir James Carmichael, prominent in the building trade, on the prospects of the availability of building materials after the war. Carmichael felt

> that the position could be safeguarded if adequate arrangements were made beforehand, but not otherwise. I was much relieved when he said that he would come in and take charge of the preparatory work for me. . . . We arranged as a first step to get a meeting of all those who at present control the supplies.

The seven departments that were concerned agreed that a committee, under Carmichael, should investigate and make arrangements.[32] Thus Addison's most cherished project in housing was launched.

Half a dozen fresh initiatives and new committees—on topics that ranged from finance and supply to Whitleyism and housing—marked the trail of Addison's first labor of inquiry and self-training. It was an important side to his first three months in office; and it was a revealing side, showing the focus of his anxieties and his thought. But it was not the only side. Much of Addison's work went into projects that had already been launched and much of the ministry's work was done by others.

Minister and ministry were caught up in many tasks through the autumn of 1917.

31. *Ibid.*, pp. 424, 430, 434–35, 436, 439, 440, 450, 460. Approval in principle was voted at WC 247, 9 October 1917, Cab. 23/4.
32. *Ibid.*, pp. 427, 429; see also F. 11509, Box 35.

6

Progress and Mounting Problems
Through December 1917

The old committees carried on. The most important of them were the Committee on Commercial and Industrial Policy, the Committee on Local Government, and the Housing Panel. Addison's new groups set to work on finance, raw materials, and government stores. The ministry's staff tackled special projects. Addison was captain of a busy team.

Among the busiest on the staff, J. L. Hammond carried his "free lance" investigation of industrial controls ever farther. His pockets bulging with notes, he stopped by Dean's Yard often; and one November day he brought in a report that, to him, announced a revolution. A study of two years' experience of the Woollens Control Board, it taught priceless lessons in the indivisibility of control.

The evolution of the Board, Hammond explained, could be dated back to early 1916, when the War Office Contracts Department decided it could not risk inflated prices for khaki. It had turned from the usual competitive tender system and had taken power to requisition factory output on a "cost plus" basis. This decision necessitated a detailed intervention by government for the first time: to determine costs, War Office accountants probed each firm's books, heard the advice of trade committees (these were, in themselves, new and necessary creations), and set up a complete costings system. Once the government set a "flat rate," Hammond noted, it created powerful incentives for efficiency: individual firms, producing below the average cost, could profit. Then came a second step. Because the costings system had to allow for the price of wool and because wool prices fluctuated widely, the War Office was driven by the logic of its own control policy and by an expected world shortage to buy the entire "home clip"—and, soon, the Australian clip and part of the South African clip. Thereupon, however, "new and delicate problems of distribution and regulation" arose. The state, now sole owner of a supply on which civilian and war industries alike depended, had to set up a "Cloth Office" to distribute wool. A Central Wool Advisory Committee followed. Protests led, in turn, to the culmination—the present Board of Control.

This, Hammond eagerly showed, for the first time "gave the industry a constitution." The Board was a model, with equal representation from government, the trade unions, and the enterprisers; the chairman was named by the Army Council and the staff was supplied by the War Office. "The Government," he said,

> keeps control from start to finish, speculative profit is excluded, and payment is made for service rendered. . . . It is generally agreed that some measure of control will be necessary after the war, if it extends only to the control of raw material. [For] those who were considering questions of priority and rationing in other industries . . . the experience of the Control Board possesses a special interest and value.[1]

C. Delisle Burns, the philosopher-economist who had just begun his work for the ministry, drew the same lessons from a broad range of data.

> General opinion is that control by the Ministry will have to be maintained for about six months after the war in order to liquidate open engagements and to direct the stocks then held to the proper consumers. The opinion of the Board of Management of the Ministry of Munitions is that control will be necessary to prevent large firms cornering materials and so delaying the return of small firms to peace output, and also in order that essential industries may be sufficiently supplied.[2]

It was urgent to bring data up to date and to convene responsible officials at once.

A. S. Comyns Carr, recently added to the staff, was as keen on insurance as Burns and Hammond were on control. Unemployment insurance, he argued, should be made universal; Health and Unemployment insurance should be administered together; administration of medical benefits

1. J. L. Hammond, "Memorandum on the Work of the Control Board in the Woollen and Worsted Industry," Box 15, Part 1.

2. C. D. Burns, "The Supply of Raw Materials for Industry in the Transition Period after the War," F. 1423, Box 15, Part 1. Burns drew on a February 1917 report to the War Cabinet on the restriction of imports, on two reports on raw materials by the committee of economists for the Board of Trade industrial engineering branch in June and July of 1917, on summaries by the War Office contracts department, and on topical memoranda from the Ministry of Munitions, the War Office, and the Board of Trade.

should be transferred. Nash, Mona Wilson, Heseltine, Greenwood, and William Beveridge examined the idea. The question of the Ministry of Health, it was decided, must come first.[3]

These separate projects of Hammond, Burns, and Comyns Carr revealed a dimension of ministry work that was far from negligible. Members of the staff were dealing with themes of the first importance.

Committee work, however, counted for much more than these individual crusades. Haldane's Coal Conservation Committee, collaborating with the new Department of Scientific and Industrial Research, had helped create a Fuel Research Board. Its other achievement, the broad plan for a national electric supply system, soon became grist for the mill of Addison's Advisory Council. Much less was obtained that year from the Adult Education Committee, despite its long sessions and voluminous papers. Their slow progress contrasted with the strides that H. A. L. Fisher was making with plans for a new Education Act. Fisher's first attempt to get parliamentary approval had failed; but he carried his case to the public, in a series of enthusiastic and crowded meetings. "Such widespread unanimity," he warned the War Cabinet, "was not likely to recur . . . the Government should seize it to push the Bill through at the earliest possible moment." Fisher was rewarded with a War Cabinet decision in November 1917 to give high priority to the bill in the next session of Parliament.[4] Here was one minister who, like Milner, sensed the value of publicity—and who, with no illusions that wartime fervor would long outlast an armistice, had resolved to strike while the iron was hot.

Three of Addison's other committees, dealing with demobilization, war pledges, and women's employment, became tangled in jurisdictional quarrels. But the progress of the Local Government Committee was a wholly different matter, thanks to Beatrice Webb.

Local Government and the Poor Law

The nominal theme was "local government"; the target was the Poor Law. The ultimate aim was to root out this law, the guardians who administered it and their punitive philosophy of deterrence, and to substitute a rationalized structure for a *new* purpose—the prevention of unemployment—grounded in the spirit of science. This was ambitious

3. F. 2773, Box 64.
4. Files 1718, 3409, 2742, 3112, Box 7. For the report on electricity, see above, p. 41, and below, pp. 190–92, 427–28. For emergence of the Department of Scientific and Industrial Research, see Marwick, *The Deluge*, pp. 228–30. For approval of education proposals, see WC 268, 8 November 1917, Cab. 3/4; see also Marwick, *The Deluge*, pp. 243–44.

enough, but success here alone would not suffice. It would not create the full "framework of prevention" for which Mrs. Webb strove; it would not bring rationality to what was an indivisible whole.

Parallel with the reform of the Poor Law, and equally important, were two other tasks: at the center, the unification of health services (basically, the creation of a Ministry of Health) and, simultaneously, the sorting out, rationally and functionally, of the tangled agencies—central and local— that handled health, unemployment, insurance, and education. The full importance which Mrs. Webb attached to the committee appointed under Sir Donald Maclean becomes clear only in this context, as part of a triple agenda. Already, the Ministry of Health reform was far advanced. Mrs. Webb was determined that the Maclean committee would not lag behind. She lashed the committee relentlessly on to its goal. To her, the old system was doubly damned: it tainted social services with the stigma of pauperism; it sinned against functionalist logic by its duplicating services. The Maclean committee seemed an ideal instrument for change, for its terms of reference included "the better co-ordination" of public assistance—exactly the definition she favored—and the ideal remedy was at hand: enactment of the views of the Minority on the Poor Law Commission of 1905–9 for the outright replacement of the Poor Law.[5] By 11 December Mrs. Webb had won. "I have piloted the Minority Report proposals through the . . . Committee," she wrote. That autumn's exhilarating work crowned "three years' hard propaganda after the three years' hard grind on the Poor Law Commission."[6]

At the start, diplomacy had helped. Sir Samuel Provis of the Local Government Board, long an antagonist of Mrs. Webb, was soon persuaded by her that his old department was "being throttled by its connection with an obsolete and emasculated Poor Law." Mollified, he named a Board representative to the committee. Mrs. Webb and Lord George Hamilton, head of the former Royal Commission on the Poor Law, were reconciled. But the documents support Mrs. Webb's final boast that the ultimate triumph was due to "innumerable argumentative memoranda with which I plied . . . the members."[7]

5. For the Maclean committee's terms of reference, see Cd. 9231, p. 36, and Cd. 8917, p. 2. See Cd. 4625, *Report of the Royal Commission on the Poor Law* (London: H.M. Stationery Office, 1909), for the minority report. See also Sidney and Beatrice Webb, *English Poor Law History*, Part II: *The Last Hundred Years* (London: Longmans, Green, 1929), pp. 469–553 and 818–20.

6. Webb, *Diaries*, pp. 98–99.

7. *Ibid.*, p. 99. See also Beatrice and Sidney Webb, *English Local Government*, note 1, pp. 489–90. On the committee with Donald Maclean—in addition to two members of the

The fifty committee documents bristle with technicalities and are fearfully impressive. Document 1 shows how Mrs. Webb took the initiative in despoiling the Poor Law Guardians of their functions. Like most of the documents, it dealt with county boroughs, and Mrs. Webb outlined four essential changes. (1) The Town Council of the county borough was to be the sole public assistance authority for that area; all of the Guardians' institutions and staff were to be transferred to it. This fitted with the committee's very first crucial decision: "that the Boards of Guardians should be abolished." Also, it would reduce duplication. (2) To give home relief in money or in kind (but *not* to care for vagrants or the able-bodied), a Public Assistance Committee would be established in each county borough. It would manage no institutions, however. The Maclean committee had already voted to keep administration of institutions and services separate from administration of assistance in the home. Instead, (3) all of the institutions and services associated with the Guardians would be put under specialized committees of the Town Council, comparable to its Education Committee. (4) A special committee should be set up to run institutions for the able-bodied; but this committee, Mrs. Webb empha-sized, would have nothing to do with public assistance as handled by the Public Assistance Committee.[8]

The strategy was obvious and logical, and much more was intended than a tidy reshuffling to avoid duplication. It was something like the dethroning of an old, crabbed, and impossibly reactionary bishop; most of all, it was like solving India's problem of the untouchables. Whatever the Board of Guardians touched it tainted, but—like the untouchables who disposed of garbage—it had one function that must be performed. The strategy was to divest the Board of all other (and, on the whole, newer) functions, assign such functions to new administrators, and then protect the new administrators and their clients—by a wall of jurisdictional separation—from contamination by the old Poor Law.

The new and progressive thing, which was to be protected at all costs, was *public assistance*. The old, hated, and disreputable but not quite

---

Poor Law Commission's majority: George Hamilton, chairman of that commission, and Samuel Provis of the Local Government Board—were Mrs. Webb, representing the view of the commission's minority; Robert Morant, A. V. Symonds of the Local Government Board, J. H. Thomas, member of Parliament and general secretary of the National Union of Railwaymen; and representatives of the Board of Education, the London County Council, and some of the local authorities.

8. See above, p. 48, for early committee votes. See Doc. 1 and the elaborations in Docs. 4 and 12, Box 88.

dispensable thing was the Poor Law for the vagrant and unredeemable unemployed.

Challenges had to be overcome—one from the Local Government Board's spokesman, another from R. C. Norman, both implicitly praising the Board of Guardians. The challengers argued against the proposed separation of home assistance from institutional medical care; they argued for the allocation of all government aid, however dispensed, to one body whose distinctive feature would be its control of public financial aid.

> It is the assistance which is public and not the health, and the services should be classified accordingly. Where the health of the community is really involved, *e.g.* in smallpox, both destitutes and others are treated alike.[9]

The committee hesitated. At its next meeting it did not vote on the four main changes proposed by Mrs. Webb. Nettled, she circulated a memorandum, which began with an unfeeling reprimand.

> I am concerned about the way in which we are, among ourselves in the Committee, continually understanding in different senses the conclusions to which the Committee is provisionally arriving. It seems to me useless to reach an apparent unanimity if we do so only by evading the sharp issues of policy upon which the Cabinet must give definite pronouncements before the Parliamentary draftsmen can even begin to prepare a Bill.

Time was running on; it was 5 October, and misconceptions must be dispelled at once. No mere transfer of Poor Law functions and institutions, from Guardians to Town Councils, was intended. The committee, instead, should get clean away from the Poor Law. The Town Council must administer the functions taken over from the Guardians "not under the Poor Law Acts . . . at all, but under the Public Health and other Acts which the Health Committee [administered]." The crucial question with which she belabored the committee was "Under *which* acts?"

It might be necessary, therefore, to rewrite existing law.

> The Town Councils will insist on knowing whether, as regards the sick poor, they are to be Poor Law Authorities or Health Authorities. . . . The Cabinet must know whether the new provision for the sick and the children is to be legal pauperism or not.

Mrs. Webb, in such event, was ready with draft amendments. But it was crucial to prevent assigning the Public Assistance Committee control of

9. Docs. 2 and 8, Box 88; see also Docs. 9 and 10.

institutions for the destitute. The alternative, that "the existing General Mixed Workhouse . . . be continued," was damned by its sheer unpopularity. Everything depended

> absolutely on cutting off the new Public Assistance Committee from all connection with the deterrent aspect of the present Poor Law. . . . If the Committee which has to dispense these cash payments to a family has the option . . . of offering it admission to an institution under its own management, . . . the Committee will use (or will be thought to use) this alternative as a deterrent. The slightest suspicion of the hated "Workhouse Test" will ruin any project of this kind.[10]

Pressing on, Mrs. Webb and J. H. Thomas tackled the problem that, at bottom, perhaps concerned her most: provision for the able-bodied. Their idea, an Employment and Training Committee, wholly outside the orbit of the Poor Law, reflected years of propaganda. The Maclean committee, she chortled, was "accepting the Minority Report—piece by piece."[11] Indeed, it adopted her ideas on transfer of duties and on care of the able-bodied.[12] In a final flurry, Mrs. Webb drafted a single clause "in substitution for all the Poor Law Statutes from 1601 down to the present," defined the duties of the proposed public health committee, penned a paragraph describing Public Assistance as a "cask with twelve holes," captioned the document "The Need for Immediate Action"—and got the committee to approve all this. Reflecting that "the time is ripe for bold constructive leadership," Mrs. Webb relaxed.[13]

Addison received the result on 19 December 1917. "My masterpiece," Mrs. Webb called it—"a unanimous report . . . embodying all the conclusions of the Minority Report of the Poor Law Commission."[14]

Not everyone was satisfied. Signing the Maclean committee report separately, Sir Robert Morant warned that the one possible result it could effect—the rational transfer of Poor Law functions—must be *preceded* by

10. See Docs. 13 and 16. Docs. 14 and 14*a*, in Box 88, are the memorandum "Under Which Acts?"

11. Webb, *Diaries*, p. 97. The Thomas-Webb memorandum (Doc. 20, Box 88) acknowledges debt to Rowntree's memorandum (above, p. 54) for "proving the certainty of new forms of able-bodied destitution after the war." See also Docs. 4 and 16, Box 88.

12. See "Minutes of Eighth Meeting," Doc. 42, Box 88, and Docs. 28, 39, 40, 45, 47, and 48. Docs. 35 and 44 deal with the able-bodied.

13. Docs. 43 and 50, Box 88; Webb, *Diaries*, p. 99.

14. *Ibid.*; F. 3400, Box 8; Cd. 8917. Document 44, on vagrants and the able-bodied, shows that detention colonies were not altogether ruled out, although this smacked of Poor Law workhouses. Details of the report are summarized, recapitulating the above items, in Sidney and Beatrice Webb, *English Local Government*, p. 490.

two equal and complementary changes in law and in central management. The full extension of all public health acts, for prevention as well as cure, was one "essential condition" of success; centralization was the other. It was vital

> that (i) the central supervision of such local services . . . (ii) the disbursement of the substantial Exchequer Grants . . . essential for securing their ubiquitous development on progressive lines, and (iii) the Central Department's approval of the local health schemes, which is the key to the attainment of conditions essential to efficient working in the various localities—shall have been vested in a Central Authority, having *all* the different main forms of medical and ancillary services within the scope of its supervision, under one Minister, i.e., a Ministry of Health with England and Wales . . . having the regular assistance of carefully constituted Advisory Councils composed of men and women versed in, and themselves exercising, the various local activities which the Ministry is to supervise.[15]

Morant had not forgotten the interdependence of the triple tasks of health reform.

None could have known that the report would await printing till May 1918; that its parent committee would never meet again; and that the Poor Law Guardians had twelve more years of life. It was, instead, a time for congratulations. For a wonder, they came from the *New Statesman*, which said the report was

> the first important project of reconstruction to emerge from Dr. Addison's Ministry: and if the others to come are of like nature, the Member for Shoreditch will not have lived in vain. With the adoption of the present scheme, the Poor Law . . . comes to an end. The Local Government Board (ceding its supervision over children to the Board of Education, and, we assume, that over Unemployment to the Ministry of Labour) becomes exclusively a Health Authority; and the case for a complete and equal merger of both the Insurance Commission and the Local Government Board in an entirely new Ministry of Health becomes at once easy and irresistible. The same Act of Parliament ought to achieve both results.[16]

15. Cd. 8917, p. 21.
16. *New Statesman*, 26 January 1918, pp. 394–96. See below, pp. 96, 184–86, for opposition and delays. For similar praise from medical journals, see Brian Abel-Smith, *The Hospitals, 1800–1948: A Study in Social Administration in England and Wales* (Cambridge, Mass.: Harvard University Press, 1964), pp. 284–86.

Commercial and Industrial Policy

An "Asquith committee" rather than a "Lloyd George committee," Lord Balfour of Burleigh's group was as different from the Maclean committee in spirit and ideology as in parentage, but its final report was, similarly, a reflection of compromise. The committee members were predominantly protectionist, but Addison termed their final report "a nasty blow for any Tariff Reform agitation." They did not call for a general protective tariff; their focus was elsewhere. As the committee analyzed Britain's trade position in 1913, the key failures were two: failure to enter newer types of manufacture and failure to keep up with competitors in organization and distribution. Lost ground could be recovered, but only if the nation overcame its inhibitions against large-scale combination and state aid. Help could take many forms: liberal depreciation allowances in income tax; a land authority, with compulsory power to acquire land for industrial growth; a commercial intelligence bureau; a Special Industries Board with funds and power to assist industry. "The individualistic methods hitherto mainly adopted should be supplemented or entirely replaced by co-operation and co-ordination": every industry should create its own representative trade association. The state, despite antagonistic public opinion, should encourage manufacturers' combinations for overseas operations. And greater domestic concentrations might follow. The nation must come to see them as "practically inevitable" and in some cases desirable.

If government helped, should government control? Back in January 1917 the chairman had conceded that some state control might be a corollary of protection to industry. But the committee was in favor of controls only over enemy imports, or for a transition period.

> Restrictive measures . . . should be kept within the narrowest possible limits and, wherever practicable, the trades concerned should be entrusted with the working of the control under Government authority. The policy of the Government should be directed towards the restoration of normal industrial conditions within the shortest possible time. We are strongly of the opinion that State control of, and restrictions upon, industry arising out of war conditions will be found to be detrimental under normal conditions and should be removed as soon as possible after the conclusion of peace.

Control of capital issues should be relaxed speedily; this was the only remedy the committee favored for a shortage of money or credit. Although favorable to state aid, the committee nevertheless cautioned against "unnecessary and wasteful expenditure by the State itself." Capital would have to come from an increase in production and savings; and the committee underscored the "vital importance" of output and productivity.

Simple and obvious to the point of being brazen, the report contained a surprise on tariff policy. The committee rejected a comprehensive tariff scheme. However, it did not reject "imperial preference," nor a limited tariff, outright. And it insisted on anti-dumping laws and protection for key industries. Nevertheless, the committee set exacting tests that any appeal for protection must meet; it warned that tariffs must never imperil export trade.[17]

The report seemed wide open to the charge of "naive self-interestedness," which came from the *New Statesman.*[18] Addison, always optimistic, was cheered by the cautious tone on tariff and by the solemn injunctions that consumer and labor interests must be kept in mind.[19] The report, in fact, exemplified a most important school of thought on the nature, aims, and methods of reconstruction. Its concepts—a coming trade war, the crucial significance of output, the pertinence of wartime gains in productivity, the need to regroup "in battalions," along with its blinkered view of state aid—reflected a whole subworld of literature and the opinions of a powerful group in government. But the Minister of Reconstruction might have difficulty in blending its counsels with those in his own Ministry's reports on local government, health, and housing. Meanwhile the cabinet made no decision.

Housing

The search for cooperation. Addison took a much more active and personal role in support of his Housing Panel than in the work of the committees just mentioned. Early in September he personally enlisted

17. All citations are from paragraphs 313–58 of Cd. 9035, the final report (which was not printed and published until December 1918; see above, p. 27). Records of the Balfour of Burleigh committee's forty-nine meetings, from 25 July 1916 through 9 November 1917, are in C.I.P. 1, Board of Trade Committee Papers, "Commercial and Industrial Policy, 1916–1917."

18. *New Statesman*, 4 May 1918, pp. 84–85. But the protectionist, W. A. S. Hewins, found the committee's work unsatisfactory. See Cd. 9033 (9 November 1916) and Hewins, *Apologia*, pp. 93, 99–100.

19. For Addison's views, see his *Diary*, 2: 453. The comments by E. E. Barry are highly pertinent; see E. Eldon Barry, *Nationalisation in British Politics: The Historical Background* (Stanford, Calif.: Stanford University Press, 1965), p. 215. As the interim report had merely been transmitted to Parliament rather than being endorsed, so the final report was held up pending discussion with the Dominions; see WC 311, 2 January 1918, Cab. 23/5.

Carmichael to secure building materials; and that same week he went to the President of the Local Government Board. But the interview dismayed him. "In the morning I saw Hayes Fisher on Building Materials and Housing," Addison wrote. "It is pitiful, after a man like Rhondda, to have a man with his parochial outlook at the L.G.B."

But a relapse into pessimism was out of the question. Lord Salisbury had just written that the emergency housing program would not brook delay; the cabinet was even then pondering housing matters; and Carmichael's new committee must have a chance, unimpeded by departmental rivalries.[20] And the Ministry of Reconstruction had just received communications that looked like overtures from the Local Government Board. The first was a note from Noel Kershaw: the Treasury objected to the Board's idea that local authorities should float wartime loans to buy building sites; the Treasury said this demand would lead to many other demands. "We could meet this with your help," said Kershaw, if the Ministry of Reconstruction would assure the Treasury "that you back this request and that you will neither put forward nor back any other Reconstruction proposal for immediate land purchase until the war is over." Kershaw stressed the need for promptness for acquiring land before the war ended. Addison had to refuse. It was a bad time to disagree with the Local Government Board, which had just sponsored an important housing conference, but Addison could not bind himself to withhold support from all other proposals.[21]

Culminating thus in Addison's reluctant refusal, the episode marked the first case of friction between the Ministry of Reconstruction and Hayes Fisher's Local Government Board. It was a bad augury for the months ahead.

The second communication from the Board was curious in several ways. Sent to Addison on 2 October, in form it was the draft of a letter to the Treasury, requesting Treasury agreement to the Board's financial proposals for housing. At the eleventh hour, Addison was asked to approve. In the margin the Board's secretary had penciled: "Will you give me the all clear on the telephone?" All this was odd. The Board and the Ministry of Reconstruction had never discussed the matter. The Board was in no position to expect acquiescence; its repute was at a new

20. For Salisbury's and Milner's urgent words on housing, see *P.D.(L.)*, vol. 26, c. 913 and 939. See Addison, *Diary*, 2: 428, 429 (and 1: 265–67, 278 for Addison's earlier experiences with Hayes Fisher); F. 1490, Box 40.

21. F. 1273, Box 30, Part 1, letter of 24 August 1917, from the Board; Addison's reply, 2 October 1917, is in F. 1279, *ibid*. F. 1265, *ibid.*, refers to the July 1917 housing conference.

low. Its latest financial terms for housing, announced in July, had brought responses from only 311 of the nation's 1,806 local authorities and had provoked sharp accusations of timidity and delay from reformers. Chilly if not arrogant, the proposed draft letter offered not even the pretense of change. "Mr. Hayes Fisher has no intention of making any announcement upon these points at the present time to the Local Authorities. . . . Assistance must vary according to the circumstances of particular cases."

Most significant was the downright rejection of the Housing Panel's plans. The Board had received a new set of them in late August (the panel, oblivious to the creation of the Ministry of Reconstruction, had pressed on). Along with Rowntree's ideas of state building and finance, and his valuation plan, the panel's new memorandum included much more. If local authorities failed to build, the state could declare them in default and could act for such areas accordingly. Even more important, the panel insisted that the country be divided into areas under "housing commissioners." Each commissioner would survey needs and assign quotas; if local authorities failed or lagged, he would organize building by the state. It was against this plan, aimed at decentralization to ensure flexibility and speed, that the Local Government Board would most continuously and resolutely object.

Hayes Fisher repulsed the panel's ideas. He was outspoken in his preference that a local authority build on any reasonable terms, rather than that the state should build and a local authority should later take over the houses at prices set by valuation. The latter alternative was "in the nature of a speculation." Moreover, building by the state would bring demands for more aid—from those "who have not yet shared in its results" nor been affected by losses on schemes already carried out. Thus the Rowntree memorandum and the panel's plan were dismissed.

As alternatives, Hayes Fisher's letter mentioned (1) an immediate capital grant, adapted to each case, or (2) a 15 per cent initial grant, based on estimated cost, plus a further and later grant for the difference between cost and officially ascertained value. To cope with rising costs and to forestall constant referrals, the Board would allow grants up to 33 per cent of the actual building cost. Thus, one way or another, 100,000 to 150,000 houses might be built by local authorities.[22]

The Board and the ministry were far apart. In this one letter we can foresee the disputes of 1918: the deadlock of February, when the Board refrained from recommending compulsory powers and offered only a 75 per cent grant; the cabinet decision, *for* the Board; the renewed contest

22. Letter of 2 October 1917, F. 1749, Box 30, Part 1.

in May; and the shock of November, when the unpreparedness of the Local Government Board led to Hayes Fisher's dismissal and Addison's appointment. At an interview with Addison on 8 October 1917, however, both departments apparently sought agreement. Hayes Fisher accepted the goal of 300,000 homes and Addison conceded some points on housing commissioners. Addison, still fearful that nothing would be done, nevertheless went the "extra mile" and accepted the idea of the 33 per cent grant for local authorities that would be willing to proceed on this basis. Doubting that the Board's proposals were adequate, he confined his campaigning to three points: (1) valuation (as Rowntree had urged) based on the comparison of normal building costs for each region at the start and end of the period, (2) the provision of government-employed architects for local authorities, and (3) the appointment of housing commissioners. "I am so deeply impressed with the immensity of the task," Addison wrote, "that I am convinced that the machinery required is of supreme importance."

"Like yourself," Hayes Fisher retorted at once, "I am deeply impressed with the immensity of the task." But he repeated his doubts that 300,000 houses would be built. He termed the Rowntree valuation ideas uncertain and impractical. He would not "set up an architectural oligarchy," and he insisted that the staff of his own department was the "real safeguard" in the matter. As for housing commissioners, he would not allow control over schemes to "pass out of the hands" of the Local Government Board, "as it must under your Panel's scheme." There matters stood; Addison, not concurring with Hayes Fisher, stood aside.[23]

Whatever had moved Addison to try cooperation and a mild line had not moved Rowntree. In September he gave Addison a sharp warning.

> I gather that . . . the Minister of Reconstruction will direct his proposals to the . . . L.G.B. . . . , and agreement will be come to. . . . Responsibility for carrying out the scheme will rest with the L.G.B. I believe that the Ministry of Reconstruction takes a very much larger view of the advantage which may be taken of the present situation, materially and permanently to raise the standard of houses . . . than is taken by the L.G.B. . . . The whole of the housing policy will be carried out by a Department which will not take that full advantage of the present opportunity which the Ministry of Reconstruction desires should be taken. For although

23. See Files 1749 and 1980, Part 1, Box 30; Addison, *Diary*, 2: 435–36 (13–17 October 1917).

the policy may be agreed to in principle, it will not actually be carried out in practice unless those responsible . . . are in full sympathy with it. The weak point in the present arrangement is that the Minister of Reconstruction acts from the outside. . . . If matters go on as at present the L.G.B. will attempt to carry out whatever housing scheme may be agreed upon with a staff which is inadequate, both in number and determination, and the unique opportunity which is now presented . . . will be lost.

The needed program, said the reformer, was like nothing the Board had done in the past, and it had

no staff at all adequate to deal with it. It is to erect in a year when conditions are particularly difficult, both as regards labor and material, four times as many houses as are ordinarily erected, superior both in design and layout to those . . . erected in the past, and through agencies which have never built houses on any large scale in the past.

Rowntree's recommendation was that a joint committee (the Minister of Reconstruction and the President of the Local Government Board) administer housing through a board of directors.[24] Lloyd George, a year later, resolved the impasse by making Addison head of the Board. Meanwhile, the Treasury, rejecting Hayes Fisher's plan, approved a fixed grant of 25 per cent.[25]

The panel and the new minister. Rowntree, like his colleagues on the Housing Panel, had been active through July and August. Interviewing builders, architects, and housing reformers and amassing data on brick output, he grappled with problems of cost, studied the financial analyses that his friend, Raymond Unwin, planner and architect, had calculated, and launched a probe of a business association that was suspected of keeping prices high. For all his suspicions of the Local Government Board, he conferred with a member of its staff, Sir Horace Munro, on possible economies.[26]

The panel had kept on meeting, as if the Reconstruction Committee had not been dissolved. In August it had found that three questions were

24. Minutes to Addison, in H. 69, Box 32; the minute of 14 September identifies the author.

25. Rowntree to Addison, 13, 14, and 25 September 1917, *ibid.* References in the 14 September document identify Rowntree as the author. For Hayes Fisher's ill luck with the Treasury and the new, lower terms he announced in February 1918, see H. 141, Box 32.

26. Minutes and summaries, Docs. H. 2, 5, 12, 14, 15, 35, 40, 43, and 44, Box 31.

unanswered. What should be the size of local authorities that handled housing outside of county boroughs? Were present data adequate? Should private builders get government aid? Distrusting small local units, the panel preferred to assign housing duties to County Councils; but it stopped short of such a departure from practice. Pondering the second question, Mrs. Webb termed the present data scanty, which helped explain why local authorities' pledges to build were vague and much too inadequate. She derived a conclusion, full of significance for the whole of housing administration, that "new, quick, authoritative machinery" was badly needed to assign to each county and county borough its quota of the 300,000 new houses. Here, perhaps, originated the "housing commissioners" idea.[27]

Should the state aid private builders? Mrs. Webb said no.

> Any proposal to make a Government Grant to speculative builders to enable them to build cottages for their own profit would arouse such a storm of public indignation and disapproval as to be quite impracticable. . . . It would be denounced in every one of the 20,000 Trade Union Branches. . . . The larger and more progressive Local Authorities would be against it, as undermining their position. . . . I think the economists would be aghast.

This "Apotheosis of the Jerry Builder" would not add one man, brick, or manager to the available resources. It would preclude good construction. It would render priority administration chaotic. Worse still, it would everywhere quicken the latent opposition against municipal building, and probably would cause *fewer* cottages to be built in the first year.

> The suggestion would distinctly weaken the Government in what is—I venture to repeat—the only method by which this task of building 300,000 cottages in a year can be accomplished. Unless the Government can quite definitely assign a quota to each Local Authority, *and quite decisively inform each such Authority that if it does not itself begin to build, within the necessary time*, the Government will itself build, we are simply wasting our time. The work will not be done. If the Government had to leave the option uncertain, open to the 300,000 or so of people whom the Census of Production found to call themselves Builders, the Government

27. A mimeographed announcement of the August 1917 meeting of Panel 4 is in Box 40, with memoranda by Mrs. Webb on "County Areas" and "Appointment of an Executive Commission." The latter body, although akin to the suggested commissioners, was urged as a fact-finding group that must report by the end of the year.

would never be able to begin. When the Government, or any Local Authority did begin, it would be opposed by those builders who had jumped in, and who would naturally protest against being competed with.

In fact, the two rival methods of supplying public need for houses—the method of public construction by Local Authorities and Government Departments and the method of relying on an artificially stimulated private enterprise—would paralyse each other and leave the Government wholly uncertain as to the result.

The panel agreed.[28] Hence their memorandum, sent to the Local Government Board in late August (as noted above), did *not* recommend grants to private builders. It also expressed favor to using larger local authorities; it urged the commissioner system; and it called for new priority machinery. It did not call for compelling local authorities to build houses.[29]

By now, Addison was at work, and a new phase in the panel's life began. Soon brought abreast of its thinking, he made himself its champion, as has been seen. By mid-October the second frustrating encounter with Hayes Fisher had angered Addison thoroughly, and the panel reinforced his mood. Lord Salisbury questioned if

> the L.G.B. have clearly grasped the magnitude and the nature of the task which confronts them. It is a task widely different in its nature from the work of inspection and from the quasi-judicial functions which they have been called upon to undertake in administering the Housing Acts in the past. Unless there is adopted some method of decentralisation in matters of detail . . . I am certain that they will find it impossible to exercise their authority satisfactorily.

It was time to learn to rely on County Councils, he added; small local authorities "carry no weight and are liable to all sorts of corruption." The panel's scheme was simpler and fairer on the financial side because it reduced uncertainty by postponing valuation until abnormal costs could be known rather than guessed. Mere amendment of the existing system,

28. See the documents of Panel 4, in Box 40, including Lord Salisbury's dissent to Mrs. Webb's views.

29. See above, pp. 88–89. Hayes Fisher left in doubt, in his letter of 2 October, which panel memorandum he had received; I identify it as the 28-page undated "Memorandum—Housing in England and Wales," in Box 30. Comments in F. 1319, Box 30, Part 1, further help identify it.

he concluded "certainly will not be adequate and . . . may conceivably end in fiasco."

> The Panel scheme is an emergency scheme. I submit it is not a failing but a merit in that it differs fundamentally from the existing law. That the State should come forward in the greatest crisis of our history with a Housing scheme on broad and unaccustomed lines in order to solve a great problem and to bear one more amongst many burdens which the war has thrown upon us is as an emergency measure reasonable but no one need fall into the mistake that it would be repeated. But to amend the existing law by tacking on to it a free grant of 15 or 30 per cent will be looked upon merely as a development which may fairly be treated as a precedent. What we want in order to meet an exceptional position is a remedy which is on the face of it exceptional and it is hoped may be unique.[30]

More and more the ministry was probing the housing question on independent lines. Addison began to seek the views of the National Housing and Town Planning Council, Britain's largest housing reform group, which had steadily lost enthusiasm for Local Government Board leadership. Addison's Committee on the Building Trade, under Carmichael, was setting a good pace. It had got Raymond Unwin to make exact estimates of the materials needed for 300,000 homes and it was planning to meet representatives from the trade.[31] If Addison wished to do battle openly with the Local Government Board he had a ready-made issue. At the Board's request, he had not published the panel's scheme. He could change his mind, publish it, and bring disagreements out into the open.

Cooperation, still. An "amazing meeting" on 20 November showed just how little ground there was for seeking compromise. Addison met the President of the Board of Agriculture, Prothero, as well as Hayes Fisher and his staff. That day, as before, Hayes Fisher backed away from the goals that seemingly had been accepted months before, and Addison was indignant.

30. See H. 212, Box 33; Addison, *Diary*, 2: 441; and memorandum, "Schemes of Panel and Local Government Board Compared," 24 October 1917, Box 30, Part 1. Earlier, Addison sent an eight-point questionnaire to the panel on housing policy; it, and the replies, although showing nothing new, reveal his process of self-education and his growing rapport with the panel. See Box 30, and especially F. 1319 in Box 30, Part 1. Maurice Bonham-Carter had charge of these exchanges.

31. F. 2532, Box 30, Part 1; F. 11509, Box 35.

The L.G.B. have stuck their heels in the ground and want to rely upon a circular letter they issued in July to the effect that "substantial financial assistance" will be provided after the war. Of course, nothing has resulted from the circular and won't, because nobody knows what they are required to do, what powers they will have or what obligations it will involve. "Substantial financial assistance" may mean little or nothing.

He also was convinced that the meeting was being held only because another, without him, had failed—other ministers would not be party to Hayes Fisher's plan to bypass Addison and Salisbury's panel altogether. Moreover, the merits of Salisbury's scheme, "which is dead against the attitude they wish to adopt," were evident to Addison.

All the Local Authorities together have never erected more than 4,000 houses in a year. The present proposal is that they should be responsible for 300,000. We therefore keep insisting that it will be quite impossible, with their existing agencies, either for the L.G.B. to satisfy themselves that the proposals are sufficient or for the Local Authorities to advise where the houses are wanted or to get the plans passed and the schemes sanctioned in time for going ahead as soon as war is over unless they appoint people to do the work beforehand. The L.G.B. apparently think they can do a job sixty times greater than before with their existing staff of "three men and a boy."

But Addison swallowed his anger. Hayes Fisher "more or less agreed" that the nation rather than the local authorities must accept responsibility, especially in rural areas. A draft would be worked out at the Board. Addison decided not to publish his panel's report.[32]

A Miscellany of Duties

There was nothing unusual in Addison's personal role in housing. He was involved in many things and in touch with all of them. A typical day might involve conferences with Morant on the Ministry of Health, with Hayes Fisher on housing, with the Scottish Secretary on forestry, and with staff members on emergency laws.[33]

32. Addison, *Diary*, 2: 447–49; Files 2860 and 3007, Box 30, Part 1, on publication. The far-reaching report of the Royal Commission on Housing in Scotland (1917) was, however, published in summary form by Addison's decision—an indirect challenge to Local Government Board caution; see Files 2350, 2860, and 3007, Box 30, Part 1.
33. Addison, *Diary*, 2: 427–28

Addison's central role in campaigning for a Ministry of Health was unavoidable; only he could meet delegations, confer with ministers, or bring pressure on Lloyd George. Early in that campaign, talking with the "approved societies" that administered insurance, he found an unforeseen obstacle: long hostile to the Poor Law, these societies feared that the Local Government Board, when it merged with the Ministry of Health, would carry Poor Law traditions into the Ministry. Addison began the slow and hard task of reassurance.[34]

Some tasks fell to Addison simply because they reached the ministerial level. Addison took liaison seriously and did what he could to put it on a regular basis. Early in his work he circularized his colleagues to learn of their after-war work and to avoid duplication, and he institutionalized the ties with the Ministry of Munitions.[35] But, though many matters could be reduced to routine, the special situation would demand the personal attention of the Minister. Thanks to conferences with Prothero of the Board of Agriculture, with Hayes Fisher, and with men from the Scottish Office, machinery for land development schemes was agreed upon.[36] The development of mineral resources, a cause for which Addison had become an enthusiast when he was at the Ministry of Munitions, now profited from his personal intervention.[37]

Ministerial work did not end there. Time had to be found for the War Cabinet and for the new and important Economic Offensive Committee of the cabinet. This body, born of Edward Carson's restless zeal, had multiple significance for present and future. In the context of *war*, its function was to parry the economic threats posed both by Germany and by the neutrals; it denounced the government's complete failure to act upon proposals outlined by the Paris Conference of 1916 and by the Balfour of Burleigh subcommittee. For the period *after* war, its proclaimed purpose was to prepare Britain for the presumed Armageddon with a competitive and powerful Germany; but its importance and functions

34. *Ibid.*, pp. 437, 442–53, 455, 466; comment by Bonar Law, *ibid.*, p. 515.

35. See F. 1405, Box 15, Part 1; F. 1066, Box 48; Addison, *Diary*, 2: 413, 426, 428 for the liaison with Munitions. Addison also suggested regular meetings on reconstruction with other ministers; see Files 1838 and 2304, Box 70, Part 1.

36. Addison, *Diary*, 2: 430. A. Daniel Hall, head of the permanent civil service at Agriculture and Fisheries, joined with Nash to draft the agreement; this was an important personal link between agencies and with the larger world of public discussion, where Sir Daniel's works on reconstruction were becoming known. For similar work on land acquisition plans for ex-soldiers, see *ibid.*, p. 440.

37. Addison, *Diary*, 2: 344, 353, 356, 358, 359–60, shows the minister's early interest in the topic and his early struggles against Treasury opposition. See also Addison, *Politics*, 2: 106–12.

transcended that limited aim. It became a vehicle for all who inveighed against piecemeal action and insisted that trade policy must be planned as a whole; it led in the fight to establish more comprehensive machinery— new structures not only for the devising but for the coordinated implementation of postwar strategy; it kept before ministers, as Balfour of Burleigh's subcommittee had done, the key problem of raw materials. Throwing his support to Carson as soon as the committee was created in September 1917, Addison specifically stressed this aspect: "the question of our requirements and possible supplies . . . was the first question to which I devoted attention on undertaking my present duties." Addison, eager for every sign that Britain was escaping old categories of thought, found an echo in the Economic Offensive Committee; one of their chief arguments for preserving an open mind toward protectionism was that war itself had rendered obsolete the old controversy between protectionism and free trade. Apart from all this, the committee acted as an advocate of continued postwar controls. In working closely with Carson, Addison was true to his own convictions about the dangers of postwar competition and the necessity for sustained control over the economy. And his beliefs on the score of finance—that Treasury refusal to sanction new issues of capital in wartime might prevent an early start by new industries, vital for trade recovery—were shared by the committee. In 1917, the bills which the committee drafted on exports and imports met harsh criticism from free-traders in Parliament, but the committee remained a thing to watch as 1918 began.[38]

No category, economic or otherwise, summed up Addison's agenda. Conferences met on the postwar use of national factories; sessions were devoted to study of commercial treaties; outside of official duty there were tasks of publicizing the "Government Programme," and duties of public speaking. Whitleyism needed support. Devolution of industrial control onto the trades had to be explained to business groups.[39]

The ministry itself needed reorganization, and Addison especially wanted a general staff or advisory council. Organized and at work by October 1917, the Advisory Council included union leaders and Labourites

38. Addison, *Diary*, 2: 435, 444. Cab. 21/108, the basic file for the Economic Offensive Committee, contains Addison's memorandum of support, G. 160 of 28 September 1917, as well as Carson's memoranda of 1917 and 1918 and supporting statements from Stanley and Montagu, emphasizing continuation of controls. For discussions and for proposals on shipping, raw materials, imports and exports, see WC 216, 15 August 1917, Cab. 23/3; WC 273, 14 November 1917, and WC 283, 27 November 1917, Cab. 23/4; and WC 312, 3 January 1918, Cab. 23/5. (Hereafter "E.O.C." will be used to refer to the Economic Offensive Committee.)

39. Addison, *Diary*, 2: 429–30, 437–39, 442, 444, 450–51.

like Ernest Bevin and J. H. Thomas, manufacturers and engineers like
W. L. Hichens, bankers and merchants like Sir Clarendon Hyde and
Alexander Roger. Years later, he still called them "as capable an industrial
staff as I believe have ever been got together." All but Thomas and Bevin
were

> eminent in Finance, commerce and industry as successful cham-
> pions of the results of individual effort; but, with the exception of
> Hichens, I think they were all more or less infected with the
> prevailing socialistic virus of national management, or of a sub-
> stantial measure of it, so far as common services are concerned.
> I believe that Hichens was the only one who was emphatic, for
> example, against that State direction of the development of power
> supplies which seemed to be inevitable if the proposals of Mr.
> Charles Merz's Power Generation Sub-Committee were to be given
> effect to.

Time—too much of it—had gone into assembling this group; and much
time also went into reshaping the secretariat along lines of the functional
subdivisions of the council.[40] Neither effort seems justified, however; the
ministry work and files reflect no results. Through it all, Addison nevertheless was learning his men and his tasks. For three months he was
utterly submerged in his work. In December he surfaced and took his
bearings.

Annual inventory

Delays and quarrels had hampered progress on forestry, war stores, war
pledges, and women's employment.

Acland's Forestry Committee had called for a single forestry authority
for the entire United Kingdom. Prothero, at Agriculture, agreed; but
Scottish representatives balked, demanding a special Scottish board. The
Development Commission entered a "definite dissent," on the basis that
the proposed authority would escape financial and parliamentary control
—and would lose the accumulated experience for which the commission

40. The ministry's final report describes the Council and the secretariat; see Cd.
9231, pp. 3–5 and 41–44, and F. 5105, Box 89. For the Council, see Addison, *Diary*, 2:
426, 431, 436, 443, 446, 457, and *Politics*, 2: 193–95. Only one meeting of the Advisory
Council is on record at the Public Record Office. Its real role in treatment of cases cannot
be reconstructed from the data preserved.

See also *Parliamentary Papers* (1918), vol. 26, Cd. 9195, "Statement by the Ministry
of Reconstruction with Regard to Advisory Bodies . . ." (printed in November 1918),
pp. 2–3.

was the official repository! Warned by Heseltine of this "storm in the departments," Addison obtained a compromise, but when he took it to the War Cabinet he received a sharp rebuke from Lord Lovat for sacrificing Acland's bold reform. The matter stood unresolved.[41]

The problem over war stores was partly that *two* new bodies had been set up, an advisory body to set policy and a second body to carry it out, for future or postwar disposal of stores. This led to trouble; but there was another hard problem: whether any new body should be created. Existing departments, actually in possession of the supplies, could dispose of them. Muddle set in at once. The War Cabinet voted for "a single Authority to dispose of all stores," but left it to the departments to define and constitute this authority. The departments, predictably, were anxious to shift postwar tasks but tenacious, meanwhile, of their control. The Ministry of Reconstruction wished to advise but not administer; the Ministry of Munitions would accept the work but not the responsibility. Treasury intervention was the last straw; in October it ruled that neither Munitions nor Reconstruction could handle the tasks; the bodies they had already set up could not deal with property but they could deal with stores! It was all too murky. A bit absurdly, Lord Salisbury's new Surplus Government Property Advisory Council (S.G.P.A.C.) began sessions; meanwhile its executive counterpart, the Disposal Board at Munitions, started in. Planned and orderly transition was the hope, but the actuality foreshadowed the fiasco of the armistice days.[42]

Bad organization accounted—at least at first sight—for other poor results. Progress on the closely linked questions of war pledges, women's employment, and civilian demobilization was hampered because a separate committee existed for each artificial part of this interdependent whole. The Women's Employment Committee, the first to see the difficulty, discovered that it could not predict how much help the women workers would need after the armistice, which was its task. It must first learn whether the unions would insist on discharging wartime female employees so as to return their jobs to union men. But this was the topic assigned to the War Pledges Committee. What, asked the women's group, was the policy? The reply was that events had knocked the bottom out of the first report on pledges and that the War Pledges Committee

41. Addison, *Diary*, 2: 428–29, 441, 454, 468; Files 814, 1400, 1588, 2391, 2490, 2741, 3270, 3045, in Box 6, and F. 1500, Box 8.

42. War Cabinet minute of 7 June 1917, in F. 804, Box 2, Part 1, and in Cab. 23/3; WC 298, Cab. 23/4. "Advisory Council for Stores," memorandum, Box 2, Part 1, *ibid.*; Files 146, 543, 804, 866, 916, 981, 1314, 1488, 2166, *ibid.*; Addison, *Diary*, 2: 459; "Minutes of First Meeting, S.G.P.A.C.," 5 December 1917, in Box 72, Part 1, Binder A.

was moribund. Back of faulty organization, however, lay grave substantive reasons for delay: the government deemed the question of pledges too dangerous to handle.

Reflecting this view, Arthur Greenwood argued that the very existence of the War Pledges Committee must remain secret.

> The question of War Pledges is undoubtedly the most delicate domestic question which we have to handle. Suppose the Committee's existence were made known; immediately it would be said that the Government were trying to evade the pledges they gave, and the volume of suspicion would be increased. This would react most unfavourably on the Ministry of Reconstruction. I have previously expressed the view that so far as Labour is concerned we have a "clean slate" and it would be disastrous to get mixed up with any hostility about the restoration of war pledges. Moreover the Government has given the pledges and the Ministry of Reconstruction must act on the assumption that they are to be fulfilled.

Nash was fully as pessimistic; indeed, he saw no solution for the deadlock on pledges—unless, just possibly, Whitleyism might come to the rescue. Nash gloomily predicted that, so long as pledges remained the "large and jagged bone of contention" dividing government and labor, committees could accomplish nothing. In fact, the cabinet continued to waver and the committees remained stalled. The delays that would add to turmoil in November 1918 were already in the making.

By contrast, army demobilization plans were almost complete. The rate of discharge (20,000 men per day, it was hoped) had been set; the order and precedence for individual discharges had been decided—not on the "first in, first out" basis that soldiers themselves preferred, but on the basis of industrial needs. An unemployment insurance provision, its importance all unsuspected, had been adopted for a one-year entitlement to benefits at a flat rate without charge. Intended only for discharged veterans, it would hastily be adopted as the system for civilian workers too, when the armistice crisis came.[43]

A survey at year's end would have to take account of many facts and of unequal progress: the disappointments on pledges, forestry, and war stores; the readiness of army demobilization; the embryonic state of work

---

43. F. 2057, Box 7; Files 2467 and 2545, Box 8; WC 274, 15 November 1917, Cab. 23/4.

by the newly appointed Committee on Trusts;[44] the unfinished task of defining the statutory termination of the war;[45] the solid research on housing, electric power, farming, and the Poor Law; and the half-won battle for a Ministry of Health. But no passive summary would do. Addison saw that he had duties more dynamic.

> My business is to be as helpful and as pushful as I can, because the war absorbs everybody's time, and people are inclined to say it must wait. . . . In substance that is why this Ministry was set up.

Accordingly his report to the cabinet that December was a call to action, a "pushful" reminder of unfinished business. Addison meant above all to identify what was *critical*; and his memorandum on emergency problems did just that.[46] Whitley Councils and industrial associations outranked all else. Of all items still undone, the first on his list was "the promotion of suitable understandings between employers and employed, so as to adjust the commitments to labour made during the war and enable labour freely and without restriction to cooperate in the necessary effort of increased Production." In the same spirit, putting "preparation of plans for post-war work" and "new manufacturing enterprises" high on his list, Addison added the phrase: "*by the Industries themselves.*"

His comments reveal an interesting relation of ends and means. Specifically, the ends might be defined as greater output and productivity, decision on trade-union practices, organization for housing, and accumulation of data; but the means to each of these ends—voluntary labor-management consultation, agreement, and self-regulation—were such indispensable necessities as to become ends in themselves. The necessity was both psychological and functional.

> It is manifest from . . . public opinion and the feeling in the different industries against centralised Government control that . . . every effort must be made to create machinery whereby the trades themselves may be competent to undertake as much of this work as possible.

Nor was this new machinery ready; Addison reported "few, if any, Whitley Councils," no systematic arrangements, and "no organisation."

44. See Addison, *Diary*, 2: 425, 427, 438, 451, 457, and documents from the Board of Trade on industrial combinations and employers' associations, in F. 4092, Box 15, Part 1, Binder 4. The result is seen in *Parliamentary Papers* (1918), vol. 13, Cd. 9236, "Report of the Committee on Trusts of the Ministry of Reconstruction."
45. Addison, *Diary*, 2: 427, 438, 442, 459.
46. *Ibid.*, pp. 424, 456–64; the latter pages discuss the report, presented on 20 December 1917. For a simultaneous report to the press, see *ibid.*, pp. 476, 607–12, and Box 40. The War Cabinet's report for 1917 (Cd. 9005, pp. 199–210) is similar.

What could be done? Addison pledged himself to negotiate for the establishment of Whitley Councils; he promised to "secure the assistance of Chambers of Commerce, the Association of Controlled Establishments and the British Industries Federation," where only employers' groups were concerned. This was "the first necessity."[47]

Second only to this, Addison stressed data collection as a means to other ends. He showed in detail how existing bodies could supply data and how the Department of Commercial Intelligence could organize and distribute them. A new body must form part of this machinery to

> advise upon the various priority issues ... and the order of the execution of work ... necessary in the restoration period. The Board of Trade, the Ministry of Labour, and the Ministry of National Service should be represented. ... These Departments, being fully acquainted with all relevant considerations ... would be enabled to deal as the executive department with the various groups of trades.

It was a good recommendation but an obvious one. The appalling thing was that it still needed to be argued.

To have grasped two urgent necessities and to have pledged himself to cope with them was not a negligible achievement. But Addison had not yet seen the third urgent necessity: a central machinery for consideration, clearance, and command. Nor had he seen that such a body must speak with the authoritative voice of the cabinet. The problem of cabinet decision was crucial and would not be solved by such occasional memoranda as his annual surveys. Piecemeal reminders were not the technique that would hold the cabinet to its duty. Judgment and decision must be institutionalized. Half a year later, the need was seen.

Work with Munitions: Beginnings of Partnership?

In all that has been said so far, the focus has been kept on Addison and his ministry. Other departments have been mentioned, primarily as they raised liaison problems for him. But no other department was negligible; and, where Churchill's Ministry of Munitions was concerned, no such subordination is thinkable. For Churchill, despite his preoccupation with victory, looked to the day when peace would come; and his parallel efforts, to ready the Ministry of Munitions, matched anything that could be seen the length and breadth of Westminster.

47. *Ibid.* See also the press release in Addison, *Diary*, 2: 610.

The work of the new Minister of Munitions on reconstruction, concentrated into the last months of 1917, took three forms: the reshaping of his ministry's central organization; stimulus to specific studies; formulation of working arrangements with the Ministry of Reconstruction.

The Council Committee. Churchill inherited a "Reconstruction Committee" of eleven key officials, set up by Addison in April 1917. He replaced that body with a Standing Committee on demobilization and reconstruction on 3 November, attaching it to his Munitions Council. To aid it he reinforced the auxiliary organization—the clerical and investigative "Reconstruction Department" set up by Addison—to do the daily work of collecting facts and preparing reports. From 15 November 1917 to the end of the war, the main Council Committee met once every week. Churchill's general directive to his new Council Committee underscored the magnitude of their task.

> You have therefore to make a great scheme, necessarily crude and bold in its outline, of what enterprise each class of munitions production is to be turned to. You have got to assume the same public credit as exists in time of war will be temporarily continued and you ought to be able to issue at 10 days' notice directions which will switch the great volume of our production on to new lines. Where it cannot be done, you will have to arrest the production of war material at the earliest point at which it can be boiled down for civil purposes, meanwhile keeping everybody paid (*i.e.*, rationed) and maintained in their existing workshop. . . . In view of the uncertainty of the situation you should not shrink from working out a very crude and general scheme which can be refined later as time permits.[48]

Special studies. Even before this top-level change had been decreed, Churchill had set his headquarters to work on specific tasks. One branch began listing the lands and hundreds of buildings controlled by the ministry; another—its task as minute as the former was geographically huge—began poring over contracts, facing that moment when some 11,000 of them would have to be terminated, searching for the elusive ideal wording of the crucial "break clause." Out and beyond the confines of Whitehall the minister's energy carried another work of reconstruction —the determination of demand: eventually, with Addison's concurrence, each of the hundreds of controlled establishments was asked to specify its

48. Churchill's memorandum, G.T. 6041 (18 October 1918), Appendix, pp. 4–5, in Cab. 24/67.

probable postwar needs for equipment and materials. And long before these inquiries, encompassing three great dimensions of reconversion, had got under way, the fourth and greatest dimension had been foreseen: the question of what to do with the whirring machines when the guns fell silent. Ultimately, when it plagued the cabinet in October, we shall term this "the problem of production"; and Churchill set that gigantic problem before all his supply departments on 30 November 1917. What should be done if an armistice was declared during peace talks? What should be done if peace were declared without prior armistice? Five questions were specified.

1. Should munitions and components actually in process of manufacture be completed?
2. Should completed munitions and components be retained at the factories?
3. Should supplies at ports of shipment be increased?
4. Should supplies already embarked proceed to the usual field depots?
5. Should the production of raw materials be continued without abatement?

From Addison, meanwhile, came other items of work. On 18 December the Minister of Reconstruction asked about national factories and the future. How should they be disposed of? What was the thinking at Munitions on this point? Fresh investigations were started.[49]

Liaison. Already a first attempt at cooperation with Addison's ministry had been made. Division of labor was, of course, the major problem. On 9 November, in an interview with Addison, it was agreed that Churchill's staff would report on four main topics: (1) national factories; (2) termination of munitions contracts; (3) use of the ministry's Area Organization in the transition period; (4) control of materials and priority.[50]

Nothing but good, it may seem, could result from all this redoubled energy and farsighted concern. A new chapter was being opened, rich with promise of fruitful cooperation and of timely results. Ultimately the outcome upheld such expectations. But the months before armistice gave little hint of eventual success. Between December 1917 and October 1918 relations were not easy; the records hint not of teamwork alone but of misunderstanding and even cross-purposes. Very early in 1918, for example, the spheres of responsibility which had been outlined in

49. *Ibid.*, pp. 23–24 (for lands and buildings), pp. 11–14 (for contracts), p. 15 (for postwar demand), p. 10 (for production policy), and pp. 28–29 for national factories.
50. *Ibid.*, pp. 5–6.

November were again explained to Addison; he was told emphatically that Churchill's Demobilisation Committee would "limit itself to considerations of the arrangements to be made and the instructions to be issued during the transitional period," while "all large questions of future policy" would be left to Addison. Although the record states that Addison agreed, the implication even so is plain that Addison did not comprehend the magnitude of the work which was being left to him. Almost defensively the Munitions records stress that "at these interviews Dr. Addison expressed no desire that the Ministry of Munitions should assume any responsibility for . . . the demobilisation of labour." In any event the staff at Munitions accordingly acted on the assumption that preparation of labor demobilization schemes rested with Addison and the Ministry of Labour, not with them. A potentially grave problem was in the making; and the first sign of it—Churchill's disclaimer in February of any responsibility for this human aspect of reconversion—seems to have come to Addison as a shock.

It may be well, at this point, to anticipate future narrative. Through most of 1918 the story of these two ministries was an odd mixture of occasional efforts at coordination and a steady pursuit of separate duties, under the misconception that the remaining tasks were being dealt with elsewhere. At first the dangers lurked undiscovered. In February massive dismissals of personnel by Munitions revealed the whole problem of demobilization and simultaneously disclosed that no ministry had plans ready to deal with it. Rising to the emergency, both ministries sought to create a large interdepartmental framework to insure coordination; but by midyear this effort had foundered on other departments' rivalries. The Ministry of Munitions returned to its own delimited view of its tasks; henceforth through September the two ministries functioned at arm's length. The problems caused by lack of coordination were compounded by other factors. For one thing, Addison's planning stressed the formation of new agencies, interdepartmental and partially non-governmental (in the spirit of devolution); but Churchill's staff clung to the assumption that their department, sufficient unto itself, would be at the center of activity and power. The lapse of time, and the sheer delay in formation and training of Addison's proposed new structures, made it increasingly difficult and unwise to use them. Hence when the armistice came, his new machinery was shunted aside, his planning went for nought, and the whole task devolved on existing departments like Churchill's ministry. The other complicating factor concerned the pace of reconversion, and the relative emphasis to be put on the merits of quick turnover to peace production, as weighed against the merits of continued full employment. As will be seen, Churchill decided in April that the former option must prevail: instead of continuing production of munitions to maintain employment, his ministry must halt all output as fast as possible. Addison seems to have been more concerned with cushioning the impact of dismissals. All these divergencies spelled trouble.

The result might have been disastrous. But, despite all the record of uncertainty, incomprehension, and disunity of plan, the situation was rescued in October and November. The causes were several: Churchill's readiness, despite his right to disavow all responsibility, to shoulder the task of helping with demobilization; his swift decision to continue production, reversing the original plan; his and Addison's fast coordination of a wide variety of measures, once armistice became imminent; the adoption of the "out-of-work" donation; and, perhaps, the assumption by both Churchill and Addison that some restrictions must be retained. The outcome, a prodigy of cooperation mingled with heroic individual effort, was the last thing that one would have predicted in view of the less than comradely relations of the previous ten months. The impulse leading in November 1917 to overtures for collaboration reasserted itself in crisis, and ministries which had taken separate paths joined in common effort.

7

The First Defeat for Housing Plans: January–June 1918

Through 1917, Addison had thought in terms of compromise. On housing, he sought for any ground of agreement with the Local Government Board that would be consistent with the needs and realities he and his panel believed to exist. In 1918 the problem of housing grew more complex. The search for a formula persisted, but without hope. New inquiries, and independent inquiries, were launched. Under Henry Hobhouse, a committee investigated financial assistance to bodies other than local authorities. Under Lord Hunter, another committee debated changes in the Increase of Rent and Mortgage (War Restrictions) Act of 1915.[1] Two dynamic housing reformers, R. L. Reiss and William Wallace, worked with Hobhouse and Hunter. Wallace, who was secretary to both committees, daily added to the fund of information by his research and reports. Meanwhile, through nationally distributed questionnaires and through special investigators, the Carmichael committee learned the scope of shortages of materials.

All this was subsidiary; the main "plot" was dominated by three episodes. In March, Addison challenged Hayes Fisher's financial proposals, until the cabinet accepted them on 18 March. In May, as Fisher's Local Government Board faced severe criticism in Commons, Addison returned to the charge. These episodes were preceded by one that, symbolically, merits front rank.

The "condition precedent." On 10 February, Addison sent the War Cabinet his memorandum on "Reconstruction Finance." An appeal for "assurance that measures essential to give the country a satisfactory start on a peace footing will not be delayed or refused sanction on the ground of expense," it put Addison's ministry firmly on record: a *joint* program of reconversion and reform was possible and imperative. Addison pointed

1. Cd. 9231, p. 40.

to seven urgent tasks, constituting the bare minimum that must be tackled *immediately* upon the conclusion of peace, at very considerable cost.

1. Housing
2. Road and railway repair
3. Land purchase: for afforestation, reclamation, and settlement of soldiers
4. Financing of essential industries
5. Extended unemployment insurance
6. A strengthened health service, local and central
7. State guarantees of credit, if banks proved hesitant, to enable manufacturers to start production

Addison met head on the view that "everything should be subordinated to the paying off of debt." He knew the argument "that there is no prospect of . . . prosperity until a considerable part of our war indebtedness has been liquidated." He threw all his force against these allegations. "By what method," he asked, "other than the development of our resources for the maximum of output in the minimum of time," could Britain "hope to pay off debt and restore the national credit?"

> Capital expenditure on every one of the subjects I have cited is as vital to efficient production as if it were invested in machinery or factory buildings. To say that the workman must be healthy and must have a house is simply to state two of the primary factors in the scheme of production which we all desire.
> . . . .
> The restoration of prosperity and public credit can only be secured if we . . . incur expenditure essential for establishing . . . the fullest means of national productivity. By all means let us pay off our debts if we can. But how can we until the conditions required for creating wealth and restoring credit are first of all restored even though the process involves a fresh drain upon our depleted credit? A discontented population and an ill-repaired machine offer . . . an improvident means of debt-extinction.

"The enormous advances in productiveness" during the war justified hope, Addison said; "improved organisation and methods and processes . . . should enable us to create wealth at a much greater rate than that to which we were accustomed before the war." Dividends in "increased health, good will, energy, and intelligence" would result. Hence,

> the restoration and development of our productive capacity to its fullest extent with the assistance of State credit and public services, wherever . . . private means and enterprise are unavailing, should be accepted for what it is . . . the condition precedent to extinguishing debt and restoring credit. . . . If support should not be given to this view, the difficulties awaiting us after peace will be too much for this or any Government. . . . If I and my colleagues concerned can count upon financial support, plans can be matured which ought to tide us over some of our most dangerous problems; but . . . in uncertainty as to whether these plans are to be given effect to, our task will become impossible.

"Of one thing I am quite sure," Addison concluded:

> It will be no defence to say that vital proposals were not enacted for want of money. Nobody will believe it. We shall be told that the money would have been forthcoming if . . . required for the war, and we shall be pressed to accept all manner of wild proposals and to devise hastily extemporised expedients which will satisfy nobody. I hope that we shall not have to . . . and spend money for reconstruction purposes in any atmosphere of panic engendered by violent agitation and well-founded discontent, but . . . this is an alternative that cannot be disregarded if our plans are laid for a half-hearted tentative scheme of Reconstruction based on the view that we cannot afford to prepare for peace.

Portentous, but as a judgment only—not a persuasive and powerful spur to daring thoughts—the memorandum never came up again that year or the next. Certainly it left no mark on the budget that was then being prepared for 1918/19, which, instead, assumed that the state's total expenditure must be kept within the bounds of predictable revenue; *without* borrowing and *without* income from the excess profits tax, all costs must be met.

But the chords of memory, seemingly benumbed, were stirred again in another world war. Twenty-six years later, almost to the day, a white-haired Viscount Addison of Stallingborough rose to counsel his peers as they debated a second reconstruction. He chose finance for his theme and a famous passage from Churchill for his text: the unforgettable evocation of the armistice and the immediate reversion to thoughts of "the money-cost." Old men forget, we are told; yet they remember with advantage. Churchill, in reminiscence on November 1918, had implicitly deplored the swift retreat from bolder visions of wartime. In 1944, Addison drew the same lessons on the score of finance; and in the Second World War he spoke with more effect. His countrymen by then had the advantage of a quarter-century's remorse over opportunities lost.

In 1918 there were fewer clear signs of like thinking. From the Office of Works, Alfred Mond responded enthusiastically: "A timid and halting policy because of financial fears . . . seems to me the most dangerous line of action any Government could adopt." Mond supported Addison's memorandum when the War Cabinet discussed it on 26 February 1918. Bonar Law met Addison on the problem.[2]

New Terms for Housing Aid?

Checked by the Treasury, which had rejected his proposals of October, Hayes Fisher came up with new terms in February 1918. His letter to his ministerial colleagues, in effect asking their endorsement, opened a new phase in the campaign for working-class housing. The state would pay 75 per cent of the estimated abnormal building cost, reducing local-authority burdens to 25 per cent—or even to zero in the case of poorer authorities. Where the burden on local rates exceeded a penny in the pound, a further grant might be made, possibly up to 100 per cent. The local Government Board plan, as he unveiled it, was threefold: (1) Announce these terms, invite local authorities to submit schemes, and "get everything ready for action"; (2) Present for enactment a bill for replacing existing local authorities by County Councils, if need be; (3) Give County Councils better facilities for housing their employees. Hayes Fisher also was thinking over aid to public utilities societies and to private firms.

Wary, the Ministry of Reconstruction staff hesitated before going into opposition. The new scheme honored the principle of using larger local

2. G.T. 3643, "Reconstruction Finance," in F. 4387, Box 70, Part 1. F. 4041, *ibid.*, shows Addison reminded the War Cabinet on 4 February that a reconstruction budget was needed. WC 354, 26 February 1918, Cab. 23/5, shows the brief discussion by the cabinet of G.T. 3643.

Vaughan Nash drafted G.T. 3643, sometimes using phrases more sweeping than those that finally were employed. Addison's bout of influenza kept him out of the cabinet session on finance; see Addison, *Diary*, 2: 491–92. H. 138, Box 32, shows that Mond had expressed similar views, in a comment on the panel's housing scheme; he went much further than the panel in favoring state building. For the discussion in World War II, see *P.D.(L.)*, vol. 130, c. 800 (15 February 1944).

units; the new terms were more definite; and no scheme backed by Prothero, Bonar Law, and the Secretary for Scotland could be lightly opposed. But Hayes Fisher's draft letter, challenging the Ministry of Reconstruction, contended that the panel scheme would give local authorities an obvious cue to shirk building: seeing that the state would build, the local councils would evade their duty. As for the conferences with Addison's staff, Hayes Fisher commented simply: "We have not reached any agreement"; and negotiations were dropped.[3]

Lord Salisbury criticized the lack of compulsory powers and the reliance on district councils—local units that were much too small and weak. The Board, unlike the panel, overlooked the need for new supervisory machinery.[4] William Wallace, Richard Reiss's new assistant at the ministry, went farther. Sharing Reiss's keenness for drastic measures and for new ideas, Wallace drew up an eighteen-page rebuttal to the Board's letter. Hayes Fisher had objected that the panel scheme threw responsibility on the state. It *must*, Wallace retorted.

> In the year 1918 we must realise that it is the duty of the State to see that homes are available for the soldiers of the State, that unemployment is prevented so far as possible, that the causes of industrial unrest are removed, that the instruments of production (as houses are) are available. That being so, there must be power given to the central authority to enforce its will on backward local authorities.

Hayes Fisher misrepresented the panel's plan, which did not relieve local authorities of all risk but only of abnormal building costs. Wallace denied that panel recommendations would lead to lax rent collection or saddle local authorities with empty houses. There were "more houses unsatisfactory for habitation now than the total" to be built. The panel's scheme would cause less delay than the Board's, he insisted; the Board offered "inadequate financial assistance of an uncertain kind at an unknown date." And it was a serious fault, in the scheme devised by the Board and the Treasury, that local authorities must raise their own housing loans. Some could not do it, and none could get loans as favorably as the state; moreover, their competition would raise interest rates all around.[5]

"The L.G.B.," Addison decided, "has not done a thing since November

---

3. H. 141, in Box 32. The Local Government Board's proposed circular to local authorities was attached.

4. Salisbury to Addison, 26 February 1918, F. 4996, Box 30, Part 2.

5. William Wallace, "The Different Methods of Assisting the Building of New Houses," 26 February 1918, Box 32.

when Hayes Fisher promised to be more active. . . . Nothing resulted from the amiable but indefinite circular of the L.G.B. last July, and now they have come forward with a request to issue another circular!" By 4 March 1918 his reply, labeled "very urgent," was speeded to the War Cabinet.

The Board's scheme would "fail to meet the essential conditions of any successful housing scheme,"[6] he held, because the Treasury note, which accompanied Hayes Fisher's memorandum, contained these two clauses:

> (5) . . . Owing to the financial exigencies of the time and the number of objects for which money will be required by the State, the assistance available must . . . be limited in amount as well as in time and one object of the Government will naturally be to secure the erection of as many houses as practicable where they are most urgently required.
>
> (6) . . . The precise date at which the execution of any schemes approved by the Board can be commenced must depend on circumstances which cannot at present be foreseen and . . . it may be necessary to give precedence to the more urgent cases even to the exclusion for the time being of the less urgent.

To meet the demands of the situation as Addison and his staff saw them, promises must be definite; duties must be mandatory and clear. Instead, "the whole thing is conditional," he expostulated. The bill that Hayes Fisher mentioned did not "impose *a duty* upon the County Councils to provide houses"; and present machinery was inadequate to deal with "inert or recalcitrant" authorities. The alternative plans—his or that of the Royal Commission on Scottish Housing—were much preferable. (Both, for example, would give the central authority effective supervision over rents, construction, and layout.) If the Board's scheme, however, were merely to be amended, Addison called for five changes:

1. Deletion of paragraphs 5 and 6 from the Treasury note.
2. Fixing a definite obligation on the local authorities to provide a sufficiency of houses.
3. Granting the Local Government Board power to act in default.
4. Providing the necessary capital by the state, at the lowest rate it could afford.
5. Restricting the Board's offer to bear 75 per cent of annual loss solely to schemes submitted within six months after the conclu-

---

6. References are to an eleven-page undated memorandum, "Housing," in F. 4784, Box 30, Part 2. It refers to G.T. 3617, 3655, 3682, and 3693, written by Hayes Fisher and other colleagues. See also Addison, *Diary*, 2: 493–94.

sion of the war and commenced within a definite period from the date of the Board's sanction.

Still favoring Rowntree's valuation, Addison pleaded that, insofar as the difference in value was due to the decline in the cost of building after the war, "the whole of this loss should be borne by the State." Again, echoing his panel, he emphasized the necessity for strengthening the staff of the Board. Thus, in the first of three communications, Addison anatomized the faults of Hayes Fisher's new terms.

A housing plan must strike a balance between economy and adequacy. Two years after the war the proportions between these values would be viewed differently. After the costs of building had soared, in 1920 and 1921, the predominant criticism was that the government had forgotten economy. In 1919, by pledging (in a formula for which neither Addison nor Hayes Fisher was responsible) to pay all expenses above those a local authority could pay by raising its rates one penny in the pound, the state had put a premium on local extravagance and had saddled itself with unlimitable debt. From that later viewpoint even Addison could find good things to say about Hayes Fisher's proposals of early 1918—compared with the generous imprudence of 1919. He avowed that the Board's proposals, like his own, contained at least a minimal incentive to economy. But in early 1918 economy held too great a sway. Addison's task of the moment, rather, was to acknowledge that his panel's plan implied higher cost, and to defend this cost as necessary.

His method was to tie housing, integrally, with every other agreed imperative of reconversion and reconstruction, in an explicit declaration of interdependence that converted the question of housing into the question of reconstruction as a whole. Slums must be cleared and slum houses must be closed for reasons of health ("Disease spreads more rapidly and there is a serious increase both in infant mortality and the general death rate"), for reasons of social peace (seven out of eight reports to the Royal Commission on Industrial Peace showed a link between slums and industrial unrest), and for reasons of food production and manufacturing output (experience with munitions showed that production lagged until housing was assured for workers). Above all, a housing effort must be recognized as "the largest single contribution to the unemployment problem."

> The necessity for providing employment concurrently with rapid demobilisation is one of the strongest arguments. . . . It will not be possible to re-establish quickly those industries for which raw

materials are scarce or have to be imported but building materials
can be produced almost entirely in this country. . . . Work might
be provided in this way for 1 million men.

That was why a program, probably not far short of half a million houses,
must be started *immediately* after the war.[7]

The cabinet, not persuaded, accepted Hayes Fisher's plan on 12 March
1918. The most that Addison, Bonar Law, and Salisbury could
accomplish was the deletion of a small part of the Treasury note, Clause
5, with its chilly forecast of limited available funds. Addison shook his
head.

> It is funny that, here am I, a life-long Radical, fighting side by side
> with a life-long Tory (Salisbury) and finding our best backer in a
> Conservative leader (Bonar Law) against a reactionary Tory
> Minister and Department (Hayes Fisher and the L.G.B.). What are
> we fighting for?

But the other limiting clause had stayed in. Like Salisbury and the panel,
Addison predicted that

> with the words . . . left in, nothing material will result. The L.G.B.
> does not propose to appoint anybody to help the Local Authorities
> in the preparatory work; mainly I suspect because Fisher is afraid
> of being accused in the House of appointing "more officials,"
> though how land and needs are to be surveyed, plans prepared and
> all the rest of it without anybody to do the work, is an oft-repeated
> question that remains unanswered.

On 18 March the Board announced its terms in a circular to the local
authorities.[8]

"The Treasury and the Local Government Board between them,"
stormed the *New Statesman*, "have . . . now ruined the plans for cottage-
building on an extensive scale, so carefully worked out by the Ministry of

7. "Notes on the Urgent Need for the Commencement of a Larger Housing Programme Immediately after the War" (F. 4994, Box 30, Part 2) was sent to the War
Cabinet on 11 March 1918 with Lord Salisbury's letter of 26 February (cited above,
p. 111). R. L. Reiss and William Wallace had used these arguments in November; see
H. 107, Box 32, and H. 164, Box 33.

8. Addison, *Diary*, 2: 493–94, and *Politics*, 2: 214–18; H. 164 and H. 173, in Box 33;
Great Britain, Local Government Board, "Annual Report" (Cd. 9157), *Parliamentary
Papers* (1918), 11: 29–30; WC 364, 12 March 1918, in Cab. 23/5.

Reconstruction and the Scottish Housing Commission." Although the shortage amounted to a million dwellings,

> the L.G.B. could not induce all the English Local Authorities . . . to aspire to build more than 150,000 cottages. It has failed, so far, to afford them the necessary powers and facilities for acquiring sites even for these hypothetical 150,000. And now . . . the Government will not, as has been contemplated, bear the whole loss . . . but only three-quarters of it—unless, indeed, the resulting burden on the rates threatens to be more than a penny in the pound, when a further dole may be made. Thus, the Local Authorities are practically told that every housing scheme they undertake will involve a rise in the local rates of a penny in the pound! . . . Very few of the inchoate schemes will result in houses.[9]

Anticlimax: Two New Challenges

May 1918 must have seemed like a month of ordeal to Hayes Fisher. Sharply criticized by local leaders and bedeviled into almost contradictory public statements, he faced an onslaught in Parliament. One reformer declared that Hayes Fisher's new terms of aid, "very different from those first expected," would lead many building societies to reconsider their earlier willingness to build housing. The Bradford City Council, which only recently had thought of erecting 10,000 houses, voted "that no local authority would be justified in undertaking the task on such uncertain terms."[10] Behind committee doors, leaders of the National Housing and Town Planning Council debated open opposition. The Board's terms, to them, fell far short of meeting the needs expressed at the conferences they had recently held; the omissions regarding town planning were serious. The Garden Cities and Town Planning Association—just at that time asking Hayes Fisher to help Public Utility Societies (on which it relied for new Garden City experiments)—reported that the Board offered no assistance.[11]

The Ministry of Reconstruction, perhaps unintentionally, added to

9. *New Statesman*, 10, no. 259 (23 March 1918): 583; see *Athenaeum*, no. 4628 (April 1918), p. 174.

10. Doc. 12, Box 37; H. 164, Box 33; *P.D.(C.)*, vol. 105 (2 May 1918), c. 1730–48 and 1803–13.

11. National Housing and Town Planning Council, "Minute Book 2" (1913–18), 19 April 1918 meeting; record of Edinburgh meeting of 16 April 1918. See also Garden Cities and Town Planning Association, "Minute Book 3" (1916–1920), pp. 158, 165, 167–69.

this conflict. It decided, after months of delay, that the report of the Housing Panel should be published. It obliquely challenged the Local Government Board on a matter affecting rural housing. The latter challenge reflected the efforts of the Board of Agriculture, whose thinking also ran counter to the caution of the Local Government Board—as Addison was quick to discern.

From the "rural section" of Addison's Advisory Council came a memorandum, "Housing Needs in Rural Areas," that he sent to the War Cabinet on 2 May. A by-product of reforms begun elsewhere, the document derived from the effort, launched in October 1917 by Prothero of Agriculture, to get land both for food production and the settlement of soldiers. Prothero's cardinal point, that the cabinet grant wider powers of compulsory land acquisition and give financial aid, would have been necessary even if there had never been a Ministry of Reconstruction, a Housing Panel, nor a Local Government Board; thus the memorandum is not a simple result of interdepartmental rivalries. In seconding Prothero's call for stronger powers and monetary aid, however, Addison's group emphatically declared "the present L.G.B. scheme will not do." The group endorsed some Housing Panel ideas; and Addison told the cabinet "I shall be glad if the question of Government responsibility for financing housing schemes could receive the further consideration of the Cabinet." Addison, clearly, was ready to reopen the contest.[12]

As vexed as Addison himself, his staff drew the gloomiest conclusions from the setback in March. Reiss even feared that if the Ministry of Health were now set up it would simply entrench Hayes Fisher's present staff more firmly in control than ever, a fatal result for housing and town planning.[13] Wallace, more energetically than before, threw himself into the Housing (Financial Assistance) Committee on the despairing rationale that—with no compulsion placed on public authorities to build houses— "the only method of securing a large building program is to grant financial assistance as widely as possible." Whatever their mood, Addison and his staff would have to face up to Hayes Fisher's draft bill, which would aid County Councils to borrow for housing their employees and would allow the Local Government Board to act without prior complaint. "A small measure of reform, useful so far as it goes"—in Reiss's view—it nevertheless did not remedy long-known defects in the law; it did not empower the Board to make orders, or investigate, or take part in local

12. F. 6409, Box 8; Cd. 9087; H. 165, Box 33; Addison, *Diary*, 2: 524–26 and 529–30.

13. H. 179, Box 33.

hearings. The Board's one weapon, the mandamus proceeding, was ineffective. The only true remedy was for the state to have the power ultimately to build. Armed with a score of such criticisms, a reconstruction official went to the ministers' conference on 31 May 1918, where the draft bill was amended and approved. Whether these were good criticisms or not, none was ever accepted. The conference of ministers, adopting Hayes Fisher's draft bill on 31 May 1918, was unanimously against compulsion of the local authorities.[14]

By comparison with the major defeat for Addison on 12 March, this defeat was minor. In the event, the bill was withdrawn by the government a month after its submission; but the Housing Act of 1919 far surpassed it, thanks partly to Addison. Thus the decisions and frictions of May were anticlimactic but they revealed that the gap between Board and ministry was still widening and that Addison's staff still retained the will to challenge.

14. Addison apparently was absent. H. 174 and H. 195, Box 33.

8

Raw Materials and Government Property: January–July 1918

Raw Materials Supply

The problem of raw materials supply was tackled in a continuous effort, within which we can discern three stages. From its first meeting in October 1917 until April 1918, the Central Materials Supply Committee tried manfully to master the data and to form recommendations. With the committee's confession on 11 April that its approach was hopeless, a new phase began, in which H. W. Garrod served as coordinator of the research and deliberation to which several new expert subcommittees devoted themselves. The submission, on 22 and 30 July, of these subcommittees' reports—among the most important contributions of the ministry to planning for successful reconversion—marked the end of the second phase; and a new phase began, in which the problems of raw materials supply merged with other tasks.

So great a topic could not long remain in isolation; other specialized themes intruded. Troublesome problems, connected with surplus government stores, arose in the new year.

The Central Materials Supply Committee

Although Addison may not have known that others had become concerned over the lack of organized current data on raw materials, he felt keenly about the topic. "It really is extraordinary how vital even small quantities of some materials are to the starting up of some industries that are now shut down."[1] He shared Sir Edward Carson's worries over British control of supply and he joined Carson's Economic Offensive

1. Addison, *Politics*, 2: 196–98, and *Diary*, 2: 425–26, 432. For C. D. Burns's earlier warning, see F. 1423, Box 15, Part 1.

Committee.[2] In October he helped create the Central Materials Supply Committee, under Sir Clarendon Hyde.[3] Realizing that liaison with all departments was crucial, he linked his efforts with the Board of Trade and the Colonial Office by a series of interlocking appointments. He explained: "The executive departments ultimately concerned with trade matters will come into it at the beginning and get men trained in the work, with a full knowledge of all that is going on."[4]

This was prudent. It was wise, moreover, to lay down the general considerations that would affect the inquiry, as Clarendon Hyde sought to do.[5] But no one foresaw the development that would soon overshadow all others. This was the sheer flow of data, and it sufficed to bring the committee to its knees.

The first reports came in quietly enough. A timber specialist enlightened the committee on "The Existing and Future Export Position of Russia"; a report on rubber was received; and tables of output and consumption began to accumulate.[6] But in January 1918 the topical reports began to surge in: on cotton, flax, and jute; sugar, coke, wool; iron (three reports) and copper (two reports). It was all valuable information. Two vast statements on trade combines, for example, gave the committee insight into a neglected side of its task.[7] But all was useless. The Central Materials Supply Committee, after all, consisted of nine overworked men, with full responsibilities elsewhere, trying to sit in judgment as a body on every question that came within its terms of reference. It was humanly impossible. In January the whole committee began to complain, and February made things worse, with reports on seven more materials.[8] Clarendon Hyde's group did not have even the satisfaction of covering the whole field; the War Office and the Board of Trade also were active in the field.

2. Addison, *Diary*, 2: 439, 444. Carson's efforts in November and December 1917 are reflected in E.O.C. 9, Box 78, Part 2, which contains G. 177, Carson's memorandum to the War Cabinet. Foreign Office inquiries are contained in F. 6046, Box 15, Part 2. The basic collection on the Economic Offensive Committee is Cab. 21/108, which contains F. 10/F/21, "Trade War." It includes documents from 20 September 1917 through 20 December 1918, of which the most pertinent to the above are three: G. 156, Carson to War Cabinet, 20 September 1917, showing the link between the E.O.C. and the Paris Economic Conference of 1916; WC 247 (9 October 1917), on the appointment of the E.O.C.; and G. 160, by Addison on 28 September 1917, stressing his concern.

3. Addison, *Diary*, 2: 425–26 and 434; earlier efforts are shown in F. 1405, Box 15, Part 1. See also F. 89, Box 39, and F. 2973, Box 15, Part 1.

4. Files 1735, 1405, 4093, Box 15, Part 1; F. 2980, Box 15, Part 2.

5. F. 3957, Box 15, Part 2.

6. F. 4384, Box 15, Part 2; F. 4032, Box 15, Part 1, and the unnumbered collection of tables.

7. F. 4040, Box 15, Part 1; Box 15, Part 2, *passim.*

8. For the minutes of January, see Files 4180, 4181, 4185, Box 15, Part 2.

Seventeen advisory committees were helping the War Office's Contracts Department.[9]

Addison's staff decided to salvage what it could. Hyde's committee should confess it had tried too much. It should confine itself to judging proposals drafted elsewhere, primarily at the Board of Trade. "The Secretary and I together," Hyde groaned, "have worked here for months until 8 o'clock at night, but the necessary detailed work cannot be done in that way." "All the work round the Ministry appears to cut into other Departments and it is deplorable," a colleague complained; "the whole place is without organisation and there is no one on the administrative staff capable remotely . . . of handling commercial and industrial problems." Only one practical work was afoot: the forming of trade committees with the Board of Trade and the Ministry of Labour. The committee unanimously—with complaints of overlapping and total lack of statistics—voted its own dissolution and the transfer of further duties to the Board of Trade. Addison accepted this action on 19 April.[10]

Nash had argued against making a drastic change.

> Even if the Board of Trade took over the whole thing they would still require an advisory committee and there seems . . . a great deal to lose by cutting off the inquiry from a Department like this which is a clearing house for all the Departments.

He was seconded by a new staff member, Professor H. W. Garrod, the slight and bushy-browed Fellow of Merton who had just joined the ministry.

> A single Government Department which could focus the problems as a whole is essential. . . . There are a number of problems which are not mere Board of Trade problems but require a fresh and unfettered view, and are . . . appropriate to the Ministry of Reconstruction as a co-ordinating department.

But Addison knew that his ministry had just been saddled with other work. Besides, the Board of Trade pledged to produce a whole series of studies—on its own controls and on those exercised by others—that would serve the ultimate end.[11]

Garrod would keep the ministry in touch with all these matters. He

9. Files 4581, 4829, Box 15, Part 2.
10. Minutes and letters, Files 4142, 4181, 4859, 5149, 5705, 5859, Box 15.
11. Addison, *Diary*, 2: 474, and *Politics*, 2: 198–200; Files 4142, 4181, 5859, Box 15.

impressed Addison and Nash as a perfect instance "of the value of pure intellect applied to no matter what."

> He brought order into what seemed like a hopeless muddle, and with delightful tranquillity beamed on those distracted problems and the perplexed persons who surrounded him. . . . Floods of data and statistics and specialised training to match seem to have availed nothing in this case until you brought in an instrument of pure intellect to edit the obscure text.[12]

Garrod had already become steeped in wartime administration through his work at Munitions since 1915; and from the fiasco of Hyde's committee he drew many new lessons. It was Garrod's plan that Addison adopted.

Henceforth Garrod would be the executive officer generally responsible for raw materials; he was to send available memoranda to *departmental* experts, who would organize three sections. These sections would be led by experienced businessmen from Munitions and from Hyde's committee. Acting in their limited fields, these sections would draft memoranda; then the three section heads would confer. Afterwards an interdepartmental conference would relate their decisions to shipping and to Allied policy. By 1 May the machinery was in motion. Ashley of the Board of Trade (who had begun a two-hour conference with Garrod by saying he could not help) stood pledged to give so many memoranda that Garrod noted: "Save for food and drugs, silver and gold, this list is I think fairly exhaustive!"[13]

The idea was to tackle first those materials that Hyde's Central Materials Supply Committee had found most important or "dangerous." Hence a Non-Ferrous Metals Conference of businessmen was speedily called, which produced reports on every one of these metals by 22 July. "Garrod is getting on well with the clearance of Materials Supply questions at last," Addison commented. Progress fed on progress. When a conference met in mid-June on ferroalloys, Garrod could hand the Birchenough Report and a Tin Committee report to the ten manufacturers present. That team, in turn, reported on 30 July.[14]

Improvisation, partnership, and Garrod's watchful eye (he was on nearly all the committees) had produced results. The ministry was well prepared for the proximate end in view: the meeting of Addison's first

12. Addison, *Politics*, 1: 177, 198–99, and *Diary*, 2: 505.
13. Files 5859, 6028, 7019, Box 15, Part 2.
14. Files 4093, 5859, 6215, 6604, 6643, 6777, in Box 15, Part 2, contain the reports and show the minutes of the many committee and subcommittee meetings; see also Addison, *Diary*, 2: 420, 522, 545, 549.

great public conference, where the government's plans would be announced to spokesmen for labor and trade. There—in Central Hall, on the first of August—an invitation to cooperate would be reinforced with the evidence of government action. Ten of fifteen planned reports had been received by that time.

Data collection, however, had never been a goal in itself. It was intended as a prologue to a penultimate phase in which—at the level of top coordination and review, involving the cabinet itself as well as select businessmen and departmental staff—a powerful Post-War Priorities Committee and an Advisory Standing Council on postwar priority would bring plans into harmony and readiness. Simultaneously at another level, within each industry and for each kind of commodity, representative trade and labor-management groups would aid in ascertaining demand and placing contracts. In the next stage the Ministry of Reconstruction would have much to do. Indeed, in the schedule that Addison envisioned (and in the much more urgent schedule that fate would impose) the ministry should already have progressed much farther than it had. But beyond that period would come the actual trial, when the new organizations (still on paper) and their detailed plans (not yet even sketched) would work with existing organizations and current data to expedite the transition to peace. By hypothesis, they would work cooperatively with the War Cabinet in that final phase. Such, at any rate, was the scheme revealed in the Birchenough Report (which will be viewed later); such were the implications of many notes by Garrod, Addison, and Nash.

Of course, there might not be a middle or penultimate period, with time for appointments and training and for a thousand separate actions of detail. The War Cabinet might act too late—or, conversely, peace might come "too soon." In fact, the latter happened, and, for good measure, the armistice weeks revealed that basic understanding and concord on the essentials of reconversion—the unstated premise of reconstruction planning, the prerequisite for its success—was lacking even in the War Cabinet. Lack of thought, lack of decision, and sometimes the simple lack of information would compound the problems derived from delay.

Then, at worst, the hard preliminary work done by the Board of Trade, the Ministry of Reconstruction, and a host of voluntary advisers would have been in vain. At best, all of the proposed new structures and the more elaborate plans would disappear, and only the finished reports would prove of use.

For the moment, however, it did not seem an unrealistic assumption that the planning and execution of raw materials policy would be orderly and grounded in fact. Nor did it seem wrong to see it as forming part of a harmonious whole. The work on raw materials had not been conceived as an isolated enterprise; rather, it was thought of as part of the tactics of reconstruction. It was on the order of a regimental enterprise—an indispensable one, admittedly, like capturing a vital bridgehead, but still only regimental. Economic recovery, as a whole, would be formed of many such actions—on shipping, on priorities, on capital. And the high strategists were to fit economic recovery into the largest context of all, into the reconstruction and reform that would endure when the transition days were forgotten. Neither the economic strategy nor the structure to put it into effect had been adopted—indeed, they were not fully planned —but Addison took heart from the achievements thus far.

Problems and Corollaries

Who touched raw materials touched the empire, and Addison was quick to sense this. On the one hand, this truism implied friction: the Colonial Office was emphatically on the scene. The noted protectionist, W. A. S. Hewins, who functioned within the orbit of the Colonial Office, had issued a weighty report on twenty raw materials. Walter Long, Colonial Secretary, headed the Committee on Trade Relations of the United Kingdom within the Empire, whose recommendations, he ensured, would come prominently before the Imperial Conference in London that summer. The Colonial Office was not alone. When the Imperial Conference added its voice to the demand for a Central Raw Materials Board, several departments drafted plans. The result was an embarrassment of blueprints, which produced discord until the "outbreak" of peace. Addison deplored the competition. It remained to be seen whether this parallelism would prove a hindrance or a help.[15]

On the other hand, Addison had his heart set on an Imperial Mineral Resources Bureau. He and Stanley induced the Imperial Conference of 1917 to favor it and the Balfour of Burleigh committee endorsed the idea that May. From other work in 1918 came more encouragement: the Non-Ferrous Metal Trades Committee gave its support. Addison provisionally constituted the Imperial Mineral Resources Bureau in June 1918 and got the Imperial War Conference to approve it. Henceforth

15. See "Imperial War Conference of 1918—Report of Committee on War Materials," by Hewins, in Box 78; CD/830, on War Office activities through the Wool Conference, Box 39; draft letter, *ca.* 30 September 1918, from Walter Long, Box 39. See below, p. 206, and G.T. 5909, Box 78, Part 2, for inquiries launched by the Imperial War Conference but not completed in time.

the empire would have one body to get and give information and advice.[16]

The ramifications of the raw materials inquiry were many. Addison saw that Carmichael's new Building Materials Supply Committee must be kept in touch with Garrod's work; and here his mind was on the long-term hopes for reform. He also saw—but with his mind on the immediate tasks of reconversion—that raw materials and shipping were two sides of the same coin. The Economic Offensive Committee had already told the cabinet that shipping must be controlled after the war. The ministry therefore tackled the question whether—and how, and especially how much—shipping should be controlled. Fielding, an experienced business-man on Addison's Advisory Council, was a mine of information on the topic. Tonnage, he warned, would in many ways have more importance in the reconstruction period than obtaining raw materials. He spoke from knowledge gained at Munitions. British *and* neutral shipping must be controlled—and not, he insisted, by any body made up of shipowners, whose interests must be minimized on any administrative body. To Addison it was very educative. He learned that it was Britain's coal that enabled her to control neutral shipping and that controls implied more controls, on and on, from freight rates right back to the prices that the domestic consumers paid. G. C. Upcott of his staff minuted:

> If there is to be control, there must be control in the public interest all the way from the original producer of the material to the final consumer of the product. The truth of this contention has been amply demonstrated during the war.

Picking up where he had started with the Shipping Controller in 1917, Addison worked through spring and summer on the tangle of emergency powers, neutral rights, tonnage needs, and shipping-control machinery. By August his staff was satisfied that a proper turnover program for shipping had been arranged.[17]

Surplus Government Property: War Stores

An important source both for raw materials and for finished or semifinished goods was the government itself. "Government stores" was a question kin to, but distinct from, the question of raw materials; somehow they

16. Addison, *Diary*, 2: 524, 527, 530–31, 545, and 550; F. 5770, Box 15, Part 2; F. 786, Box 40.

17. For the Carmichael committee, see Files 3450 and 4146, Box 3, Part 2. For shipping, see Addison, *Diary*, 2: 432, 524; Files 1121, 1218, 1907, 2812, Box 10. The wartime Committee on Neutral Tonnage, said to have saved the government £119,000,000, reported on 11 April 1918; see F. 5598, Box 10, Part 2. For E.O.C. recommendations, see WC 273, 14 November 1917, in Cab. 23/4.

were always spoken of separately. Perhaps this was because raw materials seemed the manufacturers' and merchants' concern; it looked to the side of reconstruction that involved recovery and reconversion. "Government stores," by contrast, called to mind the buildings and building equipment, the machinery and consumer items, that might go into a housing program or might help employment.

In the long run, war stores proved to be everyone's story. Hardly an agency failed to take some part in it, because most had sizable stocks for disposal; and the cabinet seemed never to escape from the task of adjudicating disputes. Beyond the armistice—into 1920, amazingly—the highest authority in government had to busy itself with this everlasting headache.

Headed straight for all these unsuspected storms was Lord Salisbury's Surplus Government Property Advisory Council, set up in 1917. The first six months of 1918 dispelled all its illusions, however, and on 1 July the disgusted S.G.P.A.C. voted to consider shutting up shop.

The council had met problems that, to put the best face on them, were at least instructive. One was the mere definition of "government property," which had seemed obvious enough. Then came a rumor that lands and buildings would be excluded—an enormous curtailment, with the government in possession of more than 87,000 properties. But this danger was weathered. Next, control of port warehouses and other transport facilities was challenged; and here the S.G.P.A.C. lost. Ironically, it met defeat at the hands of Addison and his staff, who, joined with Churchill, preferred an independent storage and transit authority on the grounds it could work more closely with the Shipping Controller. This consideration, rather than the need for tight integration with the S.G.P.A.C., weighed especially in Addison's thoughts because he and his colleagues were coming more and more to feel that questions of priority, shipping, and demand—all closely linked—would probably be crucial for the success of reconversion. The story (which will be considered again) is instructive. The defeat of the S.G.P.A.C. illustrated the very close but mercurial relationships between supply, demand, transport, priorities, and recovery. It was revealed—Salisbury's council being the injured party in this case—that no one part of this tangle could remain permanently isolated for treatment. And no agency, although settled to work with a comfortable and clear mandate, could expect an untroubled life. The S.G.P.A.C. was the victim of changing emphases. In the same way the S.G.P.A.C. wanted national factories within its terms of reference, but it lost this point as well.[18]

18. F. 3487, Box 62; S.G.P.A.C. 2 (meeting of 19 December 1917) and minutes for March, April, and May 1918 meetings, in Box 72, Part 1; Files 4916, 4954, Box 2, Part 2.

A second danger was that departments were selling their surpluses, and precisely at that time. Unilateral and uncoordinated, and without safeguards against profiteering, such sales must be challenged. The evil might still produce good, if the government saw the wisdom of putting the new Disposal Board to work at once, handling such sales in place of the departments. The S.G.P.A.C. sensed the "importance of an early start"; it voted that its own agency, the Executive Board, gradually relieve the departments of their work. But the danger persisted as long as the Executive Board lacked legality.[19]

The sure and powerful position of the wartime departments undoubtedly was the basis for these and most other complaints of the S.G.P.A.C. From the council's standpoint, each episode seemed to reveal departmental obstructionism. In all of it, we may feel, there was nothing willful, at least nothing active; but the deadlock was almost inevitable. The departments were the established and dominant powers. They could win by inertia; and their prestige and size ensured that if any contest were joined they would hold the advantage. The S.G.P.A.C., by contrast, was the challenger. It had to act and succeed promptly, lest it lose ground. Accordingly, it frequently protested the delay in getting departmental replies to its letters, for such delay doomed the S.G.P.A.C.—and, even worse, the Executive Disposal Board—to inexperience and thus to failure.[20]

The whole situation seemed to improve in March 1918 when an Order in Council defined the status and powers of the S.G.P.A.C. and the Surplus Government Property Disposal Board (S.G.P.D.B.). Heartened, Salisbury's council began circulating lists of articles for sale to all local authorities in Britain and the empire. But nothing had really changed. Departments were tardy, when not obstructive; staff was lacking; and the Treasury backed departmental control. Addison could not budge the Treasury, which held that the S.G.P.D.B. could not have executive powers: the Ministry of Reconstruction from which it stemmed was purely advisory. More and more departments were not only selling goods, but setting up their own advisory committees on future property sales. In July the S.G.P.A.C. unanimously voted to suspend operations; simultaneously, the Treasury announced that the Board of Trade would take over all of the council's responsibilities.

Negotiation and lament continued. In September, unburdening himself to Addison, Lord Salisbury could report no progress.

19. S.G.P.A.C. 3, Box 72, Part 1.
20. *Ibid.* See Recon. A/24/12 for summaries of replies and failures to reply.

Independence was the council's greatest handicap. It was inexperienced; it was new; but worst of all it stood alone. Winston Churchill put his finger on the chief flaw. Looking back from 1 November, when the whole matter erupted into cabinet-level debate, he insisted that agencies should not be created to function free of departments nor remote from parliamentary control. The principle of ministerial responsibility must and would prevail. This, he said, was why Lord Salisbury's committee could not fulfill its task.[21]

But raw materials—data, policy, procedure, and the right groups to advise and execute—were at best a part, not the whole, of economic policy. Economic policy, in turn, was but a segment of reconversion, which, when fully conceived, must cope with human demobilization too. Beyond all this was reconstruction in the full sense of a long-term program that would embrace reform. Only when every part of that vast vision had been thought through, proposed, adopted, and put in readiness for operation could the ministry truly claim to have produced a plan.

21. "D.S.P. 10," memorandum of 1 November 1918 by Winston Churchill to the War Cabinet Committee on Disposal of Surplus Property, in Cab. 27/47. See also Addison, *Diary*, 2: 459, 466–67, 522, 540–41, 547; F. 5336, Box 2, Part 2; minutes of S.G.P.A.C. for 4 March, 1 July, and 29 July 1918, and Order in Council of 4 March 1918, Box 72, Part 1. From Ministry of Munitions records, G.T. 6041, 18 October 1918, Cab. 24/67, corroborates this narrative of the difficulties of the "war stores" organizations, in its Appendix, pp. 25–27.

9

Policy and Structure:
Planning the Machinery for Reconversion
and Reform, January–July 1918

"Planning" as a science, with techniques and vocabulary all its own, had
no part in the thinking of the Ministry of Reconstruction. The planner's
penchant for seeing his tasks in their abstract form was worlds apart from
the thinking of Addison and his colleagues; equally, the tendency to
elevate procedure and machinery above substance was the opposite of
their thought. Yet as the one ministry charged with seeing reconstruction
as a whole, the ministry had to consider problems of procedure; and the
sheer weight of tasks forced the question of machinery to the fore. It
became clearer every day that substantive duties could not be fulfilled
without much greater attention to structure.

A higher framework for decision and for action—the need for this was
becoming ever more urgent, whether one considered reconversion or
reform. Between January and July of 1918, Addison and a small group of
colleagues—notably Edward Carson—became utterly convinced that
there could be no progress on details of policy without a definition of
policy as a whole, and that such definition—as well as crucial first steps of
action—absolutely required a new structure. The perception of this need,
the campaign to create new machinery, and the close relation of structure
and substance, form the theme of this chapter. But it may now be said
that, by July 1918, Addison saw the campaign through to success on both
fronts. For both reconversion and for reform, he first outlined the case for
new structures and then won cabinet approval after a hard fight. For the
work of reform, a new Home Affairs Committee at cabinet level was
authorized. For economic tasks of reconversion, three major bodies were
approved: the Post-War Priorities Committee of the cabinet (new, but
modeled on Smuts's War Priorities Committee) to settle questions of
policy, to adjudicate, and to supervise actual work; the Standing Council
on Post-War Priority to advise the preceding; and the Economic Defence

and Development Committee (E.D.D.C.), derived from Carson's Economic Offensive Committee. The first two groups were meant to go into action once the *end* of war came in sight; the first was to have broad powers to administer and decide. The E.D.D.C. differed in being more strictly deliberative; and it was to function, from the moment it was named, on matters of war *and* peace.

Though parallel achievements, these four creations arose in different ways. The Home Affairs Committee, on the side of reform, resulted from the sheer accumulation of proposals; the quantity of schemes demanding attention, rather than their kind, was the cause. The structural innovation in this case bore only a quantitative relation to the substance of issues. By contrast, the link between structure and substance was far closer on the side of economic reconversion. These agencies reflected, in their titles, and character, the specific kinds of policies to be carried out, the motives in view, and the dominant conditions of fact.

Planning for Reconversion

Priorities and Allocation

Two of the agencies which the cabinet set up, it will have been noted, were "priorities" bodies. The emphasis was no accident. To a man like Addison the first reconversion problem *was* priorities, and it sprang directly from the shortage of raw materials, which was the central fact in reconversion planning. Anticipating dearth, the government daily strove to get as much raw material as possible, to deny supplies to the enemy, and to corner all shipping. But once this problem was under control the question of priorities and allocation arose: Who in Britain was to get the accumulated supply, and in what order?

From November 1917 on, appeals from industry had reached Addison. Provisional priority certificates, to become valid with peace, were asked; and priority was sought to get materials in wartime to aid in experiments or re-tooling.[1] Addison needed no prompting. Months at the Ministry of Munitions—that great and merciless instructor—had taught him to envision problems in terms of supply, priorities, allocation, and control. He shared the beliefs of most men those days about shortages and the

1. For Vickers' request, see F. 2643, Box 70, Part 1; for other discussions, see F. 5165, Box 53, Files 4469 and 3157 in Box 54, Files 2297, 2119, 6219, and 6871 in Box 52, and Addison, *Diary*, 2: 466, 469.

prospect of chaos after the war.[2] Early in 1918 he had put his ministry's Advisory Council to work on the whole topic of regulations.

What policy was best? What machinery might best execute it? Piggott, writing from the Ministry of Munitions on 18 March, uncomfortably confessed he did not know. Was the Ministry of Reconstruction

> in a position to determine how far it would be necessary to regulate priority of production . . . ? . . . The rationing of certain . . . materials . . . must involve in consequence regulation of the order of production in those industries that are dependent on them. If, therefore, any system is proposed for . . . priority . . . I am to ask that Mr. Churchill may be informed as early as possible . . . as this will materially affect . . . demobilisation of the work of this Ministry.
>
> The problem of post-war priority appears to be fundamental to the reversion of munitions industries to commercial work.

Addison could give no answer for any particular class of materials "until the conditions of demand, supply, and transport can be estimated." But the safest general principle, in his view, "unless there is convincing evidence to the contrary," was to assume that "control will be required." Such was his reply on 5 April 1918. *The presumption*—we must note this—*was for the continuance of control.*[3]

This was just what Stanley and Carson were insisting on. Imports and exports must be controlled after the war, said Stanley, President of the Board of Trade, for one simple reason: "to prevent chaos." Restrictions "hardly less strict" than the present ones were necessary during the period of reconstruction, Carson added; "in no other way can the country hope to escape from the perils of hunger, unemployment, social disorganisation, industrial paralysis, and financial chaos."[4] Addison and Nash had their special reasons, closer to their hopes for housing and health.

> Even if materials may prove sufficient to meet the requirements of a particular industry or group of industries, it may still be necessary to institute a system of priority in order to secure the execution of

2. Examples of this outlook, so pervasive that full documentation is neither possible nor desirable, are the letters of 21 and 23 May 1918 from the Foreign Office, in Cab. 21/108.

3. F. 5165, Box 53. See the Ministry of Munitions' record of the exchange, in G.T. 6041, 18 October 1918, Cab. 24/67.

4. Discussion of the "economic offensive" is in WC 312 (3 January 1918), with comments by President Stanley of the Board of Trade; memorandum by Edward Carson, G. 190 (21 January 1918), in Cab. 21/108.

orders in accordance with the measure of their importance and urgency in the public interest.[5]

With his reply Addison enclosed a document that answered Piggott's questions—and many more: the Birchenough Report. Named after the chairman of the Advisory Council that Addison had charged with studying priorities and allocation, it was the Ministry of Reconstruction's most important—certainly its most articulate—contribution on this whole cluster of topics.

The Birchenough Report. Addison had prescribed only two assumptions for his council: "There will be a shortage of certain raw materials after the war" and "Trade organisations should be used as far as possible for the administration." The council adopted something like a mirror image of the first assumption: "Control and allocation will only be necessary and should only be applied in the case of materials of which there is either actual shortage, or a shortage of means of transport."

It was a revealing inversion. If controls and raw materials were as close-linked as men thought, and if no other argument for controls was articulately put, then Addison (not personally hostile to controls) could say positively: Because materials are short, there must be controls. And his Advisory Council (very different in outlook) could say negatively: Except where needed, controls should cease. Ernest Bevin, who wrote a dissent on the very first page of the report, stated another premise that would put a very different order on events: "Cessation of Government Control as soon as the trades demonstrate to the responsible Minister of State that they have adopted satisfactory Joint Control of the industry." No single page in all the official literature of reconstruction more perfectly juxtaposed the choices before the government: *either* a policy in which labor representation and joint control held parity with economic recovery and business enterprise *or* a drastically simplified plan in which all other purposes or principles yielded reference to recovery through orthodox stimuli to business enterprise. The majority in Birchenough's group stated its choice in two unmistakable "guiding principles": "(1) The minimum of control and interference with private enterprise that is compatible with the prevention of a general scramble for materials. (2) The cessation of control at the earliest possible moment."[6]

Did this pronouncement mark the parting of the ways? If it was even as much as the prologue to an eventual decision for runaway decontrol, then

5. F. 5165, Box 53.

6. Advisory Council, "Report upon Post-War Priority and Rationing of Materials" (printed in July 1918), in Box 52.

the moment and the document were decisive. In this case British labor, in unions and in politics, also would swing angrily to extremes; and the workers, if ever they had been willing to accept a moderate reformist program and shared control of industry, would either retreat into the defense of prewar positions of strength or make a desperate bid for supremacy. (The same result, of course, might occur anyway; or it might occur because of the mere appearance of things, misread by labor.) The chance would have been lost to ensure that reconstruction would represent authentic consensus.

Closely read and set in context, the Birchenough Report did not show an exclusive decision for a simple extreme. The Advisory Council admitted that the existing control system "on the whole . . . had fulfilled its purposes very successfully"; it recommended that control and allocation of shipping continue, at least during the early part of reconstruction. It not only endorsed the official idea of demobilizing labor only *after* materials and transport were on hand to start industry, it accepted the logical corollary: Industries should be reestablished in the order of their importance for reconstruction purposes. All of this presupposed controls. Most telling of all was the simple fact that the report proposed new machinery. It should consist of

(1) A CABINET COMMITTEE on the lines of the present Cabinet Priorities Committee. Its function would be to decide all questions of policy, to lay down the principles upon which the block allocations of materials, power and transport were to be made and to determine priority as between different industries. It would also act as a court of final appeal upon all such questions.

It should be assisted by:

(2) A STANDING COUNCIL consisting of men of high standing associated with industry, commerce and labour, together with the representatives of the Public Departments interested, such as the Treasury, the Board of Trade, the Ministries of Shipping and Labour. Its function would be to investigate and to advise the Cabinet Committee upon all questions of priority and allocation, and to administer the policy laid down by that Committee.

When the block allocations had been made to the different industries by the Standing Council, or upon its authority, their detailed allocation as between branches and members of any particular trade should be confided to

(3) TRADE ORGANISATIONS representative of each important industry concerned.

This was the report's main contribution to Addison's larger work—a three-tier structure for decision and action.

But the report also laid down principles for allocation.

(*a*) To stimulate and assist the production of food and raw materials in the British Isles to a maximum in order to economise overseas transport by restricting imports;

(*b*) To re-equip, where necessary, the country as a going concern as quickly as possible in order to maintain and increase its power of production. In this connection all the means of internal transport are of primary importance;

(*c*) To give priority to the production of goods for export in order to rectify foreign exchanges, restore or maintain our position in markets where we were already well established and to facilitate the establishment of British trade connections with markets from which enemy countries have been temporarily cut off owing to the war;

(*d*) To foster such essential industries as previous to the war were mainly or wholly in the hands of foreigners;

(*e*) To bring about the gradual restoration of pre-war conditions of life in this country. In this connection it seems to us desirable that home consumption should in the early period of reconstruction be limited as far as possible to essentials, in order to provide as large a margin as possible for export.

Of course, this was fearfully general. The Advisory Council, almost with audible relief, said a definite table of industries, in order of priority, was being prepared at the Board of Trade. Still, the lack of reference to housing, health, land, or even relief should have aroused comment.

Criticism of the Birchenough Report. A brief commentary, signed by Addison, had accompanied the report when it was sent to the Ministry of Munitions, but, as we have noted, it was an odd if not misconceived paraphrase: "Unless there is convincing evidence to the contrary, control will be required."

Churchill took an independent view. The Minister of Munitions held that if no real shortage of materials developed, "any attempt to lay down in detail the priority of execution of individual orders should . . . be" avoided. But Churchill agreed that "plans should be framed on the assumption that control both over materials and over priority of manufacture will need to continue for some time after the conclusion of peace" —but not "longer than is necessary." As for machinery, an error in the originally circulated draft of the report (not in the final copy I have quoted) was pointed out; and the correction tells us much. The original draft had mentioned, as if it were already constituted, a joint priority board that would exercise all governmental priority powers; the revision noted that "the proposal to transfer immediately to the War Priorities Committee the various existing departmental organisations is at present in abeyance." With peace, departmental powers and staffs *should* be transferred to a central authority (if one were set up), Churchill agreed. The comment showed how thoroughly the departments still exercised the actual power over priority and allocation. In conclusion, Churchill asked for a much more detailed set of principles. Plainly, some problems had not been solved. Addison had only general ideas; Churchill wanted concrete plans. Addison steadily emphasized the continuance of controls; his own Advisory Council looked toward the speediest possible decontrol. Nevertheless, for the future it was a good augury that the two key ministries were in contact, and that their ministers—each for his own reasons—assumed that controls must in fact be retained.

At the moment, Churchill's ministry was dissatisfied on one other count: Addison's plans might be helpful for the postwar or post-armistice future, but they provided no help for the *current* problem of assigning priorities, as between different firms, where materials were desired at once, or where permission was sought to initiate new types of peace production *before* war ended. It was precisely here that the Munitions staff thought they could be of special help, through their control of materials and plants, in readying Britain for postwar situations. Addison's recommendations were worse than irrelevant; they impeded such action as Munitions might otherwise be able to take on its own initiative. For, until the new agencies which Addison planned had formulated their policy, the Ministry of Munitions must wait, lest there be serious conflict; and the new agencies had, in fact, not even taken definite form. While Churchill's staff waited, applications poured in from anxious businessmen and trade associations. Caught in this situation, the Munitions staff began devising its own set of priorities. But action was not possible on any of these schemes, in part because of the lag in Addison's work, and in part because the very simplicity of the Munitions priority system put it into potential conflict with the United States' conditions of use of the materials that it supplied. America had insisted that any goods which it supplied must be used for war purposes only, rather than for producing those peacetime commodities which might pit America and Britain against each other. Setting up their system for maximum speed, the Munitions staff had been forced to disregard the question of the origin of raw materials. This tangle was not resolved before the armistice.[7]

Meanwhile, Addison's ministry pursued the problem of priorities along its own lines. They decided that, before the future controls could be determined, present controls must be known. The task of summarizing them fell to Professor Garrod.

Garrod's slant was unique. Vainly trying to compress a description of existing controls into manageable space (it ended up fourteen pages long), he squinted at the proposals for future controls with special knowledge. The report overlooked the international dimension, he said; Britain controlled many materials at the source, especially the American source. "We have really a more vital need to get our international machinery in order; if we fail . . . we may be extinguished." Garrod was willing to study further the more representative controls—the "democratic" as opposed to the "autocratic"—but meanwhile he questioned "the extent to which the existing machinery appears capable of being adjusted to or shifted across to organisations such as the projected Industrial Councils." He felt equally the desirability of early decontrol and "the inevitable evils consequent upon want of control." He thought "a very good sermon on this subject" could be based on the Shipping and Shipbuilding Report.[8]

In late May, armed with more studies, Garrod concluded that some of the trade organizations were fit to assume duties; the Standing Council should help them and should introduce trade representatives where control was still purely governmental. Sensing that the Board of Trade would not countenance deputing control powers to any bodies lower than semigovernmental bodies, he challenged such reluctance. "Our ideal should . . . undoubtedly be gradually to transfer to purely trade organisations all the work beneath the Standing Council." He felt other doubts. The new structure needed executive subcommittees, staffed by experts; they would make detailed studies. He also opposed the formation of wholly new bodies; the war had transformed the economy, and the wartime agencies must be represented. But speed was paramount: "We must have

7. Churchill to Addison, 27 April 1918, F. 5165, Box 53; GT. 6041, 18 October 1918, Appendix, pp. 18–19, in Cab. 24/67.

8. Memorandum of 24 April 1918, F. 5841, Box 90, Part 3. G. M. Young wrote a similar study; see F. 11498, Box 39. Addison, like Garrod, had been indignant at Runciman's report of November 1916 on shipping, terming it "the most invertebrate and hopeless of any memoranda presented to the Government during the war by a responsible head of a department on a great issue"; see *Politics*, 2: 10, quoted in Taylor, *English History, 1914–1945*, p. 64.

our Standing Council at once. . . . In fact our main business is to get the Standing Council together and leave it to them to get the machinery into . . . form."[9]

Garrod's many-sided appraisal was a wise commentary on substance, structure, the need for training—and the need for *speed*.

Taking Garrod's ideas to heart, Addison concluded that the present War Priorities Committee should have attached to it a Post-War Priority Section. This would ensure continuity between wartime and peacetime agencies. In this spirit he recommended close ties between the Tonnage Priority Committee and the new Standing Council.

So modified, the report went to the War Cabinet on 7 June.

Cabinet approval in July. "Immediate establishment," Addison declared, was "a matter of urgency." He showed the cabinet how much the Standing Council would have to do. Its first tasks would be to survey existing controls, devise improvements, promote use of trade organizations rather than governmental controls, and draw up a schedule of post-war priority.[10]

Clearly, judging by this description and by his emphasis, Addison looked to the Standing Council more than to any other agency for success in both reconversion and reconstruction.

Cabinet action could not be taken for granted. That week Addison had seven proposals before the cabinet: for a top-level Home Affairs Committee to clear all reform schemes; a draft bill for a Ministry of Health; a complete battery of civilian demobilization proposals, not one of which had been adopted; pay scales for army demobilization; a land-settlement scheme; plans for officers' resettlement; and the Balfour of Burleigh committee report, long since received but neither rejected nor endorsed. Some of the proposals had been stalled at the cabinet level for months. Since January the absolutely foremost plea of Carson and Addison, crucial for reconversion—that the Economic Offensive Committee be transformed into an Economic Defence and Development Committee with ample powers—had gone unanswered.[11]

9. F. 6871, Box 52.

10. Memorandum (n.d.), Doc. 94, Box 52; F. 6805, Box 52; see also Addison, *Diary*, 2: 533.

11. See WC 311 (2 January 1918) and 312 (3 January 1918) in Cab. 23/5, and WC 393 (17 April 1918) in Cab. 23/6, and Addison's memorandum (G.T. 4771) on army pay scales, handled finally by WC 431 (17 June 1918), *ibid*. See also Addison, *Diary*, 2: 489, 492–93, 509. See G.T. 4368 (27 April 1918), from the E.O.C., in Cab. 21/108. The paper "Reconstruction Finance" had been shrugged off by referral to Bonar Law, and the forestry proposals were snarled in jurisdictional tangles that the cabinet had not resolved; see WC 354 and 360, Cab. 23/5.

Addison could not afford optimism. His diary recorded weeks of futile pleading with Lloyd George for action. His fight on housing had ended in victory for Hayes Fisher. On raw materials he had lost the initiative to the departments; and on the new urgencies of civilian discharge procedures his negotiations with the Ministries of Labour and Munitions were quite bogged down. Amazingly, however, within a month he and Carson won— five times. The Economic Defence and Development Committee was set up, which approved the Birchenough Report, which the cabinet then adopted, making the Post-War Priority Council and its Standing Council official. The Home Affairs Committee was formed. A choked tangle of reform measures began to move through. How had this happened? The delay and the odd pattern of action must be explained.

The delay had many causes. In the case of Carson's plea for early establishment of the Economic Defence and Development Committee, special factors relating to the substance of policy had been involved. Although the proposal for the E.D.D.C. seemed wholly a question of machinery at first glance, Carson had coupled this proposal with demands for a clear announcement of the government's economic policy as a whole. Thus form and substance were joined, and the cabinet did not like the implied substance. Apart from the embarrassing fact that the government had no economic policy to announce, there was Carson's background. A well-known protectionist, he presumably wanted a declaration in favor of a postwar tariff. And beyond question he wished to breathe into economic policy the spirit of "trade war." His request had been resisted because of these overtones; structural reform was impeded for reasons of policy. Some of the cabinet members were doubtful and all of them knew that Parliament would suspect the worst. Parliament had reacted strongly, twice, in 1917 against exactly the kind of anti-foreign and protectionist measures which Carson strove for.

For a similar reason, action on civilian demobilization had hung fire. The whole explosive question of pledges pertaining to the unions' restrictive practices was involved, and any declaration might destroy the shaky wartime industrial truce. Another deterrent was the vague but powerful sentiment against any announcement that might smack of peace while the national will to fight must remain at top pitch. Still, despite these three specific factors, some measures that were unaffected by them had come up and been decided, piecemeal, in January, February, and March. Why had this pattern of decision not been continued?

April brought the greatest of deterrents. The last tremendous German bid for victory broke the Allied lines. All routine debates came to a stop. There were 120,000 casualties in two weeks; the dead numbered 11,000. The Ulster problem erupted and conscription for Ireland was debated for weeks. In May a political storm broke over the Maurice letter.[12] A war crisis, second to none, caused the logjam of June.

When the chance for action finally came, it came all along the line. First, the War Cabinet on 10 June set up the Economic Defence and Development and the Home Affairs committees. With these general organs for review and approval created, specific measures could benefit. For the Birchenough Report the sequel was swift. On 18 June the first meeting of the E.D.D.C. considered the report; on 2 July it recommended that the War Cabinet approve the proposed machinery; on 11 July 1918 the War Cabinet did so. The new Post-War Priorities Committee was named: General Smuts, the President of the Board of Trade, and the Ministers of Labour, Munitions, Shipping, and Reconstruction.

The Standing Council, outlined in the Birchenough Report, still had to be nominated, of course. And Addison was planning a grand conference for 1 August to explain the new priority plan. Invitations must be discussed and sent out, with new informational material, to the businessmen and trade unionists who would attend. But the priorities problem seemed well on the road to solution.[13]

Ramifications and corollaries. The trouble with victories in any of these campaigns, however hard fought, was that each gain disclosed the host of unsolved problems just beyond; and no success, even that just won on priorities, could be satisfying while uncertainties or inaction on other topics menaced the recent gains. The truth of a baffling interdependence was borne in on all. "This question of control," Churchill wrote, "affects nearly every problem connected with Reconstruction."[14] It was true all around. Munitions could not answer questions on allocation until supply and shipping answers were known. Shipping could not be estimated or precisely planned while economic policy, and diplomatic strategy itself, remained unsettled. Inter-Allied strategy was a most variable function of

---

12. WC 385 (6 April 1918), 406, and 407, in Cab. 23/6.
13. Addison, *Diary*, 2: 545–50. WC 429 (10 June 1918), in Cab. 23/6. E.D.D.C. meeting 1 (Minutes of 18 June 1918), accepting memorandum G.T. 4819 by Addison, and meeting 2 (2 July 1918) confirming same, in Cab. 27/44; see also E.D.D.C. memorandum 8 (15 June 1918), *ibid.*, summarizing G.T. 4819 (the Birchenough Report, as amended). In Ministry of Reconstruction records, see Files 6871 and 7398, Box 52.
14. Churchill to Addison, 27 April 1918, F. 5165, Box 53.

questions of postwar international controls, themselves still in dispute, and so on.

Three topics especially demonstrated how the problem of priorities branched out and overlapped: national factories, overseas and industrial demand, and storage and transit.

For one simple reason, the question of national factories was bound up with priorities problems: these factories were prime consumers of raw materials, and if retained by government they would make claims for priority in getting materials. But the factories were a huge problem in their own right. This was especially of concern to Munitions headquarters, where it was seen in early 1918 that a few factories were becoming redundant and others soon would not be needed. From firms anxious to ready themselves for postwar orders, requests for decision began to pour in. But who was to determine the whole cluster of interlocking questions, now that Salisbury's advisory council had been denied jurisdiction over factories? Churchill's staff urged on Addison, several times, that a decision must be made quickly so that negotiations might start. Otherwise, they warned, at the end of the war the government would incur great loss, possessing a large number of valuable properties that would be thrown simultaneously on the market; furthermore, any advantage of giving a prompt start to peace industry, and thus alleviating unemployment, would have been lost. Confronted in May with a specific purchase bid, Munitions asked Addison to concur that Munitions might begin negotiations for sale or lease, with power to conclude an agreement—subject to his and the Treasury's approval. Not until 10 August did Addison endorse this idea. Meanwhile the Civil War Workers' Committee added a new dimension, by suggesting the factories might be used by government to sustain employment when demobilization came. Churchill himself, in a July meeting of the Economic Defence and Development Committee, interpolated that the factories might be permanently utilized to produce war materials and perhaps execute other contracts for the government; but he had come to no definite conclusion. His staff had done much preliminary work, classifying factories by type, and coming to the important conclusion that prompt disposal—and prompt discharge of employees—should be the guiding concept. But no policy had been ratified. Only in late September did Addison make proposals on which action was finally taken.[15]

15. Addison, *Diary*, 2: 498, 533, 541; F. 7890, Box 52; E.D.D.C. memorandum 19 (4 July 1918) and minutes of meeting 2 (2 July 1918), Cab. 27/44: below, pp. 205, 281. See also G.T. 6041, 18 October 1918, Appendix, pp. 28–30, in Cab. 24/67.

"Demand" was the second ramification of priorities which became identified and came under study. To Whitehall and to businessmen, future needs and demands (not only of Britain but of its Allies and potential customers, and of war-devastated areas) must be known if sensible decisions were to follow on priorities. A unified study by one department, treating as one the many elements of the supply-demand-priorities complex, would have made the most sense; and in December this had been the idea.[16] But the situation had changed: demand was being treated separately from other factors; and unfortunately it was the business of several uncoordinated groups. As noted in chapter 6, Churchill had seen that the needs of his controlled establishments must be estimated; in February 1918 inquiries had been sent to them all. Results of this broad survey were meager, to the point of being almost unusable: only 33 per cent of firms had replied, and little could be deduced from the data. It was notable that, of 1,175 firms which did reply, few would require extensive renewal of plant, and 999 needed no new equipment. But *general* inquiry into demand had obviously failed. Much concerned, Addison and Churchill settled for a more limited effort, to determine the probable postwar situation for iron and steel.

This at least, the Ministry of Munitions staff felt, was something that they could handle competently, and alone. Churchill accordingly sent letters to overseas purchasers, explaining that he hoped definite orders could be placed before war ended; he would aid this advance work by issuing appropriate instructions to controlled establishments. In his own ministry, he assigned a special group to ascertain requirements and relate them to capacity; he put Walter Layton in charge. Layton's experience from that moment was an epitome of life in Whitehall during the war. Layton turned, naturally and characteristically, to confer with his former chief, Addison—and they found that there were five separate inquiries under way on the same topic! After much time was lost, Addison convened the five departments concerned; by early April a single Iron and Steel Committee was at work for them all. In twenty-five meetings, this committee heard dozens of witnesses and amassed data sufficient to begin shaping a report. But by then it was September. It was still impossible to make more than rough estimates; by that time, moreover, a new problem had been encountered, as large as the first. This was the whole question of subsidies. Complete revision of the wartime subsidy system was required; and this, in turn, meant that still another committee must be set up. On 30 September, that committee was in being but had not yet

16. See above, pp. 75, 104.

met. The lack of unified and powerful machinery had proved, and was still proving, serious.[17]

A nation that lived by its ships and that had invented the steam railway, Britain came naturally by the third of these ramifying problems, which was officially known as Storage and Transit. Seemingly a mere adjunct of the raw materials and surplus stores topics, the business of finding warehouse space and railway facilities was a major priority problem. With the armistice, a fierce contest for scarce and precious accommodations would break out. Already the Shipping Ministry was demanding that twelve ports be reserved for commercial purposes, with all their storage space; but the Ministry of Munitions also would desperately need to store away its munitions stocks to clear factories for peace work (and if the government produced extra munitions to create jobs, even more warehouses would be required). Three other defense ministries also were seeking storage space.

The tangle was a manifold problem: not just competition but the lack of any committee charged with laying down general policy or with reconciling the various interests. Colonel Maurice Bonham-Carter advised Addison it was "obviously the duty" of the Reconstruction Ministry to provide a proper policy, but he spelled out the production intricacies that would make priority tricky.

> On demobilisation . . . while some trades . . . could absorb a considerable number of men immediately, the bulk . . . must be converted from war to peace production and provided with raw material, sometimes of a different nature from what they are at present using, while others—at present in a state of suspended animation for the lack of material—must be supplied before they can absorb their quota. But not only is the earliest possible reestablishment of the industries . . . essential to rapid demobilisation, it is of no less importance if British trade and shipping are to hold their own against foreign competitors who may otherwise get a start of them.

Convening the twelve departments concerned, Addison heard his own S.G.P.A.C. cry that this matter was in its jurisdiction! Overriding this complaint, he and the departments conferred on 10 April but could agree

17. Minutes by Nash, 4 April 1918, in F. 4469, Box 54; for Munitions inquiries, see Layton to Addison, 29 May 1918, Files 6625 and 5761, Box 53. For general conferences, see F. 5165 in Box 53 and F. 4917, Box 90, Part 3. G.T. 6041, 18 October 1918, Appendix, pp. 15–16, summarizes the whole situation.

only to refer things to an informal committee. In September, recommendations for a solution were just coming in.[18]

If the key problem of priorities seemed nearly solved, the same was not true of these three ramifications. Policy and machinery on national factories, demand, and storage were not settled that summer.

We began this chapter by stating its general theme: the need for new comprehensive organizations. We have seen that this need was urgent, whether for reform, economic reconversion, or demobilization of personnel. The first months of 1918, I have affirmed, would show that for each of these three great areas the structure and the substance were closely interdependent. But so far we have seen proofs of this interdependence in one area only—economic reconversion—and have focused on but one part of that area, the topic of priorities. To trace the interaction of policy and structure for that topic, we have carried this segment of the story to September 1918. We must now retrace our steps. It remains to show how, for reform and also for the other human and economic sides of reconversion, this same interrelation became manifest; it remains to explain the structural changes for those areas too. We may begin conveniently with civilian demobilization, where a dramatic crisis revealed the need for coordination. To tell this story, we must revert to the beginning of 1918.

Demobilization, Discharge, and Reemployment

As with the material and impersonal side of planning for the transition period, so with the human side: demobilization and resettlement plans suffered in 1917 and 1918 from segmental treatment and delay. The great truth of interdependence was acknowledged by all but flouted in practice. Readiness was everywhere extolled but still unattained. Committees that dated back to Asquith's first acts had met, and were still meeting. But in January 1918 Nash confessed to Brade of the War Office: "Nothing is happening here. The Minister feels questions of high policy may justify postponement." Then, suddenly, the staff at Queen Anne's Gate was thunderstruck. The Ministry of Munitions had begun to discharge workers summarily and at an appalling rate. Three factors—reduction in the available shipping tonnage, a consequent drop in raw materials imports, and the cancellation of Russian orders—had led to a revision of the munitions-production program. Now, in February 1918, staff members of the Ministry of Munitions were sounding the alarm; if the trend continued, 100,000 or more women might be discharged.

18. Addison, *Diary*, 2: 509; Files 4332 and 4332A, Box 43.

As it rushed to cope with the situation, the Ministry of Munitions issued directives on discharges, employment, and benefits. These directives perturbed Greenwood, who wished to be sure that temporary policy fitted in with general demobilization plans. Addison branded it "an amazing thing that there should suddenly be a wholesale discharge of a vast number of workers without the problems raised thereby having been brought to our notice for careful examination in every possible way." He demanded clarification and was "turning on all necessary force of the Office to obtain it." Nash and Greenwood pleaded that Addison get a War Cabinet committee to convene the five departments concerned, for other industries would soon be affected. The Ministry of Munitions could not handle matters, they reasoned, and had admitted that the situation might "involve practical questions of reconstruction." This might, in fact, be the beginning of civilian demobilization. Bad precedents might be set and the Reconstruction Ministry would be responsible. In any case, the planned demobilization machinery must not be prejudiced or discredited. By 19 March, with Churchill concurring, a ministerial Committee of Four, with a broad mandate, was formed.[19]

It got nowhere. Some ministries wished to discuss only their immediate problems; most already had committees; and some were even applying policies of which Addison's staff knew nothing. On 27 March the four troubleshooters deadlocked with the Ministry of Labour's Labour Resettlement Committee. Should the Ministry of Reconstruction champion the new machinery of the Committee of Four, or yield to the Ministry of Labour? Nash interposed still another question: Had not machinery outrun policy in this case? He agreed with the Ministry of Labour: The Committee of Four simply could not act on the broad lines laid down in its mandate, and agreement on the proposals of the Civil War Workers' Demobilisation Committee was still incomplete. Addison expostulated that "war discharges don't wait until the Civil Demobilisation Committee's full reports are in." Besides, a narrowly departmental

19. For earlier work, especially by Bellhouse's Civil War Workers' Committee, see above, p. 74, and Files 241, 617, and 886, Box 40, plus Files 4793 and 2545, Box 8; Cd. 9231, pp. 19–20; Addison's, *Diary*, 2: 439–40, 446–47, and 466. See Greenwood's memorandum to Mona Wilson, 24 February 1918, F. 10752, Box 39; F. 5180, Box 90, Part 3; and *Athenaeum*, no. 4628 (April 1918), on the "alarming rate" of discharges. On 11 January 1918, the War Cabinet set up a special committee on "unemployment caused by government action," omitting the Ministry of Reconstruction; see F. 10752, Box 39. Strong protest was voiced by the War Emergency Workers' National Committee, in February 1918, on these dismissals; see minutes of its meetings for 26 February and 21 March 1918 in its files at the Trades Union Congress library, London. See also *History of the Ministry of Munitions*, 6, Part 2: 77–80.

committee was not fit; what was needed was one with "interdepartmental knowledge," which by acting and discussing would acquire experience.

It was all dismally instructive. Like Garrod's work on priorities systems, like Lord Salisbury's frustrations with the topic of "war stores," the experience of the Committee of Four on personnel demobilization was an epitome of administration in wartime London.

All the ingredients of chronic procedural dilemmas were present: the argument for speed versus the argument for departmental consensus; the argument for improvising short-term policies, somehow, versus the argument for settling long-term principles; the argument for the old and experienced—but narrow—department versus the argument for unified treatment by a broad—but untried—committee; the case for creating machinery with broad powers, and perhaps too vague a mandate, versus the argument for determining guidelines first. Efforts at compromise failed. Perhaps luckily, the flurry of civilian discharges halted when Ludendorff unleashed his attack. By midsummer all of the original impetus had been lost.[20]

The whole episode, an unplanned dress rehearsal for the panicky drama of armistice days, was full of lessons and omens. It showed the need for joint planning and full coordination. It revealed the unreadiness of many plans—a salutary warning which Addison's men heeded, as will be seen in the five reports that his Civil War Workers' Committee released in the next few months. But it also led to a decision by Churchill, logical but potentially very serious, whose importance Addison seems not to have grasped.

That decision was to shift responsibility for the whole work of demobilization and reconversion to the Ministry of Reconstruction. As Churchill put it in February, "the general application of war industry to peace industry constitutes a principal part of the work of the Ministry of Reconstruction." The munitions staff would supply data to Addison's staff, "but they alone can make a broad scheme." With this sister ministry "disclaiming responsibility for demobilisation as a whole" (as its official history states), Addison's problems were doubled.[21]

Given the setbacks and delays revealed by the February crisis over munitions discharges and by the later attempts at teamwork, Addison perhaps chose to seek compensation in harder work by a group within his own control—the Civil War Workers' Committee. Thus, though problems

20. F. 5180, Box 90, Part 3; Addison, *Diary*, 2: 519.
21. *History of the Ministry of Munitions*, 6, Part 2: 82–84.

of structure would remain unsolved, something might be salvaged in terms of policy. He had reason to resort to this approach. By April that committee had supplied him with three solid interim reports. The first report went beyond routine suggestions and took a bold view on highly controverted points. The government, it insisted first of all, must aid discharged workers, and it must aid those who were not connected directly with munitions as well as those in munitions firms. The machinery for aid should include, along with the obvious employment exchanges, the new Labour Resettlement committees and the Local Advisory committees; temporary trade committees or Whitley Councils, where founded, also should be enlisted. Action must precede an armistice; as soon as there was a reasonable prospect of peace, all these committees must ascertain the local requirements for workers. Meanwhile—on forms the C.W.W.C. suggested—the Ministry of Labour should register workers, to aid reemployment. The committee recommended a fortnight's notice or a fortnight's wages in lieu thereof. Lastly, the report stressed the restarting of industry.

> Steps should be taken by the Departments concerned to encourage Government Departments, public or semi-public bodies and private employers to place post-war contracts in advance, the contracts being arranged, if necessary, at provisional prices to be adjusted later according to revised estimates of the cost of labour, materials, and other things, or as an alternative, on a profit basis. Similar measures should be taken by the Department of Overseas Trade through their Trade Commissioners and Commercial Attachés abroad.
>
> The Government should have in readiness before the end of the war, further schemes to meet the possibility of any local or general unemployment which may prove to be more than of a temporary nature.[22]

Here was a framework sufficiently broad and certain (if well carried out) to make demobilization a fit prologue to permanent humanitarian reform. The second interim report, sent to Addison in the spring, took an uncompromising line on unemployment insurance. Challenging the distinction between war work and other work and rejecting partial

22. *Parliamentary Papers* (1918), vol. 14, "Ministry of Reconstruction—Civil War Workers' Committee—First (Interim) Report," Cd. 9117, pp. 7–8. See also *New Statesman*, 3 August 1918, p. 343.

extension to trades that had been hit especially hard by unemployment, the report insisted that

> general provision should be made for prevention of distress through unemployment by seeing that everybody is insured against unemployment. A general scheme . . . is likely to prove less controversial . . . while it makes certain, as no partial scheme would, of really covering all the ground and excluding the necessity for hastily improvised supplementary measures.

Lest the government be driven in crisis to a system of doles the committee held that the Ministry of Labour should frame proposals for general insurance, of a contributory kind, and give effect to them promptly.[23]

Parallel to these, but agreed upon in principle long before, were the plans for army demobilization. On parts of these—officers' resettlement and soldiers' out-of-work donation—Addison won a provisional success. Even this was subject, Addison foresaw, to the need for "concurrence of the Treasury—which . . . may mean a fight." But piecemeal gains here guaranteed nothing on the civilian side. Although an interim report became public in July, no others were made public. The proposed machinery was lacking; and later proposals had not been accepted even in principle. The situation was hardly better on the eve of the armistice.[24]

Surveying all these separate efforts, the Ministry of Reconstruction could take consolation only in the knowledge that it had fought hard. With the sole exception of priorities, not one of the projects—raw materials, demand, shipping, storage and transit, national factories, or civilian demobilization—had cleared the crucial stage of cabinet approval. And the lone success was imperiled as much by delay on the other projects as by its own intrinsic incompleteness.

The Need: A Plan—and Planners.

A few observers saw deeper flaws. Had every one of these bits and pieces been endorsed they would not have added up to a general economic plan. To overlook no single part of the whole economic transition, physical and human, was one task of planners; but synthesizing the whole

23. See the second interim report in *Parliamentary Papers* (1918), vol. 14, "Civil War Workers' Committee. Second, Third, Fourth, and Fifth Interim Reports," Cd. 9192, printed in November 1918. For the sequel regarding unemployment aid, see below, pp. 315, 332–34.

24. Addison, *Diary*, 2: 498, 505–7, 508, 544, 581; F. 5180, Box 90, Part 3. Addison had won approval for the idea, but not the amount, of veterans' unemployment benefit; see WC 274, 15 November 1917, Cab. 23/4, and WC 431, 17 June 1918, Cab. 23/6.

was their duty too. How did demand relate to supply, and how did shipping and storage affect each? Granted there must be a certain sequence in restarting industry, what would that sequence be in detail and which controls—for there was a bewildering variety—would ensure it? If systems of priorities were to constitute the chief controls (even this had not been decided), what precisely did "priorities" mean, for shipping, for soldiers, for munitions work, and for the manufacturers who would begin to clamor for goods, trains, and seaport space? When and how would plans for discharge, unemployment aid, and reemployment contribute to an orderly revival of trade? And could anything be deemed settled while the question of pledges was not faced?

These were questions of substance, but they could not be settled piecemeal. Nor could they be solved by *ad hoc* conferences. They must form part of a general plan; and this plan could never result from existing methods, for Whitehall was an anthill of uncoordinated if prodigious departmental effort, at the center of which an utterly war-centered cabinet did nothing to provide unity. Hence the felt need for decisions on policy in general became transmuted into a campaign for new machinery. Substance and procedure, policy and structure, were inseparable; the counterpart of the substantive need for a general plan was the need for a great power to oversee all.

It fell to Carson's Economic Offensive Committee to voice this dual need. From January to June of 1918 the committee pressed for action. The result was a dual triumph, but not the triumph that it expected. It brought into existence two new committees, but not the general plan. Fortunately the results—the Home Affairs Committee and the Economic Defence and Development Committee—were organs at the level of greatest need.

Levels of planning. A priori, one may distinguish three levels of planning. A planner might concern himself with a particular question of substantive policy—details of housing finance, for example, or a schedule of priority in shipping. The result on this primary level would be the submission of a specialized topical report, proposal, or bill. One step higher, the planner might devise a deliberative body to which such reports, of several kinds but within one group, might go. The result on the second level would be a comprehensive advisory or review committee—something like the proposed Central Raw Materials Board, or the ministerial Committee of Four, or an interdepartmental "umbrella" conference. Such groups made for coordination and perspective. Third, the planner, far up in the spidery structure of the command tower, might construct a body, with cabinet authority, to validate or judge the work done on all types of things at both lower levels. The result might be a fully empowered subcommittee of the War Cabinet.

Planning on surplus stores, raw materials, and priority involved the second level and, obviously, the first. The Standing Council and the S.G.P.A.C. were monuments to successful endeavor there. But the aim of all aims, Carson and Addison had realized, was higher still.

Carson's Economic Offensive Committee, the prime mover in effecting structural change, was prompted to demand new machinery by its concern for substance. But these concerns had a most specific content, as well as a more general side. Its records, not accidentally, bear the contemporary title "Trade War." The files bulged with appeals for protection and the heftiest documents were the translations from such German journals as *Der Wirtschaftskrieg.* Its pet projects were the import and export bills. Its favorite quotations were from the Balfour of Burleigh committee, which took a debater's pleasure in anticipating free traders and in quoting Asquith's endorsements of the 1916 protectionist and punitive inter-Allied conference at Paris.

But the narrow and intense enthusiasm for "trade war" was hardly the sole motive. Joining their memoranda to those with which Carson bombarded the War Cabinet, Addison, Montagu, and Stanley strove for the more general end of aiding reconstruction by forging a new and fit instrument; they used the E.O.C. as a sounding board for demands less divisive and no less urgent. Carson wanted to make sure of raw materials supply as part of "trade war" preparedness; so did they, for their own reasons. Carson championed bills to control imports and exports; so, out of fear of runaway inflation or of disastrous "dumping" by other nations, did they. He deplored the failure to follow up the Paris resolutions and the Balfour of Burleigh reports; so did they. All contended that prewar fiscal controversies and loyalties had subsided, so that measures hitherto damned by free traders might now get fair consideration.[25]

Had Carson's original protectionist and anti-German motives dominated the campaign launched from the Economic Offensive Committee, and had he presided alone over the final cabinet agreement to set up the E.D.D.C., the result might have been no gain at all for the broader purposes of reconstruction. But the eventual victory in the campaign for the E.D.D.C. was shaped by other advocates and their other purposes. Even

25. For papers on German economic policy, see Cab. 21/109. See G. 156 by Carson (20 September 1917), G. 158 by Stanley (4 October 1917), G. 160 by Addison (28 September 1917) and G. 161 by Montagu (8 October 1917), in Cab. 21/108.

Carson, as weeks passed, muted his protectionism and put the case for the new committee in the same general terms his colleagues used. And thus the very organ that was created, born in the service of trade war, became a weapon in a different cause. The War Cabinet, scarred by Parliament's rejection of protectionist measures in 1917, refused to endorse a specifically anti-German postwar policy.[26] The significance of the E.O.C. campaign lay not in protectionist battles won but in the gradual acceptance of the case for a new form.

Carson's most vigorous statement argued for agreement within the government on economic policy, on the grounds of restricting the resources of Germany *and* on the need to protect the Allied peoples against starvation and unemployment throughout reconstruction. It was a shrewd attempt to dispel the suspicions that the very phrase "economic offensive" evoked. The public, said Carson, perhaps thought that the government meant to inflict damage on Germany during reconstruction and afterwards, but as far as the government was concerned this policy "did not exist"! The broad aims—to secure the people against worldwide shortages, to help essential industries, to extend government aid to trading communities, and to stimulate enterprise in foreign markets— were the very aims of reconstruction. The problems of economic defense and development formed "a part—perhaps the most important part—of the problem of Reconstruction."

Carson ranged himself unequivocally with the planners in favor of continued controls.

> In our opinion restrictions hardly less drastic will be necessary during the period of Reconstruction. In no other way can the country hope to escape from the perils of hunger, unemployment, social disorganisation, industrial paralysis, and financial chaos.

He predicted the Salisbury committee would find that British industry would be beaten in a stand-up fight against the organized state-aided efforts of Germany "if it adheres rigidly to the old system of *laissez-faire* and refuses to learn the lesson that in modern commerce, as in war, the power of organized combinations pursuing a steady policy will speedily drive out of the field the unregulated competition of individual enterprise." Then came the case for a new system. Piecemeal action had prevailed thus far, but it forfeited the opportunity to enlist support and

26. See WC 273 (14 November 1917) and WC 312 (3 January 1918), in Cab. 21/108 and Cab. 23/4 and 23/5. But WC 329 (23 January 1918) accepted E.O.C. plans for postwar protection of the dyes industry; see Cab. 23/5.

enthusiasm in Britain's own people; it sowed doubt and suspicion. "The experience of our Committee has convinced me of the absolute necessity for some co-ordinating authority, such as the Minister of Reconstruction." But that minister, Carson warned, "cannot hope to exercise the influence which it is absolutely essential he should exercise . . . unless he works through, and is supported by, a Cabinet Committee representative of the various Departments which are concerned in the task of Economic Defence and Development." A new body, no less representative and no less authoritative, must be set up. Asquith's way had a new champion.

The union of substance and structure was patent. Addison emphatically agreed on the twin needs—for a general policy and a general authority.

> The experience of five months had convinced me that . . . we constantly run the risk of grave delay even in urgent matters if the work of Reconstruction has to be carried out through a sequence of individual negotiations between all the Departments severally on the one hand, and a single Department on the other. . . . The most practical course for the Cabinet to follow is to establish a small Ministerial Council on Reconstruction for which the Ministry of Reconstruction would furnish the Secretariat. The business of the Council would be to review in an orderly and progressive manner the Reconstruction Programme submitted to them item by item from the Ministry; to recommend to the War Cabinet proposals for action and allocation of executive duties following thereon; to receive reports as to the progress of measures on which they had decided; and of course to initiate proposals of their own which, having been examined by the Ministry of Reconstruction in their bearings on the general programme, would be returned to them for consideration as substantive projects. For all these purposes the Council would be reinforced by the attendance on any question of all the Ministers concerned.[27]

Walter Long, adding his support, pointed to two reports on the empire's trade relations—submitted by his committee, and still waiting. Finally, on 10 June—to consider reports, to settle minor details, to prepare major proposals for the cabinet, to prevent overlapping, and to establish a body that could follow up decisions—the Economic Defence and Development

27. "Reconstruction," memorandum of 4 February 1918, Addison to War Cabinet, in F. 4041, Box 70, Part 1. The Carson memorandum is G. 190, of 21 January 1918, in Cab. 21/108.

Committee was voted by the War Cabinet.[28] At its first meeting the E.D.D.C. accepted Addison's proposals (the Birchenough Report) for priority machinery. Not surprisingly, the first project it authorized was a full-scale report on the general basis of future economic policy![29]

Addison had double cause for rejoicing. The E.D.D.C. "would save the War Cabinet a lot of time"; it would also encourage the Home Affairs Committee, whose creation that same day had crowned his effort.

> The similar body which I have been wanting so long and which has nominally been created for Home Affairs is still only on paper and has not been called together. With the additional pressure behind it, I hope this will have better luck. At all events a number of Ministers are keen about it. This proposed committee on Economic Affairs may provide an important working model.[30]

Planning for Reform

Months had gone into creating the Home Affairs Committee. Addison suggested a council of ministers on home policy to the Prime Minister in February, and nominal approval came on March 6. But nine weeks of delay, while matters requiring decision mounted up, brought Addison to the boiling point. The draft bill for a Ministry of Health, sent to the cabinet in April after months of negotiations and disappointments, was repeatedly postponed. "Pushed out once more by war matters," Addison raged; "we must have some way of getting decisions on Home Affairs." Austen Chamberlain rejected the idea of using the Economic Offensive Committee or its successor; they would have nothing to do, he announced, "with Land, Housing, Health and such-like questions."[31] Tormented, Addison wrote Lloyd George, asking formally

> whether I can look to you for sympathy and support, or not. . . . At your request, I have undertaken a big task which is . . . a great joy to me, provided I am able to get on with it. . . . Things are now heaping up in such a way and so many matters are nearly ripe for decision that, with . . . the brusque treatment which I received

28. G.T. 4368 (27 April 1918) and G.T. 4770 (8 May 1918), in Cab. 21/108; letters from Foreign Office, 21 and 23 May 1918, in Cab. 21/108; WC 413 (17 May 1918) and 429 (10 June 1918) in Cab. 23/6.

29. Economic Defence and Development Committee, minutes of first meeting (18 June 1918), in Cab. 27/44; Addison, *Diary*, 2: 541, 542.

30. *Ibid.*, pp. 536–38.

31. *Ibid.*, pp. 439, 441, 444, 474, 533, 535 sums up E.O.C. action; pp. 536–38 explain the E.D.D.C.; pp. 489, 492–93, 509 are on the Home Affairs Committee.

from you on Thursday last, I am compelled to enquire what hope there is of my being able to deal with them.

I propose—if only as a final effort—to submit, separately from this letter, a Memorandum on the subject.

Lloyd George promised "unqualified support" if Addison "did not expect him to devote his own mind" to home affairs. The Home Affairs Committee soon came into being.

It was a body much like Asquith's Reconstruction Committee, composed of the presidents of the Local Government Board, the Board of Trade, the Board of Education, the Ministers of Labour and Reconstruction, a law officer of the Crown, the Secretary for Scotland, and the Home Secretary (in the chair). It was to meet weekly and to handle all domestic questions that involved more than one department or were of such importance that they would otherwise call for cabinet attention. It would have wide discretion in dealing finally with questions on which agreement was reached; and, best of all, there would be automatic referral from the War Cabinet.

Behind it Addison saw, or thought he saw, a tangle of politics and factionalism: hostility to the Ministry of Health; Tory maneuvers against Lloyd George; obstructionism by people like Long and Hayes Fisher on matters like Home Rule and the voting register. Nor was he happy that a month elapsed before the Home Affairs Committee actually met. But it was a good sign that at its first meeting it tackled the Ministry of Health Bill. In July, three sessions on the bill revealed a growing measure of agreement.[32]

How much had been gained by the creation of the four new committees in June and July? If the effort spent in winning cabinet sanction was a criterion, the new structures were important indeed, but there were grounds for more cautious appraisal. It was not clear that the Home Affairs Committee, the Economic Defence and Development Committee, and the Post-War Priorities Committee and its Standing Council would prove commensurate with the great task ahead. Products of specific situations, called into being to unravel a tangle of quite specific issues that had been

32. Besides George Cave (chairman and Home Secretary), the first meeting consisted of Addison, H. A. L. Fisher of Education, Hayes Fisher of the Local Government Board, and Stanley Baldwin as Joint First Secretary to the Treasury; see Cab. 26/1, minutes of first meeting, Home Affairs Committee (9 July 1918). See also Addison, *Diary*, 2: 459, 526–27, 535–42, 552–53, and 559. Hereafter "HAC" will be used to identify the Home Affairs Committee, and the source will be Cab. 26/1 unless otherwise stated.

stuck at the cabinet level, the four new bodies might prove correspondingly limited and incomplete. Even if they were perfect and fully formed (as they manifestly were not, as long as the staff for one had not yet been named), the new structures supplied only one of the three great preconditions for success. All three of these preconditions need emphasis: first, to overlook no single *part* of policy, perfecting every detail; second, to synthesize the *whole*; third, to create the *machinery* needed for action. Before June, solid work had got no further than the first precondition (and, even there, much remained undone). The four new structures represented encouraging progress, for the first time, on the third great need, but the crucial second task still remained.

Perhaps the gains of midyear brought a synthesis nearer; certainly they encouraged unified thinking. But the machinery had arrived before the plan, and it remained to be seen whether the campaign for that machinery had drained away the energies that were needed to think through a synthesis. Certainly no general plan had been formulated. The attainments of June and July, literally indispensable, were in themselves insufficient.

10

Toward Democracy and Devolution in Industry—the Alternative to State Control? January–July 1918

Fresh from his unique research, Hammond brought vivid proof for a growing national faith.

> The Control Board in the woolen and worsted trade is perhaps the most striking of all the experiments that have been made during the war. The corporate spirit it has produced, the confidence it has inspired . . . above all the example it gives of effective cooperation between employers and workpeople and the several interests engaged in the trade, are full of encouragement and instruction for those who look along some such lines as these for the improvement of the tone and power of British industry. Nobody could sit through a meeting of the Board of Control without realising that this scheme is much more than a wartime expedient and that it conveys the most significant lessons on the whole problem of industrial efficiency and industrial peace.[1]

Men such as Hammond meant to extend this living reality of wartime into the postwar period and to make it a permanent feature of British life. Control boards were far and away the clearest proof that war was teaching new lessons, demonstrating new powers, prefiguring future good. They were democratic; they were representative; and they worked. They solved huge problems and they effected huge economies. If Britain was feeling, as Hammond insisted, "a new ambition and a new confidence," these agencies were the visible proofs of the invisible cause, war. They shone with the promise of a Britain transformed. "The very machinery of a new social order," declared the *Round Table*, "is being created hour by hour in the struggle."[2]

1. See above, p. 78.
2. *Round Table* (December 1917), p. 14.

Hammond probed the cotton controls and found a true community come to life. Industry had accepted its responsibility for its own reserves of labor; highly paid workers claimed no more from unemployment funds than the lowest; the trade unions had their rightful place in administration. The foundation for everything was the agreed principle "that all sections of an industry must accept a common discipline for the sake of industry as a whole." He and Garrod and Nash probed ever wider. They studied the leather-trades control. They pestered other ministries for news. The ministry became something of a repository for the growing literature on controls, labor-management experiments, and the democratization of industry.[3] Back and forth within the ministry the documents passed, bringing news not of control boards alone but of Whitley Councils and new trade groups, bodies present and future.

It all reflected a stirring of hope throughout the nation. Practical considerations, along with emotion, played their part, for these bodies would have work to do. The Civil War Workers' Demobilisation Committee stressed that Joint Industrial Councils could help greatly in reducing the period of unemployment; the Financial Facilities Committee noted that committees from the trades could make recommendations. At point after point the proposed machinery for reconversion was to be geared to local or occupational groups outside of government. These were specific functions; none was unimportant. But a much more general function was the greatest future service of all. These new organizations were expected to serve the ends of output and industrial peace. Whitley Councils especially were looked to for just this reason. The enthusiasm and the concern of officialdom and the public bespoke the belief that increased productivity and swift resumption of trade—the preconditions for all else—depended on harmony between employers and employed.[4]

On many fronts and for many motives, therefore, the Ministry of Reconstruction joined other departments in a strenuous effort of promotion. It is a campaign hard to analyze, impossible to narrate, and not easy to judge. To underrate it would be wrong; too much was, and was thought to be, at stake. To narrate it, given mere fragments of records, is

3. "The Cotton Control Board," F. 6208, Box 67; "Memorandum on the Control of Leather," by Hammond, with Nash's comment, F. 6091, Box 71; F. 6081, Box 39. F. 3770, Box 70, Part 1, contains articles and pamphlets on Whitleyism, apparently from John Hilton of the Garton Foundation. See also the Garton Foundation's *Memorandum on the Industrial Situation after the War.*

4. See F. 6091, Box 71; Cd. 9117, pp. 7–8; Addison, *Diary*, 2: 468; Cd. 9005, pp. xvi–xvii; Ministry of Labour, *Report on the Establishment and Progress of Joint Industrial Councils*, p. 1.

out of the question. Even contemporaries found it hard to assess the movement; not only were they divided as to its intrinsic merits (as we shall see), they were alternately beset by anxiety and pessimism and swept up by joyous hope. Success would do more than anything else to bring the promised better world, but the issue was constantly in doubt.

Perhaps that was because the plan to promote devolution, democracy, interclass harmony, and cooperation between interests took such a variety of forms. These—with a warning that the forced pace of development threatened to produce new species almost momentarily—may be put into six groups.

1. *Joint Industrial Councils* (Whitley Councils) and *Provisional Drafting Committees* (meant to become Whitley Councils). Deriving from the Whitley Report, these bodies bespoke more clearly than other bodies the faith that consultation on an equal basis between workers and employers was a help or a necessity in future industrial relations.

2. *Interim Industrial Reconstruction Committees.* These belated groups differed from Whitley Councils in being planned for more temporary advisory work in the transition; sometimes they had fewer labor members.

3. *Trade committees.* The departments used this term for groups wholly or chiefly composed of businessmen, who were grouped by trade. Munitions listed seventy-nine, and the Ministry of Food two hundred such groups, which helped with advice.

4. *Trade Boards.* Set up for particular trades under the Trade Boards Act of 1909, these boards fulfilled statutory duties, such as fixing wages in (originally) exceptionally ill-paid industries. They were very much under government control.

5. *Control boards* or *standing councils.* These bodies aided a department in administering wartime regulations. Representativeness was a common feature, and often a requirement.

6. *Local reconstruction organizations.* Least ambitious and least aided, these groups often were of early origin and were highly representative of persons who were keen on reconstruction. They sometimes began as simple discussion groups but they aspired to be more, and the Ministry of Reconstruction hoped they would form nuclei of popular support.

The first three types were to be self-governing and wholly unofficial organizations, unlike the fourth and fifth types, which were oriented to government. The fourth, with a clear prewar statutory basis and very narrow scope, seemed hardly to belong in the list at all; in practice, however, a surprising trend arose to encourage Trade Boards to become broader and freer groups, like Whitley Councils.

There were other differences. First, it must be clear that, in men's hopes, Whitley Councils stood above all the rest. If wartime control boards were the most vivid examples of present success, Whitley Councils were the chosen instruments of greatest promise for the future. Second, if one took a sharp ideological line, Whitley Councils and trade committees should never have been spoken of in the same breath. The essence of the former was labor's equal role, bespeaking a new worker-oriented concept of industrial democracy; they were a tacit judgment on existing capitalism. Trade committees, however, carried no such connotations; they implied merely that industry needed more unified organization. To insurgent labor and to guild socialists, of course, both groups were capitalist-dominated obstacles to true workers' control. (In contrast, Addison spoke of the two types almost interchangeably. To the reconstruction staff, both types were examples of the wider organization that industry needed. Both rested on the faith that harmony of interests and a greater sense of public obligation would grow with experience—but the reconstruction men were liberals.)

The historical origins differed for each type, and their departmental "sponsors" also were different. The Board of Trade supervised Trade Boards; the Ministry of Labour increasingly took charge of Whitley Councils; the Ministry of Reconstruction alone cared for the second and the sixth types, and busied itself with forming a network of new trade committees. These differences assumed historical importance when they caused repeated frictions and delays.

It is necessary to insist on these differences if only because the departments did, but experience blurred all clear distinctions. When an organization began it was very hard to be sure what it would develop into. A group whose nucleus was predominantly businessmen, but with some laborers, might gain more workers' representatives and blossom into a Joint Industrial Council, as intended; or it might remain one-sided and best be treated as a trade committee. Such were the realities that the government's organizers met—a kind of Lewis Carroll croquet in which "chosen instruments" developed refractory lives of their own.

Despite all diversities, some similarities marked the whole campaign. The problems that were encountered were much alike: questions of constitution, clashes of jurisdiction, the wearisome slowness of founding and the uncertainty of survival. Broadly speaking, campaigns for most types went through similar stages: prior inquiry as to group interest;

establishment; and first steps in training. For most types there was another similarity: incompleteness and unreadiness as the war ended. But there were inequalities here: control boards *lived*; some Whitley Councils *existed* and others had *approached* establishment; but the groups in Addison's charge lagged far behind the others.

By the end of 1918 the government had reported the existence of twenty Whitley Councils, nineteen provisional drafting committees, and thirty-six Interim Industrial Reconstruction Committees. This is the measure of the effort put forth. Of these achievements, Whitley Councils claim first attention.[5]

The Crux of Reconstruction: Reconciling the Preconditions

As war opened new depths of feeling the familiar ideas of Whitleyism came to mean more. In 1916 Cavendish-Bentinck joined J. R. Clynes and J. J. Mallon in a study of works committees, and B. Seebohm Rowntree began a lifetime of advocacy. Covering individualism and laissez-faire with shame, war cleared the stage for a new system. There was hope, too, in the words of the presidential address that year to the Trades Union Congress. Harry Gosling told his audience:

> We hope for something better than a mere avoidance of unemployment and strikes. We are tired of war in the industrial field. The British workman cannot quietly submit to an autocratic government of the conditions of his own life. He will not take "Prussianism" lying down. ... Would it not be possible for the employers ... to put their businesses on a new footing by admitting the workmen to some participation, not in profits but in control? ... Believe me, we shall never get any lasting industrial peace except on the lines of democracy.

Coming in this context, the Whitley Reports stirred and divided men to a peculiar degree. Herbert Samuel thought them "the most important of any that have so far reached us from the Reconstruction Committee."[6]

5. Cd. 9231, pp. 7–8.

6. *P.D.(C.)*, vol. 96, c. 1612 (27 July 1917); *ibid.*, c. 2175–76; Gosling's address is quoted in B. C. Roberts, *The Trades Union Congress, 1868–1921* (Cambridge, Mass.: Harvard University Press, 1958), p. 284. See also Theodor Plaut, *Die Enstehung des Whitleyismus* (Jena, 1930), chap. 1; Leonard D. White, *Whitley Councils in the British Civil Service* (Chicago: University of Chicago Press, 1933), pp. 4–5; *Athenaeum*, no. 4618 (June 1917), p. 288; Ministry of Labour, *Joint Industrial Councils*, p. 15. For precedents of 1911–13, see Barry, *Nationalisation in British Politics*, p. 214.

An archbishops' conference endorsed the idea, as did Asquith and Lloyd George, J. L. Hammond, Neville Chamberlain, and a host of anxious "reconstructionists." From Bristol, London, and elsewhere the local reconstruction groups sent encomiums.[7] As magazines passed judgment, the *Nation* half convinced itself that Whitleyism brought industrial peace within the realm of the possible—one of the few beliefs that the *Economist* shared with it. From the ranks of labor, Clynes saw Whitleyism as the alternative to a condition of perpetual revolt; John Murphy and others of the left wing saw it as outright betrayal.[8]

Why did men care? The answer reaches to the heart of the whole vast unofficial literature on reconstruction. Whitleyism was there, in every major book, and endorsed in every segment of that literature but one. The peculiar nature of the applause for Whitleyism, half fervor and half despair, speaks volumes about the fears that beset sober men. Beyond the armistice they foresaw two kinds of war: between nations and economies (the competitive war for world markets) and within Britain itself (fratricidal war between labor and capital). The first of these wars could not be avoided; it must be won. Defeat would be synonymous with disaster and would, at the minimum, cost Britain her hopes for a better national life. For the sake of survival and for the fulfillment of costly reforms, competitive fitness (which, practically speaking, meant higher output and efficiency) was essential.

The other war could not be won. It must lead to the ruin of a program that was dependent on cooperation and consensus. It must never be allowed to start. Prevention—indeed, more than prevention (a mere grudging truce would not meet the need)—must be achieved. What was required was nothing short of the replacement of present strife by a new

7. Report of Archbishops' Conference, in Lucy Gardner, ed., *Some Christian Essentials of Reconstruction* (London, 1920), pp. 192–93; speech of Asquith in Birmingham, December 11, 1917; "Jason" [J. L. Hammond], *Past and Future* (London, 1918), pp. 112–14; H. J. Jennings, *The Coming Economic Crisis* (London, 1918), pp. 99–100 (citing Neville Chamberlain); Bristol Association for Industrial Reconstruction, *Report of a Conference* (Bristol, 1918), pp. 13–16; London Industrial Reconstruction Council, *Reconstruction Handbook* (London, 1918), pp. 7–9; F. T. Woods, *A New Fellowship in Industry* (London, 1918), p. 3; Leonard J. Reid, *The Great Alternative* (London, 1918), pp. 84–85; "Report on the Reconstruction of Industry," published for the Devon and Cornwall Association for Industrial and Commercial Reconstruction, in F. 8447, Box 71, Part 2.

8. *The Nation*, 21 (1 September 1917): 550–51. See also *New Statesman*, 27 October 1917, p. 75, 1 June 1918, pp. 164–66, and 15 June 1918, p. 202; *Athenaeum*, no. 4628 (April 1918), p. 174, and no. 4630 (June 1918), p. 270; *Economist*, 7 July 1917, p. 3; Clynes in D. H. S. Cranage, ed., *The War and Unity* (Cambridge, 1919), pp. 125–31; for Murphy and others, see Barry, *Nationalisation in British Politics*, pp. 214–18, 232, n. 33.

order of things, in which all parties gave of their best at a new and higher level of partnership.

Whitley Councils held promise of serving both needs. They would gird a united Britain to meet world challenges by a superior productivity born of common endeavor and they would make industrial strife unnecessary by basing policy on free agreement between equals. Whitleyism's supreme merit, as its advocates saw it, was that the system relied not on exhortation but on a new structure of power in which labor had an *equal* share. Labor would yield nothing to preachment alone, but it would respond to the prospect of equal power.

The stakes could not be overestimated. To reconcile labor to higher output was the very crux of reconstruction. Only from a much greater fund of national wealth could new housing be built, welfare programs financed, and the war debt paid. "Increased production," declared the *Round Table*, was "the necessary basis for *every* advance." But just as necessary was the removal of industrial unrest—"an absolute postulate of progress"—and these two preconditions clashed. Workers suspected all talk of increased output as the feared forerunner of an attack on wage rates. Even a verbal campaign for higher production would unleash a system of "ca' canny"—deliberate slowdown—or a wave of angry strikes, which would be fatal to reconstruction. This was the danger in any simple initiative for output alone. Contrariwise, in the workers' singleminded demand for the redemption of pledges there was equal danger, for a literal restoration of old trade-union rules menaced output. These prewar practices were restrictive. Redemption, however, was pledged; without it, the *Athenaeum* warned, "industrial peace will be as remote as ever." The impasse seemed complete.[9] Precisely here, where society's imperative need for higher output clashed with labor's suspicions, Whitleyism promised to break the deadlock. Whitley Councils could calm these fears by putting workers in the seats of power too.

9. *Round Table*, 7 (March 1916): 234, 238, 252; *Athenaeum*, no. 4635 (6 November 1918), pp. 457–58, 460–62. See also Jennings, *The Coming Economic Crisis*, pp. 94–98, 109–10; Woods, *A New Fellowship*, pp. 2–3; Reid, *The Great Alternative*, pp. 85–86; Alan Bullock, *The Life and Times of Ernest Bevin* (London, 1960), 1: 64–66; William Dawson, ed., *After-War Problems* (London, 1917), p. 13; A. W. Kirkaldy, ed., *Industry and Finance* (London, 1917), pp. 15, 20, 144–49; Lucy Gardner, ed., *Some Christian Essentials*, p. 30; Lucy Gardner, ed., *The Hope for Society* (London, 1917), pp. 23–47, 113; W. C. Dampier Whetham, *The War and the Nation* (London, 1917), pp. 26, 28, 31–32, 131–42, 162, 277–92; J. A. Hobson, *Democracy after the War* (London, 1917), pp. 171–78, 182; Thomas C. Evans, *Democracy and Reconstruction* (Manchester, 1919), p. 45; Lord Beveridge, *Power and Influence* (London, 1953), p. 123, n. 1; Labour Co-partnership Association (London), *Papers*, no. 3, pp. 7–8; Paul U. Kellogg and Arthur Gleason, *British Labor and the War* (New York, 1919), p. 133.

Some writers thought that the Joint Industrial Councils solved still a third problem: how to maintain controls and yet avoid rule by Whitehall. The dilemma was real. On the one hand, as the majority of writers conceded, no return to laissez-faire could be tolerated; at least for the transition months, some curbs were indispensable. On the other hand, this concession was grudging; spokesmen for government rule were few. As J. L. Hammond wrote:

> If State control was not too popular before the war, it would be difficult to find language that would do justice to its unpopularity today. . . . It is not by State control that democracy will find a safe place in the industrial system.

Thanks to Mars, he saw a clear alternative: "The war has taught us that there is a type of relationship between the State and industry which avoids the evils of a crippling State control . . . and the dangerous power of a trust."[10] Devolution of economic functions onto nongovernmental bodies, where employer and employee would meet and vote: this was the popular new middle way; and Whitley Councils were its favored embodiment.

This third argument for Whitleyism was neither universal nor uniform. Not all who used it held the same attitude toward controls or saw the link between Whitleyism and the control question in the same light. At one extreme of opinion, a few men were determined on maintenance of controls and agreed that Whitley Councils were the preferable means for administering them. This was the position of those most opposed in principle to laissez-faire. It clearly implied that if there could not be devolution there must be state control. (Ernest Bevin, in his dissent to the Birchenough Report, exemplified this view.) For others—closer to the middle range of the spectrum—controls were necessary and/or inevitable, but *only* in the nonbureaucratic form of a Whitley Council or a kindred trade organization: only Whitleyism could make controls tolerable. For still others the real affinity was between devolution and *de*control, and Whitley Councils would be the first step toward the end of restraint. At this same end of the spectrum, it may be, were some who disliked conceding labor a share of power but accepted this side of Whitleyism as the price business must pay for its first victory over officialdom. Such lukewarm converts perhaps looked to a later day, when the partnership, its function served, could be disbanded.

Ulterior motives, then, differed. As men took contrasting views on the

10. "Jason," *Past and Future*, p. 105. See also *Economist*, 85 (1 December 1917), p. 867; Henry Jones, *The Principles of Citizenship* (London, 1919), pp. 1, 12.

control question, they endorsed Whitleyism for different and even potentially opposite reasons. The diversity was ominous. Agreement on the controls question (one is inclined to insist: "consensus *for* controls") would be immensely valuable. But for the moment the chorus of endorsement was the main fact.

The Left held apart from this consensus. To Leftists in or beyond the ranks of organized labor the primacy of output and of a postwar trade war were not self-evident truths; the redemption of society from within, not the preservation of an old society by triumphs abroad, came first. Thus one key argument for Whitleyism held no appeal for the left. And the second argument, by its very nature, could bring no response: the idea of industrial peace violated the tenet of ineradicable class conflict; and the underlying premise—trust—seemed sinister, ludicrous, or both. Whitleyism demanded mutual confidence, at least confidence sufficient to give the experiment a substantial trial. To the skeptics on labor's left wing, however, the worker could trust his government or his employer only if he ignored the whole of his bitter wartime experiences. And trust would be fatal to the temper by which labor could truly triumph, through its own militancy and union.

The government's stand was not in doubt. They had heard Addison's strong endorsement of Whitleyism—one of his first reports to the cabinet as Minister of Reconstruction—in which he optimistically listed many tasks and questions which he hoped to refer to the Whitley Councils for action or advice. They listened while Shackleton, of the Ministry of Labour, canvassed the main objections—partly from advocates of national guilds ("who fear the adoption of the Whitley Report would tend to improve industrial relations"), and partly from highly organized industries like the cotton trade ("where satisfactory machinery had been evolved and where Government interference was not welcomed"), but they noted his opinion that practical difficulties could be surmounted. They heard from a Ministry of Munitions official that the report had already stimulated formation of shop committees, including some in national factories. On 9 October 1917, they voted approval of the Whitley Report. Soon, the Ministry of Munitions held a major conference on works committees and the Ministry of Labour and the Ministry of Reconstruction joined forces to build new joint councils. The cabinet lavished encomiums in its Annual Report:

> The establishment of Industrial Councils will mark a new era in industry, as it will enable the principal industries to regulate their

own affairs through representative bodies . . . and to give joint advice to the Government . . . as to how far further State interference by means of legislation is or is not desirable. It will also associate the workers with the employers in the solution of the difficult problems of the reconstruction period, which can only be successfully dealt with by all concerned . . . co-operating to work out the best method of coping with them.[11]

Addison took to Whitleyism with all his heart. He and Rowntree, while they were at the Ministry of Munitions, helped set up joint committees; later, when he joined the reconstruction staff, Addison was delighted to find Greenwood and Zimmern already at work in the same cause. His diary abounds with references to Whitley Councils. "Properly backed up," he reasoned, they could "transform the outlook in British industry in the course of a few years."[12] Losing not a moment, Addison devoted his first public speech as minister to the case for joint councils. He explicitly linked them to the desire for devolution and to the need to win labor's consent for the introduction of new technology. He cheered his staff on: "The more we can get the Whitley principle adopted, the better."

Greenwood and Hammond needed encouragement. Speaking that December in Manchester, they faced an audience that was dominated by shop stewards who were intensely suspicious of the Whitley reports. The two men found considerable support, but they joined in a warning.

> The Ministry of Reconstruction will labour under considerable difficulties because of the suspicion with which all proposals made by the Government will be regarded. . . . Any proposal emanating from the Government will encounter a very serious body of prejudice and suspicion. . . . There is evidently a violent and uncompromising spirit in the workman's world, and it is important to keep this in mind in urging the Whitley Policy.

It was the advice that Zimmern had given in 1916 and Mrs. Webb in 1917, but Addison pressed on. In January 1918 he helped launch the Pottery Council, the first of the Whitley Councils.[13]

11. See WC 247, 9 October 1917, Cab. 23/4; War Cabinet, "Annual Report for 1917," Cd. 9005, pp. 100–101; National War Aims Committee, *Looking Forward : Lloyd George's Message* (London, 1918), pp. 11–12; F. 11498, Box 39, for the Munitions conference; Seymour, *The Whitley Council Scheme*, pp. 16–22, and Ministry of Labour, *Joint Industrial Councils*, pp. 3–25.

12. Addison, *Diary*, 1: 250, and 2: 424, 426, 430, 580.

13. *Ibid.*, 2: 450–53, 460–64; Files 3913 and 7249, Box 71, Part 3, and F. 43, Box 71, Part 1. For other work by Addison, see *Diary*, 2: 469–72, 479, and F. 4469, Box 54; Ministry of Labour, *Joint Industrial Councils*, p. 30.

Cooperation and specialization. A great impetus resulted from the meeting of Stanley, Roberts (Minister of Labour), and Addison with six of Britain's most distinguished bankers and industrialists, who represented the Federation of British Industries, the Association of Controlled Firms, and the Association of Chambers of Commerce. Although this January meeting focused on trade committees rather than on Joint Industrial Councils, the optimistic response from the businessmen helped Whitleyism too. The resultant decision was to set up a working body of nine men —from the ministries, the three business groups, and from the Trades Union Congress. From this moment, Whitley Councils became the Ministry of Labour's "show." Addison was to concentrate on "trade organisations," but he saw the decision as a gain for all of these linked causes. Now worried at slow progress, now submerging his doubts in redoubled efforts, he spoke to more meetings and watched as joint councils grew. One was set up for the leather trade, another for the building trades; more trade committees that might become Whitley Councils came nearer establishment.[14]

Progress and problems to June 1918. Half a year's work taught many lessons. Nomenclature and identification were persistent problems, as many groups applied for Whitley Council status without meeting the specifications. Could the Maritime Board evolve into a Whitley Council? Might the National Chamber of Trade, representing thousands of retail merchants—or the National Employers' Federation—qualify as they were then constituted? Ernest Benn, for all his keenness on trade organization, counseled that "the less we have to do with the National Employers' Federation the better." Could one joint body represent the whole chemical industry? Officials decided against this.[15]

Would the departments cooperate? Whitleyism would gain immensely if the government used the council; and the Ministry of Labour had pledged that

> the Councils will be recognised as the official standing Consultative Committees to the Government on all future questions affecting the industries which they represent, and that they will be the normal channel through which the opinion and experience of an industry will be sought on all questions with which the industry is concerned.

But the Board of Trade had strong misgivings: the new forms—either trade committees or Whitley Councils—might "promote Trade Combina-

---

14. Cd. 9005, pp. 206–7; Addison, *Diary*, 2: 475–79, 485, 499, 524, 539, 541, 547.
15. Files 3128 and 5969, Box 71, Part 3; Addison, *Diary*, 2: 470, 479, 521.

tions or Rings." A persistent, reasonable doubt, it deterred the Board from conferring powers on the councils.

More and more, Whitehall would reveal the same disquiet. Could it be right for Whitley Councils, or groups like them, to gain power without responsibility and without subordination? Must the rule not prevail, instead, that power belonged only where popular election or ministerial responsibility justified it? Unless devolutionists came up with answers to these questions the whole program would be blocked. The government, of course, might publicly offer "to leave the industries to ration themselves"; lip service could always be continued. Officials might call for action, realizing that unless the new groups found practical work and gained official recognition, devolution would be stillborn. But the problem defied solution. The risk grew that devolution would remain only a hope.[16]

Interim Industrial Reconstruction Committees and Trade Groups

Addison was as keen for trade committees and I.I.R.C.'s as he was for Whitley Councils. At Munitions he had set up a committee of chemical manufacturers to report on postwar needs—and had incurred the wrath of the *New Statesman* for his pains. To help on employers' association questions, he brought Ernest J. Benn into the ministry. It seemed an odd choice—a "businessman's businessman," bursting with enthusiasm for the capitalist system and the free-enterprise spirit, set down amid Greenwood, Hammond, Reiss, and Nash. But Benn's task would be different, just as trade committees were different. Their aim was not industrial democracy but higher efficiency through centralization—to the ultimate end of success in the trade war. Sheer utility was their rationale. A small, manageable number of responsible bodies must be formed, simply because the government, as Addison noted, could not "make arrangements with thousands of separate individuals. . . . Unless we can get the Trade Associations well established, we shall be involved in much unnecessary turmoil after the war."[17]

A third kind of group, uniquely the charge of the Ministry of Reconstruction, fell somewhere between the clearly distinct trade committees and Whitley Councils. These, the Interim Industrial Reconstruction

16. Ministry of Labour, *Joint Industrial Councils*, p. 11; F. 3873, Box 71, Part 3; F. 539, Box 71, Part 1; Cd. 9005, pp. 205–6; *Athenaeum*, no. 4627 (March 1918), p. 154.

17. Cd. 8882, submitted 1 November 1917 (see *Parliamentary Papers*, 1917–18, vol. 18), prompted the comment in the *New Statesman*, 6 October 1917, p. 3. See also Addison, *Diary*, 2: 426, 444, 468, 476.

Committees, were embryonic Whitley Councils—at least in intent. But Addison's staff found it hard to keep categories straight. There were complaints of overlapping from the Ministry of Labour, and Benn found he had to confer weekly with that Ministry lest its campaign for Whitley Councils be hampered. To pacify the departments and to clear the air, an official announcement declared that the "trade organisation" campaign was meant simply

> to promote in as many industries as possible representative organ-
> isations to advise the Government as to the views and needs of the
> industries . . . during the Reconstruction period. The creation of
> the organisations . . . is not intended in any way to prejudice the
> formation of Joint Industrial Councils, but is designed as an
> emergency measure to facilitate the transition . . . and to expedite
> the establishment of permanent Industrial Councils.[18]

Such frictions were easily predictable. A more interesting problem, with a revealing finale, arose when Roberts' Ministry suggested that the government rely not on the new trade committees but on the established Trade Boards. Benn felt Trade Boards would not fill the bill and he urged that new I.I.R.C.'s be formed. Arthur Greenwood dissented:

> I thought it was agreed that Trade Boards *should* be used where they
> existed, just as Boards of Control or other joint bodies already
> existing would be used. I do not think you could get a more
> representative body.

Nash agreed with Greenwood: "Our best plan will always be to make use of existing joint bodies as far as possible." [19] He spoke more prophetically than he knew: only the existing bodies came into play with any effect in the critical phase of the transition period. Was this a warning that the whole crusade for new forms was energy ill spent?

Outside of government there were other difficulties. Some manufac-turers' groups balked at trade-union representation. Addison, eager for Whitley principles, strove and argued. In rare unison, his staff counseled acquiescence. "I agree with Mr. Greenwood," said Ernest Benn—and hastily penciled "for the moment!" Addison yielded, accepting a com-mittee that included only industrialists.[20]

18. Cd. 9005, pp. 206–7.
19. F. 5879, Box 71, Part 3; Files 1193 and 10485, Box 90.
20. Paper 1 (23 July 1918), Box 52; F. 4469, Box 54.

One objection touched fundamental policy. The Machine Tool and Engineering Association refused cooperation, viewing the committees as a first step toward postwar control. "It is the unanimous opinion of the trade," their deputation said, "that the Government should relax control as soon as possible." It was a grave issue, and Addison's answer was too quick: "The possibility of getting away from Government control depended upon the form of representative body to whom the Government could hand it over." This was as near as Addison ever came to the position that Whitleyism and the trade-committee schemes were *alternatives* to state control. But it was unauthorized; the government's decision on control had not been made. And if Addison was here making policy, he was making it ambiguously. His answer might suggest a clear presumption in favor of maximal state control until bodies exactly fit for devolution had been formed. This would be a strong line, mightily encouraging the growth of truly representative groups; or it might encourage hopes that if token organizations were formed, government would speedily decontrol.[21]

Rich in problems, poor in results—so Addison judged the story by May 1918. He had conferred, exhorted, lectured; his staff had slaved. The Board of Trade had pledged to utilize trade committees; the interdepartmental Trade Organization Section was taking part; advisers (ranging from Ernest Bevin and J. H. Thomas to spokesmen for the Federation of British Industries) were hard at work. But the creation of new committees lagged. The National Chamber of Trade, the object of propaganda for many months, was—and remained—uncommitted. Declarations of intent from the steel and iron trades and the cotton and woolens trades were good as far as they went; on paper, the total of exploratory conferences was impressive. By one count, eighteen committees had been formed; by another, twelve Interim Industrial Reconstruction Committees existed. But apart from discrepancies in figures was the disturbing fact that the totals included Trade Boards (no gain in *new* bodies there). Some groups were mere "Provisional Drafting Committees."

By June another difficulty began to dwarf all others: finding work, assigning it to the groups, and briefing them on their tasks. Starting the councils and committees was as nothing compared with the task of keeping them alive. No one doubted that all prior progress would prove useless if this effort fell through. Unless trade committees and others

21. F. 3157, Box 54.

knew officially where they stood and what they were to do, and unless they had the solid, continuing satisfaction of doing such work and seeing results, they would perish. Hence, from the start, planners had been fertile in ideas for committee work; hence Benn had early produced a memorandum on "Organisation *and Work* of Interim Industrial Reconstruction Committees."

Vaughan Nash perhaps put the need clearest of all. In a rare analytical mood, while proposing to Addison a "general plan for being in readiness with the necessary organisations for control of materials during the transition period," Nash got to the heart of this problem. His minute of 18 April spoke volumes by assuming

> that we shall have to fall back in the main on the existing control agencies, but that Advisory Committees of a representative kind from the trade (if possible including workmen) shall be associated with them. Let the whole of the existing control machinery be examined with this in view, its weak points brought out and . . . opinion sought as to improvements. At the same time collect patterns of existing advisory committees . . . and existing methods of ascertaining requirements and rationing. This survey is now in hand and can be expedited.
>
> As Interim Councils and Industrial Councils are formed, let them get into touch with the existing control machinery and train on for taking part in the work of transition control. Some of them may be capable of this, others may not, but the majority will be, and can and ought to be used. . . . I regard it as a *sine qua non* of smooth operating after the War that there should be this period of apprenticeship during the War.
>
> . . . Some of the present controls may kick against admitting newcomers to their counsels. But if the policy is right it can be supported by the authority of the War Cabinet and carried through.[22]

Some might regard Nash's minute as a confession of defeat: the millennial hope for a completely new, nonofficial control system—the vision of industry reconstituted democratically from top to bottom—was being abandoned. The "autonomous bodies" were being drawn into the deadly orbit of Whitehall. But it is just as possible to interpret Nash's

22. F. 3116, Box 70, Part 1; Addison, *Diary*, 2: 474–77, 553; F. 5468, Box 71, Part 2; Files 3873, 3913, 5879, 5909, 10697, 5704, Box 71, Part 3; F. 7723, Box 88; F. 4687, Box 90, Part 1; Paper 1, Box 52; F. 2541, Box 8.

plan as a highly intelligent adjustment to the course of events, which sacrificed some things temporarily in order to realize essentials; and his entire minute bespoke realistic concern for practical experience. In this view, Nash's proposals indicated how a deteriorating situation might be saved in time.[23]

Benn brought the whole matter to a head in late April, asking the ministry's advisory committees to prepare memoranda that trade committees might study. The departments must be asked again to use the new groups. "This matter is urgent," he insisted; groups were meeting and "it is important that they should be able to get to work at once on definite questions."[24]

Hindsight leaves no doubt that this campaign never did succeed. For Whitley Councils, which also were proving hard to start,[25] the delay was not fatal; their work reached far into the future. But trade committees had no margin of time. They must help with immediate reconversion work; they must be ready before the armistice. But by 11 November few of them —and by 1 October (the true deadline) altogether too few—had been formed. Such as existed often were untrained. The tasks set for them were unperformed, or were done hastily by war agencies. Insofar as the period of demobilization was precisely the time of greatest need—and such was the case for all groups save Whitley Councils—the verdict must be failure. The failure, which is historical fact, prompts many questions. Much effort had been squandered and many hopes had been raised; was the campaign worth it? Did the campaign represent a reasonable choice that had been freakishly overtaken by events? Or was it a bad idea, a hopeless dream from the start? Was it not inevitable that experimental methods, utilizing untried groups in a complicated process of consultation, must either fail or (before proper trial) be shunted aside by the cabinet and by departments accustomed to having their own way?

Hindsight supplies no answer. What was wise, what was possible, and what might have been done even then to rescue matters are things that history does not disclose. But it is certain that amid those closest to the unsatisfactory progress of events in 1918 the gravest doubts about the whole project had arisen; and those who still determined to carry on with it were not working effectively.

23. For the proposed work and Benn's memorandum, see Files 982 and 7716, Box 71, Part 1; Files 5468 and 8447, Box 71, Part 2; F. 6411, Box 71, Part 3; Seymour, *The Whitley Council Scheme*, p. 22; Ministry of Labour, *Joint Industrial Councils*, pp. 14–15; Nash's memorandum, in F. 5812, Box 71, Part 1.

24. F. 6388, Box 71, Part 2.

25. Board of Trade *Journal*, 7 February 1918; F. 4705, Box 71, Part 2.

Awareness and alarm were not matched by speed. Well-phrased and earnest memoranda were exchanged. "We want," wrote Garrod,

> to give these Committees definite pieces of practical work. We want to see that their enquiries and results are coordinated with the work of other bodies . . . that they do not build on the air . . . that their Reconstruction fits into what may be called the Government framework.

Nothing happened. On 15 July Addison ordered Nash to "give your immediate and personal attention to the delays which have occurred in the preparation of memoranda setting out details of the work which we should invite Interim Reconstruction Committees or other Trade Bodies to consider."

> We stand in danger of being seriously discredited if, having called these bodies into being, we leave them for any length of time without thoroughly responsible work. It is now several weeks since I first called for the preparation of these Memoranda.

But only in late August did an "information series" (thin documents of obvious suggestions, which could have gone out in January) appear.[26]

So many difficulties had plagued the entire effort that, it seems, the planners were foolish to have persisted. That they carried on is a measure of their conviction: to them it was not enough that right results be achieved, regardless of method. Right results, instead, must be based on the right method, which was a method of consultation and consent. Indeed— almost by definition, within their philosophy—*only* an outcome founded on consent could be right. But the story of the trade committees was also a measure of their faults: tardiness, faltering, and overoptimism.

Was not the whole campaign for all types of "representative joint bodies" a history of retreats and retractions? At first, hopes were pinned on industrial councils; then, as they failed to form fast enough, makeshift trade committees, including employers and employees, became the new hope. Soon the government ceased to insist on the joint character of even these and instead chose to recognize bodies that represented only employers. Then the Board of Trade denied official status or powers to council and committee; and Nash took the final step of conceding that they must "fall back in the main on the existing control agencies."

26. Files 6683 and 5516, Box 71, Part 1. For conflict with another department on publication, see F. 4962, Box 71, Part 2. Greenwood commented on the Ministry of Labour guides to the Whitley Councils: F. 7716, Box 71, Part 1.

Local Reconstruction Organizations

Certainly, these same ills beset the plans to garner public support. It had looked easy, and reconstruction folk at first were optimistic. The air was full of talk on after-war conditions; the nation's reform groups were mobilizing, conferring, lobbying; and friends abounded. From Stoke-on-Trent the mayor had written Addison, as soon as the ministry was formed, to describe the city's reconstruction group; he followed up with memoranda on housing, industrial growth, and land. In Cardiff a "Reconstruction Council" had launched specialized investigations and volunteered to do more. The Welsh National Association, Hammond found, was just the sort that should be encouraged and given genuine work. The Devon and Cornwall Association for Industrial and Commercial Reconstruction had a series of major local conferences to its credit, led by Major Waldorf Astor (eventually Addison's second-in-command at the Ministry of Health in 1919). It lustily supported Whitley Council ideas. Here were friends for the asking.

Addison knew the ministry needed friends. C. D. Burns, J. L. Hammond, and—above all—Arthur Greenwood felt there was

> a great need for voluntary local bodies thinking about Reconstruction as it affects their locality. . . . It would be worthwhile for the Minister to publish a statement on . . . the sort of problems which they might consider. . . . Their advice might be asked in much the same way as advice is to be asked from Industrial Councils and Interim Committees.

In June he worried over the complete inaction to date. "There is not enough public knowledge of Reconstruction problems or policy; and . . . the majority are as yet hardly aware of the difficulties of the period immediately after the war." Again there were committees, subcommittees, drafts; not until September was there so much as a report. By then, there was a "Birmingham Reconstruction League," a group in Hereford, and an Association for Industrial Reconstruction in Bristol. All suffered from the slowness at Queen Anne's Gate.[27]

Greenwood's judgment was sound. The ministry needed these local committees, as surely as they needed it. Whether for lack of time and personnel or for some other cause, the ministry did not put forth an effort to build these local organizations while the time was ripe.

27. Files 3212, 7260, 7261, 10640A, and 10659, Box 70, Part 1; Files 7219 and 7416, Box 70, Part 2; F. 8447, Box 71, Part 2; Addison, *Diary*, 2: 489–90, 548.

The vision of a self-regulating economic community, unhampered by the limitations of the state but guided and restrained by a keen sense of the common good, informed the labors of men like Greenwood, Benn, Hammond, Burns, and Addison. Realistic or not, their hope was a fact. It is equally a fact that efforts to ensure the realization were not adequate in the moment of time that was generally viewed as decisive.

Devolution: Symbol and Test

Ministry and government alike had accepted successful devolution as a test of success in reconstruction as a whole. Politically, it was unwise to give critics so convenient a target; but was it, in fact, a fair or necessary test? And what would it prove? Was the failure of devolution (for, with the exception of Whitley Councils, the crusade for devolution was heading for failure) truly a symbol—perhaps even a cause—for failure in general? Or had it never been central?

A good case can be made that reconstructionists exaggerated the necessity of devolution. Perfectly adequate results could have been and were being achieved by departmental bureaucracy. Decentralization and amateurism might prove handicaps, especially in reconversion, in which speedy decision was of the essence. A reconstruction effort that built houses, kept prices stable, raised the standard of life, combated ill health, and conquered unemployment would be no less a triumph for failing the devolutionist test.

If reconstructionists erred only in entertaining false but harmless hopes, failure in devolution was irrelevant. This first critique is exculpation as much as censure.

But what of the time spent? A second and much more serious critique is that the effort that was squandered on councils and committees should instead have gone into thinking through solutions to some of the severe dilemmas. High costs amid high prices—this was one daunting case: the cost and inflationary pressure of expensive reform programs, which must be launched at a time of undesirably high prices. Compared with such tasks or with the hard choice between "restrictive practices" and efficient modernization, the devolution campaign looks like a lazy man's course of least resistance: suitably strenuous without requiring painful thought. So seen, devolution (otherwise irrelevant) becomes a real impediment. Emphasis on this luxury jeopardized essentials. And devolution was given too central a place in organization; postwar controls were geared in principle to these trades committees and Whitley Councils. Even where these bodies existed they were at best merely tolerable as minor adjuncts. It was folly to base anything major upon them, and criminal folly to link the whole of reconversion to amateur, fledgling, inchoate groups.

Reconstructionists could retort, first, that the right policy on such controversial topics as wages and priorities could not be proclaimed by fiat. Any solution would entail sacrifice and compromise. Just as no policy could be known to be right without consultation, no compromise could be known to be genuine unless it was explicitly ratified—which implied a mechanism for real consent. Devolution rested on the simple axiom that acceptance was every bit as important as correctness. The very concept of a "right" policy presupposed the means to find the acceptable middle ground of shared sacrifice. Regarding controls only, there was a second rationale: Because labor and capital both suspected Whitehall, devolution emerged as the lesser evil, the one form in which controls would be tolerable.

So minded, reconstruction's planners held the devolution campaign well worth the effort. It would be a bold critic who would today dispute their logic. Nowadays the economic necessity for a combined program that would limit prices, incomes, and wages seems patent; in essentials it was as needful then. But restraint sits well only if it is self-imposed—only if those who acquiesce have some unmistakable proof that other interests bow equally to the yoke. Acknowledge the need, and the machinery follows. Acknowledge that wages and prices and incomes must be controlled, and the case for consultation and consent is made.

But in that case, devolution *was* central and the test *is* fair. Frankly, tests for the merit of reconstruction planning are welcome, for they are rare; and this one is especially fitting. Other campaigns passed to other departments, or went through a cabinet mangling that absolved the ministry. But this campaign ran its course within reconstruction agencies, from 1916 to its inglorious end, which had now come in sight. It was the agencies' responsibility and, it seemed, their failure.

From such a reckoning the planners were rescued, where their own logic condemned them, by the illogicality of events. When devolution broke down officialdom came to the rescue; somehow, without devolution, the essentials of reconversion were saved. And (sufficient plea in extenuation!) the bulk of the program for reform was enacted in 1919. Thus, although accident retrieved the chance for success, one may nevertheless deem the blunders on devolution a judgment. They symbolized faults that pervaded and menaced reconstruction. This censure stands, even if much of reconstruction be counted a success and even if the fiasco of devolution wrought minimal harm.

The campaign revealed the basic fault, not of failing effort or speed, but of a persistent infatuation with innovations and overelaborate schemes. The planners put obstacles in their own path, and not in this case alone. Their system for priorities seems too complex, their proposals for raw-materials procedures too cumbersome. Their campaigns too often ignored the rough, imperfect, but decidedly competent existing bodies. Oddly, the rather happy results of the swift, unplanned rescue at armistice time underscore the point. The measure of their fault was provided, curiously, both by the failure of their own efforts and by the success that others achieved.

One cannot say they should not have tried; errors of method do not condemn an essential idea. The argument for devolution was good.

11

Eve of the Armistice:
August and September 1918

Dramatic events marked the two-month period before the news of peace overtures reached London. Addison met industrial and trade leaders from all of Britain to explain reconversion plans. The controversy over a Central Raw Materials Board moved toward climax. The Standing Council on Post-War Priority was named. Long-sought agreements on land-settlement programs and on the Ministry of Health Bill were reached. Housing finance took a fateful turn. But August and September were also months of holidays. Garrod and Gardiner left for vacation in Scotland; Addison joined his family in Lincolnshire; and this lull offers us a chance to assess both the achievements and the unfinished business at Dean's Yard and at Queen Anne's Gate.

The Status of Reports

In March 1918 "Sardonyx" had surveyed the government's progress for the *New Statesman* and had rated it low.

> The friction and the lack of co-ordination between Ministries is becoming more and more pronounced. Perhaps this explains somewhat the total failure of the Ministry of Reconstruction (which obviously depends in a peculiar degree on the sympathetic attention of other Departments) to accomplish anything whatever. It does not wholly explain the failure, part of which is easily explicable by the sole fact that the staffing of the Ministry of Reconstruction has been a series of jobs from top to bottom, with a resulting incompetence possibly unique even in the annals of British government. In the matter of reconstruction one thing, and only one thing, has been actually done, and that is the full working-out of the scheme for military demobilisation. But this immense affair was accomplished

by the first Reconstruction Committee in 1916, and Mr. Asquith set his signature to it just before he left office. The vast reconstituted body presided over by Dr. Addison has so far reached nowhere. No recommendation has been made as to the demobilisation of the millions of civilian war-workers. No recommendation has been made as to housing; indeed, housing had gone all to pieces. A Report has been prepared as to the compulsory purchase of land for housing; but it is a silly Report and will assuredly be shelved. No recommendation has been made as to railways. No recommendation has been made as to the restoration of Trade Union conditions. No recommendation has been made as to raw materials—unless the Non-Ferrous Metals Act is to be counted! No recommendation has been made as to Government factories. The Electric Power business is being held up. The Ministry of Health has not materialised. The Whitley Report is stranded. True, one trade committee has been constituted in accordance with it in the Potteries—but as this trade committee instantly took on the complexion of a trade protection association, authority smiles not on it. In short, the record of the Reconstruction Ministry up to date can be accurately expressed as 0. Within the Ministry there are about one hundred committees— perhaps more. I know of one which has met once in the nine months of it existence.[1]

Here was both a judgment and a method of judgment: a measurement of what had been achieved by the progress of paper work. The appraisal may have been faulty but the scale was clear. Maximal attainment would be shown by cabinet approval plus legislative enactment (or, in cases of a different sort, by approval plus full administrative implementation). Short of this, a measure or report that had cleared the ministry and reached the cabinet would spell good but inadequate success. Dangerously low on the scale of readiness would be reports sent from the Ministry of Reconstruction to other departments but not returned; worst of all were those that still lingered within the ministry. Ignoring topical divisions and grouping reports by their position along this administrative scale, what perspective do we get of 1 October?

Of roughly fifty reports or recommendations, just under one-half had been sent to the cabinet. Just under one-third of the fifty had been acted on there—favorably in twelve cases out of sixteen. The twenty-seven that

1. *New Statesman*, 30 March 1918, p. 615. See *Athenaeum*, no. 4627 (March 1918), p. 129.

had not yet been sent on to the cabinet and the ten that had been sent to it but had not yet been considered represented a backlog of thirty-seven items of unfinished business.

Three recommendations from official reconstruction bodies had run the entire gauntlet and become law: the Trade Boards Act of 1918, which owed much to the Women's Committee of the Civil War Workers' Committee; the Tithe Act of 1918, and the Corn Production Act of 1917 —both deriving from the work of the Selborne committee, named by Asquith. Of course there was the Fisher Education Bill of 1918, a landmark in its field, and the measure Fisher had persuaded the cabinet to adopt, on pensions for teachers, but these were not achievements of the reconstruction staff.[2]

Nine of the adopted measures had called for administrative action rather than legislation. Farthest along, in terms of departmental follow-up, were the Whitley committee's proposals for industry, energetically handled by the Ministry of Labour, and the Balfour of Burleigh committee's plan for new organizations to aid overseas trading, on which the Board of Trade was far advanced. Implementation was less adequate for seven other approved measures. In principle, the extension of Whitley principles to the civil service had been sanctioned, but no council yet existed. Acland's controversial forestry plans had weathered a departmental storm, but the Treasury grant of interim aid, which would assure their success, lay months in the future. The general plan for army demobilization, although approved months earlier, still awaited attention in its crucial details: the registering and withdrawal of pivotal men. A Fuel Research Board had been set up, but its record is not known. Three of the poorly implemented items, discreditably, were responsibilities of the Ministry of Reconstruction: the program to create and train Interim Industrial Reconstruction Committees (noted in chapter 10), the Standing Council on Post-War Priority, sanctioned but not staffed, and Lord Salisbury's ill-fated Surplus Government Property Advisory Council, with its auxiliary Disposal Board. Thus in only two cases was administration clearly up to need.[3]

2. For the Corn Production Act and Tithe Act, see Cd. 9231, pp. 23–24; Cd. 8508; and above, p. 31; for Trade Boards Act, see WC 402 of 1 May 1918 in Cab. 23/6, citing G.T. 4332.

3. For Whitley Councils, see above, p. 164; for overseas marketing, see above, p. 102. For the extension of Whitleyism to the government, see WC 438 of 1 July 1918 in Cab. 23/7, citing memoranda G. 213 and 214 by Milner (Cab. 24/5). For Forestry, see G. 189 by Ministry of Reconstruction, 27 December 1917, in Cab. 24/4, and WC 455 of 7 August 1918 in Cab. 23/7, citing G. 215, 216, G.T. 5063 and 5121; for the Fuel Research Board, see Cd. 9231, pp. 8–9.

As against the approvals, one proposal for legislation—the Ministry's alternative housing program, rival to that of the Local Government Board —had been rejected. Three administrative proposals had been rejected or dropped: those for housing commissioners, for various kinds of housing design, and for a labor "clearinghouse."[4]

A pessimist would find much to comment on in this record; a fore-sighted man would find cause for gloom in the fact that any such list of action on policies proposed and reports presented took no account of policies *not* devised and needs *un*anticipated. But even if we confine our attention to what had been thought of, an appalling number of items was held up in the cabinet itself. The list includes questions of wage rates and war pledges, plans for land-settlement and small holdings, schemes for electric power, and the entire list of the Civil War Workers' committee recommendations. It embraces the bill for a Ministry of Health, the plan for officers' resettlement, and a permanent system of industrial arbitration. Nor had the broader recommendations of the Selborne committee, reaching far beyond the Corn Production Acts, won through.

Three other measures, which had cleared the Ministry of Reconstruction, also seemed to be jammed at the doors of 10 Downing Street: proposals for a more liberal policy on new issues of capital, which would speed reconversion; for recommended improvements in the law on departmental orders, submitted in February by the Acquisition of Powers Committee; and Leslie Scott's drastic scheme for a single sanctioning authority to speed the acquisition of land.[5]

Still not out of committee were numerous reports that were stuck at the ministry itself; and nine were not minor. In October, proposals for anti-dumping laws and the report of a housing committee on Public Utility Societies would be published. In November, reports on the building industry, the valuation of land, and financial facilities would come out, along with a report from the Civil War Workers' Committee. December would bring reports from the Engineering (New Industries) Committee, Haldane's Machinery of Government group, and the group on rent.[6] This general state of affairs interprets itself.

4. For the housing commissioners, see above, pp. 90–93; for housing design, the rejection of proposals is in F. 6294, Box 34, Part 2; for the clearinghouse, see F. 4962, Box 71, Part 2, and F. 3081, Box 71, Part 1.

5. Where the minutes of the Home Affairs Committee (Cab. 26/1) or the War Cabinet (23/4–7) do not make it clear that the item was submitted at the cabinet level, Cd. 9231 establishes the point.

6. See Cmd. 445 on anti-dumping laws and Cd. 9223 on Public Utility Societies (also Box 37). Cd. 9197 deals with the building industry, Cd. 9228 with financial

Reconversion, Recovery, Reform: Progress by Fields

Was the plan as a *whole* anywhere near readiness? For the parts on which action must come first, was the condition satisfactory even if decision lagged on others? To answer this it does no good to fix the *disjecta membra* of individual reports along the paper trail through Whitehall. Distinctions of time, distinctions of type—above all a synoptic view—are called for.

Documents supply no instant answer. No single statement for all of the plans survives to serve as a checklist. But the whole can be reconstructed thanks to Addison's far-ranging chats with Lloyd George and his drafts of electioneering programs. The result is anything but an index to *need*; it is a summary of tasks known. It shows what men wished and anticipated at a rare moment of pause. The truer agenda and the real needs—the unforeseen tasks—jut from the logjam of agenda and frantic working papers after October came, when the time for forethought had passed. Such as they are, however, the reconstructed "agenda" establish a rough sequence and order of priority *by field*. They fall into three parts: permanent reforms, the least urgent that year; permanent economic policy; and immediate economic policy and plans both for demobilization and resettlement—the most urgent of all.

Permanent Reforms

Housing, land settlement, a Ministry of Health, Whitleyism, education, and an end to the Poor Law—to make life better and to make industry less unjust, these were the "big six" the ministry counted on. Some lesser programs flanked these (Trade Boards, industrial arbitration, forestry). Also of intrinsic importance were several items that were linked with the immediate tasks of demobilization—such as broader unemployment insurance and better labor exchanges. Although by-products of transitional programs, they would (it was hoped) become permanent reforms.

Homes for workers. Housing, foremost in importance, ranked low on the scale of achievement. It was here the Ministry's one major defeat had occurred, and the midyear lull brought a second setback. Ironically, the Home Affairs Committee provided the stage. The Local Government Board was under attack. Herbert Samuel frankly told the House of

---

facilities, and Cd. 9229 with the valuation of land; Cd. 9228 is the fifth report of the Civil War Workers' Committee. Reports issued in December were Cd. 9226 on engineering (new industries), Cd. 9230 on the machinery of government, and Cd. 9235 on rent and mortgage interest.

Commons that the government was poorly prepared. Arnold Rowntree pressed the Board to publicize the results of local authorities' response to the 18 March circular; George Cadbury voiced his disappointment, as spokesman for Birmingham's Borough Council.[7] Challenged without, the Board chose to rally its friends within Whitehall.

Hayes Fisher sent the cabinet a memorandum in which two cabinet colleagues, Walter Long and Prothero, joined him. It was nothing less than an accusation against the Ministry of Reconstruction for stirring up self-interested local opposition to the Board's announced financial terms. More than 200 local authorities, Hayes Fisher reported, had responded favorably to the 18 March circular—proof enough, he implied, of their willingness to go ahead with the assistance offered. But others, predictably, had sought to obtain more favorable terms and had been "assisted by rumours which have been spread that under pressure better terms might be obtained." He cited the Municipal Corporation Association and a conference of Yorkshire and Lancashire county boroughs as the lobbyists who were pleading that all local losses be held to a "one penny" limit. Such special pleading, said Hayes Fisher, struck at the root of the state–local partnership, destroying economy. But if the Government held firm, most of the local authorities would accept the terms and would build. He asked that a housing bill on his announced terms be issued early.

Lloyd George directed Hayes Fisher and Addison to confer and he deputed Walter Long to oversee the conference. Reconciliation failed. On 1 August Addison retorted in his own memorandum. The important point in the returns, he insisted, was not that 225 local authorities had agreed to build but that 1,581 had *not* agreed to build. He utterly disbelieved Hayes Fisher's faith that private enterprise would make a substantial contribution in houses built; the lack of fixed deadlines and of compulsion to build were fatal shortcomings. Addison, fearful he was being quoted in favor of the L.G.B. bill, recorded his dissent explicitly. Either the terms must be altered or it must be announced that the state would act upon default, and thereafter impose a rate on the local authorities.

> It will be a lasting disgrace if on demobilisation adequate preparations are not in hand to secure that all returning soldiers and sailors can obtain a decent home; and they must be able to obtain it in their own district if they so wish.

7. *P.D.(C.)*, vol. 109 (7 August 1918), c. 1438; minutes of 11 September 1918 meeting of the Housing (Financial Assistance) Committee, Box 37.

Hayes Fisher next day took the whole matter to the Home Affairs Committee. He gave them to understand that he, Long, and Addison had accepted the Board's policy, and he asked ratification of a circular to local authorities on those lines: it would tell them they could "not expect any material modification" in the announced aid. Just two minutes before this, Addison had been outvoted on the proposal to submit the Ministry of Health Bill at once; he walked out. Hayes Fisher's statement was approved; the L.G.B. draft bill was endorsed.

Hayes Fisher provided an epilogue. His summary memorandum, explicitly a reply to Addison, alleged two causes for local authorities' delays: the complexities of procedure and *deliberate* delay by the local authorities, which aimed at exacting easier terms. Hayes Fisher rejected any idea of state coercion.

> Most local authorities can be induced to do what is necessary. . . . The time to take drastic powers is when that majority have shewn the way to the less enlightened and when it will be clearly seen that coercion will be limited to the few defaulters. . . . This . . . is a better policy than uniting in a formidable opposition the various local authorities. . . .
>
> I am opposed to house building by the State as undesirable in itself and uneconomical in practice.[8]

Ministries defeated in the cabinet could retreat onto home ground. Bested in the open plain, where department fought department, the Ministry of Reconstruction prepared for the next campaign in the fast-nesses of its committees. Five of these kept energy and purpose alive until autumn. The five committees tackled "housing banks," control of rent, house design, supply of building materials, and financial assistance by government to building societies.

The Housing (Financial Assistance) Committee had originated, as all five had, well before this clash. Especially concerned with the role of Public Utility Societies (societies registered under the Industrial and Provident Societies Acts, limited by their rules to a 5 per cent maximum annual interest or dividend), Reiss had set out to find how these societies and other private builders could help with housing. Interestingly, Kershaw

8. Home Affairs Committee meeting 8, 2 August 1918; G.T. 5231, 26 July 1918, memorandum on housing by Long, Fisher, and Prothero, Cab. 24/59; G.T. 5282, 1 August 1918, memorandum by Addison regarding G.T. 5231, *ibid.*; F. 7758, Box 30, Part 2; Addison, *Diary*, 2: 561; G.T. 5314, 2 August 1918, memorandum by Hayes Fisher regarding G.T. 5282, in Cab. 24/60.

had encouraged this start; ultimately, both Addison and Hayes Fisher helped bring the committee into being. Of enormous help to the committee were the expert aid it could draw on and the running start that Reiss, Wallace, and Rowntree gave it. In unorthodox liaison with the main groups of Public Utility Societies, these men circulated a list of all existing plans of aid. Predictably, the first meeting resoundingly voted in favor of disregarding precedents, declared its willingness to defy risk, and plumped for undisguised and lavish subsidies. Loans to the societies should be at the lowest rate the state could afford; repayment periods should be extended; and local authorities should have power not only to loan but to get land compulsorily for the societies.[9]

A warning against overlapping by the L.G.B. representative at the first meeting showed the wide gulf between the Board's and the committee's approach. In fact, the very existence of the housing committee implied dissatisfaction with the Board; its work was cheered on precisely by those who feared that present Board policy would give no help to Public Utility Societies. Protests from *The Builder* and from Birmingham's housing and town planning committee underscored the point. Hayes Fisher's own words, full of discouragement to the societies, were reprinted and circulated by Reiss or Wallace to remove any doubt that existing aid was insufficient. Raymond Unwin, a key figure in both housing reform and town planning, took the Treasury, the Board, and the Board's Advisory Housing Conference to task in a devastating analysis that was supported by lengthy statistics. The official terms of aid, he concluded, would offer local authorities a financial inducement to *delay* raising rents until after the transition period; there was no special inducement to economy. The error lay in basing valuation on "net rental revenue" and "eighteen years' purchase of that net revenue"; the consequence would be a depression of rents (as far as local authorities' houses were concerned), which would be a standing discouragement to any private initiative in housing. A remedy was possible, Unwin felt: Through proper financial terms, private enterprise—including Public Utility Societies and those who invested in them—could be induced to build, so as to give an alternative standard of rents and values. He judged the new plans of Salisbury and Rowntree free from these flaws. Reiss and Wallace, meanwhile, had calculated that the societies would find it impossible to make any profit under the present terms. The fifth meeting, on 24 July, produced tentative decisions that soon were

9. For the origins, see above, p. 107 and Cd. 9231, p. 40, and Files 3945A, 3945, 5877, and 5923, and H. 173 in Box 30, Part 3. Minutes of the first meeting are in Doc. 13, Box 37.

embodied in an interim report "for departmental use only and not to be published." It was to be ready if the Board's circular of 18 March was abandoned. This was under consideration when peace overtures came in October.[10]

What did it all prove? For one thing, that in some men's minds were workable formulas of aid that would bring private builders and societies into the housing campaign. For another, that the Ministry of Reconstruction, as far as housing was concerned, was acting very much like an "alternative government," framing its own measures. With 1919 opportunity would come, and the Housing Act of 1919 shows how far this other option prevailed. But such meditations on the fringes of battle did not obscure the fact that the Local Government Board held the field.

Similarly, the "housing banks" question was taken up in June by a subcommittee. By 8 August it was revising a draft report, but the report was not ready for submission on 1 October.[11]

Rent was under control, but would it remain so? In March 1918 the *New Statesman* gave warning:

> The Rent Restriction Act is due to expire six months after peace, when cottage rents in some places will bound up by ten shillings a week. We suggest that no Government will venture, when the time comes, to allow this to happen. Yet this Government, apparently, cannot think so far ahead.

But in fact the ministry was already deeply concerned. Bonham-Carter and Nash advised Addison that the case for inquiry into the act was "strong and urgent." Negotiations took time, because of extraordinary demands for group representation. By 17 September the committee (named in May) had in hand its chairman's view, backed by Wallace's calculations, that some rents must go up, to encourage both municipal and private building. But deliberations were far from over when the armistice came in sight.[12]

The Women's Advisory Committee on Housing had a special task, the study of design, but its fate was like that of the others—friction and delay.

10. See Dickinson's comments in Doc. 13, Box 37. Critiques and Hayes Fisher's words are in H. 178, 167, and 165, Box 33; analyses are in Docs. 18 and 28, Box 37; see also F. 6897, Box 30, Part 2. Doc. 34, Box 37, contains minutes of the fifth meeting and the report.

11. Documents 4–12, Box 36.

12. *New Statesman*, 23 March 1918, p. 583. See Wallace's H. 130 in Box 32, and Docs. 9, 14, 22, 24, 25, 46, 49–50 in Box 38. The committee's report, Cd. 9235, was dated 31 December 1918.

When its first interim report was ready—dealing with architects' designs, submitted in an L.G.B. contest—the Board protested its publication. Furious that the ministry had been bypassed, Reiss pleaded for publication. The net result was delay, all around. The report came out only in October, shorn of criticisms strong enough to constitute an attack on the L.G.B.[13]

For help on the crucial problem of building materials supply, Addison looked to Carmichael's committee. Reports came in, through 1918, on timber supply, combinations of merchants, and material needs. Himself in the building trade and the key man at Munitions for all its construction, Carmichael kept the committee closely in touch with professional and trade organizations. Eventually he would recommend setting up a central building industry committee to control bricks, cement, timber, prices, and priorities. But that still lay ahead, at the end of September.[14]

Housing apart, there were no notable setbacks. Nor were there impressive gains.

Local government and a Ministry of Health. Addison knew that the creation of the Ministry of Health in fact involved a triple task: the task of integration itself, bringing all health activities under one direction; severance from the Poor Law, whose philosophy and organization alike must be laid to rest; and changes in local government, both in structure and spirit, to complement all this and fulfill the work. But these substantive goals, he came to see, would never be reached until a basis—procedural and psychological—was laid. The procedural basis seemed assured, once the Home Affairs Committee came into being. The psychological basis required much more time, but by July 1918 he judged that it was laid.

The hardest task had been to dispel doubts about the "Poor Law taint." In more than a score of talks with the Labour Party, Scottish representatives, physicians, and the approved societies, Addison convinced his listeners that the new ministry would drop that legacy from the past. Here, the problem had been to show that the government meant business and would not compromise. Morant had the opposite kind of task: to deal with the approved societies that handled insurance (whose interests were rooted in that past) and to demonstrate that—although doing away with separate insurance commissioners as such—the government intended to

13. F. 6294, Box 34, Part 2, and H. 188, Box 33, include a copy of the report (Cd. 9166).

14. Files 4654 and 6810, Box 35, and H. 187, Box 33; see Addison, *Politics*, 2: 218–19; Addison, *Diary*, 2: 466, 480, 495, 596; and the eventual report, Cd. 9197.

reach a fair compromise with the societies. Addison took a sympathetic and admiring view of Morant's enormous efforts.

> Many and many a time Morant was inclined to despair. He said more than once: "You will never get it through, Addison; they will be too many for you." But, whenever any fresh obstacles . . . had to be overcome, Morant would work like a slave. . . . It was due more to him than to anyone else that we received the wholehearted confidence and support of the Approved Societies under the Insurance Act.

Blocked since July 1917 by Lloyd George's doubts, the whole project came before the Home Affairs Committee on 9 July 1918—at its very first meeting. Objections had cost a year.

But opposition did not stop at the committee's door. In the draft of the Ministry of Health Bill, which Addison was defending, almost everything came up for debate: the long list of powers to be transferred; the Consultative Council, through which Addison wished to sound and rally the doctors of the country; and the explicit declaration against the Poor Law. Even the omission of two words from the title, "Local Government," was challenged. Lines formed at once. Addison was for the anti-Poor Law declaration, which some trade unions adamantly insisted on. The L.G.B. spokesmen, resisting change, fought to insert the omitted words. Sessions grew numerous; delegation after delegation trooped through; Addison beat a calculated retreat, hoping to preserve the substance by making verbal concessions. He agreed that the words "Local Government" would be added, although this would increase the fears of a continued link with the Poor Law. To appease the Boards of Guardians he acquiesced when the statement on the Poor Law was dropped from the bill, but he insisted that a declaration on that topic, independent of the bill, be given by the government. By such concessions he hoped for agreement on the powers to be transferred, and he was rewarded when most of them were accepted. Aided by deputations of Britain's most distinguished physicians, he won approval for an advisory council. But his highest hope, for submission and adoption of a bill that year, was defeated by the sheer delays involved. Although the bill was approved in principle on 2 August, it could only be introduced *pro forma* that year; actual passage came in 1919.

It had been a wrangle all the way. Doctors' delegations had voiced the keenest disappointment at the delays. They and the trade unions, hot for dissociation from the Poor Law, felt the very words "Local Government" in the title hinted that officialdom clung to that hated precedent. But the Local Government Board had dislodged the anti-Poor Law declaration, thus winning a rearguard skirmish. Meanwhile a conflict arose on the publication of the report by the Local Government Committee that Mrs. Webb had backed. The link to Poor Law questions was patent. "The vested interests," Maclean said, "are naturally hard at work and the only way to combat them is to get public opinion on the move." For publication, Heseltine argued that "its opponents have got" the report "and its friends have a good deal of leeway to make up." Addison made the report public knowledge, with a congratulation to Maclean for "splendid work."[15]

Despite all the heartaches it was a good outcome. The strategy made sense: to introduce the bill, and simultaneously to pledge to deal strongly with the Poor Law on the lines set out in Maclean's committee report. Each reform implied the other. As the *New Statesman* commented, integration at the top was not enough; as the *Athenaeum* said, the Maclean proposals for local change implied a ministry at the center.[16]

Labor reforms: Trade Boards and Joint Industrial Councils. The campaign for more Trade Boards spelled pure gain. Recommendations from Addison's staff to the Ministry of Labour helped shape the Trade Boards Act of 1918, which the *New Statesman* hailed as the biggest reconstruction measure yet passed.[17] Whitley Councils were also growing in number; some had taken part in Addison's conference of 1 August. The cabinet, probing gingerly at the plan for such councils in the civil service, had accepted Whitleyism in principle; not far off was the decision to go ahead.[18] The extension of Whitleyism to government itself was the one great milestone that was passed that summer, in what looked like a long campaign. The trend, at least, was clear.

15. Addison, *Diary*, 2: 482, 484, 492, 498, 499, 501, 509, 515–16, 532, 534–35, 538–40, 543, 546, 552, 555, 559–64, 568; Addison, *Politics*, 2: 221–32. For complaints on delay and premature rejoicing, see *Athenaeum*, no. 4628 (April 1918), p. 174, *New Statesman*, 9 March 1918, pp. 538–39, and 20 July 1918, pp. 304–5. See F. 3400, Box 8, and Cab. 26/1 for sessions of the Home Affairs Committee in July–September 1918, citing pertinent memoranda. See also Bernard M. Allen, *Sir Robert Morant: A Great Public Servant* (London: Macmillan, 1934), pp. 294–304.

16. *New Statesman*, 9 March 1918, pp. 535, 538–39; see also *ibid.*, 30 March 1918, p. 607, and *Athenaeum*, no. 4627 (March 1918), pp. 138–39. For professional opinion and public discussion both on the hospital services and the Ministry of Health, see Abel-Smith, *The Hospitals*, pp. 286–88.

17. See 8 and 9 Geo. V., c. 32; *New Statesman*, 27 July 1918, p. 232; F. 10485, Box 90, Part 1; WC 402 of 1 May 1918, in Cab. 23/6.

18. See above, p. 177; see Cab. 23/7 for 1 July 1918 decision of WC 438. See also G. 213 and 214 of June, cited therein, in Cab. 24/5.

Dr. Christopher Addison   Photo by Stuart Black
Minister of Reconstruction, 1917–18

Arthur Greenwood   Photo by W. Scott

Vaughan Nash   Photo by Fabric Photos

Robert Morant   Photo by Langfier

Viscount Rhondda

Eric Geddes

James Carmichael

Jan Smuts

Photo by Vandyk

A shell factory in 1916

HARVEST HOME, 1918.

WITH MR. PUNCH'S JOYOUS CONGRATULATIONS TO THE MINISTER OF AGRICULTURE.

A LEVY ON PATRIOTISM.

THE BEST BRICK-LAID SCHEMES . . .

Sir Alfred Mond. "STOP WORK!"

[The Minister of Health has fixed a limit to the Government's Housing Schemes.]

Labor reforms: wages, hours, insurance, arbitration. To Addison, the provision of minimum wages and proper working conditions, especially for women and unskilled workers, was a test by which government should be measured. A start had been made with some industrial surveys that reflected the growing faith in the reduction of hours as an aid to health and efficiency. In 1917 and 1918 minutes had been exchanged on revising the insurance acts. But none of this had been followed up by Addison's group, except for some recommendations from the Civil War Workers' Committee—ostensibly for transitional weeks only. On these topics, the ministry had little to say.[19] Few omissions seem more serious. It was precisely on these issues that labor disputes erupted in 1919. How much might have been rescued by foresight!

The ministry had not shirked its duty, however, where industrial arbitration was concerned. A report on it was being circulated. Belatedly, legislative action would follow—in 1919.

Another question, pledges, held implications for every part of labor reform. Wages, hours, tenure, seniority: all were involved. Inaction and indecision reigned here as well. The entire matter will be reexamined when measures for reconversion are reviewed (below).

Forestry, farms, and the land. In the great wishing-well that was reconstruction, some men saw the reflection of their own visions of a revived countryside and an England of prosperous farms. From such men—Selborne, Scott, and Acland at first, then Prothero and Hall—derived that part of the reconstruction agenda that promised land to the soldier, new forests for the nation, and drastic changes in land laws.

Affinities, manmade and technical as well as obvious and natural, linked all these separate projects. Every one of the programs implied a more vigorous state, manhandling vested rights, where need be, for the nation's good. Each was integrally linked, in its sponsor's eyes, with recovery from a postwar slump, for each made its contribution to employment. Each was linked somehow with the housing campaign. Each would require fresh answers to difficult questions of finance. And each had begun far back in Asquith's time. But in mid-1918 they were moving down separate paths to contrasting fates.

19. See Addison, *Diary*, 2: 555; "Industrial survey" papers, F. 11193, Box 90; papers on industrial insurance, Files 77, 136, 2773, Box 64. Belatedly Addison made recommendations in September 1918 for an "Annual Holiday" and for a general eight-hour day, forwarding recommendations from his Adult Education Committee; there is no record of substantial discussion of these. See his G.T. 5837 and 5838, Cab. 24/65.

Plans for the settlement of veterans on the land had taken definite form by May. On 15 May the plans won a hearing by the cabinet, which referred them to a committee. By October Addison felt agreement had been reached on such crucial matters as financing and empowering local authorities to acquire land. The drafting and approval of specific bills still lay in the future.[20]

The cabinet had intervened more pointedly when forestry was involved. As we have noted, Acland's idea of a single forestry commission had jarred sensibilities from Whitehall to John o' Groats. The Development Commission was furious at having its jurisdiction threatened and its reputation affronted; Scottish officials fumed at the very thought of unified control. For once, Addison had sought to appease. Redrafting his own Forestry Committee's plan, with concessions all around, he had forwarded a compromise proposal to the cabinet. This done, he clamored for cabinet action; but it was with very mixed feelings that he reported it on 7 June 1918: "They are, at last, going over my Memorandum . . . of the 22nd of December last year; and I must say they are doing the job very thoroughly." Cabinet members (who could be categorized many ways) divided into "departmental" men and "new agency" men. Barnes and Curzon, to whom the whole matter had been referred, were by chance "new agency men," and because of them the cabinet was urged to reverse Addison's conciliatory adjustment. With an unflattering glance at "the more cautious proposals of the Minister of Reconstruction admittedly framed on grounds of political expediency . . . to conciliate national sentiment and disarm formidable opposition," they supported Acland's idea of an independent central authority. They added that "a forestry department would work a vast improvement in a single generation." Addison, who shared these hopes, now found himself in the odd position of writing memoranda to contest a decision that was favorable to his own committee. When the vote went against him the anomalies did not end. The cabinet thought it had given a clear decision for Acland's plan, but in fact it had not; and soon Addison had to plead that a "decision"—which had gone against him—be clarified and strengthened!

For a minor program, forestry took up an amazing amount of the cabinet's time. That year and the next it created jurisdictional snarls that

20. See Addison, *Diary*, 2: 508, 515, 522, 524–26, 529–30, 546, 560, 570, 571–73, and (for the sequel) 576 and 597–98, as well as *Politics*, 2: 209–14. See WC 412, 15 May 1918, Cab. 23/6. For Addison's assertion that on 23 July 1918 the cabinet declared "Soldiers' Settlement, Housing, Land, etc., as well as Afforestation were suitable subjects for acquisition and that compulsory powers must be available," I found no corroboration.

only ministers could unravel; and its very successes bred further trouble. Quite exceptionally, it received a Treasury grant that antedated the formal establishment of the Forestry Commission. The result, where only support and expedition had been intended, was that new doubts affected its status. Addison's embarrassing skirmish in mid-1918 foreshadowed the oddities to come.[21]

Two programs, two contrasting paths; and Leslie Scott's proposals traced yet a third. His committee hacked at its huge topic—"the law and practice relating to the acquisition and valuation of land for public purposes"—and produced its first report, a mammoth discourse, in early 1918. The central idea—a single, special, permanent sanctioning authority under close parliamentary control, to study and authorize all acquisition of land for whatever public purpose—delighted some reformers. Complexities, delays, and legal costs, terribly burdensome to housing schemes, would be swept away; four existing methods of acquisition—"an intolerable state of affairs"—would give way to one. R. L. Reiss happily told readers of the *Athenaeum* that "the effect of the War has been to produce much greater unanimity than would have been thought possible four years ago." But Reiss spoke too soon. He and other enthusiasts for housing plans or for land settlement might proclaim that speedier land purchase was essential, but the cabinet did not act. Nor did Scott's second report, on the valuation of land, fare any better. Not until mid-December did either report reach the Home Affairs Committee; and delay persisted, in fact, halfway through 1919. The departments held on to their acquisition powers; legal officers frowned. Even the Minister of Reconstruction, once he became Minister of Health, found reasons to object.[22]

Thus not a single part of the interlocking reforms for land and farm was fully ready. For measures so long contemplated and in principle so accepted, this was a poor showing; for measures that Addison counted on to provide real help with transition difficulties, this was downright bad. A pessimist, surveying all the area of reform, could note that law reform ideas had been dropped, and that Haldane's Machinery of Government Committee had not finished its work; he could add that conscription of wealth, mentioned once in cabinet, had not been studied by Addison's

21. Addison, *Diary*, 2: 541; Files 4153, 6503, 7265, and 5864, Box 6, Part 2; WC 411, in Cab. 23/6, and WC 455 of 7 August 1918, in Cab. 23/7, citing G. 215, G. 216 and G.T. 5063 and 5121, in Cab. 24/5 and 24/57–58.

22. See Cd. 8998 (the first report) and Cd. 9229 (the second report); papers in Box 33; Addison, *Diary*, 2: 456; and review by "R.L.R." in *Athenaeum*, no. 4628 (April 1918), pp. 183–86; "land settlement" files of Ministry of Agriculture and Fisheries, no. L 2759/IG.

ministry at all; he could find progress where H. A. L. Fisher was in charge, notable changes where Prothero had taken the lead, but nothing established in that entire range—housing, land, forestry, insurance, and the rest—where the Ministry of Reconstruction was responsible.

Nothing visible on the eve of armistice suggested for a moment that, in 1919, every major reform that had been proposed by the ministry would become law.

Permanent Economic Policy

Reformed or not, Britain must make her difficult way in the competitive postwar world. For farm and factory, commerce and finance, long-term plans were essential. Where did they stand, on the eve of armistice?

Goals seemed obvious. Britain must produce more goods, more efficiently. Britain must perfect her methods of marketing, to meet the competition of neutrals and her belated allies. The Ministry of Reconstruction added something to this crude consensus, but not much. Addison, who shared with the Board of Trade an undefined duty to plan permanent economic policy, added that *new* goods and whole new industries also would be required, and he showed more concern than others for tapping new sources of energy. His special attention was on the preconditions of success, while he agreed on the main targets. The result of his work was a program that incorporated the general consensus and extended it a bit farther.

Addison's program. To Addison the current catchwords—output, efficiency, power—meant specific things. (*a*) They meant unity and organization in each major trade. His annual report had termed this "the first necessity." The conference of August 1918 renewed that plea.[23] (*b*) Efficiency and output required improved transport. Reports were in on the standardization of railway equipment and on the development of light railways. Opening a much grander vista, Addison had sought a general inquiry into the future of railways, including the matter of ownership. He conferred frequently with Bonar Law and Stanley on the overall topic in July 1918—but the subject, and his data on it, were turned over that month to a select committee of the House of Commons.[24] No decision had been taken, at any level. (*c*) Greater output implied greater energy, in the sense of physical power. New fuels could be found and present facilities could be bettered. Addison inherited the work of the Asquith committee on electrical power (as noted). The differing plans of the

23. Addison, *Diary*, 2: 456–64, and Cd. 9005, pp. 199–210.
24. Cd. 9231, p. 16; Cd. 9084; Addison, *Diary*, 2: 541, 548–49, and *Politics*, 2: 210–11.

Parsons committee, the Williamson committee, and Lord Haldane's group were all under study; and Addison, who had set his Advisory Council to studying each plan, especially directed its attention to the Williamson report.

All the committees had agreed on the enormous promise and value of electric power and all had favored extension in facilities and unification in management. But disagreement was still strong on other points—notably on the plan for electricity commissioners who would be subordinate to the Board of Trade, which clashed with the idea of a more independent statutory commission. Friends of parliamentary control rallied to the former alternative while the latter alternative recommended itself to those who wished the new system to be modeled on commercial undertakings. There was debate, too, about the degree of control in general: champions of public power clashed with the foes of nationalization. The dispute drew in one group and agency after another, from Addison's Advisory Council, through the Economic Defence and Development Committee, to a special committee of the War Cabinet itself. Tempers grew short, and with good reason. Prompt action, if successful, would send output soaring and make every task of reconstruction easier; but action must be *very* prompt, because the necessary preliminary work clearly would be immense. And the risk of misguided action also caused worry. There was a real possibility, if state aid were given in the wrong form, that it would perpetuate existing inefficiencies and defeat the whole purpose. The whole problem—the chance on the one hand of attaining a goal vital for all of reconstruction, and the risk by one misstep of undermining everything—was perfectly epitomized for the Electricity Supply Committee of the cabinet in one eloquent memorandum on "the urgency of certain new power stations."

> Unless new Power Stations are ready or well in hand for after-the-war demands, it will be difficult to check the installation of further private generating stations. . . . From the point of view of intelligent labour, all hangs upon the rapid restoration of industry after the War. Every energy should be bent to making the maximum profits out of industry, and as rapidly as possible. It is the only source from which money will be forthcoming to pay War taxation, good wages to labour, and to provide better housing accommodation, health conditions and educational facilities for the working classes. In this work of reconstruction . . . a sound system of electrical power supply to industry must play a primary part.

By the end of August the War Cabinet seemingly was moving ahead, taking the initiative from the Board of Trade and the Ministry of Reconstruction alike. In any event the ministry's Advisory Council did not make up its mind and issue a report until 14 October.[25] In the definitive action, which came only in late 1919, the Ministry of Reconstruction agencies played little part.

Petroleum and coal were alternatives, of course. To seek out new power resources within the empire, Addison had campaigned more successfully for a Fuel Research Board. That Board, at least, was now set up.[26] (d) Addison perhaps foresaw that the day of British preeminence in the great staple industries was over. He had established the Engineering (New Industries) Committee in late 1917, but its report, finished in July, met a snag. Greenwood and C. D. Burns charged that labor interests were overlooked. Not until January 1919 did it appear in print.[27] (e) To make new goods and more goods would profit nothing if marketing techniques were unchanged. Addison therefore seconded the efforts of the Board of Trade to aid overseas trading, as the Balfour of Burleigh committee had urged. Addison endorsed the reorganization of consular services. At the Board of Trade and the Foreign Office, a thorough change was under way.[28]

(f) One project, concerning "key" or "special" industries, had a rationale all its own, which bore no relation to competitive success in export trade. The few industries that conventionally went by that name— the strategically essential industries—were, almost by definition, uneconomical and uncompetitive duplicates of industries that flourished in other nations. But they were vital for the sake of self-sufficiency in war. On this topic, Addison's mind was made up. Thanks to his work at the Ministry of Munitions he deemed it proved beyond dispute that key industries absolutely must be protected, as part of any serious long-term economic policy. He personally argued the case for them; his ministry devoted one of its Information Series pamphlets to the topic. But the

25. Notations by Nash, Barter, and R. Walter, October–November 1918, in Box 83; Memorandum WC.WPC.ESC 1, in Box 83. Minutes of E.D.D.C. meeting of 20 November 1918, and the report by the Ministry of Reconstruction's Advisory Council of Chairmen. See Cd. 9072, 9062, 8880, and Cmd. 93, and Addison, *Diary*, 2: 544, and *Politics*, 2: 211–12. The Haldane, Parsons, and Williamson committee reports are compared thoroughly with the views of the Advisory Council (the "Birchenough Report") in Henry Self and Elizabeth Watson, *Electricity Supply in Great Britain: Its Development and Organization* (London: Allen & Unwin, 1952), pp. 32–42.

26. Cd. 9231, pp. 8–9.

27. Addison, *Diary*, 2: 414, 419; F. 7716, Box 71, Part 1; Cd. 9226.

28. Cd. 8815.

question remained whether the measures in hand would meet the need. A special report put this question before Addison's Advisory Council, which concluded that

> the new department of "Industries and Manufactures" of the Board of Trade . . . set up since the date of the Balfour of Burleigh report, together with the new Board of Trade Advisory Council, do in fact provide in essentials the machinery which Lord Balfour's Committee had in view. . . . Any other machinery could only be justified by the failure of the existing machinery to produce results.

Still dissatisfied, Addison went against the advice of his chairmen and urged the E.D.D.C. to favor, instead, an *independent* industries board, to stand above politics and above departments as well. His lengthy memorandum showed why this should be done, and, under his commentary (seemingly a quibble about structure), the real complexity and inwardness of the policy question was revealed. Addison traced the evolving thought of the Balfour of Burleigh committee. It too had begun thinking of a few selected enterprises as key industries, from the narrow standpoint of self-sufficiency and munitions needs; but its final report had abandoned such distinctions and had recommended attention to *all* industries. In the last analysis, no simple dividing line could be drawn between "essential" and "nonessential" industries; and certainly any such line failed to correspond to the line between industries that would need or seek assistance and those that would not. Every board, then, would have to possess very wide discretion. It would operate, largely, in an experimental field.

Addison, who had meant to deal only with a question of structure, thought he had shown the superiority of an independent Board. But had he not revealed something much more profound? Whether he saw it or not, he hinted at a truth that had been revealed by war but was vastly important for industry in peace: The traditional concept of key industries was too narrow; where whole economies fought against each other, every industry was essential and *any* industry might therefore require aid. But surely the interdependence of industries outlasted a war; surely the case for aid could be valid anywhere, and no *a priori* exclusion should be decreed. This was the logical conclusion to which his practical argument led, but what a challenge it implied to assumptions of laissez-faire!

Addison passed on to a digression that showed the growth of his thought. He took as his point of departure the National Liberal Federation's recent vote for *complete* confiscation of profits, where the state gave aid. The whole question of "state-aided profits" arose naturally, Addison knew, and he saw that the Federation had thought it logical, in the interest of protecting free trade, to vote for confiscation by the state. But he dissented vigorously: "We often do things which are logically inconsistent, but which are found to work."

> I am not one of those who entertain an abstract fear of extending the State's participation in the promotion or conduct of trade and industry, and in many directions I think the War has shown—in none more strikingly than in the special industries . . .—that individual effort alone has not . . . secured an efficient maintenance of some essential industries.

But he opposed total confiscation, above all, where research and inventiveness figured largely in the results. The principle of reward was still valid. Excess-profits duty, where it restricted this, had been harmful: "Actual and fairly recent experience does not encourage the view that the State can best promote industrial enterprise by eliminating private profit"! The man who would pen *Practical Socialism* in the 1920's did not hesitate to defend a pragmatic compromise with business profit, where it worked.

Ultimately, though after the 1 October deadline, his challenge to the Board of Trade came up, and lost. The Board of Trade remained in control of the situation, though not without debate. Much later, its launching of a special inquiry into key industries reflected credit on Addison's basic arguments. Meanwhile, some kind of action to protect key or special industries seemed assured.

But what of the kindred problem of "dumping," by which any and all British firms might be menaced? There was unanimity that foreign nations should not be allowed to dump their goods on the British market at prices below those in their domestic markets for the same goods. But could measures be found that stopped short of outright protectionism, and that did not subsidize inefficiency? Would not such favoritism automatically hurt other British interests—consumers and labor, for instance? The Economic Defence and Development Committee wrestled with the matter, and so did Addison's staff. Data on other nations' laws were compiled; Gardiner collated the views of departmental committees; and the Advisory Council reported in favor of special duties on goods where dumping was proved. J. J. Mallon interposed with a sharp objection: No attention had been paid to the question of "sweated goods," and it was imperative that British workers be protected against these. Addison agreed. But neither the main report on dumping nor the clarification on sweated goods was ready before the crisis period of October.[29]

On all this—transport, power, unity in trade, marketing, aid to new industries and key industries, and a *tremendous revival in agriculture*—the ministry pinned its hopes. The farming program may have passed for implementation, long since, to the Board of Agriculture and Fisheries but its place on Addison's agenda was unchanged. Addison and Prothero spoke with one voice on every major reform for the countryside, and their common message was the same that Lord Selborne had put before the nation in 1917. With the gospel of Whitleyism, the great commandments of the Selborne report completed the circle of the ministry's national plan.

Some humdrum corollaries also came Addison's way. Finance and its ramifications must be studied—not with the thought that fiscal policy could be a powerful lever in the government's hand but simply because financial questions complicated life. Accordingly, Addison sponsored the Committee on Currency and Foreign Exchanges, under Lord Cunliffe of the Treasury, the Committee on Financial Risks, to deal with trading in shares, and the Committee on Financial Facilities, under Sir Richard Vassar-Smith. By October, only Cunliffe's committee had reported. A cabinet decision had not even been asked.[30]

All this work was important but it hardly broke new ground. Contemporaries, moreover, were perfectly aware that it did not add up to a clear or complete program.

Disunity, indecision, delay: economic plans outside Addison's Ministry. In July the British Empire Producers' Organization deplored the Government's "continued delay in deciding upon and making public the Economic Policy under which these industries are to be carried on after the war." The British Engineers' Association angrily commented that the Balfour of Burleigh recommendations, which it endorsed, had been available for months.[31] The files of the Economic Offensive Committee and the E.D.D.C. bulged with the same complaint *within* the government. Confronted with immediate proposals at the very first E.D.D.C. meeting, Alfred Mond had protested that they should discuss the "general basis of our economic policy before deciding detailed points, such as . . . had come

29. See Files 3349, 5104, and 7781, Box 90, Part 3; Cd. 9231, pp. 14–15; Binder 1, Box 78, Part 1. See also the minutes of E.D.D.C. meeting 7 (20 August 1918), and E.D.D.C. Memorandum 41, "Special Industries," by Addison, 24 September 1918, in Cab. 27/44. Not till 4 November did Addison issue his statement on "dumping" (E.D.D.C. Memorandum 63, *ibid.*).

30. Cd. 9231, pp. 13–14; Files 775 and 9245, Box 56; Cd. 9227, 9224, and 9182.

31. Cab. 21/108, especially letters of 23 and 31 July 1918.

under notice at this meeting." Back and forth went the memoranda (Mond's among others), between the committee, the Board of Trade, the Ministry of Reconstruction, and the Ministry of Shipping, but no decision was taken before the armistice became imminent. The committee's duality of purpose caused delay; it had to think of short-term transition policy and thus take account of a rapidly changing specific situation, simultaneously with determining general policy for the long term. Moreover, departments were working at cross-purposes. On export bans,

> one sort of difficulty was due to different departments wishing to pursue different policies. . . . The Foreign Office, for political reasons, might want an embargo on certain goods, while such a policy might cut across the views of the Treasury for exchange reasons, or the Ministry of Information for reasons of propaganda, or the Board of Trade for commercial reasons, or the Ministry of Shipping for reasons of tonnage.[32]

Plainly, policy also was in flux on tariffs. In June 1918 a Foreign Office spokesman went out of his way to describe the Paris Economic Conference of 1916 as a mere stage. (He meant to reassure American merchants who might fear that British policy would be not only punitively anti-German but anti-American as well.) But had the Paris conference really been repudiated ? Other papers suggested a fixed intent to take over Germany's overseas resources, and, indeed, to use the inter-Allied controls for this end after the war. Nor was alliance and "hands across the sea" the decreed choice. There was a hint, directed at a bill just passed by the United States Senate, that measures might speedily be needed against American competition.[33]

Thus far the E.D.D.C. had been little more than a mirror of indecision. If policy was to be formulated anywhere, however, this was the logical place. There were signs of a better trend. Mond sketched one synthesis, and the Board of Trade supplied another on 10 August; significantly, both were discussed without provoking major dissent. Mond's "outline scheme" reflected the impact of the war, almost to the point of caricature. "National security is of greater importance than national wealth"; self-sufficiency must be maximized; present alliances must become a "permanent bond of Union." The government must "buy British," prevent dumping, and

32. Minutes of E.D.D.C. meetings 1, 2, 4, and 7, July–August 1918, and E.D.D.C. Memorandum 34, in Cab. 27/44.
33. E.D.D.C. Memoranda 5 (June 1918) and 7 (13 June 1918), and minutes of E.D.D.C. meeting 6 (13 August 1918), in Cab. 27/44.

shelter a list of essential industries (so numerous one wonders if anything was omitted). True, there were corollaries: Consumers must not be exploited; "no fresh burdens should be imposed on the poor"; the state would have to insist on a specified quantity and quality of production, and reserve the right to control. Such comments were standard. Mond closed with a sharp warning about German preparation for the coming "economic war."

In contrast, Britain's vulnerability was not the first or the only point in the postwar economic policy contained in a seven-page memorandum from the Board of Trade. The Board put as much emphasis on other reasons for careful planning: the needs of reconstruction, the value of unity with the Dominions and the Allies on peace terms, and the urgency of dispelling business uncertainty. In principle, the Board distinguished "security" from "development." The former implied merely a few obvious measures, but "development" took up most of the paper. In transport, "development" implied that the railways of Great Britain should thereafter be worked under public control as a unified system; it also implied a strong system to coordinate port facilities and to aid rural traffic by light railways. Ocean transport, it was hinted, should come under much stronger control. "Industrial power," second only to transport, must be increased by continuing the studies on water power and on coal, and most of all by adopting the Williamson report on electricity. "Intelligence, invention, and research" came next: Commercial intelligence must be strengthened by new machinery; patent laws must be amended; and invention must be aided. Industry must learn to standardize. "Improved trade organisation" was recognized as a thorny subject. Fortunately, the promotion of Whitley Councils was already part of the government's policy,

> but if our industries are to hold their own in competition after the war, a very much greater development of co-operation and organisa-tion will be necessary for common purposes, *e.g.* buying, selling, and export organisation, and even complete fusion of interests, than has been prevalent in the past or than would have met with public approval . . . before the war.

Hindrances to planning were confessed. A policy on tariffs could not be recommended, for several reasons: There was at present no general agreement on the subject; high prices after the war would make it very difficult to defend any increased costs; and, candidly, Britain's industrial house must first be put in order lest protectionism subsidize inefficiency and deter the proper reorganization of industry. The authors added that any plan must depend, externally, on the way the war ended and, internally, on the continuance of the coalition. With all its limitations admitted, this memorandum was the fullest discussion at hand; and it is small wonder the E.D.D.C. seized on it.[34] Had peace not come so much sooner than expected, the last touches might have been put on a genuine plan. But midway in October all efforts were turned to short-range tasks. Neither policy paper came before the E.D.D.C. again.

As we weigh the merits and the shortcomings of the plans by the Ministry of Reconstruction it is well to remember that Addison took a full part in the sessions of the Economic Defence and Development Committee and that he had every right to expect that his colleagues there—especially the heads of the Board of Trade—would play a primary role. Still, some duties lay especially heavy upon Addison. More than others, he may have been obligated to demonstrate how the rival claims of reform, domestic demand, efficiency, overseas competition, and financial solvency could be reconciled. The ministry, however, appears to have prepared no such presentation; within the crucial period before the armistice, no paper was written that even hinted at a problem of reconciliation. There was, nevertheless, clear evidence—even in the ministry's own documents—that the problem existed.

Cunliffe's committee, for example, termed it imperative that conditions for return to the gold standard "be restored without delay."

> Unless the machinery which long experience has shown to be the only effective remedy for an adverse balance of trade and an undue growth of credit is once more brought into play, there will be grave danger of a progressive credit expansion which will result in a foreign drain of gold menacing the convertibility of our note issue and so jeopardising the international trade position of the country.

But this thinking implied that the government should cease borrowing as soon as possible after the war; it meant that note issue must be curtailed; and it meant that international claims must be accorded parity if not priority. Surely, then, domestic industry would be denied the special credit and preferential treatment that the new developmental plans presumed. Addison's own memorandum, "Reconstruction Finance," patently was at odds with this. A private correspondent warned Addison

34. Minutes of E.D.D.C. meetings 1, 4, 6, 7, June–September 1918, and E.D.D.C. Memoranda 18 (2 July 1918) by Mond and 33 (10 August 1918) from the Board of Trade, in Cab. 27/44.

that the Cunliffe committee's ideas aimed "a serious blow at Reconstruction," inviting Britain to a Barmecide feast.[35]

Which broad policy would prevail? There were no agreed answers and there was little serious discussion. And thus things stood on a wide range of crucially important questions. Would there be a special law to curb profiteering? Should tariffs rise generally? Would imperial preference triumph? Would changes be decided piecemeal—and, if so, which changes and on what basis? What did "decontrol" mean? Granted that restraints would generally be relaxed, what would the exceptions be?

At the cabinet level, indecision—or, more often, inattention—was the rule. In the circumstances this was no crime, but it was less pardonable that the cabinet's advisers had not set out the alternatives so plainly that the cabinet might be better able to decide. Plentiful individual suggestions and a lively exploratory debate in the E.D.D.C. could not conceal the fact that nothing authoritative had been pronounced. This was one gaping defect; the other defect was incompleteness.

Several Ministry of Reconstruction committees had not reported, and in only two cases (fuel research and the reorganization of aids to marketing) had real action followed the reports. Furthermore, even if a report had been made and a decision reached, detailed implementation had almost never got under way.

Within the limited scope of the official work in progress, such criticisms apply. But why should we accept this handful of minor measures as a full economic policy? Surely the perspective of 1919, let alone that of later years, proves that nothing near the complete list of hard decisions and indispensable topics had been attempted. Railways and their nationalization, the future of coal, the restraint on inflation (if price limitation was to be tried), definition of the tolerable level of budgetary deficit, and the relation of abnormal wartime costs, wages, and prices to ultimate desirable levels—all these remained, at least at the high interdepartmental level, not simply undecided but unstudied. How could the new drive for integration within industry be reconciled with the growing fear of powerful trusts? What formula could adjust the measures aimed at self-sufficiency with those aimed at the revival of export trade? These topics became the agenda of 1919; and so far no clear pronouncement had come forth.

To these strictures officialdom could perhaps have offered two answers, and it did offer one. Its proclaimed defense was that, under a regime of devolution, self-regulation by all the interests would produce decisions.

35. F. 775, Box 56; Cd. 9182.

The merits of this answer were not self-evident; in any case, it was doubtful that preparation was adequate to give devolution a fair trial. The second rejoinder (if it can be legitimate to supply one where the government did not) is that the soundness of prewar practices and the adaptability of private enterprise were presumed, save in a limited number of cases where government therefore would intervene. Assuredly, the official's plans (or lack thereof) make most sense if they are conceived as adaptations at a few points to a tried and sturdy organism. Had war changed Britain so little? Had war left the conditions for world trade so intact that no drastic departures were called for? From the very wording of the official papers an opposite case could be made.

The goals, as we noted above, seemed obvious. Targets were easy to state, but how to reach them? Incantation and generalities would not do; and thus far the government had not supplied much else. It was in this area—planning for a permanent economic policy—that Addison and his colleagues showed up worst.

Reconversion

Perhaps, after all, it was in the six-month transition period from war to peace that Addison's chief duty would lie. How clear were his goals and plans for that special time? How much of the machinery was fully ready? The tasks at that time would range from demobilizing a huge armed force and more than three million workers in the industrial army to the dismantling of war enterprises. There must be speedy action on pledges, priorities, wages, unemployment pay, government workshops and supplies, imports and exports, and foreign relief. What was the state of readiness by 1 October?

Addison knew, for each part of reconversion and demobilization, the policy he wanted. For each part he had a plan, and each plan had gained approval, at least by the cabinet's auxiliary committees, and often by the cabinet itself. This was the case for the whole of the civilian demobilization question, as well as for national factories, raw materials organization, pledges, priorities, and the government's supply organization. The cabinet itself had spoken on the last two items; implicitly, it had endorsed a general line on decontrol. The great needs now were implementation and precision.

Decontrol. The Birchenough Report on priorities had called for "cessation of control at the earliest possible moment," which was exactly the tone of Addison's talk to his special public conference on 1 August. He declared his hearty sympathy with the expressed desire of industry "to get rid as soon as possible of what is known as Government control of industry." But even Birchenough's group acknowledged many limiting factors that would justify interim controls; and Addison had reminded his audience that "prevention of a general scramble for materials" was necessary. Also, he had spoken of release from *government* control, which was very different from saying control would not be exercised at all. Ernest Bevin's blunt insistence on decontrol only *after* representative joint bodies existed was very much on record; and Addison himself had said, at least once, that decontrol was contingent in precisely this way. Nor did others speak more univocally. At the conference in August, two businessmen called for speedy decontrol without qualifications, but three other businessmen put the emphasis the other way round and claimed support from their branches of industry. By contrast, Mond wrote a memorandum cautioning that continued controls might have a disastrous effect on the reestablishment of normal industry. To Mond, obviously, the government's declarations carried the threat of excessive control.[36] From all this it was obvious that policy lacked precision. Moreover, even so negative a process as decontrol would entail many specific actions. Controls took many forms, each requiring a distinct decision. Some forms —notably bans on imports and exports—would prove so necessary or popular as to require exceptions to any general rule; and even if decontrol were the sole aim, it must occur in stages, which raised the whole question of principles to guide the sequence. An apparently settled policy, on closer examination, disclosed a decision that was not a decision.

Decontrol did not stand alone. Logically and functionally it overlapped with the priorities question and with the program for trade organization.

Representative bodies in industry and trade. Support for Whitleyism had been settled a year before; campaigns to organize trade committees had been sanctioned almost as long. But chapter 10 made it plain that the progress with Whitley Councils, though solid, was slow; and the campaign for trade committees was in a sorry state. Few of the committees existed; none was trained; still fewer were informed. Not one was truly linked with government, ready to play the integrated role that had been so loudly promised. Implementation had gone nowhere near far enough.[37]

The need for action before the armistice, strong enough for such groups, was overwhelming where central organizations within the

36. Addison, *Diary*, 2: 560, 568–70, 577; Files 7792, 7890, and 11061, Box 52; draft memorandum to War Cabinet, Box 78; E.D.D.C. Memoranda 8 (15 June 1918), 15 (2 July), and 39 by Addison, and Memorandum 10 (25 June 1918) by Mond, Cab. 27/44; and minutes of E.D.D.C. meetings 1 (18 June 1918) and 2 (2 July 1918), *ibid.*

37. See above, pp. 164–72.

government were concerned. New bodies must arise—or so Addison insisted—to handle supply, and government stores, and priorities.

Priorities. With the adoption of the Birchenough Report the cabinet approved the establishment of a postwar priorities counterpart to Smuts's War Priorities Committee, and a representative Standing Council on Post-War Priority; and it defined their tasks. The cabinet group had now been named. Its advisory Standing Council meant much to Addison, who set great store by such lay groups. To present the idea to unionists and businessmen, Addison called the largest public meeting he ever held: a conference on 1 August, at Central Hall, with representatives of fifty-one industries. Spokesmen were there for employers and labor from all the Joint Industrial Councils and Interim Reconstruction Committees.

On the positive side, this was undeniably a two-way conference. Addison explained the plans for priority and allocation, and workers and employers spoke up from the floor. Addison stressed the central role of the Standing Council: its first duty would be to draft a schedule for handling priority certificates so as to assist transition. He was frank in his appeal for cooperation:

> Unless we get a proper working relation established here and now with the trade committees which have the knowledge of the facts . . . there will be such a scramble . . . as will be disastrous to the rapid recommencement of prosperous work.

This was a large order, but Birchenough invited the audience to "put their backs into it."

> If the return to a normal state of affairs is to be made smoothly and successfully the trades must do the work themselves. We have all been brought up in an atmosphere of individualism . . . we have reached a stage when we must fight in battalions.

Addison was pleased at the friendly and helpful spirit, but the meeting set up no organization, and he had to select spokesmen and assign duties. At the end of September, after conferences with six business groups, Addison happily concluded that nominations for the council could go to Smuts's committee.

His optimism was excessive. The council had neither staff nor data. It needed special training, and history was to allow no time for this. Even had the council been designed to *administer* a prearranged schedule these handicaps would have been crippling, but it was meant to *devise* a schedule, as its first task. This, indeed, would have been its greatest contribution. As it happened, the council was officially set up only on 15 October. By that date all hopes for a carefully drafted priority schedule, based on a thorough survey of existing controls, had been abandoned.[38]

The faults we have seen under the above three headings compounded each other. Policy on decontrol was too vague; it could gain precision only if (among many other things) a priorities schedule had been exactly outlined, but the council for this job existed only on paper. The new trade organizations were locked with the Standing Council in a mutually poisonous interdependence. Because the former were few or embryonic, they could not advise the council; without an effective council, the trade organizations and Whitley Councils would lack direction and work.

It was not a good situation, and high hopes had made it even worse. The enthusiasm for devolution compounded the problems, prolonging processes that were difficult enough in themselves. Between aim and decision it interposed several steps (forming committees, training committees, and linking the committees to Whitehall) that took time—just when time had vanished. The months of August and September had been put to wrong use.

Supply : raw materials. Fear of shortages spurred everyone, but not in the same way. Some searched for policy; others began to compile data; Addison strove to create a new central organization for raw material supplies. Wisely or not, he turned from the existing investigative bodies; they had no administrative competence, he thought, and they lacked cabinet status. In early September Garrod sketched plans for a new Board. It was a late start—perhaps altogether too late—and, worse still, Long and Hewins at the Colonial Office also were drafting plans. Although Garrod and Hewins came to agreement on plans by 30 September, their ministers broke into disagreement during October. Addison's plan lost to Long's.

Planning for this organization by the Ministry of Reconstruction appears to have been slow; certainly it was highly ambitious. Garrod envisioned a complex ministerial committee, perhaps even on a statutory basis. He had wanted General Smuts, head of the Standing Council on Post-War Priority (and of many full-time wartime committees), to be chairman of the Central Raw Materials Board. He intended that representatives of the Foreign, Colonial, and Indian offices should meet with men

38. Addison, *Diary*, as cited in note 35 above; see below, pp. 251–52. For summaries of views in the trades on postwar controls, see E. H. M. Lloyd, *Experiments in State Control at the War Office and the Ministry of Food* (London: Humphrey Milford, 1924), pp. 110, 153–54.

from the Board of Trade, the Ministry of Reconstruction, and the Standing Council on Post-War Priority. Somehow, this body was supposed to negotiate with the Dominions, appoint expert assessors, arrange purchases and aid private buying ("in consultation with the departments concerned"), and simultaneously review the broad issues of policy. The very loftiness of the concept condemned it, at this late date. It is arguable whether, in general and over its whole career, the Ministry of Reconstruction aimed too high and hoped for too much, but in this instance the impracticality was patent. Structures much simpler were the need of the hour—drastically new structures ought not to have been contemplated at all. The time had passed for anything but a system that utilized the tried machinery and departed from it as little as possible.[39]

Just as belated, and just as ambitious, was another plan—for a new Central Non-Ferrous Metals Committee. It was distinctive chiefly in reflecting the traders' restiveness under government control: its main tasks and powers would devolve on business representatives. If what business wanted was a share of power, the scheme was ideal, for the proposed committee would "appoint and supervise the rationing authorities . . . adjudicate within the trade associations . . . receive all applications for shipping space," and approve all applications and carry on such investigations as it wished. But if business wanted *speed*, the thing was hopeless. After September little was heard of it.[40]

Supply: government property. In a gigantic memorandum of protest, Lord Salisbury's Surplus Government Property Advisory Council unburdened itself to Addison in September: "Owing to hindrances over which we have had no control we have not been able to make satisfactory progress." "The unresponsive attitude of some Departments" (the Board of Trade had ignored the council) and "the paralysing effect of uncertainty, indecision and protracted delay" were bad enough. Worse still, "combating for the right to work" had taken the time needed "to put us in a position many months ago to devote our energies to our formidable task." The Disposal Board, its only executive, had been delayed; the Order in Council that empowered it remained a dead letter. All the same, in ten months the council had dealt advisorily with half a million pounds' worth of property, had negotiated with foreign governments, and had studied British stocks from Belgium to Suez. But by 1 October it was not ready.[41]

It was another failure but not a case for blame. The reasonable view,

---

39. Addison, *Diary*, 2: 561; F. 7572, Box 53; F. 8040, Box 15, Part 2.
40. Files 5859, 6215, and 8040, Box 15, Part 2; Cd. 9231, paragraph 21.
41. Draft of Interim Report, Box 72.

from longer range, is that no one ever solved the surplus stores problem and that probably it was insoluble. Long after 1919 the fighting services were still deadlocked with the Ministry of Munitions and the Ministry of Supply, which suffered from the same obstruction that had crippled the S.G.P.A.C. If such great departments, with the prestige of giant wartime operations, could not succeed, and if the cabinet itself was bedeviled long after the armistice by these disputes, what chance had Lord Salisbury's tiny council? If it was a failure the failure reflects rather the intractability of the problem than delay or defect in the ministry. Regardless, the fact of unpreparedness was very grim.

National factories. Addison's ministry was better prepared with recommendations on the 242 establishments the Ministry of Munitions directly managed or whose workers it paid. Here, however, was a theme that was destined for controversy. In 1919 no thought came quicker to the minds of discharged munitions workers than the idea that they should be reemployed in national factories, producing articles for peacetime uses. And time and again the topic came onto War Cabinet agenda in the year after the war.

Addison followed the lead of the Ministry of Munitions. In late September 1918, Addison recommended to the Economic Defence and Development Committee that sixteen or twenty plants remain publicly owned (although they might be leased to private firms). These he classified as category A, the first of four groups. The eighty-five plants in category B would return to private ownership. The dominant principle, Addison said—with an eye to unemployment problems during the transition period—was that "firms should be encouraged to prepare plans in advance"; therefore, negotiations for return should begin at once. Addison stressed that, alternatively, these eighty-five plants might be used by the state or by local authorities, perhaps for power generation or for agricultural industries. The twenty-five establishments in category C could be used for storage, and the 115 plants in category D might be returned to their owners. On 24 September the E.D.D.C. adopted Addison's plan, which the War Cabinet approved on 9 October.

It was a plan, though without a clear rationale.[42] Still, in terms of a timetable, it was not overly delayed.

42. G.T. 5351, in Cab. 24/60 and in Box 77, also cited in minutes of E.D.D.C. meeting 9 (24 September 1918), Cab. 27/44; D.M. 18 and 20, Box 77; F. 7890, Box 52; WC 483, 9 October 1918, Cab. 23/8; G.T. 6041, 18 October 1918, Appendix, pp. 28–30. See also A. C. Pigou, *Aspects of British Economic History, 1918–1925* (London: Macmillan, 1948), pp. 124–25.

Demand and shipping. On the physical side of reconversion, Addison's staff identified three other problems: ascertaining overseas demand, especially from the Dominions; defining the Allies' requirements; and estimating shipping resources and needs. On the first problem, policy formulation and data collection alike suffered from delay all year long, and basic decisions were still unmade by October.[43] Happily, a sound program for shipping during the transition period was now ready. At the Economic Defence and Development Committee the Shipping Controller confidently reported that the present level of shipbuilding would create ample tonnage. The powers of his department would not lapse until one year after the war had ended; and the current regulations under those powers, which otherwise would lapse, were extended by an E.D.D.C. recommendation at his request. Maclay, the Shipping Controller, brought exceedingly good news. Probably there would be "no serious tonnage problem after the War. . . . There ought to be no particular difficulty in lifting within a comparatively short period from the cessation of hostilities all the raw materials which are . . . essential to the reconstruction of industry."[44] Thus a prime cause for anxiety would disappear!

The Allies' requirements were still not known. The E.D.D.C. agreed that data must be compiled and it passed the task to the Foreign Office on 17 September. (Interestingly, the committee did *not* create the new organization of manufacturers, which Addison had recommended for the placing in Britain of orders on behalf of the Allies; it feared friction and resentment among manufacturers.[45] Devolution had lost again, perhaps because it seemed next door to jobbery.) On one topic, domestic demand, Addison supplied nothing. He knew that, under the spur of Churchill's commands, the Ministry of Munitions was paying close attention to the needs of its controlled establishments; and he counted on the "Iron and Steel Committee," formed in the spring, to determine demand, supply, and capacity for that industry. Addison's reliance on the Munitions staff was understandable: they were far closer to the industrial realities than he; they could use a working force—in the London headquarters alone— of 18,000 employees, while his ministry never had over 800 on its roster. Still, the partnership was ironic in view of Addison's tendency to grouse about the curse of departmentalism. A *de facto* division of labor had grown

43. See above, pp. 74–76, 103–4, 140–42; F. 8050, Box 53.
44. Minutes of E.D.D.C. meetings 3 (9 July 1918) and 12 (22 October 1918), and E.D.D.C. Memoranda 13 and 22, Cab. 27/44.
45. G.T. 5217, "Allied Post-War Requirements," by Addison, cited in minutes of E.D.D.C. meeting 8 (17 September 1918), Cab. 27/44; F. 7890, Box 52.

up, in which the good will and expertness of many a maligned ministry made all the difference.

In any case, policy and details for physical reconversion were being shaped.

Demobilization: the armed forces. The human side, the other great dimension of Addison's reconversion task, fell naturally into two parts. Policy for the fighting services had been wholly decided, although it was far from implementation. Policy for civilian workers had been proposed but it still lacked cabinet approval.

By mid-1918 the government, as we have noted, was well prepared for the discharge of soldiers and sailors—if "preparation" means the possession of a plan. Since 1917, indeed, it was accepted that soldiers and sailors would be released in terms of their occupations and in the order of need, rather than in terms of length of service. "Need" embraced economic revival and the demobilization process itself: that is, some men and some firms and industries were held to be especially important in "starting up" the economy. Other men, by virtue of their training and prewar positions, were considered "demobilizers" (e.g., civil servants in labor exchanges). "Pivotal" men (those linked with either kind of need) would be discharged first.

It was a thoroughly bad plan, as disastrously remote from the elemental desires of fighting men as it was from the national instinct for what was fair. To make things worse, preparations and the collection of data had been neglected; as late as 21 August 1918, preliminary steps and the selection of pivotal men were discouraged lest an undesirable "peace atmosphere" result. For a scheme so complicated, these delays virtually ensured that the system would break down. The War Cabinet itself was beginning to feel doubts in August. Haig had long ago gone on record against pivotalism, but no change was made. Eventually, a system that was wide open to the charge—in Churchill's words—of "humbug and jobbery" would be swept away by the mutinous outcry of the soldiers themselves. In this case, the government would have done better to have had no plan at all.[46]

Demobilization: civilian employees. To Addison, the topic of civilian demobilization was so important that he had devoted his first staff meeting to it alone. The dread "General Post" for over three million

46. Addison to Nash, 15 November 1917, F. 2545, Box 8; WC 274 (15 November 1917), Cab. 23/4; WC 431 (17 June 1918), and WC 462 (21 August 1918), Cab. 23/7; WC 393 (17 April 1918), Cab. 23/6. For Churchill's comment, see G.T. 6874, 21 February 1919, Cab. 24/75.

workers continued to hold his attention. But neither the cabinet nor the Home Affairs Committee had taken decisions; as a whole, the topic had not even come up there. The psychology of war accounted for the delay. When one small part of the problem had come before the cabinet in April, the mere possibility that an announcement might soften public morale had stopped discussion at once. Ludendorff's offensive silenced debate. Four months later a similar comment from Smuts again swept peace topics from the agenda. As late as 27 September, Sir Eric Geddes was predicting a renewed submarine offensive. It was for such reasons that the cabinet discussion commenced in earnest only on 23 October. Meanwhile the interdepartmental talks, launched by Churchill and Addison in spring, had ended fruitlessly. On the eve of the armistice Addison had to reprint afresh, for his cabinet colleagues, all the policy recommendations of his Civil War Workers' Committee.[47]

But at least that committee had done its work; and for good measure it had combated inertia by issuing new reports and exhortations in August and September. It had already sent in three reports. Its fourth report spelled out arrangements for cessation of war work, underscoring the points made earlier. (*a*) Arms production should continue on a half-time basis, supplemented by war bonuses. (*b*) Discharged workers should be transferred to "other work of national importance," which state financial aid might encourage municipalities to undertake. (*c*) Unemployment benefits should be augmented (a most advanced idea) according to the number of dependents and the current cost of living. All such measures should be *general*, not for munitions workers alone.

These proposals were known within the government. A confused but energetic discussion began, particularly on insurance. It was all inconclusive, however, and the committee—well aware that its plans implied prior arrangement that would take time—returned (in a fifth report that September) to stress the urgency of action. The "war pledges" question must be settled; schemes for postwar work must be prepared at once, so that contracts could be signed; employment exchanges must be strengthened. Employers under government contracts ought to be given more time to fulfill their obligations.[48] These reports went well beyond generalities; they made choices between detailed alternatives; they recommended

47. WC 393 (17 April 1918), Cab. 23/6; WC 462 (21 August 1918), Cab. 23/7; WC 479A (27 September 1918), Cab. 23/14; and WC 487 (16 October 1918), Cab. 23/8; Memorandum D.C. 1 (31 October 1918), by Addison, Cab. 27/42; G.T. 6047 (19 October 1918), by Addison (discussed below, pp. 271–75).

48. Cd. 9192; Files 539 and 7716, Box 71, Part 1; Addison, *Diary*, 2: 544, 576, 577; Cd. 9231, pp. 20–22.

specifics. This was all to the good. They repeated the case for putting demobilization in the larger context of a constructive recovery program. They largely fulfilled the ministry's duty to plan. And three of the reports had appeared in time.

The work of the Civil War Workers' Committee is one proof, among many, that reconstruction officials had not been content to leave matters at the level of a vague rhetorical promise. They not only called for change but spelled out the nature of that change in a lengthy list of detailed and sometimes far advanced measures. The well-understood program of Whitleyism, the civilian demobilization plans, the sustained campaign for Poor Law reform and a Ministry of Health, and most eloquently the close reasoning and precision of the case for a bold attack on workers' housing, demonstrate beyond cavil that the officials within the government had not avoided direct consideration of the objects of social policy or of the means to reach attainable objects. Planners had done more than this. They had foreseen, and plainly had been moved by, the hardships that demobilization and reconstruction could bring.

Basic Needs: Prior Action and Synoptic Review

By their very thoroughness and precision, however, these reports showed what a world of implementation still remained. They showed, on page after page, the need for complete and early action of the most specific kind. To turn then to the records of the Cabinet and of the Home Affairs Committee, and to see these recommendations unheeded (let alone adopted) until late October, is to take the measure of unreadiness. And yet there was an even greater flaw. The committee's ideas presumed that the government would accept the duty of providing employment and that it would not flinch from subsidy, the placing of orders, underwriting local authorities' expenses, and from all supportive measures. The committee presumed that the government would have solved the pledges question, that it would possess the data needed to formulate an industrial policy, and that it would have formulated one! But none of these prerequisites was provided in time. On 23 October Sir Stephenson Kent put it flatly: "The problem of demobilisation could not be solved until the Government made up its mind as to its industrial policy."[49]

Aid from a Colleague: Plans at Munitions

At least one other department felt equally bound to prepare for reconversion; the Ministry of Munitions completed its preparations and reports

49. Minutes of Home Affairs Committee meeting 15 (23 October 1918).

just in time. The report on 30 September from its Council Committee on Demobilisation and Reconstruction amounted to a huge harvest: recommendations on contracts, stores, national factories, controls; plans for labor demobilization; special arrangements for iron and steel; policies for engineering and chemical trades; and data and background analyses on all of this. (Addison may have felt almost parental pride, for he had set this work going at Munitions in April 1917.) But there was a catch. At the Ministry of Munitions—as its official history phrases it—the assumption was that, as a temporary department, it would have no ultimate responsibility for demobilization; that duty rested with the Ministers of Reconstruction and of Labour. As we have seen, Churchill said this most plainly in February 1918.

> Although the Ministry of Munitions necessarily must deal with the questions of day to day discharges . . . and must continually be studying the methods by which the situation arising on peace is to be tided over, I am of opinion that the general application of war industry to peace industry constitutes a principal part of the work of the Ministry of Reconstruction. We should supply them with the data obtained from our knowledge of the particular firms and industries under our control and with suggestions as to alternative forms of production. . . . But they alone can make a broad scheme.

With this understanding Churchill's Munitions Council Committee on Demobilisation and Reconstruction confined itself, where civilian labor demobilization was concerned, merely to data collection.

Labour displacement. Data from their samples suggested that the dislocations at armistice would be less troublesome than had been feared inasmuch as two-thirds of the engineering force was at its normal work. Broader studies indicated that, at war's end, the chemical and metal trades would have 2,228,000 males and 870,000 females at work—90 per cent on government tasks. Of this 3,098,000 total, about 1,891,000 persons would be employed on products adaptable for peace purposes. If pledges were rigidly carried out and all dilutees removed, total displacement might reach 1,025,000 males and 571,000 females. The pledges, of course, were the great unknown; but possibly 1,000,000 munitions workers would have to change jobs in any case. If the pledges were enforced, the figures would be increased by 500,000 men and 100,000 women.

Even though not as bad as feared, these predictions were alarming. They fully explain why, in the furious cabinet exchanges of October 1918, Churchill angrily resisted the speedy restoration of prewar trade-union practices. For the heart of that "restoration" question was the status of the wartime "dilutees"—the workers who had been allowed to take on munitions jobs despite their lack of prewar union status (thus "diluting" the proportion of union members in the factory). Restoration of prewar rules would automatically make dilutees ineligible to hold their wartime jobs; the result could be an immediate enormous increase in the number of unemployed.

Eventually, by insisting on restoration of prewar practices, Addison would clash with Churchill in that October debate. But in April, oddly, the Ministry of Reconstruction—specifically, its Civil War Workers' Committee—complemented the planning at Munitions and tended to confirm Churchill in his plan to terminate munitions work at the earliest moment. Inasmuch as that plan was one of the main ingredients in the October crisis, this interrelationship must be spelled out.

In the spring, anticipating the day of armistice, Munitions planners faced the broad choice between antagonistic policies—gradual and delayed termination of work, or immediate stoppage without regard to the effect on workers; but they faced these antagonistic policies with some trepidation. They "recognised that the interests of Labour must be considered"; seemingly, this consideration dictated the choice of a gradual slowdown. But Churchill's staff preferred a quick stoppage, partly to avoid wasting raw materials on munitions, and partly to free plants for postwar work. As they wavered, it came to their attention that the Civil War Workers' Committee plans provided comprehensive and generous unemployment aid to all discharged munitions workers, and for their dependents. As the Munitions report puts it, "the [Munitions Council] Committee were fortified in their opinion by the knowledge that the Civil War-workers Demobilisation Committee were actively engaged in the preparation of a scheme for the payment of unemployment allowances to workpeople during . . . industrial demobilisation." This was encouragement enough: with such aid as a cushion against the loss of munitions jobs, rapid termination of munitions contracts was made feasible.

Accordingly, Addison was asked to concur in a plan for immediate termination when war stopped; he was reminded by Munitions that "to continue production of munitions for which there is no future demand, even though it may assist in some measure in dealing with . . . employment . . . must necessarily have the effect of utilising . . . material which will be

urgently required for commercial industry, and thus delay the change over
. . . to the products of commerce." On 6 April 1918 Nash replied for
Addison.

> While the Minister concurs in the general principle of discontinuing
> as soon as possible any production of munitions for which there is
> no future demand, he does so on the assumption that Mr. Churchill
> has in mind a scheme of demobilisation under which it hoped, by
> the placing of new contracts and by ensuring materials for their
> execution, to facilitate the transition from munitions work to other
> forms of production.

The exchange of views was highly illustrative. It showed the near-
incompatibility of policies dominated by labor considerations, and policies
dominated by concern for rapid industrial revival; it showed how the two
imperatives, economy in raw materials and maintenance of industrial
peace founded on humane treatment, could conflict; it showed how
anxious the Munitions staff were to get on with their immediate production tasks, by counting on others for plans to cope with personnel needs,
just as it showed how Addison was uneasy about the human impact of a
swift termination. But at the moment, it was the misunderstanding on
their several duties that worried the Munitions men. Addison seemingly
did not or would not accept or understand that Churchill looked on
demobilization as the Ministry of Reconstruction's task. Finally the
Minister of Munitions won Addison's consent to a revised formulation—
that Addison concurred on rapid termination, "on the assumption that he
may rely upon Mr. Churchill's co-operation in the preparation of a scheme
of demobilisation." Churchill thereupon went ahead, his assumption
confirmed: "plans for terminating contracts must be framed on the broad
principle that materials, manufacturing capacity, and labor should be
diverted at the earliest possible moment from the production of useless
munitions to peace industry." Or, as Churchill put it on 1 October 1918,
"The manufacture of munitions should not continue for a single day
longer than is absolutely necessary and economically justifiable." Thus
the manufacture of shells, shell components, trench warfare munitions,
explosives, and the like "would cease within two to four weeks of giving
notice to terminate." For heavier equipment, production on a reduced
scale would continue only as necessary to complete articles in manufacture
that could not economically be scrapped. This might not mean that all
laborers in lighter munitions would hit the labor market at once, for
contracts would doubtless be ended gradually. The Munitions staff kept

in close touch with the Civil War Workers' Committee, and generally accepted its framework.[50]

The main plan at Munitions. Demobilization of personnel, as thoroughly as it had been studied, took up few of the thirty-two pages of fine print in the final report from Munitions. A mere list of other headings would be formidable; the details were nothing short of a dissertation on wartime controls and the problems of reconstruction. More important was the fact that the Munitions people knew exactly where they stood. They knew which plans were ready, which ones must be completed without delay, and which decisions must be made at once. On 30 September 1918, with all this information in hand, the Munitions Council Committee was ready to report. The essence may be stated here, although the full statement was not given to the cabinet until mid-October.[51]

1. Basic principles had been determined for the demobilization of the Ministry of Munitions and of its workers. Data were on hand —far from perfect, but the best likely to be found—relative to postwar demand.
2. Problems of priorities, disposal of government property, termination of contracts, and supply had been thoroughly examined.
3. Many detailed recommendations were ready on controls, prices, and administrative machinery. As regards steel, however, the final decisions had not been made; a complex plan for State purchase and import of steel, offering a guaranteed price and controlling in turn the manufacturers' selling price, still awaited approval. Subsidy—the most critical question of all, touching every part of this giant industry—might be continued, or might not; the question was still under study.
4. Many emergency powers, it had been found, must still be used by the Minister of Munitions in the transition period; a number of these required the cabinet's reaffirmation. Churchill's advisers, who deemed this crucial, spelled out the case under seven headings: termination of contracts for supply of munitions; disposal of stores and machinery; arrangements for disposal or use of the national factories; control of materials during the transitional period; special arrangements with the iron and steel

---

50. *History of the Ministry of Munitions*, vol. 6: *Man Power and Dilution*, Part 2: "The Control of Industrial Man Power, 1917–18" (London, 1922), pp. 82–84.
51. G.T. 6041, "Demobilisation of Munitions Industries," by Winston Churchill, 18 October 1918, Cab. 24/67, together with 1 October 1918 report of the Munitions Council Committee on Demobilisation and Reconstruction. See especially p. 12.

trade, to secure continuous output; reinstatement of peace industry; demobilization of civilian munitions labor.

5. A cabinet decision was needed at once on five substantive points.

a) The postwar use of national factories. The wider question—what *products* these factories should make—had not been answered either.

b) The exact level of output that the War Office would need.

c) The relative priority to be assigned to various forms of industry. This complex and undecided matter hinged, it was ominously added, on advice to be given by the Standing Council on Post-War Priority; but Addison had not yet set up this body.

d) Creation of a Ministry of Supply, or a firm decision *not* to create one.

e) Appointment of a powerful "Director-General of Civil Demobilisation," and retention of Munitions staff to help him.

6. As a matter of urgency, there must be precise and authoritative definition "of the respective responsibilities of the Minister of Reconstruction, the Minister of Labour and the Minister of Munitions," for the demobilization of civilian labor.[52]

The Council Committee of Churchill's ministry understandably stressed how much still had to be done. Their report dwelled on the unsatisfactory results of the inquiries launched in late 1917: surveys of lands and buildings, still imperfect; inadequate replies on postwar needs for equipment and materials; unreadiness of a detailed scheme of priorities, either in the form that they had started, or in the form that Addison's Standing Council—for the simple reason that it still existed in name only—was to have prepared. Indirectly too they criticized other ministries for not dealing with the question of redeployment of labor, and censured Addison for slowness in dealing with national factories, which had prevented their negotiating with firms on problems of lease or sale. Nevertheless, despite these negative points, they supplied the best and most useful summary produced in Whitehall. It told just where things stood. It showed just what the cabinet must now do.

But as an index to the state of governmental readiness it revealed something different. It was appalling that the general division of labor on

52. G.T. 5863 from Churchill, "Industrial Demobilisation," 1 October 1918, Cab. 24/65; see below, pp. 278–80, for list of emergency powers needed.

demobilization still needed to be made clear, and deplorable that so many questions had not been decided at all at the top level. The broad "lesson," delay at the center, was the same that could be learned from Addison's work. Ministries, as advisers and planners, had done their work; the cabinet had still to decide.

The Economic Defence and Development Committee, of course, had been set up just to speed this process. In nine sessions, through 24 September, it had sent on for approval the plan for the Post-War Priorities Committee and its Standing Council, had authorized study of Allied post-war needs, and endorsed Addison's ideas on national factories. But only the first of these had passed the cabinet. It had opened discussions on postwar policy in general, on shipping in particular, and on inter-Allied postwar economic controls. But these plans were not ready for submission to the cabinet; the prickly topic of imports and exports still produced only disagreement. As late as 24 October such matters were still under debate. In mid-October it would still be possible for a Munitions official to ask, "Is it the policy of the Government to attempt to cripple Germany's trade after the war?" And the Shipping Controller himself would ask his colleagues in mid-October "to settle definitely on what hypotheses we are going to work"![53]

Needs Seen and Unforeseen

As October opened, men like Addison, Churchill, Roberts, and Stanley knew which items on their agenda had been fulfilled; they knew which were still delayed by unpreparedness within their ministries or by indecision higher up. This awareness was valuable. Addison understood just which items were jammed at the cabinet's door and which ones had not cleared the E.D.D.C. or the Home Affairs Committee. He knew that his own ministry had not finished work on the electricity question, had not forwarded proposals on annual holidays, had not spelled out the details on safeguards against "dumping," nor put its final case for a Central Raw Materials Board. And he recognized that several committees on finance, housing, and education had not even reported. He and Greenwood worried especially about pledges and the reinstatement of workers:

> Winston, at the last moment, is making himself troublesome by plunging in on the Pledges Bill . . . and has now circulated to the

53. Minutes of E.D.D.C. meetings, Cab. 27/44, and memoranda, *ibid.*, on the themes: commercial policy, Memoranda 5, 7, 14, 22, 34; inter-Allied controls, Memorandum 37; shipping, Memoranda 13, 22; economic policy in general, Memoranda 5, 10, 18, 27, 33, 41. The October comments are from Memoranda 42 and 50.

Cabinet, without consulting anybody else, a half-completed result.

...

The Ministry of Labour is letting loose Industrial Councils on war pledges at a most inconvenient time to us. The Bill has not been introduced yet and there is no clear Government policy.[54]

Yet these were troubles *within* the scope of foreseen tasks. What of those not foreseen?

There was, in fact, a whole series of questions that had not been faced, which in October and November would suddenly spring to everyone's mind. What should be the national minimum wage, and how would it affect the intricate system of wage differentials? What was the real strength of consumer demand at home, and how would its strength or weakness promote Britain's indispensable recovery of a share in world markets? Would temporary factors, such as a worldwide shipping shortage, protect Britain from underselling by American and Japanese steel producers? Was blockade of Germany compatible with the revival of British manufacture? Was it more costly to subsidize workers through unemployment donations or to subsidize business firms through state grants and government orders? Was a swift price slump, unimpeded by government, the truly practical and merciful way to end business uncertainties and allow revival to commence, or was it merely a way to line the pockets of speculative importers? If prices were to be maintained for a time, what relation should the new prices bear to the exceptionally high prices of wartime? Could business, aware that prices must eventually fall, be moved by any inducement to resume production and take risks? Should the government sustain demand and employment by entering into peacetime production, or would this discourage enterprise? Would insurance and unemployment donations remove the stimulus to work— and at what level, in any case, should they be set?

Once the cabinet found itself fairly caught in the troubles of demobilization and depression, these questions seemed obvious, even if their answers were not. It was around *them* that the anxious conferences, through the spring of 1919, talked their quarrelsome way. This half-year also brought to the fore three questions so concrete, so obvious, and so dangerous that the lack of prepared answers seems incredible: the question of finance and exact costs, the question of the railways, and the question of coal.

Perhaps these questions were foreseen but avoided, but three other

54. Addison, *Diary*, 2: 508 and 569; Greenwood to Barter, 13 September 1918, in F. 7716, Box 71, Part 1.

216

needs seem really to have been overlooked. (1) Measures of reform, tasks of reconversion, and aims of permanent economic policy had to be co-ordinated, and machinery had to be created to keep them so. Not even at the level of words and ideas had the coordination of measures been done, and the structure for the latter plainly did not exist—unless one counted the cabinet, which at this point seemed pathetically uninformed. To his credit, Mond had demanded in July that the E.D.D.C. face the need for an all-powerful committee of ministers to see the whole task through,[55] but his initiative was lost. (2) The appointment of a "czar" for demobilization of personnel was not even mentioned till mid-October; then it seemed obvious to all. (3) Consensus and comprehension must not be left to chance. Just as the forming of plans on which no one acted was useless, so the formal approval of plans by a cabinet that had not understood and therefore had not truly accepted or agreed left a dangerous gap. The mind of the cabinet had to be prepared, and the mind of the nation. It was an elemental truth, but perhaps, in the midst of war, it would have done no good to have grasped it.

The failures of foresight could easily be multiplied—one has the rest of 1918 and all of 1919 to work with—but there is no need to round the list. The point is that the situation in October should be judged by needs broader than those the planners saw.

The most critical shortcomings, in retrospect, seem to have numbered thirteen. (1) International understandings had not been attempted and were not even minimally planned. (2) Machinery and personnel to cope with the demobilization of personnel were seriously incomplete or unavailable. (3) Major questions of insurance, wages, prices, hours of work, and unemployment donations still went unanswered at the cabinet level. (4) No financial policy had been determined, let alone the kind that bespoke a fixed will to carry reconstruction through. (5) Irresolution on the war pledges sustained labor's suspicions and thus endangered every hope. (6) Staff, legal powers, and detailed arrangements for housing, farm settlement, and land reform fell far short of what was needed to prosecute these reforms speedily and also make them serve the cause of reconversion. (7) Rapport with labor was not recognized as a critical need. (8) New machinery, even where it existed, was untried and untrained, and the departments showed little disposition to welcome it. (9) The hope of a more democratized industrial order was heavily mortgaged by the fact

---

55. E.D.D.C. Memorandum 27 (23 July 1918), Cab. 27/44. In general, one author notes, at this time "there was no coordinating committee . . . to supervise the work of the rest throughout the civil sphere"; John Ehrman, *Cabinet Government and War*, p. 97.

that Whitley Councils and lesser committees did not blanket the country and they lacked authority and experience. (10) Predictive "lore" and machinery were so inadequate that sudden fleeting economic changes could cause panic and throw plans into disarray. (11) There was no clear and complete set of permanent economic goals to serve as a guide. (12) The cabinet did not truly understand such goals and plans as existed. (13) There was no organized system to assure national support.

Some of this could be, and some of it was, retrieved; but public endorsement and understanding could not be arranged by a committee summoned into emergency session. Moreover, public support could not be ignored. It might be the indispensable factor in transforming proposals into law. Moreover, the enthusiasm to match Britain's wartime economic miracles with equal prodigies after the war—and this, all sober observers agreed, *was* indispensable—could not be improvised. Opinion grows slowly; faith and the will for new sacrifices must rise from deep sources. Where the government could not create, had time and war made Britain ready for reconstruction? The ministry badly needed allies. Did it have them?

12

Mars and the Millennium: War, Reform, and Fate

Was British opinion united in its views on reconstruction? Did public attitudes augur well for Addison's ministry? On the eve of the armistice, what was the state of British thought?

All these questions were implied in the government's purpose and program; they were implicit, too, in Addison's growing attention to the drafting of election platforms and his search for public support, which became more and more strongly marked in the last six months of 1918. But the questions transcend such narrow limits. For us, who now seek to write the story of reconstruction and to put it into context, they become questions far broader, requiring a survey of national opinion as a whole, to measure the impact of war on a nation's mind.

An answer may conveniently begin with men like Sir Daniel Hall, author of *Agriculture after the War*. Sir Daniel knew of the Ministry of Reconstruction and had worked with it; he had served with Selborne's committee in 1916. As he labored at the Board of Agriculture to restore greatness to Britain's farming, so he saw colleagues at work up and down Whitehall, each of their departments a vehicle for reform whether in housing, education, labor relations, or health. He confessed that the war years had converted him into a far more hopeful advocate of direct state initiative for major and rapid agricultural advance. Above all, he saw England astir, its concern for the postwar era reflected in a vast new literature of reconstruction. From his vantage point he summed up the state of British opinion confidently: "We all know . . . that a great effort at Reconstruction is before us."

Had Sir Daniel spoken for himself alone, his appraisal would mean little. But—if literary output and articulate statement are any measure of public thought—he spoke for the largest single segment of British opinion.

The huge wartime literature on reconstruction was produced by many groups, but its largest part was written by those whom I term the "reconstructionists"; and Sir Daniel's confident remark exactly caught the optimistic mood of his reconstructionist colleagues. For one of the two most distinctive traits of this group was their conviction that a great era of reform was imminent. The other trait was their remarkable agreement, on program, with the kind of reconstruction that men like Addison planned. Both traits went a long way to justify Sir Daniel's confidence. For Addison, the very existence of a group sharing these convictions was encouraging, but its sheer size and (to all appearances) its preeminence meant even more. That these were the traits of Britain's most numerous body of opinion was vastly promising.

It is with these "reconstructionists" whom Sir Daniel Hall symbolized, I feel, that an inquiry into Addison's chances for public support ought to start. They were his most likely allies; their message, their program, their numbers, and the force of their argument are therefore all essential subjects for investigation. Although they bore no current common name, they are no less distinctive for all that. They were joined by shared convictions; they achieved a remarkable identity on program; they shared a broad humanism of outlook which precluded any definition of reconstruction in narrowly commercial terms. They united in an emphasis on postwar industrial cooperation—as a good in itself, as a cherished hope, and as a simple functional necessity—which precluded equally a reconstruction based on industrial autocracy or on class triumph. These beliefs, and their outspoken refusal to adopt the dogmas either of laissez-faire or of socialism, marked them off from other groups and identified them as heirs to a progressive liberalism, strongly favorable to labor, eclectic in regard to program. Their roster covers many fields and includes famous names: J. L. Hammond, B. S. Rowntree, and J. H. Whitley; the agriculturists C. S. Orwin and Christopher Turnor; the architect Raymond Unwin; churchmen such as L. George Buchanan and Samuel Keeble; Sir Joseph Compton-Rickett, frequent commentator on economic issues; Arthur Greenwood, Lord Haldane, and the economist S. J. Chapman, at work within the government; Lionel Curtis of the *Round Table*; Albert Mansbridge, of the Workers' Educational Association; William Dawson, the historian; Alfred Zimmern; A. L. Smith, the Master of Balliol; Edward Wood, later Lord Halifax; W. C. Dampier-Whetham, the scientist; Patrick Geddes and Henry Aldridge, champions of town planning and of housing reform. In party terms, they ranged from Conservative to Liberal and Labour, but it was characteristic of them to speak in other than partisan ways, and no single organization—although they led and figured in many—encompassed them all.

To Addison, labels hardly mattered; but what potentially made a world of difference for him was that the group which came closest to seeing reconstruction as he saw it was, to all appearances, the largest vocal element in Britain as war came to a close. Quantity, however, was far from the only measure of the public support that the reconstructionists represented. They wrote with zeal, with powerful conviction and a persuasive rhetoric; they marshaled impressive argument heavy with the data of wartime fact. And as a group they preached great themes: the imminence of a great opportunity, the plasticity of a nation ready for change, the emergence of much greater unity, the need for steadfastness and bold thought. In all these qualitative ways, the reconstructionists constituted a wartime augury of great promise for the postwar success of reform plans.

To our first question, then, the existence and traits of the reconstructionists supplied a partial answer: the ministry did have allies, numerous and articulate. Subsequent pages will elaborate these points. But one other trait of the reconstructionists must be taken into account first, and it raises a question of a wholly different order: the question of the relation between war and reform. That question, as noted in chapter 1, transcends time; it has occasioned a considerable scholarly literature; and, independently of our duty to trace the course of reconstruction, it is also our duty to consider that great question. Hence we must consider what the reconstructionists said (and, as they thought, proved) concerning the service of war to reform.

Reconstructionists claimed to know, not merely *that* a great new era of reform was imminent, but *why* it was imminent: War was the cause. Scholars have debated the question, for and against; but the reconstructionists were not in doubt. From every aspect of the war their writings drew rich and hopeful lessons, applicable to future reform; in the war and because of it they saw a new spirit of cooperation and a national confidence in new powers, based on wartime experience, which could supply reconstruction with crucial preconditions of morale and technique. To them, war served reform both objectively, by the sheer momentum of trends that it began, and subjectively by the creation of a new mentality and a new purpose. Long before World War II produced the concept of a "national planning consensus," these writers declared that the war itself had produced a broad agreement on measures of reform. For us, therefore, the reconstructionist works have a dual significance. They figure as functional elements in the narrative, influencing reconstruction and its chances. But they also supply argument and data on the puzzling inter-relations of war and reform, transcending the limits of 1918 and 1919. We must read their works with both these aspects in mind.

But it will not do to examine their works alone. For the reconstructionists did not speak for a united country, nor did they monopolize the literature on reconstruction. Other Britons had also studied the same evidence, with very different results. No less than four separate groups, as will be noted, can be distinguished. Of this, Addison and his colleagues were fully aware; and no scholar since, pondering the relations between war and opinion and reform, dare ignore what this diversity of opinion means. These other Britons had also labored to measure, to preach, and to observe; they too had scanned doubtful skies to discern the future—but they lacked Sir Daniel's faith. More than a few of them doubted, and some denied, that war was bringing good along with evil. Their views, as well as his, were present forces; they too mirrored current reality and perhaps caught part of the truth on war and reform. Sir Daniel and his like were a part of public opinion, not the whole.

War and the Prospects of Reform: Reconstructionist Views

"Since August, 1914, England has . . . broken with her past and entered an entirely new epoch. Today can never be as yesterday." William Dawson spoke for all reconstructionists.[1] They explained why: clearing men's minds, revealing new powers, exposing past wrongs, quickening comradeship and social conscience, war seemed already to have exercised an "awful ministry for good."[2] Its twofold legacy, for Hammond, was "a new ambition" and "a new confidence." War not only exalted Britain's aims, it showed the way and forged the means to attain them.[3] Above all, war was "full of guidance and instruction"; war *taught*. This war, Hammond had said, had shown that "there is no such word as impossible,

---

1. Alfred D. Hall, *Agriculture after the War* (London, 1916), p. 130; William Dawson, ed., *After-War Problems* (London: G. Allen & Unwin, 1917), p. 7 (hereafter cited as Dawson); Alfred Hopkinson, *Rebuilding Britain* (London, 1918), pp. 157, 167; "Jason" [J. L. Hammond], *Past and Future* (London, 1918), pp. 34–35 and *passim*; Albert Mansbridge, *The Trodden Road* (London, 1940), pp. 90–91; Henry Cecil, *Brightest England* (London, 1919); W. C. Dampier-Whetham, *The War and the Nation* (London, 1917); The Marquess of Crewe, ed., *Problems of Reconstruction* (London: T. Fisher Unwin, 1918), p. 8 (hereafter cited as Crewe, *Problems*).

2. Dawson, p. 10, and most of the sources cited in note 1, above.

3. "Jason," pp. 34–35; *Round Table* (December 1917), p. 4.

and that resolution and imagination can surmount difficulties thought insuperable." This was his great reason for believing that 1918 need not repeat the grim chronicle of 1815. Over the range of material circumstance and psychological change, he and other reconstructionists found proofs.[4]

The "*star shell*" *of war.* None of the reconstructionists was in doubt where to begin. Exposure itself was war's first service to reform.[5] War bared a calamitous dependence on foreign sources for food. Eventually, the toll of the submarine—sending thirty-four ships to the bottom in one day—brought the country's sugar reserves down to a few hours' supply; but the discovery had already prompted outcry, and led to restudy of every part of agriculture.[6] And once the U-boat interdicted timber imports, forestry gained attention. On topic after topic, from industrial research through physical fitness to education in science, publicists stung national pride with revelations of German superiority or

4. "Jason," pp. 34–35, 126; H. Sanderson Furniss, ed., *The Industrial Outlook* (London: Chatto & Windus, 1917), p. 14; see above, pp. 57–58, 78–79, 154–55.

5. George Lloyd and Edward Wood, *The Great Opportunity* (London, 1918), pp. 1–2, 13, 20–25, 82.

6. A. D. Hall in Crewe, *Problems*, pp. 164–67; J. M. Connell, ed., *Problems of Reconstruction* (Lewes: Baxter, 1919), pp. 62–68 (hereafter cited as Connell, *Problems*); Sanderson Furniss, chap. 6, especially pp. 250–54; Dampier-Whetham, pp. 50–54; Hall, pp. 1–17, 118–19; W. B. Worsfold, *The War and Social Reform* (London, 1919), pp. 32–33, 40–41, 56–76; S. J. Hurwitz, *State Intervention in Great Britain* (New York: Columbia University Press, 1949), pp. 209–10; H. J. Jennings, *The Coming Economic Crisis* (London, 1918), p. 52; A. M. Gollin, *Proconsul in Politics: A Study of Lord Milner in Opposition and in Power* (New York: Macmillan, 1964), pp. 415–46; Mancur Olson, Jr., *The Economics of the Wartime Shortage* (Durham, N.C.: Duke University Press, 1963), pp. 23, 42–44, 77–78, 96–99, citing numerous government reports; Christopher Addison, *A Policy for British Agriculture* (London, 1939), p. 205. For Churchill's stress on shipping, leading to his plea on 16 November 1916 to abandon minor measures and turn drastically to state intervention, see *P.D.(C.)*, vol. 87, c. 1106–8; for reactions to the revealed dependence on foreign imports, see John W. Wheeler-Bennett, *John Anderson: Viscount Waverley* (London: Macmillan, 1962), pp. 37–38. But Lord Ernle stressed that, among the uninformed, complacency about food supply persisted through 1916; see Prothero, *From Whippingham to Westminster*, pp. 290–91. See also R. C. K. Ensor, *England, 1870–1914* (Oxford, 1936), pp. 511–12; F. E. Green, *The Awakening of England* (London, 1918), *passim*; Dawson, pp. 128–31, 166, 186; S. E. Keeble, *Towards the New Era* (London, 1919), p. 33; Victor Branford and Patrick Geddes, *The Coming Polity* (London, 1919), pp. 309–10; A. W. Ashby, *The Rural Problem* (London, 1918); George Radford, *The State as Farmer* (London, 1916); J. H. C. Johnston, *A National Agricultural Policy* (London, 1915); Asa Briggs, *Social Thought and Social Action* (London, 1961), pp. 138–39. For the government's policy, compare Cd. 9231, p. 25, and the Verney Report (to which Vaughan Nash contributed) as summarized in P. Ford and G. Ford, *A Breviate of Parliamentary Papers, 1900–1916* (Oxford: Basil Blackwell, 1957), pp. 74–76.

British neglect.[7] "In two years," said one writer, war "accomplished what we land reformers failed to achieve in a long life's agitation"; and half a dozen reformers concurred.[8] Kellaway of the Ministry of Munitions, Addison's close friend, surveyed the entire range of vital materials and industries, whose value had remained unsuspected till the Germans attacked. He quoted the Prime Minister: The war had been like a star shell illuminating the dark places in the nation's life and industry.[9]

Malefactor, reformer, teacher. Exposure was not the sole means by which war allegedly promoted reform. Not only where it bared evils, but where it intensified or created them, war could indirectly produce benefits. Munitions work, the very symbol of war, epitomized that. The development of new centers of munitions production brought a desperate housing shortage, an ominous rise in women's work, and a shocking increase in child labor. But at least the nation learned that it must employ women workers; against prejudice and against determined opposition by the skilled trade unionists, as Millicent Fawcett bitterly commented, the door of the munitions plant became a new door of escape from domestic serfdom.

> The freeing of women from these shackles has only been accomplished at the price of a world war on an unprecedented scale. It may well be said, "At a great price bought I this freedom." There has been nothing like it in industrial history since the Black Death . . . broke down villeinage and serfdom.

7. Ian Hamilton, *The Millennium?* (London, 1919), pp. 16, 25; Keeble, pp. 32–34; Dawson, pp. 104–6, 277, 248; Worsfold, pp. 32–41; Lucy Gardner, ed., *The Hope for Society* (London, 1917), pp. 13, 162 (hereafter cited as Gardner, *Hope*); W. A. Robson, *Public Enterprise* (London, 1937), pp. 225–29; A. H. Unwin, *Labour and Afforestation* (London, 1920), pp. 2, 8; "Jason," pp. 37, 41, 56–60; Henry Birchenough, *Elementary Education* (London, 1938), p. 186; "Memorial on the Neglect of Science," London *Times*, 2 February 1916; British Electricity Authority, *Electricity Supply, 1882–1948* (London, n.d.), pp. 4–6. For revelations of faulty stockpiling policies regarding cotton, see Sir Charles Macara, *Social and Industrial Reform*, 7th ed. (Manchester: Sherratt & Hughes, 1919), p. ix; for discussion in general on the deficiencies of education, and particularly in the sciences, see above, pp. 16–17.

8. Gardner, *Hope*, pp. 13, 150–54; Dawson, pp. 105–10, 140, 185, 207, 248; Connell, *Problems*, pp. 5–6; Bristol Association for Industrial Reconstruction, *Report of a Conference* (Bristol, 1918), p. 17; J. J. Robinson, *National Reconstruction* (London: Hurst & Blackett, 1918), pp. 57–58; John Whitley, *Works Committees and Industrial Councils* (Manchester: Longmans, Green, 1920), pp. 2–3.

9. Henry Kellaway, in *Ministry of Munitions Journal* (December, 1918), pp. 369–70. But, where hospital organization and medical care were concerned, the effect in wartime was exposure without adequate action. Standards of care for civilians seriously declined, judging by informed comment; only after war was serious reform attempted. See Abel-Smith, *The Hospitals*, chaps. 16–18.

Even more reformers pointed to another fact. Public outcry stirred the Ministry of Munitions to take action. Soon it was building houses for workers; it was requiring that contractors provide amenities within the plants; it was inspecting sanitary facilities. By the end of the war, 867 canteens had been set up with the ministry's sponsorship. Moreover, the ministry soon appointed a "Health of Munitions Workers Committee"— headed, ironically, by the Quaker pacifist B. Seebohm Rowntree—and then indeed it seemed that the ministry, once a chief offender, had become an accessory to reform. For Rowntree's committee produced a treasure of studies on fatigue, short hours, efficiency, and morale. In its reports, reformers found an arsenal of timely arguments for shorter hours and better pay. Now, this service of war was different in kind. The others seem automatic and objective; but here the gain was not in evils exposed, or material benefits reaped; it was rather in what men soon called "a *lesson* of war": in this case, the lesson that shorter working hours spelled higher output.

The point deserves emphasis. War here performed a service, not through the dead weight of impersonal and inarticulate forces, but through the active intervention of men's minds. For the very concept of a lesson implies human recognition. Change brought benefit, not because of the force of new circumstances alone, but because of such factors as human interpretation, human will, and the inherited enveloping context of society and its humanitarian conscience. So it was for all alleged "lessons," and the fact helps to put in truer light the supposedly mechanical relation between war and reform. In all cases, human interpretation played a part.

The lesson derived in this instance was simple but encouraging: efficiency and reform had been proved "inseparable" and "almost identical." This was the point that Addison had stressed to the cabinet in his memorandum on "Reconstruction Finance," and such reconstructionists as William Dawson echoed and elaborated his thought.

> For not only is all social reform in essence a question of national efficiency, but the great social changes and ameliorations which are vital to any real renewal of England will unquestionably make great demands upon the nation's material resources . . . and these demands in turn will be successfully met just in the measure that the productive forces of the country . . . are developed with greater energy, concentration, and intelligence than ever before. . . .

Reformers valued this and other lessons, more than war's more fleeting benefits. The emergency housing program at the munitions centers, the

rise in total pay, the forces that sustained full employment for the
moment, would not last; but such lessons would outlive the war. And
best of all, they could be transferred. As the final report of the Health of
Munitions Workers Committee proclaimed, "the principles underlying
right action at the present time are permanent."[10]

A new confidence. One lesson transcended all: the lesson of power.
Everywhere Hammond found "new and unsuspected powers": the newly
discovered efficiency of women workers, the increased output of labor, the
spectacular gains from the Corn Production Act. The war, he exclaimed,
"removed the word 'impossible' from the language of politics." From
shell output alone, the *Nation* caught "a fascinating glimpse of our
industrial possibilities." The greatest corollary appeared in one exultant
phrase: "War overwhelmed the economists." Four years of war, the
Athenaeum judged, had indeed transformed views on "interference" with
economic law. Housing champions rejoiced; henceforth no plea of
poverty would stand. The state was spending £5,000,000 a day; twenty
days' such spending would rehouse every dweller of every slum.[11]

10. William Dawson and Millicent Fawcett in Dawson, pp. 13, 140, and see also
pp. 196, 207; Keeble, pp. 25–31; Hurwitz, pp. 84, 113–15, 135–36, 211, 214, 219, and
197, n. 4; Worsfold, pp. 50, 194–97; Gardner, *Hope*, pp. 127–40; Crewe, *Problems*, pp.
151–62; Hamilton, p. 16; R. L. Outhwaite, *The Land or Revolution* (London, 1917),
pp. 93–94; "Jason," pp. 120–22; Millicent Fawcett, "Equal Pay for Equal Work,"
Economic Journal, 28 (March 1918): 1–6; A. J. P. Taylor, *English History, 1914–1945*
(Oxford: Oxford University Press, 1965), p. 37; Lord Leverhulme, *The Six-Hour Day*
(London, 1918), p. 3; Dudley Sommer, *Haldane of Cloan* (London, 1960), p. 337;
Briggs, p. 117 ff. See Great Britain, *Parliamentary Papers* (1918), "Industrial Health
and Efficiency: Final Report of the Health of Munitions Workers Committee," Cd.
9065, cited in Abrams, *The Failure of Social Reform*, p. 48. For discussion of the Health
of Munitions Workers Committee reports, see especially Irene O. Andrews, *Economic
Effects of the War upon Women and Children in Great Britain* (New York: Oxford
University Press, 1918), pp. 141–44; and Adelaide M. Anderson, *Women in the Factory*
(New York: E. P. Dutton, 1922), pp. 224–49. For legislative and administrative enforce-
ment of higher welfare standards, see Godfrey Ince, *The Ministry of Labour and National
Service* (London: Allen & Unwin, 1960), p. 141, and George Newman, *The Building of a
Nation's Health*, pp. 372–75, stressing the Factory Act of 1916 as a landmark. For
balanced comments on harm and aid alike, see Marwick, *The Deluge*, pp. 16–17, 113–19.

11. *The Nation*, 30 June 1917, p. 311; Connell, *Problems*, p. 57; Brougham Villiers,
England and the New Era (London, 1920), pp. 95–97; Hopkinson, pp. 136–37; "Jason,"
pp. 11, 34–35, 149; A. D. Hall in Crewe, *Problems*, pp. 169–71; Dawson, pp. 124–25,
144, 152, 156, 191, 209; Dampier-Whetham, p. 26; Thomas C. Evans, *Democracy and
Reconstruction* (Manchester, 1919), p. 51; Green, pp. 321–23; Outhwaite, pp. 12–13;
Addison, *Diary*, 1: 35 and 2: 580; N. B. Dearle, *The Labor Cost of the World War to
Great Britain, 1914–1922* (New Haven, 1940), p. 74; Branford and Geddes, p. 149;
Athenaeum, no. 4634 (June 1918), pp. 425–46; Keeble, pp. 3, 22, 25, 30; John Hilton in
Huntly Carter, ed., *Industrial Reconstruction* (London: T. Fisher Unwin, 1917), pp.
95–96; A. W. Kirkaldy, ed., *Industry and Finance* (London: Pitman & Sons, 1917),

Behind the lesson of power stood complex lessons of technique. Of these, three formulas for reconciling labor to higher output were paramount: the doctrine of economic control; Whitley Councils, the key to industrial peace; and unity of economic organization. On *modes* of control opinion divided, but all groups denounced planlessness; all favored keeping some controls, at least for the transition. A minority favored governmental priorities; for them, one man pleaded, "We must come to believe in the State," and he took wartime experience as his proof. Wartime facts supported them in detail: state initiative had unified a major industry and saved the banks; the state had caused a spectacular farm revival.[12] Some of the reconstructionists (Sir Daniel Hall, and W. C. Dampier-Whetham, notably) took this line. But J. L. Hammond, whose criticism of state bureaucracy has already been seen, was infinitely more typical. For him and many others, the true solution lay along the lines of a transfer of functions to broadly representative but voluntary groups. In general, devolution—especially in the form of Whitley Councils—became a cornerstone of reconstructionist hopes.[13]

Birchenough voiced another tenet: "We must fight in battalions." The Lord Mayor of London spoke of an emerging second industrial revolution, a "new era of various forms of co-operation." Hammond and others

pp. 24–145; Anderson, *Women in the Factory*, pp. 224–49; Andrews, *Economic Effects*, pp. 42–43. Mancur Olson stresses the factor of additional labor resources, in stimulating food output; see his *Economics of the Wartime Shortage*, pp. 98–99. The National Housing and Town Planning Council, citing wartime experience to show that the state could aid housing, is mentioned in Henry Aldridge, *National Housing Manual* (London, 1923), Part 2, pp. 145–48.

12. Dampier-Whetham, pp. 15, 30–33, 92–98, 106, 162, 198, 268, 277, 293–94; Crewe, *Problems*, pp. 55–59; Briggs, p. 115; Keeble, p. 35; Dawson, pp. 120–26; [Anon.], *After War: A Future Policy* (London, 1918), pp. 11–12; Hall, pp. 10–13, 112–16; Green, pp. 324, 339–59; Gardner, *Hope*, pp. 34, 100; "Jason," pp. 126, 156; Worsfold, pp. 43–66; Webb MSS, II, fol. 422, in Passfield Memorial Library of the London School of Economics; Sanderson Furniss, p. 6; J. A. Hobson, *Democracy after the War* (London: Allen & Unwin, 1917), pp. 164–65. Regarding the banks, see Marwick, *The Deluge*, pp. 163–64. Lord Ernle, asserting that agricultural output rose prodigiously, adds the reminder that administrative measures, rather than the Corn Production Act of 1917, were the cause of this increase; see Prothero, *From Whippingham to Westminster*, pp. 307–8.

13. "Jason," pp. 112–14; Keeble, pp. 17–20; Dampier-Whetham, p. 33; Briggs, pp. 147–49; Sanderson Furniss, pp. 391, 398–99; Lucy Gardner, ed., *Some Christian Essentials of Reconstruction* (London: Bell, 1920), pp. 192–93 (hereafter cited as Gardner, *Christian Essentials*); D. H. S. Cranage, ed., *The War and Unity* (Cambridge, 1919), pp. 122–31; *Economist*, 1 December 1917; W. L. Hichens, in Huntly Carter, *The Limits of State Industrial Control* (London, T. Fisher Unwin: 1919), pp. 65–67. See above, pp. 48, 76–77, 101, 155, 158–63.

echoed the thought.[14] Associated effort, breaking from the tradition of competitive individualism, must be the keynote of economic enterprise. War, men said, had taught all these lessons by concrete example. War made these truths visible: a modern economy must have consultative machinery, must grant new functions to labor, must not leave cooperation to chance.[15]

But "lessons," one may object, invariably imply learners—willing learners. They imply the capacity both to learn and to remember. Unlike the material contributions which the war had made to progress and which might carry over into postwar years simply by inertia and force of circumstance, lessons would require human transmitters. And human links might fail. What did reconstructionists say to this? Had war created the necessary psychological preconditions for success?

The answer, so far as the reconstructionists' own mentality was concerned, was not in doubt. Their writings show a zeal and firm purpose which would continue beyond the war. Although they were reporters—and this factual dimension of their writings is very important—they were not neutral reporters. The lessons that they voiced were communicated, not in classroom tones, but often in a torrent of conviction and eloquence. But what of the nation as a whole?

Rhetoric and the national mind. From the reconstructionist literature one may derive a many-sided, positive, but in one respect highly qualified answer. They spoke often of Britain's "moral transformation." Some of them held that the war, shaking old dogmatisms and deepening both its knowledge and its moral purpose, had created a "new national mind." A war in which traditional doctrines and cherished party principles had often been jettisoned in favor of pragmatic results had produced a new receptivity to ideas; a war which conferred higher status on the worker and revealed

14. E. J. B. Benn, *Trade as a Science* (London, 1916); "Jason," pp. 42–43, 153–57, 161; Dampier-Whetham, pp. 15, 30, 91–92, 116–17, 123–36, 142–44, 160–64; Green, pp. 236–38; Dawson, pp. 124–29, 134–39; *Round Table* (December 1917), p. 14; J. M. Rees, *Trusts in British Industry* (London, 1920), pp. 245, 251; "Oxon.," *Reconstructors and Reconstruction* (Oxford, 1919), pp. 43–54; *Athenaeum*, no. 4629 (May 1918), pp. 218–20, and no. 4631 (July 1918), pp. 299–300; Leverhulme, pp. 190–92; *After the War*, pp. 11–17; William Beveridge, *Power and Influence* (London: Hodder & Stoughton, 1953), p. 214; Evans, pp. 57–58.

15. Briggs, p. 156; Beveridge, pp. 117–18; Dampier-Whetham, p. 30; Edward Cadbury and Ernest Benn in Carter, *Industrial Outlook*, pp. 70–82; Sanderson Furniss, pp. 401–2 (bibliography); John Hargrave, *The Great War Brings It Home* (London, 1919); Tawney, "Abolition of Economic Controls," p. 15; London *Times*, 25 November 1917; Ernest J. P. Benn, *Trade Parliaments and Their Work* (London: Nisbet, 1918), *passim*.

his vital national role had quickened the nation's sympathy with labor. In general, the war was said to have instilled a much greater willingness to sacrifice; above all it was held to have created a new unity, transcending class differences, and a "new vision of fellowship" that might "transform class antagonism into class alliance."[16] Although it is easy to smile at these views as exaggerations, it is harder to deny the evidence on which they rested. The number of strikes did drop markedly below the prewar average; the cooperation of labor leaders in government work, and in facilitating settlement of disputes, is also significant. And the literature of the war years revealed a trend that gave credibility to the concept of a reconstruction of national thought. A revulsion against individualism, laissez-faire and "private-mindedness" began early; the change dated from the first great outcry against profiteering (that "whiplash across the face") in 1915. The stress on cooperation and collectivism, as ideals too long neglected, rose through the war years. The growing demand for a redefinition of industry and work as national service is one sign.

But the reconstructionists did not contend that the improvements in national purpose and attitude justified relaxation and complacency. War had created a change in the national mentality, far more favorable to reform—but not sufficiently favorable to obviate the need for preachment and exhortation.

The reconstructionist literature has a rhetorical side, tinged with anxiety as well as buoyed up with the thought of great opportunity. This rhetorical dimension to their writings deserves attention, for it reveals that success was not viewed as certain. Real perils—mass unemployment, the pressure of a gigantic war debt, the uncertainties of trade war—were all foreseen. Nor was social revolution dismissed from thought. The soldier and the worker—fearsome figures ready to meet half-measures or betrayal with violence—are not absent from the literature. Although the predominant attitude toward labor and the fighting man is one of gratitude, respect, and atonement, some reconstructionists held that Mars made reform not merely possible and morally obligatory, but imperative. To forestall such dangers by sustaining the national mood of sacrifice and

16. Dampier-Whetham, p. 114; Gardner, *Hope*, pp. 21, 103–10, 148; Green, pp. 311–14; Dawson, p. 149; Crewe, *Problems*, pp. 24–28, 31, 51–52; Keeble, pp. 7, 15, 24, 33; Leverhulme, p. 15; A. E. Zimmern, *Nationality and Government* (London, 1918), pp. 244–45; Cranage, pp. 109, 120–23; J. J. Robinson, pp. 67–68; "Jason," pp. viii, 31–32, 98–99; Briggs, p. 133; Branford and Geddes, pp. vi, 323–24; Worsfold, pp. 53–58; Hopkinson, p. 152; Hall, pp. 129–31; Robert Cecil, *The New Outlook* (London, 1919), p. 13; Harry Gosling, *Up and Down Stream* (London, 1927), p. 130; Garton Foundation, *Memorandum on the Industrial Situation* (London, 1916); Sanderson Furniss, pp. 106–7.

insuring justice to the fallen, exhortation had a natural place. And rhetoric was some testimony, also, to the inherent uncertainty of a program that relied on "lessons of the war." Aldridge's comment—"Time will tell if we have learned these lessons"—underscores the point; the possibility of failure was acknowledged.[17] Lessons, encouraging though they were, nevertheless by their nature needed continuous reinforcement; if reconstruction depended on Britain's remembering the lessons of war, then preachment and reminder were necessary. Rhetoric was thus functional.

Sober appraisal of all these perils produced, in the reconstructionists, neither gloomy fatalism nor fearful appeasement. Voluntarists and men of hope, they responded by redoubling their efforts so that promising psychological trends would not lack encouragement. Rhetoric, thus seen, was both a measure of obstacles perceived, and a realistic necessity if obstacles were to be overcome.

For their convictions, reconstructionists found realistic support in several conditions of fact. Reforms, first of all, were becoming law. The list of wartime enactments included the Corn Production Act with its minimum wage clause, the establishment of the Ministry of Labour, new laws aiding the amalgamation of labor unions, extension of workmen's compensation benefits, the adoption of dependents' benefits, and a huge extension in the coverage of national insurance, without even counting the rules beneficial to woman workers which the Ministry of Munitions was enforcing on its contractors. War not only put an educator, wonder of wonders, in charge of the Board of Education, but carried a bold Education Act through Parliament; and it put the finishing touches on democratic electoral reform. Second, government was energetically planning further reforms. Third, unofficial organizations were continuously and intensely active. Fourth, reform now enjoyed that immense asset, an agreed program.

Practical consensus. Book after book revealed the same precepts and programs. All reconstructionist works preached the commandments of

17. "Jason," pp. 9, 12, 26, 31–35, 99, 136–38, 171; Hall, pp. 112–14, 130–31; Mansbridge, pp. 90–91; Lloyd and Wood, pp. 2–4, 100; Dawson, pp. 10–13, 111, 188–89, 242–46; Crewe, *Problems*, pp. 55–59; Keeble, pp. 18–20; J. A. Hobson, pp. 37–38, 133; Leonard T. Hobhouse, *Questions of War and Peace* (London, 1916), p. 31; "Demos," *The Meaning of Reconstruction* (London: Athenaeum Literary Department, 1918), pp. iii, 4–5; John Oxenham, "*Inasmuch*" : *Some Thoughts concerning the Wreckage of the War* (London: Methuen, 1918), pp. 3–4, 19–21; Outhwaite, *passim*; Gardner, *Some Christian Essentials*, p. 112; Gardner, *Hope*, pp. 115, 141–43; Briggs, pp. 136–37; Sanderson Furniss, pp. 58, 181.

advance preparation, of close rapport with labor, and of positive assumption of duties by the state. All emphasized the same preconditions of success: high taxes, industrial peace, continuation of priorities, heightened productivity, and sustained high employment. At the level of detailed measures, they agreed on program, duplicating the huge agenda in work after work: state housing for workers; a Ministry of Health; elimination of the Poor Law system; and a new welfare program emphasizing preventive medicine, augmented pensions, greater child care; expansion of the schools; state aid to full employment; a new start in agriculture, with guarantees of decent wages as well as measures to insure profit and higher output; Whitley Councils, trade committees, electrification, improved transport, and the rest. But the authors who listed these parts saw them in their interrelations. The reconstructionists had grasped the basic concept of interdependence.

As some of them saw, consensus counted even more than breadth of program. Surveying the list of measures, one writer declared that "not a single one divides us on party lines." [18]

Reformers mobilize. Private archives and the newspapers showed also a sharp increase in unofficial group work. Local committees formed to publicize all of reconstruction; a major foundation took up the Whitleyite cause; delegations demanded a Ministry of Health. The Federation of British Industries, the Housing Organisation Society, and the Royal Institute of British Architects collaborated with more than thirty other groups on new housing goals. Every year of the war, great reform conferences were held. The nation's greatest housing societies—the Garden Cities and Town Planning Association and the National Housing and Town Planning Council—at first buckled under the strain, then emerged new-modeled to fight as never before. They took the case for workers' housing to the offices of the Local Government Board, meeting every minister in succession who headed that department: Walter Long, Rhondda, Hayes Fisher, Sir Auckland Geddes, and Christopher Addison. Broadly sharing the government's purposes, they sought to encourage its bolder spirits, favoring Addison over Hayes Fisher where it could be discreetly done. With like-minded organizations they set up public

18. The most representative are works by Dampier-Whetham, Cranage, Keeble, Connell, Hopkinson, Evans, Dawson, Worsfold, "Jason," and Hall. Representative statements are in the compendious works edited by Crewe, Cromer, Sanderson Furniss, Carter and Gardner. See Briggs, pp. 116, 151. For the growing consensus in the medical profession in favor of the Ministry of Health and against the Poor Law, see Abel-Smith, *The Hospitals*, pp. 278–82, 284–89.

exhibits, lobbied in Parliament, and supplied private volunteers who worked with official committees and gave expert advice.[19]

Addison's allies. In the reconstructionists' numbers, solid factuality and rhetorical power, and in the national context which gave them heart, one can thus take the first measure of war's aid to reform. In them and in the ranks of Britain's reform organizations one can reckon the stoutest forces in Addison's cause. Had only such as these spoken for the British public, one could not doubt that the ministry would get all the support that it needed. Had they stood alone, and had no data pointed instead to other and even adverse effects of war, the link between Mars and the millennium, via public opinion, would be beyond dispute.

Dissenters

But the existence of four other distinct groups, each plausibly citing wartime proofs of its creed, told otherwise. Each was a potential rival to the reconstructionists. They ranged from the "Productioneers" on the right, who reduced reconstruction to a Cato's sermon on coming trade war,[20] to that coterie of esthetes on the fringe of labor's far left, writers hardly within politics who disdained material goals and called instead for reconstructing the human spirit. Between these two extremes stood Asquith's band of Liberals, and most of the spokesmen of labor. How did each group, by lining up for or against the government, affect the chances for successful reform? How did each group see, illuminate, and affect the link between war and reform?

Labor groups. Workers and their leaders saw promise in the war, but much menace too. They ended up less hopeful of the chances for reform, and more impressed by war's harmful effects.

Often at one with the reconstructionists on questions of immediate program, most spokesmen for labor simply did not think that government would, or that capitalist society could, live up to their promises. "It is only

19. See Minute Books of the National Housing and Town Planning Council and of the Garden Cities and Town Planning Association for the years 1915–19, as well as Briggs, p. 123; Crewe, *Problems*, pp. 23, 183–97; *New Statesman*, 13 October 1917, p. 27; Alan Bullock, *The Life and Times of Ernest Bevin* (London, 1960), 1: 68–72; *Journal of the Royal Institute of British Architects* (3d series), 22: 308; 23: 52, 155, 173, 213–14; 24: 3; 25: 1, 8–9, 36, 66–70, 121–42, 171–75, 186–87, 207–8, 261–62; 26: 22–23, 196–97. This journal lists the deputations, conferences, and discussions of its own committees and officers, and of other housing groups for 1915 through 1919.

20. Hopkinson, p. 58; Worsfold, pp. 25, 69, 121; Edward Saunders, *A Self-supporting Empire* (London, 1918); Thomas Farrow and W. W. Crotch, *The Coming Trade War* (London, 1916); [anon.] *Victory or Free Trade?* (London, 1917); Samuel Turner, *From War to Work* (London: Nisbet, 1918); Herbert Gray and Samuel Turner, *Eclipse or Empire?* (London: Nisbet, 1918).

power they will yield to," Bevin told the Triple Alliance. It was precisely the questions of power and trust that sundered many laborites from the reconstructionists. Of course there were other signs and causes of divergence: outside the range of reconstructionist proposals, labor had its own demands, notably for a capital levy and for the nationalization of railways and mines. But what opened a gulf was not the occasional specific step beyond the general short-term consensus, but a pervasive fear. The combined influences of preconceptions, past history, and wartime experience bred a deep skepticism toward several key reconstructionist tenets: class harmony, productivity, "equal sacrifice." Moreover, the new wartime controls that awoke others' enthusiasm moved labor to distrustful demands for more worker representation. And even where—as with Whitley Councils—the enthusiasm for a new experiment prevailed over defensiveness and suspicion, new and different kinds of doubt might still arise. Thus the Whitley Councils were welcomed and strongly endorsed by numerous spokesmen for the workers, but the very merit and attractiveness of the plan seem to have prompted doubt that the government would endow the councils with work and power. Philip Snowden spoke for many: "Through this war the working classes have sacrificed, perhaps for a generation, the hope for further social reforms." For others, the thought of reform arrested or postponed was not the grimmest possibility. The armistice was widely expected to unleash an employers' attack on wages, with government connivance. Suspicion and pessimism, in the ranks of labor, sure to be politically expressed (political opposition, indeed, was the lesser danger), boded ill.[21]

Nevertheless the gulf can be exaggerated. War had built a bridge between reconstructionists, government planners, and labor. On the

21. Bullock, 1: 48–49, 60–66, 75–79, 97; Dawson, pp. 167, 184; Beveridge, p. 162; B. Sacks, "The Independent Labour Party," *University of New Mexico Bulletin*, no. 358 (1 August 1940); Ruskin College, *The State and Industry* (London, 1918), pp. 51–52; M. Beer, *A History of British Socialism* (London, 1918), 2: 376; *New Statesman*, 13 March 1915, 23 January 1916, and 16 March, 2 November, 14 December 1918; Fabian Research Department, *How to Pay for the War* (London, 1917), pp. xii–xiii, 53–85, 149–50, 183–87; Labour Party, *The Old Age Pensioner* (London, 1918), pp. 4–5, *Nationalism and State Control* (London, 1918), pp. 1–3, and *Paying for the War* (London, 1918); Alexander Clayton, *The Rise and Decline of Socialism in Great Britain* (London, 1926), pp. 173–74; Arthur Henderson, *The Aims of Labour* (London, 1917), p. 28; Paul Kellogg and Arthur Gleason, *British Labor and the War* (New York, 1919), pp. 47–48, 112–14, 125–37; H. M. Hyndman, "The Railway Problem Solved," *Nineteenth Century and After*, 80 (November 1916): 1023–39; *Labour Year Book* (London: Labour Party, 1916), pp. 13–14, 104; Robert Williams, *The New Labour Outlook* (London, 1921), pp. 70–72, 78; G. D. H. Cole, *Organised Labour* (London, 1924), pp. 9, 83–84, 110; W. A. Orton, *Labour in Transition* (London, 1921), pp. 64–69, 115–16, 162–64; Gardner, *Hope*,

dangers of planlessness, their minds met. On questions of housing, controls, "pledges," and much else, most of the arguments that Sidney Webb favored had been presented by Addison's staff. The crucial importance of heightened production and greater efficiency had been stressed by MacDonald and by Sidney Webb in the Labour Party Conference of June 1918 and in its famed publication, *Labour and the New Social Order*, just as the Minister of Reconstruction had emphasized it to the War Cabinet. There were other signs of convergence. When the Labour Party Conference defended its demands with the argument that "We know we can keep employment steady," it repeated a major reconstructionist "lesson of the war." The reconstructionists came near the men of labor on the question of reconstruction finance; some labor spokesmen edged near to them. Common work was a factor in this rapprochement: Bevin, Gosling, the Webbs, Barnes, Clynes, Henderson, and many a trade unionist or Fabian helped in Addison's work. H. A. L. Fisher remembered, to the year of his death, how Ernest Bevin turned out the dockers of Bristol to hear and cheer one of Fisher's speeches in the campaign for educational reform. Contact and *de facto* partnership over two years promised united pressure for some reforms.[22]

Far different was labor's left wing. Many convictions alienated it from party men and job-oriented union leaders: utter distrust of government, hatred for compromise and capitalism, contempt for labor's officialdom.

p. 134; Labour Party, *Report . . . to the November 14, 1918, Emergency Conference* (London, 1918), pp. 1–2; *Labour Manifesto* (London, 1918); Arthur Gleason, *What the Workers Want* (New York, 1920), p. 38.

Also pertinent are Ralph Miliband, *Parliamentary Socialism* (London, 1961), pp. 59–62; A. Morton and G. Tate, *The British Labour Movement* (London, 1956), pp. 260–70; Sidney and Beatrice Webb, *History of Trade Unionism* (London, 1920), p. 635; S. G. Hobson, *Pilgrim to the Left* (New York, 1938), p. 191; Mary Hamilton, *Mary Macarthur* (New York, 1926), pp. 134, 148, 155, 160.

22. See, e.g., the participation of Arthur Henderson, Bevin, and Sidney Webb in work on forestry and on rent and other controls (pp. 10–11, 97–98, 107, above), and in B. C. Roberts, *The Trades Union Congress*, p. 310. Arguments between the champions of nationalization, on the one hand, and labor spokesmen for Whitleyism and for a great increase in output as a basis for reconstruction, as given in the Labour Party, *Report of the Eighteenth Annual Conference of the Labour Party, London: June 1918* (London: Labour Party, 1918), pp. 43–46, are well presented in E. Eldon Barry, *Nationalisation in British Politics: The Historical Background* (Stanford, Calif.: Stanford University Press, 1965), pp. 201–5, 214–19. For Bristol reception of the educational reform campaign, see H. A. L. Fisher, *An Unfinished Autobiography* (London: Oxford University Press, 1940), pp. 94–95. On Sidney Webb's concern for output and his public appeal to the trade unions not to return to obsolete practices, see G. D. H. Cole, *Trade Unionism and Munitions*, p. 214. On the rather favorable reception among some physicians to Webb's proposals for health service reorganization, see Abel-Smith, *The Hospitals*, pp. 286–87.

Such estrangement and suspicion among shop stewards, militant champions of nationalization, Guild Socialists, and opponents of war cannot be attributed to wish or dogma alone. Deportations, conscription, clashes with government which were reflected in the rise of a new leadership and in unauthorized strikes, were not cerebral cogitation but wartime fact; and these were the events, as leftists saw it, that disclosed the true meaning of the war. Profiteering scandals and crises of production confirmed their apocalyptic economics.[23] Nearby them, in common revulsion against war and against regimented industry, stood another band: the esthetes, archindividualistic and often apolitical, who turned to spiritual values and the pursuit of beauty but who agreed that uncompromising opposition to the established order of things was richly justified. The wartime alliance of such kindred "spirits of revolt" is interesting, at least, for it foreshadows the mood of the twenties;[24] but for the prospects of governmental reconstruction it was far less menacing than another odd but real affinity.

23. Gardner, *Hope*, p. 93; Dampier-Whetham, pp. 20–23, 185–98; Sidney Webb, in Crewe, *Problems*, pp. 146–69; 14 November 1918 Labour Party emergency conference; *Labour Problems after the War* (London, 1917); Labour Manifesto; Labour Party, *The War Aims of the British People* (London, 1917), pp. 17–18; Clayton, *Rise*, pp. 166–67; Bullock, 1: 77–85; Margaret Cole, *Beatrice Webb* (New York, 1946), pp. 146–51, and *The Story of Fabian Socialism* (Stanford, 1961), p. 169; the Webbs, *Trade Unionism*, pp. 646–50; Chushichi Tsuzuki, *H. M. Hyndman and British Socialism* (Oxford, 1961), pp. 222–23, 244–45.

24. Bullock, 1: 75; David Kirkwood, *My Life of Revolt* (London, 1935), pp. 99–101, 112, 118–22, 126–62; S. G. Hobson, p. 182; Labour Party, *War Pledges* (London, 1918); Morton and Tate, pp. 262–71; J. T. Murphy, *New Horizons* (London, 1941), pp. 51–53, 70–72, 79–80; Mary Hamilton, pp. 157–59; Sacks, pp. 14–15, 22; R. Williams, pp. 69–75; Orton, pp. 49–50, 55, 73–75, 81–85, 90, 96–99, 118, 124, 142–43; Hurwitz, pp. 243–80; Tsuzuki, pp. 229–30, 235; Joint Committee on Labour Problems, *The Problem of Demobilisation* (London, 1916); S. G. Hobson, *Guild Principles* (London, 1918), pp. 9, 15, 28, 45–46, 69–71; G. D. H. Cole, *Self-government in Industry* (London, 1918), *passim*; N. B. Reckitt and C. E. Bechhofer, *The Meaning of National Guilds* (London, 1918), *passim*; Fenner Brockway, *Inside the Left* (London, 1947), p. 44; Niles Carpenter, *Guild Socialism* (New York, 1922), pp. 142–47, 150, 206–7; S. G. Hobson, *National Guilds and the State* (London, 1919), chap. 1; A. R. Orage, *Alphabet of Economics* (London, 1917), p. 153; Carter Goodrich, *The Frontier of Control* (New York, 1920), pp. 226, 255; Ruskin College, *Some Problems of Urban and Rural Industry* (Birmingham, 1917), p. 33, and *The State and Industry*, pp. 52–57; *New Age*, 1 November 1917 ("Notes of the Week"). See also G. D. H. Cole: *Guild Socialism Restated* (London, 1920), chap. 1; *Chaos and Order in Industry* (London, 1920); and *A History of Socialist Thought* (New York: St. Martin's Press, 1958), 3: 212–44, and 4: 7, 25; and Cole and William Mellor, *The Meaning of Industrial Freedom* (London, 1918). Statements from the esthetes are particularly notable in Crewe, *Problems*—for their distrust of the state and their insistence on the role of artists, in an essentially spiritual reconstruction, see pp. 52, 56–59, 211–314. For enthusiastic proclamations of a "new era," matching the reconstructionists in fervor but implying a socialist content, see Fred Henderson, *The New Faith* (Norwich, 1915), *passim*; Austin Harrison, *Before and Now* (London, 1919), pp. 168, 238–39, 223–24, 259.

Intellectuals of the left articulated the resentments of labor's rank and file. They bespoke its disbelief in class harmony; they furnished trenchant argument against Whitleyism. These affinities, culminating in demands for workers' control, presaged the strife of 1919.

A left wing, destined to lead militant opposition in industry as well as in politics, seemed not merely a bad omen but a portent of disaster. Some reconstructionists seem to have cherished the hope that argument, even here, might promote cooperation or at least allay fears sufficiently to give official reconstruction a chance. As other writers strove to win support from labor in general, so a few reconstructionists, to win the left wing, spoke to it in terms of common interests and shared beliefs. Hobson and Hammond argued that their two groups had a common stake in higher output, even if that cause was advocated by others for the wrong reasons. There were in fact affinities between some reconstructionists and some labor leftists which made all categories doubtful. Both groups detested and denounced mere commercial plans for postwar action; both yearned for a free and democratic economy, untainted by old wrongs; both hailed the dawn of a new day for the working man. Britain was still at that historic watershed where a man could be both liberal and laborite in many basic things; and it is plain that such men as Hammond and Hobson were in fact fighting on two fronts—trying to shape the plan of reconstruction in as pro-labor an image as possible, and trying to win support throughout labor for a plan so amended and redeemed. Perhaps some of the left wavered.

But on the whole the left remained determinedly hostile. It stood in the opposition to government plans. And the left wing showed that war had worked *against* as well as *for* national unity and reform.[25]

25. Affinities between these groups are suggested in Hobson, *Guild Principles*, pp. 28–29; Crewe, *Problems*, pp. 211–12, 268–69; Reckitt and Bechhofer, pp. xii, 15–18, 22–24, 45–46; Bertrand Russell, *Principles of Social Reconstruction* (London, 1916), pp. 120–21, 222–23, 234–36; Carpenter, *Guild Socialism*, pp. 84, 145–48; Cole, *Self-government*, pp. 1, 5, 91–92, 119–22. For links with the rank and file, see *Fabian News*, especially for February and March, 1918; Russell, pp. 138–39, 242–43; Hobson, *Guild Principles*, p. 28; Carpenter, p. 194; Morton and Tate, pp. 260–76; Murphy, *New Horizons*, pp. 54–65; Kirkwood, pp. 96–101, 110–13; Orton, pp. 93–96; Reckitt and Bechhofer, pp. 144–49, 221–25; Beer, *A History of British Socialism*, 2: 375, 393–94; Cole, *Self-government*, pp. 23–33, 43–44, 53–62, 139–40; Miliband, *Parliamentary Socialism*, pp. 53–58; Goodrich, pp. 7–14; G. D. H. Cole, *History of the Labour Party from 1914* (London, 1948), pp. 42, 54; Branko Pribicevic, *The Shop Stewards' Movement and Workers' Control, 1910–1922* (London, 1958), pp. 147–65; S. G. Hobson, *National Guilds*, pp. 226–71. For views of the parliamentary committee and of the left wing on Whitleyism, see Barry, *Nationalisation in British Politics*, pp. 215–17 and p. 232, note 33, as well as Roberts, *The Trades Union Congress*, pp. 288–90.

Asquithians and reconstruction. "War is fatal to liberalism," wrote Churchill. In general, war seemed the negation of all that liberals stood for. World War I interrupted programs of educational development and thwarted tax and land reforms; its statism challenged the whole liberal tradition. And one specific group of liberals had special cause to dissent from praise of Mars's service to reform. For Asquith's Liberals—the third distinct group with whom we must deal—war had meant disunity and the gall of Coalition triumph. War might therefore have cast them in a negative role; either by its disastrous effect on party unity, or by some more profound and fated logic, it might have weakened dangerously the unity on which reconstruction depended.

Astoundingly, their election program of 1918 endorsed virtually all the official and reconstructionist agenda. The document, adopted at Manchester by the General Committee of the National Liberal Federation, was one of the best statements of the reconstructionist consensus, even reflecting some labor thought. The workers "must be given a full share in determining the conditions that affect their own lives"; a minimum wage should be established, and made a first charge on industry; antitrust laws were to be strengthened, a comprehensive public health service established, and five million houses built in a five-year period. Prewar trade-union conditions must be fully restored; local authorities should be granted fuller powers of land acquisition; some of the burden of rates should be shifted to land values; Whitley Councils must not only be promoted, but endowed with substantial powers. It went so far as to endorse the state's *building* of houses, if local efforts failed; and it called for national control of monopolies such as railroads, canals, and coal mines, "with a view to ultimate national ownership if further experience proves it to be desirable."[26]

This official document, from the National Liberal Federation meeting of September, suggested only unity: unity within the Asquithian Liberals; unity between them, the Coalition, the government, and the reconstructionists. Had war truly had this unifying effect?

The concealed truth was that the war moved some Liberals to new and advanced positions on reform, moved some to pessimism and moved

26. Beveridge, *Power and Influence*, p. 113; Liberal Party, *Housing and Liberal Policy* and *Liberalism and Industry* (London, 1918); National Liberal Federation, *Proceedings in Connection with the Meeting of the General Committee Held at Manchester, September 26–27, 1918* (London: Liberal Publication Department, 1918) (hereafter cited as NLFGC), pp. 6–10, 91, 94–99. See also Gilbert Murray, *The Way Forward* (London: Allen & Unwin, 1917), *passim*.

others not at all. Taken at face value, the Liberal platform, like a flat page under strong sunlight, showed no shadings. But this was the surface. A closer look, in the flickering light cast by the debates at the September meeting, disclosed a prism of paradoxes. The Liberals' guiding group approved controls, but reluctantly and in narrow terms. In detail it backed costly reform; in principle it stressed economy. A motion from the floor of the meeting assailed the platform as hostile to controls; the motion was a clear sign of Liberal discord,[27] and so was the narrow margin by which it lost: 182 to 158. For Liberal ambivalence and disunity, there was a wartime background. Asquith, who had named the first Reconstruction Committee and had stirred housing zealots into action, was of the same party as Herbert Samuel, who derided the Ministry of Reconstruction as a "ministry for overlapping"; and Samuel headed the parliamentary Committee on National Expenditure, the darling of the economy-minded press. Of two Liberal authors of books on reconstruction, Leonard Reid and George Radford, one indicted trade-union restrictions and the other sought to rebuild liberalism on laborite lines. Liberal audiences, at official conferences in 1917 and 1918, heard the Corn Production Act damned as a "dole for landlords" and hailed as a miracle of democratic efficiency. They listened to liturgies of nineteenth-century economic fundamentalism and to demands for the capital levy. One speaker told them that "our businessmen will not be able to restore our industries if you insist on keeping them in shackles. . . . The strong and deep-seated objection to bureaucratic rule is based on four years' experience." But another speaker prophesied bloodshed if the state did "less for life than it does for capital." Runciman, who declared that "no more violent and decisive blow has been struck at State socialism . . . than our experience during the present war," waxed eloquent over the benefits of state aid to agriculture. Asquith's speeches ranged almost as far.[28]

In retrospect, the most interesting persons in all this divided group are

27. *NLFGC*, pp. 30–33, 41–49, 82–84.
28. *Ibid.*, pp. 40–42, 128–34; Liberal Party pamphlets, nos. 10, 11, 13; Ernest Benn, *The Trade of Tomorrow* (London, 1918), p. 22; Leonard J. Reid, *The Great Alternative* (London, 1918), *passim*; George Radford, *Liberalism for Short* (London, 1917), pp. 13, 23–26, 40–55, 89; Charlotte Leubuscher, *Liberalismus und Protektionismus in der englischen Wirtschaftspolitik seit dem Kriege* (Jena: Fischer, 1927), *passim*; Hopkinson, pp. 103–5, 133–35; *Economist*, 26 January 1918, p. 111; *P.D.(C.)*, vol. 96, c. 1613–17; Murray, *The Way Forward*, pp. 35–36; London *Daily News*, 21 August 1915; Liberal Conference (Huddersfield), *Towards Democracy* (Huddersfield, 1918), 1: 1–26, 35, 70–86, and 2: 1–23, 71–77, 103–11; Trevor Wilson, *The Downfall of the Liberal Party, 1914–1935* (London: Collins, 1966), pp. 131 ff.; Charlotte Mendelsohn, *Wandlungen des liberalen England durch die Kriegswirtschaft* (Tübingen: Mohr, 1921), pp. 99–114.

those Liberals who adumbrated the "economy drive" of 1921. By their speeches for retrenchment and against bureaucracy they disclosed that, even in wartime, a strong undertow of laissez-faire orthodoxy ran counter to the wartime tide of State intervention and reform. For the scholar of intellectual history, here was proof that old dogmas silently resisted the new "teachings" of war. But indeed there is proof of something else. War itself may have been—as some of these contemporaries said—the *cause* for their resistance to these more popular currents of opinion. The circumstantial proof is obvious. By multiplying resentments against restraint— in the hearts of workingmen, liberals, and Everyman—war bred opposition against state controls; and for liberals of the older school especially, it confirmed their economic orthodoxy. As Professor Hurwitz and others have contended, "economic laws" were overcome but temporarily, so far as many were concerned; their grip on men's minds was weakened, not broken.[29] From Addison's standpoint, here were enemies indeed.

Variety then—in all things save immediate conclusions on program— was the keynote of liberal opinion: variety of conclusions, variety of rationales, variety in use of wartime "proofs." Some advanced liberal reformers claimed vindication by the facts of war, for their radical interventionism; the war, they held, had cured them of old dogmatisms and taught them to be bold. Conservative Liberals claimed the support of wartime evidence, for opposite conclusions. But Liberals showed greater variety than this, where the relevance of war to reform was concerned. There were those who insisted that the correlation between war and reform was inverse; those who declared the correlation nil; and those who ignored it.

Immobilism and skepticism. The Radicals who wrote land value taxation (a prewar demand) into the 1918 Liberal program, like the Labour Party conferences which called for nationalization (an old cry), testified, by example if not by words, to some historic continuities; their actions went far to belie the influence of war. Even where timely references to war ornamented an old proposal and an old rationale, it is the prewar origins that impress one. Addison's espousal of the Ministry of Health is pertinent here. He defended it by citing wartime revelations of physical fitness among conscripts—but also he stressed the prewar roots of the problem; and indeed the proposal of a Ministry of Health dated back to the 1870's. For intellectual history it is important to consider that war did not, in even one instance, initiate any reform idea; every proposal that I have

29. Hurwitz, pp. 164, 195, 65, n. 11; *NLF*, pp. 33, 84; Hopkinson, pp. 133–35.

found had a pedigree reaching back, sometimes far back, into Britain's history. Arthur Marwick's recent comment is sound: the war created no new body of knowledge or theory; it added "a violent awareness" of need, and provided a more favorable level of social practice.

From the Liberals' own debates on election programs, two votes throw further light on the strength of older teachings. Rent control, a wartime measure that was no direct affront to basic dogma, was endorsed. But further food subsidies were disapproved; against this wartime departure from the cherished tenet of Free Trade, the enthusiasts for "war's lessons" and the resisters could and did vote, *unanimously*. Both measures were wartime policies, and both involved state intervention; the distinction cannot be drawn in those terms. The real cleavage was not to be found in terms of receptivity or resistance to new ideas and "lessons of the war," nor was it the line between friend and foe of reform. The quality and the ideological or moral importance of the measure made the difference. Devotion to a cherished partisan principle survived the wartime drift toward protectionism.[30]

Such evidence suggests that, objectively, there was no correlation between war and reform, and certainly no constant relation between men's openness to "war experience" and men's zeal for change. The same negative conclusions that one is forced to, today, were voiced then.

In wartime, there were those who dissented explicitly from the optimistic trust in war's lessons and its benefits. It was not only Liberals who declared that the correlation between war and reform was inverse. We have heard Snowden's pessimistic cry, proof enough that some laborites felt war was doing terrible harm to reform. Asquith had echoed such doubts, in a lament for long-planned educational reform and the prewar "Land Campaign": "These things we had already in hand when the great cataclysm . . . arrested for years the advance of social reform." Addison had at first, as we have noted, assumed that war would blight reform. Another Liberal pessimist found "the debris of a great war" deposited on "the threshold of every door opening into reform." J. H. B.

30. Hobhouse, *Questions*, pp. 8–11, 31; Evans, p. 57; NLFGC, pp. 30–31, 40–52, 62, 88–93; Liberal Party pamphlet no. 13; Frederick Verinder, *Free Trade and Land Values* (London, 1916), pp. 1–4, 14; Marwick, *The Deluge*, p. 242, citing Addison's statement of 26 February 1919 in the House of Commons. This statement is in *P.D.(C.)*, vol. 112, c. 1828–30. "Lessons of the war" had been anticipated, too. Prewar warnings on food supply are cited in Mancur Olson, *Economics of the Wartime Shortage*, pp. 39–41; the relation of working hours to both health and efficiency had been observed before the war, as mentioned in Anderson, *Women in the Factory*, p. 241. For continuity of economic theory, see review of S. J. Chapman's text, *Outlines of Political Economy*, in *Economic Journal*, 28 (March, 1918): 99–100.

Masterman put little trust in the current belief that English opinion had been transformed by the unsettling effect of war; he argued that the war, on the contrary, had shown that the ordered fabric of society was stronger than men had expected—and from this he inferred that inertia would reassert itself. Masterman doubted, even more strongly, that the unity of purpose evoked by the war would survive into peacetime. A storm of class conflict was in the making, he feared: "Irritation and resentment are held in check for the moment by the appalling danger that overhangs our national life, but we should be living in a fool's paradise if we imagined that an orgy of universal benevolence would follow the return of peace."

Liberals, perhaps more than other groups, revealed how war could engender a general skepticism, undirected but paralyzing. H. A. L. Fisher saw the current hopes as mere mass hysteria, on a par with the famed belief in the Russian soldiery, tramping in their nonexistent battalions across Britain. McKinnon Wood denied altogether that the conditions of peace would bear any resemblance to those of wartime, and he accordingly rejected out of hand the concept of "lessons of war"; so did the economist Alfred Marshall, who likewise felt that the analogies of war to peace were too farfetched. Men of such nearly academic detachment, suspending judgment on what the future would bring, were probably rare compared with those other Liberals who saw war as the destroyer of their party; they were still rarer than those Liberals and Radicals, humanitarian, tolerant, and individualistic, who saw war as the henchman of bigotry.[31]

All these dissenters raise serious and valuable doubts, as one looks back, about the connection between war, public opinion, and reform. They were emphatically right in rejecting the notion of war's automatic aid to reform. They were sometimes right on war's specific disservices to progress. They were wrong in their final assessment of the net result when harm and aid were weighed together. But all this, in 1918, was of secondary importance. What counted then was the similarity between the Liberal program and the government's program. At the time of the armistice, most Liberals stood in the ranks of reform.

31. Verinder, pp. 3–4, and *idem, Land, Labour and Taxation* (London 1916), pp. 1–5, 9–10; Gardner, *Hope*, pp. 176–77; H. A. L. Fisher, *Political Prophecies* (Oxford, 1919), pp. 3–4; *NLF*, p. 30; Robertson, p. 181; Reid, pp. 11, 42–44; Dawson, p. 184; A. Marshall in *ibid.*, pp. 316–17; Masterman in Crewe, *Problems*, pp. 29–30; A. L. Bowley in Carter, p. 225. For a present-day view, emphasizing the effect of war in delaying land reform and extension of insurance, see Gilbert, *Evolution of National Insurance*, pp. 264, 446. For similar left-wing views, see Outhwaite, pp. 60, 83–86, 95–96, 113; Russell, p. 76, and *idem, Justice in War-Time* (Chicago, 1916), *passim.* The group that wholly ignored war's impact is typified by Montague Fordham and his writings.

Trade warriors. The "productioneers," as I term the fourth distinct opinion group, stood just to the right of the reconstructionists. They were distinguished chiefly by their preoccupation with postwar trade rivalry and the means to win it. "Productioneers" shared the beliefs of several other groups, especially those of the reconstructionists. They stressed output and productivity; but that was part of the reconstructionist creed. They shared the reconstructionists' optimistic reading of the influence of war, but agreed with many of the older Liberals on fundamentals of profit and the central role of management; but they also showed a passion for change which, though totally different in content, was like the zeal otherwise found on the far left. In endorsing Whitleyism, heralding the "new era," and preaching the organizational lessons of the war, they were second to none.[32]

Yet the productioneer was different. Another spirit moved him, toward another goal. No productioneer ever spoke the thought that seemed self-evident to the reconstructionists: "Humanity comes before output." Sir Daniel Hall was as ardent for output and efficiency as any productioneer. But when he called for "rendering the countryside a more efficient system of production," he sundered himself forever from the productioneers by insisting that efficiency was only a *means* ("or else we ought not to be at war today"). He put his economic argument in the larger context which was the hallmark of the reconstructionist.

> . . . Greater efficiency is the necessary basis. Unless the new farming can earn more out of the land than the old, we shall have no margin whereby to attain our end, which is life. . . . All our sacrifices will be in vain unless we draw nearer to giving every man his share in the imponderables—freedom, society, recreation, the indulgence in

32. Reid, pp. 55–59, 71–76, 80–86, 93–94, 105–7, 125–32, 167–68; J. T. Peddie, *Economic Reconstruction* (London, 1918), pp. 51–64, 215; Leverhulme, pp. 3, 15, 17–27, 99, 114–15, 145–72; Lord Leverhulme, *Reconstruction after War* (Port Sunlight, 1919), pp. 20, 31–32; A. O. Richardson, *Britain's Awakening* (London, 1916), *passim*; Dawson, pp. 170, 183; Jennings, pp. 52, 110; W. L. Jordan, *On Payment of the National Debt* (London, 1919), pp. 1–4; Sidney Barwise, *Never Again* (Derby, 1916), pp. 15–17, 20, 28; J. Ellis Barker, *Great Problems of British Statesmanship* (London, 1917), pp. 234, 280–94, and idem, *Economic Statesmanship* (London, 1918), pp. 181–82; Gray and Turner, *Eclipse or Empire*, pp. 5–20, 24–27, 49, 81–93, 105–117; Turner, *From War to Work*, pp. 9–10, 12–40, 101–7; Alfred Vago, *A Better England* (London, 1918), pp. 10–14, 25; Cecil Walton, *The Great Debenture* (Glasgow, 1918), pp. 5–10, 58–59, idem, *Never Again* (Glasgow, n.d.), pp. 3–7; [Anon.], *After War: A Future Policy* (London: St. Catherine's Press, n.d.), pp. 2–5, 9, 15; "Clarity" [pseud.], *Our Future* (London: Thomas Murphy, 1917), pp. xiii–vi, 163–65; and statements in Huntly Carter, *The Limits of State Industrial Control*, pp. 107–10, 155–57.

a soul. Let us pay what need be paid for life in efficiency or labor, provided it be life that we purchase.[33]

The productioneers' concessions to labor were calculated means to industrial ends, not "goods" in themselves; a few productioneers—revealingly—refused to pay the price, at least where the restoration of restrictive practices was concerned. Also, most productioneers saw tasks in material terms: "It is a question of machinery and organisation," said one. And almost all productioneers brushed laissez-faire and internationalism aside with contempt, in a burst of chauvinist protectionism. Alone among the groups, they adopted not Woodrow Wilson but Australia's nationalistic W. S. Hughes as their hero. Their most distinctive trait was their unshakable belief in an impending, tremendous, trade war. They saw it in the ruthlessly nationalistic spirit of war itself, which dominated their minds, and they declared that victory depended first and last on output. To productioneers, seemingly, productivity and superiority in export were not the preconditions of reconstruction's success, but reconstruction itself. "Trade is the great thing," said H. J. Jennings; "it is indeed, when we come back to bedrock, the only thing."[34]

The productioneers spelled a double threat. They might capture public opinion, and certainly the simplicity and conventionality of their views gave them an advantage. They preached no doctrine of equality, rejected nationalization, and often exalted the man of business. They did not hesitate to cater to anti-Germanism. They thus tapped the mightiest emotions unleashed by war. Lenient terms for Germany, said one, would be "altruism indistinguishable from lunacy." And they could appeal to wartime fact (as persuasively as any other group); they could use the stories of unpreparedness and warn of commercial weakness. For their pet ideas—subsidy for key industries and anti-dumping laws—they had ample wartime precedent; stories of wartime prodigies of production were perfect grist for their mill. War, having put the defense of reforms

33. Keeble, p. 26; Webb MSS, fols. 299–317; Dampier-Whetham, pp. 32, 252–53; Crewe, *Problems*, pp. 53–54, 132–33, 169–71; Cd. 9107, pp. 20–21. But see Turner, p. 31, and *After War*, pp. 9–10.
34. "Oxon.," *Reconstructors and Reconstruction*, pp. 40–42, 60; Barker, *Great Principles*, pp. 234–47, 294–339; "Clarity," pp. 5, 30–31, 36; Walton, *Never Again*, pp. 21–33; Reid, p. 85; Barker, *Economic Statesmanship*, pp. 38–70; Gray and Turner, pp. 24–68, 90–98, 111–18, 124; *After War*, pp. 5–10; Turner, pp. 1–2, 27–56, 60–63, 67; Vago, pp. 5–7, 25; Peddie, pp. 25, 51; Jennings, pp. 53–67; Barwise, pp. 3, 15–25; W. Cunningham, *Personal Ideals and Social Principles* (London, 1919), pp. 20–21; Richardson, pp. 29, 45–50. But see Reid, pp. 140–53, and Dawson, pp. 337–39, for rejections of protection.

in quasi-military terms (housing *for physical fitness*, improved farming for *self-sufficiency*), especially favored this group. Furthermore, their influence would denature or menace true reconstruction, as defined by reconstructionists. Against the productioneers' protectionism, labor might join many free-trade Liberals and go into angry opposition.[35] Moreover, if productioneers simply succeeded in imposing their own priorities, production output and tariffs would come before the campaigns on housing and health and before the redemption of the trade-union rules; and labor would turn violent in protest.

Unable to achieve their own program, however, but able to thwart others', productioneers seemed to prove that war worked for the undoing as well as for the advance of reform. By their own lights and evident zeal they were earnest reformers, ardently hopeful that the promise of war would be realized. Their books, second only to those of the reconstructionists in number, had been the earliest to appear;[36] ironically, they were the firstborn of Mars's children.

Agreements and affinities. Between all the groups ran lines of attraction and repulsion. Liberals were linked with the extreme left by a common hostility to bureaucrat and censor. Distrust of laborite solutions brought right-wing Liberals closer to the productioneers, despite their fundamental opposition on tariffs. In a different combination, the moderate Liberals and the Radicals in their ranks shared a nostalgia for old slogans—in utter contrast to the productioneers and reconstructionists with their gospel of all things made new. Most conservative of all, of course, was the thinking of the trade unions and the stereotyped dogma of the left wing.

Larger groupings hinted of possible alignments after the war. Liberals, productioneers, and reconstructionists deplored the prospect of class strife, on which the left wing pinned its hopes. But if reconstructionists and much of labor clashed on this point, they dreamed alike of a Britain egalitarian and emancipated from poverty. Other affinities appeared—only to dissolve. Reconstructionists, advanced Liberals, and most of labor shared an approach that was humanistic and very critical of capitalism,

35. Bullock, 1: 61; Fabian Research Department, *How to Pay*, p. vii, and *The War Aims*, p. 15; Villiers, pp. 133–34.

36. Barwise, pp. 1–30; Jennings, pp. 67–75; Gray and Turner, p. 5; Richardson, pp. 25–37, 66–67; Peddie, pp. 24–25; Reid, p. 53; *After War*, pp. 3–4; Turner, pp. 26–28; "Clarity," pp. 1–7; C. R. Enock, *Can We Set the World in Order?* (London, 1916), p. 194. For the wartime "militarization" of reform concepts, see A. D. Hall, pp. 1–17, 99; Hopkinson, pp. 147–55; Dawson, pp. 166, 189–90; Enock, pp. 108–13; Ensor, pp. 511–12; Mowat, *Britain between the Wars*, pp. 131–32; and Plummer, pp. 40, 252–58.

but a gulf separated this trio from the productioneers, who saw problems as merely technical. A workable alignment, obviously, would combine Greenwood's and Addison's dreams. But lastly, against the apostles of hope stood the pessimists, recruited across the political spectrum. They formed a phalanx, shielded against faith by several negativisms: skepticism of war's "benefits," doubts of the coalition's good faith, and pervasive contempt for politicians and the parliamentary game. Between some businessmen, many labor extremists, and a few right-wing Liberals, these beliefs disclosed an affinity that is odd—anywhere save in human thought.[37] The resulting kaleidoscope of shifting, converging, separating ideas and attitudes is a plain warning against any view that war had worked with single influence toward a single end.

On every level, from first premises to details, the ranks of opinion divided and re-formed. The unseemly dispute beneath the coveted gonfalon of reform never ceased. Debaters and prophets alike were hurried on toward the armistice, which came sooner than any foresaw. About them, as they searched for auguries of the future, peace burst like a thunderclap.

Assessment at Dawn

What was the net meaning of all these tendencies, for the chances of postwar reform?

War had heightened the probability of a successful reconstruction. After full allowance for all diverse opinion is made, the power of the reform impulse was strong in December 1918. On Christmas Day, 1918, Haldane wrote cheerfully to Esher: "There are all the indications of a wholly new school of thought which is laying hold of the people."[38] This favorable condition, however, was not due to unanimity among the nation or its intellectuals (no such inhuman—or un-British—monstrosity had come about); nor was the strength of reform due to any single, constant influence of war on the circumstances of life or on men's minds, any more than it was due to any uniformly favorable trend line. This situation cannot be traced with confidence to objective or "intrinsic" factors; the many men, then and since, who so hypostatized or projected their hopes

---

37. *How to Pay*, p. xii; Gray and Turner, pp. 96–110; *Economist*, 1 December 1917, p. 867; Reid, pp. 6–17, 110–11; Outhwaite, pp. 59–80; Robinson, pp. 67–68; *Towards Democracy*, 1: 16–17, 2: 67–69, 98–99; Verinder, pp. 1–2; O. Wihl, *Parliament for Reconstruction* (Manchester, 1919), pp. 4–24, 46–47.

38. Haldane to Esher, 26 December 1918, Haldane Papers, fol. 103.

(or their fears) revealed only their humanity, not their vision. War's effects were not univocally favorable. And war's influence (as we have seen many times above) invariably depended on the men who judged it—dogma, preference, personality, and interpretation mediated between experience and response. This truth is the single and sufficient rejoinder to any notions, past and present, about the determinative effects of war. The high likelihood of successful reform rested on an aggregate of circumstances: reconstructionists outnumbered other schools of thought; most Britons seemed to agree with them; government thinking and plans put a basis of evident realism behind its forecasts; the state, devising a huge program within a kind of reformers' consensus, tipped the balance of forces toward substantial reconstruction; and fate and history, bequeathing a goodly if impermanent legacy on the world scene and a goodly precedent from wartime, smiled on reconstruction for the moment. Somehow, against all partisan logic and pride, another circumstance worked for good: For all their debate, most members of most groups had, paradoxically, converged on questions of the immediate program. It augured well that the war ended with this wide agreement on details.

The outcome was not certain. Government might falter—as it did, many times. The combined tasks of the armistice, peacemaking, demobilization, and reconstruction might prompt disastrous haste. The effort, conscious and sustained, to understand labor's viewpoint and to shape a program of reconstruction fit for labor to accept, might prove to be inadequate, or might never be given a chance. Planners and higher officials alike had been well aware of the deep divisions within British society and had understood that the many-sided and various impact of war had not produced among workingmen the same attitudes and consensus which prevailed among the reconstructionists and within government. To cope both with labor's needs and labor's distrust, Whitleyism had been pushed to the fore, and urged on business as well as on labor; the case for redemption of pledges, against all standard economic logic, had been stated and would continue to be. The very breadth of the official reform program—a program that was planned for over two years, repledged in the election, and enacted in 1919—testifies to the determination to show in deeds that labor had something to gain by reconstruction along government lines. All this might not prove sufficient. Labor, with its suspicions and its memories, its grievances old and new, and its prideful sense of new power, might erupt in devastating strikes before the Coalition faith had been given a chance. Business might demand freedom, and receive chaos. Also, time was sure to bring swift change; and new circumstances, introducing new moods and issues, might join a fated revulsion of feeling to dispel the indispensable will. War had guaranteed nothing, but the probabilities remained. Judged by the balance of factors in November 1918, war in this sense "favored" reform.

The answer to Addison's question was thus encouraging: the government had allies; a reform impulse was strong in the land. This chapter, however, with its survey of opinion, has raised two other questions, one explicit and the other implied: What did men think about the effects of War? And who was right?

Verdict without jurisdiction. Lord Acton insisted on his right, as historian, to play the hanging judge. With no such conviction and without the slightest right, I conclude that each disputant group was right. They were right, not simply subjectively—by expressing accurately what war meant for them—but in one important objective sense as well: each group caught some actual aspect of the war. Back of every group sentiment and conclusion lay some reality. War had had effects as multiple as the reactions that men voiced. All groups, further, were right by another test: the arguments of each were rational, persuasive, and circumstantial. Nevertheless, no group was wholly right and no contemporary assessment was wholly sound, whether on the likelihood of reform or on the net impact of war. The reconstructionists, who caught the truth of many a specific service which war did for reform, and who concurred on a policy which in fact did make sense, were wrong when they created the impression of unalloyed benefit (which the wisest of them were careful not to do); they were seriously wrong in overrating—as more than a few of them did—the readiness of a united Britain for innovation and sacrifice. The productioneers were fundamentally wrong in assuming that a merely commercial or material reconstruction would satisfy the ranks of labor. Some of the labor spokesmen overrated the possibility of reaching victory for their own special program by independent action; some of them underrated the gains that cooperation might bring and the harm that violent opposition could do. The whole truth on the whole impact of war escaped them, as it escapes us.

Homage to freedom. But how colorless, in the end, all such calculations and general judgments are! Summary pales beside the iridescent variety of thought. For four years war gave arguments for every cause, speaking to men's hopes and fears on every side. With fine impartiality the deity of war offered his evidence to all, with freedom to use and distort. War had split some parties but united left and right; it clapped reformers in jail but pushed their reforms through the cabinet. Capricious and inconclusive, war was not fate; and the "fate" men may have seen in it existed only in their minds. Men's minds made free with Mars's teaching as the red god did with men. To the last, interpreters illustrated man's power to rework actuality into the preconceived pattern of his dreams. The whole is one vast testimony to the ambiguity of experience and the autonomy of the human mind.

13

Reconversion, Demobilization, Decontrol
4 October to 4 November 1918

Garrod and Gardiner were to have no rest; in Scotland as October began, they received an important telegram: Bulgaria had sued for an armistice. Preparations for an early peace must begin.

Addison was already at Queen Anne's Gate. At Munitions, Churchill sprang into action. A report from his council told him that *much* must be done, at once. Four tasks were primary, basic, and urgent: clarifying the division of labor between Munitions and other ministries for demobilization; extending vital powers that legally extended only to the end of the war; clarifying the question of state-property disposal; and deciding on continued governmental production of munitions and of peacetime commodities, if any. The question of "production"—a commonplace word, for a world of uncommon trouble—now entered the story. Churchill rushed to the cabinet a plea for prompt action and decision.[1] Three of the most hectic months in British history had begun.

Men, ships, and machines: each of these must be thought of, if the shift to peace was to be effected at all. To each of these realities there corresponded a question of policy that must be answered.

1. The question of "pledges": should peacetime jobs be governed by the trade unions' prewar rules, as promised by government?
2. The question of "production": what commodities should be made, in what sort of order, and by whom—and for what purposes and under what conditions of prices, subsidies, and control?
3. The question of "shipping": was enough available, and could it be organized on time?

1. G.T. 5863, "Industrial Demobilisation," by W. S. Churchill, 1 October 1918, Cab. 24/65.

Around these three questions, most of them enormously complicated, government debate and action swirled from October through December 1918. They identify the themes which give some order to three months of bedlam, and in this chapter each will be discussed separately where possible. It was with shipping and raw materials that Addison dealt; at the Ministry of Reconstruction for the first two weeks of October, these claimed first attention.

Ships and Shortages, 10–31 October

Back in London, Garrod found a flurry of activity. Addison was convening an emergency meeting of department heads on immediate supply requirements. Actual shortages were to be identified, before anything else; the running battle with Walter Long over the Central Raw Materials Board would have to wait. Garrod himself was to hurry to the Ministry of Shipping. There, on 11 October, he got reassuring news: It would be easy to fill vacant space on the ships under the ministry's control, but there would be problems of priority among materials.

Addison was told the same thing. He had met that day with John Anderson (who was well on his way to becoming the immensely grave "Jehovah" of civil service fame). To shape the best policy from the point of view of reconstruction, Anderson asked, "Can you give us any indication of the lines on which we ought to work?" Not for some weeks, Anderson felt, would the permanent departments possess such information. Addison doubtless made a mental note to bring Anderson onto his staff as soon as the cherished Ministry of Health came into being (which he did, in 1919), but now he turned to retrieving an urgent situation. To all the heads of "controls" and to many departments, he rushed a letter on Saturday, 12 October.

> I have found it necessary to get together, on Monday next, a small meeting of persons concerned with the supply of the more essential raw materials . . . to consider how the programme of supply would be affected by the event of either an armistice, or of peace. . . . I should regard it as a personal favour if you could make it convenient to come and give me the benefit of your advice. . . . The question . . . is one of very great urgency.

Monday morning, before the conference, Garrod briefed his minister:

> The events of the last few days have brought an armistice within the range of practical possibility. . . . A considerable amount of

tonnage would be made available. . . . Some directions should be
given to the Shipping Controller as to the priority to be assigned to
different classes of materials for importation.

"*I.e.*, not Ford Motor cars," he interpolated testily! He turned to
particulars with an aside that dismissed months of prior work and hope.

> The determination of what may be called a Scientific Priority
> belongs to our Standing Council when it gets together. Meantime
> . . . we must work with makeshifts. We want to know . . . today:—
> (1) what commodities there are in which an armistice would mean
> a substantial reduction of imports, and the probable amount . . .
> (2) in what industries which are a vital concern the stocks are at
> present lowest and most in need of replenishing.

Above all, was it possible "to furnish in the rough a revision of the 1919
program for the principal materials which will show in the rough the
modifications which would be desirable during, say, two months of
armistice"? [2]

The Departments Meet and Act

Answering Addison's call that afternoon were Ball of Timber Supply;
W. H. Beveridge from the Ministry of Food; Vernet, the Paper Controller; Robinson of Ships; Currier from the War Office; and W. T.
Layton and three Ministry of Munitions colleagues. That day—14
October— they agreed it was practicable "to try and shape . . . an armistice
programme of imports" and they agreed to furnish the figures to Addison
within three days. The second conference was set for 18 October. [3]

In the next three days Garrod confirmed his reputation for indefatigable
genius. A host of minutes, jottings on telephone calls, and draft reports
tell the story of his action at Queen Anne's Gate and of his many trips to
offices concerned. For the second conference, on Friday, 18 October,
Garrod not only had assembled an even larger group but could point to
several prodigies of departmental cooperation. A memorandum from
Timber Supply was ready, complete with the request for authorization to
act; the War Office's Directorate of Raw Materials, the Paper Controller,
the Admiralty, and the Ministry of Food had prepared summaries and

---

2. Minute by Garrod to Addison, 10 October 1918, and attached documents, in
Box 39; "urgent and confidential" letter from Addison to ministers, 12 October 1918,
and minute by Garrod to Minister, 14 October 1918, in F. 8428, Box 15, Part 2; F.
9357, Box 15, Part 2.
3. Minute by Garrod for Secretary, F. 8428, Box 15, Part 2.

warnings on the continued need for control. In all, the memoranda covered wool, jute, nonferrous metals, hemp, flax, and leather—and Garrod and Gardiner had produced a three-page summary of all this. With the Ministry of Reconstruction's abstract the basis for discussion, a three-man interdepartmental committee was formed at once: Chapman of the Board of Trade, Robinson of Shipping, and Garrod. They were to study the data, get more data, and prepare the way for decisions.[4] For ten days Garrod, Chapman, and Robinson kept in close touch, going over reports together. The record from 28 October on shows their success.

One of the dreaded shortages never materialized. Maclay, the Shipping Controller, repeated as fact, in mid-October, what he had rightly foretold in July.

> The Committee was proceeding on two assumptions which could not be justified. One of these was the shortage of tonnage, the other ... of raw materials. ... After the cessation of hostilities the supply of tonnage would be equal to any real demand.

Abundant shipping, an immense reassurance, steadied these harried men through anxious days. Summing up other reports, the Standing Council on Post-War Priority issued a very cheering Tonnage Peace Budget.[5]

The Standing Council (to digress a moment) was on the stage but not in its destined central role. Its documents were reprints from others'; there was no sign of the authoritative and deliberative function that might have vindicated the months spent on its creation. Garrod's wry comment on "scientific priority" was a warning. Had the moment passed when new and independent instruments would be tolerated?

For Addison, this question was neither minor nor isolated. He had many such proposed systems at stake. His campaign for a single, new authority on raw materials had been interrupted, not stopped.

When the October crisis broke, Long's rival proposal was up for cabinet hearing. Addison challenged it, above all for its lack of relation to unofficial trade groups. Unable to pen a reply, he got the item postponed; but it would have to be faced, and soon. Garrod was pessimistic as he sat down to write a defense of Addison's ideas. "We shall have to abandon the idea of a Statutory Board," he conceded.[6] Perhaps he thought that *every* battle for *every* new body would be lost.

4. F. 9357, Box 15, Part 2; same, Box 52, Part 2.
5. Minutes of E.D.D.C. meeting 12 (22 October 1918), Cab. 27/44; P.W.P. Memorandum 15, Tonnage Peace Budget, in F. 9357, Box 15, Part 2.
6. Garrod to Minister, 10 October 1918, Box 39.

The fiasco of "war stores." The history of the Surplus Government Property Advisory Council was an ill omen for all fledgling bodies. Trying to soldier on, it found that the departments were in control of everything on its agenda. The Disposal Board (its executive) confessed impotence and disclaimed all responsibility. On 10 October the council's patience gave out.

> The Surplus Government Property Advisory Council desires to express to the War Cabinet its dismay and dissatisfaction that, although appointed in November . . . its powers, functions and responsibilities still remain indefinite. . . . It has not been possible . . . to proceed satisfactorily with the work.
>
> The Council, having made repeated efforts to obtain a definite decision as to its duties and responsibilities, disavows all responsibility for the present unsatisfactory position, and further expresses the opinion that the existing system whereby each Government Department is dealing independently with its own Surplus Property and Stores will be wasteful, extravagant, and unsatisfactory under the conditions that are now arising and will prevail after the war in connection with the sale of the vast quantities of stores which will become surplus to Government requirements.

The majority still argued, despite everything, for a single, central authority, but this was something the cabinet must choose. The council, as one of its members said, "had been rendered anomalous and undignified. . . . It would only be a waste of time to continue in office. . . . After eleven months of hindered work the organisation is unprepared on the eve of events which may lead to peace." The council voted to suspend all its meetings, forthwith.[7]

Proposed new machinery on raw materials. Addison wanted more than the present makeshifts; nothing less than an authoritative superagency of ministers, supported by a full and expert staff, would do. Opinion had crystallized in favor of a central body, but none yet existed to give prompt effect to the many recommendations now in hand. The reports on iron and steel, timber, and asbestos still awaited action; the reports due soon—on textiles, hides and skins, wool, and cotton—would redouble the need for decision. Stanley's proposal for a Board to "examine the position" would not equip Britain to face a forthcoming inter-Allied conference with precise schemes. Long's idea—a Committee of Ministers to work with the departments—had among other faults the basic defect of inadequate

7. S.G.P.A.C. minutes 164–203, Box 72, Part 1, and Appendix.

provision for a special, unified staff; it would add little to the fragmented departmental framework. And it would wholly lack executive power. In contrast, Addison implied, his own proposal took account of the task in its actual dimensions. A central Board would have to shape schemes for international allocation and for negotiating with the Dominions and the Allies; it must be an international clearinghouse for materials; it must acquire materials, and thus must have full powers for their acquisition. He proposed a two-level agency: (1) a Board of Ministers, or at least Under-Secretaries, from the Foreign Office and Colonial Office, the India Office, the Board of Trade, the Ministry of Reconstruction, and the Standing Council on Post-War Priority; (2) an expert Board of Assessors, drawn from all these and from the Ministries of Munitions, Food, Shipping, and Agriculture, the Wool and Cotton Control Boards, and the proposed Non-Ferrous Metals Central Committee. The President of the Board of Trade should be in charge. The whole proposal, "E.D.D.C. 47," was sent to the Economic Defence and Development Committee, which never formally considered it.[8]

Meanwhile, the War Cabinet acted. On 18 October, with only Long's proposal before it, the War Cabinet established (over protests from Stanley) a committee of ministers to consider the raw materials cited by the Imperial War Conference; to decide what action was needed to insure that necessary supplies were available for the United Kingdom; and to make arrangements for action with the Departments directly concerned with the supply.[9] Thus originated the Raw Materials Board, which took charge within ten days. Long was to outline its working rules.

Should Long's victory be challenged? Addison had not been consulted; neither his nor Stanley's memoranda has been read; the E.D.D.C., where these memoranda lay, had been bypassed. A Board lacking expert staff and with no powers of its own had been set up. Earlier, Garrod had dismissed Long's plan as too slight for comment. Addison turned to Garrod.

Acquiescence. Garrod now spoke differently. Experts might still be added; trade representation might be arranged. Addison could get the E.D.D.C. to urge improvements. "The great thing is to get some kind of Board, whether his or ours, going at once."

---

8. E.D.D.C. Memorandum 47 (n.d.), by Addison, "A Central Raw Materials Board," in Cab. 27/44 and in F. 8524, Box 15, Part 2 ,with dates 14 and 17 October 1918 crossed out. Long's proposal, "Raw Materials," G.T. 5909 (5 October 1918), is in Cab. 24/66.

9. WC 489, minutes (18 October 1918), Cab. 23/8, citing only G.T. 5909.

Long's draft of working rules, when received, put this accommodating mood to a severe test. Long proposed that each material be disposed of at a single meeting, without consulting the Dominions; no new policy should be contemplated; two ministers would constitute a quorum. As Garrod saw it, Long contemplated

> for the first period of the Board's activity a much narrower scope than is suggested by the terms of reference approved. . . . His object no doubt is to take decisions . . . one by one so that something may, at all costs, be ready either for an inter-allied conference or for a peace conference. He seems to me to be rather scrapping certain wide and important functions of the Board in favor of immediate production.

But it was now 25 October. "We ought to fall in with this view," said Garrod, "for the reason that the more elaborate organisation proposed by ourselves must take a very considerable time to get together."[10]

It was an argument that reduced to rubble every long-nurtured scheme for building an expert, unified, reconstruction apparatus; but none of the overworked officials in those incredible weeks could have ignored it.

Ministers had just realized that the armistice was truly upon them, and the discovery sent them into a paroxysm of panic and flailing motion. Civilian demobilization not only was not under way, but the chief demobilizer had not even been named. The cabinet's omissions had caught up with it. Suddenly, every postponed question moved from the penumbra of deferrable things into the sharp light of immediate duty. There was no Ministry of Supply; in name, a dozen departments were in charge of property, but there was no one to give signals to them all. More than two hundred national factories had to be disposed of—or kept running—and there was no short way to do either. "Pledges," which could not wait, produced only furious disagreement. Meanwhile, a new wave of strikes was rumored. The necessary emergency powers were still being listed, although a full list should long have been ready, for Parliament to approve their extension; there was no decision on emergency imports and exports, nor on inter-Allied plans, needs, and machinery. Ministers not only did not know what to cooperate toward or on; save through the cabinet, they could not even learn *how* to cooperate; but the cabinet had become a bear garden. If indecision made trouble, decision sometimes made worse

10. Minute by Garrod to Minister (19 October 1918), Box 39; CD/740, "Rules of Procedure (Provisionally Laid down by the Chairman)," Box 39; note by Garrod to Addison (25 October 1918), Box 39.

trouble: when the cabinet deadlocked, men did not know which way to move; when ministerial shouting matches brought cabinet action, the result more often than not was a new effort at improvisation or inquiry, not clear choice between matured plans. Addison, who had worked his staff to exhaustion producing a memorandum on pledges, another on emergency legislation, and a ten-page report on demobilization and reemployment, also was battling around the clock on raw materials, shipping, the Ministry of Health, surplus property, and the appointment of a labor demobilizer. He was appalled at the specter of unreadiness on housing. He could appreciate Garrod's reluctant decision that "the great thing" was "to get some kind of Board" going at once.

Rather than appeal to the cabinet, he partially followed Garrod's advice to go along with the makeshift plan. He would raise his objections in the sessions of the Raw Materials Board. At the very first session, on 28 October, he challenged the rules and the structure. Long based his defense on "the need for prompt action." Addison put his basic objection: It was wrong "to leave executive action after the war in the hands of the Departments which at present exercise control." He proposed the establishment of a raw materials executive, responsible to a minister; the executive would consult the Board on matters of policy. Long merely asked Addison to provide the next session with a memorandum in this sense, and the meeting then turned to other business![11]

Two days later, the battle lost, Addison suggested a counterweight to departmental influence: an administrative panel, attached to the Board, to make recommendations and supply information and expert advice. In the most direct challenge of all, he said the panel should take the administrative action required by Board decisions. He referred explicitly to his own "E.D.D.C. 47" in justification. Surprisingly, he found support. Montagu was partly in favor; Islington concurred that the Board should have a full-time staff. Unaccountably, Addison fumbled midway in the debate. Austen Chamberlain, sharply objecting to "anything in the nature of a new department," thereupon recommended that "as each article is reached, the responsible authority should present proposals to the Board." Addison commented that "this suggestion was in effect the proposal he had in mind"—and withdrew the amendment he had offered![12]

11. CD/756, "Minutes of First Meeting of Raw Materials Board" (28 October 1918), Box 39.
12. "Raw Materials—Memorandum by Dr. Addison" (29 October 1918), Box 39; CD/771, "Minutes of the Second Meeting of the Raw Materials Board" (30 October 1918), and F. 7841, Box 39.

Addison's staff was dazed; it was not (and is not) clear what had happened. In the Ministry of Reconstruction's copy of the minutes of that meeting, a very large question mark was penciled in the margin, fifty years ago. Addison, sure he could gain something, kept arguing with Long and Austen Chamberlain. Finally, Walter Long yielded sufficiently to give the Board's secretariat broader scope. It would ask the departments, after each Board decision on a commodity, to state the action they intended, and the secretariat should eventually ask what had been done. (The secretariat, in fact, was two men.) This was the net difference Addison's campaign for a separate, expert staff had made.[13]

The entire episode, meaningless for the substance of reconstruction, stands nonetheless as a monument: to the staying power and prestige of the departments, to the impatience of a cabinet more concerned with cutting Gordian knots than with perfecting forms, to Addison and his qualities. Stubbornness, misplaced zeal, confusion between form and substance—all these are hinted, and a pride still smarting from May 1917 and too ready to see personal affront in minor or necessary change.

The Central Raw Materials Board in Action

But the data were in, and this was grounds for pride. And from its very first meeting the Board took positive action on them, through nine meetings and thirty-five reports on materials from asbestos to zinc. Lord Islington voiced the conviction that spurred them on.

> Once hostilities are terminated, the question of raw materials will become the most vital in the whole scheme of civil reconstruction, and if well conceived and timely measures are not taken, the problem of unemployment may become acute, restoration will be hampered, and the revival of our export trade delayed.

Questionnaires to all departments and controls were the first order of business. Dispatched and answered with speed, they typically asked half a dozen basic questions. Thus on 9 November the Board got answers to its "aluminium ores" questionnaire of the previous day.

> 1. Do the recommendations of the subcommittee appointed by the Ministry of Reconstruction represent the views of the Ministry of Munitions?
>
> [*They*] *represent the view of the Ministry of Munitions Department charged with dealing with Aluminium.*

13. CD/776 and CD/796, "Minutes of Third and Fourth Meetings of the Raw Materials Board" (4 and 6 November 1918), and memoranda from Long, Islington, and others, in Box 39.

2. If so, what steps are being taken in each case to give effect to them, and in particular to carry out the proposal to safeguard the importation of French bauxite? Do you consider these steps adequate? If not, what further measures do you suggest?

The proposed legislation referred to has not ... been actually brought forward by the French Government at present, and no trouble has so far arisen. ... It would seem sufficient if a careful watch were kept on any proposed legislation in France ... so that the necessary diplomatic action could be taken in case of need.

3. How much bauxite, with the necessary percentage of alumina and silica, do you consider the United Kingdom can derive from British sources after the war?

... Deposits of suitable bauxite exist in India capable of producing much more than the requirements of this country, but they have not hitherto been developed.

4. Will any emergency legislation be needed in the United Kingdom after the war?

It is difficult to gauge the possible demands after the war, and it would seem prudent that any Hoarding Order issued in respect of metals should be made to apply to Aluminium.

5. How much Government Control after the war do you think necessary and for how long?

No government control after the war would seem necessary.

6. What is your view as to anti-dumping legislation?

The very large increase in output that has taken place in America during the ... War seems to me to render anti-dumping legislation advisable.[14]

Board sessions were short and simple. A meeting might deal with five commodities, such as aluminum, copper, jute, mica, and zinc. Informal discussions, after the departmental spokesman had been heard, culminated with results that were shaped by the findings: the Board might recommend further study, conclude that no further action was needed, make recommendations to the department, or undertake further work itself. The situations varied enormously. A serious shortage was feared in timber, as in hides and skins, but for rubber, tungsten, and molybdenum the problem was a surplus.[15] The departments' views on controls showed some

14. Islington to Barter, 8 November 1918, and CD/790.MG., Box 39.
15. All minutes of meetings from 28 October to 2 December 1918 and all documents are in Box 39.

correlation, and some surprises. The Timber Controller held it impracticable to let the trade purchase its own supply during the first year of peace; he said the trade favored centralized government purchase for a time. The leather and hides trades allegedly wanted controls for the next two years. The Food Controller asked that international controls be kept lest food prices soar. For cotton, the Board of Trade predicted that without controls the reentry of enemy powers into the market would "cause a frantic rush for cotton and a still further rise of prices." Of the five cases for which no shortage was reported, the response for four (spelter, zinc, oil, and aluminum) was negative regarding extended control or emergency legislation; this was the predictable thing. Replies for oil, asbestos, and wool recommended continuation of controls only for six months. For commercial and industrial opinion, the report declared that the Wool Council, "completely representative of the wool trades," had

> voted that it is desirable to release all restrictions on the wool trade as soon as possible. On this point the twenty-three representatives of employers were unanimous. The ten Labour representatives would have preferred to maintain a system of control.

A. H. Goldfinch thought that almost all internal wool controls could go by mid-1919. For foreign trade, however, control on supplies to enemy lands would be difficult, and provision for the Allies would probably not be needed. He listed seven types of control powers to keep.

Surprisingly, the rubber and tin exports group, though confident of a surplus, wanted control machinery kept. For tungsten, copper, and molybdenum, controls were favored to prevent hoarding. No situation was simple: a surplus might exist now, but a shortage might develop six months later; price controls might be dropped, but export controls often were indispensable. No report called flatly for ending all control at once on the commodity concerned. State *aid* was several times asked.[16]

So spoke the departments and controls; what of the Board? Ultimately the Raw Materials Board agreed with the departments in *all* cases; hence the Board's decisions showed no uniformity, for the departments' had not. It approved keeping the existing controls (usually for six months) on cotton, mica, tungsten, tin, molybdenum, asbestos, hides, skins, and wool. It endorsed state purchase of American zinc, backed departments which asked for state purchase of timber, and endorsed the pleas for hoarding orders, anti-dumping laws, and import-export bills—as it had seconded state aid to build copper and zinc plants. This habit of concurring, which

16. Box 39.

in these cases worked for state action, could work the other way—as when the Board, agreeing with a department on a brief continuation of controls, tacitly accepted the department's decision for eventual decontrol. This was so for wool, where the Board knew the Wool Council's intentions. Like the departments, moreover, the Board tended to confine its favor to hoarding orders or export licenses (as with mica, aluminum, and other ores), not price controls.

The Board was not passive. Eight reports were returned to the departments; reinvestigation was ordered in two cases. The members argued with one another. When Slade of the Admiralty proposed the continuance of control, claiming support from the trade, Austen Chamberlain doubted that control was possible or desirable in view of competitive buying from other countries. In all the documents this was the only strong statement against control by a Board member—announcing, as it happened, the tone that Chamberlain maintained through 1919. More often the Treasury was associated with such views. Goldfinch, an advocate of the centralized control in force for hides and skins, declared that "the Treasury were anxious to get rid of all controls as soon as the military necessity for them ceased." Keynes, with pregnant asides on the problem of vanishing foreign credits, reported the Treasury's opposition to timber purchases.[17]

Board members showed a special understanding of the worldwide ramifications of their task and of the opportunities to put diplomacy to work. Because of them, British officials in Paris were kept advised (for instance) of cotton controls, which the United States reportedly opposed. The global implications were striking: the policy for spelter and zinc dictated that German domination of Belgian industry be blocked; France's reconstruction plans must be watched lest her bauxite exports to Britain stop; decisions on leather must wait while the future of the Washington Hides Executive hung in the balance; and if the War Office did not buy her entire crop, India might ban all exports of hides and skins.[18]

"Raw materials," so easy to misconstrue as a simple matter of purchase orders, had turned out to be a major enterprise. It affected the whole structure of statutory controls, touched dozens of departments, meshed or clashed with policy in other fields, and reached round the globe itself. To Addison, Stanley, Long, and their colleagues, the miracle was that it had been dealt with at all.

17. Minutes of third and eighth meetings (4 and 27 November 1918) for Treasury views; for other documents, see Box 39.
18. Box 39.

How had the process affected controls? There had not been an explicit or general decision to decontrol. Yet in some cases the larger apparatus of wartime control (in recommendations, at any rate) had been exchanged for simpler restrictions. In other cases a time limit had been set on the life of departmental powers. In still other cases, decontrol would result automatically, whether from statutory limits or from decisions by the controls. Wherever controls were kept, continuation was contingent upon the persistence of a shortage or the continued threat of monopoly or foreign competition. New governmental powers sometimes had been asked, and sometimes granted, but there was never a hint of a general strengthening of controls, for "peace purposes" or any other aim. The Ministry of Reconstruction, if it contemplated a different result, had had no effect; its influence, save as a purveyor of data, was nil. The initiative lay with the departments; the follow-up almost always rested with them.

The ministry had done useful parallel work in one area, shipping—by now, happily, not a matter of anxiety. On 30 October Garrod brought data to a special conference with men from the Ministry of Shipping and the Board of Trade. The new, expanded program of raw materials imports, as submitted to the Ministry of Reconstruction, would require 3,000,000 more tons of shipping in the first six months; but (a phenomenal finding!) "probably there would be four million tons available to meet this demand." There and then the Ministry of Shipping pledged to frame, at once, a schedule showing the tonnage and routes needed to bring the desired commodities in on time.[19] But this routine and easy accomplishment was among the least of the ministry's tasks. By now it was busy on everything at once. So indeed was everyone.

Paying for Delay

Every department felt the momentum of four years grinding to a stop. A startled Minister of Munitions suddenly realized that his enormous output might no longer be needed, and his vast holdings might become redundant overnight. His 3,106,000 employees would become one huge nightmare. The Minister of Labour, with 5,000 persons in training, had just been handed the responsibility for all civilian demobilization: Churchill's three million, and more. With trainees who must be dismissed and dismissed workers who must be employed, what was he to do? The War Office was paying £1,000,000 a day to its contracting firms; what did "reconstruction" call for here?

19. Minute by Garrod, 31 October 1918; see also his 28 October 1918 note transmitting data, in F. 9357, Box 15, Part 2.

Between 5 and 15 October, it dawned on Whitehall that there were no answers to these questions. In that fortnight, there had been only one cabinet decision: on national factories (which dealt only with ownership, not use). "There is no 'Government policy,'" W. L. Hichens was told.[20] This was the accusation made by Stephenson Kent a week later, and very near the truth. There was policy in the form of abundant recommendations—Addison, Churchill's staff, the Ministry of Labour, and men at the Board of Trade had not failed their duty—but decisions had not been readied: decisions, signals, and machinery.

On twenty-some topics general directives and clear signals were needed at once: fulfillment or termination of war contracts; retention or termination of priority orders and allocations; use of national factories; price levels; other controls; release of curbs on credit and on the issue of shares; surplus government property; raw materials for Britain, the Allies, and Dominions; interim exports and imports; priority in port facilities; industrial training; and tenure, wages, short-term work, allowances, holidays, out-of-work donations, insurance entitlement for war-industry workers—and policy on "pledges," which would affect each of these. In the most obvious and gigantic duty, demobilizing the forces, four indispensable steps were still unauthorized: withdrawal from the forces of all pivotal men; opening the civil service to veterans; the turnabout of transport; and definition of terminal pay, allowances, and entitlement to unemployment aid. Worse still, the very preconditions for a beginning were lacking in part (for example, decisions on administrative powers and emergency legislation). The staggering total of over twenty undecided questions was in fact a minimal list, confined to what represented *instant* need; it omitted all the arrears on health, housing, land settlement, the Poor Law, and every other stalled reform. These arrears must wait. It was, moreover, only a substantive list, which meant that, parallel to every item, was another task of structure and staffing, needed but unsanctioned. One such decision alone—the immediate appointment of a director-general for civilian labor—was indescribably crucial. Such was the condition of unreadiness and indecision in the government in early October, when the prospect of armistice became real.

All men therefore turned to the cabinet. The first to sound the alarm, after Addison, was Churchill. His memorandum of 1 October, which we have already seen, demanded four answers, without which his ministry would be helpless. On 3 October he ripped the whole question of pledges wide open.

20. Hichens, in G.T. 6057 (14 October 1918), Cab. 24/67.

The Fight on "Pledges": Peace or Productivity?

Churchill denounced the unions' prewar restrictive practices as "anachronistic." Britain ought not to tolerate them, in the light of what she had learned.[21]

His colleagues exploded. Against Churchill's reasoning and his conclusions, Addison, Roberts, and Horne retorted that the government had no choice: it had pledged that the unions' restrictive practices would be restored, and it must act—at once, and unmistakably—to acknowledge and redeem those pledges. All three men shared Churchill's knowledge that the restrictive practices would hamper Britain in her future trade position. Regardless of the economic merits of the case against restrictive practices, however, the government must take this initiative, to show good faith. Alarmed to his depths, and urged on by Nash, Addison at once put Greenwood to drafting a retort.

> There is no half-way house between repudiation and fulfilment ... repudiation is unthinkable ... the honour of the Government is deeply involved.
>
> Almost every avenue towards industrial reconstruction is at present a *cul-de-sac*, blocked by the restoration question.... The future of women in industry, the place of the semi-skilled worker, the development of improved methods, increased productivity, all depend ... upon the attitude of the trade unions of skilled workers, which will be determined by the action of the Government with regard to its obligation to give them the right to restoration of pre-war practices. *Labour resettlement hinges upon the intentions of the skilled unions*, and unless ... carried through smoothly ... re-establishment of industry ... will be perilously delayed and ... industrial discontent ... more than probable.
>
> ... If the Government does not, ... the Government will ... have to face the stubborn opposition of the skilled unions, smarting under a sense of injustice.... If the Government grants to the skilled unions the power to enforce restoration, then alternative agreements may be reached which will not hamper industrial progress.... The skilled workers do not desire ... to insist on literal restoration, but [only as] a bargaining weapon to be used in obtaining new labour conditions. The unions, I believe, fully realise that the far-reaching character of the industrial changes ... make it

21. Churchill's G.T. 5863 (1 October 1918), Cab. 24/65; WC 482 (3 October 1918), Cab. 23/8.

imperative that trade union rules should be adapted to the new circumstances. But . . . to attempt to preserve the more efficient methods of production introduced during the War by withholding from the skilled trades legislation to which . . . they were entitled, will end in disaster.

Addison pressed his large round signature into this memorandum, hard; but, even so, Greenwood would have gone further. The draft he sent Addison (which Addison softened) would have decreed the restoration of prewar practices by government fiat.[22]

In total contrast, Stephenson Kent would have made a clean break.

Government must either implement its pledges or give *in lieu thereof* a constructive policy on liberal and far-reaching lines which will meet to some extent the aspirations which Labour has so often expressed. . . . The second alternative should be adopted.

Agreeing that labor was demanding restoration of prewar practices purely for bargaining purposes, so as to contract out of literal terms, Kent objected that such a bilateral process of bargaining between capital and labor would take too long and—worse still—would leave the matter to "haggling between competitive interests." "Decisions affecting the nation as a whole cannot be made by sectional interests." But he acknowledged that labor was insistent and could point to an inexcusable year of delay. The pledges were very "definite and comprehensive." This was Addison's basic point when the cabinet shook with debate on 16 October: "The Government had given pledges on numerous occasions which they were morally bound to make good."

The Government might, at any moment, find themselves concluding an armistice, and difficulties would immediately arise with the Trade Unions. They would insist they had agreed to dilution for war-work only, and would refuse to work on material which was intended for use in the reconstruction period. . . . The Draft Bill should be discussed with representatives of the employers and the Trade Unions, and a definite undertaking should be given in advance that the Government fully intended to redeem its pledges by Act of Parliament. On the basis of such an undertaking he thought it might be possible to secure some compromise during the

22. Addison, *Diary*, 2: 579–82; F. 8495, Box 71, Part 1; G.T. 5992 (14 October 1918), Cab. 24/66, by Addison; articles by Arthur Greenwood ["Appius Claudius"] in *Athenaeum*, no. 4635 (November 1918), pp. 457–58, 460–62, 469–70.

armistice period. The employers themselves were anxious that some understanding should be come to with the Trade Unions, as they were held up in discussing post-war conditions of production by the unredeemed pledges.

The Minister of Labour, Roberts, wholly agreed: "Without a Bill there could be no negotiation with the Trade Unions." He had found that

> employers were equally keen with the men to obtain a Bill. . . . He had recently pledged himself to a deputation from the Trade Union Congress to do his utmost to secure the passage of such a Bill. Wherever he went he found the Government's delay in this matter to be one of the most active causes of industrial unrest, and further delay would tend to rally the reasonable elements among the workmen to the support of extremists.

Churchill denied that such pressure was widespread. Within the last few days he had met no opposition when he had explained to bodies of workmen that it was impossible to redeem the government's pledge.

> The War Cabinet was being asked to approve a Bill which was absurd and vicious. It was a Bill to entrench a number of small and close corporations in restraint of trade, and would probably meet with the resistance of the great majority of the unskilled and women workers. When hostilities ceased, the State would be faced with the enormous task of bringing the armies home and of transferring the labour of women, and during that period the Government must retain control of industrial conditions.

There was an infinitely superior alternative:

> He should like to see an attempt made by the Government to come to terms with Labour for a reconstruction period of, say, two years, during which special conditions of control would be in force. This might be done by a National Conference, at which problems of wages and conditions of production might be examined, and a charter for Labour drawn up. If such a charter were secured and given a trial, he was satisfied that the resulting material prosperity during the transition period would be so great that there would not be the slightest desire on the part of anyone to revert to *pre*-war conditions.

If a bill were proceeded with, ministers who believed in it should be put in charge; he did not.

The Secretary of State for Air also felt "the dominating issue should be to preserve the great progress in productive methods brought about by the war." The task was to *explain* "the Government's concern to encourage industrial conditions in the future which would provide large production, abundant employment, and a decent level of life for the workers." But Shackleton grimly hung on to redemption. Fulfillment was the wish of the employers as well, he insisted. He spoke from the Ministry of Labour's experience about the division in labor.

> There were three groups of workmen, whose attitude varied: the extremists, who would be delighted if no Bill were forthcoming, and who could then point to the Government repudiation of solemn pledges; a second group, consisting of Trade Unions who had been reluctant to give up *pre*-war practices; and a third group, who had met the Government fairly generously. If Mr. Churchill's advice were taken, the Government would be giving the best treatment to those who had helped them least.

There was no decision that day. In Lloyd George's absence, the cabinet session merely authorized informal inquiries. That evening Addison tackled the Prime Minister on pledges and other urgent issues but he felt the interview was spoiled by Churchill, who "stamped up and down the room indulging in outbursts of irrelevant stuff, brilliant perhaps . . . but entirely unthought-out." Another minister was as perturbed as Addison. To express his "profound difference" from Churchill's views, Montagu declared that the government promises were as solemn as a treaty: "We have no other course but to redeem our pledges unless those to whom they were made release us from them." The government could enter negotiations with clean hands only if it declared for restoration, "unless those to whom they were made are willing to confer on substituting better conditions." If it was true that labor's restrictive practices were the absurd and vicious bulwarks that entrenched "close corporations," the government must tell this to the unions. Without a bill, negotiations would never begin.[23]

Alternatives, thus, were defined. Controversy over pledges would sputter on through the rest of the month. Infidelity was worse than inefficiency, said one side: the former meant certain ruin; the latter was speculative and improbable. Redemption was less important than reconstruction, came the retort: the former ignored the lessons of the war;

23. Addison, *Diary*, 2: 578–79; WC 487 (16 October 1918), Cab. 23/8; Montagu's G.T. 6056 (18 October 1918) and Kent's G.T. 6024 (16 October 1918), Cab. 24/67.

the latter depended on converting the lessons into a permanent basis for prosperity and reform.

The storm over pledges, which was not resolved until redemption was publicly announced on 6 November, revealed something ultimate. It disclosed the utter dependency of reconstruction upon an industrial truce. It revealed a state whose life demanded an adjustment, never final and secure but always imperative, between the organized power within government and the organized power without.

The debate showed that *delay* was not simply caused by the quantity of problems alone. Consensus, where it existed, could triumph over that obstacle. Where agreement among ministers was discovered, decisions and action might swiftly follow. But *disagreement* on policy and purpose was a far more serious obstacle, and "pledges" was just such a case. And yet another cause for delay was now about to become evident: lack of complete prior study, and lack of sufficient time and talk to produce consensus.

"Production" was of the latter sort: a question half seen, a problem not even identified, its ramifications hardly anticipated. It embraced five types of decisions: what peacetime commodities to produce; what balance to keep between them and war goods; what to make *first*; how to deploy men and materials accordingly; and *all the implications*, administrative and logistical and financial, *of these four questions.* So the problem may be anatomized and defined. But in early October, that definition was lacking; that, indeed, was the trouble; and it is precisely the cabinet's slow and sickening descent, into a full understanding of the problem, that calls for study.

The discovery began contemporaneously with the emergence of the other urgent questions already reviewed—shipping and pledges. While Addison was rushing to deal with questions of tonnage, and while the question of pledges was provoking debate, Churchill first introduced the question of "production" to the cabinet. But significantly even he did not see it in its full dimensions.

"Production": The Fight for Precise Signals

Churchill, the first to demand answers, had not raised the hardest or most urgent questions. On 1 October his dilemma was simple: Was he right in aiming at the earliest possible halt in war production and did responsibility lie with others for the huge unemployment that would immediately result?

> It would appear that it is [my] duty to bring the manufacture of useless munitions to an end at the earliest possible moment, and

that it rests entirely with the Minister of Labour, and with the Minister of Reconstruction . . . to make the necessary arrangements for dealing with the labour thereby thrown out of employment. This is the sense in which the Minister of Munitions is at present proceeding.

He defended his assumption that "the manufacture of munitions should not continue for a single day longer than is absolutely necessary and economically justifiable." The Minister of Reconstruction had agreed; besides,

> to act otherwise . . . would involve the waste on the production of useless munitions of materials that will be urgently required for all kinds of commercial and industrial work. . . . Action on these lines . . . will in the end lead to the most rapid transfer of labour and of manufacturing capacity to the normal products of peace.

He also defended his ministry's view that (contrary to general hopes) the national factories could not "be depended upon to provide employment for more than a very small fraction of the number of workpeople at present engaged in them."

> Those who offer this suggestion do not usually take into account the fact that to convert a large national factory to the manufacture of some industrial product would take from three to nine months. During this period a certain number of skilled workmen would be employed, but there would be little or no employment for the large body of semi-skilled and unskilled workpeople attached to the factory.

But Churchill was not defending inaction. For one thing, whatever was decided, he would have many decisions to make on specific stoppages of production. The great bulk of munitions production could be cut short, and many articles scrapped, but for "motor vehicles, aero-engines, optical instruments, and possibly guns, it will be more economical to complete the articles that have passed a certain stage in manufacture." The latter category would entail much work and many decisions.

Churchill admitted four borderline cases in which he would share the work. (*a*) His ministry would for a time control most of the materials required by industry. (*b*) For private firms under contract to Munitions, he must assist the transfer to peacetime industry. (*c*) For unemployed civilians the guiding principle was that "the responsibility for the preparation of plans for the transfer of labour from one place to another, for the payment of any necessary unemployment allowances, for the registration of unemployed workpeople and of applications for labour on the part of employers, would seem to fall on the Minister of Reconstruction and the Minister of Labour." But Munitions was obligated to supply those ministries with data on the volume of labor to be discharged and the kinds of work to which it might be diverted. Churchill, by requesting a demarcation of duties, implied that he might help further. (*d*) For national factories, although he plainly wished to dispose of them to private firms, there was another course.

> If the Government would determine what articles the State, as such, would consider itself justified in manufacturing in national factories, or would even lay down the general principle that it is open to the State to manufacture any articles used in bulk by the Imperial Government, or required by Dominion Governments or local authorities, it would be a comparatively simple matter for the Ministry of Munitions to make recommendations for the post-war use of some of the National factories at present under its control.

Churchill's memorandum of 1 October showed that comprehension and alarm were at a low stage.[24] The answers that he requested were ones that, *if* demobilization came, he must have. He had simply presented some general assumptions—which needed confirmation, so that planning could continue—on a contingency not yet instant. But the premise, that demobilization was not yet upon them, was falsified within a fortnight.

Some were appalled that no decisions had been taken. Hichens exclaimed, "We shall be landed in a hopeless and disastrous muddle." It was the unpreparedness that worried him. Others were more fearful that decision would be made—too soon, and in the wrong direction—or had already been made. Roberts, the Minister of Labour, was appalled by the thought that Churchill intended massive and immediate dismissals. Consequently he asked the government to decide at once on the questions of discharge benefits, notice to labor exchanges, and the order of discharge, so that reemployment could be speeded.[25] It was a protest, not against Churchill's economic rationale, but against the human hardships and industrial unrest that were sure to result. The hard questions had begun to be asked.

24. G.T. 5863; Stanley's G.T. 6004 (15 October 1918), Cab. 24/67.
25. G.T. 5847 (11 October 1918), by Roberts, Stanley's G.T. 5957 (11 October 1918), and Hichens' G.T. 6057, in Cab. 24/66.

The Cause for Indecision

Why had the cabinet done nothing? After the first wrangle on pledges, two weeks elapsed without so much as a discussion on reconstruction or demobilization. Surely the first answer is that the ministers could not believe that peace was upon them. Wilson, the Chief of the Imperial General Staff, told them on 1 October that 187 German divisions were holding the line; orderly retreat was the most that could be predicted. On 16 October Wilson declared there was "nothing in the present situation to warrant the assumption that the present military situation justified the Germans in giving in."

On 1 October Churchill's talk in the cabinet had focused on plans for continued war. Food and munitions were being reckoned far into 1919. (Only a month earlier he had actually been in doubt that the next year would bring an end; should he, Churchill asked his colleagues, aim "to force the War to a successful conclusion in 1919 or . . . aim at a conclusion in 1920"?) Moreover, the war did not taper off; it rose to a crescendo. In fifteen days of September fighting, an unprecedented 10,000 tons of ammunition had been used; and this fact had set Churchill thinking, not of less munitions production, but of more. For all the cabinet, the outlook was still basically what it had been for four years. On 16 October the problems of shipping and of troop transport were still the military problems of bringing men and supplies *to* the front; alarms about the decline in coal production were *war* anxieties. Moreover, the meaning of the interchange of notes with the Central Powers was not clear. For one thing, the discussion was of *armistice* terms, not peace terms. For another thing, the terms of armistice were so uncertain, as late as 24 October, that the need to gird for renewed war still held priority.[26]

But by then the possibility of peace could not be ignored, and the debate on demobilization had become a storm. It had begun in earnest on 16 October, parallel to the continuing discussion of warfare. Somewhere in the previous fortnight, peace had ceased to be incredible, become likely, and at last imminent. But it was the end of the war that had come, not the end of delay. Ministers seemed to have awakened not to deeds but to bewilderment. Now they must face up; they did not know how to cope. The cabinet had not really heard its own members' reports; it had no idea it was so far behind. There was a benumbed first moment, then

---

26. WC 480 (1 October 1918) and 487 (16 October 1918), Cab. 23/8. Milner stressed how the conclusion of the war had caught all the ministers by surprise; see Alfred Milner, *Questions of the Hour* (London: Thomas Nelson, 1925), p. 14.

weeks while the cabinet thrashed about. The prospect of peace, which once caused disbelief, now produced consternation.

Momentum Recaptured

A memorandum from the Minister of Labour, on 15 October, revived the will to act. Very simply, Roberts passed the frightening range of intolerably delayed questions in review. Men and machines, now even more of a problem than materials, were involved in them all: machines to be stopped—and then restarted; men to be freed—and then given work. Sharply Roberts brought things to a point: Policy *must* be determined; nothing, otherwise, could begin to move. Staff and premises for demobilization must immediately be found. The most essential step was "the appointment of a sub-committee of the War Cabinet with full powers to take the necessary measures and review the whole situation." Roberts had shown a way out and he warned that there was no other: "The ordinary course of departmental action cannot work."

The next day two major necessities of reconstruction at last got onto the agenda: pledges and profiteering. On the 17th the War Cabinet considered government property disposal and directed Chamberlain to find the best way. On the 18th it created the framework for decision on raw materials—Walter Long's committee, fully empowered to authorize departments to act.[27]

Movement, finally, had begun. True agreement—even agreement on makeshifts—was still remote; a world of problems had not been faced. Items had merely been referred; those, like pledges, that provoked inconclusive wrangles had merely been adjourned. Nevertheless it was a start. Addison did not like what he saw on pledges or on raw materials, but now he recognized his cue.

Addison's Memorandum of 19 October

Twelve days of strenuous work culminated in the Ministry of Reconstruction's ten-page, secret memorandum to the War Cabinet, "Demobilisation and Employment." G.T. 6047 of 19 October 1918 was both an alarm on work undone and a detailed blueprint for action required at once.

Into memorandum A, covering demobilization for civilians and for the forces, Addison sought to compress every specific recommendation

27. WC 487, 488, 489 (16, 17, 19 October 1918), Cab. 23/8; Roberts' G.T. 6001 (15 October 1918), Cab. 24/67.

from his staff and from colleagues elsewhere, repeating proposals long made but updating them to fit the present. He prefaced it with a statement of "governing considerations."

> 1. He assumed that "if an armistice is concluded it will be of such a character that the possibility of a further outbreak of hostilities may be disregarded."
>
> 2. The dismantling of the machinery of war production and the reestablishment of peace industry, however, would take a considerable time.
>
> 3. Hence "interim measures . . . to avert unemployment and distress and to assist the resumption of normal industry" were obligatory.
>
> 4. Cost must be faced in the spirit of his memorandum of February, "Reconstruction Finance," and in no other way. "We may be confronted with serious social dangers if the problems . . . are approached in any niggardly or hesitating manner."

He reminded all that "the State, for its own imperative purposes, has destroyed in great part certain principal industries in the engineering trade and has effectually prevented the possibility of immediate reemployment in them." There was hope, not too distant, that "after twelve months there should be abundant opportunity for employment, if tonnage is available to the extent anticipated." There was another overriding recommendation: At the earliest safe moment, new issues of capital should be permitted, especially for export trades.

On "demobilisation and resettlement," an administrative problem of "almost unexampled magnitude," Addison put one need first.

> A Director-General of the civil side . . . should be appointed without delay . . . authorised to take into his service such sections of the staff of departments concerned with war services . . . as he may deem necessary. The Director-General should be directly responsible to the Ministry of Labour and should be represented on the proposed Raw Materials Board and on the Standing Priority Council.

Addison knew the man he wanted—Stephenson Kent—and had pressed Lloyd George to name him; and he had half won the even harder campaign to persuade Kent. He talked with former Munitions colleagues until they too supported Kent for the job.[28]

28. Addison, *Diary*, 2: 578–79.

In twelve points Addison summed up the items of utmost urgency for civilian resettlement. (1) The War Office must list, and withdraw from any other work, men of the employment exchanges staff. (2) Employment exchanges and their local advisers should immediately ascertain where workers were needed and what the demands, not only of businessmen but of public authorities, were likely to be. (3) Now that the withdrawal of demobilizers and pivotal men from the army had been decided, ample staff and facilities must make this decision effective. (4) Blank forms, already devised, must be circulated at once to help war workers get new jobs or resume old ones. (5) Inquiry must establish the proportion of women workers who desired or were required to continue working. (6) Juvenile Advisory Committees and Choice of Employment Committees must be extended; and (7) to cope better with this problem, the school-leaving age should be raised temporarily to fifteen.

Next, Addison followed his Civil War Workers' Committee onto disputed ground. (8) Under the 1917 Munitions of War Act, discharged workers were entitled to a week's notice or a week's extra pay in lieu thereof. "This will stand. I recommend that during the four weeks following discharge, the workers, if unemployed, should receive a weekly payment of 30 shillings under the usual conditions, and that supplementary allowances be paid" (subject to proof of dependence). (9) During the first six months after the armistice, "all work-people should be entitled to free unemployment benefit (under the usual conditions), for a maximum period of not less than ten weeks"—at 20 shillings per week, or such flat rate as veterans were given, with supplements for dependent children. Munitions workers, when their four weeks at 30 shillings had ended, should come under this scheme. Back of these two points stood the full-scale policy paper that Arthur Greenwood had managed to hammer out; but Addison hurried on.[29]

(10) There should be maintenance grants for unemployed juvenile workers if they attended educational or work centers (which, he added, needed to be set up). (11) Every war worker should be issued a free railway pass. (12) The Ministry of Food should promptly be advised how to cope with a changing population distribution.

A program that changed a whole nation's life and involved a budget of millions of pounds resolved into a dozen components, one of which virtually put through a revolution in national insurance. Here was cause to marvel, but Addison had no thought of this. He turned to half a dozen

29. Greenwood's appendix I to G.T. 6047, 19 October 1918, Cab. 24/67.

key points pertaining to the armed forces. Almost as many items required decision here: (13) by the War Office and the Treasury on the amounts of war gratuity and terminal gratuities; (14) by the cabinet on out-of-work donations, where only the principle had been sanctioned—and where Addison raised the proposed rate to 20 shillings for men; and (15) by the cabinet on land-settlement schemes, where a fully outlined plan was ready for implementation.

The minister, it must be said, had done more than reiterate demands made long ago; this was no rehash. He and Greenwood had walked the length of Whitehall to find where every project stood, and they spoke with accurate current knowledge. Addison therefore (16) asked cabinet approval of the bill dealing with demobilized apprentices, adding that it was being drafted that day on the lines approved by the Home Affairs Committee. (17) The original bill on out-of-work donations would have to be redrafted. (18) The whole question of transport facilities and port accommodations must be investigated with French and Belgian authorities. But action, not investigation, was the need where officers' resettlement was concerned; all this had been referred to Smuts, Milner, and Addison on 17 April, and they were ready to report. (19) "All permanent appointments in the Civil Service," they held, should be reserved for a year for ex-officers and ex-soldiers. Buried in the Treasury committee, this must go to the cabinet at once. (20) University training at government expense, with grants and maintenance, should follow the plans that had been recommended months ago.

Weightier if possible than Memorandum A, Part B of G.T. 6047 dealt with "provision of employment," in which one item was foremost: There must be a Ministry of Supply. Addison agreed that it must be based on Munitions. As a logical corollary, on which all reconversion hinged, he saw that the production question must be *precisely* answered. This was Churchill's greatest need, as Addison also saw: Armaments goals must be *specified* to clarify "the destination of several Government factories."

Nine "armistice arrangements" were crucial. (1) Like Churchill, Addison put "breaking contracts" at the head of his list. Over 11,000 agreements must be dealt with. Munitions and other departments must have discretion to use the break clause. (2) "Short-time" work should be coupled with wide distribution of government contracts. (3) Departments must release raw materials to firms to help in building up stocks and preparing patterns, gauges, and machinery. (4) Manufacturers badly needed machine tools. Redistribution by Munitions must be sanctioned.

(5) The short heading, Regular Peacetime Orders for Business, embraced several imperatives.

a) Departments should liberate firms to accept ordinary contracts, and actively help obtain them.

b) Priority regulations must be changed, but with care for the needs of overseas governments, public authorities, and devastated countries.

c) Departments should take immediate steps to formulate requirements and should encourage employers and public bodies to place orders, if need be *at provisional prices*.

(6) For national factories, he also advocated many policies in one. Munitions had a plan, on lines approved by the E.D.D.C. and the cabinet but modified for swift lease or sale, with which Addison concurred, but he put his emphasis elsewhere. *Governmental* requirements must be quickly compiled; some factories, he stressed, *were* reserved by the cabinet "for the manufacture of Government or public requirements"—and they should be so used. "During the transition period such manufacture should be carried on . . . *wherever* it appears to be required for securing employment."

Freedom to borrow had been denied in war, but (7) these curbs must be eased to permit action on housing, road work, land reclamation—and on *power stations* (he asked for an early decision on the electricity reports). He reminded the cabinet it should (8) decide on surplus stores, set up a Raw Materials Board, name a storage executive, and maintain Allied transport systems after the end of hostilities—each item in itself a weighty thing. (9) He demanded bills (without which the transitional situation would become impossible) to prolong the Shipping Controller's powers and to give government power over imports and exports. He wholly (and foolishly?) endorsed the Birchenough committee on "release from control."

> The Standing Council on Priority has now been established to deal with . . . priority and bulk allocation, and I should like the confirmation . . . of the principle . . . that at the earliest moment at which it may be safe, we should release materials from the operation of control orders.

That was G.T. 6047. It was not the only document that reviewed the entire scope of production, demobilization, and reconversion; there were

Churchill's two documents and Roberts' memorandum of 15 October. G.T. 6047 was simply the greatest. And it was not the only contribution Addison made that month: there were papers on pledges and insurance and raw materials and industrial reform and emergency legislation and surplus property, issued amid endless conferences and cabinet meetings, and tiffs with Lloyd George. It was Addison's greatest single service to reconstruction, in a crisis when it could count most.

G.T. 6047 has been valuable ever since, as it was useful then. It serves, precisely as it was intended, to sum up the problems; it still serves as an accusing register of ghastly delay, and perhaps was so recognized then. The memorandum served and serves as a checklist for progress and failure.

But it was drafted that October with three aims: to ask every vital question; to "focus the mass of anticipatory work into specific proposals for action by . . . departments"; to spur the cabinet. It had accomplished the first two aims. It showed precisely what must be answered, exactly who must carry out decisions. But Addison had noted the hardest problem of all.

> We at the Ministry are well prepared . . . and have been for some time. . . . The difficulty is that decisions by the Cabinet are badly wanted on many questions that have been before them for a long time but which have constantly been postponed, and the Departments cannot act until they are dealt with.[30]

Two Weeks of Cabinet Delay

Addison pressed Lloyd George to call the ministers together. On the morning of 24 October, after Wilson's reply to the Germans was read, he urged the Prime Minister once more. Thereupon a meeting was called for that afternoon—to deal, Addison hoped, with demobilization proposals. The session dashed his hopes.

> This lasted rather over an hour, and I have never attended a meeting . . . more utterly disorderly. . . . As a result of much shouting and making long speeches, Winston got the urgency of the munition problem attended to. L.G. was in his most impatient and

---

30. Addison, *Diary*, 2: 577, 581–83; G.T. 6047 (19 October 1918), Cab. 24/67. On national factories policy as decided by the cabinet, see G.T. 6041, 18 October 1918, Appendix, pp. 29–30.

illogical mood, and had clearly not taken the trouble to find out what was involved. . . . . There was another wrangle on the Pledges Bill, Roberts and I insisting on its being dealt with. . . . I came away feeling exceedingly angry.[31]

It was right that he felt this way, and it was very useful. If inarticulate crisis is to find a human voice it must call on apoplexy and hysteria to make men oracles of a present need. Addison's anger brought decision closer by several days.

There was, however, another perspective on the meeting. Admittedly, Addison's G.T. 6047 received scandalous treatment but three other documents fared better. Churchill's G.T. 6041 (thirty-two pages from the ministerial Reconstruction Committee, plus three pages merely listing the powers needed, *plus* Churchill's own message) loomed above the others.[32] But so did Churchill's problems, and the document disclosed them all. First, and unbelievably, the problem of existence: He had not yet learned whether his ministry was to continue. "At the threshold of any arrangement which may be made by the Ministry of Munitions for the disposition or transformation of the national factories" stood the choice between two alternatives: (*a*) termination and dismantling, all within a few months after peace, or (*b*) a permanent Ministry of Supply. Until this was decided (for the latter alternative, he hoped), no action or decision would make sense. The second problem was equally fantastic: Until the cabinet's decision of 9 October on national factories, Churchill had considered that his responsibilities at Munitions "were completely discharged when he furnished to the Minister of Reconstruction all the information in his power." Now, one month (as we know) before the signing of the armistice, he learned that the biggest single task of turn-over in Britain fell immediately on him! Any amount of recrimination and disclaimer would have been justified, but Churchill was not that kind of man. He bit on the bullet and faced the problem of means.

The Ministry of Reconstruction, said Churchill, was not equal to the need. Politely, he recorded that he had kept in the closest touch and accord with Addison. But the Minister of Reconstruction had no executive power, and "some authority to conclude bargains in this field should be vested in some Minister." Churchill was willing to do this, but there was a condition: One person—he insisted it must be Stephenson Kent—must

31. Addison, *Diary*, 2: 581–82, and *Politics*, 2: 259.
32. Churchill's G.T. 6041 (18 October 1918), Cab. 24/67.

absorb all of the departments which dealt with the demobilization of civilian labor. The personnel side must be surgically separated.

No diversity or duplication of action should be tolerated at this time. . . . The Minister, whoever he may be, who is charged with the commercial and business aspects of the transformation of our industries from a war to a peace basis should not be burdened with the intricate study of the labour problems which are simultaneously involved.

Churchill's staff classified the powers his ministry needed under seven heads. Addison had helped draft it (as Churchill seemed not to know); its likeness to G.T. 6047 was patent on at least seven points.

1. *Termination of contracts.* Only Treasury approval of financial settlements were needed; otherwise, this power was complete.

Manufacture should stop, as soon as possible, save where victory required production. A month's notice (or a month's pay at a generous flat rate) should be given. Full powers were immediately needed here.

2. *Disposal of stores.* The ministry was coping now, but for the enormous task ahead its machinery must be greatly strengthened. It alone —no "advisory council" or separate department—must do the job.

Large quantities of materials have been delivered to contractors to enable them to carry out their contracts, and plant and machinery have, in many cases, been installed in their works on terms which form part of the contracts themselves. It seems inconceivable that any other body than the Ministry of Munitions, who have been in constant relations with these firms, and on whose behalf the articles to be disposed of have been manufactured, should be responsible for disposing of the property thus accumulated. . . . The outside area organisation of the Ministry is exceedingly well adapted to the decentralisation of this kind of work. Through this organisation many of the difficulties connected with the disposal of material, etc. could be settled locally. The materials could, in fact, be sold where they lie, thus saving transport and unnecessary handling.

3. *National factories.* The minister had power to sell; he should "also be empowered to maintain a national factory in temporary activity should he consider it desirable . . . and be at liberty, in consultation with the Ministry of Reconstruction, to prepare plans for turning over national factories to the production of commodities required in bulk by the Government or by public bodies."

4. *Control of materials during the transitional period.* Basic action, only just taken, was reported: "The War Priorities Committee on Tuesday 15th October . . . decided that during the transitional period and until further arrangements were made, the control by the Government of various kinds of materials should continue to be exercised by the Departments in which it was at present vested." His departments would thus keep functioning; they would aim at speeding materials to useful industries.

5. *Special arrangements required with the iron and steel trade.* No argument was needed to prove that this was a category unto itself. A full stop to munitions output automatically meant that the output of blast furnaces and rolling mills must be reallocated. The crucial point was that during the war it had been "necessary to grant subsidies in order to maintain a uniform price of steel for munitions production." The government unquestionably would be compelled to maintain output of steel for peace purposes. This meant immediate decision on arrangements so that "output of the fundamental forms of steel and iron is not checked," "manufacturers are not placed in a position to enhance prices," "abnormal speculative movements of price are avoided," and so that, in the transition, the product would be distributed according to the government's allocation. Churchill needed authority, both to negotiate and to issue instructions on manufacturing for peacetime purposes. This might "involve a guarantee on the part of the State to indemnify makers of steel and iron stocks against loss, or a continuance of the sale of imported ore at a fixed price, or even the purchase and holding of the surplus stocks" by the state.

For a moment, the tone rose. "These powers are urgently required and may have to be exercised at very short notice. . . . They can only be exercised by the Minister of Munitions who, at the present time, has complete control of the iron and steel industry."

6. *Reinstatement of peacetime industry, particularly in the engineering and chemical trades.* Sure that he would also be asked to help here, Churchill asked for the power to act, subject to Treasury sanction.

7. *Civilian munitions labor.* Accepting Addison's plan for a Director-General of Civil Demobilisation under Roberts, Churchill simply urged that the Munitions Labour Department be kept intact. Churchill clung to this document, forcing it before the cabinet on the 24th. But Lloyd George expostulated that it was impossible to foretell whether armistice negotiations would succeed. The probabilities of peace might be very high, but "so long as there was any possibility of hostilities being resumed, it would not do to dismantle factories or turn them entirely on to peace products. . . . The Government had to be ready for either contingency."

One could not balance forever "on the one hand" and "on the other hand." Chamberlain, groping toward an understanding, thought out loud: There must be no slackening until the cabinet's orders were given, but there must be preparation for instant change. Yes, there was a distinction between products for war and for peace, but perhaps Churchill should "carry the preliminary processes . . . up to the point where civilian and war production began to diverge, and keep it at that neutral point"! The main thing was that

> every legitimate effort should be made to prevent unemployment and its accompanying demoralisation. It was far better to run the risk of manufacturing commodities which would not be required, and to resolve them into their elements later, than to have multitudes in receipt of unemployment benefit.

Churchill should get full authority to act at his discretion.

Gradually everyone joined in: Churchill, Addison, Horne, Stevenson, Roberts, Geddes. Whether to believe in peace; *how much* to believe in it. Whether, abstractly, it was better to pay men for doing nothing (and save materials), or to keep men producing what might prove useless (and save neither money nor materials). Whether the crucial question was the state of reserve supplies, or instead the inherent nature of the product, or the length of the manufacturing process. Whether those ideal products existed "which had an ambiguous value and could be used in either peace or war" (which would halve their problems). Whether (to be honest) anyone but Churchill and his staff had the slightest competence to judge. Everything was asked. The Prime Minister threw in a total irrelevancy: How much had war depleted the labor reservoir? Addison more pertinently estimated that 500,000 persons would require special provision in the transitional period. Talk overflowed into the topic of personnel demobilization. New questions arose. Geddes expatiated on the hard work ahead if employment exchanges were to prove adequate. Glad that at least that point had been made, Addison grumbled that

> the only person present in the room who had read the proposals [G.T. 6047] at all was Auckland Geddes, who did give me some assistance when I urged that a combination of the Labour Departments to provide machinery for civil demobilisation was an initial requisite. I got that sanctioned in principle, anyhow.

When the vote came in that cabinet session of 24 October, Addison gained more than this one point, however. Nominally, all decisions were a victory for Churchill and his immediate cause, but Addison could benefit from them all and he had in fact championed most of them. The first of the five decisions was a triumph for Churchill: approval of all the recommendations in his ministry's G.T. 6041, together with full sanction for the powers requested in that memorandum. Now the Ministry of Munitions could act. This was no loss for Addison or for anyone else. Second, an additional Secretary was authorized for the Ministry of Labour, to handle civilian demobilization; to Addison, this was not as good as the actual naming of Stephenson Kent (Lloyd George was flatly against this) but the principle was won. The transfer of other departments' labor machinery to the Ministry of Labour was the third decision, in keeping with G.T. 6041 and G.T. 6047. Addison himself was authorized, with Churchill, to prepare schemes for using national factories on public peacetime requirements: another victory. Addison and Roberts, lastly, were asked to specify the powers the cabinet should give them to handle demobilization. This apparent gain irritated Addison. The need was not for powers but for clear answers to specific questions, such as pledges and discharge payments, as he promptly told the cabinet. What galled him most was that, shouldered aside by Munitions' problems, he and his memorandum had got nowhere.[33]

To make matters even worse for him, the entire pledges wrangle wracked the meeting. Strong objections were raised against redeeming the pledges. "If the pledges were to be kept, not a single dilutee could be employed on work done before the war by skilled men"; and thousands of women must be summarily fired. The ranks of the unemployed would increase by half a million. "It would be infinitely better for the Government to bring forward an advanced programme of industrial betterment." Lloyd George squirmed and looked for a way out: Were trade unionists entitled to anything more than the guarantee of protection against loss of employment because an unskilled man was in their place? If there was work—for skilled and unskilled, or perhaps just for the skilled—would not this suffice? "However irrational it might appear," Roberts countered, "nothing short of the statutory fulfilment of the pledges would satisfy the men. By this means they meant to increase their bargaining power." Addison forecast that "if the men obtained the bill . . . they would be willing to enter into bargains with the employers for the continuance of the dilutees"; and unless promises were honored, "the Government would lay up for itself a mass of trouble." Barnes favored postponing the bill. For the bill and against it, the cases were beautifully set out.

33. G.T. 6136 (29 October 1918), Cab. 24/68; Addison, *Diary*, 2: 581–82.

Mr. Barnes thought it would be worth while making a serious conciliatory effort by calling a Conference of masters and men, putting before them frankly the difficulties which confronted the Government, and appealing to them to support the larger policy indicated by Mr. Churchill.

... Mr. Chamberlain supported the suggestion of a Conference. He thought there would be great difficulty in passing the proposed Bill through the House of Commons, because the Bill in effect was one to legalise what everyone knew to be intolerable industrial practices.

No decision was reached; and Addison was contemptuous.

Winston put forward a lot of unpractical nonsense about Housing as a substitute for the redemption of War Pledges which L.G. himself scoffed at. Fancy the gauge makers, tool setters and hosts more being satisfied with cottage building by someone else![34]

Indecision that day was a fearful augury. Addison had just issued a 7,000-word summary of utterly essential emergency legislation. If not even one issue of principle could be faced, what would happen to these lapsing laws and regulations in all their intricate detail?[35]

He sent Lloyd George, on 25 October, "a last request" that the proposals be decided in a systematic and comprehensive way.

The course adopted yesterday was to take hold of one section of the proposals on which I had previously reached agreement with the Ministry of Munitions ... and ignore other parts ... which are essential even to them. ... It makes my task quite impossible. ... It is ... not possible for me to express to you ... the measure of my disappointment, notwithstanding definite pledges to the contrary, at the disregard and lack of support which I seem to receive from you in this vital matter.

Over the weekend Addison made up his mind: "I would not any longer be a party to drift." Lloyd George was in France, but Addison told Bonar Law "the present position was utterly intolerable."

I must have a Cabinet Committee appointed with full authority to deal with the business, to sit from day to day, if necessary; that I

---

34. *Ibid.*; WC 491 (24 October 1918), Cab. 23/8; Roberts' G.T. 6150 (31 October 1918), Cab. 24/68.

35. G.T. 6051 (19 October 1918) and 6111 (23 October 1918), Cab. 24/67–68. For the memorandum on emergency laws (G.T. 6051), see below, pp. 308–9.

must get a decision on pledges, and that, unless it were in favour of the Government redeeming its pledges to the trade unions, I could not possibly remain, and if I went out on such an issue it would certainly mean that every Labour Member would have to leave the Government, and that I was finally determined, unless these matters were . . . dealt with forthwith, that I should do so.

On 29 October Bonar Law took Addison's second message to the Prime Minister: "Unless, with regard to these . . . matters which I have placed before the War Cabinet and some of which are long outstanding, I am placed in a position within the next few days to obtain decisions and action upon them, nothing can save this country from chaos and disaster."

That day, things took a turn for the better. The cabinet asked Smuts to convene a conference of the ministers especially involved to consider forming a cabinet committee on demobilization and resettlement and to cite any powers the departments might need at once. The next day, 30 October, at its 493d session, the War Cabinet finally voted that Smuts, Austen Chamberlain, and Barnes should "meet with the authority and powers of the War Cabinet, to dispose of demobilisation questions."

That morning, Addison learned the vital news from Smuts: "They had decided to set up a Cabinet Committee to deal with my business to sit daily."

> This was something accomplished. I insisted that they should take my memorandum beginning at the beginning and work right through it. We met on Thursday, the 31st, at 11 o'clock for the first time.[36]

The Demobilisation Committee (they were back to Asquith's form, although nobody noticed) tackled the two items Addison had put foremost: pledges, and payments of discharge and unemployment benefit. But the next day, Friday, 1 November, the latter item occasioned a clash.

> The Treasury had a deputation across to see me, ——— was in his most insolent mood as to my proposal as to out-of-work benefit. He suggested that we might possibly concede 14s. to insured munition workers. I am not going to stand up in the House of Commons and attempt to justify 14s. under present conditions! What also about the multitude of people who will be thrown out of work who are not classified as munitions workers? I stamped upon the suggestion.

36. Addison, *Diary*, 2: 584–86, and *Politics*, 2: 259–62; WC 492, 493 (29, 30 October 1918), Cab. 23/8.

Thoroughly provoked, Addison told the Treasury spokesman that if he "were to go to the Tommies in the trenches and tell them he thought 14/– would be enough for them to live on if they could not get a job after demobilisation, he would probably be strung up to the nearest post and would deserve it."

On Saturday there was trouble in the new Demobilisation Committee too. Someone doubted its competence to decide on the out-of-work donation. But Addison refused to reopen that question.

> I flatly declined to join in . . . and said that, unless this Cabinet Committee was competent to decide it, I would go no farther. That brought them up to scratch, and they agreed to settle it.

But the committee felt unable to decide upon pledges, and Addison telegraphed Lloyd George.

> War Cabinet which has been sitting daily on Demobilisation matters states that it has no authority to deal with the Pledges question. An immediate decision must be taken, as the issue will arise as soon as material is released for post-war work. Material is now available and ought to be released. Will you please cable Cabinet Committee authority to deal with this matter? If you cannot do so, I propose coming over myself on Monday, so that my own position in this matter may be determined.

On Monday, 4 November, "full authority was received and from that day onwards we got on swimmingly." [37]

37. Addison, *Diary*, 2: 584–86, and *Politics*, 2: 260–62.

14

Reconversion, Demobilization, Decontrol
November–December 1918

November 4 was full of activity and good news. Smuts's Demobilisation Committee finally took up the question of pledges. The war pledges bill was almost ready in the drafting department. The Demobilisation Committee authorized steps to facilitate officers' qualification for entry into the civil service. The committee endorsed the unemployment donation proposals of Addison, Churchill, and Roberts, brushing aside the Treasury protest that "rates paid should be low enough to insure that persons receiving the benefit would spare no effort to get employment." Austen Chamberlain brought "surplus stores" closer to a solution, on Addison's lines: authority should be vested in Munitions, aided by an advisory committee like Salisbury's (this, Addison complained, was where they had started, and should have been done long before). At his ministry the Advisory Council, going down G.T. 6047 item by item, heard the good news on raw materials: There would be ample steel both for useful and useless work. Except in isolated instances the difficulty in regard to raw materials would not be very great.[1] Hayes Fisher left the Local Government Board, but not without a circumstantial and worrisome critique of the Ministry of Reconstruction; few at Queen Anne's Gate regretted this resignation.[2] Addison managed to forward a carefully redrafted war pledges bill[3] and Birchenough's report on anti-dumping laws, with a minute of his own.[4]

Tuesday, the 5th, was even better. The Economic Defence and

1. Addison, *Diary*, 2: 593: "Advisory Council, Meeting of Chairmen—Note XXIII" (4 November 1918), F. 6813, Box 90, Part 3; Austen Chamberlain's G.T. 6204, Cab. 24/69.
2. Addison, *Diary*, 2: 586–89; Files 8505 and 8891, Box 30, Part 2.
3. Addison, *Diary*, 2: 588–89.
4. Box 78, Part 1.

Development Committee voted for a workable postwar system of inter-Allied controls, ending months of debate. Addison could introduce the Ministry of Health bill next day; he would have next Tuesday to speak to the House. "Smuts' Committee," he heard, "would go on sitting daily to deal with my business as long as I wanted." Meanwhile the cause of Whitleyism was advanced to the very doors of government—and was being suavely ushered in. On the idea of Joint Industrial Councils in the civil service, Stanley Baldwin commented: "It was a novel proposition, but the Treasury had decided to fall in with the proposal and try to make it a success."[5]

From Churchill's ministry, meanwhile, came reports of titanic striving. The Munitions Council, working with a newly established Demobilisation Board, cleared the way for action by formulating several governing assumptions.

> A Ministry of National Supply will be created . . . ; equipment and munitions will be maintained . . . sufficient to place in the Field an army of 50 Divisions six months after the declaration of war; . . . expenditure by the Ministry . . . will be defrayed by the Treasury and the requisite Cabinet authority will be forthcoming; . . . labour considerations must be considered . . . a prime object.

That done, specific instructions followed: ministry boards of management were to confer; the principal trades must be convened; restrictions on machine-tool manufacture must be removed. Huge orders on behalf of Indian railways were placed (they amounted eventually to more than £21,000,000). Unemployment benefits and short-time work were decided on. Clear and specific, at last, came a directive that cut to the heart of the problem of "production."

> On the signing of an effective armistice, the supply of materials will be cut off, but articles in process of manufacture will be completed provided that more than X per cent of their cost has already been spent upon them. . . . The object . . . will not be preparation for war, . . . the presumption being against the re-opening of hostilities.

Within two days Churchill's staff determined what to do with national factories: shell factories, which were only on loan to the government, would be returned to their owners; projectile factories would not be released until army requirements were known. Churchill reasoned that

5. Addison, *Diary*, 2: 587; HAC 16 (30 October 1918).

it was better to do this rather than face a mass of unemployed. . . . The country would realise that the emergency . . . was no less serious than the emergency of war. . . . People would be prepared to give the Government three or four months in which to turn around.

He still faced perils. He was acting on wartime powers, due to expire soon; he still had to beg the cabinet to extend them.[6] But the outlook at Munitions had been transformed in just eleven days.

Retrospect. What had happened and was happening was a rescue operation, and nothing else; it could not possibly be mistaken for the triumph of reform. Not a single reform measure had been passed. Nor had this manful improvisation advanced economic recovery a single step. It could not be mistaken, either, for true reconstruction.

Reconstruction as it had been planned—careful, scientific, supervised by superagencies, ratified by new decentralized councils, and resting on broad consent—had disappeared. Addison had hoped that new surveys would be made so that reconstruction would reflect current data; instead, the cabinet and the Raw Materials Board perforce assumed that the available data were correct, and plunged ahead. Yet in that tumult Addison expressed no real regret. He knew of course that the Standing Council on Post-War Priority, shaped for a deliberative role, was not functioning as intended; its first task, a preset system of priorities and allocation, could never be accomplished. He knew the Raw Materials Board was only a coordinating committee, over departments that held real sway. In the rush to get something ready all power had either reverted to the departments or had been whirled into the maelstrom at Downing Street. Looking back he could trace, over the month of October, the wild swing: from cabinet inattention, through a first instinctive and dangerous centralization when awakening came, to a choice—sensible in principle but not yet vindicated—for delegation. He knew that the ratification of Churchill's plans, even more than Long's victory on raw materials, compromised his ministry. But no resentment or dejection showed. Once a basis for action had been won, Addison threw his energies into the work.

6. Demobilisation Committee Memorandum 6 (4 November 1918), Box 78; G.T. 6200 (5 November 1918), Cab. 24/67; F. 4917, Box 90, Part 3; Walter to Nash, 11 December 1918, Box 90, Part 3, on follow-up. All minutes of Demobilisation Committee sessions are in Cab. 27/41 and all their memoranda in Cab. 27/42; therefore no individual citations of location will be made. For the policy on national factories as the cabinet authorized it, see G.T. 6041, 18 October 1918, Appendix, pp. 28–30, Cab. 24/67.

On the Threshold: 6–12 November

Work with Smuts on the Demobilisation Committee was tremendously exciting.

> From November 6 onwards the Committee practically left things to Smuts and me, and every day, and practically all day, we sat in an upper room at Whitehall Gardens deciding things by the score. . . . Our room was the scene of deputations in and out all the time.[7] Smuts divided the work into sections and we slaved away. . . . One of the tasks . . . was to go through the plans for providing work, and cross-examine each department on their preparedness—Roads, Timber-felling, Government Factories, and many more.

Unhappily, the report of the Local Government Board verified Addison's worst fears: for housing "there were practically no plans prepared and nothing upon which work could be begun for several months." He thought Smuts's comment "brief and merciless."[8]

But the Standing Council on Post-War Priority was hard at work. It met four times that week and Addison thought it made "magnificent progress" through the entire month. Its first act was to

> review the various controls . . . to get in hand the simplification of proceedings with regard to speeding up the transfer from war to peace. . . . With a multitude of war priority orders, people have to get permits for the different materials . . . often from quite different departments, until there is a network of procedure to go through which constitutes, rightly enough, an elaborate series of obstacles during war, but which, when war demands cease, makes expeditious resumption of peace-work an impossibility. . . . Smuts agreed upon a comprehensive amalgamation.[9]

On 6 November good news abounded. Lloyd George personally took up the question of war pledges—no more waiting for committees. He, Balfour, and Addison, with the original Labour Party signatories, agreed to announce redemption next week. Addison himself had the glory of introducing the Ministry of Health Bill to the Commons on 7 November— "a year and eight months," he recalled, "since Rhondda sent in his memorandum 'on the urgent need for a Ministry of Health.'" In his

7. Addison, *Diary*, 2: 587.
8. Addison, *Politics*, 2: 262.
9. *Ibid.*, p. 263; Addison, *Diary*, 2: 590–91; chairmen's meeting, cited in note 1; F. 8040, Box 15, Part 2.

speech to the House of Commons, Addison put stress on the "Declaration on the Poor Law" to show that this reform too was included within the plan for improvements at the center. He termed it a pledge to follow the proposals of Maclean's committee.

> The Report of the Local Government Committee, presided over by Sir Donald Maclean, on the transfer of functions of Poor Law Authorities has been carefully considered by the Government . . . the Government accept the recommendations of the Committee, that all services relating to the care and treatment of the sick and infirm should not be administered as part of the Poor Law but should be made a part of the general health services of the country. . . . the Government regard it as a matter of urgency that effect should be given to these recommendations as soon as possible.

On that same day Lloyd George asked Addison to be the first Minister of Health. That night the overjoyed Minister of Reconstruction wrote in his diary: "I hope . . . that this great matter is at last on the way to fulfilment."[10]

The cabinet sliced through departmental tangles, finally approving Acland's dream of an independent forestry authority. With wonderful illogic it ordered a supplementary estimate from the Treasury while the new forestry group still had no more than interim status. On 8 November it hacked at another Gordian knot and voted for a Ministry of Supply.[11] Delegation to the Demobilisation Committee seemed also to be paying off, at least while Smuts was in charge. It approved Stephenson Kent to take charge of all demobilization. It directed studies of the articles needed by the government that national factories might produce. It launched its own probe—Smuts and Addison taking personal charge—into "public requirements" for stimulating industry by showing the exact demands of local and central authority.[12]

That Saturday and Sunday Addison's mind and heart were far from the details of reconstruction policy. In common with millions of Britons

10. Addison, *Diary*, 2: 587–88, and *Politics*, 2: 230; F. 8495, Box 71, Part 1, citing Shackleton's G.T. 5740, Cab. 24/64; G.T. 5992. For the Poor Law, see also G.T. 6126, 6148, and 6222, Cab. 24/68 and 69; WC 497 and 500 (7 and 8 November 1918), Cab. 23/8. For Addison's announcement on the Ministry of Health, and the pledge of acceptance of the Maclean Committee views on the Poor Law, see *P.D.(C.)* vol. 110, c. 2338–40 (7 November 1918). For the favorable reaction by such leading physicians as Dr. Bernard Dawson, see Abel-Smith, *The Hospitals*, p. 289.

11. WC 497 and 500 (7 and 8 November 1918), Cab. 23/8.

12. D.C. 6 (6 November 1918), D.C. 7 (7 November), and D.C. 8 (14 November).

he turned his thoughts toward Europe—to the rumors and contradictions that weekend about the abdication of the Kaiser and the death of the Crown Prince. On Monday, 11 November, the hope that had seemed "almost too good to believe" became fact: the Germans had accepted the armistice.

> Downing Street was packed from end to end with a cheering crowd
> . . . not only the inhabitants of most of the Government offices, but as it seemed, the whole of London simultaneously downed tools and rushed into the streets—taxi-cabs, motors, lorries, buses and vehicles of every description were commandeered by joyful crowds . . . cheering, whistling, singing, rejoicing.[13]

Winston Churchill looked from his window and saw an eternity come to an end.

> The minutes passed. . . . And then suddenly the first stroke of the chime. I looked again at the broad street beneath me. It was deserted. From the portals of one of the large hotels absorbed by Government Departments darted the slight figure of a girl clerk, distractedly gesticulating while another stroke of Big Ben resounded. Then from all sides men and women came scurrying into the street. Streams of people poured out of all the buildings. The bells of London began to clash. . . . The tumult grew . . . like a gale. . . . The chains which had held the world . . . had snapped upon a few strokes of the clock.

Pensive, Churchill walked to Downing Street. There the cabinet discussed arrangements for marching into Germany; the lifetime that was just ending required its last rites. Then to the new era: "Mr. Churchill read a draft of his proposals in regard to the output of munitions and the gradual discharge of certain munitions workers, for communication to the press." The draft was approved.[14]

Report to Parliament. Stopping at Queen Anne's Gate next day, Addison learned that the shipping people would be able to go ahead at once with a new program. He pocketed his notes and walked across Parliament Square. His report to the Commons on the state of reconstruction measures lasted *two hours.*[15]

13. Addison, *Diary*, 2: 592.

14. Churchill, *The World Crisis, 1916–1918* (London: Thornton Butterworth, 1927, 1929), 4: 542–43.

15. Addison, *Diary*, 2: 591, and *Politics*, 2: 263; *P.D.(C.)*, vol. 110 (1918), c. 2589–628.

Addison had first to dispel any illusions about reconversion. Encouragingly, even in the metal and chemical trades, heavily involved in munitions work, 70 per cent of the men and 40 per cent of women were doing work for which there would be a continuing civilian demand; but peacetime work must be found for another 1,000,000 workers. The conversion of factories might prove "not a matter of days but of months." To cope with these problems and with those of 3,000,000 or more veterans, fast action had been needed. (*a*) With no time to set up ideally desirable machinery, they had fallen back on "an amalgamation of those war services . . . already dealing with this class of problem." (*b*) The Minister of Labour had set up 260 local committees to help demobilization. (*c*) The speedy release of demobilizers had been asked. (*d*) Unemployment insurance, no easy problem, was being solved for now on a *non*-contributory basis. (Addison here followed Greenwood's thinking, shown in G.T. 6047: the wide scope of munitions work and the national dimensions of demobilization precluded all narrow systems based on insurance paid by munitions workers.) (*e*) Grants for training juvenile workers had been approved. Fisher, in fact, had so impressed the Demobilisation Committee that it ordered the Treasury to grant up to £25,000 for six months' continuance of the work. (*f*) As for armed forces demobilization, Addison rehearsed the general system of early releases; then he turned to welfare measures: small holdings and allotments, reservation of civil service posts for veterans, officers' training at state expense—all approved. (*g*) On industrial reconversion, he reported the administrative changes (a storage executive and the creation of a Ministry of Supply) and the encouraging news on shipping and raw materials. Here he brought in the work of the Carmichael committee, which he counted on to expedite housing. Far too hopefully, he alleged—as seemed true at that moment— "We are now well ahead in our preparations" for the production of building materials.

Pointed questions interrupted his discussion of price and allocation policy. "It was proposed to release iron and steel forthwith," he answered, but a subsidy and maximum price for them must be maintained; a priority system could not be dispensed with, at home or abroad, although (he claimed) trade opinion would guide the policy. (*h*) On trade groups, Addison used phrases that, against the background of 1918, showed how far these bodies were from present usefulness: "In due time I hope that they will undertake the responsibilities" for priority. Hurrying, Addison came to his chosen climax: devolution and Whitleyism. "All our efforts will be in vain . . . unless we have industrial peace." Government prescription could not succeed by itself; representative decentralized organizations were the key. Because of "a lot of spade work of a very unattractive kind during the last twelve months," industrial councils and committees for about fifty industries now gave grounds for hope.

When he had finished there was some talk—much as in July 1917—against "giving away presents" to the electorate, and some grousing against new ministries. But Carson congratulated the minister.

> I know well the amount of time and attention and anxiety that he has given, . . . for many many months past, . . . looking forward to the great day which we now have. . . . I wish him well in all his efforts, and I do not believe there is any Member of this House . . . who will not give him all the assistance that he can in building up once more the great trade of this country.[16]

A New World?

More work came to fruition next day. On pledges, decision came at last. Smuts cut through the neatly balancing arguments for and against restoring prewar practices: if a bill for restoration of these rules was not introduced, "it would be impossible to make any real headway with Reconstruction." On 13 November, the price for continued industrial peace was paid, and the unionized skilled workers were given back a measure of control over the terms of work; a crowded meeting of employers and trade unionists heard the Prime Minister and A. J. Balfour commit the government "up to the hilt" on pledges. Not only a war pledges bill but a bill fixing wage rates for six months would be introduced. With this announcement, much was changed—seemingly for the better. Workers' anxieties for the prewar safeguards were diminished; fears for the immediate security of wage levels may have subsided. The wage rates soon were fixed by the Wages (Temporary Regulation) Act, passed on 21 November 1918—and they were fixed at wartime levels. Moreover, since these rates were *minima*, the stage was set for strike action to obtain increases. The act, significantly, gave workers once more the right to strike.[17]

16. *P.D.(C.)*, vol. 110 (1918), c. 2619–20; Addison, *Diary*, 2: 595.

17. Addison, *Diary*, 2: 587–88. See also Lord Askwith, *Industrial Problems and Disputes* (New York: Harcourt, Brace, 1921), pp. 460, 463–64. See also G. D. H. Cole, *Trade Unionism and Munitions*, p. 175, for the events of November 1918, and *ibid.*, pp. 190–96 for the protracted negotiations between employers and unions leading to the enactment of an agreed measure on restoration of prewar practices, in August 1919. The act is 9 and 10 Geo. V, c. 42. Regarding the Wages (Temporary Regulation) Act of

On that same day, 13 November, Smuts and Addison sent the War Cabinet a report that showed how many men each reconstruction scheme would employ.

1. A one-year program of road repair (first installment in the Road Board's ten-year program) could absorb 150,000 men in the first year, for £30,000,000. However, Treasury sanction for the state's £24,000,000 share, and the swift return of pivotal men, were prerequisites.
2. Land reclamation, to put 200,000 men to work quickly, was so important that all aid to the Board of Agriculture and the Development Commission were urged, plus £1,000,000 from the Treasury and the necessary amendment of existing law.
3. Forestry work would employ few men.
4. Scholarships and maintenance grants, costing £910,000, would benefit some 15,000 ex-officers.
5. Facts on housing and public works were not ready.[18]

This last item, an ill omen, was no surprise. Addison took it as one more proof that the Local Government Board was many months behind. Far from wasting time on fault-finding, however, he snatched at more encouraging signs from the Local Government Board. He personally endorsed their plea to the War Cabinet to help local authorities get on with the job. Numerous councils stood ready with electricity and water schemes that totaled £19,000,000—mighty stimuli to enterprise and employment.

> In a number of cases the works can be put in hand as soon as the present restrictions are withdrawn. . . . Local Authorities will be slow to move until assured that . . . the necessary money will be available. . . . Unless the Treasury are prepared to make an early announcement . . . there will be a serious risk of nullifying the efforts which the Local Government Board have made.[19]

Times had changed, when Addison had become a spokesman for the Local Government Board, eager and ready to move!

November 1918, attributed to the Ministry of Reconstruction, see Alan G. B. Fisher, *Some Problems of Wages and Their Regulation in Great Britain since 1918* (London: P. S. King, 1926), pp. 19–23.

18. Addison, *Diary*, 2: 586–87, 595, and *Politics*, 2: 262; G.T. 6277 (14 November 1918) and 6277A (3 December 1918), Cab. 24/69.

19. G.T. 6307 (16 November 1918), Cab. 24/70.

Times indeed were changing, sometimes with electric swiftness. On Armistice Day the Ministry of Munitions had telegraphed hundreds of contracting firms with instructions on the termination of manufacture and the discharge notices for hundreds of thousands of employees. There were, of course, niceties and qualifications in what it said.

1. There should, as far as possible, be no immediate general discharge of munitions workers; however,
2. All workers who wished to withdraw and all who could be absorbed elsewhere should be released at once.
3. Production for eleven categories (guns and gun ammunition, machine guns, small arms, small-arms ammunition, trench mortars, bombs, aerial bombs, aircraft and aircraft engines, pyrotechnic stores, and stores therefor) should be reduced by (*a*) abolishing overtime and (*b*) wherever possible suspending the system of payment by results and shifting to time work, with reduction of the work week where possible.
4. Work on a "time work" basis must be regularized, staying at least at one-half the present level, with short-time arrangements dictated by the ministry and with *reimbursements by the state to employers who paid their workers for time lost.*
5. To speed the issue of railway passes to all, employers might give them out direct.[20]

Government, in this instance, was keeping pace with the growing demand for change, but just barely. Change was demanded, by both left and right. In a report of 13 November, the Ministry of Labour found impatience throughout the ranks of labor with the control that had been in force during the war. From the other end of the political spectrum, Addison faced the same passionate mood, ready to strike at every reminder of the wartime past. It was his task to pilot through Commons the "Termination of War" bill—a bill that, expressing the view then prevalent in Whitehall, implied the possibility of considerable extensions of wartime rules. Even the possibility was anathema. Addison confronted sharp demands for the outright abolition of controls, together with angry warnings that the people opposed anything like wartime regulation. Addison temporized and placated his critics, reassuring them that the bill also empowered the government to end controls early.[21] But inasmuch as

20. *History of the Ministry of Munitions*, 6, part 2: 83ff.
21. Ministry of Labour report through 3 November 1918, G.T. 6323, Cab. 24/70; *P.D.(C.)*, vol. 110 (1918), c. 3145; see, in general, c. 3127–46, 3307, 3475–78.

he did not capitulate, he failed to satisfy his challengers. Amid the enthusiasts for change, he seemed like one from the past, busying himself with unpopular agenda inherited from a bygone age. The danger was not in change itself—with the armistice, change had become an irresistible law of life; the danger was in change unguided, subject to every mood and whim. Reconstruction, in any planned and coordinated sense, would be in peril if such moods and pressures prevailed. The prime need was for a cabinet that was thoroughly informed, resolute in purpose, constantly attentive, and continuously active.

Delays and reversals. Perhaps from sheer reluctance to recognize dangers, Addison was slow to note signs of a new slackness in the cabinet. Sessions, daily or more often since 1916, now came at five- to seven-day intervals, and when the cabinet met it did not act. From 12 November to 6 December there were only three positive decisions on reconstruction. Two of these—export-import controls and land settlement—soon came unstuck; the third—the eight-hour day—had been added to the agenda by workers' agitation after the armistice.[22] Addison's and Smuts's plea for local work schemes, ignored for weeks, got back on the agenda only in December. Local authorities' borrowing powers were not freed, and new appeals were necessary.[23]

Hard work became harder, because the special committees set up in June, precisely to make plans ready on time and to expedite cabinet action, had not come up to expectations. Both the Home Affairs Committee and the Economic Defence and Development Committee belied the hopes that Addison had pinned on them. The Home Affairs Committee, useless in October, held just one session in November—and that topic was off the point! In December, worse would come. There would be only one session, and it would decide to postpone major plans on land acquisition and on the continuance of emergency legislation.[24] In the period of the armistice crisis, the E.D.D.C. was little better. It met more often, but results were few. In October it should have handled many questions, especially four urgent ones: inter-Allied machinery to control imports; extension of the Shipping Controller's powers; the form of license control, and the choice of an administrative authority, where both imports and exports were concerned; and tariff policy. The backlog of greater but less urgent questions included the questions of protection for British shipping, policy on railways and coal, definition of key industries,

22. WC 507 and 510 (28 November and 6 December 1918), Cab. 23/8.
23. G.T. 6307 (13 November 1918), Cab. 24/70.
24. HAC 18 (18 December 1918).

and synthesis of the whole of economic policy. Five October meetings, however, produced only decisions on sugar tariffs and on an import-export bill. In November the tendency to mere referral persisted. It was frustrating to Addison, who wanted thorough discussion of electric power questions. He let the E.D.D.C. know that he was doubtful about the Williamson report on electricity—and was told to confer with Stanley. Meanwhile Stanley's idea of interim appointments of electricity commissioners was approved. On "special industries" Addison got the same treatment.[25] Much was decided by the E.D.D.C., or at least reviewed, but almost wholly in *external* policy: foreign investment, blockade policy, protection against dumping, Allied controls and postwar requirements, foreign relief and reconstruction. No help here for *internal* problems. These two committees, set up in midyear to clear away obstacles, were proving no substitute for War Cabinet attention and deeds.[26]

All too soon, moreover, Addison learned how unreliable some of the first "successes" of improvisation actually were. Where juvenile employment was concerned, implementation became deadlocked between two rival ministries. Training for ex-officers lagged because, though the policy was already approved, the authorization had not covered fine points of execution.[27] But must the cabinet decide even the details, and then maintain supervision as well? Was this a fatal flaw in all new schemes, that only the enactment of a completely elaborated plan—eliminating the need for departmental ingenuity and overriding departmental jealousies— would meet the need? The cabinet simply could not take time to decide on details; but the example of the debate on "production," which had to be threshed out completely in cabinet, seemed to preach the dismaying lesson that only cabinet sanction of exact details could release the springs of action.

Smuts's committee. The Demobilisation Committee was the outstanding exception to the sorry spectacle in November. Meeting seven times in a fortnight, it played its twin roles—adviser and judge—to the hilt. On 14 November it speeded Addison's list of demobilization and reconstruction schemes to the cabinet; the next day it reviewed the £80,000,000 "war gratuities" for veterans, and sent the measure on; it got a subcommittee to rush in a report on unemployment donations for temporary civil servants

25. E.D.D.C. meetings of 8, 15, 22, 24, and 29 October 1918, and of 5 and 20 November 1918, Cab. 27/44.
26. See above, pp. 151–53.
27. G.T. 6308 (16 November 1918), Cab. 24/70; D.C. Memorandum 22 (27 November 1918) by Addison.

and voted favorably upon it, as Addison wished. Earlier decisions to deny out-of-work donations to Dominion and colonial soldiers and sailors who were not paid from imperial funds and to soldiers and sailors who had been discharged or transferred to the Reserve before demobilization were reversed, partly at Addison's suggestion. For twelve months veterans might receive an out-of-work donation, to a maximum twenty-six weeks; for six months civilian workers might receive a donation, to a maximum of thirteen weeks. The Exchequer, not the recipient, should pay the cost to the National Health Insurance Fund. Meanwhile, over Treasury protest, the committee had pushed for instant payment of unemployment donations to the armed forces. Equally important—and this meant urgently important—Addison's idea of promoting local public works was sanctioned, with a strong recommendation that the Treasury ease the restraints on loans.[28]

Some things the committee did not solve; others, which it thought had been decided, returned for judgment. Addison's proposals on veterans' reemployment, which would have granted restoration to specific pre-service jobs, proved too thorny. A new cry (new for November—Addison had demanded this for months) arose for a superagency to get business started by helping firms get peace orders; employers were floundering. Addison got the workers' perspective on this when a deputation from Woolwich Arsenal saw him; meanwhile, Sir Arthur Duckham, closer to employers, had been set to work by the Board of Trade and Munitions to coordinate the job. Stanley was ready with a small interdepartmental committee, under Duckham. He was so concerned that he espoused ideas that affronted others: state assumption of risk for firms that agreed to place orders to replenish stock; a state promise to pay the difference between present and future costs if local authorities would buy now rather than wait for prices to fall. On the face of it, such expediting was vital, but Auckland Geddes challenged the initiative: There was no need for another new, special body. But Smuts thought the need was self-evident.

> The Local Authorities were wanting certain things, but in the new situation they did not know where to place their orders. The Ministry of Munitions had the machinery . . . for meeting the needs of local authorities, but had not got the orders.

28. D.C./U.D. 3 and 4 (15 November 1918); Doc. 10, Civilian Resettlement Coordination Committee, Box 78; Addison, *Diary*, 2: 595–96.

It was a dual dilemma, financial and administrative, and the whole thing was postponed.[29] A whole month had elapsed, however, since the cabinet learned it was precisely such questions that it must face!

Not even Smuts's committee had filled the gap at the top, where machinery to *coordinate reconversion as a whole* was still lacking. The Federation of British Industries asked for it in November—as Mond had proposed it in August. In December the cost of such oversights would escape no one.[30]

The paradox that delay as well as fluid change marked this period must be insisted on, but misunderstanding is likely. The delay was of a fortnight, perhaps three weeks, after armistice. It was, however, the delay of neither stagnation nor complacency. Ministers were fearfully busy; in fact, sessions such as those Smuts chaired ate up their energy. Every man had his department to manage, and an appalling amount of new work. One new chief in labor administration came so near despair from overwork that only the alcoholic intervention of two colleagues kept him from suicide.

Inaction was not the sole danger—action also could cause trouble, as Addison saw that month. Land-settlement plans were suddenly upset, in the spirit of haste.[31] The crucial Carmichael plan for building materials came under blistering attack from Kent, and Addison leaped to rescue what he could.[32] Agreements for paying temporary civil servants were unilaterally undercut by the Treasury. Addison, who had won assent that "the Government must act as a model employer," protested with Auckland Geddes against confusion worse confounded by this "grave injustice."[33] Plans for the out-of-work donation, barely ratified, came unstuck. The cabinet's decision to appoint a Ministry of Supply, basing it on the existing Ministry of Munitions, killed the long-suffering Surplus Government Property Advisory Council. They went out of business with a final complaint.

> If the advice of the Council as to the separate Ministry had been taken in time it would have proved the better course, but . . . as the Government had left the solution of the question until hostilities were actually at an end, there was a great deal to be said in favor of the decision to utilise an existing Ministry with a good establish-

29. Addison, *Diary*, 2: 595–96; D.C. 12.
30. D.C. 23 (27 November 1918), Box 78, Part 1.
31. Addison, *Diary*, 2: 598.
32. *Ibid.*, p. 596.
33. D.C. 9, 10, 20, and 21.

ment.... The Council had been able to undertake only a fraction of what might have been done ... but they had done their best.[34]

Speed, Solvency, Fear

Behind the delays and reversals stood four portentous causes. The setbacks and frustrations that they had already caused were bad, but these causes were a still greater threat. There was no time limit to their operation and there was no area of reconstruction that they might not touch.

Solvency. Unemployment donations, discharges of civil staff, land-settlement plans, like the painful irresolution on local public works and war gratuities, all reflected a new concern: *cost*. Even the Demobilisation Committee, forwarding to demobilization and reconstruction schemes only seventy-two hours after the armistice, shrank from endorsing its budget because it "was affected by the general post-war financial policy of the Government." Winston Churchill caught it exactly:

> A new set of conditions began to rule from eleven o'clock onwards. The money-cost, which had never been considered by us to be a factor capable of limiting the supply of the armies, asserted a claim to priority from the moment the fighting stopped.[35]

Speed. Always a recognized necessity and therefore built into the reconstruction plans, speed was rapidly becoming a wrecking force inside it. Protests already were rising toward the angry roar of December. Troop restiveness was disturbing. Testy letters from the Federation of British Industries, for swift declaration of policy and for instant doses of interim aid, exposed unmet needs only too painfully. The *Nation*, the *Athenaeum*, and the *New Statesman* struck without mercy at the injustice of demobilization and the unreadiness of economic plans.[36] However critics differed in philosophy, their common effect was to discredit carefully elaborated schemes precisely *because* of their complexity. This was especially true when a scheme was criticized both for complexity and for pitting governmental requirements against the shouted claims of business enterprise. This was the argument that threw the Carmichael system into jeopardy, and struck it down in December. Speed was the consideration that

---

34. See below, p. 312, on unemployment donation. For the S.G.P.A.C., see Minute 204–9 (18 November 1918), Box 72, Part 1, Binder 1.

35. Churchill, *World Crisis*, 5: 32–33.

36. G.T. 6396 (23 November 1918), Cab. 24/70; *New Statesman*, 5 October, pp. 2–3, 26 October, pp. 64–66, 9 November, p. 103, 16 November, pp. 132–33, 23 November, pp. 146–47, 30 November, pp. 172–73, 28 December 1918, pp. 253–54.

prevailed against official plans for continued output by national factories: such state production—whatever the workers hoped—deferred the prompt resumption of private industry, and trebled the uncertainty among private producers. Speed was the decisive argument against Addison's land-settlement plans and for Prothero's eleventh-hour proposal. It was a factor both old and new: a need long seen, a need redoubled and amplified once peace had come. Once acknowledged, speed brought perilous changes in mentality and in action. Garrod, only *one day* after the armistice, discouraged the use of Interim Industrial Reconstruction Committees as aids to the Standing Council. Officially their help with demobilization was still welcomed.

> These bodies have always been informed that during the Reconstruction period their advice and assistance would constantly be needed by Government departments, and we are very anxious that as much use as possible should be made of them.

But the truth was soon faced that the essence of success in demobilization, the "rapid obtaining of names," would be jeopardized by taking time to consult the I.I.R.C.'s. Such logic applied to the whole field of devolution —I.I.R.C.'s, trade groups, Whitley Councils, all.[37]

Probably the greatest impact of the new impatience, however, was on economic reconversion rather than on army demobilization. Paradoxically, by grasping the nettle the government was making its own plight worse. First, any government success in cutting production (fulfilling part of the plan) would automatically create enormous demands from the unemployed simply by swelling their ranks; at the same time it would redouble the pleas for aid from businessmen, who were clamoring for the termination of war work! New headaches were thus inherent in success. Second, no decision brought savings—almost every remedy for unemployment, like most of the stimuli aimed at accelerating business enterprise, involved huge outlays. What had been begun in the name of economy, to save money by halting expenditures on war, created problems of unemployment that then defeated the purpose.

Addison had no way out. Speed had been his plea—for the sake of reconstruction plans. Now speed was a different argument; heedless of his careful plans, it often rushed directly against them. His colleagues could no longer be accused of inattention or unconcern—on the contrary!

37. F. 7716, Box 71, Part 1; Files 10563 and 10093, Box 71, Parts 2 and 3.

Fear. It was not humanitarianism alone or zeal for efficiency that moved them; they were afraid. Lloyd George told the War Cabinet it was important that

> the public in England should realise more fully what Bolshevism meant in practice. France was more secure against Bolshevism, owing to the existence of a large population of peasant proprietors. Here we had a great, inflammable, industrial population, and it was very desirable that our industrial population should know how industrial workers had suffered equally with the rest . . . of Russia in the hands of the Bolsheviks.[38]

No such alarm shows in the entire War Cabinet files beforehand; and it appeared on *the third day of peace.*

Two days before, Mond had printed his "Suggestions to Prevent the Spread of Revolutionary Ideas in the United Kingdom." Roberts, circulating the draft Wages (Temporary Regulations) Bill, warned that a lowering of wage standards would cause serious unrest. The usual reports on "pacifism and revolutionary organisations" began to report now a mounting fascination in labor with signs that "the revolution" had burst aflame through central Europe.[39] Lloyd George, hearing that the prompt discharge of miners was not certain, told Milner:

> Unless the supplies of coal . . . were increased, it was not impossible that there might be a revolution. . . . The spirit of lawlessness was apparent, and none could say what might happen if . . . there was no coal in the East end in December.[40]

Truculent demands for the eight-hour day, on behalf of locomotive drivers and firemen, took the form of a flat ultimatum: the eight hours must be recognized *during the next few days* "or there must be a trial of strength—there was no more room for argument."[41] By 6 December the ultimate calamity of a railway strike seemed imminent.

Sir Thomas Munro put "a growing and grave difficulty" in words that Churchill rushed to his colleagues.

> It is bluntly put that the Government have used and praised the workers while the war was still to win, and now that it is won no consideration is being shown. Strong criticism is also directed

38. WC 502 (14 November 1918), Cab. 23/8.
39. G.T. 6270 (12 November 1918), Cab. 24/69; G.T. 6275 (13 November), Cab. 24/69; G.T. 6377 (to 20 November), Cab. 24/70.
40. G.T. 6374 (25 November 1918), Cab. 24/70.
41. WC 507 (28 November 1918), Cab. 23/8.

against . . . using well equipped factories as storehouses instead of adapting them to peace industries. . . . The workers say that the Government were spending millions per day to win the war, and now that the war has been won through the exertions of the people, they grudge the much smaller expenditure that would keep the workers in comfort.

Small comfort to Addison and Greenwood that these had been their very words ten months before! Munro's forecast also repeated theirs.

A dangerous situation may arise. . . . I am especially apprehensive of the attitude of discharged sailors and soldiers who are banded together in an association which is insistent on its demands and most aggressive.

Stephenson Kent, worried about grave unrest among women munitions workers, spoke the felt priorities of the day: "Suspicion and unrest among the workers now form the most dangerous feature of the situation."[42]

International Questions

Intrinsically nowhere near as worrisome, international questions also made for pervasive delay, if only because they absorbed so many ministers' time. The archives for November bulge with the records of old and new international tasks. Merely to scan them, fifty years later, produces a sympathetic sag of weariness. The list of world and allied complications seemed interminable.

The details on the Allies' postwar requirements still had not been catalogued. Addison, whose July memorandum had made a start, found that Sir Arthur Steel-Maitland had urged other plans on the E.D.D.C. at the end of October. Two other key issues were not decided: machinery for common action in wartorn areas and a control policy for raw materials. To judge by an Economic Offensive Committee memorandum, the number of implied tasks approached the impossible: (*a*) decision on priority between the claims of neutrals, enemies, and the Allies; (*b*) agreement on the possessor country's rights to help itself first; (*c*) formation of trade committees and statistical bureaus; (*d*) formation or extension of government export licensing machinery; (*e*) definition of policy, estimates of short-term targets, and pooling of information; (*f*) decision on internal and inter-Allied controls. The E.O.C. recommended controls

42. Munro's G.T. 6427 (3 December 1918), Cab. 24/71; Kent's G.T. 6479 (14 December 1918), Cab. 24/71.

on eleven major commodities but it warned that the global scheme could not be

> turned into a permanent industrial control without a complete change of commercial and industrial opinion throughout the world. It would involve . . . a degree of State control strongly repugnant to current opinion, and most unlikely to be realised in the near future.[43]

This *was* a major topic—what would happen to this whole structure? The Foreign Office answered with undiplomatic zeal that amounted to bad form. Over the whole existing organization (Allied Maritime Council, raw materials and finance councils, and the rest), said they, a new General Economic Board should be made supreme. In any case, the whole inter-Allied organization should be maintained until the peace, and its various control components should be strengthened; the enemy should be made to accept this, and surrender all shipping thereto. Although the aim was negative (to terminate Britain's duties to her Allies, secure war-debt cancellation, and get back to "normal trade conditions"), the result would be positive; the proposed General Economic Council must continue in force in peacetime. Business hostility to controls must be faced down.

> Our time is short. We cannot count upon a long period . . . to elaborate detailed plans. . . . We cannot be certain of the effect . . . of a sudden reduction of control, while it is certain that any such removal would alarm very large sections of labour opinion just at the very moment when the withdrawal of war pressure, and possible examples of serious popular disturbances in Germany will be exposing every Allied country to a recrudescence of Bolshevism.

In defense, out came the whole case for controls, formulated sixteen months before by Montagu and later repeated by Burns and Addison.

> On the troubled morning after the termination of hostilities, a sudden relaxation of control would leave the world, not a more or less even plane over which supplies could easily find their own level, but a series of depressions and pockets of varying depths into which supplies would at first flow very unevenly and even violently. . . . Such anomalies . . . could not fail to produce the most acute suffering and discontent throughout Europe.

The paper predicted a rapidly worsening financial situation for Britain. It shrewdly forecast that a swift resumption of export trade at high prices,

43. E.O.C. 56, Box 78, and Cab. 21/108.

though desirable by many economic tests, would strip the home market of supplies—which would stir political trouble and imperil the work of reconstruction. Moreover, the document acknowledged that exporters must not be allowed to profiteer; political reasons here entered into consideration, cutting athwart the normal calculations of recovery.[44] The Foreign Office had discerned a fundamental truth: the goals that Britain sought were contradictory. Victory in competitive world trade, stability in finance, decontrol and abundance at home, were all deemed desirable; and all were incompatible. The cabinet would face hard choices.

World Trade Policy and International Organization: A Digression

That was just the trouble: every problem of this nation of traders bristled with contradictions and difficulties. Speed warred with solvency. Recovery by sales overseas would worsen workers' plight at home. Everyone wanted exporters to get busy, but without profiteering; yet anti-profiteering measures could easily kill initiative. Now was the time to carry through lasting worldwide controls, but the weeks it would take to negotiate them would imperil a situation already bad. (Ultimately, therefore, the E.D.D.C. voted to keep the imperfect bodies rather than follow the Foreign Office proposal.)[45]

There was, in addition, the problem of the United States, and particularly the problem of Thomas Woodrow Wilson. On 9 November the President was reported to be under the impression that

> our aims in connection with this machinery are bound up with economic boycott of Germany. This of course is not so. All American economic representatives here cordially agree with us in believing that the continuance of this economic machinery during the armistice period temporarily is essential in order to prevent trade dislocations fatal to the well-being of every civilised country, quite independently of any idea of discriminating against our present enemies.

This mood, which Colonel House shared, was one more block to formal conferences on new machinery. Not a step could be taken without

44. E.D.D.C. 51 (21 October 1918) and 55, Cab. 27/44 and Box 78, Part 2; F. 9166, Box 90, Part 3.

45. E.D.D.C. 12 (26 October 1918), and 16 (14 November 1918), Cab. 27/44 and Box 78, Part 2.

America's consent.[46] And no sufficient step *was* taken. In January the chairman of a special conference ruefully summed up "just how much—or rather how little—had been done."[47]

What were Britain's goals? Was no item of overseas trade beyond dispute? In April, when the Ludendorff offensive had simplified all views, the basic premise of a trade war had seemed agreed upon. Surely, then, curbs on alien investments seemed within a consensus that also included restrictions on import and export and—*a fortiori*—an airtight blockade on Germany. But now, the wartime anti-German stance was weakening. When Stanley proposed to curb alien interests, Maclay hit back hard, and the committee swung to his view. "As regards the restriction of Foreign Capital in British Shipping, the measure . . . would be actually injurious. . . . There was much to be said against restricting the investment of foreign capital in other British industries." The E.D.D.C., only nine days after armistice, approved a rather permissive policy on blockade—without one punitive word on Germany! The overriding concern was to speed the turnover to peace work. The stern morality and lively fears of wartime confronted now the indulgent profit motives of peace; the guardians of the state—diplomats and generals—faced the leaders of the economy. The outright clash in 1919 over the continued blockade of Germany was in the making.[48] If antagonism was waning, so the wartime assumptions of comradeship, never secure, were more doubtful than ever. The Webb-Pomerene bill in the United States Senate had prompted warnings of a concerted American export drive, and, accordingly, Addison's anti-dumping plan was sent to the Board of Trade for action. The Federation of British Industries added its cry for imperial preference. As Carson had said, commerce is "neither war nor friendliness, [but] . . . a thing entirely apart."[49]

Was nothing settled? Could it not at least be stipulated that controls were needed, whatever their long-term fate or aim? Business increasingly said no; a consistent line of E.D.D.C. recommendations said yes. On 25 November Addison stolidly defended his wartime stand, firing like a good but deaf soldier into the new stillness.

> It is necessary to set up some machine which will insure that the urgent requirements of this Country and the Allies are provided for before less pressing needs, and that if shortage of supply should

46. E.D.D.C. Memoranda 66 and 74 (7 and 19 November 1918), Cab. 27/44.
47. "Minutes of a Meeting . . . 9 January 1919," F. 9166, Box 90, Part 3.
48. E.D.D.C. 15 (5 November 1918), Cab. 27/44.
49. G. 190 (21 January 1918), Cab. 21/108.

occur, the available stock shall be reserved for those purposes which are of the greatest national importance. . . . During the Reconstruction period it will be necessary to control the export of certain materials and commodities of which the supply is limited.[50]

External planning was beset by many such controversies, and by some larger uncertainties. Should Britain cut free from its world obligation? So the Foreign Office had hinted; nevertheless in regard to the starving peoples of Europe, the E.D.D.C. accepted the view that the "responsibility of revictualling the world lay with the victors." Austen Chamberlain, however, moved to set a limit at the very next meeting: "His Majesty's Government did not propose to undertake the distribution of food in enemy countries." All other questions were referred.[51] In foreign affairs, all questions seemed held over to December.

Relaxation of Controls

Delays and their causes encircled the government with taunting critics. Only decontrol announcements won applause, which Addison almost encouraged. With an eagerness to please that makes his later adherence to Labour puzzling, he told Commons on 15 November:

> What have we done? The Armistice was declared on Monday. On Tuesday we released a considerable number of things, and we have released more every day since then, and at the Standing Council on Priority, which is composed almost exclusively of merchants, traders and business men, and is sitting daily with the sole purpose of getting rid of any embarrassing regulations which may be in restraint of the development of trade, we have released various commodities, and they were released in every case within a few hours of their recommendations. I am content that we should be judged on our record since Tuesday morning last as to whether we intend to continue embarrassing Orders any longer than the state of affairs compels. . . . I am just as anxious as the Hon. Member . . . that we should get rid of these embarrassing restrictions as fast as we can.

A note of 31 December reveals no alarm.

> Within a fortnight or less from the Declaration of the Armistice, we had got agreement with the industries and departments con-

50. F. 7890, Box 52; see his G.T. 5217 (23 July 1918), Cab. 24/59; F. 9166, Box 90, Part 3.
51. E.D.D.C. meeting 16 (14 November 1918), Cab. 27/44.

cerned, whereby steel and non-ferrous metals were liberated, and had got rid of many other control orders. We secured the amalgamation under one Department (the Board of Trade) of (1) the Imports Restriction Department; (2) War Trade Department; (3) Priority Department of the Ministry of Munitions and (4) Export Licensing Department, and made a clean sweep of all the priority certificates required, except with regard to specified cases of urgent importance, such as Merchant Shipping Construction, Locomotive Building, etc.

What had been done? Less than the flat word "decontrol" connotes. The ministerial orders and regulations, tying firms to manufacture *for war*, were being scrapped. The framework and procedure was being unified— a task of simplification, not equivalent to laissez-faire. Basic statutes were not repealed; many could (and some would) long continue—the phrase "termination of hostilities" permitted retention until 1920 or 1921, as it proved. There was a world of potential difference between releasing firms from duties incident to defeating Germany, and stripping the government of power to win the battle for reconstruction. Amalgamation of controls had aims and effects that were best summarized by Addison: "It was impossible to ask manufacturers to run from one place to another to get permits, and the simplifications arranged will be an infinite relief to industry." [52] This was no commitment to general decontrol in principle. Moreover, the documents from the Foreign Office show that it continued to assume into December that there would be both an international Allied structure of economic controls, and a powerful system of national controls to work with it. Other specific proofs of intent could be multiplied. The Ministry of Munitions, in its summary on 18 October 1918, showed that it was presumed that controls would be kept, their administration remaining in the wartime departments. The ministry presumed at that time that it must set up a Factories Branch to manage such national factories as remained under control; it noted that the termination of the war (in line with a January 1918 report by Mr. Justice Atkins) would legally come at that remote date when the belligerents exchanged ratifications; and not until then would emergency legislation lapse. As for priorities, the ministry's Reconstruction Department termed it "inconceivable" that the whole system under the Defence of the Realm Act should be dropped during reconstruction, as it would "still be necessary to direct materials and manufacturing capacity into the most useful channels." Power to

52. *P.D.(C.)*, vol. 110 (1918), c. 3145. Addison, *Diary*, 2: 590–92, and *Politics*, 2: 263.

investigate costs must be kept for the same reason, at least concerning contracts not finally settled; indeed it was urged that this power might be made permanent, "if for no other purpose than as a necessary corrective to excessive prices which might otherwise be charged by the Trusts which are at present growing up under Government approval." To retain some check on fluctuations, price control was also recommended where the ministry held large stocks of materials; control of materials "for some considerable period after the cessation of hostilities" was urged "with a view to allocation to the most urgent post-war needs of the community."

Addison had been even more outspoken than this, in his 19 October 1918 memorandum, "The Continuance of Emergency Legislation." At the wish of a Select Committee of the House, he had got together a compilation of departmental plans and preferences. As for government stocks of materials, first of all, he held it

> almost inevitable that such control, though perhaps in a modified form, will require to be continued during the period immediately following the cessation of hostilities. . . . Most of the arguments adduced by the War Office . . . are also applicable to the case of the Ministry of Munitions. . . . Manufacturers have adapted themselves to a certain amount of control, and the relaxation of that control cannot be accomplished hurriedly or abruptly without creating great confusion. Further, for the purposes of Reconstruction, it may still be necessary to retain the power of controlling the supply of materials, with a view to their diversion into the most useful channels, in order to meet the most urgent post-war needs of the community.

This was almost the exact wording in the Munitions statement; and, like the Munitions staff, Addison urged the continuance of powers (under Orders based on Regulations 2B, 2BB, 2E, and 7) to investigate costs, especially for contracts already made. He defended retention of Regulation 8, for taking any factory or plant, and for directing or restricting work in any factory. In particular as to Regulation 8A

> it would be most inexpedient, and indeed disastrous, that the control which is being exercised by the Ministry of Munitions . . . should be precipitately relaxed, and it is suggested that the continuation of this Regulation for a considerable period after the cessation of hostilities is essential. . . . The maintenance of this Regulation is also considered important from another point of view.

... It is Regulation 8A which forms the main foundation of priority control.

It is inconceivable that this system of priority in manufacture can be altogether abandoned during the considerable period of reconstruction which must follow the cessation of hostilities, for there will of necessity continue to be a shortage of essential materials of many description, and the Government will probably desire to retain the power to direct the manufacturing capacity of the country into the most useful channels.

Both the priority and materials controls might require fresh legislation, if present types of controls were dropped. As to continued government control of coal, he insisted "a further extension . . . might be necessary in the event of nationalisation being strongly supported by the miners with a threat to strike, which the country could not stand during the period of reconstruction." Iron ore mines should also remain under control to help government allocate supplies, maintain prices, and obviate possibilities of labor troubles. On other topics, additional arguments supported Addison's case for controls: shortage of raw materials, the probable large size of the postwar army, and the dangers of profiteering.[53]

In November and well into December, action seems to have remained within the framework of these premises. The hint of danger lay, not in present actions or in a conscious reversal of intent, but in the growth of pressures that would extend the present trend line too far.

Back to politics. On 25 November Parliament was dissolved. A national election, the first since 1910, was scheduled for 14 December.

One technical result of the dissolution worried some of the ministers: their emergency powers were in doubt. Churchill, the week before the armistice, pointed to the danger to his ministry. A. D. Hall of the Board of Agriculture, forwarding a full-scale plan for reviving farms and making jobs, added a plea to grant the powers implied. The uncertainty of powers for Shipping Control appalled the E.D.D.C.[54] Charged with identifying necessary emergency powers and legislation—a task too huge for quick

53. See Standing Council recommendations in D.C. 27 (P.W.P. 30) (12 November 1918), Box 78, Part 1, and Thomas Gardiner's 12 January note in F. 11061, Box 52. For Foreign Office views, see above, pp. 303–4, and documents cited in notes 46 and 47 to this chapter. See also the London *Times*, 26 November 1918, and P.W.P. 43, Cab. 33/4. For Addison and his rationale for controls, see G.T. 6051, 19 October 1918, Cab. 24/67. For proof that Churchill's staff presumed the continuance of controls, see G.T. 6041, 18 October 1918, p. 2, and Appendix thereto, pp. 2–3, 7–9.

54. E.D.D.C. 18 (17 December 1918) and Memorandum 76 (28 November 1918), Cab. 27/44.

performance—Lord Cave's committee and its parliamentary counterpart failed to compile them in time; the list was needed in October, but even December brought no solution. Concern on this score clearly showed that the government had not the least plan of surrendering to laissez-faire.[55]

To some ministers' dismay, further, no bill had actually cleared Parliament for land settlement, housing, acquisition of land, electricity supply, transport—or even pledges. Insistent and obvious needs—for example, a clear decision on unemployment donations—were unmet. To the more discerning, however, the worst omens were of a subtler kind: the delays and blunders which showed that the cabinet did not yet grasp the issues before it, either in their dimensions or their inner logic; the near-impossibility of improvising machinery to coordinate and command; the brutal power of impatience. What, if anything, could be done?

The cabinet might intervene and save reconstructionist plans. It might intervene and wreck them. It might set up a new group with delegated powers, capable of wreck or rescue. It might leave the departments to cope. It might evade and do nothing. These five paths lay open to the government. In December, it took all of them.

December 1918: Anxiety Takes Command

Smuts's committee started the month briskly. On 2 December it approved Addison's summary of costs for present schemes—lengthy even if still incomplete. Under "reconstruction finance" he had listed:

1. Housing subsidies for seven years: (*a*) £26,500,000 for capital subsidies to building houses in 1919 and 1920; (*b*) £14,000,000 further subsidies for these houses, to cover loss of economic rent.
2. Training and apprenticeship: £3,500,000.
3. Roads: first year, £30,000,000, plus £1,000,000 for land reclamation, and £6,000,000 to train ex-officers. A total of £37,000,000 to follow up his and Smuts's interim report of 14 November, which Addison had thought was *already* endorsed.
4. Adult education: £170,000 in addition to Fisher's funds.
5. Forestry: for ten years, £2,357,000, followed by £5,917,000 for the next decade.
6. Out-of-work donation: between £20,000,000 and £30,000,000.
7. War gratuities for warrant officers and other ranks: £80,000,000.

55. G. 233, Cab. 24/5.

It was all highly provisional. Costs were not reckoned for the Ministry of Health. Estimates were impossible for the Development Commission, electric power, aid to special industries, repatriation of Dominion workers, grants for veterans' civil liabilities, for officers' war gratuities, and for the Ministry of Munitions. These eight items might greatly alter the totals. Even so, the minimal figures reached £148,917,000. The value of Addison's tabulation was lessened by the fact that the recommendations of his Financial Risks Committee were not available. Their views on excess profits tax, if adopted, could affect revenue decidedly, forcing retrenchment throughout the reconstruction budget. To add to the uncertainty, there was the Treasury pressure for economy. An attempt to cut costs had already been made with the Treasury. The road program was reduced with an unspoken prayer that unemployment would be small; and the entire list of costs had been ratified only with the Treasury proviso that figures were maxima, not to be spent unless exigencies required it. Erosion had started.[56]

Smuts's committee was becoming a mirror of the worries of a bedeviled government. It is well to follow their sessions, in all their variety, through the next few days. On 4 December, Stephenson Kent told the committee about the fearful pressures on him as Director-General of Civil Demobilisation.

> The principal trouble he had to contend with was the deputations of disgruntled munition workers which arrived at Richmond Terrace. The chief grievance of these workers was that no consideration had been given to their claim for turning munition factories into peace factories. . . . Another factor which contributed to the dangerous state of affairs which now existed was that the out-of-work donation was not considered enough. . . . On the other hand, Ireland had said the whole unemployment donation scheme was a failure owing to the fact that everyone there would endeavour to be unemployed. . . . the Government should make a statement guaranteeing that manufacturers would find a market for their goods, or at any rate that their stocks would be absorbed, and the manufacturers would not be the losers. This would greatly ease the situation. . . . It had been expected the cotton industry would absorb a large number of the women munition-workers. The contrary had been the case, and a deadlock [was] reached in that

56. G.T. 6277a (3 December 1918), Cab. 24/69.

industry between employers and employed. The employers had been asked to give a 40 per cent. rise on a falling market.

Sir James Stevenson had a recommendation that stood out for its sheer unacceptability.

> If only the workpeople would realise it, the quickest way to transform the munition factories into producing peace articles was to discharge the workers now. There was no known way of doing this without a certain amount of unemployment. He was being pressed to continue the manufacture of useless munitions in order not to create unemployment. . . . The unemployment donation should be increased. Real unemployment had not started yet, but would be at its worst between the 15th January and the 15th March. They had therefore six weeks in which to put their house in order.

The entire matter was simply referred, that day, but the session decided several other matters. It made up its mind on machinery to speed the departmental liquidation of contracts and to help with the absorption of labor. It rejected Duckham's idea of a separate industrial demobilization committee but it voted to put him and Inchcape in charge of a subcommittee. This "permanent subcommittee" was to have an executive staff. Inchcape, for the Treasury, proposed allowing issues of fresh capital as aids to the Local Government Board, to electricity programs, and to roadbuilding, which the committee gladly accepted on 5 December.[57]

The next day, under strong cabinet pressure to produce recommendations, Smuts's group again wrestled with the topic of "unemployment donations"—or tried to. For all its earnestness, the session rambled: a testimony to the perplexities of the day, and to the interdependence of all reconversion. Symonds pushed Local Government Board problems to the fore. While yesterday's approval for local loans would help, outright subsidy to housing was also needed—and he stressed the relation of this idea to the topic of the day, suggesting that it "would be better that the money should be spent on these objectives" rather than go to increase the unemployment donation. Then it was Stevenson's turn to raise another close-linked question. Government was continuing to produce; if this did not stop, more would be paid to employers than would be spent for the unemployed. It was a revealing comment. Even those agreed on the value of economy could not agree on *how* to economize. On the official topic of the agenda, rough proposals were at hand, drawn from Addison's G.T.

57. D.C. meetings of 4 and 5 December 1918, Cab. 27/41.

6047: a weekly allowance of 24 shillings for men, with comparable allowances for women and juveniles. But this improvised suggestion roused objection from departments with more complicated long-matured plans, as all improvisations did. The National Insurance Commission had a different plan; the Ministry of Labour saw peril, in Addison's suggestion, to its future scheme, which would be *contributory*; and the Treasury of course wanted economy and clung to "deterrence" philosophies. Recent action made things worse: The Committee of Production had just awarded 5 shillings more for men in industry, thus compromising the 24-shilling standard by which Addison sought to show generosity and good faith. Vague approval for an increase was voted.[58] Then, midway in their business, Smuts's group adjourned.

But most of the members convened again that same Friday afternoon, at 10 Downing Street for the cabinet session. The cabinet's agenda were huge: work schemes (approved straightaway), army demobilization, out-of-work donation, priority licenses, elections, and police action (to cope with processions of munitions workers that were crowding into Richmond Terrace and Downing Street). And the eight-hour-day demand had got on the agenda; the unions' ferocity had paid handsomely. The Prime Minister, long voluble on Bolshevism, now lectured on a different theme.

> The public were coming to the conclusion that it was a question not whether the men could stand the physical strain of a longer day, but that the working classes were entitled to the same sort of leisure as the middle classes. The workmen said that they were not going to be working machines but that they required time to enjoy life as well.

Should the eight-hour day for railwaymen, then, be accepted? At the very least, acquiescence in their demand would cost £20,000,000. Objecters stressed that if the question had been presented directly to the private railway firms, implying that the cost must be met from their private resources and revenues, the firms would have been forced to reject the idea at once; for, to meet the extra cost, 40 per cent would have had to be added to their freight charges. The fact that the question was instead posed for the state made an important difference (state control, then as later, eased concessions by permitting costs to be spread). Eric Geddes totaled up the actual cost: with the £50,000,000 pay increases actually granted in war, this eight-hour day would amount to a 150 per cent

58. D.C. meeting (6 December 1918), Cab. 27/41.

gain, over prewar income, for railway workers. But the railwaymen won. The War Cabinet accepted the eight-hour day for them, in principle. Then the cabinet turned to the agenda heaped before them. "The position of releasing men from the army was very unsatisfactory," Lloyd George began.

> We had in France an army of 2,000,000 men, and at the outside 300,000 of these men were required for the army of occupation in Germany. He would like to know what steps were being taken in order to demobilise the remainder at the earliest possible moment.
>
> General Smuts said that authority had been given for demobilisers and pivotal men to be released up to the number of 150,000. This number was in addition to the coal miners ordered to be released.
>
> The Prime Minister said that in spite of the fact that authority had been given for the release of these men, his information was that this was taking place only in very small numbers. If these men could be brought home, peace industries could be started immediately.

The ministers' comments and responses were only marginally helpful. Stephenson Kent identified transport in France as the limiting factor; it held returns to 700 per day. Weir reported he had demobilized air cadets on his own responsibility. Smuts showed that the "slip men" policy, soon to be odious, was in operation. As he explained it, "An agreement had been arrived at with the Army Council by which officers and men who had prewar employment waiting for them, or whose training had been interrupted, should be demobilised at the earliest possible moment, in addition to the pivotal men."

Since the armistice, only 50,000 men had been demobilized, and dispersal stations were still unopened. Stephenson Kent explained the delays best.

> The Ministry of Labour had only had permission to set up the machinery for releasing the pivotal men at the end of October, and the names of the pivotal men required by the different employers were only just beginning to come in now. We had suffered from endeavouring to keep down the peace atmosphere of the nation until the armistice was signed.

The technique of delegation, therefore, was given another try. The Demobilisation Committee was voted "authority to deal with the question," with "full powers to give orders on behalf of the War Cabinet."

Next on the agenda came the out-of-work donation, which was swiftly decided. If the Chancellor of the Exchequer concurred, a raise would be given, of not over 5 shillings. Then priority licenses. Many ministers felt abolition would help. Addison "understood that the trade had plenty of orders which they could execute as soon as licenses affecting materials were withdrawn." Symonds suggested that abolition of licenses would speed production of items for Local Government Board housing. The Demobilisation Committee accordingly was given power "to cancel trade licenses, when and where they thought fit." In these two cases the cabinet had given specific answers, beneficial presumably to reconversion and reconstruction alike.[59]

The decisions of 6 December. Back in session again that afternoon, the Demobilisation Committee followed these clear signals from the cabinet. It approved abolition, with Addison's consent, of priority regulations for manufacture. It approved relaxation of import and export bans, and—in the spirit of simplifying and reducing control—it ratified Addison's plan to combine all priority departments (save for Building Licenses) under the Board of Trade.

How important were these decisions of 6 December? Had Smuts's committee dealt a death blow to lasting prosperity and to reform? What it had done looked simple: a step toward unification, and two partial modifications of systems that in any case had been shaped by war conditions and needs. No general decision for total decontrol had been proposed, much less adopted. But did not this small cluster of decisions imperil the whole future of controls and put all reconstruction in danger? There is reason to think so.

For one thing, there was contemporary protest. The Standing Council on Post-War Priority charged that, in the relaxation of export bans, an essential safeguard—indeed the only one now workable—had been omitted. By voicing a critique, the Standing Council alerts us to the possibility that a major blunder had occurred. But even where the Council did not protest, there are grounds for suspicion. In the conditions which the Council and all others accepted, two dangerous flaws were revealed: the outright impossibility, as men then saw it, of perpetuating the existing controls in their wartime form, and the serious lack of any complete schedule of peacetime priorities. The criticism and the general discussion call for thorough examination.

But in advance of detailed analysis, an abstract comment is necessary. Logically the wartime system of controls, it seems, should not have been

59. WC 510 (6 December 1918), Cab. 23/8.

abandoned even in part—whatever its faults—until a true and effective substitute had replaced it. Logic alone, not even to speak of the eloquent lessons of wartime experience, would seem to dictate that some system of controls should always be in effect.

Did cabinet and committee ignore this logic (if it be logic) and consciously throw away the chance for retaining any controls whatsoever, thus deciding a general and fateful question within the form of decisions on mere detail? In retrospect it strongly appears that this was the result. There was no such vote, however; on the contrary, the decisions of 6 December nominally left a body of controls in existence, transferring them for simpler administration to the Board of Trade—a consolidation of authority which, if proving anything, proves the desire to make controls effective. There was then no intent to settle the permanent question of general controls, there and then; the logic of retention was not ignored. Wormald, a manufacturer who worked closely with the Ministry of Munitions, stressed that the government should reserve the right to confer priority on any contract "in the national interest." The Deputy Controller of that ministry's Priority Department acknowledged that "in many trades no postwar priority is necessary," but he added "this is no ground for abolishing priority altogether."[60] Given these pronouncements of December 1918, how can one account for what may have been a tragic misstep?

The men who acted in December 1918—even those who saw the crucial importance of retaining some controls for the sake of reconstruction —can be understood best if we realize that they were moved by other, and narrower, thoughts. First, they wished to expedite recovery and therefore wished to speed revival of overseas trade; concentrating on this smaller and more concrete goal, they were willing to make an exception for the sake of export in the general fabric of restriction, especially since most of them felt that basic controlling authority was retained. Second, they agreed with the widespread view that the form and complexity of existing export bans and systems of priority precluded a simple continuance of the wartime methods. Thus they did not approach the question of modification fearfully as one might today, avoiding any change that might undermine the ultimate capacity to control. To them modification was commercially beneficial, pragmatically necessary, and safe.

The Standing Council dissented from none of this thinking in principle. It agreed that export bans should be partially relaxed, within a system of residual controls. Accepting the view that exports should be allowed, save

60. G.P. 6 and G.P. 7 (13 December 1918), Cab. 33/23.

where military reasons or shortages forbade, the Council had indeed tailored its recommendations to allow for this purpose—thus falling in with a tendency that it could not control. But the Standing Council had a distinctive viewpoint on the *type* of controls that might work. The Council contended that, in relaxing imports while retaining control in the form of a *priority* system, the cabinet and the Demobilisation Committee had overlooked the question of effectiveness. It was a technical impossibility to rely on *wartime* priority or allocation devices, because many materials had now been released; and it was on governmental control of materials that the wartime systems depended. Furthermore, a prerequisite essential to the working of any priority system was lacking: a prepared set of peacetime priorities, worked out with due attention to the purposes of business, relief, and reform. Only this would solve questions of precedence. The Standing Council had been meant to devise this but had never done so; the armistice, as noted, had come before it buckled down to work. Here was a crippling handicap, just in itself. Therefore the Council had proposed an alternative: devolution of the task of supervision, onto industry. "The essential needs of this country can be met ... if it is left to Traders and Manufacturers voluntarily to regulate the order of production and distribution on certain general lines ... already promulgated ... by the Ministry of Reconstruction."

Over this alternative system, the Standing Council would stand guard. The Council pledged to secure manufacturers' voluntary adherence to an order of precedence in production. Moreover, for safety's sake it wished the official 1917 "Order as to Priority" to be kept, along with the apparatus of export licenses. This much of the Standing Council's proposal had been accepted by Smuts's committee (sufficient proof that they did not join any stampede for decontrol).[61] But the Standing Council also wished one further element of control. It wished to keep in its own hands all specific decisions on import and export; such power would be subject only to the Post-War Priorities Committee. In the Council's view this safeguard was crucial. But it was this last element that had been omitted by the decisions of 6 December.

In summary, it appears that fate either put desirable options out of reach or dealt harshly with those that remained. The best system was not in readiness; the next best—the existing wartime system—was not acceptable, for plausible enough reasons; the makeshift which the Standing Council offered, a system utilizing business groups, would have been

61. D.C. meeting (6 December 1918), Box 78, Part 2; see D.C. Memorandum 31 by Standing Council on Postwar Priority.

very imperfect; and even that makeshift was weakened by the decision actually made. The whole episode shows that the future of control was handicapped by the absence of an agreed broad system of detailed priorities, by the very weakness of substitutes proposed, and by the narrow concentration of ministers on the revival of trade.

The above analysis suggests, but does not demonstrate, that a major blunder had occurred. The future of controls may, or may not, have been damaged beyond repair. The presumption is that these changes were decidedly harmful; for Birchenough had made it clear in November that proper handling of materials shortages depended upon supervision by a "very strong Priority Council" which he had thought was being set up; and Addison had counted, in his fight for Carmichael's licensing plan, on the Post-War Priorities Committee and its Council to maintain precedence. Disruption could not be to the good.

Whether or not one can be certain about the impact of these events on future controls, it was perfectly clear that the future of the Standing Council itself was bleak. Reduced to errand-boy status from the moment of its birth, it had bid for a major role, and had lost. Devolution had also lost again. At once the Board of Trade, drawing into its orbit all the priority departments, took the logical next step: it offered the Standing Council a place on the new Import-Export Advisory Council of the Board. If the Standing Council had any representations to make, it could make them there. Gardiner voiced the alarm in the Ministry of Reconstruction: "The Standing Council and its policy will be absolutely at the mercy of the Board of Trade." Addison protested to the Demobilisation Committee:

> The Board of Trade may propose to relax restrictions . . . which the Council consider imperative. . . . They desire to be assured that in such circumstances the prohibitions will not be relaxed until they shall have an opportunity of laying a note of their objections before the Demobilisation Committee.

There was no reply.

For the Standing Council, by which Addison had set such great store, December did not pronounce irrevocable doom; the possibility still seemed open that it might find a lasting and significant role. Premonitions did not turn into dismal certainties for it until January—when it became clear that the Council was ignored and impotent, and when the Board of Trade showed that it had no intent of using such priority powers as it had been given.[62] But for other schemes that Addison cherished, December was not so merciful.

Background for three defeats. The Demobilisation Committee became something like a place of execution for his plans; and Addison in retrospect viewed Smuts's successor—Eric Geddes—as the executioner. More than a change of persons was involved. There was "a clamour for dramatic things" at election time, he recalled. The times required Geddes to play the part, "not of an economist, but a hustler."[63]

Certainly there was clamor—and for good reason; but it had its ironic side. Although Addison subsequently deplored it, much of the cry in that month for speedy resolute action paid tribute to him and his staff. Colleagues were now repeating his arguments, at last recognizing their soundness. The trouble was that in December the argument for speed jeopardized his, and all other, matured and complicated plans.

Had Addison been content with the pleasure of implied compliment and imitation, December's arguments would have given him much ground to feel vindicated. Who had said, more emphatically than Addison and his ministry's staff, that the workers feared a long period of joblessness which would be "used to reduce wages" when the existing act lapsed? The reconstruction officials had been the first to call for short time, greater unemployment donations, and the use of national factories in peacetime work. But now these were the words of Stephenson Kent; it was Kent who flourished memoranda while the government delayed. Kent had become transmitter of labor views—demanding speedier action on industrial training (a potent cause of unrest), denouncing the deadlock on pledges (still a factor), looking to industrial councils for ultimate solutions —who also reported business difficulties. Few trades, he declared, were ready to absorb workers, and buyers were reluctant to buy at the top of a falling market. Kent became the voice of financial daring, declaring there was no alternative to government-financed stockpiling. "It is impracticable for the Government to withdraw its support from industry at this moment; the risk . . . is too great." Hesitation "might very easily bring about a social upheaval, and unemployment would not be tolerated." The government must subsidize manufacturers who produced for inventory and allow liberal depreciation allowances as a credit against the excess

62. Files 11061 and 11131, Box 52. For Birchenough's comment, see "Advisory Council. Meeting of Chairmen. Note XXIII" (4 November 1918), F. 6813, Box 90, Part 3; for Addison's stress on the Standing Council, see D.C. 29 (3 December 1918), Cab. 27/42. For comment by Charles Merz on Board of Trade intentions in January 1919, see Cab. 33/1.

63. Addison, *Politics*, 2: 213, 219.

profits duty. Kent even echoed Addison's year-long plea for a general body to coordinate all reconversion processes, and particularly to help firms liquidate their contracts and readapt.

But the problem of unemployment, and the fury of the jobless, brought him to desperation. Things had come to such a pass at Kent's office that his most difficult problem was not the workers' grievances but the number of workers' delegations that came to voice them. They simply made it impossible to do any work. Worse yet, they exposed a series of unresolved and nearly insoluble conflicts. Skilled unions wanted their prewar jobs and practices; veterans wanted guaranteed jobs, and *veterans' preference* for the very jobs that were covered by the pledges. There was also a deadlock on the terms of work. Many employers refused to reduce working hours and clung to "payment by results." Workers insisted on shorter hours and—with Kent's help—fought to reverse the wartime system and revert to time work. On national factories, Kent marveled at the "diametrically opposed points of view."

> The workpeople feel that the State is a better employer than the private manufacturer and protest with vigour against being turned out of Government employment when a demand exists for . . . which the National Factories . . . could well be adapted. . . . The confidence of the manufacturing community will be seriously shaken and private enterprise will be checked if there is any prospect of Government competition on a large scale.

He clutched at the hope of a middle course—temporary use of the factories—as had been asked two months earlier by Addison (as Kent had noted).[64]

Kent's arguments were reasonable and rested on solid fact; they pointed to genuine problems; they restated the case for promptness, which Addison had long ago had to present without such eloquent support. If the vindication of Addison and his arguments, alone, had been at stake, then all of Kent's agitation would have been to the good. Addison might have rejoiced that his nominee for the Director-General's position was repeating his arguments and citing his memoranda. But the agitation was turning into a critique of Addison's own proposals. The argument for speed told against his plans, and specifically against Carmichael's plan for handling building materials.

Housing plans attacked. If Stephenson Kent saw few solutions to most dilemmas, of one step Kent was sure: The Carmichael committee's plans

64. G.T. 6479, Cab. 24/71.

must be scrapped. For one thing, he said, the proposed forty-five-man Central Building Industry Committee was "not suited to the exercise of executive functions" and would take many weeks, if not months, to set up. Carmichael's plan looked good on paper: a thoroughly representative body to reorganize the trade, stimulate the output of materials, allocate them, issue building permits, control timber and bricks. It was all too complex, and Kent offered an alternative. A simple priority system, said Kent, would halt any price rise. The need for making jobs *now* was paramount.

> The whole of the building license restrictions should be abandoned immediately and . . . the only control . . . should be . . . of the principal building materials. . . . We run a serious risk of reducing the amount of labour which can be employed during the transition period. . . . There is no other trade or industry capable of affecting the employment market in the immediate future to anything like the same extent as the building trade, and . . . all branches of this industry should be restored to their full development as rapidly as possible.

Addison, Rowntree, and Nash had seen this point long ago, which now was being turned against them. Unfortunately, to men in a hurry Kent made sense. Carmichael envisioned a special permit and committee system, along with detailed tenders and plans (how could a system be kept *under control*, and aimed steadily at building *workers'* houses, otherwise?); but this complication would "restrict general demands in order to meet a special building programme which may never materialise; . . . a multiplicity of comparatively small contracts will be held up all over the country, and these are the best, and indeed the only immediate, cure for unemployment." With 10,600 building-trade workers out of jobs, with brickyards being closed down and brick production 60 per cent down from prewar averages, Kent redoubled his pleas and asked for guarantees of brick prices. He quoted the unions themselves for *unrestricted* resumption of building.[65] Here was the crux: a campaign *to house workers* was pledged and planned, but the impressive need of the moment was to *employ* workers, on *any* kind of building and in fact on any job at all. It was the dilemma of 1919, the tragedy of 1920.

Another colleague, and a distinguished reformer at that, spoke out against Carmichael's plan. H. Llewellyn Smith—long the friend of Nash and currently secretary at the Board of Trade—joined the opposition. "It

65. Kent's D.C. 39 (27 November 1918) and D.C. 40 (14 December 1918).

would be wise to suspend the granting of permits or priority certificates for buildings or building materials altogether," rather than maintain the entire priority machinery to cover a small percentage of work. Smith, working with the momentum of recent simplifications and knowing the mood of the harassed, overworked Demobilisation Committee, suggested that the question of authority for licensing be allowed to solve itself: "There will be no such licenses." More positively, he favored retaining timber and brick price controls and reserving the right to resume priority controls. He offered his department and the aid of a full, expert staff to other departments in promoting materials output.[66]

With Smuts's support, Addison began "a passionate fight" for the Carmichael plan—but with leaden heart. He knew that the government, because of delays at the Local Government Board, was in a weak position to resist the clamor of firms that wanted materials immediately. Either the government must vindicate its claims to priority for workers' public housing, by proving its readiness and capacity to use materials at once, or it must yield to those who could say "We are ready to use the material, the Government is not." And the government was not ready. Furthermore, he felt he could count on little help from personnel at the Local Government Board, still resentful of his fight against Hayes Fisher—a fight that he had felt bound to wage, for the sake of housing. Unpreparedness, that general danger against which he had warned, now was hurting the program about which he cared the most. He must, however, do the best possible. He knew that Carmichael's group did not view the licensing system as a detail, but as fundamental—"a *sine qua non* of efficient control under the new organization proposed." Addison, who characteristically overrated the power of factual argument, sent in one memorandum of his own and then set Carmichael's group to work on 10 December. They soon offered a compromise: houses that cost up to £1,000 might be built without a license. They pleaded with interrogators—Chapman of the Board of Trade, and men from the Demobilisation Committee—that their Central Committee would work quickly, through existing agencies. As for proposed regional committees, a key point and perhaps a wise one, but vulnerable, these could be set up in a month. By 17 December belated rejoinders had been cranked out at Queen Anne's Gate, thanks to Garrod and Carmichael. Garrod authored several compromises: automatic approval below £1,000; unlicensed maintenance and repair work; a time limit of a fortnight on scrutiny of applications by the regional committee, approval to be automatic thereafter; concurrent scrutiny by the regional committee and the

66. D.C. Memorandum 38 (13 December 1918).

local authority, to save time. Garrod tried to reassure Addison: Carmichael's committee gave employment a paramount place and built the local employment exchanges into its regional bodies; hence "the idea of delay seems to me a bogey." Everything Kent wanted could be done within Carmichael's scheme, he said. Carmichael's revised proposals went a long way "to meet Sir Stephenson Kent's difficulty with regard to employment which may well prove the determining factor in reaching a decision about the Carmichael Committee."[67]

Workers' jobs or workers' houses? Here was the problem of the government in a nutshell, and the menace to two years of reconstruction work. Kent, Churchill, Smith, Roberts, Stanley—and Addison himself—had created an atmosphere of alarm and haste, and it was in such an atmosphere that the fate of carefully laid plans would be decided. Roberts had already felt the pressures, when a snap judgment on the unemployment donation undercut his ministry's campaign. Addison still smarted over setbacks on raw materials and the Standing Council. When the demand was increasingly strong for the quick solution and the simple answer, his work was in jeopardy. Ignorance was on the aggressive against knowledge: men who did not know what many months of study had disclosed were rushing to decree answers because they could not afford to neglect any aid against unemployment.

Housing Plans Defeated

Carmichael covered ten pages with the case for building licenses and permits. The permit system

> would prevent undue raising of prices by unnecessary competition for materials; . . . would secure the fullest . . . employment of building labour by close touch with local Labour exchanges; . . . is designed to adapt itself to varying conditions in all localities; by decentralisation . . . would cause the most extensive local interest in saving unnecessary transport . . . and developing local resources; . . . could be set up and operate within 4 weeks.

The building industry wished and approved his system: "This in fact is the only form of control they will willingly submit to." The alternative "free list" system, favored by Smith and Kent, would in Carmichael's view precipitate

> a scramble for uncontrolled materials and prices would increase enormously. Labour unrest, due to suspicion of profiteering would

67. Addison, *Politics*, 2: 219; and his D.C. 29 (3 December 1918), Cab. 27/42.

follow, and the industry as a whole would be convulsed, and the object aimed at—full employment—might not be attained. We understand control of bricks, cement and timber only is proposed. Prices of all other materials would tend to rise, say 15/ or 20/ at least before control would likely to be imposed. Should these conditions mature it would increase the cost of a workman's cottage costing today £500 by £25 to £30, or 4d. to 6d. additional weekly rent, or put another way—for 300,000 cottages, an extra cost of $7\frac{1}{2}$ to 9 million pounds. The complaint of the system of permit by license . . . during the War results from the requirement of license plus priority, plus control of materials, plus centralisation. Our proposals involve no priority of materials, but decentralisation with consequent local incentive to local production.

Garrod and Addison recognized that here was a test case for the philosophy of devolution. Carmichael had spoken with almost naive trust:

The best machinery . . . was thought to be . . . a body representative of the whole Building Industry of the country. It was thought that this proposal was in consonance with the expressed Cabinet policy that the guidance and control of the various industries should be left as much as possible to the representatives of the industries concerned.

And Addison's basic strategy of reliance on self-restraint and long-term wisdom in industry, here supported by the industry's own clear choice, also was at stake.

The Building Industry is extremely anxious that prices should not soar to undue heights, with the consequent unrest and dislocation. While removal of all measures of control might operate favourably for a short time in high prices and high profits, the Building Industry prefers to take a longer view and to have a reasonable measure of regularisation to tide it over the transition period. It is also anxious that the whole resources of the country should not, on account of high prices, be restricted to Government subsidised operation. It feels that, if all measure of regulation is removed, prices will be extremely high, and that the only works which may be able to proceed will be Government Subsidised operations. It fears that the result of this may be an enormous and unnecessary sacrifice of the Government subsidies, and the leaving of the Building Industry thereafter in a state of chaos and unrest.[68]

68. Addison, *Diary*, 2: 597; F. 11007, Box 35; F. 10661, Box 30, Part 3; D.C. 42.

By 20 December Addison had approved circulation of the memorandum. But that same Friday the cause was lost. The Demobilisation Committee studied memoranda from Kent and from H. L. Smith, but not Carmichael's paper; it merely heard Carmichael briefly on the industry's fear of shortages and high prices. Then "Mr. Churchill advocated sweeping away the impediments which confronted anyone who wanted to build, but . . . suggested a maximum price . . . for bricks." Addison, weakly, commented that he had attended a meeting of the Central Materials Supply Committee, and "was impressed with the unanimous opinion of that body that some sort of control should still be exercised. For this reason he hesitated to advocate the withdrawal of all restrictions." Geddes' Demobilisation Committee voted removal of "all existing restrictions on building" but continuance of government control of prices for bricks, cement, and timber.[69]

Other housing items were on the agenda for 20 December, but to Addison nothing compared with the defeat of Carmichael's plan. Years later he described the scene.

> Every one of us who knew anything about the subject vehemently protested. Carmichael was almost in tears and prophesied with literal accuracy what would happen. . . . I have scarcely known anything which created more widespread disgust than this reckless scrapping of all the arrangements Carmichael had made for fostering local production all over the country.[70]

In retrospect, the defeat seems more a symbol of volcanic forces at work than a deathblow to housing. It is possible to see much else in the meeting of 20 December—things both better and worse than the one episode that dismayed Addison and Carmichael. In a second decision, the Demobilisation Committee on that day empowered the Ministry of Munitions to place large orders for bricks, for the government's use. This was surely a gain. In a third decision, it decided the terms of state aid to housing built by local authorities. That decision, only slightly discussed at the time, has been famous ever since; for it established the formula of the "penny-rate" limit on the costs that the local authorities must bear.

Ever since, the formula has been criticized; but, even before the criticism can be understood, the general background of public housing finance must be explained. Public housing then and later involved a

69. D.C. meeting (20 December 1918), Box 78.
70. Addison, *Politics*, 2: 219, and *Diary*, 2: 597.

partnership, with both the state—that is, the Treasury—and the local authority bearing portions of the cost. For each partner, the coming housing campaign would involve additional costs: the Treasury must find additional money by loans or taxes, the local authorities must obtain the money by increasing the rates on local property. The proportion, to which the local authority must raise its rates so as to pay its share for the houses built in its area, would depend on a formula devised by the government. The "penny-rate" limit put a ceiling on that local proportion—an absolute limit stated in money terms, that is, not proportional to the costliness of the houses. This "penny-rate" formula assured the local authorities that the government would pay any cost, beyond the amount that would be produced locally by raising rates "one penny in the pound." The formula was a flat, unconditional and seemingly permanent guarantee to a local authority and to its rate-paying residents that their financial burden would be both predictable and light.

Two and one-half years later, when the concern for economy reached its heights, critics in 1921 denounced this formula as a witless concession to imprudence and as a virtual invitation to extravagance and poor management; as they saw it, it removed all incentives to economy and sent housing costs soaring. Then and earlier the Treasury flinched at this limitless claim on the Exchequer. Moreover, the critics blamed Addison for this extravagance; and they associated him with the folly of the "penny-rate" formula. On this charge, more than anything else, Addison was driven from office in 1921.

Now it is true that the penny-rate formula, adopted on 20 December 1918, was carried over in 1919 into the Housing Act—an act known to history as "the Addison Act." In that legitimate sense, he is linked with the formula. But he was not its author, and the financial terms which he favored for housing were those which Rowntree had drafted, with their built-in safeguards for economy and careful management.

Rather—to return to the session of 20 December—it was the President of the Local Government Board, Sir Auckland Geddes, who moved the fateful proviso that "the burden on the local authorities . . . be limited in all cases to the produce of a 1d. rate, any deficit in excess of this being a charge upon the Exchequer."[71] Geddes patently thought that nothing less than this generous guarantee would thaw the icy reluctance of town and county councils around the nation. Not anticipating the outcry of 1921, some observers looked on it as the happy culmination of the trend that

71. G.T. 6497 (December 1918), Cab. 24/71; D.C. meeting (20 December).

Nash had started, in Asquith's time. On 20 December the proposal passed without a single recorded dissent.

A Fortnight of Defeats

Two days before Carmichael met defeat the Home Affairs Committee had awakened long enough to thwart another long-matured Addison plan. The successful rival, a £20,000,000 scheme for land purchases for resettling ex-servicemen, involved different financing: outright purchase, not lease. In November Prothero had nearly stampeded the cabinet into this choice with the simple argument that there was no time to get enough land, quickly enough, any other way. "The guarantee of a large sum now was the only thing which could save what now amounted to an emergency situation." Trying a second time, he finally convinced the Home Affairs Committee in December that the state should buy land outright. It seemed a triumph for boldness and fulfillment, but Addison opposed it to the last (in odd company with the conservative chairman, Lord Cave, and the Treasury) not because economy was an end in itself but because eventually *others* would think so. "As people came to realise our straitened financial position, the movement would be brought to a stop." Realistic foresight had dictated his own plan, for the payment of small rent charges. "We went out of our way to provide against a time of postwar reaction by designing a scheme which would enormously diminish the capital commitments." Ever afterward this episode, which "effectually torpedoed . . . hard work by practical men," epitomized for Addison "the clamour for dramatic things at the General Election in December." [72]

To Addison, who loved the land, this was not minor. Nor did he underrate the harm Llewellyn Smith had done the Standing Council. This priority body, a fledgling, was no match for the Board of Trade at any time; now even the Demobilisation Committee favored the Board, not the Council, as the heir to priority powers. Addison knew the Council had been overrun by events at its birth. Thomas Gardiner told the story.

> One of the tasks entrusted to the Council on its inception was "To survey the existing machinery of . . . allocation and control of materials, and see . . . what modifications are desirable, and to what extent Government controls may be devolved upon organisations of the Trades themselves." The sudden cessation of hostilities

72. Addison, *Diary*, 2: 599; *Politics*, 2: 213–14; G.T. 6373, Cab. 24/70, citing G. 225, in Cab. 24/5. Addison in July 1921 clarified the origins of the "penny-rate" formula, reminding Commons of the alternative that his ministry had originally preferred; see *P.D.(C.)*, 144: c. 2498–99.

precluded even a preliminary survey of the situation, and the Council gave directions through the Departments concerned that the various Control Boards, etc., should continue to operate for the time being but should deal as sympathetically as the circumstances permitted with individual applications for materials. . . .

. . . It was . . . decided to concentrate attention on increasing the shipping facilities available for the importation of raw materials of which the shortage was acute.

In December the Standing Council was reduced to writing the departments to ask what controls the departments exercised! It also tried for the last time to assert a role, informing all controls that

an effort should now be made to deal with . . . supply on a broader basis and they desire each 'Control' forthwith to get into touch with trade bodies representative of each industry which absorbs a substantial proportion of the materials . . . controlled, . . . ascertaining whether the needs of each Trade are supplied. . . . You should as a first step call a conference at an early date of the representatives of those Industrial Councils . . . and Interim Industrial Reconstruction Committees referred to on the accompanying list . . . the Board of Trade, the Ministry of Labour, and the Ministry of Reconstruction should be invited to attend any conference that may be arranged. . . .

Departments and controls simply shrugged off Gardiner's request. Or else they claimed to be in touch, already, with the kind of representative council that Gardiner had named; indeed in one case the control itself now claimed to have superseded the trade committee. Plainly, power now lay with the departments. The responses also suggested that decontrol had begun to defeat the Ministry of Reconstruction's purposes: one control agency explained that it would no longer consult Whitley Councils *because control would end soon*, and therefore "no useful purpose would be served." Departmentalism and decontrol were rising as the Standing Council and devolution sank.

The Council had other troubles, derived from the reshuffling of cabinet-level committees in December. It was to have been linked with the Post-War Priorities Committee of the cabinet itself, and might thus have gained authority. But that parent committee was dissolved early in December, and the Council was put under the Demobilisation Committee, which had just gained a new chairman, Sir Eric Geddes, who seemingly knew little about the Council. Meanwhile the Demobilisation Committee had tentatively set up an operative council of its own. Swift positive action might have solved this problem; but action was slow, and when it came was negative.[73]

Meanwhile matters more weighty than the fate of two new committees were at stake. By now, deeds as well as delay had produced evil as well as good. Would action speed the work or harm it? Would action be postponed, once more?

Assessment amid Changes

To follow the action on housing, land-settlement, and the Standing Council, we have moved far into December, departing from strict sequence. We have seen that these events, and the general context of impatience, raised major questions. The answers to those questions lay in Downing Street and Whitehall Gardens, at the very center of government. To the center, and to the earlier days of December, we must therefore return. The election campaign, beginning in November, continued to dominate the first two weeks of December. Polling took place on 14 December. Ballots from servicemen kept coming in for a fortnight, however, and it was not until 28 December that the huge electoral triumph for the Coalition—and especially for the Conservatives within it—became known. Meanwhile the cabinet met, on 17 and 19 December; and the Demobilisation Committee, now under Geddes, met on 20 December in a session that we have studied only so far as housing was concerned. These three sessions, which have bypassed or examined only in part, must now be looked into.

The cabinet, on 17 December, toyed with the problem of demobilization. Smuts had resigned as chairman of the Demobilisation Committee. Lloyd George fumbled with the question of finding a successor; his own idea was "to have some one person appointed . . . to act as the co-ordinating centre of the Government's policy, . . . to have supreme authority within the limits of certain main principles" laid down by the War Cabinet. The difficulty was that "no one person seemed to be in complete touch with the whole problem." Churchill objected that

> there were serious objections to the appointment of any one
> Minister in a position to give orders to other Ministers and

73. D.C. meeting (6 December 1918), Box 78, Part 2; D.C. Memorandum 31; Smith's D.C. Memorandum 33, Box 78, Part 1; Addison to committee, 17 December 1918, Cab. 27/42; F. 10464, Box 52. For a summary of changes at cabinet level, see memoranda of 13 November and 10 December 1918 in Cab. 33/3.

Departments. Such a system would tend to weaken Ministerial responsibility. It would be preferable to have a Cabinet Committee of four or five Ministers drawn from the Departments specially involved in demobilisation, with a chairman. . . . Inasmuch as principles of high policy were involved, . . . Underneath this Cabinet Committee would be a Committee of Experts. He was not sure that the War Cabinet fully appreciated the extent and number of the decisions already taken.

Addison and Churchill, convinced that prices were the dilemma of the moment, came to the same conclusion: unforeseen financial risks must be faced, and nowhere but at the top. Addison said

> the problem was not merely or mainly administrative, but financial. Manufacturers were holding back because of the uncertainty as regards prices and the fear of having presently to unload their goods on a falling market. . . . Some issues raised far-reaching questions of political principle which could only be decided by the War Cabinet. . . . Rendering financial assistance to manufacturers prepared to work to stock was one of these.

Churchill too favored government subsidy to firms that were willing, under the current adverse circumstances, to produce for inventory. But Lloyd George balked. "Was it absolutely impossible that industry should be made to work quickly on natural lines?" Kent and Symonds spoke for promptness: 10,000 men in the building trade were drawing unemployment benefits because bricks had not been ordered. The Local Government Board was preparing orders, but bricks currently cost two to three times the 1914 amount.

Two days afterwards Lloyd George had made up his mind. On 19 December he announced to the ministers that Geddes had agreed to take Smuts's post. Geddes would be

> charged with the co-ordination of the efforts of the Departments dealing with demobilisation, and would represent the War Cabinet and be armed with its authority. No doubt, in the case of any conflict of principle or large issue of disputed policy, he would bring the matter before the War Cabinet. Subject to that, he would have the same power as a representative of the Cabinet, would act in conjunction with the Departments, and consult with them with a view to complete co-ordination. It was very urgent that the machinery should be working swiftly and smoothly. There was an unjustifiable feeling abroad that demobilisation was proceeding very slowly.

Churchill's protest that work should go through the Ministry of Munitions, "the natural centre" of demobilization, failed. And so the decision stood, dissolving Smuts's committee and placing "Sir Eric Geddes, as representing and with the authority of the War Cabinet, in charge of the coordination of demobilisation and the rehabilitation of industry, with full power to take decisions on their behalf, and to summon meetings of the Heads of all Departments concerned in this question." [74]

The campaign for a powerful and single coordinator had belatedly won, but in most other ways this decision represented a loss. The change measured the government's impatience and desperation, not its wisdom. Geddes had not the same grasp as others, for all his undoubted energy and success in his field; the new system did not ensure he would be properly advised. In any case, it was a *new* system. Its lack of training, data, and understanding would soon be attested in the frenzied weeks of January and February, which would culminate in a fresh try under new leadership when recovery and troop return alike had stalled. The existing machinery suffered not merely dismantling or dismissal but disruption.

The results became clear in 1919. In December, however, Geddes acted with decision on those things he bothered to tackle. (1) Building-license proposals were dropped, as was noted above. (2) The Ministry of Munitions was empowered to order large quantities of bricks, consulting the Local Government Board first, with preference for government orders over those of private builders. (3) Auckland Geddes' proposal, limiting local authorities' housing costs to the produce of a penny rate, was approved. It was what Eric Geddes *would* do that was ambiguous. Pressures were rising fast. Already the "slip men" (veterans who had got an employer's certificate of an available job) were being granted early demobilization, a pure concession to discontent. The Federation of British Industries begged for protection, in a new tone of alarm, as a flood of American goods hit the British market. And still, as the Federation complained, no economic policy had been announced. [75] Geddes' colleagues were baffled. Two of them clashed on the idea of the swift sale of government ships. In obvious bewilderment, Clynes wrote a memorandum on "the future of food control." The ministers' confusion was one of the many uncertainties as 1918 ended. [76]

---

74. WC 512 and 513 (17 and 19 December 1918), Cab. 23/8.
75. D.C. meeting (6 December 1918); G.T. 6346 (23 November 1918), Cab. 24/70; Federation of British Industries, letter (20 December 1918) in Cab. 21/108.
76. On ships, G.T. 6543 (23 December 1918) by Maclay, and 6558 (27 December 1918) by Barnes, Cab. 24/72; on food, G.T. 6579 (1 January 1919), Cab. 24/72.

Addison tried to read the future in the election results. When the voting boxes were opened at Shoreditch town hall on Saturday, 28 December, he found he had beaten his closest opponent by 6,100 votes. But what did the national results mean? Disconcertingly, "the majority for the Coalition was greater than anyone expected and certainly more than we liked. . . . The thing I do not like is this great block of Conservatives"; but, on reflection, Addison felt "it is altogether to the good that Labour has come up so well."[77]

It also was hard to assess the present or render judgment on the past. Reconversion had been tackled manfully. The best achievements were those of the Ministry of Munitions, making emergency decisions for the gradual reduction of output, swiftly adapting its plans for iron and steel so that prices could be adjusted in stages, placing its new orders to help with employment and recovery. Of all things done in November and December, probably one single decision by Churchill—to stay in production—helped most. One cannot overemphasize this. Churchill had intended to stop production at once; his swift reversal of plan, providing continued employment at the Ministry of Munitions, may have done more than anything else to avert disaster. Decisions elsewhere, however, on other topics, were enormous helps: to permit local authorities to borrow; to keep wages at wartime level; to give, and indeed to give generously, an unemployment donation.

This donation, mentioned only briefly so far, deserves full discussion. It became at once a main prop to incomes throughout the transition crisis. By its nature and its scale (29 shillings each week), it did what no existing insurance schemes—with their weekly benefits of 7 or 11 shillings—would do. Moreover, it had a most unusual and instructive origin.

It was apparently a complete innovation. The department in charge of unemployment relief had planned nothing of the sort. The Ministry of Labour had been intent rather on broadening the established system of unemployment *insurance*. The distinction between the insurance which was planned, and the "out-of-work donation" which was improvised in the emergency, is fundamental. The insurance system would be contributory; the insured worker would pay his contribution and be entitled to benefits, while those without payments to their credit would get nothing. The donation system was non-contributory, and would be open to all discharged employees. There were important implications. The insurance system necessarily favored those who were more continuously employed,

77. Addison, *Diary*, 2: 528, 597, 602.

and had credits; the donation system helped all equally—unfair to the more skilled and the more steadily employed, perhaps, but generous to the less skilled and to the irregularly employed, which was the important thing. At the end of the war the latter category—notably the munitions workers drawn belatedly into war plants—was probably the more numerous, and certainly included those more in need of help. Those covered by insurance, moreover, tended to be the better paid; the introduction of the donation helped those with least resources. There was another vital difference: with the donation was introduced the principle of additional payments for dependents, proportional to the number of dependents. Again the effect was to render aid where need was greater.

If not planned, how had this system come into being? If insurance did not imply allowances for dependents, how had they been grafted onto the system? The answer seems to prove that the disruptive impact of war could for once be beneficial. Sir Frank Tillyard, long a civil servant with the Ministry of Labour, states that at the end of the war the Ministry of Labour still had no plan ready for civilians. Its plan for servicemen, providing both donation and allowances, had been ready for some time; the principle of a free grant had been decided in December 1915. But the armistice caught the ministry by surprise. With small staff and with numerous applications suddenly coming in for aid, it had to devise something "as simple and straightforward as possible." Thus it was quickly decided that the form and terms of aid for soldier and civilian should be basically the same; and similarly the dependents' allowances—unprecedented and illogical by the test of past law and practice—came into effect too. The civilian system was assimilated to the military model, in a pattern that prevailed to the end of civilian donation in November 1919.

Arthur Greenwood, with Addison's full support, had added emphatic words to produce this effect. Magisterially summing up the past legislation, he made six points.

1. For some ten million workers, no provision existed.
2. "To pass through Parliament a comprehensive measure of unemployment insurance, and to make the necessary administrative arrangements, would be a matter of months. . . . This method is ruled out of court . . . during the months of transition."
3. "The principle of the out-of-work donation adopted for soldiers, etc., should be extended to the civilian population, by the distribution of free policies operative in the first instance, for six months from the commencement of an armistice."

4. "Such a scheme would need to be universal. . . . Any attempt to limit it to munition workers would create insuperable practical difficulties, and public opinion would probably demand the wider scheme."

5. Precedents for allowances existed in the plan for soldiers and in the cotton industry's unemployment scheme; the allowances would prevent widespread hardships, especially if they bore— as they must—some relation to the cost of living.

6. Although the improvisation would admittedly create difficulties in the way of a general contributory scheme, nevertheless "the Government cannot face the armistice and transition periods without some such provision."

Greenwood's service is thus established beyond dispute. So was the merit of the Civil War Workers' Committee, whose work here came to fruition at last. What does the story tell about the department? The initial unreadiness was hardly to its credit; but the ministry did recognize the new situation and act boldly along new lines. After an embarrassing start, moreover, it turned the episode into a success story— in Sir Frank's words, "an interesting experiment in unadulterated bureaucracy."

> No Act of Parliament was passed to prescribe the persons to whom or the conditions on which it was to be paid. A vote of the House of Commons and a single line in the Finance Act, 1919, authorised the Ministry of Labour to spend a prescribed sum, and the details of administration were left in its hands.[78]

Departmentalism, so often the villain of the reconstruction story, here shows in a better light.

Of such achievements, a substantial list could be made. To those who knew the state of things on 15 October, this was a creditable performance, if also a sad reminder of the cabinet's unpreparedness. Against these good signs, it was disappointing that the progress of several investigations had slowed or stopped. Topics of reform, as well as reconversion, were

---

78. Sir Frank Tillyard, *Unemployment Insurance in Great Britain* (London: Bank Publishing Co., 1949), pp. 36–45; Greenwood's Appendix I to G.T. 6047 (19 October 1918), Cab. 24/67; Karl de Schweinitz, *England's Road to Social Security* (Philadelphia: University of Pennsylvania Press, 1943), p. 218; for emphasis on the plans of Bellhouse's Civil War Workers' Committee on which Churchill's staff relied, see the *History of the Ministry of Munitions*, 6, Part 2: 83.

involved: land acquisition, new plans for taxation of land and revision of the local rates system, rent control, women's employment, adult education, and policy toward trusts. Publication of one committee's report had been blocked by Hayes Fisher's objection; another committee, on rent increases, was too divided to produce a report; reports on adult education and on trusts were slowed by the fact that their key men, Arthur Greenwood and John Hilton, became swamped with emergency work at armistice time.[79] If this was regrettable, it was far more disturbing—so far as the revival of the economy and the resumption of normal employment went— that the expected good results were nowhere visible, and Churchill warned that 15 January would bring massive dismissals. Easily the worst feature, however, was that so much was still undecided. In terms of many basic choices, Kent's complaint of 5 December still applied: "We are not ready with a new practical program of reconstruction which will either immediately absorb some considerable proportion of the workpeople discharged or by providing orders . . . prevent the mass discharges that must otherwise take place." Whether to subsidize civilian production; whether to scrap controls; whether to let prices slump; whether to underwrite departmental and local authority purchases; whether to end exchange supports; whether to let foreign goods flood in; whether, for army discharges, to break free from "pivotalism." If the government was to help, these unresolved questions were the logical place to start. As yet, the effort at reconversion and demobilization was neither a clear failure nor a clear success.

This short-range work of demobilization and reconversion was only one dimension of reconstruction, but Addison considered it crucial. For him, the interim period might prove decisive for many plans which would come after. And four blatantly bad situations, already compromising early reconversion, therefore made him worry for the long term: in housing, finance, controls, and emergency legislation.

79. Submitted late in 1918 were two reports of Leslie Scott's committee: Cmd. 156, "Third Report of the Acquisition and Valuation of Land Committee," and Cmd. 424, "Fourth Report of the Acquisition and Valuation of Land Committee," in Great Britain, *Parliamentary Papers* (1919), vol. 29. On them, see F. 10886, Box 89. Regarding Hobhouse's committee which studied aid to Public Utility Societies, see F. 8820, 8891, and 8777 in Box 30, Part 2; F. 9248, Box 30, Part 3; H. 234, Box 33; *P.D.(L.)*, vol. 31, c. 950–54; papers 66 and 78–87, Box 37; Great Britain, *Parliamentary Papers* (1919), vol. 10, "Final Report of the Housing (Financial Assistance) Committee," Cd. 9238. On rent restriction, see Box 38, and papers 14, 62–65, Box 39. See also Great Britain, *Parliamentary Papers* (1918), vol. 13, "Report of the Committee on Trusts," Cd. 9236, and vol. 14, "Report of the Women's Employment Committee," Cd. 9239; *ibid.* (1919), vol. 10, "Final Report of the Adult Education Committee," Cmd. 321.

(*a*) Emergency controls, delegated to Cave's committee, had been shuffled in and out of the Home Affairs Committee, and Parliament as well. A list of desired powers, already grown gigantic, proved that decontrol had not triumphed, but was still not ready for action. (*b*) Meanwhile signs suggested that the decision on controls was heading the wrong way. Addison worried over the applause that greeted every announcement of relaxation: "If even the *Morning Post* gave me its blessing . . . we may have been too prompt and thorough in what we have done." Gardiner sketched the control situation on 18 December, and his wording was ominous: no survey of needs of priorities would be made "until it shall have been established in which cases the retention of control is likely to prove necessary."[80] It was the case *for* control that had to be proved; the presupposition was beginning to favor *de*control. Twenty-nine control orders on materials had vanished, by Ministry of Munitions order in November and December, of the forty-four materials covered. The powers that were linked with them and the laws that underlay them still stood; but the trend spoke volumes. (*c*) Financial questions lingered. Addison got his Financial Risks Committee report on 21 December, too late for prompt action on its idea of a 20 per cent cut in the excess profits duty.[81] Despite many warnings, no general budget existed.

But it was the housing situation that most dismayed Addison. (*d*) Brick supplies were short; public works had not started; the Carmichael plan had been scrapped. These—the legacy from Hayes Fisher, the results of snap judgment by Sir Eric Geddes' Demobilisation Committee —were the features that Addison was struck by, in the department that he was about to take over. There was, in fact, another side. The brief interlude, when Sir Auckland Geddes was head of the Local Government Board, saw an amazing change begin. Sir Auckland ended the period of waiting, and made the choice for not only the "penny-rate" financial formula, but for the appointment of housing commissioners—the very thing that Salisbury's panel had wanted. He also demanded that his Board be empowered to replace uncooperative local authorities with others, and be authorized to build where local groups did not act. He had drawn up a long list of powers, including controversial demands in the area of land acquisition. It was the sort of root-and-branch reform that Addison would see through to enactment in 1919. But in December 1918 Addison could only feel aghast at "the utterly bare field that the Local

80. Addison, *Diary*, 2: F. 11131, Box 52; 596; HAC (18 December 1918), citing G.T. 6397.

81. G.T. 6553 (21 December 1918), Cab. 24/72.

Government Board presents." He concluded that "the whole thing must be begun as from the grass."[82]

Addison, furthermore, had lost the central role he had briefly enjoyed. The ministry was passing from the scene; the odd interlude when minister and ministry performed duties at the cabinet level was over. Eric Geddes, taking over demobilization, symbolized the future; henceforth such men, and such emergency groups, would hold the center of things. Geddes moved in at Queen Anne's Gate, displacing Addison and his ministry. Nash and Addison arranged for the transfer of the ministry's papers— and all their plans for future work—to the executive departments. But Addison neither recorded any lament about this change nor predicted the doom of reform. He knew that Geddes and Chamberlain had challenged Scott's proposals for land laws and that others criticized Sir Auckland Geddes' housing crusade. Perhaps Addison felt that detailed pledges on forestry, housing, health, and land—and that greatest of pledges, the election campaign—assured a better future.

He avoided complacency, however. Talking to the Prime Minister, Addison declared that the election had made the P.M. master of the situation. But the temper of the people was short: the Prime Minister should assume he had only six months to act.[83]

82. *Politics*, 2: 219–20; Addison, *Diary*, 2: 586–87, 597. Auckland Geddes' circular letter of 14 November 1918 to the local authorities, urging them to act on housing, is reprinted in Great Britain, *Parliamentary Papers* (1919), vol. 24, "Forty-eighth Annual Report of the Local Government Board, 1918–1919," Cmd. 413, as Appendix 1.

83. Addison, *Diary*, 2: 600, 603. On Scott's Cd. 8998 for Land Acquisition, see the comments in Geddes' G.T. 6501 (18 December 1918), Mond's G.T. 6552 (23 December 1918), and Austen Chamberlain's G.T. 6556, Cab. 24/72, as well as Leslie Scott's reply, G.T. 6577 (n.d.), *ibid.*; and see HAC (18 December 1918).

15

Cabinet and Ministries:
January–June 1919

January marked no pause. The Ministry of Munitions, in full operation with all its old energy, employed its thousands, administered its raw materials, fixed its prices. At his new post, Secretary for War Winston Churchill bent to the task of reversing demobilization policy and accelerating its pace. The Ministry of Health, long past the milestone of approval, took shape. The Local Government Board became a beehive, buzzing with housing plans. Acland threw himself and his Interim Forestry Authority forward on faith alone, ignoring its total lack of legal sanction. In ministry after ministry prosaic legislative drafting was enlivened by an atmosphere of excitement and haste. Geddes' new Coordination of Demobilisation Section attacked a mingled agenda of reconversion and reform. Up and down Whitehall plans were made, debated, scrapped, and remade; memoranda drifted like leaves; committees and agencies formed, battled, disappeared. Tasks foreseen and new—in short, the work of reconstruction—occupied men everywhere.

Everywhere except at the Ministry of Reconstruction. A dismal pall hung over the staff; they had one major task—dissolution. The minister, Sir Auckland Geddes, told Nash to

> wind up the business of the Ministry of Reconstruction as soon as possible. The files should be sent either to the Offices most concerned or to the War Cabinet Secretariat. The winding up should be effected by the end of the financial year.

January saw the end, too, of the Standing Council on Post-War Priority, which Addison had counted on to administer controls. At Queen Anne's Gate, where the Ministry of Reconstruction had functioned for over a year, a new crew moved in; the old staff departed. Sir Auckland's assistant took over Nash's work; Nash went back to the Development Commission.

With him went E. H. E. Havelock, who one day would succeed Nash as the Commission's Permanent Secretary. Five men followed Addison to the Local Government Board: Heseltine, Wallace, Percy Barter, Rowntree, and Carmichael. Ernest Benn returned to his publishing firm, Garrod to Merton College, Gardiner to the Treasury. Reiss undertook a lifetime work of building Welwyn Garden City. Greenwood and Burns were asked to remain.

Papers, too, went their several ways to the *permanent* departments. A few reports trickled in until midyear; most unsatisfactorily, at least ten were in committee as 1919 began. The Committee on Trusts reported on 24 April; the gigantic report of the Adult Education Committee, produced by a terribly overworked Arthur Greenwood at great risk to his health, came in on 29 July. The planned series of reconstruction pamphlets remained incomplete; Geddes called a halt in midyear. In the thickening gloom the final report had to be written. A disingenuous document, concealing many unfulfilled tasks, Cd. 9231 must have been distasteful to write. By the time it appeared, members of Parliament were demanding, and obtaining, a pledge that the ministry would soon be liquidated.[1]

Addison: Retrospect and Prospect

In this context Addison dropped in to say his good-byes. He knew the shortcomings of his own effort, the frustrations and defeats caused by others. Better than anyone else he knew how many polished schemes had given way to improvisations, how many structures of his devising had been bypassed. Plaintive requests still coming in from Interim Industrial Reconstruction Committees and local reconstruction organizations told nothing he did not know about the collapse of the plans for devolution and organized support. But as he faced his Council for the last time, he spoke of success, not failure.

> It was a matter which that Ministry might well feel proud of that 19/20ths of their schemes had been accepted by the Government without alteration. The Government had recognised the value of the work done, and were unanimous that such a body should be continued permanently on the same lines as the Ministry of

1. Cd. 9231; Geddes to Nash, 14 January 1919, F. 10886, Box 89; Great Britain, *Parliamentary Papers* (1919), vol. 10, "Final Report of the Adult Education Committee," Cmd. 321; for pamphlets and letters of 21 and 26 August, see Box 76; for the Committee on Trusts, see "Reconstruction Pamphlet" by John Hilton, and "Report of the Committee on Trusts," Cd. 9236; *P.D.(C.)*, vol. 119 (13 August 1919): 1287, 116: 1207–9, and 118: 946.

Reconstruction as at present constituted. . . . The existence of the Ministry had proved the advantage of having a body to go into questions from an outside point of view which was impossible in the case of an ordinary Government Department.

How much of this was simply the gallantry and gratitude the occasion required? Did his words reflect only the perennial optimism for which Addison was long remembered? Less than two years later he would speak of his service in reconstruction as "the bitterest experience which any man could have"; had he stifled all personal feelings in order to do the proper thing?[2] Perhaps; but I think three other explanations suggest that he was truly speaking his mind. First, the performance of tremendous short-term duties in the three months of crisis, through December, may have taken on the dimensions of success. He had fought every minute to make the results even better, but he may have realized it was a triumph to have accomplished as much. Second, he could see that not a single reform had been shelved. With the promises made to the public and personally to him, he could reasonably expect fulfillment. Third, he was already caught up in the work of fulfillment. In the leadership of the Local Government Board, the prosecution of the nation's greatest housing campaign, and the creation of the Ministry of Health Addison was utterly engrossed. The Ministry of Reconstruction was becalmed, but its former chief had been promoted to a new command.

Here was no post limited to advisory powers; it was a complete, operating department. Here was no life of impotence, of tugging at other men's sleeves, but full executive power. Here one was builder and doer.

It is a thousand pities that Addison's published diary goes no further than December 1918; what a story of redoubled effort it could tell! But even the public documents show a minister, out from the backwater where his old vessel awaited dismantling, liberated into the main current of reconstruction.

Part I

Reform: The Local Government Board

The Ministry of Health Bill, having moved through an acquiescent Home Affairs Committee, stood ready for the War Cabinet's approval. The new

2. Addison, *Diary*, 2: 594–95, 600; F. 10902, Box 90, Part 1, "Chairman's Note No. XXX" of Advisory Council; R. J. Minney, *Viscount Addison: Leader of the Lords* (London: Odhams Press, 1958), p. 173.

terms for housing aid, in a circular that swept the negativism of 1918 into oblivion, had gone to every local authority in the land. Carmichael, in the dust of defeat not two months before, had been raised up to head the entire housing campaign. Conferences and deputations, now *welcomed* to the Board, had met with Addison. And all this by 7 February! In the first of his weekly reports, Addison summed it all up, letting these facts speak for themselves.[3]

No need to proclaim the transformation that had begun. To all who knew the past it was clear that the long deadlock at the Local Government Board had been broken. And this was only the first report, in a remarkable month that culminated with submission of both the new Housing Bill and the new Land Acquisition Bill on 1 March. In five February messages Addison rapped out the details of progress. On 14 February there was news of a mammoth housing conference, where Addison met the County Councils Association, the Association of Municipal Corporations, the Association of Urban District Councils and Rural District Councils, and the avant-garde group from the National Housing and Town Planning Council. The applause there for the financial terms—the famous "penny-rate" guarantee—augured well for energetic work. Health matters also were sharing the limelight at last. Sir George Newman was named Principal Medical Officer of the Board. Addison met with the National Health Insurance Commission on tuberculosis problems in London; he issued new regulations for the compulsory notification of diseases.[4]

Midway in February, details on housing were rushed to the cabinet: 1,026 local authorities had indicated readiness to build; a special new Housing Department had been formed; the country had been divided into eight housing areas, where housing commissioners (the staff that Rowntree and Salisbury had fought for) would be in charge; production of materials was being tackled; financial aid to Public Utility Societies was being cleared; a manual had been prepared for layout and design; house fittings had been standardized and orders for them were being arranged. As for legislation, "very important modifications and extensions of law relating to housing" were necessary; a new housing bill would be ready in a fortnight.[5]

In two more reports the next week, Addison outlined the problem of landlords and tenants, submitting a comprehensive bill his ministry had

3. G.T. 6769, Cab. 24/74. For Addison's circular letter of 6 February 1919 on housing, see Cmd. 413, Appendix No. 2.
4. G.T. 6810, Cab. 24/75.
5. G. 235, Cab. 24/5.

drafted in 1918. He told of memoranda sent to local councils on the influenza menace and of meeting the Labour Housing Association. With immense satisfaction he reported that the Ministry of Health bill had been introduced into Parliament.[6]

Intruding emergencies. Before that record month was over Addison—like everyone else—had been caught up in U.A.S.T., Auckland Geddes' crash program on "unemployment and the state of trade." This huge effort of survey and command had been dumped in Geddes' lap by the Prime Minister, as will be seen, after a hectic conference that revealed the appalling logjam in Whitehall and the stagnation of trade. Addison's reports to Geddes were another measure of Board work. His inspectors had visited *483 counties and districts*; in "public works," projects worth £500,000 already were under way; they found sanctioned projects, worth £11,000,000 more, ready to go. The findings, spelled out in page after page of tabulations, led Addison to redouble his pleas that the Treasury embargo on loans be lifted forthwith.[7] The new panic over unemployment, it seemed, might strengthen Addison's case—and help the whole program of housing.

There were other proofs of the new force of Local Government Board leadership: tenders had been received from local authorities for two billion bricks;[8] the Acquisition of Land Bill was progressing parallel to the Housing Bill. In the immediate present, however, the workless men dominated all thoughts. And at the heart of this situation was a specific question, which concerned Addison's Board deeply: the "out-of-work donation," Britain's drastic innovation in "outdoor relief."

Born of armistice necessities, as we have seen, the donation was no less vital because it broke with all precedents of the prewar years. Until other measures or programs got under way it was the one sure thing in the government's repertoire. Addison therefore took time on 13 February to alert the Demobilisation Committee that the donations would stop within a fortnight. Details (the topic bristles with technicalities) must be bypassed, but the force of the Local Government Board's argument cannot be overlooked. Major Waldorf Astor and A. V. Symonds, speaking for Addison, set themselves dead against any return to the old machinery. They drove the 1905 Unemployed Workmen Act from discussion with

6. G.T. 6836 and 6872, Cab. 24/75.
7. See G. 237 and supporting documents: "Unemployment and the State of Trade. An inquiry into the question of rehabilitating trade and providing employment, undertaken by the Minister of Reconstruction and National Service at the request of the Prime Minister. Sir Auckland Geddes' Report" (14 March 1919), Cab. 27/58.
8. G.T. 6766 (30 January 1919), Cab. 24/74.

the simple reminder that it smacked of the old Poor Law. And they had an alternative: use the local authorities on public works representing *genuine* projects and employing *all* types of laboring men.

The debate had dual meaning. It showed first that—by alerting other men to the imminent lapse of the donation—Addison's spokesmen were striving to prevent all the hardships which a lapse might produce. At that level they appeared willing to settle for mere extension of the donation system. But it was plainly revealed, secondly, that they preferred instead to create work, rather than merely alleviate suffering among the unemployed. Their real aim was not to extend the donation but to substitute something better. They were using the moment as a steppingstone toward a program of made work; and they saw this program as an aid to two causes, not just one.

Addison's men found a swift response to their idea: Horne, Kent, Geddes—in fact, all the Demobilisation Committee—put employment ahead of everything else; they agreed that Poor Law options were not to be thought of. Astor and Symonds exploited the chance to hammer at Treasury limitations: the local authorities *must* gain freedom to borrow or all their readiness would come to nought. The discussion was significant in many ways: it prompted a further probe into brick production, still a major obstacle to house building; it highlighted the link between finance and action, crucial both for public works and for housing; it revealed that—*for that time*—relief of joblessness, the great cry, worked to help Addison's housing scheme.[9]

Pause for assessment. Addison did not slacken his pace as a new month began, but the first week of March is a convenient moment for review. Several things were clear. (1) Public works were hampered by credit problems, by Local Government Board unpreparedness dating from 1918, and by the uncertain price situation. (2) The housing effort was badly handicapped by the unreadiness of plans as 1919 opened, and by the discouraging influence of Hayes Fisher's earlier words: only 52 of more than 1,800 authorities had submitted housing schemes; their proposals were for building a little over 10,000 houses; final sanction had not been given to a single scheme. Brick production was a major worry. By one estimate, predictable output would nowhere meet the need. Before the war annual production averaged 3,600 million bricks; in 1918 it was down by five-sixths; and the Local Government Board scheme alone, ignoring all private or governmental construction, would take 6,000 million bricks.

9. Minutes of fourth meeting, Demobilisation Committee (13 February 1919), Cab. 27/49.

Other hindrances were the shortage of skilled men (a crippling factor, just beginning to be sensed), the delays and costs resulting from the unamended Lands Clauses Acts, and lack of surveys of need.[10]

One kind of problem, however—official reluctance—did not arise. The housing pledge was holding good. Auckland Geddes cut through committee haggling with the curt reminder that "a million new houses were required at the present time"; and he was representative.[11] Indeed the cabinet itself, in January, invited Addison to outline all current housing needs.[12] There was opposition, of course, which had raised its head in December, when Sir Auckland Geddes was at the Local Government Board; now Addison's plans evoked some protests.[13] He brushed some aside and turned others to advantage. He made it perfectly clear, in retort to one protest, that if necessary his Board intended to handle the construction itself. To remove all doubt he explicitly announced that he was carrying out "the policy which I ventured to recommend in August 1917." Lest any might misconstrue what this meant, he circulated details of the Housing Bill weeks before it was complete—nothing less than a writing into law of the whole reform Salisbury, Rowntree, and Addison's staff had championed for two fruitless years. It was all there: a positive duty of house-building, imposed on Local Authorities; power to simplify schemes and to relax bye-laws; power to enter into possession of land without meeting terms of the Lands Clauses Acts; repeal of the obligation to hold local enquiries; power to buy for sale or lease, not just for construction; power to acquire and improve existing houses; aid to Housing Societies; power to replace laggard minor Authorities by the County Council without formal proof of default; power for the Board to provide houses and recover costs from defaulting Authorities.[14]

Addison had labored to make sure his colleagues knew exactly what they were being asked to accept. Ready and willing they were, or at least professed to be; he was determined they should be ready, willing, and *informed.*

10. See G. 235, "Housing: The Present Position," by Addison (February 1919), Cab. 24/5. For bricks, see G.T. 6293, minutes of second meeting on unemployment and the state of trade (App. 3 to G. 237, Cab. 27/58), as well as minutes of sixth meeting, Demobilisation Committee (13 February 1919), Cab. 27/49. For other difficulties, see these documents and App. 43 and 44 to G. 237.

11. *Ibid.*

12. WC 518 (22 January 1919), Cab. 23/9.

13. See above, p. 337, and G.T. 6618 by Walter Long (7 January 1919), Cab. 24/73.

14. Addison in WC 534 (19 February 1919), Cab. 23/9, responding to Mond's G.T. 6793 of 13 February 1919, in Cab. 24/74; Addison's G. 235, cited in note 10 above.

So much for retrospect. On 1 March the Housing Bill, fully drafted, reached the cabinet.[15] It could have met a March storm of opposition. The Electricity Bill was being challenged clause by clause; the Acquisition of Land Bill barely survived a month of merciless critique; but the Housing Bill got nothing but applause.

High tide. The War Cabinet did not receive the Housing Bill; it snatched at it. Ministers knew all the hardships; they saw precedent and moderation crumpled beneath line after line; and they embraced it all. Austen Chamberlain, though already the voice of economy on other matters, even suggested writing stronger compulsions into the bill. The Prime Minister—then as ever the prime mover—looked unflinchingly at a probable cost of £20,000,000 to £40,000,000 per year and counted it cheap.

> Russia had gone almost completely over to Bolshevism, and we had consoled ourselves with the thought that they were only a half-civilised race; but now even in Germany, whose people were without exception the best educated in Europe, prospects are very black. . . . In a short time we might have three-quarters of Europe converted to Bolshevism. None would be left but France and Great Britain. . . . Great Britain would hold out, but only if the people were given a sense of confidence—only if they were made to believe that things were being done for them. We had promised them reforms time and again, but little had been done. We must give them the conviction this time that we meant it, and we must give them that conviction quickly. We could not afford to wait until prices went down. If nothing were done, the people themselves would break down prices. . . .
>
> We were 300,000 houses below our normal level, and that level was itself far below what it should be. . . . People were saying, "When the Government wanted to build factories to produce shells, they had overcome all difficulties; . . . When it came to the question of providing houses, the Government was still talking, and meanwhile people were without houses." That was actually the case, and it was necessary for the State to . . . grapple fairly with the problem at issue. . . . He could foresee the possibility that this country might have to stand alone for social order and common sense against anarchy, as we had stood for freedom against despotism. So long as we could persuade the people that we were prepared

---

15. G.T. 6911 and 6931, Cab. 24/76.

to help them and to meet them in their aspirations . . . the sane and steady leaders amongst the workers would have an easy victory over the Bolsheviks among them.

The total cost for all reforms had been put at £71,000,000. "Even if it cost 100,000,000*l.*, what was that compared with the stability of the State?"

Chamberlain warned that heavy taxation must one day be faced, but he concurred completely. Housing, the first and biggest problem, must be pushed on immediately, "at whatever cost to the State." Cabinet ministers actually vied in proposing new powers; they probed to see if the bill was big enough for the job. Why was not power given to clear slums? Should not the Board have power to make surveys?

Usually Addison's answer was that such powers were provided, but twice (and it must have been marvelous to watch) the cabinet outdid Addison in boldness. His draft allowed local authorities six months to submit a housing scheme; the cabinet substituted three months. Where the Board's ability to cope with local default seemed unclear, the cabinet conferred full powers to compel the local authority to prepare adequate plans. For once the cabinet was fully seized of a situation. The members competed like schoolboys to offer helpful suggestions. Had transport been thought of? Addison should confer with the electricity commissioners and the new Ministry of Transport. Had possibilities of repair, rather than new construction, been overlooked? Would the new housing commissioners be strong enough? Finally satisfied, the War Cabinet gave its blessing. The bill was accepted in principle and referred to a committee (with Addison in charge); it need not come back to the cabinet again.[16]

Next day at the committee meeting, every clause—including those the cabinet had reinforced—went through. Addison's Board gained compulsory powers; town planning procedures were speeded; financial aid to Public Utility Societies made its way at last into the draft: an epochal bill could go to the waiting House of Commons committee that day.[17] Only a little later, Geddes clinched two vital matters: "The money required for the housing scheme should be given the very highest degree of priority by the Treasury"; and to encourage prompt contracting it was announced that if restrictions had to be imposed later, they would not affect contracts already made. He added his personal authority.

16. WC 539 (3 March 1919) and 541 (4 March 1919), Cab. 23/9.
17. Minutes, War Cabinet Housing Bill Committee (5 March 1919), Cab. 27/56.

The Housing Scheme is the most conspicuous, as well as the most urgent, item in the Government programme, and it is of the greatest importance that there should be no avoidable delay in the provision of sites and materials in anticipation of the commencement of actual building operations.[18]

On 18 March the Housing Bill was introduced into the Commons.

Reform: Land Settlement and Acquisition

On 1 March the Acquisition of Land Bill and the Land Settlement Bill were ready; the cabinet took them up at once. They were in every sense companion measures to the Housing Bill; even without the Housing Bill they would have made it a banner week for reform. But they met much more criticism. Born of the same spirit and rationale that produced the Housing Bill, both bills complemented it many ways. Why did enthusiasm for the former not speed them through? The answer may be a clue to crisis motives and to the resistances that set limits to reform.

Neither measure promised the same massive relief to unemployment as housing; both shared this fault. Beyond this were individual reasons. The Acquisition of Land Bill, from Leslie Scott's group, raised many objections. It affronted the inherently conservative legal profession. It offended advocates of decentralization by proposing a single sanctioning authority for all public acquisition of land. This change also offended the departments, jealous of their powers; on this point, ultimately, even the Ministers of Reconstruction—Geddes in December and Addison from his new vantage point in 1919—objected.[19] The Home Affairs Committee had held the measure over from December; a measure so apparently revolutionary, said some, should await a new government.[20]

The first consideration by the War Cabinet began with a chilling report: the Lord Chancellor "opposed the whole plan." Spotting references to valuation clauses of the 1910 Finance Act—a vivid reminder of prewar storms—ministers flinched; reading on, they found clauses on "betterment," the very Waterloo of land law. An eye to the Coalition, some muttered about "opening up vast and very controversial issues of social policy." Because the bill overlapped other pending measures, and referral was a way out, the cabinet launched the proposal on a stormy passage through committee.[21]

18. G. 237, p. 11, Cab. 27/58.
19. Auckland Geddes' G.T. 6501 (18 December 1918), Cab. 24/72.
20. Home Affairs Committee (18 December 1918).
21. WC 539 (3 March 1919), Cab. 23/9.

Against the Land Settlement Bill, in contrast, there was only one argument: cost. The Board of Agriculture intended to settle 100,000 men on the land that year, and every man meant a subsidy. The cost was impossible to reckon. But back of the measure stood a man of determination, Edmund Prothero, and back of him a mighty department, with a phenomenal record of wartime triumphs. Prothero—Lord Ernle, as he had now become—wisely admitted everything. "No time could be worse than the present for settling men on the land." Agricultural costs still were very heavy, while prices of produce were coming down. For his part—acknowledging that Lloyd George and Addison felt differently— he was willing to exclude civilians from the plan, but he was adamant about soldiers. "Land settlement for ex-service men is a national duty, and the State must be prepared to bear a considerable part of the cost." Prothero stirred guilty consciences with the history of delay: No decision had been reached until 31 December 1918; but the urgency of the situation had been put on record in October 1917 and underscored twice in May 1918. Sure of his moral position, Ernle took the offensive. He catalogued the preparations already taken: invitations to landowners for help, surveys of ecclesiastical land, interviews with army applicants in France. The chosen instruments, county councils, had been alerted; a reorganized Board of Agriculture stood ready.

Prothero won the first skirmish. Mollified by the exclusion of civilians, Bonar Law and the Chancellor of the Exchequer echoed Ernle: "In the case of ex-soldiers, we were pledged." From that moment it was certain that a huge program would go through, but sticky questions of detail remained. Auckland Geddes held out for aid to civilians. Lloyd George was of two minds (when, one might ask, was this not true of Lloyd George?). On the one hand he said Balfour's success in Ireland was an argument for inclusive aid. After all, "the policy here advocated was the same."

> In Ireland Mr. Balfour had found a condition of social disorder, chronic trouble, poverty, and misery, . . . and he had developed a large scheme for settling labourers on the land. . . . There was no doubt that Ireland had benefited thereby.

"It was not an economic scheme," he reminded them—and was off grandly into a survey of France, Russia, Bolshevism, and the state on the brink of anarchy, leaving considerations of economy far behind. Conceivably, he might have prevailed—if the case had been simple, and if he had not been of two minds. But the case was not simple. The strongest preference was not for mere land ("small holdings") but for land with untied cottages—cottages, of course, that would have to be built by the state. Thus new dimensions were added to cost. Second, there was no necessity to do the whole thing at once (resettling civilians had *not* been pledged), and there was wisdom in postponing this task until land prices fell. And there was the question of subsidy: clause 25 offered Treasury grants to landowners who adapted land for small holdings.

With this arose the question of equality, and the Prime Minister revealed the other side of his thinking.

If this was allowed in the case of landowners, it would be claimed also for industries. The Federation of British Industries had already made the suggestion that the State should recoup them for any losses they suffered in restarting industry.

Ernle protested that unless this generosity was shown, landowners could not afford to cooperate. Besides, they would get only what the local authorities would get, and this was the same in principle as the present safeguard against losses on account of the war. Now it was the more conservative ministers who veered; they wanted economy but they sympathized with landowners, and they knew the temper and composition of the new Parliament. They favored generous subsidy. But Lloyd George scented danger. Would not County Councils also demand total safeguards, with their new housing duties? Would not industry clamor? Would not private contractors, with their entire market preempted by the state under the new housing law, insist on the same? Munro chimed in: Clause 25 would be denounced in Scotland as "preferential treatment for landlords."[22]

Out went clause 25. Nevertheless, Ernle's bill moved safely into committee. There, for a wonder, the exclusion of civilians was reversed! Over Treasury objections, munitions workers were included. Broadening the program still more, the committee redefined "small holding" to include a site with a provided house.[23] It was fully aware of what this meant: the land-settlement program would become a housing program, at trebled or quadrupled cost. Back went the bill to the cabinet on 21 March. In consternation the Chancellor of the Exchequer, Austen Chamberlain, exclaimed that "the Committee had reversed all the decisions of the

22. WC 539 and 540 (3 March 1919), Cab. 23/9; Ernle's G.T. 6716 (21 January 1919), Cab. 24/74; text of bill, G.T. 6791 (14 February 1919), Cab. 24/74.
23. Minutes of first meeting, Land Acquisition Bill and Land Settlement (Facilities) Bill Committee, G.T. 6988 (8 March 1919), Cab. 27/63.

Government." He floundered, searching for rebuttals, while Ernle blandly declared that the War Cabinet "had decided that the Bill should be extended in its general application to all classes of the community"—as doubtful an assertion as tongue could utter.

For one thing, Chamberlain still insisted, the original plan of 1918 was limited to £20,000,000; for another, it had allowed for a cheaper method—annuity payment—of relieving the current budget. It had been a scheme for land sites *alone*; extension beyond servicemen had *not* been agreed upon. Aghast, Chamberlain pointed to the enormous consequences of redefining "small holdings" to include a house. Did the ministers understand? Budgetarily, this transferred the burden to the state. As long as housing was left where it stood—a problem for the Local Government Board and a cost to the local authorities—the Treasury's share was practicable, but use the term "small holdings" and the whole burden of rural housing, by the Small Holdings Act, fell upon the government.

The point seems trivial but it was the entering wedge of the analysis that finally cut across all of the cabinet's intentions; it was the clue to the mood of 1920 and 1921. Now it did not prevail. The cabinet was not even a quarter of the way toward the autumnal mood of economy. Nor did it yield when Chamberlain stated his case.

> He was already alarmed at the extent of the borrowing which the Government had to undertake at the present moment. Before any new borrowing was undertaken they must provide for the renewal of repayable debt already incurred. 1,500,000,000*l.* must be renewed before the end of next year, of which 900,000,000*l.* were in Treasury Bills which would have to be renewed four times over in the course of the year. . . . He regarded the financial position as one of extreme gravity.

Ernle was more than a match for Chamberlain. He argued suavely that his plan—tiny holdings with houses attached—would save on land costs; they were popular; and they met the demand, which was in fact for just such cottage holdings as supplements to farm wages. Then he trumped Chamberlain with a laconic reference to the Prime Minister's "emphatic appeal" for land settlement. Fisher sided with Ernle. Bonar Law moved toward compromise: Let the bill be general, but with preference for ex-servicemen. At this point Addison walked in. He minimized the problem; his Board and Ernle's could iron out problems of overlapping; there would be no practical difficulties. Ernle observed mildly that he had no objection to this view. His case was won. In a clear choice between limitation and near recklessness, between economy and optimism, the cabinet voted the Land Settlement (Facilities) Bill through. There would be veterans' preference, but no restriction.[24]

Meanwhile, what of the Acquisition of Land Bill? It deserved strenuous support. It was not merely the third leg of the housing–land settlement–land purchase tripod; it was fundamental to the success of the new Ministry of Ways and Communications, to electrical power reform—and indeed wherever a department might have to make good a claim to land. Ernle, in fact, had put the case for a hard-hitting all-round land reform; he cited public and professional endorsement of Leslie Scott's 1917 report. But departmental self-interest muted Addison and Geddes. In the event, the brunt of the committee battle fell on Leslie Scott.

There is no need to follow Scott into that complex three-day debate; and the end product—the Acquisition of Land (Assessment of Computation) Bill of 1919—can be viewed later. In survey, however, the first thing to stress is that this bill became a bill on *procedures* alone—not a grant of new powers, not a radical redefinition of values, not an assault on such hugely important questions as betterment and injurious affection, but merely a device to speed the use of powers then held. Scott's committee had intended much more; the original bill had treated "betterment," by making owners pay for unearned gains that resulted from socially increased land values; but this cause was lost at once. "With a view to the whole question . . . being considered comprehensively as a separate measure" (decades later as it proved), that clause had been dropped. It would be misleading, however, to picture a cabal of traditionalists pitted against Scott, a lone crusader. The divisions in committee occurred on technical and practical grounds more often than on radicalism or innovation. Leslie Scott was not an ideologue assailing property rights; indeed, in advocating that values be reckoned as between "a willing buyer and a willing seller" he was championing *owners*. The committee quickly retorted that "a willing seller" would mean much greater costs to government buyers. On the other hand, no one in the committee defended the Lands Clauses Acts of 1844; this bulwark of property, with its crippling delays, had not a friend.

Another detail accentuates this truth, and suggests where the true conservatism lay. This was the sensitive question of hiring at high salaries, as government's official valuers, part-time men with private practices—as against full-time civil servants. Scott and the entire committee were

24. WC 549 (21 March 1919), Cab. 23/9.

strong for private, part-time men. Admittedly, such valuers could be accused of bias, but they would be reliable, and as highly paid preeminent professionals they would give the system the prestige and skill that were needed for success. If conservatism figured, it came from outside, in the form of a letter from Lloyd George, declaring to the Lord Chancellor "with profound disappointment" that

> the Bill was supposed to be one to facilitate acquisition of land for most urgent public purposes, speedily and at a fair price. It has been transformed into a Bill which will be represented as making sure that the landlord gets a good price, that the lawyers get their pickings, and that there should be no undue hurry in the completion of the transaction.
>
> To entrust the valuation of land to a man whose future prosperity and even livelihood depends on the goodwill of owners of land, is to guarantee an interest and bias in favour of the landlord against the State. . . .
>
> . . . these methods in the past . . . have rendered all housing schemes barren. It is owing to these that land producing only a few shillings an acre fetches hundreds of pounds per acre the moment it is requisitioned to build houses for the workmen whose labour has created the adjoining wealth.
>
> . . . the results of the West Leyton election will suffice as a warning to those who have drawn wrong deductions from the overwhelming majority of the last election. Mason's record . . . marked him down as a reactionary. I beg you to assist in making these Bills a reality. . . . The country is in no mood to tolerate reactionaries, high or low.

Lloyd George flatly vetoed the idea. Ernle argued that the salary of valuers would be "saved ten times over by saving the expenses of the Lands Clauses Acts," but purity and appeasement overrode the merits of the case. Back and forth the bill went—three times before the cabinet. Its approval, on 19 March, had an ambiguous result: some uncompromising features were retained and some controversial clauses were dropped.[25] Still irresolute, the cabinet launched a belated study of a more radical

25. Cab. 27/63, as cited in note 23 above, and G.T. 6988 and 6989, Cab. 24/76. The bill itself, G.T. 6910 (1 March 1919), is in Cab. 24/76. For other citations, see WC 539, 540, 541, 543, 545, 546, 549, Cab. 23/9–10. Lloyd George's letter of 15 March 1919 to the Lord Chancellor is reprinted in Beaverbrook, *Men and Power*, pp. 394–95.

change. At the end of May the larger issue was still in doubt.[26] Unappeased, Leslie Scott bided his time.

Reform: Addison and the Ministry of Health

Although he had no time to spare, Addison had watched both measures anxiously. The land settlement bill—though drafted by the Board of Agriculture—was his in spirit; Scott's proposals were his own, and vital for housing. Addison's warnings that drastic land reform was "the real basis for the scheme" had not sufficed;[27] therefore in May he led, with Lloyd George's encouragement, the demand for a simplified and strengthened process for compulsory acquisition of land. "He could not imagine anything more dilatory than some of the present methods of acquiring land compulsorily." Scott's recommendations, "more expeditious and far less costly," were backed by the law society and the land companies.[28] For the moment, he could only hope that the pledges of broader reform would bear fruit. He was preoccupied with an enormous amount of other work.

Some of it was pleasurable beyond expression. The Ministry of Health Bill (his pet) came before the Home Affairs Committee on 6 February. That committee, his creation, had nevertheless become in 1918 the graveyard of his hopes; through its very last session in December, it was the sounding board for hostile views. But between December and its first session of 1919 a world of change had occurred. Every one of Addison's ideas for the Ministry of Health Bill now went through. Powers and duties of whatever sort, if they appeared related to Health, were approved and were added—and only health matters (that is, nothing redolent of the Poor Law) would be his charge when any revision of poor relief was made. This was a straight victory for Addison and for the Friendly Societies. Gratifyingly, one of the old members was there to grumble that this was a reversal of last year's committee decision.[29]

Addison's next report, for March and April, stopped just short of boasting, but the facts spoke for themselves. Addison's staff had

26. See WC 549, 577, 602, Cab. 23/9–11, and meetings 25, 33, and 35, Home Affairs Committee (31 March and 8 and 18 July 1919), as well as Addison's G.T. 7298 (20 May 1919), Cab. 24/79. For land-value duties of 1910, see G. 239 (31 March 1919) by N. Warren Fisher and H. P. Hamilton, Cab. 24/5.

27. Addison's G. 235 (above, note 10), p. 3, and statements to third U.A.S.T. session (G.T. 6923), Cab. 27/58 and 23/76.

28. Addison's G.T. 7298 (above, note 26); for Lloyd George's concern, see minutes of meeting 25 of Home Affairs Committee (31 March 1919).

29. Minutes, Home Affairs Committee meeting 19 (6 February 1919); the bill is G.T. 6734 (3 February 1919), Cab. 24/74.

completed the central machinery for the new campaign; terms for aid to the Public Utility Societies were finally agreed upon. The Housing Bill passed its second reading with strong support. All but one housing commissioner had been appointed and the others were at work with their staff. The Ministry of Munitions was following through on brick production. As against an inheritance of 56 schemes, 693 had now been submitted; they were still in their first stage, but were expected to produce 100,000 houses. At Buckingham Palace the King had addressed members of the Rural District Councils and Urban District Councils Associations, the National Housing and Town Planning Council, the County Councils Association, the Association of Municipal Corporations, and the London County Council. Conferences had been held on influenza, malaria, venereal disease, and tuberculosis. To cap it all, Morant and John Anderson had come in as a team to head the new ministry, the bill for which had just been sent, unscathed, from Commons to Lords.[30]

Morant alone was a battalion; hearing of the appointment, Haldane wrote him, "This gives the Health Ministry a chance."[31] Morant *plus* Anderson, the fastest coming man in the civil service, was a triumph. Characteristically, it was the perfectionist Morant who sounded the only gloomy note. He resented the time it had cost to spur Addison into fighting for Anderson's appointment—three precious months when he and Anderson might have been "getting things ready beforehand." Besides, he wrote Haldane, "Addison is a queer chaotically minded person with no belief in clear organisation, and things will therefore be fearfully difficult. But one can but try."

If the staffing had turned out marvelously—and with Carmichael, Newman, Morant, Anderson, Reiss, Wallace, Barter, and Heseltine, who could deny it?—it was a success for many determined men. Morant, aching to make the ministry a success and then push on to reshuffling *local* administration, which he deemed crucial, had nevertheless refused to come without Anderson. And Newman had refused to come without Morant. It was not, then, by accident that the head of the medical staff of the Board of Education and the National Health Insurance Commission's chief—Newman and Morant—came together, in an ideal working unification.[32]

30. G.T. 7162 (26 April 1919), Cab. 24/78.
31. B. M. Allen, *Sir Robert Morant* (London: Macmillan, 1934), pp. 304–9.
32. Violet Markham, "Sir Robert Morant: Some Personal Reminiscences," *Public Administration*, 28 (Winter 1950): 255–57; Morant to Haldane, 26 March 1919, Haldane MSS, vol. 5914, fol. 119; George Newman, *The Building of a Nation's Health* (London: Macmillan, 1939), pp. 122–25.

It was the substance of policy, as much as the ministry itself, that delighted the housing reformers. Freed at last from the "Hayes Fisher atmosphere" of 1918, the National Housing and Town Planning Council exploded with praise.[33]

Reform: Other Projects Are Cleared

Whitleyism, electric power, forestry, and health insurance also progressed in that half-year. The cabinet built Whitley Councils into the civil service[34] and watched as the Ministry of Labour raised the total in industry from twenty-one to more than fifty.[35] Acland, already fully at work, with no statutory basis whatever, fought for a permanent forestry commission. The cabinet and its committees heard (or endured?) this prickly and pugnacious reformer, agreed that by now the problem with his bastard but sturdy Interim Authority was "how to regularize the situation," and yielded. Despite bureaucracy, despite Scots pride, there would be a central authority for all Great Britain.[36]

Here were two victories for the work begun by Asquith and championed by Addison. Educational allowances for servicemen were successes for Addison and H. A. L. Fisher jointly.[37] Addison, however, did not have a hand in every reform nor did he win every time. Health insurance, for example, made small progress: There were plans to raise the income limit (then £160) to £250 for recipients (otherwise a million persons might lose eligibility); this passed, but nothing else was done.[38] As for unemployment aid, the out-of-work donation was maintained; nevertheless, though experts look on this as epochal, it represented no change since December.[39] Potentially vast reforms in wages and hours, which Addison's memorandum of September 1918 had failed to effect, gained new impetus from the great National Industrial Conference of workmen and employers

---

33. National Housing and Town Planning Council, Minute Book 3, reports of 23 and 24 January, 16 May, and 31 July 1919, and *Annual Report* for 1918–19; *Jubilee Yearbook* (1960) of the National Housing and Town Planning Council.

34. WC 534 (19 February 1919), 550, and 579, in Cab. 23/9–11.

35. *Ibid.*; see also Ince, *The Ministry of Labour*, pp. 118–21.

36. Home Affairs Committee, meetings 25 and 26; G.T. 6913 (13 March 1919), Cab. 24/76; WC 549 (21 March 1919) and 567 (14 May 1919), Cab. 23/9–10.

37. WC 584 (24 June 1919), Cab. 23/11.

38. Minutes of meetings 28 and 30, Home Affairs Committee (16 and 28 May 1919).

39. Home Affairs Committee, meetings 20 and 22 (21 February and 10 March 1919); Demobilisation Committee, sixth meeting (13 February 1919), Cab. 27/49; G.T. 6943 by Auckland Geddes, Cab. 24/76; Report on Industrial Conference by Robert Horne, G.T. 7057 (31 March 1919), Cab. 24/77; WC 538, 550, 554, 572, 574, Cab. 23/9–10.

in February; but, as will be seen, Addison had little to do with this.[40]

Nor was he the prime mover for transport and electric power, which were independently pushed, one by Sir Eric Geddes and the other by Stanley of the Board of Trade. To Addison, however, they belonged in any catalogue of reform, and high on the list. Akin in their rationales and overlapping down to their fine print, they differed from other measures in one vital way: they had no tinge of duty, conscience, or pledges—only the prospect of glorious power. This guaranteed a brawl. Dutiful reforms might glide through on boredom and sufferance, but these splendid ministerial fiefdoms were worth fighting for. Even had they not smoldered with the dynamite of nationalization, a battle was assured. It took just one sentence to initiate it. Geddes' bill for the Ministry of Ways and Communications, in one tiny clause, gave him the power over merchant ships. This clause, challenging both the Board of Trade and the Ministry of Shipping, ringed Geddes with enemies. Leviathan and Behemoth roared and smote. Geddes had to fight the redoubtable John Anderson, acting for the Ministry of Shipping, and also the experienced Sir Hubert Llewellyn Smith, acting for Stanley of the Board of Trade. Against Geddes' bid for maritime authority, these two men evoked a ghostly fleet of enraged shipowners, hinting at a disastrous conflict that would surpass the Spithead mutiny. "No vested interest in the House of Commons," intoned the First Lord, was "so powerful as the shipping interest." Valiant for their ministers, Anderson and Llewellyn Smith, those two simple seafarers from Whitehall, defended the deep. Sir Eric was stopped at the water's edge.

Nor did he win powers on the land, but here the conflict grew many-sided. Just as Geddes faced opposition to his transport bill, so Llewellyn Smith had to fight opposition to his bill which would give control over electricity to the Board of Trade. Llewellyn Smith immediately found himself fighting on two fronts, for his proposal encroached on the Ministry of Munitions and the local authorities—forces in being—and encroached on the proposed Ministry of Ways and Communications. If Sir Eric had fought giants, Sir Hubert fought the world. The question of railways was the center of the crossfire. These, which Geddes meant to control through his new ministry, Sir Hubert

40. Addison, "Reconstruction and Industrial Conditions" (based on the Report of the Adult Education Committee, Cd. 9107), G.T. 5838 (28 September 1918), Cab. 24/65.

meant to control through the Board of Trade so far as electricity was involved. To show that electricity (and, to that extent, railways) must be controlled by a broad authority like the Board of Trade, Sir Hubert began with the remark that "the supply of electrical power was overwhelmingly an industrial problem." At once Sir Eric countered. Twenty per cent of electricity must be for railways alone; much of the remainder would go for tramway traction. In retort, Llewellyn Smith put the Board of Trade's case more fully: Electric supply should be handled by electricity commissioners "responsible to a Department . . . concerned with the general interests of electrical users as a whole"—rather than by one consumer, as represented by Geddes' ministry. Also, he warned, Geddes' bid for jurisdiction would founder on municipal authorities' resistance. Better to let the Board of Trade bill, based on the Williamson committee report, prevail.

Churchill bluntly and unflatteringly intervened against Llewellyn Smith: "The Ministry of Munitions in three years had multiplied enormously the electrical power supply of the country as compared with thirty years under the Board of Trade"! Lloyd George concurred. Geddes swung behind these temporary allies, charging that the Board of Trade bill concerned only generating—it conferred no power to transmit; but for technical reasons electricity must be controlled through the distribution points. He scoffed at the alleged clash of interest between railways and the trading community; the contrary was the case. Addison joined in, favoring control of electricity by the Ministry of Supply—a third choice! He rejected the Board of Trade proposal. Geddes won a poor victory: Ways and Communications should control electricity, for now at least, but only if the Board of Trade agreed; and the Board was encouraged to rush its bill forward.

The ministers boggled at two clauses in Geddes' bill, for acquiring and taking possession of railways. Was the government going to nationalize the railways? Sir Eric did not say no. True, the power to take possession was limited by his bill to two years, and the power served more purposes than nationalization.

> Under the Defence of the Realm Act, the Board of Trade had power to take possession of the railways. This merely enabled the new Minister to continue the powers for two years which had been exercised during the war. Otherwise so soon as the Defence of the Realm Act lapsed, there would be no power at all to control railways.

So long as the government's pledge to guarantee the railways their prewar profits still held, the power to control them must be kept. But Austen Chamberlain worried about the "big question."

> The War Cabinet at the moment had no policy in the matter; some kind of control must continue, and it was possible that nationalisation was the right policy; but the Select Committee pondering nationalisation had not yet reported.

Lloyd George dwelled on the complications, as will be seen later. In the end, he asked that the question not be pressed but that for now the powers be kept. So it was decided; powers over tramways, air travel, and shipping were deleted, but otherwise the Ways and Communications Bill passed.[41]

With fewer changes, but not without a struggle, the Electricity (Supply) Bill went through the cabinet later. This time Geddes and the Board of Trade—together for once—had to contend with the Treasury, which was appalled at the thought of yet another £50,000,000 for loans. But the main issues had been settled in the first battle.[42]

It had been a confusing fracas. Compared with the wider scene of cabinet work from January through June, however, it was clarity itself.

Part II

The Cabinet in 1919: Context for Reconstruction

Not simple chaos but chaos compounded, the cabinet's record is almost unendurably fascinating. The reforms, pledged and unpledged, which we have noted so far, formed only part of that record. There was, in fact, everything on the agenda; and the mere task of categorizing is enormous.

Thus, for example, even a first glance discloses such topics as relief, training for veterans and for munitions workers, minimum wages, training for unemployed women, "pivotalism," maximum hours, food crises and food control, war bonuses, and rent restrictions. All these individual themes appeared in the record and beviled the cabinet. Discouraging in their multitude, they all have at least some unity. All derive from the demobilization process, and all may be grouped under the heading "unemployment." But once we consider the hard fact of the

41. WC 534 (19 February 1919), Cab. 23/9, citing G.T. 6801, 6809, 6812, and 6832, Cab. 24/75. See also commentary by Philip S. Bagwell, *The Railwaymen: The History of the National Union of Railwaymen* (London: Allen & Unwin, 1963), pp. 406–8.
42. WC 550 (31 March 1919), 556 (14 April 1919), and 562 (5 May 1919), Cab. 23/9–10; the bill is G.T. 6926 (3 March 1919), Cab. 24/76.

economic slump, a whole jumble of new issues is introduced: prices, national factories, shipyards, decontrol, raw materials, profiteering, nationalization, and coal. For such topics the official general phrase "U.A.S.T." ("Unemployment and the State of Trade") was used; but it is simply too bland. It fails to reflect the conflict which made of early 1919 a continuous period of economic storm. For the state of trade was complicated by many a suspenseful wage negotiation and marked often by strikes. Strikes and a pitched battle in Glasgow; strikes in coal; threats of walkouts at the docks, railways, and mines; the ultimate threat of a Triple Alliance strike, on 27 February; strikes, before July came, in Lancashire mines, among shipbuilders, and among engineers. For all this, how pallid is the official term "Unrest"! Through a lifetime thereafter ministers would be likely to question whether that banal term was adequate to describe a situation where the cabinet, midway through its meeting, might be interrupted with the news that Glasgow, coal, and rails had all reached the strike stage in the last twenty minutes. What they *did* ponder then, and without sleep, was the Triple Alliance, and the great strike that did not come that year but was expected daily. Even this outline omits reparations, Versailles, Prinkipo, the Supreme Economic Council, the League of Nations, the United States Senate, the agony of the Caucasus, and Siberia—the outside world that kept breaking in. For six months and more it was all a kind of nightmare traffic jam in a railway yard greater than the world had ever seen. These many distinct topics, running through the first half of 1919, define the tracks, glutted by endlessly incoming traffic.

The actuality was still more complex. Across these parallel topical lines, three great events cut transversely, raising many issues at once: the Sankey Commission; the National Industrial Conference, bringing workmen and employers face to face with ministers from February on; the all-embracing survey by Sir Auckland Geddes in February and March. One clutches at such episodes, hoping that they promise, not only relief from the unmanageable task of narrating each topic separately, but a chance to identify turning points, and to give the whole a beginning, middle, and end.

It is true that there appear to be four discernible periods. (1) January was a time of brewing storm, while the government remained comparatively inattentive and lethargic. (2) The end of January, when rumors of coal and rail strikes and actual reports of the Glasgow riot broke into the cabinet, seems to mark the start of a second stage and the beginning of real crisis. (3) At the end of February several events—the ultimatum by the Triple Alliance, the decision to hold the National Industrial Conference, the launching of Geddes' "U.A.S.T." inquiry, the start of the Sankey Commission—define a moment of cabinet awakening and resolution. From that high point a kind of plateau extends to late March, when the interim Sankey Commission report, and the next session of the Industrial Conference, suggest another turning point. (4) Again on 16 April and 28 May, the cabinet's responses to the Industrial Conference seem to be useful landmarks. Such periodization is not wholly wrong, but there is danger in stressing these episodes. From other events, for example, one could derive a different outline. The reversal of demobilization policy, in mid-January, tended to reduce tension. This change, when "pivotalism" was scrapped, removed the armed forces' discontent as a major component of unrest, converting February and March *pro tanto* into months of ebbtide. Indeed, the very concept of a landmark or a turning point, however plausible, can be misleading. If it suggests order, where chaos prevailed, if it suggests resolution, where no solutions were attained, above all if the concept suggests the situation became anything less than explosive, it must be abandoned. The main merit of such episodes is that, briefly, they brought the cabinet above the ruck of detail and thus furnished ministers—and History—a glimpse of the whole.

Toward comprehension? Such synoptic views were precious; but they came late. Through most of January the approach was *ad hoc*. The cabinet's reliance on Sir Eric Geddes and his Co-ordination of Demobilisation Section falsely sustained optimism. Sir Eric's group was not, in fact, at grips with the situation. It took the uproar in the army camps to destroy complacency. In their thousands, soldiers demonstrated—first at coastal camps, then in London. "We won the war; give us our tickets" was the slogan. "Get on or get out, Geddes," was the refrain. Five days' study of pivotalism, before Churchill took over the War Office, convinced him (with an assist from the Folkestone mutiny) and then convinced the cabinet to put speed before everything. He deplored the lawless spectacle, but he understood it.

> Life had been lifted to a strange intensity by the war spell. Under that influence, men and women had been appreciably exalted above death and pain, and nothing had been too hard to bear. . . . But now the spell was broken: too late for some purposes, too soon for others, too suddenly for all! . . . Links of imperative need, links of discipline, links of brute force . . . every one had snapped upon a few strokes of the clock. . . . The dire need and the high cause which

had cemented the alliance of twenty-seven States and held their workers and their warriors in intensifying comradeship had vanished in a flash.[43]

Soon the remedy was applied, and 10,000 soldiers were released each day;[44] but by then the cabinet had realized that piecemeal deeds and present means would not do. Sir Eric gave way to Sir Auckland at the Demobilisation Committee.[45] Concentrated, all-out effort superseded past methods in the cabinet. Even the dullest could now see that a greater and more pervasive evil than army discontent had come upon them: trade was at a standstill.[46]

Labor throbbed with indignation. Women workers, seeing industrial training launched for men, charged that nothing was being done for the women.[47] Housing was worse than ever; rent increases were rumored; members of Parliament badgered Bonar Law with news of evictions.[48] The total of unemployed jumped above 1,000,000 ("increasing every day," Horne told his colleagues).[49] Here was the vocal human side to stagnation in trade.

What were the causes? No one was in a mood for detached analysis, but some of the roots of this dual crisis were obvious. The very success of demobilization daily pushed thousands into the labor exchanges. To make matters worse, munitions employees were not quitting. Those who had jobs and sought pay increases, which had come so easily in wartime, found employers dead set against them.[50] For this nationwide palsy of enterprise, falling prices also were a cause. Anyone who produced for stock, at current wages and current costs for materials, was a fool; anyone who committed himself to deliver, or who invested in plant (which is to say any employer who took on more employees!), was gambling against all

43. Winston Churchill, *The World Crisis, 1916–1918*, 4, Part 2: 542, and *The World Crisis: The Aftermath*, 5: 29–30, and 52–60; C. W. Mowat, *Britain between the Wars, 1918–1940* (London: Methuen, 1955), pp. 22–23; WC 514 (8 January 1919) and 521 (28 January 1919), Cab. 23/9; G.T. 6674 (15 January 1919) by Churchill, Cab. 24/73. Papers in Cab. 33/1 and 33/2 indicate the chaos, and inactivity, in Sir Eric Geddes' committee on demobilization.

44. Churchill, *The Aftermath*, pp. 60–66; Mowat, p. 23.

45. WC 523 (31 January 1919), Cab. 23/9.

46. G.T. 6601 (4 January 1919), Cab. 24/73; Stanley in WC 514 (8 January 1919), Cab. 23/9.

47. Home Affairs Committee, meeting 20 (21 February 1919); see D.M. 6 (13 February 1919), Cab. 27/49.

48. G.T. 6817 (16 February 1919), Cab. 24/75; Home Affairs Committee, meeting 20 (21 February 1919).

49. Home Affairs Committee, meeting 20 (21 February 1919).

50. G.T. 6825 (17 February 1919), Cab. 24/75.

expert opinion and current evidence. The price situation minimized the value of government decisions to sell the national factories; who wanted them in that uncertainty?[51] Nor would it help to pass the War Pledges Bill; entitlement to a job in a firm that was not producing was an empty right. Pessimism about taxes also retarded initiative; the excess profits duty cast shadows of uncertainty. Business still did not know whether government intended a capital levy.[52] Government's cut in the subsidy to iron and steel, on 15 January, deepened the gloom and augured worse for April, when the subsidy would end.[53]

This amounts to saying that the government itself, with its timidities and oversights and irresolutions, was a major cause of crisis. The bill was being rendered for the inattention of 1918 and the frenzied makeshifts of armistice time, for the nullity of Eric Geddes' leadership, for the optimistic assumptions of natural rebound. Of course, the state could employ and manufacture, but it was as sure as anything that this would guarantee future loss to the state. Not even the government could escape the logic of falling prices.[54] All this the ministers knew; they saw, too, that palliatives did not work. Industrial training and administrative reshuffling made no visible difference;[55] the unemployment donation and soldiers' war bonus were inadequate.[56] If we can judge by debates, moreover, what the ministers did *not* know was equally bothersome. Roberts speculated that if the state undertook manufacturing, no good would come. "If you embarked on trade you had got to be a monopolist. If the Government entered into trade, stagnation would remain and unemployment would become greater than it was to-day."

But others defended the usefulness of government workshops. For and against the plans to sell national shipyards, the pros and cons balanced just as exasperatingly.[57]

Even the obvious was debated. Mond's plan to throw his Office of Works immediately into building (which he vowed would create many jobs) was opposed by rival departments.[58] Amazingly, the out-of-work donation had its foes. Auckland Geddes insisted that it kept people

51. Demobilisation Committee (8 January 1919), Cab. 27/49; WC 514 and 533, Cab. 23/9; G.T. 6782 (11 February 1919), Cab. 24/74.

52. G.T. 6689 (21 January 1919) and 6759 (7 February 1919), Cab. 24/73 and 24/74.

53. G.T. 6722 (15 January 1919), Cab. 24/74.

54. WC 514 (8 January 1919), Cab. 23/9.

55. *Ibid.*; Demobilisation Committee, meeting 4 (16 January 1919), Cab. 27/49.

56. WC 520 (28 January 1919), Cab. 23/9, for the bonus; for the unemployment donation, see the sources in note 98 below.

57. WC 514 (8 January 1919), Cab. 23/9.

58. G.T. 6793 (13 February 1919), Cab. 24/74.

unemployed, and Kent agreed. "Continuance of today's scale would bring disaster. The high sum paid acted as a deterrent to employment, and this was especially the case among the women."[59]

The point of all this is not that, somehow, a solution was distilled from the details—far from it! The point is that *occasionally* the cabinet rose to a larger view, of which these details were the parts. It had to. The greatest point of all was that the cabinet *must act*. It was no good continually discovering that past patchwork had been bad—or that inquiries into items the government might produce, or the forming of new ministries, or the "reparations" cure which was recommended would all take too much time.[60] There must be an attempt at something. The miners were at explosion point. Lloyd George reported them "firmly convinced that they could hold up the community and prevent the distribution of food." For his part, he seriously suggested withholding food from mining districts. On 7 February the cabinet's discussion revealed that the ministers fully expected a showdown and were bracing to fight.[61] Churchill's memoranda on Bolshevism were hardly needed; violence in Glasgow seemed warning enough.[62]

Auckland Geddes struck one spark; Lloyd George struck another. Geddes proposed an immediate and complete inquiry, from scratch, into every phase of the economy; Lloyd George confronted eighteen key ministers on 17 February with the fact that "trade in the country was more or less at a standstill." He at once asked for a summary of what the ministries were doing; he got recapitulation of problems, revelation of departmental tangles, but no resolution. If there was a consensus, it was a deep anxiety about foreign competition (India and the crown colonies had placed orders with America, not Britain) and a tendency to favor decontrol.

Professor Chapman of the Board of Trade voiced this most clearly: "Government . . . should remove as far as possible the obstacles . . . in the way of the attaining of a new natural level of prices. If this could be obtained, trade would restart itself." Chamberlain was more circumstantial: the Treasury hoped for relaxation of the blockade, so that neutrals could buy British goods, but

> he viewed with some dismay the general relaxation of import restrictions, on account of the exchange position. If we spent much

59. Home Affairs Committee, meeting 20 (21 February 1919).
60. For reparations, see G.T. 6822, Cab. 24/75.
61. WC 531 (12 February 1919), Cab. 23/15; WC 529 (7 February 1919), Cab. 23/9.
62. G.T. 6857, 7086, 7092, Cab. 24/75 and 24/77.

money in buying things that were not necessary, we should have great difficulty in getting things that were absolutely necessary for the rehabilitation of industry owing to the extraordinary difficulties of exchange . . . created by the war. The importation of raw materials was good: the importation of fully-manufactured goods should be avoided.

Sir Eric, Sir Auckland, and Montagu blamed the indecision itself.

British trade would never be restored so long as the present uncertainty continued. It was not of so much consequence whether control was removed or not, so long as the trading community knew what was going to be done. It was the uncertainty . . . that was killing the industry.

Dissatisfied, the Prime Minister found only one thing clear: "There was a great deal which required searching investigation." Some *one* minister must take charge of all questions that affected the reconstitution of British trade. (Addison doubtless suppressed a pardonable "I told you so.") Sir Auckland, as Minister of Reconstruction, was given broad powers to coordinate the effort and was told to survey the entire situation, with the full authority of the War Cabinet. He was to report remedies and to give decisions. Meanwhile, relaxation of controls, wherever feasible, was to continue.[63]

Toward action? Sir Auckland Geddes' first inquiry. As Minister of National Service, Geddes had handled one of the toughest assignments of the war; as President of the Local Government Board in late 1918, he had used his brief tenure to turn crusted hesitation into bold and farsighted decision. On whatever topic, his memoranda carried authority; and now he had charge of the inquiry he had demanded. A few days later he put before the cabinet his first appraisal, which even today is the most articulate and crisp analysis the records hold. "Inconsistent policies" were the cause of many difficulties, he began. They included:

1. The orthodox financial (gold standard) policy
2. The Federation of British Industries' (back to 1914) trade policy
3. The social (better Britain) policy
4. The Imperial policy.

63. G.T. 6820 (17 February 1919), "Minutes of a Conference . . . on Unemployment and the State of Trade," Cab. 24/75; Auckland Geddes' earlier proposal, G.T. 6779 (Cab. 24/75) is discussed in WC 533.

The Treasury's policy—the first of these four—he judged "undoubtedly sound," if the cabinet's one aim was the earliest possible return to the gold standard. Its essence would be retrenchment: paying the debt, deflating the currency, and returning to the 1914 purchasing power of money. But he held it "a most doubtful policy . . . in view of the huge volume of indebtedness" the state had incurred at war values. The "back to 1914" policy—return to the prewar trade conditions, with the state carrying all burdens and making good all losses—seemed to him "as incompatible with the financial policy as it is with the social and imperial policies."[64] Geddes summarized the "social policy" (housing, land settlement, education) without adverse criticism, but emphasized its premise: "The State shall freely invest large sums of capital in improvements which will give an indirect return in the future and in the meantime seeks to find employment for vast numbers of persons on State works."

The imperial policy (his pet, one suspects) flowed from a view of the entire empire as an undeveloped unit; it would require massive migration within the empire. Geddes passed along his own judgment: The government was pledged to the hilt to support the "social" policy; by implication, it *must* therefore adopt some of the "imperial policy." For "if large sums of capital are locked up in slow maturing investments (e.g. housing), the trade of the country must be reduced and emigration on a large scale is a necessity." Protection, perhaps by tariff, must follow; otherwise some industries would be crushed by foreign competition.

And then the two crucial points:

> The general financial policy of the country seems to me to require urgent consideration in the light of Government election pledges. They appear to me to be quite incompatible with action along the lines required by the orthodox financial policy. Be this as it may, of one thing I am quite certain. The present lack of real agreement on policy makes it quite useless to hope for speedy action in any direction. I would sooner adopt the worst of the four policies and stick to it than continue the present pull devil, pull baker between Departments which is preventing decisive action in any direction.[65]

On 25 February, just before Lloyd George walked in to a second emergency conference with his key men, he read Geddes' paper—and

64. G.T. 6841 and 6878 (18 and 19 February 1919), Cab. 24/75.
65. G.T. 6880 (*ca.* 21 February 1919), by Geddes (Cab. 24/75), citing first, second, and third U.A.S.T. conferences of 17–20 February 1919, G.T. 6820, 6835, and 6843, Cab. 24/75.

reacted strongly. Cutting in to Geddes' opening statement, he objected: he "did not really see where the clash came in." He had not been shown that policies were inconsistent, and he doubted that lack of capital was the root cause. Geddes tried again.

> There is no doubt that the Government is pledged by every possible election pledge to the social policy. But that carries with it . . . certain things which I do not think are perhaps fully recognised by all Departments. . . . Just so long as that capital is locked up will it be unavailable for trade purposes. . . . We should recognise that the trade position of this country cannot be what it was before the war, and the country cannot carry the food population which it did carry before. We have had during the last four years by recruitment what is, in so far as its social effects are concerned, really the same as emigration on a great scale. We have had the places of those who have gone filled, and a social reorganisation has taken place which has profoundly modified the whole conditions as they existed in 1914. It seems to me that with this social policy—I have looked at it carefully, and I think there is no doubt about it—we cannot possibly hope for years to come to carry the food population which this country did carry before, because the development must be slow if we are to get the agricultural development which is necessary to produce the food in this country. It is not going to happen this year or next year; it will be a matter of slow development. The development of the agricultural policy, the production in our own country, seems to me to be essential if we are to carry the population, and for this reason, that the markets of the world are entirely transformed, so far as trade is concerned, from what they were before the war. We cannot possibly have the same sort of markets. Central Europe is practically shut out. Our Allies, France, Italy, and so on, are not in a position to pay for goods that they receive from us to a great extent. They owe us amounts of money which it is likely they will never pay for in food, and the trade position cannot go back. Therefore it seems to me that what we have to recognise is that the minute we embark upon this social policy—as we have embarked— we have done two things: really we have made it essential that there should be great emigration, and we have also recognised the fact that trade is not going to go back—the conditions and the organisation of trade and industry in this country cannot go back to a pre-war state. Take building alone. In my view, what we are doing there

366

is to create a position in which private enterprise, at all events in connection with smaller houses, is politically impossible. We have had houses built now at a perfectly different rate, a much higher rate, perhaps more than twice as high. The rent that is going to be paid for those houses is going to be kept down in the meantime to a level very near what the old economic rent was, but not quite. If it were conceivable that labour was going to give up the high rates of wages, it might be conceived that the cost of building would go down, but I do not think it is conceivable that labour will do that. Therefore I think we may assume that the cost of building is not going back to the old level. If new houses are to be put upon an economic level for their cost of production there will be at once an enormous rise in the rents of the houses built upon the old scales of cost. I do not think there is any chance whatever of that increased return upon the original owner's capital, regarded as unearned increment, being accepted politically. I think the result of a sudden jump in building, the change in prices, the change in policy, will be that we have absolutely destroyed the basis upon which our industry —particularly in house-building—was built up, and it seems to me on this policy we are going straight to the nationalisation of building. It may be a good thing or it may be a bad thing, but it is clearly a great departure from anything that we have had before.

Geddes was dismayed that "we have got these various things being recommended, pressed, and carried out, without there being any agreement between the departments and the fundamental ideas that underlie their policies." Therefore, "we have clashed everywhere."

Was there a lack of capital? Several said no; "It is only that business is nervous." Chamberlain retorted: "There is an abundance of capital for [resumption of trade] if you do not want capital for anything else, but there is not sufficient capital for all that we want to do." Bonar Law thought the focus wrong.

Ultimately there will be a shortage of trade. Meanwhile firms have spent so much in excess profits duty that they have not the courage, with that big burden . . . to go to the public and ask for big sums of money.

But Lloyd George resisted these long views; he doubted that the shortage existed at present.

> Supposing the war had gone on for another year . . . could not we have borrowed the necessary 2,000,000,000*l*.? We were spending money freely on public works, so if you create a sort of prosperity there is no doubt you could find the money.

Jabbing at one minister after another, he extracted their estimates of what they could spend that year: perhaps £25,000,000 for housing, £15,000,000 for land settlement, and so on. "That is 71,000,000*l*. altogether. I want to know why this problem should be such an appalling one for a nation which has been finding 2,000,000,000*l*.!" Chamberlain cried: "How have I to meet that?" The Prime Minister's vague reply provoked Chamberlain.

> We cannot live by taking one another's washing. What we want to do is to get a healthy trade started. This is far more important than stocking a great lot of expensive relief work. If you could get the business to move, the rest would follow.

"71,000,000*l*. to be raised in the course of a year is not going to stop business," the Prime Minister said; "there is plenty of money, and if there were business and confidence on other grounds business would start. I say there is no incompatibility between these two things." He listened while Bonar Law said that now there were special difficulties, whereas in wartime the government had ample money—five to six billion pounds—because it came from war profits; but the Prime Minister did not yield.

> All I know is this. I always used to hear from Mr. McKenna, when he was Chancellor of the Exchequer, that we could not borrow beyond the 31st March, and that then there would be an end. Then he brought it up to September.

Geddes yielded; Lloyd George pushed on. "Really the biggest item" was *building*. Stanley, backing Lloyd George, discounted its cost.

> You get that back in the better work the people will do. Then when you come to electricity, the scheme there is to provide cheaper power. That is all for the development of industry and to make . . . railways more efficient and make more money.

This looked too simple for Bonar Law, who agreed with Sir Auckland that "trying to get rid of the inflation" was the big question. If, in addition to coping with wages and expenses and markets, "you want to get back to the gold standard business, it is obvious you cannot do it. Inflation must be kept up." Geddes agreed: "We have to keep inflation, and we have to realise it."

Chamberlain tried to put the Treasury's problem in a few words: Deflation, even if desired, would be very hard to attain, but what did "inflation" mean?

> What happens then? At the present time we maintain the dollar exchange in New York, as we maintain other exchanges, by artificial means. The Government buys exchange and sells exchange. In other words, it subsidises the importer from those countries and to some extent penalises the exporters to those countries. If we let the exchange go, import would become more difficult and export would become easier. Does Mr. Bonar Law contemplate that it is the proper policy for us to pursue to let the exchanges go? If we do, then of course gold will be shipped.

It was all very well for Bonar Law to insist on keeping up the exchange, but this was increasingly harder, with Congress hostile and the United States Treasury reluctant. In retort, Bonar Law could only emphasize that America also would suffer if the exchange fell. He added: "Whether we like it or not, it is obvious you cannot stop inflation if you have to go on borrowing money; and you can do nothing else if we are to go on with our policy at all." Undeniably, Chamberlain said, and as for social reforms "the Prime Minister knows I agree with the policy." If, however, export trade did not revive, it would be no real compensation to be "spending an enormous amount of money on housing."

Leo Amery urged plans for massive emigration. Then he and Stanley reopened the question of export trade, and found no cheer. At present, necessities of the blockade prevented sales. In the long run, said Amery, it would be found

> that the old market for British industry on the Continent and in neutral countries no longer exists. . . . We are in fact no longer the sort of country that can compete industrially in the open market except in certain industries. . . . It really comes to this, that we can both carry out our social reform and develop an immense trade, but mainly if not almost entirely within the Empire.

The Empire must be peopled as the American West had been, and British industry would flourish. Otherwise (he became prophetic)

> you will find England cannot reabsorb the men who emigrated for the war, unless it is prepared to come back to the pre-war wages and pre-war conditions of labour; in fact, we should have to be the old

European competitive England instead of what it is now, an England almost on the American basis of high wages.

But Lloyd George would not have it (what Prime Minister relishes the thought of telling his electorate that they must leave?). Churchill, Addison, and others felt the country would face a growing *shortage* of labor. Plainly, Lloyd George wanted quick, specific, and workable (or if need be, just quick) measures. His impatience stemmed directly from the crisis in coal. Only four days before, he had met the executive committee of the Miners' Federation—men whose strike threat made an ultimate contest for survival imminent; he needed answers at once. The Prime Minister therefore sought to return to details but Geddes interposed:

> It will help us if you would state what the policy is. You wish to discourage emigration, and you wish to retain the inflation. Is it to be taken as the policy of the Government that all the money that is required for these social improvements is to be found? Is that to be a first charge?

"It is not merely that we are pledged," Lloyd George replied, "I want to look ahead and see how we can guarantee the peace of this country."

> Nothing struck me more, in the conversations I had with the miners, than the part this plays in the general irritation which has made them unreasonable. . . . A well-to-do man went to remonstrate with the miners. One of them, a fairly educated man and a Scotsman, said "Do you know the place I live in?" He lives in one of those houses that are back-to-back, with all the sewage brought right through the living room, and he has all his children living in that place. He said "Supposing your children lived in those conditions, what would happen to you?" The well-to-do man said frankly "I should be a Bolshevik." Confidence is the thing you want to restore, and you will get no confidence until there is a certain contentment in the labour world. I believe the introduction of a series of Bills we are preparing now one after the other, showing real determination on our part to deal with it—not sham Bills, but real Bills—will have a great effect in quieting labour. It is their conviction that they have come in vain to the doors of Parliament, and that promises made by one party or another have only produced measures that did nothing. The Town Planning Bill has not produced three houses; the Small Holdings and Allotments Bill has not produced anything substantial—they have not made a real

change. That is the kind of thing that has made them feel "Well, it is no good going to Parliament, we must trust to our own power," and they strike, and a strike may end in a revolution. You have first of all to give confidence in the Government to the people, for the Government means as much for them as it does for the well-to-do classes. Until you do that it is no use trying to build up trade in this country.

"I agree that our housing problem has got into such a condition that it is a source of danger to the stability of the State," Chamberlain said.

We have got to deal with that problem, in accordance with the programme which we took to the electors, on broad and generous lines, and go ahead with it as fast as we can, with due regard to carrying it out properly. I think that ought to be the first charge on the public resources which we have. Then in their order come the other things. For example the land settlement of ex-soldiers. That is a special thing, and that ought to come first. We ought to go on with these things in what measure we can, and do all the departments would ask us to do. At the same time, we cannot have both a tremendous development at home and all the development we should like to have abroad.

The question of the hour was different, however; even when social reforms had the effect of making jobs, it was still different. "Far more important than these Government schemes from the point of view of unemployment is the setting to work of trade," which the government still had not solved. The cabinet could and did all concur in rejecting the Federation of British Industries' program. "The most extreme thing I have seen in that line," said Geddes. "It is incompatible with anything," said Bonar Law. "Quite absurd," Chamberlain agreed; "I told them they were asking the impossible, and that no Government would listen to such demands." Churchill favored placing government orders and underwriting losses on manufacture; these measures would ease the turnover for "a comparatively small amount of money."

Pros and cons were chorused, and Lloyd George tried again.

There are here four business men in front of me who are engaged in trade. . . . I will hand over to them for the moment the British Empire as a concern. . . . Would they feel any despair about finding sufficient employment for everybody in this country provided the right course were taken to set the machine going? . . . What course would they adopt in order to set the machine going?

Inverforth and Illingworth answered, "Restore confidence." Sir Eric Geddes spoke for retaining a wartime attitude toward costs.

> You must be prepared to spend money and treat it as part of war expenditure in order to employ people. The best way to employ them is upon the schemes which we are all agreed are essential—these social schemes. I think during that period you will have to allow people to get out of the country or employ them, because you cannot keep giving them doles and keep them contented.

This done, trade would revive—"there is no reason why it should not"—but guaranteeing business against loss would be fatal. The short-term remedy was to lower prices, partly by reassurances on excess profits and partly by further decontrol.

Stanley jumped in.

> Get rid of the controls first of all, get rid of all the restrictions, and get trade and industry back to where they were, so far as general principles are concerned. We should at least know where we were then. We should have the responsibility back upon tens of thousands of people in industry, and upon them will be the responsibility for the development of our trade and industry. I should sweep away the controls, and leave only so much of the restrictions as is absolutely necessary in the opinion of the Supreme War Council to deal with the question of blockade. There, again, I should be liberal in order to get some of the trade going again. So far as the financial aspects of the problem are concerned, I should get rid of the excess profits duty. So long as that exists you cannot expect capital to venture into new enterprise. The margin of profits is so small that it is not really good enough for capital to be risked.

Horne, Minister of Labour, felt that none of the suggestions was quick enough.

> Operations should take place now in order to prevent the amount of unemployment which we must foresee for some months to come, at any rate; otherwise you may have a state of affairs in which employment is not worth giving at the end of that period. The situation is going to be serious, and it is already serious. Unemployment last week mounted up out of all proportion to the previous week.

Specifically, he endorsed government orders, even at the present prices. It would be cheaper than the unemployment donation; and hesitancy, "a menace to the State, . . . may end in disaster. . . . Every private manufacturer and every man with an order to place was holding back, saying 'If the State are holding back under these conditions what about us?'"

Lloyd George came to as much of a conclusion as the discussion warranted. Blandly he thanked the ministers for confirming his view that "there is no real apprehension as to the future of British trade and British industry"! As for specifics,

> First of all, there are these restrictions. I have heard so much on that point from almost every quarter that I feel confident that, even if there is no substance in it, the mere apprehension . . . is acting as a kind of bogey, and we shall not advance . . . until something has been done to ease matters in respect of restrictions.

Although Lloyd George cautioned that this must be an international process, partly hinging on his work at Paris, he nevertheless instructed Stanley to list the British commodities that were awaiting export (rumored to value £100,000,000). Second, on government orders, he agreed with Horne: government must take some risks. Commons permitting, Lloyd George wished anticipatory orders placed by the Ministry of Supply; he wanted houses begun at once, and public works pushed. Third, the excess profits question must be settled. Fourth, one must "give confidence to Labour as well."

> That is a much more difficult business, because they are thoroughly rattled and are greatly suspicious. Personally, I think a good deal has happened in the past which justifies their suspicion. Take the sort of stupid thing the shipbuilders did in Glasgow, trying to rob them of their five minutes at the beginning of the day. That is the kind of thing that annoys and exasperates them. Then take Smillie and the miners. We all know what has happened in the past, but it is no good telling them that that is ancient history. It is in their bones, and you have to win back their confidence. Until we get that confidence back we shall get unrest. Unrest is one element, and lack of confidence on the part of Capital is another. Capital will not go on spending money and taking risks when they do not know whether in the course of the next three or four months there will be some sort of upheaval which may involve them in bankruptcy. Therefore we have got to do our best to win them back, too. We will try and

settle these immediate disputes, and if we cannot we shall have to fight the thing through. It may be a good thing, because Labour is getting unreasonable in some respects. I thought they were very unreasonable yesterday when they refused to give an extra fourteen days for investigation. It may be necessary to take a firm and strong line to bring them to reason. Still, we must do more than that, and I am sure that the introduction of these measures will show that we are prepared to deal on a large scale with the real grievances of theirs, the housing, the way in which they have been kept away from the land, the depopulation of this country, where the fathers of these people have been driven away from their homes, the divorce of the people from the land in a way which you have not got in any other country in the world, and the lack of social amenities of the villages, raising what they call their standard of life—and anybody who has seen their wretched cottages knows what that means without any definition—all these things have to be dealt with.

Those who had bills should bring them forward at once.

You must give the people a horizon, or they will look at their wretched surroundings, and once they lose hope there is nothing but revolution and trouble. You must tell the people something of that sort in order to show that we are not merely talking. They are getting sick of talking.[66]

Decontrol, orders, tax amendment, reform: Lloyd George had chosen four specific points of attack. Such, seemingly, were the results of the session of 25 February. Were there more?

Had the government chosen between the four competing policies Geddes had seen? Clearly not. Had it, at a lower level, faced the hard questions of subsidizing manufactures or production by the state? Not formally; but inaction meant negation. There were no subsidies, in the event, save for rails, freight, food, and mines, areas not negligible. As for productive use of state factories, two lines of thought had begun in January: (*a*) government must not compete with private industry, for fear of discouraging it (Sir Eric Geddes championed this principle); (*b*) if only for political reasons, preference in purchase must be offered to the co-operatives and unions. Offers of factories, and actual agreements, were

---

66. "Shorthand Notes of a Conference . . . February 25th, 1919, on Unemployment and the State of Trade," G.T. 6887 (26 February 1919), Cab. 24/75.

made, but they came to nothing.[67] Meanwhile, reports convinced the cabinet there was no distinct group of products for exclusive governmental use that the state could efficiently make. Not one national factory, without considerable delay for retooling, was fit to turn out such supplies. Among industrial commodities generally, not a case was advanced in which state production would not be at the expense of private industry. Whether one hewed to Sir Eric's principle or simply tried to make jobs, two conclusions followed.

> Any manufacturing capacity set up by the Government would simply transfer the work from one plant in one district to another plant in another district. There would be no addition to the amount of labour employed in the country, except that caused by the construction of any additional plant. . . . It does not appear that there is any satisfactory middle course between the taking over a whole industry in the country to be run as a Government monopoly and the present system of purchasing Government requirements from the trade. Any intermediate course would miss the advantages both of a monopoly and a minimum economic cost of production.[68]

That clinched it. The factories would be sold.

But there was progress on other mandates: government orders were placed, reforms jostled through Parliament, excess profits duty was cut. As for the fourth imperative, decontrol, between mid-February and 11 March six Munitions Control Orders were suspended or revoked, making fifty-two materials that were decontrolled. Although seven large categories remained under control, terminal dates (April or May) were fixed for fertilizers, iron and steel, new machine tools, carbon and coke. Nineteen of forty Board of Trade Control Orders had been revoked, with early abolition set for nearly all. Cotton control had been abolished. Building licenses for cheaper houses were no longer needed.[69] The situation was not uniform, however. Restraints on production, on use, and on dealing in materials were being freed first, and most emphatically, as in armistice time; but food, coal, rails, and some materials were controlled and would remain so for more than a year. Although many exports and imports were free, a merchants' panic that spring produced new import barriers.

---

67. WC 514 (8 January 1919) and 565 (9 May 1919), Cab. 23/9 and 23/10; *History of the Ministry of Munitions*, 7: *The Control of Materials*, Part 1, 80–81.
68. G.T. 6881 (22 February 1919), Cab. 24/75; WC 533 and 543, Cab. 23/9.
69. App. 17 and 19, G. 237, Cab. 27/58; G.T. 6820, Cab. 24/75.

In Whitehall, last year's emphasis on retaining basic powers was weakening.[70]

Such had been the conference of 25 February and such were its sequels. Events in late March would force another strategy session, but that event must wait. Three other February events, ranking with the ministerial conference, merit attention: the Sankey Commission, the Geddes inquiry, and the National Industrial Conference.

Whitleyism—perhaps. Extending invitations to almost one thousand representatives of business and labor, the government called together a "National Industrial Conference" in late February. This Conference met in plenary session on 27 February and 4 April 1919; there were numerous sessions, between and after those dates, of the Provisional Joint Committee of masters and men, which the Conference had established. From it came the stimulus to renewed governmental activity, culminating on 18 August 1919 in Sir Robert Horne's submission to the House of Commons of two major bills, one for a 48-hour work week, the other for a commission to determine minimum wages. At that moment, with the principle of a minimum wage accepted by the cabinet, the campaign for Whitleyism seemed on the brink of lasting victory. The probabilities seemed strong that, in exchange for governmental action on wages and hours and several other proposals of the Provisional Joint Committee, the representatives of employers and employed would rapidly create what the cabinet had emphasized most strongly: a new permanent body, to be called a National Industrial Council, representing both capital and labor. Things went awry. The Conference's wide scope, the apparent breadth and unanimity of support for its proposals from within its own ranks, and the government's seeming alacrity in response, all make the subsequent decline and disintegration something of a puzzle. By October 1919, recriminations between government and the spokesmen of labor had replaced the earlier cooperation. From then until the resignation of the entire Provisional Joint Committee in July 1921, the story is hard to trace; and, long before, the Conference had lost importance.

Nonetheless, one may begin with the premise that the Conference had symbolic importance and might have had substantial results. Furthermore, whatever the obscurities of the sequel, the initiation of the Conference is not hard to explain. In the context of 1919 it made perfect sense to call a

---

70. G. 233, "Committee on Home Affairs. Continuance of Emergency Legislation after the Termination of the War. Report" (January 1919), Cab. 24/5, ratified by Home Affairs Committee 24 March 1919.

meeting of employers and employed; union officials and ministers alike had invoked the spirit of Whitleyism again and again.

The proposal had come, in late January, from the National Alliance of Employers and Employed, via the Federation of British Industries.[71] At the first session at Central Hall, on 27 February 1919, Sir Robert Horne spoke to an audience of five hundred workers' representatives—Ernest Bevin, J. H. Thomas, Clynes and Arthur Henderson among them—and three hundred representatives of employers. Their meeting, Horne began, had "no parallel in history." He put the emphasis on Whitleyism from the start. Hopeful that a true national Whitley Council might be created by this body, he spoke of the signs of progress so far in the cause of Whitleyism: twenty-six Joint Councils already formed, and twenty-four more in preparation. There were speeches, severely critical, from labor spokesmen. Government unpreparedness for reconstruction was attacked; the nation's continued ignorance of cabinet intentions was stressed. The state, many of them held, must conscript wealth. The Prime Minister made the closing speech. He put most emphasis on efficiency and cooperation. He reiterated that the cabinet was open to suggestion; they were willing, for example, to aid a cooperative to take over and run a national factory. But greater productivity alone could create that margin which spelled decent living for all; and, to achieve this, suspicion and recrimination must give way to the teamwork that had been shown in war. All these speeches, no doubt, had helped; but the great question was whether there would be any action. From this standpoint, the final vote augured well. Despite Ernest Bevin, who charged that the Conference had been called "to sidetrack the efforts of men and women who were struggling for better conditions at the moment," all sides of the Conference gave a resounding endorsement to a motion for cooperation.[72]

Both sides set to work. Each was to prepare a memorandum, and help set up a Provisional Joint Committee, to represent both sides equally.

71. G.T. 6799 (12 February 1919), Cab. 24/74. For the stress on introduction of Whitley Councils, as an item to which the government was pledged, see comments by the union leader J. H. Thomas, in G.T. 7021, Cab. 24/77; see also favorable comments by Sir Auckland Geddes in G.T. 6943 (5 March 1919), Cab. 24/76.

72. London *Times*, 28 February 1919, p. 12; Mowat, *Britain between the Wars*, pp. 36–37; WC 553 (8 April 1919), Cab. 23/10; Horne's G.T. 7057 and 7057A (31 March 1919), Cab. 24/77; Roberts, *The Trades Union Congress*, pp. 317–18; Arthur Gleason, *What the Workers Want*, pp. 70–79, 317–38; Allen Hutt, *The Post-War History of the British Working Class* (London: Victor Gollancz, 1937), pp. 22–24; *The Annual Register* (1919), pp. 41–42; Mary Agnes Hamilton, *Arthur Henderson: A Biography* (London: Heinemann, 1938), pp. 210–13; Alan Fisher, *Some Problems of Wages*, pp. 54–71; Gregory Blaxland, *J. H. Thomas: A Life for Unity* (London: Frederick Muller, 1964), p. 122.

Together they were to present proposals for action. By 26 March, the memorandum from the labor side was ready. Part of it was a magnificent summation of "The Causes of Unrest." It spared no indictment and conceded no point of principle:

> The mass of the working class is now firmly convinced that production for private profit is not an equitable basis on which to build, and that a vast extension of public ownership and democratic control of industry is urgently necessary. It is no longer possible for organised Labour to be controlled by force or compulsion of any kind. . . .
>
> It is not enough merely to tinker with particular grievances or to endeavour to reconstruct the old system by slight adjustments. . . . It is essential to question the whole basis on which our industry has been conducted and to endeavour to find . . . some other motive which will serve better as the foundation of a democratic system. . . . The motive of public service should be the dominant motive throughout the whole industrial system, and the problem in industry at the present day is that of bringing home to every person engaged in industry the feeling that he is the servant, not of any particular class or person, but of the community as a whole. This cannot be done so long as industry continues to be conducted for private profit, and the widest possible extension of public ownership and democratic control of industry is therefore the first necessary condition of the removal of industrial unrest.

But the peroration could be read two ways, for all this uncompromising wording. "If unrest is to be prevented from assuming dangerous forms, an adequate assurance must be given immediately to the workers that the whole problem is being taken courageously in hand." Here were words that implied giving the government a chance. Indeed the peroration contained the telltale word "gradual." And the text of the labor memorandum dwelled on a wide range of specific demands—difficult enough, but amounting to a melioristic program rather than a defiant manifesto of intent to attack the existing order. These demands included housing (to be built by the state), prevention of unemployment by a regularized system of spending, a permanent unemployment donation, a minimum wage, and a system of maximum hours; these figured as largely as demands for state production and for price control.[73]

73. "The Causes of Unrest," Appendix to G.T. 7057, Cab. 24/77. See also National Industrial Conference, "Report of the Provisional Joint Committee Presented to the Meeting of the National Industrial Conference, Central Hall, 4th April, 1919," Cmd.

Now, the National Industrial Conference may—if one wishes—be considered a gigantic hoax, within a deliberate policy of bidding for time. Certainly it was called in the light of the Triple Alliance threat of a great strike. Those who so view it can point to other evidence from later in the year. The government did not nationalize, did not go into production, did not reverse decontrol; it was girding—and had been since early February —against strikes, and twice that year it threw the whole apparatus of the state against them.[74] It did not enact a general minimum wage nor set a permanent ceiling on hours; its anti-profiteering measure of 1919 came nowhere near the prosecution—or execution—that was asked. For some, these facts will close the case. If anything less than total equals nil, this result judges itself; and if state responsibility is the whole story, the result must be condemnation. The Industrial Conference may be dismissed as pointless, or remembered as proof of reactionary cunning, but until the whole is seen, no verdict should be returned.

In a study that tests the fulfillment of reconstruction plans, and therefore states the context for this test, the first thing to note is that the government, from the start, took at least a part of the demands most seriously. Reporting very fully to the cabinet, Horne emphasized four demands from the representative joint committee of the Conference: a 48-hour week, a minimum wage in *all* industries (to be fixed by a commission that should be set up at once), a national joint industrial council, and extension of the Wages (Interim Regulation) Act to 21 November 1919, thus keeping wages where they were on Armistice Day. On unemployment measures, the demands were emphatic and numerous: short time, state construction of houses, increase of out-of-work aid, greater access to education; and government should stabilize work by postponing some contracts to times of falling trade.

Three facts impress me.

    1. The Conference put valuable *new* items on the top-priority agenda of 1919. They added to the program of reconstruction, or

---

139, as well as Cmd. 501, with same author, title, and content but including the labor members' memorandum on "The Causes of Unrest," both in *Parliamentary Papers* (1919), vol. 24. The prewar precedent for the Conference is noted in Barry, *Nationalisation in British Politics*, pp. 214–15, and in Lord Askwith, *Industrial Problems and Disputes* (New York: Harcourt, Brace, 1920), pp. 178–86.

74. Explanatory Note, Records of the Industrial Unrest Committee (from the Tube and Omnibus Strike of February to the Railway Strike of September 1919), Cab. 27/59. For the view that the Conference was an element in a stalling technique, see for example G. D. H. Cole, *A History of the Labour Party from 1914* (London: Routledge & Kegan Paul, 1948), pp. 89–90; John T. Murphy, *Preparing for Power* (London: Jonathan Cape, 1934), p. 182, and *New Horizons*, p. 82.

rescued from neglect, four demands—wages, hours, normalized demand, and permanent unemployment relief. Their stress on wages and hours was highly significant; the Glasgow demonstrations, as well as much of the miners' and railwaymen's demands, revolved around this. Furthermore, the idea that the state could and should normalize demand deserved emphasis, and was relatively new. The idea of unemployment aid, though not new, needed the support that the Conference gave; ministers were wavering in their concern for it.

2. The Conference's stress on joint consultation, along with their insistence that wages be determined by the joint committee from their own ranks, and along with the simple fact that they proposed setting up a permanent Joint Industrial Conference, revived the flagging cause of Whitleyism. Not that labor smiled on Whitley Councils; G. D. H. Cole, the resolute guild socialist who had become secretary for the workers' side, ensured that the labor memorandum would not compromise on this. But the practical emphasis, however grudging, and the Conference's very example put it in line with the declared philosophy of the government—and, truth to tell, put it in line with the one means by which reconstruction might really come about.

3. Horne came out strongly for the report. He stressed that the committee, made up equally of employers and workers, was unanimous. The Prime Minister allegedly had received the report most favorably, and endorsed every word of it.

The government was now ready to do two of the things demanded, Horne told his colleagues: stabilize wages for six months more, and help set up the National Industrial Conference. Bonar Law concurred. Personally favorable to *all* these demands, Horne quoted a leading employer: "The country had been so near the precipice within the last few weeks that the only way to convince Labour that Government was sympathetic was to accept the Report and introduce the necessary legislation as soon as possible."

On 4 April the National Industrial Conference met again in plenary session. It was a meeting that could prove decisive, for far more than this sudden experiment in Whitleyism. J. H. Thomas of the railwaymen rose with a question: had the Provisional Joint Committee considered any proposal to give workers an effective voice in management and control? Significantly, the answer came from the Secretary of the Labour Party—Arthur Henderson, who had seen Lloyd George in Paris that week and had heard the Prime Minister declare his favor for the committee report. There had not been time to go into this question, Henderson explained; it was labor's view that proposals on it would be made for transmittal to the proposed National Industrial Council when that body was formed.

Henderson, in fact, dominated the session. Far more than Horne, he took the initiative. From every evidence, he foresaw a dual threat to the causes which the Conference symbolized. There was danger that labor criticism and labor abstention might block the whole effort; and so he personally moved that the Conference "welcomed" the Provisional Joint Committee's report, and agreed to submit it to the constituency organizations as soon as the government officially declared readiness to proceed at once with the legislation and other steps necessary to carry the report into effect; he further moved "that the Provisional Joint Committee remain in being until the National Industrial Council and the Standing Committee have been brought into operation." But there was another danger— government betrayal, or government inaction—and Henderson threw his whole personal force into a warning against that. Both business and labor, he declared, had stopped short of pressing their extreme claims; the government was now the pivot on which the whole issue turned. Government must adopt the report, and adopt it as a whole; it was no good going to the constituent organizations, he warned, unless the government had said, "We are willing to discharge to the very full all the obligations resting upon us as a Government." "It was not sympathy they wanted, but Acts of Parliament," he warned—and then concluded with a promise: "If the Government were prepared to introduce their Bills immediately, his Committee would work equally hard to give effect to their part of the work, and to bring into being the National Council with all speed possible."

After a seconding speech from the employers' side, Henderson's resolution was declared carried. It was Horne's turn to speak.

He was not, Horne declared, in a position to give on that day the government's complete adhesion to all details of the report. But he quoted Lloyd George ("The Government would give their immediate and sympathetic consideration") and said that he believed these words. He added that the cabinet would have preferred the establishment first of a National Industrial Council, to which the Prime Minister could come and deal with the items on the report; but the Conference had decided against that, and implicitly Horne accepted. Then he listed the items to which the government, as he put it, could give immediate assent: housing, transport, forestry, allocation of governmental orders, extension of Trade

Boards. The government could and did pledge its aid to the organization of the National Industrial Council, he said; and he announced—amid cheers—that the cabinet would extend the Wages (Temporary Regulations) Act to 21 November 1919. A proposal for the 48-hour work week had been made by Great Britain at the Paris Conference that week. Lastly, in contrast to this matter-of-fact statement, something different:

> They had lived near to great and wonderful deeds. They had examples in the persons of those who had fought and died in order that this country . . . might be preserved. It was for them to make the country worthy of those sacrifices, and themselves to be worthy of it in their turn.

On 16 April, Horne recapitulated the committee recommendations to the War Cabinet. He foresaw some problems. So far as the 48-hour week was concerned, "there were obvious difficulties in meeting the case of farm workers, seamen, and domestic servants," and any bill must allow for exemptions and variations there. As for a legal minimum wage, he felt the public was ripe for a pronouncement of that sort. The committee wanted the immediate appointment of a commission, obligated to report within three months. The third long-range proposal—Whitleyism itself—had taken more definite shape: a National Industrial Council, composed of two hundred representatives of employers and two hundred representatives of workmen, would be chosen by methods which each side would devise; it would meet twice a year, and would also work through subcommittees. The government would pay expenses but would not have its own representatives on the Council.

To all this, Horne was personally favorable. He had drafted a letter by which the Prime Minister could indicate general approval of these three recommendations.

In the discussion, both Long and Lloyd George suggested that agricultural labor might have to be exempted from the 48-hour week. Churchill put his emphasis on the value of wage minima; "the real answer of ordered society to Bolshevism was the frank recognition of minimum standards and open access to the highest posts in industry." Thereupon the War Cabinet approved Horne's reply, including a reference to agriculture. The Minister of Labour carried the answer back to the Provisional Joint Committee.

After several conferences, Horne reported progress on 29 May. Some of his doubts about the minimum wage, he declared, had been removed. At first he had thought it would be impossible to meet the Provisional

Joint Committee's requirement that there must be an *immediate* announcement on the minimum wage. But he had arrived at a compromise with the committee. A bill would be passed. Its preamble would admit the expediency of fixing minimum rates, and would provide for the appointment of a commission to inquire concerning the proper bases for such minima; the commission would take account of the cost of living, of the granting of exemptions, and the methods for varying the rates. The government's hands, he emphasized, would still be free when the report of this commission was received. As to the maximum-hours provision Horne told his cabinet colleagues that the Board of Agriculture now did not object to being included with other industries in a 48-hour week, so long as there was some elasticity where this rule applied to agricultural labor. Still Horne stressed that, in talking later with the Provisional Joint Committee, he would try to exclude agricultural and commercial workers. The War Cabinet approved his proposals: to go ahead with the already drafted "Minimum Rates of Wages Commission" bill; to prepare a 48-hour week bill, for industrial workers only; and to report accordingly to the joint committee. The general principle of a minimum wage bill had held firm.[75]

One searches the whole history of reconstruction, to and beyond the point of utter weariness, for a turning point. Month after month from 1916, one watches the onward current, waiting for it to slow, veer, or stop. With what result? Until now, many a false sign of check; each time, a revival; acceleration here, aimless eddying there; apparent dissipation of force after the armistice, then the fuller tide of early 1919 refuting all portents. Of course one knows the outcome—or thinks one does. Hindsight, discouraging the belief that all might yet go well, spurs rather a search for that crisis when

> Earth felt the wound, and Nature from her seat,
> Sighing through all her works, gave signs of woe
> That all was lost.

But still those hopes, that men had learned to live by in wartime, assert themselves. And it was precisely such an assemblage as this, and such a

75. WC 553, 557, and 573 (3 and 16 April and 29 May 1919), Cab. 23/10; sources cited in note 72 of this chapter; Mary Hamilton, *Arthur Henderson*, pp. 213–15; Alan Fisher, *Some Problems of Wages*, pp. 55–73; London *Times*, 4 and 27 March, 4, 5, and 11 April 1919. See *ibid.*, 6 May 1919, p. 17, for Horne's description of the Wages (Temporary Regulation) Extension Bill as a measure desired by the National Industrial Conference. For the 27 February 1919 "Memorandum of Causes of and Remedies for Labour Unrest," see Gleason, *What the Workers Want*, pp. 371–93.

new initiative as an industrial conference might begin, on which those hopes centered. If the circle of suspicion were to be broken, if something new were to come to the rescue of reconstruction, here was one—perhaps the last—clear chance. The cabinet had been forthcoming; the response outside had seemed promising. Had the need called forth its chosen instrument?

Into May, the work of the National Industrial Conference supplied no clear sign. But, on the one hand, employers and workmen within the Conference had risen to the occasion and presented a program both broad and unanimous; on the other hand, the government had agreed to much and had ruled out little. On some things the War Cabinet had hedged; but, weighing attitudes as shown in cabinet sessions together with public words, I feel the falling action of the drama had not begun. If hearts were already hardened against a concession or compromise, on either side, this truth was not yet evident. It was a discouraging sign that the miners, railwaymen, and transport workers, as well as the Amalgamated Society of Engineers, were not officially represented; there was danger, further, in the insistence by the labor side of the Conference that the cabinet's response must be immediate and *complete*; and there was danger in the cabinet's reservations about hours and the general wage. Eventually, the whole effort foundered; later in the year, serious obstacles emerged, and forward movement stopped. But so far the portents were not hopelessly bad.

Our focus is still on spring. The Sankey Commission and the Geddes inquiry, then in progress, tell more about the context for reconstruction.

The Sankey Commission: coal and nationalization. The story of the Commission, often and fully told, needs no narrative here, but it is a judgment on reconstruction and a factor in it. It exposed a huge gap in Addison's planning, for it revealed there was nothing in his work that coped with the questions the Commission raised. For another thing, the Sankey Commission first helped, then hindered, the general climate for reform success—raising hopes and then dashing them. This is not to say that either the miners or the government were to blame, nor to raise the topic of nationalization: it was simply the undeniable effect.

Little else that is relevant to reconstruction in general is clear from official records. They are voluminous and they show beyond doubt that no minister declared himself convinced by the miners' case for nationalization. They show that Churchill, who had discomfited his colleagues by speaking for railway nationalization in December, drew the line at nationalizing the coal mines. They show (this matter came to a head in

July and August) that the cabinet, though still divided, was in a mood to announce its disapproval of nationalization even at the cost of a strike. The records leave doubt whether this cabinet, as a whole, ever intended to nationalize anything—or even had an open mind on nationalization. Churchill, clearly, was not against it, although he did not make a fight in the cabinet. Geddes either had not ruled it out or positively favored it, for transport, judging by the debate on his new ministry. Lloyd George either was wavering, or preferred to conceal his disapproval, when he replied to Montagu—as noted—on 19 February.[76] The record from that date—when Chamberlain had said "They had no policy . . . and had never considered it" and was not contradicted—until August discloses no campaign inside the government against it—and none for it. In August the government rejected nationalization and offered compromises; most labor spokesmen took this as betrayal.

The result was a decisive change of climate that was deeply hurtful to reconstruction plans. But this lay ahead. The net impression, overwhelmingly, is that, until July, the cabinet did not turn its full mind to the matter.[77]

Geddes' second inquiry. Meanwhile Sir Auckland Geddes had been probing unemployment and the state of trade, a mingled task of analysis and decision. It was more of the former, his colleagues may have felt, for the net result of labors truly Herculean was a superb survey—which even today is the best government paper (and the *only* compendious one) on it all. But it ran to 171 pages and it told of things to do, not of things done. Even its "Summary of Decisions" cited more items under study than accomplished. Historians find it useful, but colleagues who hoped for superdeeds by a superminister (as earlier they had hoped in passing the responsibility to Smuts and Sir Eric) found it more than a disappointment: it meant a dangerous delay. The final report, finished about 22 April and printed in early May, came two months after Geddes had been put to work.

An interim report, however, packed with forty-seven major recommendations, reached the cabinet on 3 April. And what was done? It challenges belief, but the fact is that only one of these recommendations was acted on that day: the Board of Trade was told to absorb several small departments that competed with its control of commerce and was

76. Records of the Industrial Unrest Committee (February–September 1919), Cab. 27/59.
77. WC 553, 557, and 573, cited in note 75 of this chapter; and sources cited in note 72 of this chapter.

permitted to take control of the raw materials in the government's account that were required by private business. Paltry and trite (such internal reshuffling had been done or at least ordered many times), this response suggested that no level of government held the clue to action. Delegation to Geddes had not worked, having produced only suggestions; departments could not cope, or Geddes' inquiry would not have been called for; and the cabinet paltered.[78]

What was left is a monument to history. Geddes' report is a manful attempt to identify causes and give specific remedies. He traced the trade stagnation to many causes: war strain, limitations on capital, Bolshevism, and German propaganda, but most of all to uncertainty—uncertainty about labor relations, uncertainty about government action on foreign trade and prices of raw materials, uncertainty about confiscation of capital, nationalization, or heavy new taxes. Business worried about all these; but workers looked forward to "new houses, less work, more wages, or a combination of all three." Geddes then turned to contributory causes, pairing them with his suggestions.

1. Expenditure was high, on war services (which could not be cut without causing destitution) and on reconstruction schemes (to which the government was pledged). This worked as a deterrent to enterprise, forcing the Treasury to borrow and thus reducing the capital available for business. However, the expenses and controls could not be ended.

Therefore the Treasury must develop a control over capital "that shall be intelligent, rapid in decision, and accessible" (and "not suspect by commercial men," he added), and this system must be *publicized*.

2. Although inflation had cut working capital 50 per cent in value, it must continue.

Therefore the Treasury must delay deflation, and even permit a slight further inflation, but review the whole topic in six months' time.

3. Although the present support of foreign exchanges (notably the American exchange) penalized the British trader who competed with American exports, adjustments must be delicate.

Therefore the cabinet was to decide whether the political or other advantages of exchange support outweighed its "manifest commercial disadvantages."

78. Auckland Geddes' report, G. 237 (May 1919), Cab. 27/58.

4. A new tax proposal had been devised, less hampering to industry than the prevailing 80 per cent excess profits duty.

Therefore the budget statement announcing a new system must be made on the earliest possible day.

5. Departments must cease their delay and must settle their accounts with firms, paying as much as possible immediately.

6. Although business requests for aid were not only numerous but inherently as reasonable as the present expense on unemployment benefits, the government should withhold such direct assistance unless the goods were for the government itself. It should place the latter kind of order "freely to the full limits of its requirements." All aid must be publicized in full (the clamor against "profiteers" was on everyone's mind) and should be screened by an interdepartmental committee.

7. Although the financial risks in holding stocks were being augmented by falling prices for raw materials, and inaction would cause many difficulties to merchants, some concessions had been made.

Therefore no further action was recommended.

8. Intolerably, overseas trade was handled by seven overlapping departments: the transfer of many functions to the new Ministry of Transport would streamline the Board of Trade and permit it to formulate policies and foster trade.

Therefore the Board of Trade should absorb the overlapping agencies or functions; and consular services must be coordinated.

9. Because the government held vast stocks of crucial materials, and there was danger of selling at the wrong price,

Therefore the government must define the anticipated postwar price and endeavor to force each material down to that level, while keeping reserves to defeat any hold-up by merchants. Prices should favor British users. The basic intention was "to provide British industry with cheap raw material."

10. Although it had been agreed that raw materials should be freely imported, British industry could not yet meet foreign imports competitively, and the situation must not be allowed to jeopardize pivotal or wholly new industries.

Therefore foreign manufactures should be excluded if they were not necessary for British consumption, or if British industry required protection; and the Board of Trade should study methods to maintain "industries which it is the policy of the Government to foster."

11. Although, in general, export trade was vital and would best be served by a removal of all restrictions, there were serious practical difficulties, especially because the blockade must be maintained until peace was secured.

Therefore the commercial community should be fully informed of the reasons for not ending restrictions. (Nevertheless, Geddes held that "we must advance as rapidly as possible" in the direction of removing restrictions on export. He urged a much more open policy for neutrals outside the blockade area, and called for prompt study of export possibilities within the blockade area. In particular, he called for the maximum development of Empire trade, with favored treatment to British traders.)

12. Because the domestic market had special advantages as long as British industry remained unequal to facing competition overseas, and because the obvious remedy—great reconstruction schemes at home—had been held up by financial questions,

Therefore "the money required for the Housing Scheme should be given the very highest degree of priority by the Treasury"; contractors should be told that future control would not affect present contracts; and housing needs must be thoroughly surveyed. A broad policy for land drainage, forestry, and public works should be framed to secure maximum employment. The Local Government Board had already been authorized to sanction local loans to the value of £6,000,000.

As a whole, then, Geddes counted on "the social policy" and freer overseas trade within a context of price maintenance and continued controls. He relied on the state to promote housing, to place orders for British goods, to keep employment normalized, to keep raw materials cheap, and to resist the clamors for subsidies and for laissez-faire. Geddes' program was not very different from the Prime Minister's suggestions.

Sir Auckland felt his inquiry proved three lessons: "there had not been a clear coherent Government policy with regard to trade"; administrative snares hampered progress; and centralization under the Board of Trade was essential. Also convinced that Britain must "secure the maximum of freedom with the minimum of delay," he held the Treasury much to blame: regulations, unwisely exercised, might damage the basis of national prosperity beyond repair.

In truth, Geddes' report preached many lessons. Like every rescue attempt from December on, it taught that clarity of aim, coordination, publicity, and centralization were imperative. And because these themes had been the burden of Addison's song, it preached the folly or tragedy of passing him by. It taught that state initiative and risk-taking were indispensable—messages Addison had long preached. It duplicated Addison's exhortation to spend liberally on reconstruction, as a key measure of employment and recovery.

Implicitly he supplied other lessons, chiefly of Britain's problems—Sir Auckland had written something of a pathologist's report. First, the dilemma he entitled "The Wage Problem."

> The general financial position of the country is one of great difficulty. Daily expenditure on war services is still very high, only about 1,000,000*l*. less than it was at the end of October. It is impossible to reduce it materially until normal trade restarts without producing widespread hardship and destitution. It is equally impossible for normal trade to be resumed without large capital sums being made available. The dilemma is obvious. The solution must be to reduce Government expenditure on war services at such a rate that the sum of the wage element in the reduced expenditure and the increased wage payments on account of new civil business remains constant. ... Government reconstruction ... is similar in kind to war expenditure, and therefore enters into the problem, which in its complete form is to keep constant the sum of the diminishing wage element in war expenditure, including unemployment benefit, plus the increasing wage element in reconstruction expenditure, plus the increase of wage payments on account of the new civil business. The need of stabilising in this way the weekly payments to the wage-earning classes adds to the difficulty of the financial position, and undoubtedly is retarding the rehabilitation of trade. If the Treasury were in a position to cease borrowing to meet its residuary war expenditure and had not to find money for reconstruction, it could, with advantage, end its control of internal capital issues, though it would still require to maintain its control over the emigration of capital. As things are, the control must continue, but equally that control must be highly intelligent, rapid in decision, and of such a character that it is not suspect by commercial men. This is absolutely vital.

Second, the incubus of inflation.

> It is impossible immediately to get rid of inflation, even if it were desirable. Rapid deflation would certainly lead to a sharp fall in

terms of currency in the wages it would be possible to pay. The social results, in the present temper of the country, would, in my opinion, be disastrous. The difficulty of finding an immediate solution for the business problems arising from inflation is therefore extreme.

Finally, there were the special difficulties of world trade due to the war: the sheer chaos after four years' conflict and interruption; the impoverishment of former customers; the outstripping of Britain by Japan and America. If much of this was in Addison's papers for 1917 and 1918, there were significant differences. Geddes' report said not a word about devolution and Whitleyism; but by this time Addison also had brushed aside the idea of using Whitley Councils to help with trade revival.[79] It was a dismal epitaph for three years' hopes!

Necessity dictated another departure from Addison's approach. He had made much of the need for elaborate independent surveys, well in advance and scientifically based on new data, as a preliminary for action. Initially, Geddes had proposed a tripartite investigation, with independent experts preparing one report. Ruefully concluding that this would take many months, Geddes did the next best thing: like Long, Smuts, Sir Eric, and Lloyd George before him, he sounded his colleagues and forged his own estimate. His change epitomized the impact of emergency circumstances upon reconstruction.

Effects intended and unintended. What would be the impact of Geddes' report? First responses suggested nil: the cabinet's single action, on centralization under the Board of Trade, amounted simply to referral. By 22 April, however, the list of adopted recommendations was substantial. Support had been withdrawn from the American exchange; the government was selling its stocks, carefully watching for the proper opportunity to depress the prices of raw materials; transshipment was being expedited, to revive the *entrepôt* trade; and housing had been given the highest Treasury priority.

On controls and subsidies, action followed a dual policy that is not easy to label: some controls were being terminated; terminal dates for other controls had been announced; but subsidies—save for a few key industries—had been decisively rejected. Geddes' doubts about subsidies had been overcome by the unswerving opponent of such aid, Professor

79. G.T. 6925 (27 February 1919) and G. 237 and 237A, Cab. 27/58, especially pp. 2 and 8 regarding problems and fears in the woolen and cotton trades.

S. J. Chapman of the Board of Trade. On Chapman's recommendation, the U.A.S.T. conference voted that

> It was unnecessary and undesirable for the Government to take any steps, by way of subsidies or otherwise, for stimulating the cotton industry. This was to be regarded as typifying a general principle, which should not be departed from without specific War Cabinet authorisation on individual application.

On the face of it, the label for all this was not "pro-business," for many firms' anguished demands for subsidies had been spurned, but surely the policy qualified as "laissez-faire"? Seen in isolation, yes; but in the larger context of policy toward trade abroad, labels again become unreliable. Questions of imports and exports, which troubled the War Cabinet most, are therefore a prime test of Geddes' influence, a major clue to government thought. By 1 May it was clear that all his trade recommendations had been adopted: Empire trade was to be unrestrained and Empire products were to be favored by government purchasers; and foreign imports were unrestricted, save for manufactured goods (a broad exception, much more than an entering wedge, for protectionism). Exports outside the blockade area were freed; those within the area almost so. Not without a major battle against blockade officialdom, and a protest from wool merchants, had these choices on export prevailed. They were proof that specific interests could and would be resisted, and proof, in the former case, that wartime purposes (focusing on Germany) were yielding to a belief that England must make her way by normal trade. Choices between competing values, at least in this area, had finally been made.

Had a choice also been made between the value known as reconstruction (in Geddes' lexicon, the "social policy") and the value of trade revival? How, for example, might Geddes' report affect housing? Officially, the answer was partly specific, partly general, and altogether affirmative: housing had the highest priority; all the adopted measures would produce the economic health by which all reforms might be financed. In short, nothing had been decided against reconstruction. But one senses other, and negative, effects. Persistent decontrol would allow inflation that could badly hurt reconstruction; decontrol would make—had made—it nearly impossible to give a simple priority for working-class housing. Besides, there was a negative implication in the very motive of U.A.S.T. As Geddes said:

> Our main object at the present time should be to adopt such a policy as would stimulate employment.... Government was paying vast

sums in unemployment donation, and if by a change in policy unemployment could be reduced, an economy would be effected for the State.

Geddes here spoke in *support* of the housing program, specifically; but what if unemployment ended? What if other means showed a higher capacity to absorb the unemployed? Absorptive value was indeed the test of tests, but it needed no speculative eye to see that state-financed housing for workers was not inherently the most effective means by this standard. Geddes had already voiced concern that Addison's estimates did not meet the need; moreover, by barring state aid to the private builder, the government had reduced such absorptive value as Addison's campaign possessed.[80] The overtones in Geddes' statement—specifically his obvious relish for any "economy for the State"—also were serious. And another bad omen was the decision for the export of railway materials. This was a plain case, some critics said, of denying a strong domestic need; hence exports, however useful for restarting overseas trade, should be curbed. But export of these materials was approved, in a clear demonstration of the overriding concern for exporting and for creating jobs.[81]

Things left undone were auguries too. Geddes listed no decision on seven of his recommendations, such as control of capital, resistance to deflation, and settlement of government accounts. Was this a sign that government energy at last was flagging?

In Geddes' report and the sequel of action and inaction, then, one can find much: proof, by default, that another clear opportunity for a high-level synthesis of policy had been lost; hints of side effects that boded ill for reconstruction, but balanced by an explicit endorsement of reform plans; and abundant proof, for good or ill, of preoccupation with other aims.

Government Policy: The Context for Reconstruction

Geddes and his colleagues, in ten sessions that ran from February into April, had made their contribution to government policy. They had not made that decisive choice between policies that Geddes wished, nor was it a reasoned program such as might satisfy one looking back from today, but it was a sizable parcel of specific recommendations. Almost none of it, however, was new. If anything creative or different were to be added—and it does appear that Britain much needed it—then it would have had

80. G.T. 6923 and 6924 (February 1919), Cab. 27/58.
81. *Ibid.*

to come from the National Industrial Conference. Almost regardless of the nature of the proposal, a genuinely new idea put forward with support from both sides of that conference would have helped a nation riven by suspicion and shaken by strikes. The Conference, however, had settled down to wages, hours, and Whitleyism—good things, to be sure, but not the inspired remedy or that rally of all interests that, in depressed hindsight, one feels was needed. Hampered from the start by the absence of some of the most militant large unions, the Conference would soon halt its work; and with it the hope that had stirred Whitley in 1916 would flicker out.

With all possibilities explored, and apparently exhausted, what can be said of the result for recovery and reform?

Strategy and tactics for recovery. The government now had an economic policy, of sorts. It had been constructed by a process which was the opposite of deductive. Specific given options were canvassed first, and larger rationales—if conscious at all—came after, or often remained unarticulated. But if the primacy of tactics and details is remembered, both strategy and tactics can be identified. There were important implications and corollaries, so far as two other matters, controls and reforms, were concerned. These too must be examined.

The government's tactics had now been chosen: maximize exports; make the most of the Empire, as a market; import raw materials, and force their prices down; keep competitive manufactures out, relaxing restrictions on them only gradually; cut government staffs; liberate private capital—that is, permit borrowing; prevent deflation; maintain the out-of-work donation and also pensions and bonuses, until private industry revived; keep rails and mines under control, and subsidized as well—along with foodstuffs. By inference, the broad strategy rested on four positive premises. (1) Salvation ultimately depended on Britain's scoring export triumphs wherever opportunity might be created or found. (2) Meanwhile, state purchases and the government's reconstruction program would normalize employment and keep prices high, thereby at least avoiding convulsions or further depression and at best encouraging business enterprise. (3) If only for psychological reasons, controls should be dropped wherever possible. (4) Fundamentally, private initiative would begin to take up the slack.

Some things, one infers, had not seemed needed or had been rejected for reasons psychological, political, or dogmatic. They may be called the negative premises of the strategy: The state need not deploy its vast economic resources on a wartime scale, taking over production in one or more major areas; Nationalization need not be tried; Deflation and retrenchment also must be ruled out.

Above or beyond the tactics and strategy were some clearly articulated aims: to employ men, to stimulate risk-taking, to create new allurements of profit, and to underwrite living costs of the poor for the interim. Perhaps (surely, I feel) another aim was sought, although not yet articulate: to hold the state's costs to the total already assumed. At least from August on, there is no doubt of this aim; by then it had begun to appear as an end in itself. But even now, in May 1919, that motive was present.

Control and decontrol. Decontrol was a fact in the entire situation. It reached far. On 29 April the announcements of orders suspended or revoked covered three closely printed foolscap pages—187 orders in all, for 107 commodities or raw materials. Slated for removal on 1 June were 38 more orders, which affected 15 materials. Many items stood for vast categories, such as iron and steel, agricultural implements, and motor engines. The exceptions, which still were under control, were 14: clinical thermometers, Egyptian cotton, flax, flaxseed, fuel and gas, glass, hay and straw, leather and leather materials, petrol, pitwood timber, potash, tungsten ores, turpentine substitute, and (in part) wool.[82]

Orders of this type told only part of the story. They involved sale and distribution, and some manufacturing processes. But the control system as a whole also involved allocation, priority, subsidy, import bans, and export restrictions. Imports and exports, as noted, were attaining freedom, save for foodstuffs and a small group of key industries. Priorities had vanished by 31 December. Building licensing had been relaxed, building permits done away with, and building prices were left uncontrolled.

The confusion and negativism of January, when Sir Eric Geddes was nominally in charge of the Demobilisation Section of the cabinet as successor to Smuts, had contributed greatly to this developing pattern. Geddes took action that affected both the substance of control and the structure inherited to administer it.

As to machinery, committees, and structure, the broad effect of his regime may be suggested by four propositions. (1) Some machinery for controls had been retained from 1918. (2) The committees intended for that purpose never got a chance to function, either because Geddes was against them or because the reigning confusion denied them a chance to take hold. (3) In the event, Geddes either presided over their dissolution,

82. G. 237A, Cab. 27/58. Details on decontrol of materials are given very fully, though not always with dates, in the *History of the Ministry of Munitions*, 7, Part 1: 72–86.

or transferred them to the Board of Trade. (4) Although presumably those which were transferred were to be put to work by the Board of Trade, the Board was strongly opposed in general to the continuance of controls —and the net result was that even these committees remained nullities.

One can follow this development in the closely related stories of the Standing Council on Post-War Priority and of Sir Arthur Duckham's Committee on Industrial Transition. Each was set up during Smuts's day. Each, in close contact with Smuts's busy Post-War Priorities Committee and his Demobilisation Committee, might be expected to acquire important functions. But the departure of Smuts from the Demobilisation Committee, and the abolition of the Post-War Priorities Committee as such, left them stranded. Organizational lines had been snapped. In January 1919 informal inquiries showed that the Board of Trade was against the continuation of priorities machinery and that it thought priority itself unnecessary. Although one official protested on 10 January that the Standing Council had been meant to discuss *all* matters involving priorities and allocation, and to coordinate the departments' work, Sir Eric Geddes nevertheless told his colleagues on 13 January that "the necessity for emergency organisations in the shape of Committees had now ceased"; Stanley and Auckland Geddes concurred. Perforce, the chairman of the Standing Council yielded, noting that priority had practically been done away with anyhow. Sir Eric Geddes commented that the initial assumptions which had made priorities seem necessary—shortage of manufacturing capacity, materials, and shipping, and a great rush of orders—had not been realized; "control has now been removed almost entirely." Birchenough, the Standing Council's chairman, still wavered; he asked Thomas Gardiner for a report on the situation. Noting a "somewhat insistent cry for the removal of Control generally," Gardiner summed up the situation in mid-January.

> Priority, insofar as it was associated with the control of raw materials, practically disappeared with the abolition or relaxation of controls of Materials. Priority as regards order of manufacture still remains, but the Council passed a resolution yesterday recommending that, except in very special cases, no fresh priority certificate should be issued after January 15th and that all certificates . . . should cease to be operative on March 1st.

He was not persuaded, personally, that the Standing Council should disband; he spoke of the demand by some businessmen for continued controls, alleged that the Council might help industry protect itself against undue continuance of control; he put in a word for the efficiency that some controls had shown. But Sir Eric Geddes insisted on the departmental method, where controls were concerned; and it was at this moment that he decided to transfer the Standing Council, and all matters relating to trade bodies, to the Board of Trade. This act prompted a section of the Standing Council to vote for its own dissolution, on 23 January. The Civil Industry Priority Committee meanwhile had closed down; and Long's Raw Materials Board ceased to function. In its last action it reported on 11 January 1919 that "supplies were fully assured" for six major raw materials, and that the departments could handle the rest.

These decisions, especially those of Sir Eric Geddes, involved structural reshuffling rather than action on the substance of controls; but the net effect of transfer and dissolution was to terminate the bodies with a will to act, and to transfer matters to a department disinclined to act. By 10 February the Minister of Munitions canceled its long-standing wartime "Priority of Work" order. Decontrol, so far as many existing orders were concerned, thus was progressing fast.[83]

Other records, however, revealed an opposite side of the story of decontrol. One sensitive gauge was the Home Affairs Committee—then, as throughout 1919, "almost a Cabinet within a Cabinet"—and its treatment of emergency legislation and emergency powers.[84] When the committee first deputized Lord Cave to list the wartime powers whose continuance was desired, Cave found Whitehall fertile in suggestions for continued controls. This was counter to the wishes of his group, which felt that "all emergency legislation, and especially all exceptional administrative powers, ought to be dispensed with as soon as it is possible to do so consistently with safeguarding the national security and public interests of a distinctively emergency character." They agreed, however, that the Courts (Emergency Powers) Acts (1914–17) must remain, and then they turned to the departments' wishes.

The Office of Works wanted to keep Defence of the Realm Act (D.O.R.A.) Regulation 2AB, by which it took possession of land; others wished 2B kept—for taking possession of war materials, food, and stores—

83. G.T. 6820, pp. 1–2. So far as the fate of the Standing Council is concerned, as summarized above, see Files 11061 and 11131, Box 52; for action of Sir Eric Geddes' group, see P.W.P. 58, Box 52 and D.M. 53, Box 78, Part 3, and minutes of 11, 13, and 16 January 1919 meetings, Box 78, Part 3, and in Cab. 27/49. Liaison between this group and the departments is recorded in Cab. 33/1 and 33/2, where the files plainly indicate the chaotic conditions. For the Civil Industry Priority Committee, see F. 9699, Box 52, and Addison, *Diary*, 2: 425, 469. For the Raw Materials Board, see G.T. 6835 (18 February 1919), Box 78, and F. 7841, Box 39.

84. Hans Daalder, *Cabinet Reform in Britain, 1914–1963*, p. 56.

at least for the industries under control. Regulation 2E was to stand, giving power to regulate manufacturing and dealings in war materials, food, and stores ("an essential part of the machinery of control," the explanation ran). The same for 2F–2J on food control, and for 2JJ by which the Board of Trade held powers to encourage, maintain, or regulate the supply of articles required for the public or for defense (although this was henceforth confined to nine major categories). So too for 2JJJ, concerning road transport.

Under Regulation 2L[*], power to enter on and cultivate land for food supply was requested—but it would be superseded by similar powers, under the Corn Production Act of 1917, when war regulations ceased. (An asterisk has been supplied to denote powers dropped with departmental consent in March 1919, as shown by G. 242 and Home Affairs committee records.) Under 6A, power was to be kept to exempt firms from the 1901 Factories and Workshops Act. The power given by Regulation 7[*], to requisition factory output for arms, ammunition, food, clothing, stores and equipment, also was requested—as "an essential and important part of the system of control of materials." Also, 7C, 7D, 7E, 30E, 41B, and 41D were to stay, for Treasury control of exchange and currency. For the Admiralty, Army, and Ministry of Munitions, Regulations 8 and 8A[*] were continued, authorizing the possession and use of any factory, and requiring factory work to follow official directives (as far as they were needed for maintaining existing orders but no farther). Continuance for six months of 8AA was asked, for banning the establishment of all retail trade without a license. As for mines, 9G, the basis of Board of Trade coal control, and 9GG[*], for control of other mines, were to be kept. Regulation 15C, the very basis of economy through cost accounting, by which agencies could require firms to maintain accounts, was on the list of requested powers. The prime means for shipping and port control— 39BB, 39BBB, and 39C—were asked for, along with 42C, for the discipline of civilians enrolled in government work.

Against its stated preferences, the Cave committee accepted, with modifications and with the assumption that only a year's continuance was involved, all these requests. A series of emergency laws (on the war loan and income tax, for example—on which the Treasury would decide) was left unaffected. Where mere extension would not suffice, the committee pointed to the need for new enactments: on wages awards, restoration of prewar practices, export controls, rent and mortgage restraint, and the munitions acts. All this happened in December 1918 and January 1919. On 24 March the parent committee accepted these proposals, in effect giving all these regulations another year of life. On 28 May it accepted the extension of the Courts (Emergency Powers) Act of 1917, and broadened its coverage to include all pre-1914 contracts. The intent was to block litigation that would inflict serious hardship.

This time, however, the recommended three-year extension was refused; the historian H. A. L. Fisher, chairman of the Home Affairs Committee, thought "it should be the policy of the Government to allow war-time legislation to lapse and return to normal procedure as soon as possible." An extraordinary proposal to pay allowances to producers and traders for losses due to the war or to the armistice also was vetoed. Fisher and Stanley Baldwin agreed that "if the principle of Government compensation was accepted at all it was impossible to say where it would end."[85] These decisions in May suggested a new mood, less open to control or expense, as did the second report of Cave's committee adopted also in May. The very departments that had asked for continuance agreed, in May, to the termination of some controls: 2L, 7, 8A, 8CC, 8D, and 9GG were dropped. The trend against decontrol was working, but the controls themselves—as powers given by statute and regulation—in many cases still stood, with another year of life assured.[86]

Control, like decontrol, was part of the situation—in fact as well as in law. Controls, in the strict official sense of specific departmental orders, remained for eighteen classes of goods and properties until 1920. Coal mines, railways, hides, and pitwood were among these, as well as food-stuffs, which meant a complete system of price controls, subsidies, and wage agreements for milk, wheat, bread, fish, meat, sugar, and flour mills. Many of these would stay until October 1920 or the spring of 1921.[87]

"Control" had other and broader meanings, such as import restrictions. Trade with Germany was still forbidden. Absolute freedom from wartime import restrictions was not approved until September 1919, and soon thereafter a new wave of protectionism—as in the spring—made itself felt. In this sense "control" also comprised five other types of state action: the practice of subsidy, far from abandoned; the possession and careful sale of huge stocks; protection for key industries; bullion and capital controls of many sorts; and ceilings on rent and on mortgage interest, destined for

85. Home Affairs Committee meetings of 18 December 1918, 24 March, 8, 23, and 30 May 1919; G. 233; G. 242, second report by the same committee (12 May 1919), Cab. 24/5, and memoranda therein.

86. G. 242 and meetings of 23 and 30 May (cited above, n. 85).

87. A. C. Pigou, *Aspects of British Economic History, 1918–1925* (London: Macmillan, 1948), pp. 24–25, 83, 119–40; E. V. Morgan, *Studies in British Financial Policy, 1914–1925* (London: Macmillan, 1952), pp. 60–66.

long lives. Shipping stayed under control until 1920. In the sounder sense of state action for and over the economy, "control" still held many salients on a disputed battlefield. Theoretical sovereignty, in the form of statutes, was still—if circumspectly—claimed, but much vital territory had been surrendered. In general, the liberties of enterprise had retaken ground for the great and profitable productive interests. Restrictions on production and on usage and dealing in industrial materials had been the first to go. The foes of such restriction meant this to be permanent: "The intention," Sir Auckland Geddes instructed a colleague, "was that control orders should be revoked and not merely suspended."[88]

Why had decontrol been able to progress, where it had? Dogma played its part, as had governmental convenience, appeasement of business and Parliament, and (in the current and conventional terms) economic good sense. Devotion to orthodox principle, which Professor Tawney so brilliantly stressed, was a constant motive for many. To them, in Professor Pigou's words, the dominant intent was to "liberate" the economy from that "thoroughly abominable thing," governmental control.[89] H. A. L. Fisher voiced the principle, and Auckland Geddes had found the Forestry Bill a case of intolerable centralization "at a time when we are moving toward decentralisation of all executive functions." Chapman had called for decontrol, general and rapid. Inverforth, foe to all positive state action, penned one predictable memorandum after another against state production and for swift liberation of private business. The Birchenough Report, like Cave's committee reports, began with this premise. The Demobilisation Section affirmed that controls "should be got rid of at the earliest possible moment."[90] Sir Auckland spoke out against "the feeling in industry that Government would assist in its rehabilitation. . . . The first essential was to make it clear to industry that industry must help itself."[91]

Orthodoxy sometimes appealed to current proof. Bringing experience to the aid of dogma, some ministers insisted that state control and state manufacturing were discredited by the results.[92] But another facet is revealed here: they *always* met opposition. Stevenson challenged Stanley, on the value of national factories. Lord Pirrie praised the success of national

---

88. G.T. 7002 (minutes of eighth U.A.S.T. conference), Cab. 27/58.

89. Tawney, "Abolition of Economic Controls," pp. 1–2, 14, 26, 29–30; Pigou, *Aspects of British Economic History*, pp. 24–25.

90. Geddes' comment in Home Affairs Committee (4 April 1919); fourth meeting, Demobilisation Committee (16 January 1919), Cab. 27/49; D.M. 53 (11 January 1919), Box 78, Part 3; see G.T. 6887, p. 12, for a typical Inverforth statement.

91. Minutes of 18 February 1919 meeting, Box 77.

92. Examples in WC 514 and 534.

shipyards. Sir Eric Geddes lauded state operation of railways. Winston Churchill trumpeted: "The achievements of the Ministry of Munitions constitute the greatest argument for State Socialism that has ever been produced."[93]

It was not dogma alone, then, that moved ministers (including Churchill) to piecemeal decisions for decontrol; "convenience of the government" was another motive. Stanley had argued that decontrol would put "the responsibility back upon tens of thousands of people in industry." Later, Fisher contended that "every control made difficulties, and the Government already had their hands full in this respect."[94] It was a pragmatic consideration, implying an *ad hoc* approach; both men could and did champion state aid or control, in the next breath. But it worked powerfully on the government, which more and more felt itself isolated and was less and less inclined to add to its burdens.

For Lloyd George, the value of decontrol was psychological: "Even if there is no substance in it, the mere apprehension" about controls made decontrol a prime means for relieving business uncertainty. Thus every mention of uncertainty, and there were many, became an argument for decontrol as a placebo. There was, or seemed, a kind of economic good sense in decontrol. If businessmen declared their uncertainty and fears, and if advisers put stress on this psychological ingredient of the slump, then any decontrol that helped remove doubts was useful, along with government subsidies, import bans, and reconstruction schemes that held the lure of profit and protected demand. If falling prices were the problem, decontrol—with its promise of rising prices—might be the answer. All the more did this reasoning prevail because raw materials supply, ever the strongest argument for control, seemed assured. One dare not overlook this. The abundance of raw materials, together with the fact that they were *in* the country rather than obtained from overseas, formed a double argument, inasmuch as most governmental wartime restraint had depended on absolute control of scarce raw materials as they arrived. This "control at the throat" was what had made priorities, allocations, orders, price controls, quality control, and all the rest effective and possible. With raw materials plentiful, the government need not, and *could* not, control as before.[95] Or so it seemed. As Keynes noted, a complete system of controls

93. *Ibid.*; Trevor Wilson, *The Downfall of the Liberal Party, 1914–1935* (London: Collins, 1966), p. 196.

94. G.T. 6887, p. 14; Fisher in the Home Affairs Committee (6 August 1919).

95. G.T. 6887, p. 16; an exemplary statement on materials supply is in *ibid.*, p. 2. For the importance of "control at the throat," see E. H. M. Lloyd, *Experiments in State Control at the War Office and the Ministry of Food* (London, 1924), p. 299.

would have been thought impossible in 1914; and minds had not changed that much.[96]

Thus the varied patterns of control and decontrol reflected a variety of motives, not simple devotion to decontrol or laissez-faire as an ideal. The whole point of voluminous cabinet discussions is missed if the ministers' concern with *many* factors and *many* aims is overlooked. For recovery, they tried many remedies, as they identified many ills: shortage of capital, fear and uncertainty, falling prices, poor administrative coordination, suspicion between social classes, and inadequate orders from the state. Decontrol was but one of these remedies.

The mixture of motives and results was well shown when consideration began on the future of food control. The Food Controller was under dual pressure, from his own Consumers' Council and from Clynes of the Parliamentary Labour Party, to make food control permanent. The Controller had moved toward decontrol as quickly as possible; he proposed that his ministry end and that its functions go to other departments ("There were certain powers which were being exercised and certain experience which had been accumulated, which should not be dissipated"). He knew the cooperatives and the Labour Party would oppose him. On the other hand, "undoubtedly by far the greatest body of opinion in the House of Commons was in favor of abolishing all control." Chamberlain interjected that, to be effective, food control must include "a thorough system of control of prices, control of distribution, and purchase of raw materials"; but such complete control must come to an end. The government must state that "control as we had known it during the war was only possible on the most extensive scale" and that the government "did not mean to attempt it." Curzon, H. A. L. Fisher, *and Addison* agreed.

As Addison saw it, there was only one possible answer: If prices were to be controlled, then production and distribution also must be controlled; but "the Government would not undertake" any system so total. Ministers seemed unanimous. Just then, however, Beveridge introduced a new consideration.

> Until quite recently decontrol had been going very smoothly, and had invariably led to a reduction in prices; but a tendency the other way had now set in, possibly owing to purchases on German and Austrian account.

Geddes declared this a point of great importance. Indeed it was: the six-months' decline in prices was over. This "tendency the other way," which Beveridge noted, was the beginning of a hugely important

96 J. M. Keynes, cited in Morris Ginsberg, ed., *Law and Opinion in England in the Twentieth Century* (London: Stevens, 1959), p. 159.

eighteen-month trend. Geddes, foreseeing a great stringency in supplies, held that the Food Controller must tell Commons clearly that such a danger existed, and therefore "all control would not be removed until the danger was passed."

This single argument trumped the others. The cabinet decided to announce that the Ministry of Food would be demobilized "as soon as [i.e., not until] the need for control came to an end." [97] It was not far from the thinking that had shaped 1917 and 1918.

Schemes for reform. Neither the trend toward decontrol nor the general economic policy was seen as incompatible with reconstruction as it had been planned, pledged, and approved. The record shows that—far from having passed into limbo—reform schemes were an integral part of the context, and a growing part as well.

Rent ceilings were being maintained; grants for the blind had been added; the principle of a minimum-wage bill had been accepted; details of women's emancipation were being implemented; the problem of unemployment aid had been referred to the National Industrial Conference (whose existence and expenses the government had endorsed) while the out-of-work donation was continued. Wages had been extended at the wartime level, for a second time. The bills for electric power and a Ministry of Transport were going to Parliament. Not content with the reforms passed in wartime, Fisher was aiding veterans to gain a university education at government expense; the way was being prepared for establishment of the University Grants Committee. Entitlement to health insurance had been broadened.[98] And these measures were in addition to the Housing Bill, the Whitley Council program, and bills for land and forest and farm.

Labor and the government. The worker had replaced the mutinous soldier as the prime force ministers reckoned with. The entire program of reform and interim aid can (if one wishes) be explained on these grounds; and it is certain that such reforms were the government's main response to that force. From week to week ministers never ceased to ask what the workingman would do—and what government could do in response.

97. WC 562, Cab. 23/10.

98. For rents, see minutes of Home Affairs Committee (21 and 28 February 1919); for grants to the blind, *ibid.* (28 May 1919); for Whitley Councils, WC 550 (March 1919); for minimum wages, WC 579 and G. 247, Cab. 24/5, and sources cited above, notes 72 and 75; for women's emancipation, Home Affairs Committee (16 and 28 May 1919); for unemployment aid, *ibid.* (10 March 1919), and WC 554, 572, 574. For wage extensions, see Ginsberg, *Law and Opinion in England*, pp. 217–18. For education grants, see Fisher, *An Unfinished Autobiography*, pp. 106–9, 115–17, and Marwick, *The Deluge*, p. 245.

Ministers were concerned, not simply about strikes, but about *the* strike —the great, expected reckoning with the Triple Alliance. With 34 per cent of laborers unemployed, with labor exchanges strained beyond capacity, and with donations going to almost a million into May, the fears never disappeared.[99] On 19 March Lloyd George forecast that miners would strike if (as he anticipated) the Sankey Commission did not report for nationalization of the mines. Bonar Law met many hours with the heads of the Triple Alliance and the Miners' Federation on 22 March.[100]

But Armageddon—even Armageddon Feared—is not the whole of the story; nor will simple references to massed monoliths and a head-on collision capture the cabinet's view. The cabinet thought, or hoped, that labor was not united; even where it feared there was unity, the ministers' attitude was a complex result of many different calculations and convictions. Ministers declared that labor was divided and that this division spelled hope but required caution. Counseling acquiescence to a set of demands he thought wholly unjustified, Bonar Law put the problem tersely: "The Trade Union organisation was the only thing between us and anarchy, and if the Trade Union organisation was against us the position would be hopeless." Ministers must compromise or "the whole of the Trade Union movement would be against the Government."[101] When a shipping strike seemed near, a major consideration was that the government must stand by the unions.[102] Support to labor leaders and the moderates, however irrational or costly the immediate demand, had been the keynote—from the very first cabinet debate on pledges, when a spokesman had tipped the scales by saying

> Failure to fulfil the pledges would be tantamount to throwing over the accredited leaders of the Unions, who would be charged with having betrayed the men. The upshot would be the destruction of organised Trade Unionism, and a great stimulus to the extremists.[103]

Beveridge had met Lloyd George's idea of withholding food from mining areas by the same decisive logic: "This would unite Labour against Government, unite anarchists and constitutionalists."[104]

Such considerations dictated caution and accommodation. So did

99. WC 554; for the figures, see "Weekly Appreciation No. 10" (12 March 1919), by the Co-ordination of Demobilisation Section, Cab. 33/7.
100. WC 546A (19 March 1919), Cab. 23/15; Bonar Law's meetings, G.T. 7021 and 7023, Cab. 24/77.
101. WC 525, Cab. 23/9.
102. WC 538, Cab. 23/9.
103. WC 491.
104. WC 531.

another: the merits of each case—especially as the public saw them. The government thus concluded it could not oppose the eight-hour day in principle; it admitted its position against railwaymen's wage demands was weak.[105] Suppose, however, caution did not work and the open hand of cooperation was rejected? The government had offered a permanent National Industrial Conference, but it knew that labor suspected Whitleyism. Government was administering costly reforms, but knew that articulate laborites denounced the reforms as inadequate.[106] If its caution and cooperation failed to achieve peace, the government would fight, and not always unwillingly. Bonar Law pondered the miners' claims, heard a forecast that the Triple Alliance strike would not come at once, inferred that public support would be on the government's side, and concluded that this might be a good strike to face up to. (It was even Addison's mood at times; as for reinstatement of total controls or reduction of unemployment aid, he said that the public outcry might as well be faced now.)[107] Ministers spoke in terms of labor versus the community, of a threat to the latter's very existence; and they prepared accordingly. The whole of Britain would have to be fed; huge populations must go onto a straight unemployment donation; transport must be secured. Quietly, Lloyd George ordered the Home Secretary to prepare a list of needed measures. The Industrial Unrest Committee, born of February's emergencies, met six times between 12 and 27 March, at the height of the crisis.[108] Armageddon was not ruled out.

But a different policy bore the emphasis (call it appeasement, ransom, compromise, or fulfillment). Pledges and the eight-hour day had been accepted, the wartime rate extended, the National Industrial Conference formed and given work. Reform bills were being passed; out-of-work donation, at a scale unmatched by pensions or prewar unemployment benefits, was in effect. (Looking back, the Webbs spoke of the 1919 atmosphere as one of "indulgence and generosity.") Workers were being offered a voice in the control of mines.[109] The costs were fully understood.

105. WC 510, 547A.
106. G.T. 7057; G.T. 7070 (2 April 1919), Cab. 24/77.
107. WC 529; Addison in the Home Affairs Committee (21 February 1919).
108. WC 538, 547, 531A, 546A; summary on the Industrial Unrest Committee, Cab. 27/59.
109. Sidney and Beatrice Webb, *English Poor Law History* (London: Longmans, Green, 1922), 2, Part 2: 827–29; WC 546 and 547; John Thomas Murphy, *Preparing for Power* (London: Jonathan Cape, 1934), pp. 180–81. Murphy notes that railwaymen got a reduction to a 48-hour week, engineering and shipbuilding workers to a 47-hour week, and cotton workers a reduction from a 55-hour to a 48 hour-week. The eight-hour shift was granted to iron and steel workers.

The eight-hour day would add £20,000,000, at least, to the wage bill—over and above the £50,000,000 granted in wartime, when weekly railway wages had gone from 25 to 33 shillings and farm wages from 18 to 30 or even 40 shillings. The full demand by railwaymen, who wanted their wartime gains made permanent, would cost an additional £120,000,000, and other industries were expected to follow suit. Lloyd George's question, however, contained its own answer: "What is £100,000,000 to the security of the State?"[110]

The labor question touched everything: nationalization, health insurance, national shipyards, and unemployment benefit (it "prevents a convulsion throughout the State," said Horne).[111] Based on the assumption that the extreme left was unappeasable—and not worth appeasing—and on the gamble that matters of hours and wages were the chief concern of the rest of labor, based also on trust in moderate leadership and in trade unionism itself, the government's multiple attitude made labor's response a critical factor. As June began, however, no predictions of that response could be confident.

We have identified above four aspects of ministerial policy and attitudes. We have seen, first, the recovery program; we noted, second, a mixture of control and decontrol; we verified that reforms, old and new, figured in government policy; and we found that labor questions evoked varying and complex responses. Our aim was to see what composite pattern, if any, had emerged by late spring 1919. What sort of pattern was there, and what name does it deserve?

Labels. On the government's policy and motives, many verdicts could be rendered. I prefer to term the policy a patchwork pragmatic response to varied pressures, part wise, part foolish—anything but dogmatic, singleminded, consistent, or reactionary. It surely reflected the desire to placate a House of Commons whose hostility to expense, controls, and bureaucracy already figured in cabinet talks as a worrisome fact of life.[112] It revealed a powerful, though not yet predominant or united, resistance to nationalization, to radical change in land laws, to overall control of electric power, to drastic innovations in taxation, and to vigorous campaigns against "profiteering."

Sir Auckland complained that "the general inclination of the people was to avoid work"—and voted to extend the out-of-work donation.[113]

110. WC 510, 536, 539, 546, 547A.
111. WC 534, 554, 556, 565; Home Affairs Committee (16 and 30 May 1919); G.T. 7225 (19 May 1919), Cab. 24/79.
112. WC 569 (19 May 1919), Cab. 23/10.
113. Home Affairs Committee (21 February 1919).

Now showing an employer's psychology on strikes (the government would be accused of "giving away the pass," Bonar Law predicted—and voted for the concession anyhow), now deploring the heightened wage bill, now yielding to frantic pleas from business that import bans be reimposed, ministers in calculation or in sympathy took the line on trade policy and controls that many businessmen wished.[114] But on each case there were sharp and outspoken divisions within the cabinet, and divisions within many ministers—if we can judge by the fact that few ministers followed a set consistent line. Not even the most seemingly acceptable platitude escaped some challenge. Sir Auckland Geddes, for example, seemed to capture the thought of his colleagues when he made one remark against an energetic probe of profiteering. He argued that any inquiry into profits might stir up something more harmful than labor unrest—namely, capital unrest. One imagines a murmur of instant assent, around the cabinet table. Yet Mond, the highly business-minded minister who could boast that he alone had campaigned against nationalization in the election campaign, was the one who clamored for that inquiry.[115]

No pressure group got all it wanted, no ideologist saw his doctrine fulfilled. The cabinet turned down the pleas of wool traders for continued control and of the cotton firms for subsidy. It deleted aid to private constructors from the Housing Bill. It ridiculed the Federation of British Industries and rejected its most ardent plea, for underwriting production costs. It held fast to Treasury controls of several types, against Commons and business organs alike. It yielded to strike threats or legislated for workers' housing over protests of the interests concerned. Only a very bold person would insist that the cabinet judged each case on its merits, but certainly it judged very few cases by dogma.

The line of policy (if the concept has application) zigzagged by almost any test: not clearly pro-business or anti-business, not pro-labor or anti-labor; certainly not, taken as a whole, pro-business and anti-labor simultaneously; and not clearly decontrol, let alone laissez-faire; not clearly either retrenchment or "deficit spending," at least not in motive. Government policy did not correlate uniformly with any of these distinctions. Several explanations apply. For one thing, "correlations" were not simple and univocal: the line of decontrol was not the simple and undisputed line of advantage for all business, nor did business opinion hold

114. Bonar Law in WC 525; for imports see E. V. Francis, *Britain's Economic Strategy* (London: Jonathan Cape, 1939), pp. 32–33.
115. WC 575; Mond's proposal, G.T. 6834 (21 February 1919), Cab. 24/75; for similar views by Addison and Lloyd George, see WC 562 and G.T. 6820.

singly to it. And this was so for another reason: interests were hugely varied and contradictory. Aiding manufacturers by forcing raw materials prices down, the government hurt the dealers in raw materials, badly. Subsidizing the railways, the government penalized the coastwise shipping trade. Banning some exports and allowing others, or curbing some imports and permitting others, the government invariably made things worse for some and better for others, proprietors and workers. And ministers were perfectly aware that this also held good for "labor questions." The restoration of prewar practices helped the established unionist, especially the *employed* union member, but it hurt some veterans and it implied dismissal for women workers and thousands of munitions employees. State construction of buildings promised jobs and homes for many, but this met resistance from others. Insurance proposals troubled the workers' Friendly Societies and their vested interests. Most of all, wage questions automatically pitted the best-paid and highest skilled workers against the rest of labor. The problem of safeguarding the hard-won advantages of skilled unionists, in peace almost as much as in war, was beyond the government's ingenuity.

By ideological tests, the plight of foreign and military policies is thought-provoking. Allegedly reactionary, they were the first target for retrenchment. Not until July did motives of economy become a threat to expenditure in general, but economy had already cast a shadow over two plans: *not* the reconstruction schemes but the British presence in Russia and the concomitantly huge military establishment. In March, Churchill voiced his alarm: Retrenchment and the priority for trade revival were destroying the plan to hold the Caucasus and protect Denikin.[116] His battle with the Treasury put him in strange alliance with organized labor, the Federation of British Industries, and Christopher Addison. The economy drive, gaining force, focused first on these rather than on domestic expenses. It makes one think.

So far we have sought to find ideological, indeed almost moral, labels for the government's policy.

Moral criticism is important. There are other kinds. The government's policy was also vulnerable on grounds of efficacy and prudence. In retrospect, inflation seems its gravest blind spot. Runaway prices would cripple land settlement and housing alike. They would deter local authorities, would rob current grants of their meaning, would discourage Commons from generosity. Prices would carry the forces of opposition

116. WC 542 (6 March 1919), Cab. 23/9.

upward with them, until the citadel—the very principle of the housing subsidy—was stormed. They would strain taxpayer and Treasury until a phalanx formed, in Whitehall and out, against every cost. They would menace recovery, overpricing British goods on the world market. They would rob unemployment aid and wage rises of half their value. In turn, this would guarantee furious outcries from the workers.

Inflation had a twin, or a second face: full employment at high wages, portentous for both good and ill. It was a vital dike against an ocean of unrest; but all that went into sustaining it meant that less was left for the housing campaign. At the level of cabinet debate, the prevailing high wages and abundant jobs removed the housing campaign's greatest rationale, inasmuch as it was no longer needed to relieve mass unemployment. Still more important, high wages and full employment made it easy and attractive for building workers to find other jobs, especially the plummy jobs of the private contractor. The latter's profit margin and his power to raise wages (simply by upgrading, the easiest way to circumvent wage limits) far surpassed the possibilities in any mere government housing project; by nature, the margin on *workers'* homes was slim. This was Addison's most intractable dilemma, but the difficulty was compounded by a condition that can be traced much farther back. There were not enough building workers, and never had been; and only when it was too late did everyone see that war, driving some to the trenches and inviting others into jobs less "seasonal" and better paid than construction work, had made matters much worse. Later, the unions' resistance to change, plus the immobility of workers, would hinder recruitment.

Inflation and full employment, then as later, brought other handicaps to a nation that could not live unto itself or beyond its means, in a state of euphoria amid inefficiency and waste. These two factors removed incentives to economy and efficiency in general, for employer and employee alike. Independent even of these causes, it was recognized (by Horne and Keynes, for example) that productivity was low. More than housing suffered from this inefficiency; recovery of overseas trade was also threatened.[117]

Other weaknesses also were significant. To some extent the government reckoned on reparations. Moreover, it reckoned on the continued prostration of rivals on the Continent, in both manufacturing and farming. Its estimate of a long and painful recovery in European agriculture accounted for the government's willingness to underwrite 1919's cereal planting and

117. J. M. Keynes, *The Economic Consequences of the Peace*, pp. 231–32; "The Labour Situation," G.T. 8388 (22 October 1919), Cab. 24/90.

this estimate underlay the whole attempt—gallant, humanitarian, but almost incredible—to make England a land of prospering farms as well as factories.[118]

As a whole, the government's venture assumed that a nation that must export and compete could again triumph overseas. For a fully employed, high-cost, high-wage nation that was stripped of its financial armor but determined to live a fuller life without drastic provisions for superior efficiency, this was much to gamble.

From Addison's Viewpoint

For someone seeking vindication, the evidence lay everywhere. That the Ministry of Reconstruction's reports had been studied was satisfying; that legislation mirrored them was even more satisfying. And imitation was a grand, implied compliment: nothing ratified the work of Addison's ministry as much as this. Early that year his colleagues, in two crash programs to investigate and to expedite, duplicated his efforts and (still better) recapitulated his findings. They did this, of course, with innocent surprise; they preached his lessons and repeated his pleas as discoveries of their own. (Caught up in other work, they had never watched *how* he did things—those who will not study history, one recalls, are condemned to repeat it.) None did this better than the hastily assembled crew of Sir Eric Geddes' Co-ordination of Demobilisation Section. Dunnell, Merz, and Rhys Rhys-Williams, called in from the defunct War Priorities Committee, found themselves in the noisy environment of local authorities, trade unions, building contractors, and employers' associations.[119]

One man above all others followed Addison's pattern most closely: the dynamic center of the Section, Rhys-Williams, wounded early in the war and busy since with duties from Whitehall to Batu. His memoranda rose above the babel of indecision in a clear call for state aid, and state control. He urged price controls for bricks and building materials, in unconscious tribute to Carmichael's plan. He took up Addison's cry, all unaware, for a central cabinet committee to handle outstanding questions immediately.[120] Like Addison, he recommended that export licensing be coordinated between the Board of Trade and the Standing Council on Post-War Priority. He spoke up for financial aid to interrupted apprenticeships and for other schooling, for subsidies to forestry and land settlement, and

118. WC 549 (21 March 1919), Cab. 23/9.
119. Chambers of Commerce resolutions, Recon/A/46/Pt. 3, Box 78; F. 9166, Box 90, Part 3; "The General Industrial Position," a memorandum in Box 78.
120. D.M. 60 (18 January 1919) and 59 (17 January 1919), Box 77.

especially for a bold housing scheme.[121] He and his colleagues stumbled upon the same needs Greenwood and Addison had found—for studies of financial stringencies and for rapport with the trades concerned. Their new surveys emulated Addison's example.[122] In this man's work, as in the cabinet's faithful adoption of Addison's chosen reforms, the record of early 1919 provided a testimonial to Addison and to his Ministry of Reconstruction.

In June 1919, as he turned fifty, Addison tasted it all—accomplishment, gratification, praise. He became Minister of Health formally; his Housing Bill cleared its crucial reading; his ministry was drawn up behind him. But this was for the last time for many years. Mercifully, the cries of failure and the humiliation of 1921 were hidden from him. Within one month, however, he was faced head-on with those rocklike obstacles and enveloped in the changed general mood that he would never escape.

Meanwhile, much has been said of Parliament. In 1919 it was indeed active.

121. D.M. 23 and 43 (1 and 10 January 1919), Box 77, and parallel documents; minutes (8, 13 and 20 January 1919) of the Demobilisation Committee, Box 77.

122. Minutes of first, seventh, and eleventh meetings of the Demobilisation Committee, *ibid.*, and memoranda D.M. 13, 48, and 66.

16

Legislative Response:
The Ministry Justified?

In 1919 legislators frequently said that they were ratifying a great and unified program of national reconstruction. Most often they cited five measures: a Ministry of Health, a Ministry of Transport, a Housing and Town Planning Act, a new law on assessment of land values, and new statutory facilities for land settlement. These measures, kindred in spirit and interdependent in fact, were hailed as the fulfillment of the pledges for reform.[1]

The Main Program

The Ministry of Transport Act

For roads, harbors, canals, tramways, and railways, this measure centralized power in a single ministry. It owed little to Addison's ministry, which issued no report on the topic. But his Advisory Council had at one time studied transport and had referred its data and views to a select committee of the House of Commons. Geddes took up the task.

The debate on the Ministry of Transport bill proved to be one of the stormiest in all of 1919. When first introduced (with the title, eventually amended, "Ministry of Ways and Communications") the bill provoked horrified cries from conservatives; after amendment in May, the accusations—angry charges of betrayal or of cowardice—came from radical liberals and from labor.

Such changes, in the public debate, may reflect an actual change of governmental intent, perhaps forced by pressure groups or by Tory members of Parliament. Or they may show that government, acting in haste, first produced a draft with unintended wide implications of

1. See *P.D.(C.)*, vol. 114, c. 1773–74, 2321, 2322, 2341–42; vol. 119, c. 223, 243, 268–69, 842–43; see also Cd. 9087, p. 11, Cd. 8881, p. 5, and G.T. 6880 and 6887.

nationalization, then used amendment to clarify its purpose. Or the tumult may reveal—if one assumes the cabinet was buying time to overcome strike threats, by a pretense of boldness—that it was all a charade to delude a hopeful public up to the moment for opportune retreat. Conceivably, however, change was more apparent than real, and the whole uproar revealed exaggerated first impressions.

What is certain, in any case, is that the broad wording of the original bill quickened hopes in labor and among radicals, and inspired fears among railway owners and Tories, and on the same ground: that nationalization was the intended result, and would be achieved by the bill. Lines formed accordingly, at first. In the major policy debates, and then in Standing Committee B, Labour Party members supported Sir Eric Geddes. In opposition, railway interests mounted a powerful propaganda offensive; the bill was denounced in the press as a monstrosity of collectivism, dictatorship, and bureaucracy. The strongest attack was centered on Clause 4. This clause—alarming, as we have seen, to some of the cabinet —would indeed have empowered the Minister of Ways and Communications, on the face of it, to acquire any transport facility: docks, roads, railways, and canals. Was this not nationalization? *The Times,* terming this "A Revolution in Transport," drew the strongest conclusions from Geddes' comment that this was "the cold bath" that the country must be prepared to take. To defeat Clause 4, alarmed Unionist M.P.'s pressed for direct discussion; reportedly, Bonar Law took the extraordinary step of threatening to resign if these fellow Tories persisted. Abruptly, on 6 May, the Home Secretary (Shortt) rose in Standing Committee B to move the complete deletion of Clause 4. This motion passed; a substitute clause, hinted at on that day, was not added; other amendments, which soon followed, curbed the minister's powers considerably. From that moment, there was no possibility that the bill could be used to nationalize the railways; but had there ever been such a possibility?

Government spokesmen denied that nationalization could be effected without an explicit parliamentary vote; the aim of the bill, said they, was and always had been to give the minister time to study and to think, and meanwhile to ensure that the railways remained under control for the two years during which they would be subsidized. It was a "two years' bill," said Geddes. Without control there would be chaos, Bonar Law insisted; this was a bill for control, and control of this type was the only alternative to nationalization. The outcome, one historian has said with considerable justification, was "a much mutilated Bill, a pale shadow of its original robust self"; but my own impression is that the government had not decided for nationalization but emphatically desired unification and control, and got a measure which served that goal. The statute, passed on 15 August 1919, concentrated all existing powers in the new minister's hands, gave him for two years the power to control any railway (including power to "take possession"), and conferred limited powers to establish services and make loans.

It must be emphasized that, in the narrow sense, neither the measure nor its dramatic career throw light on Addison's wartime planning. But the parliamentary interlude is not wholly irrelevant. It suggests an upsurge of contrary pressures, and a curtailment of plans, which if proved would be most germane to the postwar story of reconstruction.[2]

The Acquisition of Land (Assessment of Compensation) Act

If the Transport Act reveals the least Ministry of Reconstruction influence, the Land Acquisition Bill is at the opposite extreme, reflecting the precise wording of Leslie Scott's committee.

Paragraph 1 of the new act set up a Reference Committee, which would name a panel of official arbitrators, expert in land valuation, with power to settle disputed cases. By supplanting juries, justices, and surveyors with one system, and by requiring that the adjudicator be skilled, the act exactly met the specifications of Leslie Scott's committee.[3] But Scott wished the panel to be a permanent Sanctioning Authority, of private men. Instead Parliament required that valuers have civil service status. Paragraph 2 of the statute followed Scott, forbidding any additional allowance resulting from the fact that acquisition would be compulsory, and banning additional compensation resulting from special suitability of the land to public use. Parliament concurred that compensation should be based on the "reasonable cost of equivalent reinstatement."[4] Similarly,

2. The statute is 9 and 10 Geo. V, c. 50. See Cd. 9231, p. 16; London *Times*, 28 February, 5 March, 3 April, 7 and 8 and 14–16 May, 13 and 14 June, and 14 August 1919; Philip Bagwell, *The Railwaymen*, pp. 405–8; W. E. Simnett, *Railway Amalgamation in Great Britain* (London: Railway Gazette, 1923), pp. 23–26; G.T. 6832, in Cab. 24/75, in which Austen Chamberlain criticized the bill for its nationalizing features; and WC 534 (19 February 1919), Cab. 23/9.

Most pertinent and illuminating, of all the long debates in Commons, are the following: *P.D.(C.)*, vol. 113, c. 1761–1867 (second reading, 17 March 1919, esp. c. 1768–70 where the case for unified control was strongest put by government); vol. 114, c. 2285, for Leslie Scott's criticism; vol. 117, c. 809–923 (1 July 1919, and especially c. 823 for Labour Party charges of betrayal), c. 1007–28 (2 July, and especially Leslie Scott's attempts to block any lingering possibility of nationalization, c. 1033–61), c. 1647–79, and c. 2083–2132 (10 July 1919 debate on the third reading, culminating in Bonar Law's defense of unification and control).

3. Compare Cd. 9229, pp. 14–15, with 9 and 10 Geo. V, c. 57.

4. Cd. 9229, paragraphs 9 and 10.

at first glance, Parliament also concurred with Scott on the formula for reckoning land values; but this agreement was only apparent, not real. The basis for computing the value of a parcel of land, as the statute finally put it, was "the amount which the land, if sold in the open market, by a willing seller, might be expected to realise." But this wording, it will be recalled, had split the cabinet committee; and in Parliament Scott again challenged it. He charged that, unless the clause included the words "and a willing buyer," a world of difference in law would result. A Parliament allegedly biased for property rights nevertheless voted down this safeguard to landowners.[5]

By contrast, many sections closely followed Scott's words. The Reference Committee, it was stated, could make regulations; the standard definitions of "consequential injury" and "compensation for disturbance" need not govern. The parties' right to witnesses was curtailed. The value of all interests in a property should be assessed in separate awards (here, Parliament reinstated Scott's wording), and the assessing tribunals' discretion would be absolute about costs and those who should bear them; a deadline for presenting claims was set. More stringent than Scott's provisions, the act required that lawsuit costs fall on the claimant if he lost and virtually required the public authority to pay in the opposite case. In affirming that official findings of fact were final and in allowing referral of questions of law to the high court, the correspondence was almost exact. But on a disputed point—referral to the Inland Revenue Valuation Department, where Lloyd George's pledges several years earlier were angrily quoted and misquoted—Parliament went beyond the committee, even accepting the inland revenue commissioner's assessment as decisive.

One looks, of course, for agreement, but the omissions are surprising. The proposal for the public authority to share in "betterment" is lacking, as is its twin, "injurious affection." Leslie Scott proved that these omissions were serious *by moving the rejection of the government bill* (just after the Attorney-General's flattering speech). Scott dwelt on other flaws as well: the failure to replace the Lands Clauses Acts and the requirement that the local authority treat concerning all interests in the property. Acland, the zealous forestry champion, loosed a quiverful of accusations against the government. Supporting Scott's resolution, he asked why the burden of acquiring all interests, or taking title instead of easements, had been imposed; why public agencies had been denied permission to withdraw from acquisition proceedings; why "accommodation works" had

5. Cd. 9229, paragraphs 13 and 8, and n. 5, p. 9; *P.D.(C.)*, vol. 114, c. 2288.

been left out; why surplus lands could not be sold. Unyielding as a Sherwood oak, he asked Commons to condemn the "small and unworthy way" the government had chosen to deal with the land.

Scott and Acland—one a keen Tory from the Unionist Social Reform Committee, the other a staunch Asquith Liberal—were echoed by several Coalition Liberals. It was a mixed crew who fought against the government. For one hostile amendment (eventually defeated), Liberals like Benn, Josiah Wedgwood, and Maclean voted in company with Labour Party members, Scott, and Sir Edward Carson. Grounds for criticism were diverse, even puzzling. The Labour Party opposition, given their hostility to profits and private property, is consistent and understandable enough. But Leslie Scott was more complex: he denounced the government for timidity on the land bill, yet he had strenuously opposed the Ministry of Transport out of fear that it might bring nationalization; and in the debates on land acquisition Scott expressed alarm that the bill might subject small property owners to a "forced sale." The context in that debate shows that his concern for property rights was strong; he carried it to the length of insisting that properties compulsorily taken must be separately assessed, and—over protests from Labour members—he forced this amendment successfully on the government. Sir Donald MacLean is another critic who defies easy interpretation. A strong Free Trader, with little love for government expense and no love for bureaucracy, he had sarcastically congratulated the government when its Electricity (Supply) Bill was introduced—on the ground that it was the last such interventionist measure. But he, almost more than any other man, fought steadily against the government's Land Acquisition Bill.

Above all, what united these diverse men was the question of price. The cost of land, said Maclean, was "the basis of how these measures"— housing, land settlement, transport, and forestry—"are going to work. The country will not stand the burden which the present measure seeks to impose on communities and on Public Utilities Societies, of buying land at a market price which largely represents the blood value of the war." Accordingly he backed an amendment to base land valuations on Inland Revenue assessment, thus making the price which government must pay equal to the value reckoned for tax purposes. The amendment lost, but not before Scott and Wedgwood had joined in supporting it. One member of Parliament—raising charges akin to those made later about the Electricity Bill—alleged that the government's intransigence reflected a bargain with the Coalition Conservatives, by which the Housing Bill got through on the understanding that landowners' property values would not be tampered with. Several members charged betrayal of government pledges, branding the bill a "reactionary measure" and "a bill for profiteering." Maclean vented his anger in a motion which declared that the bill set up "an unnecessary and expensive staff of valuers" and failed to "establish the principle that the value on which land is taxed should also be the value at which it may be acquired for public purposes." The hidden intent, he charged, was to scrap the great machinery of land reform which had been set up before the war.

Behind the scenes, some men within government echoed him. Lloyd George's protest to the Lord Chancellor has been seen. Addison was trying to launch broader reforms covering questions of compensation and betterment.[6] Official defenders were hard pressed. To meet the charge that not one iota had been added to existing powers of land acquisition, government spokesmen retorted that further reforms would tackle fundamental change. They held that this act did much and that the Housing and Land Settlement bills would add more.[7]

What shall be made of this bill—the one most obviously patterned on a Reconstruction Committee report, yet the only one whose strongest critic was its author? In 1941 Leslie Scott, now Lord Justice Scott, told a wartime audience that "the great Lands Clauses Consolidation Act of 1845 is still law to-day." Perhaps this is the first point to grasp: with the 1919 statute, the rivulet of government law reform ran dry. A change that was useful in expediting acquisition had been effected, but nothing more. Continuing, the Lord Justice remarked that the 1845 act had been shaped to protect the rights of individuals, and, save for the slight modification "in favor of the nation" by the act of 1919, the balance still tipped that way.[8] Most critics would agree that an unequaled chance to deal once and for all with compensation and betterment had been lost; the 1945 and 1964 Labour government's fight for the "development charge" suggests the same. Housing reformers have claimed that the costs of public housing and interwar London transport would have been saved, and easily, had compensation for betterment been eradicated in 1919.

6. *Ibid.*, c. 2281 and 2288 (see his similar view on the Ministry of Transport Bill, c. 2285); for Acland, *ibid.*, c. 2297–98, 2302–5, 2311. For other criticisms, see *ibid.*, c. 2327, 2347, 2353–54, 2358–62, and *ibid.*, vol. 116, c. 1172–73, and *ibid.*, vol. 117, c. 177–293, 417–18, and 2155–96. For Addison's attempts, see HAC 35, Cab. 26/1, and his G.T. 7298 (20 May 1919), Cab. 24/79.

7. *Ibid.*, c. 2327, 2347, 2353–54, 2358–62; the rejoinders are in c. 2371, 2372, 2376, 2378, and 2379.

8. Oxford Conference of the Town and Country Planning Association (Spring 1941), *Replanning Britain*, ed. F. E. Towndrow (London: Faber & Faber, n.d.), p. 116.

Legislative Response: The Ministry Justified?

The Land Settlement (Facilities) Bill

Board of Agriculture spokesmen reminded Commons to read this bill (for putting more men on farms) in the context of the land, housing, and transport bills. They ascribed it to the Selborne committee. Critics made the same reference, deploring the delay of two years since that committee reported. These comments were at once true and misleading.

The origins of the bill were in fact diverse. Lord Selborne's group outlined a huge and comprehensive policy, but often in general terms. Nor was it the sole influence on the bill; other committees, and the continuing work of Prothero's Board, shaped the 1919 measure. Specific features clarify the origins of the 1919 measure. The bill provided for extending credit facilities, so that tools, seeds, trees, and livestock might be bought; in like vein the Selborne Report had noted the need for capital to aid building and had recommended aid (through Public Utility Societies) for industrial equipment of farm land.[9] If this feature illustrated the influence of Selborne's committee, another feature disclosed a debt, instead, to Lord Salisbury's housing panel. This concerned recoupment of losses incurred by councils. Under the bill, County Councils might borrow from the Public Works Loan Commissioners, both to acquire land and to equip farms; they would be repaid in part annually, and in 1926 for the whole loss. The Salisbury panel had urged the same: repayment in stages, ultimately covering the entire loss due to land acquisition and to falling prices for labor and materials. Prothero had stressed his bill's similarity to the forthcoming housing provisions; the latter also went back to Salisbury's panel.[10] Rather different is the case of financial arrangements: the bill allowed County Councils to buy, if they chose, in consideration of a perpetual annuity (which had dismayed Addison). Leslie Scott's committee had considered the idea of a perpetual rent charge on the land, but had rejected it.[11]

Parallelisms in detail nevertheless can mislead—the *contrast* between the bill and the Selborne committee's report is general and strong. The act is essentially an amendment of the Small Holdings and Allotments Act of 1908; it clarified and extended County Council powers and gave some default powers to the state; its aim was to get men *onto* farms. Infinitely more ambitious, the Selborne committee struck out toward a bold policy of national agricultural planning, national control, and even national

9. *P.D.(C.)*, vol. 114, c. 2576–77, 2611–12, 2639; cf. Cd. 9231, p. 25. Compare Cd. 8506 with 9 and 10 Geo. V, c. 59.
10. Compare Cd. 9087, paragraph 21, with the statute.
11. Compare Cd. 9229, paragraph 22, with the statute.

management. It sought primarily to get more *out of* the soil. Prothero had no illusions in early 1919 about early gains in output or productivity; his plea was not for efficiency but for fulfillment and justice.[12] The contrast was basic.

Thus far the attempt to trace Ministry of Reconstruction influence reveals no single pattern, although it shows that Addison's ministry was in no instance irrelevant.

The Ministry of Health Act

This landmark of 1919 owed a great deal to Dr. Addison but little to his ministry. His stubborn fight is recorded not only in his diary but in the Home Affairs Committee and the cabinet. It is plain that a host of others took part—Sir George Newman, the heads of the Friendly Societies, Lord Rhondda, and many distinguished physicians (often carefully coached by Addison). Of course there was a Local Government Committee under the Ministry of Reconstruction—the famed Maclean committee, formed under Lloyd George and bullied by the exultant Beatrice Webb—but it offers negative evidence on origins. It turned aside from its mandate, which might have led directly to a Ministry of Health ("to secure the better co-ordination of Public Assistance"); instead, it reported on the transfer of Poor Law functions to other bodies at the *local* level only. Admittedly, this is not the whole truth; implicit in the Maclean committee report was a further work of central reshuffling and consolidation, which meant, practically, a Ministry of Health; and Morant stressed this point. But it was as keen individual enthusiasts, not as members of the Ministry of Reconstruction, that Morant, Addison, and many others got the Ministry of Health definitely onto the agenda in 1917.

Still, the negative results of detective work in no way minimize the value of the bill. "Brief, simple and comprehensive"—as Sir George Newman said—it opened a way for many additional reforms. The bill stands as a culmination of fifty years' propaganda work and an epitome of the public support and organized campaigning that had been stimulated by war. With it, the unification of *health* measures and the *insurance* system helped to bring the latter more closely into a true single policy. With it, the medical staff for the first time gained equality with civil servants in what was basically a common task. With it, private professionalism was joined with governmental experience; and the first chairman

12. Compare Cd. 8506, especially paragraph 56, with the statute and the Small Holdings Act; see also WC 505 and 539, and G.T. 6910.

of its medical consultative committee was one of the nation's greatest physicians, Sir Bertram Dawson.[13]

The Housing and Town Planning Act

No proposal surpassed the Housing Bill in universal and immediate appeal; of all the measures passed in 1919, this was what men meant when they spoke of a new and better England. Here culminated the best features of three years of reconstruction work—Vaughan Nash's lone initiative of 1916, Salisbury's aggressive panel, Rowntree's sober and devastating memoranda, the work of Wallace and Reiss, and Addison's mingled diplomacy and outraged dissent. It is also the monument to the Royal Commission on Housing in Scotland, to the Health of Munitions Workers' Committee, to dozens and dozens of meetings of the National Housing and Town Planning Council that never gave up hope, to many silent services by the Royal Institute of British Architects, and to vociferous protest from the War Emergency Workers' National Committee. The Garden Cities and Town Planning Association, for all its factional trouble, also made a contribution. And even (professionals would say "especially") the Local Government Board gave its help, for it had sponsored the Tudor Walters committee, whose recommendations on design and standard still win praise today; by its own force that committee put workers' housing policy permanently on a new plane.

The great changes effected by the Housing Act of 1919 are almost too simply and easily put, and of these the greatest is so simple as almost to seem unimportant: housing of the working classes became a duty of the state. The statute envisioned housing activity *by government*, a clear break with the prewar past; then, private enterprise had been responsible for 90 per cent of such building. Now a partnership of the central government and the local authorities would be in the business of housing. The premise of governmental responsibility and action had been common ground to all wartime reform groups. It was adopted here, once and for all—a principle that, as it proved, was the greatest and most enduring consequence of the act. In effect, as A. J. P. Taylor notes, housing became a social service; later governments might differ in the methods they used, but they accepted the task. Three other changes ranked as major, by any test. First, the act put the great bulk of building costs on the central

13. George Newman, *The Building of a Nation's Health* (London: Macmillan, 1939), pp. 118, 122–25. The statute is 9 and 10 Geo. V, c. 21. See also Marwick, *The Deluge*, p. 242, citing Arthur Newsholme, *The Ministry of Health* (London: G. P. Putnam's Sons, 1926), pp. 93, 137–38, 150–51.

government. Second, it made housing a *duty* of the local authority. Third, it gave the central government power to act in default, where the local authority proved incompetent or unwilling. It is small wonder that, forty years later, one historian made it the cornerstone of his eulogy to liberalism. "One thing has been forgotten," said R. B. McCallum:

> The pledge was honored, the great development begun, the whole standard and quality of housing for the people raised. . . . In it [the Housing Bill] the empirical social democratic Liberalism which arose in 1906 had its greatest social triumph.

It was the work, he added, of a *Liberal* Prime Minister and a *Liberal* Minister of Health.[14]

Details again merit attention and throw light on origins. Direct subsidy to private builders was ruled out, in conformance with the Salisbury panel and House of Commons opinion. But the financial provision for local authorities departed from Rowntree's plan, which the panel favored. Rowntree had spoken of a five-year period, after which prices probably would have reached their normal level; in the interim the state would provide the entire cost of building, would *own* the houses, and then would transfer them to local-authority ownership at a price that would allow for the price decline as well as for depreciation. Instead, the act fixed ownership in the local authorities; it provided *annual* state payments, not a final reckoning after five years. And, of course, the famous "penny-rate" limit—dear to many local councils, adumbrated by Hayes Fisher, and adopted by Sir Auckland Geddes—is there: from the state's payments to local authorities would be deducted "a sum not exceeding the estimated annual produce of a rate of one penny in the pound levied in the area chargeable . . . with the schemes."

What of aid to other builders? It had been seriously questioned whether Public Utility Societies should get help: the Treasury demurred, Hayes Fisher's administration refused, and the Hobhouse committee under Addison (strongly favoring aid) had trouble merely getting its report published.[15] Surprisingly, the statute went almost all the way: as Hobhouse's committee wished, local authorities gained power to lease land for Public Utility Societies and were authorized not only to make

14. Taylor, *English History, 1914–1945*, pp. 146–47; R. B. McCallum, in Morris Ginsberg, ed., *Law and Opinion*, p. 75. The statute is 9 and 10 Geo. V, c. 35.

15. Files 8820, 8891, 8777, in Box 30, Part 2; H. 234, Box 33; paper 66, Binder 2, and papers 78–87, Box 37; F. 9248, Box 30, Part 3. See *P.D.(L.)*, vol. 31, c. 950–54; see Final Report of the Housing (Financial Assistance) Committee (headed by Hobhouse) in *Parliamentary Papers* (1919), vol. 10, Cd. 9238.

money advances to them but to "guarantee loans and loan stock, make grants outright, and take up shares of loan stock" in the societies. Aid by the government was less generous. The Hobhouse committee had suggested state grants, upon completion, up to 75 per cent of the difference between excess costs and the estimated value, this grant to go to Public Utility Societies and to housing trusts (registered semiprivate bodies that were limited in profits and interest rates)—along with cheap fifty-year loans up to 80 per cent of estimated values. The statute, which provided no state grant, authorized the state to pay 30 per cent of loan charges and to make fifty-year loans for 75 per cent of the costs of land and development. The statute also extended aid to residents, actual or potential, to buy houses, and raised the previous £400 limit to £500. Such provisions met many Hobhouse committee demands, and exceeded what the cabinet committee had allowed.[16]

For the cases in which Parliament surpassed the cabinet in liberality, the National Housing and Town Planning Council claimed credit. Much that the council held indispensable was accepted, after Sir Auckland brought a new spirit and Addison took hold. These successes included the penny-rate limit, the expedition of local plans by the omission of formal inquiries, the control of bricks and of coal supply and prices, raising the design standards, and the system of housing commissioners. The council failed in its efforts for brick price control and for state production of fittings (and had opposed the Carmichael plan from the start). On the crucial provision to make town planning *obligatory*, it had not yielded.

> For the first time since the war we measured strength with the Government and, despite the unwillingness of Dr. Addison . . . were able to secure such overwhelming support in the House of Commons Committee Room that the acceptance of the Clause by the Government was rendered inevitable. The fact that the Clause was defeated in the House of Lords caused anxiety . . . but here again our friends in the House of Commons rendered invaluable aid, and the Government accepting through Dr. Addison in the final stages . . . earned our warm thanks by standing firmly by the principles of the Clause, with the result that the battle for obligatory planning is clearly won.[17]

16. Cd. 9223, paragraphs 10 and 13; compare with the statute and with the discussion in Cab. 27/56; see also Cd. 9238, paragraphs 40, 46, and 48.
17. National Housing and Town Planning Council, Minute Book 2 (1913–18), report of meeting on 28–29 September 1918; Minute Book 3 (1918–23): minutes of special joint meeting, 29 November–1 December 1918; minutes of rural Sub-Committee

Whatever the realities in Westminster corridors, the council was right in holding this clause a great improvement. Nothing like it had been done since 1909, when a committee, packed with the council's allies, forced through an amendment that limited the number of houses per acre. The 1919 imposition of a duty ranked with, or outranked, that clause as a landmark in British planning history.

"The housing reformers have got what they wanted," said one professional journal, and the council rejoiced.

> The year has been marked by the passing of an Act which promises . . . to transform the activities of Local Authorities so far as housing and town planning are concerned. . . . Until the Act of 1919 . . . the housing duties to be performed by Local Authorities were not adequately defined . . . and as a result the pace of progress . . . was disappointingly slow.
>
> It has needed the earthquake shock of war to bring the nation to the recognition of the truth, which the Council has always maintained . . . that it is the duty of the community acting through self-governing bodies to take the necessary action . . . however drastic. . . . The history of the housing and town planning development of this period is indissolubly bound up with the efforts of the Council and we can therefore regard the passing of the Act of 1919 as memorable in our history in a specially intimate sense.[18]

In housing there were no neutrals; everyone was partisan. Hence those who had won found no praise too high for the act. Those who had both won and lost were of two minds.

The Garden Cities and Town Planning Association is a prime example. As active as the council, its companion and rival, and as keen for all that was done, the association had reached for more. To build housing was imperative, and it agreed with the council on every provision necessary to this end; accordingly, it hailed every feature of the act. Town planning also was imperative (the association stressed this point, if possible, even more than the council); accordingly, it also had fought for, and exulted in, the obligatory town planning clause. But "garden cities" was their great dream; the association was the true and zealous heir of Ebenezer Howard and the ever imperiled "garden city" idea.

---

meeting, 23 January 1919; minutes of meeting of the General Committee, 24 January 1919; minutes of quarterly meeting, 16 May 1919; and *Annual Report* for 1918–19 (attached to General Committee minutes for 31 July 1919).

18. National Housing and Town Planning Council, *Annual Report* for 1918–19.

The truth is that these three concepts—building, town planning, and garden city development—represent three sectors, each more advanced than the preceding, along the spectrum of housing reform. Consensus, achieved on the first two sectors, did not extend to the third. But were not all three compatible—and could not all three have been achieved by unity at this supreme moment? We cannot know. Instead, two easily predictable things happened. (1) The association split in 1916–17, the desperate champions of garden city planning hiving off into a special group to propagandize for "new towns." (2) Within the association, and outside, the fight for three intrinsically compatible ideas developed into a choice between them. The great names of this splendid association temporarily stood on opposing sides: Reiss and Norman Macfadyen, Patrick Abercrombie, G. D. H. Cole, F. J. Osborn, and C. L. Purdom were *for* garden cities and *against* the senior leaders, threatening tragedy. Then Rowntree knocked heads together. Insisting that mass housing and not the creation of garden cities must be the great aim, placating all until the dissident groups were merged by common consent, he helped bring the association back into the main battle in time. Nevertheless, mixed feelings were the inevitable result: although many rejoiced, some members deplored the act's failure to promote garden cities in any way. A few, such as Reiss, went further. Of course they were not hostile to mass housing; nevertheless they saw with clarity (the zealot's gift, which no statesman can afford) that the garden city idea would perish without their efforts; and therefore they took a lonely way. At a time when all was state initiative, they perforce adopted private means. Reiss, for example, helped form the Welwyn Garden City Corporation, and gave his life to it.[19]

Addison got nearly all he asked, but a later generation of critics says he should have asked for more. In general scholars and reformers have praised the 1919 act for its boldness and its principles but find serious faults in details. In their most unanimous critique they rightly charge that planning, as contrasted with mere construction, did not benefit, as had been hoped. The clause that obligated councils to plan proved but "the shadow of a shadow of planning policy."[20] Then too, the very generality

19. Garden City and Town Planning Association, Minute Book 3 (1916–20), pp. 175–316; see especially pp. 183–84, 190, 194–95, 225–26, 236, 242–43, and 278–91; action and attitudes on the 1919 act are in *ibid.*, pp. 273, 284–85, and 291. See also *New Towns after the War* (London: J. M. Dent & Sons, 1918), *passim*, and C. L. Purdom's eloquent *Decentralisation and Satellite Towns*, National Housing and Town Planning Council Pamphlet 14 (1938).

20. Ginsberg, *Land and Opinion*, p. 128.

and apparently generous scope of the powers granted to local authorities produced an unexpected result; they engendered that interwar anomaly by which planning, although decreed in general, could easily be subverted in detail. The act encouraged a municipality to put an area under "interim development control," which was meant to be a blanket ban on unauthorized construction, but the controls were so tentative and vague that they gave leeway for a private contractor to build in the designated area and risk the possibility (which proved to be remote) of being stopped.[21]

Moreover, the act proved inadequate in empowering a local authority to build. The power was conferred only inside its boundaries; too often the only available land lay outside. Amendment of this point took several years. In still another way the 1919 act showed that geographic scope had been one of its blind spots. Inter-council cooperation had been facilitated by the act, but the provision was not enough; such joint work was increasingly seen as a prime need, but it progressed slowly. The fight for regionalism had to wait—and, it seems, still waits—for another day.[22] Nor did the attack on slums make headway; the act was a measure for building *new* houses, not for rehabilitating or razing old ones. A medical inspector, visiting 5,000 pre-1914 homes between the wars, found not one that was equipped with a bath. Tudor Walters' reports and council schemes had meant nothing here.[23]

This inspector's critique might have been made in 1919. But the chief criticisms depend rather on forty years' evolution. They reflect the soaring aims and heightened anxieties of planners who witnessed traffic evils and ribbon development that few had foreseen, who watched as a countryside was ravaged by "cities in flood," and who grasped weapons that broke in their hands. The master of concision, F. J. Osborn, who in 1941 summed up the bitter learnings of the interwar years, wrote an implicit commentary on 1919 when he listed "the key ideas of modern planning": "loosening out of over-built areas, defense of the right to a family house and garden, relief of traffic loads rather than a tame acceptance of inevitable increase, better placing of industry and business,

21. Charles M. Haar, ed., *Law and Land: Anglo-American Planning Practice* (Cambridge, Mass.: Harvard University Press, 1964), p. 218; National Housing and Town Planning Council Memorandum 11, by W. S. Cameron, "Problems Arising under Interim Development Control" (1937).

22. National Housing and Town Planning Council Memorandum 20, by A. H. Prince, "Rural Planning" (1938), and memorandum 27, by Patrick Abercrombie.

23. J. M. Mackintosh, *Trends of Opinion about the Public Health, 1901–1951* (London: Oxford University Press, 1953), p. 103; C. L. Mowat, *England between the Wars, 1918–1940* (London: Methuen, 1955), pp. 507–8.

prevention of endless encroachment on green areas around the city."[24] Of these five ideas, only the second was served by the "Addison Act."

Nor was reorganization of the building industry as a whole even attempted. Professor Marian Bowley has argued that economies of large-scale production, standardization of design, and innovations in use of materials as well as in construction were urgently needed, especially for workers' houses. She finds a major obstacle to such improvements in what she calls *the system*—architects, builders, and local authorities, interlocking in defense of traditionalism. The whole problem of housing should have been recognized as a production problem, even if that recognition implied a frontal attack on "the system." Administratively, something to this end was tried, under Addison. Legislatively, Parliament did not see or did not tackle the question at all.

All these subsequent criticisms seem valid. In failing to provide for these needs, the 1919 Housing Act was deficient.

Where it had faced housing problems, however, the Parliament of 1919 had not flinched. The word for its financial provisions—the center of four years' debate—was pronounced by Professor Bowley: "heroic."[25]

Other Statutes

The Forestry Act

Supported by Addison and originated by Asquith, this bill provided for eight forestry commissioners who would promote afforestation and production of timber. Gaining the powers of the Board of Agriculture and Fisheries, the commissioners also acquired powers to lease, sell, exchange and hold land, to manage holdings and build or plant on them, to buy and sell timber, to make grants and loans, and to aid research. Also, they might acquire land by compulsion.

24. F. J. Osborn, "Problems of Decentralization," in Oxford Conference (cited above, note 8), p. 86, and Purdom, *Decentralisation and Satellite Towns*.

25. Marian Bowley, *Housing and the State, 1919–1944* (London: Allen & Unwin, 1945), p. 18; elsewhere, Professor Bowley notes other virtues of the act, notably its provision of a subsidy proportionate to need; see pp. 19–23, *ibid.* See also Marwick, *The Deluge*, p. 274; William Ashworth, *The Genesis of Modern British Town Planning* (London: Routledge & Kegan Paul, 1954), pp. 199–201, 206–7; and Mowat, *England between the Wars*, pp. 43–44. See also J. B. Cullingworth, *Town and Country Planning in England and Wales* (London: Allen & Unwin, 1964), pp. 18–20. For the question of modernized production and the traditionalist "system," see Marian Bowley, *The British Building Industry: Four Studies in Response and Resistance to Change* (Cambridge: Cambridge University Press, 1966), pp. xii, 37, 184–85, 350, 362.

Acland had not fought the clans of the north and the disgruntled civil servants of Dean's Yard in vain. Concurrently, ten-year plans to afforest 200,000 acres were announced—the exact program his committee asked. Suavely, Griffith-Boscawen assigned all credit to the Reconstruction Committee, and Acland graciously admitted, "what is proposed . . . does largely follow the Report of the Reconstruction Committee."[26]

The Electricity (Supply) Act

Much work, many committees, and a number of specific compromises lay behind the Electricity (Supply) Bill, which the government placed before Commons in May 1919. The whole topic of electrical power had been seriously debated—and it was small wonder. The war, forcing construction of many ordnance plants, had put a premium on developing new power facilities, widely dispersed; electricity seemed ideally fitted to meet the need. Between 1914 and 1918, private and municipal plant capacity grew from 1,100,000 to 2,200,000 kilowatts; in the new munitions factories, 95 per cent of the machinery was powered by electricity. But war revealed the inadequacy of Britain's power system, to all informed observers; and war—which had forced the continued use, or reinstatement, of many obsolete generating systems—left a general impression of inefficiency and overdue reform. Hence, within the great general debate on reconstruction, there swirled a four years' debate on the reorganization of electricity supply. Private firms, local authorities, great complexes like the London County Council, private regional associations of producers, and professional associations—all joined in. Some participants had indeed been active in the discussion well before the war, for this was no new issue; some had espoused, on the eve of war, reforms which came near adoption. But most of them had pushed on, by 1918, toward conclusions well beyond the prewar emphasis on voluntary cooperation and mere local coordination.

The official signs of all this wartime debate were the reports of the Haldane, Parsons, and Williamson committees, and of Addison's Advisory Council. By no means unanimous, these reports nevertheless all represented an advance; and the Williamson committee, together with the Advisory Council, put particularly heavy emphasis on central super-

26. Compare 9 and 10 Geo. V, c. 58, with Acland's two reports, in Cd. 8881. The debate is in *P.D.(C.)*, vol. 119, c. 219–78 (5 August 1919); see the attacks in the *New Statesman* during January and February 1919 (12: pp. 319–20, 348–49, 365–66, 372–73, 443).

vision and direction—reform from the top down, backed by powers of compulsion. Discussion had revealed several great choices: (*a*) between localism and unification; (*b*) between the method of voluntary cooperation and private initiative, and the method of legal compulsion; (*c*) between a maximal program of new construction, and a minimal program of linking the existing systems; (*d*) between the alternatives of private, municipal, and national ownership. Moreover, for schemes which presumed central direction, a fifth choice was posed: (*e*) establishment of a basically independent electricity authority, subject only to Parliament and chiefly composed of technical experts; or the subordination of any electricity authority to a regular department such as the Board of Trade. Proposals combining almost all these choices, in great variety, had been offered.

The Williamson committee flatly opposed any reliance on "a large number of small areas" operated by separate authorities, terming it "incompatible with anything that can now be accepted as a technically sound system." It declared that mere interconnection of existing supply stations could not meet the current requirement: "A comprehensive system for the generation of electricity, and, where necessary, reorganizing its supply, should be established as soon as possible." It found a "general consensus" for the creation of one central authority to regulate generation and distribution. Hence it called for prompt establishment of a board of Electricity Commissioners, to whom all powers of governmental bodies should be transferred; but even this, the committee said, would not be enough. The new commissioners should have positive powers of initiative, including "the *encouragement* of the supply and distribution of electricity." In general, said Williamson's group, generating stations and main transmission lines should be publicly owned. To facilitate all these aims, regional consolidation was favored: the Electricity Commissioners should devise large new electricity districts and set up, for each, a District Electricity Board—the structural key to their scheme. These district boards should acquire all generating and main transmission within their districts (excepting stations for private supply), develop supply, erect new stations where necessary, and acquire surplus power sources. Costs of construction and development, they stressed, must be paid by the *national* exchequer. Thus, combination, regionalism, public ownership, and powerful central control were the keynotes of their plan.

The Williamson committee was the creature of the Board of Trade. Understandably then, it decided the question of "independence *vs.* departmental subordination" in favor of the latter, and recommended that the commissioners be responsible to the Board of Trade.

Briefly, Addison had opposed the combined forces of the Williamson committee and the Board of Trade. He favored not the Board but the proposed new Ministry of Supply as the responsible department; this ministry, to be based on the Ministry of Munitions, presumably would inherit the dynamism and experience of the war agency. Addison further charged that Williamson's plan stopped short of true unification. It relied too much on coordinating schemes which remained essentially local; it involved a cumbersome and inadequate financial scheme, part local rather than wholly national; it maintained a link with the local ratepayer, whose parochialism would prevent vigorous action. For emphasis, Addison quoted the alternative plan of his own Advisory Council. A highly conservative group, opposed to nationalization, this Advisory Council nonetheless favored state action on electricity, because the situation was so exceptional. State aid, said the council, should work through one consolidated system rather than through separate corporations or local authorities. But Addison's effort failed. He was simply referred to a conference with Stanley, President of the Board of Trade; and Stanley did not budge. The dispute shifted, as seen, to the War Cabinet; and Stanley won.

The Williamson Report, though unsatisfactory to Addison, was a rather bold scheme; and the government bill modeled on it was a genuine reform measure. One might have expected that the new consensus in favor of reform would have carried it through; for the bill provided that Electricity Commissioners be named, that they in turn set up District Electricity Boards, and that all generation and main transmission be transferred to the boards. The boards were also to have compulsory purchase rights and could ban the establishment or extension of stations by existing firms. These District Boards were to be broadly representative of labor, consumers, and local authorities. The Electricity Commissioners could require local enterprisers to give reasonable facilities of supply, under penalty; they were to have power to borrow capital. A large financial expenditure for new construction was planned. Shortt, the Home Secretary, claimed that the Electricity Commissioners would have controlling power over the nation's entire electricity supply.

One might have expected, too, that several compromises—for the bill was a blend of boldness and concessions—would have disarmed opposition: the majority on the District Boards was to be chosen by existing undertakers, proportionately to their holdings; the rights of existing undertakings were not to be altered by the District Boards without their consent (unless the Board of Trade gave specific authorization); local enterprises, so far as distribution was concerned, were left untouched. The Commissioners were not empowered to build generating stations or to engage directly in electricity supply.

But the bill was massacred in Parliament. What happened can only be described as a general onslaught, followed by complete capitulation. Private interests and local authorities joined in stripping the District Boards of their powers and in destroying the financial clauses of the bill. The voice of Sir Archibald Williamson, protesting that government had not adopted his committee's plan for generous national financial aid, was drowned in clamor from the other side. If he warned that government was not laying an adequate basis, critics charged that it was attempting too much. The familiar outcry against bureaucracy and extravagance prevailed. The bill was amended to favor private firms, where compensation for compulsory acquisition was concerned. Powers of enforcement were cut out, or confined to cases of voluntary acceptance. Structurally, the entire plan was altered: in place of District Boards set up by the Electricity Commissioners in the name of public control and in accordance with a general plan, a drastic amendment provided that "Joint Electricity Authorities" might be created, by agreement among a district's interests; and even then such authorities would have only the powers which the constituent groups allowed. The whole priority was reversed. The state would not plan, holding the initiative; the local—and in effect private or parochial—"joint electricity authority" would draw up plans, and the central commissioners would have only a limited power to modify. Even when all these changes were made in Commons, the House of Lords went further. So drastic were the amendments and criticisms there that, finally, nearly all the disputed clauses were dropped, and a very minor and incomplete bill was passed. Thus the Electricity (Supply) Act of 1919 simply sanctioned the appointment of a central group (the Electricity Commissioners) with meager powers for coordinating existing schemes, for advising and collecting data, and for planning voluntary schemes of local reorganization. The statute spelled out the terms on which Joint Electricity Authorities might be formed—thus putting the stamp of law on voluntary cooperation of local interests. Delay and permissiveness were the keynotes. The idea of electricity reorganization from the top had been lost. Abashed, government spokesmen in December 1919 could cover their retreat only by describing it as a "postponement"; the controverted clauses would be reintroduced next term.

Why had the government yielded? What could rationalize the change? Pressure-group opposition was intense and well organized. The radical

Liberal, Colonel Wedgwood, charged that the Home Secretary had capitulated to railroad interests in June, to exempt their generating stations from the operation of the District Boards—a charge all the more interesting in view of kindred accusations of the government's "humiliating climb-down" in favor of vested interests on the Ministry of Transport bill. "Government have now dropped down on the side of private enterprise," declared Major Barnes of the Labour Party. Such men, who had voted consistently in committee for the original bolder plan, denounced the amendments as a betrayal by the very Coalition ministers whom they had supported. This reversal in 1919 raises major questions; and the government's subsequent behavior—reviving the Electricity Bill in 1920, and then withdrawing it—adds color to the accusations.

The consequence in 1919 was a measure that promised no forceful solution to the problems of unification or modernization, and left matters to voluntary effort among well-entrenched groups. It was a victory, as one authority puts it, only for vested interests; for the centralizer, the socialist, and the prudent, it was a defeat.[27]

The Industrial Courts Act

The historian of industrial conciliation, Ian Sharp, finds this act a victory for Whitleyism. In its fourth report the Whitley committee favored *voluntary* machinery—much as in the statute; it rejected compulsory arbitration in any form. Enactment did not come in 1918; meanwhile, during the delay, employers strongly criticized the Wages (Temporary Regulation) Act. Altering its course, the government introduced the Industrial Courts Bill in a first draft that made tribunal decisions "legally

27. Compare the Williamson committee report (Cd. 9062) and the statute (9 and 10 Geo. V, c. 100) with the Advisory Council report (Cmd. 93) and with Ministry of Reconstruction comment (Box 83); compare Stanley's G.T. 6248 (8 November 1918) with Addison's G.T. 6322. Thorough and accurate comparisons of proposals, bill, and final statute are made in Self and Watson, *Electricity Supply in Great Britain*, pp. 32–48, and in H. H. Ballin, *The Organisation of Electricity Supply in Great Britain* (London: Electrical Press, 1946), pp. 98–141. For drafts of the Electricity (Supply) Bill, see G.T. 6926 (3 March 1919) and G.T. 7093 (9 April 1919), Cab. 24/76. Of many discussions in Commons, the most enlightening are in the following: *P.D.(C.)*, vol. 116, c. 2129, an attack on the amount of money grant, as extravagance; vol. 117, c. 459–92, especially Williamson's critique, c. 464–46 and 485–86; vol. 121, c. 1197 ff., 1481 ff., 1669, 1847 ff. (especially c. 1486 of 24 November 1919, for Josiah Wedgwood's accusation of a deal with railway firms); vol. 123, c. 1101 ff., 1301 ff. (especially c. 1108, 1111, 1115, dealing with charges of government's reversal of course). Indications of government intent to introduce a new electricity bill are found in Cab. 23/20 as follows: p. 3 (9 February 1920), p. 4 (31 March 1920); see also HAC (30 November 1920), Cab. 26/3.

binding" throughout the trade for four months. Then, facing strong labor objections, the government dropped this clause. Thus, finally, the act resembled the Whitley ideas, with a permanent tribunal (the Standing Industrial Court) and independent powers of inquiry. There was no provision for enforcing whatever awards were made, as Professor Mowat notes, but powers were extended to threatened as well as actual disputes. The Standing Industrial Court, Sharp declared, "can justly claim [on the basis of statistics on its work] to have been the most important single agency in the inter-war period for the settlement of trade disputes within the voluntary principle." Asquith's committee had left a small but durable mark. Wartime compulsion was dropped.[28]

There were other measures that year, most of them patchwork on existing law or little more than afterthoughts. But there was a promise of more in 1920: fundamental changes in land law, decisions on the Poor Law, new progress in health insurance, and extended unemployment insurance. The last measure was enacted as promised, but the others must have been scheduled on a Greek, not a British, calendar.

Parliament in 1919

"So far as the House of Commons went," Sir Arthur Griffith-Boscawen recalled, "we got on well enough; the Coupon Parliament would in fact pass anything which the Government proposed and was equally ready to repeal the same measures two or three years later"! Thanks to an imminent Derby Day, Sir Arthur's bill for land settlement went through unopposed.

> The highly complicated and controversial Addison Housing Bill also went through at express speed. The fact is that we were all committed to a great program of social reform; in the words of the Prime Minister, we were to "create a new Heaven and a new Earth". . . . We were to build "homes for heroes". . . . Hence we embarked on these great schemes which, unhappily, later on we found we could not afford. . . . Parliament in the days of poverty had to repeal measures which it had passed only a year or two before in the days of factitious prosperity.[29]

28. I. G. Sharp (*Industrial Conciliation and Arbitration in Great Britain* [London: Allen & Unwin, 1950], pp. 348–49, 361–63) discusses 9 and 10 Geo. V, c. 69, as do Mowat (*Britain between the Wars*, pp. 29–30) and W. H. Wickwar (*The Public Services* [London, 1938], pp. 33, 174–80, and 203).

29. Arthur Griffith-Boscawen, *Memories* (London: J. Murray, 1925), pp. 216–17.

17

Commitments, Hesitations, Failures
July 1919–July 1921

A cabinet adviser spoke one language; housing reformers spoke another. "The interim trade policy now in operation expires on September 1st," wrote S. J. Chapman; "the results hoped for have been attained. Trade has restarted and employment is rapidly improving."[1] Thus calmly he began a résumé of discussions held at Criccieth with Lloyd George on 16 July 1919; smoothly he related achievements to comprehensive new plans. Far different, however, was the alert sent by the National Housing and Town Planning Council to its members:

> An attack of an embittered kind against the policy embodied in the Act of July 1919 . . . was being made to convince both Parliament and the general public that the Ministry of Health and the Local Authorities were neither competent nor willing to perform their duties. . . . This attack was rendered more dangerous by the regrettable delays which had occurred in entering upon the work of construction.[2]

Chapman spoke as if the success of transition policies cleared the way for continued progress; the Council lived in daily fear that the early gains would be undone.

One document concerns July; the other, December. Together they suggest a turning point, the end of a great, hopeful period. Now it is certain that between July and December 1919 the time of troubles for the housing campaign had begun. Perhaps in that half-year the critical moment for everything had occurred, and the falling action had begun. The Council's records leave no doubt that housing champions had gone

1. Cab. 21/159.
2. NHTPC, Minute Book 3, *Annual Report.*

on the defensive; their fund appeals in 1920 disclose the terrible cost.[3] But their rally succeeded: the housing campaign went on, ever more bedeviled and expensive but with new stratagems and powers. Not in December 1919, not even in the new emergencies of July and October 1920, was doom pronounced. The replacement of Addison in March 1921 and the reversal of policy that July unmistakably marked the end; until then a neither-nor policy—of mounting criticism and wretched achievements but also of strenuous endeavors and rallies—left both fulfillment and failure in doubt.

The least certain value of these contrasting documents, then, lies in their chronology; rather, they serve to bracket the extremes of mood. One was complacent about the past, confident of a margin for deliberate stabilization in the future; the other poised over an abyss that could engulf the past and even the future. Even more than this, they typified differences in focus. To the Council, housing reforms were everything, the redeeming significance of the war, the essence of reconstruction. Chapman did not minimize reforms; nor did Sir Maurice Hankey, who was with him at Criccieth. Hankey's far-ranging analysis ("Towards a National Policy") made reform integral, stressing measures for a healthy and productive population.[4] But for Chapman and Hankey, economic revival was primary, and trade was at its heart. Government, Parliament, and the public then and henceforth would tend to divide into the groups symbolized by Chapman and those typified by the Council: the latter group accepting reforms as the end and measure of policy; the former looking first to efficiency, finance, and export. The Chapman group might hold—and long affirm—that its means to prosperity were also the means for successful reform. But a precondition is by nature a limit. In the fateful interplay between the reconstruction program and its preconditions lies much of the history from mid-1919 to the moment of defeat in mid-1921. At first the prevailing policies in trade, finance, and fiscal policy seemed to be fit preconditions for continuance of reform; thereafter, as doubts grew in early 1920, new but still compatible preconditions were sought for; eventually the search for possible and adequate trade and fiscal policies turned in a new direction, without regard for their consistency with reform; the new policies ceased to be preconditions for reform, and proved to be limits on it. Finally the Geddes economy ax gleamed—a precondition, it was thought, for solvency, but accepted at the cost of reform.

3. NHTPC entries for 1920, *ibid.*
4. Cab. 21/159.

It follows that, because there were these two groups and because there was this dualism between reform and its preconditions, our narrative and our attention must be directed first to one, and then to another, level of governmental action. At one time it will focus on Addison's ministry, closest in spirit to those who yearned for reform; at another time it will shift to the cabinet and to that broader field of debate where all issues were confronted and where all purposes competed. These two fields or levels were markedly different. Addison, his aims set, fought within narrow compass; his task was to meet a set of problems peculiar to the housing campaign. His was a kind of hand-to-hand combat at the very front line. The cabinet, like any GHQ, lived for many purposes; it weighed considerations weightier and more diverse than Addison's. At and between each level, the last act was played out.

Housing: The First Response to New Obstacles

Addison's staff was keen and fully organized; his legal powers were greater than any that Britain had ever before offered for housing; his subsidy was the acme of financial generosity. But he lacked a terribly important asset: time. As early as August 1, the cry resounded that nothing but emergency construction would do; the Office of Works urged that all existing housing schemes be given to it for completion; houses or cottages presently held should be offered at once to local authorities. The proposal was sensible, and much of it was adopted,[5] but the peremptoriness of the demand illustrates the impatience, unreasonableness, or naiveté in which Addison had to work. Housing always takes time; an anxious and needful nation was not prepared to wait.

It was a storm warning, no more. In September, Addison's staff received applications for 582 sites, which brought the total to 5,105; on the 46,000 acres involved, an estimated 460,000 houses would be built.[6] "We may safely claim," he reported, "to have mastered our first great difficulty of securing and approving sites."[7]

Then came the storm. By October, his colleagues were both angry and worried; by 27 October, Addison himself acknowledged the facts: "The present position of the National Housing Scheme is far from satisfactory. . . . Causes of serious delay . . . can only be removed by drastic action." Of the nation's £5,900,000 expenditure on construction, less than one-

5. HAC (5 August 1919); WC 505 (1 August 1919), Cab. 23/11.
6. G.T. 8402 (23 October 1919), Cab. 24/90.
7. C.P. 3 (27 October 1919), Cab. 24/92.

seventh went for houses.[8] The Minister of Labour called for complete control of building; reporting workingmen's grievances on housing, he did not hesitate to call them justified. Austen Chamberlain rushed in with suggestions. Mond flatly declared, on the anniversary of the armistice, that "the scheme is breaking down." Two days later the same charge was made openly in the House of Lords. Meeting in an emergency session with Treasury and Ministry of Labour chiefs, Chamberlain found no easy solution; they could only agree that "the position is a very grave one."[9] A dozen memoranda were on the table by the time a thoroughly alarmed cabinet met to discuss remedies.[10]

I think that, for Addison, neither the criticism nor the clash of proposals represented the worst side of the situation (they came with public life); rather, he sensed that the causes were ineradicable. He knew what high prices would do and were already doing; moreover, he knew that the labor shortage was critical and that the building trade unions would not budge. Then and there the sickening realization came that the housing campaign might fail. The shortage of money and materials had been foreseen, but few had foreseen that the number of workingmen would be quite inadequate, that the organized trades could block recruitment, and would want to. Since July Addison had negotiated with the building trade operatives, without result.[11] When the Minister of Labour reported

8. *Ibid.*

9. C.P. 107 (11 November 1918), Cab. 24/93; G.T. 8272 and 8354 (16 October 1919), Cab. 24/90; Cab. 7 (14 November 1919), Cab. 23/18; C.P. 74 (7 November 1919), Cab. 24/92.

Changes in official abbreviated headings for cabinet meetings, records and memoranda necessitate an explanation here, to distinguish past use of the abbreviation "Cab." from usage in this chapter. With the adoption of a new system on 4 November 1919, the abbreviated heading "WC" to designate a War Cabinet meeting and its serial number ceased to be used; starting that day, the cabinet session was designated by the abbreviated heading "Cab." followed by the number showing the meeting's place in the sequence, with a further number in parentheses to show the year. Thus "Cab. 1 (19)" designates the first meeting of the cabinet in 1919 under the new system. In this chapter, where the abbreviation "Cab." is followed by a single number, the reference is to the minutes of a particular cabinet meeting; but where—as in previous chapters—the abbreviation "Cab." is followed by two sets of numbers divided by a diagonal line (as in Cab. 24/67), the reference is to a cabinet memorandum, the first number designating the class list and the second number, following the diagonal, designating the volume in the series.

At the same time, in November 1919, the "G.T." memorandum series was terminated, the last volume being Cab. 24/93; most memoranda thereafter were designated by the abbreviated heading "C.P.," meaning "cabinet paper." See Public Record Office, *The Records of the Cabinet Office to 1922*, Public Record Office Handbook no. 11 (London: H.M. Stationery Office, 1966), pp. 5–12.

10. Cab. 7, 14 November 1919.

11. *Ibid.*

soaring wage rates in other types of building and complained that "the willingness of private individuals to pay excessive rates gains for them a vicious priority over public housing schemes," Addison knew this was true. Addison quarreled with Lloyd George behind the scenes. In anger and reproach, he wrote of a unique opportunity imperiled by weakness at the top.

> We have been compelled to work under restrictions imposed by the Cabinet itself, against my repeated advice. . . . My proposals with regard to (1) direct building, (2) the restriction of unnecessary building, and (3) finance—all vital matters—were emasculated by the Cabinet.[12]

Still, remedies must be sifted and tried. It did no good to join Chamberlain and Shackleton in lament ("Our whole building programme is being jeopardised by the trade selfishness of masters and men. . . . All housing schemes will become absolutely uneconomical"). This path led too easily to a destination only too clear. "The time would come when the Government would simply have to say that they could not go on," Shackleton concluded; and Chamberlain insisted the whole scheme must be recast to protect the government against its inability to meet even the present liabilities.[13] Addison would not admit this.

A disillusioned cabinet heard that, to 8 November, only 43,299 houses had been approved (approval was the final step before building began)—this against an agreed target of 500,000 required houses. It accepted the explanation that local authorities had not proved equal to the task, and therefore listened to the idea of a subsidy to stimulate private building contractors, which had many advocates. Amid misgivings ("this was a reversion to the system of private enterprise which had actually broken down before the War"), such subsidy was approved, but as a supplement only; the present state scheme "must not be thrown over." Carmichael suggested experimentation with steel-frame houses, concrete blocks, and other new methods and materials. Someone proposed that the Prime Minister address masters, men, and local authorities on their responsibilities ("nothing but pressure of public opinion would induce the building trade to take up a more reasonable attitude").

Addison endorsed all of these measures, proposed half a dozen changes, and put the accent on finance. Many authorities, he held, faced great difficulties in raising loans; some, especially those too high in rateable

12. R. J. Minney, *Viscount Addison: Leader of the Lords* (London: Odhams Press, 1958), pp. 170–72; G.T. 8388 (22 October 1919), Cab. 24/90.
13. C.P. 74.

value to qualify for Public Works Loans, were "floundering about . . . quite unable to raise the money themselves." No matter what else was done, "the State would have to help materially in financing some of the Local Authorities, or else in the localities concerned no houses would be built."

The cabinet cooperated fully. It approved private subsidies, up to £150 for as many as 100,000 houses (if built in twelve months). It endorsed agreements already reached with the building trades by Addison (who had launched talks without awaiting approval); it sanctioned work in rural areas by Ernle's ministry. It granted power to ban demolition, and power for Addison—even where local authorities were not in default—to prescribe the works they must build and pay for (a half-gain, this, it applied only to conversions and emergency accommodation). All these things were approved, even though it meant rushing a new bill to a vocally critical Parliament. The Prime Minister would address masters and men, plead for removal of prewar restrictions, and ask for the training of new recruits. All this might help.[14]

Nevertheless there were serious limits in the response and ominous overtones in the enveloping debate. Chamberlain's memoranda attacked the very idea of control: "The tendency of control . . . must be to increase costs. . . . The more controls we have . . . the more difficult it becomes for trade to resume its natural course." He was quite prepared to tell the country that "we cannot go on like this!"[15] Shackleton, representing the Ministry of Labour, was not so drastic. He did think there was some value in a licensing system. But he saw no real solution, for—as he put it— there was no incentive whatever to economy on government contracts; there were bound to be further advances in wages, whatever one did. As for the obvious theoretical solutions—greater recruitment into the building trade, and union acceptance of "dilution" whereby jobs would become open to the semi-trained, diluting the number of fully qualified union men on the job—he simply had to scoff. The unions had proved too conservative for this.[16]

In the cabinet debate the Treasury pleaded near-impossibilities. To help the poorest authorities it must pay £60,000,000 by September 1920,

14. Cab. 7 (14 November) and 8 (20 November 1919), Cab. 23/18. The basis for action was Addison's memorandum, C.P. 94 (11 November 1919), in Cab. 27/66 and in Cab. 24/93. The entire record of all memoranda and of subcommittee minutes on this crisis is in Cab. 27/66.

15. C.P. 73 (7 November 1919), and G.T. 8354 (16 October 1919), Cab. 24/92 and 90.

16. C.P. 74 (7 November 1919), Cab. 24/92.

and £160,000,000 by September 1922—from a local loans fund of £15,000,000 (i.e., from new money, but City opinion was that "at the present moment the Government could not borrow any more money"). Addison lost. The cabinet concurred that local authorities must not be encouraged to think they would get additional state assistance; such aid must be only a last resort after local authorities had exhausted every other method. The Treasury's idea of giving special, guaranteed status to new local authorities' bonds was to be studied, but Addison himself must swallow the pill of announcing in Commons that

> Local Authorities were entirely incorrect if they believed that the State was in a better position than they were to undertake the financial responsibility for raising money to carry out their housing schemes; in fact the Local Authorities . . . were in a better position for this than the State, whose credit had been so heavily drawn upon by the War.

Worse still, Addison doubted that the scheme for local authorities' bonds would succeed.[17]

No emergency proposal had ruffled Addison's colleagues so much as his idea of a ban on nonessential building. "During the past three months contracts have been [lavishly] placed," he charged, for places of amusement and factory and shop extensions throughout the country.

> They are being pressed forward . . . regardless of cost, the Contractors being permitted in many cases to give 2d or 3d per hour or even more in excess of the district rate to building labour, and thereby attracting them from Housing. . . . Three weeks ago the number of brick-layers on one of our housing schemes dropped from 160 to 42 in one week from this cause.[18]

Retorts were vehement. "The State ought to give every encouragement and impetus to the re-opening of trade and industry." Priority for factories, even entailing demolition of houses, brought employment to some districts. With 72,000 places needed in schools at once, school construction must not stop. These objections had point. The means necessary to produce ample houses might contradict the means that would revive industry; the recovery of enterprise and the building of schools might block the housing campaign. Indeed there was conflict between the goals that the government sought, as well as the means; basic values also were in conflict. Perplexed, the cabinet gravely passed the problem to a com-

17. Minutes of cabinet meeting 8 (20 November 1919), Cab. 23/18.
18. C.P. 94 (11 November 1919), Cab. 27/66.

mittee, with a revealing directive: "to reconcile the moral with the economical aspect of the question." The phrasing was uncomfortably apt. "Morality" dictated the fulfillment of housing pledges; the "economical aspect" seemed to require measures which undercut the housing campaign. The cabinet's directive was not only an apt summary of immediate obstacles to housing; it was a near comic epitome of the problem of reconstruction.[19]

On the Housing (Additional Powers) Act of December 1919, every positive decision left its mark. The subsidy to private contractors (businessmen, unions, and cooperatives alike) was a victory in itself. Of the 213,821 homes built under the "Addison Acts," private builders accounted for 39,186, or 18 per cent.[20] Desperate pleading by Addison got the Public Utility Societies' aid raised from 30 per cent to 50 per cent, at the last minute. But nothing could conceal the fact that the elation of July was gone forever. The minister was on the defensive; the unresolved tangle of purposes and policies held mortal danger for the housing campaign. And against the half-dozen cases where the cabinet had given Addison exactly what he wanted, the list of defeats must be reckoned. He wanted some hard-pressed authorities made eligible for Public Works Loans by altering the standard of entitlement. He wanted to make the profits of private builders deductible from income tax. He wanted the government to contribute to union insurance funds, in proportion to the recruits accepted. He wanted a private subsidy of £160, not £150. Especially, he wanted the government to guarantee local bonds. On all these financial proposals he lost.

If the Treasury's arguments meant anything, this was not simply aid denied this time but a door that had closed forever. Moreover, Addison's failure to get full default powers, covering *all* cases, ranked as a defeat. The cabinet was rigorously negative on the alleged "hardship cases" of financially distressed local authorities; once a list was compiled of those whose inability had been completely proved, the list would be considered "absolutely final"—and left to the Chancellor's discretion. This was a bad omen, but how good were the better ones? The ban on luxury building might not work. Local authority bonds might not find purchasers. The crucial appeal for dilution might fail.

19. Cab. 8 (20 November 1919), Cab. 32/18.
20. C.P. 236 (2 December 1919) and Memorandum C.H.C. 8 (3 December 1919), Cab. 27/66; C. L. Mowat, *Britain between the Wars, 1918–1940* (London: Methuen, 1955), pp. 509–10; Marian Bowley, *Housing and the State*, p. 23; see also Table II, *ibid.*, p. 24.

Present facts completed the outlook, and all were dismal. *Not one house* had been completed. Although sites sufficient for 460,000 houses had been approved, the totals were much worse for subsequent processing steps: housing plans for only 31,101 units had been approved through October—for contract tenders, even fewer.[21] Local authorities were completely dismayed; private building, once productive of many houses, had been killed by high costs and state competition; and it was a humiliating fact that Ministry of Health housing schemes "came last instead of first." Very recently, state housing had seemed the one great means for reviving employment; now all was reversed, and (to quote Addison) "The effect of this abundant employment in building . . . is directly responsible for an inflation of the tenders for housing."[22]

For the moment, the two worst auguries concerned inflation and dilution. The cabinet, exhausting its ingenuity on the housing crisis, had done many things, but nothing that was calculated to halt the general rise in prices. But what good would increased wage rates do if continued inflation made them obsolete? What would private subsidies avail if contractors found costs pushing against profit margins? Investors, even now, feared inflation too much to buy government stocks; the response to the Victory Loan was unnervingly weak. The Treasury itself could not borrow. If inflation lasted, what hope for new loans or for local bonds—or for persuading the Treasury to raise a subsidy?

Dilution, if anything, was worse. Addison spoke from experience: "In conjunction with high cost, this is the most serious issue of all." Months earlier he had asked the Joint Industrial Council to help increase the number of workmen; in November he concluded that "neither masters nor men are disposed to render any real assistance." The government simply could not meet the needs of the housing program "unless there is a rapid augmentation of the building labour . . . coupled with improved production."[23]

After the fact, knowing that generous offers and guarantees by the government (in the months to come) failed to overcome the conservatism and vested interests of the building unions, one asks if short-term solutions were even possible. Why, after all, should the unions budge? They knew that men had been leaving the trade by thousands; they knew the seasonal character of employment; they saw hard-won and indispensable safeguards

21. C.P. 158, Cab. 24/93; Christopher Addison, *The Betrayal of the Slums* (London: Herbert Jenkins, 1922), pp. 25–27.
22. C.P. 94 and 236, Cab. 27/66.
23. C.P. 94.

in every restrictive practice, and above all in their control of recruitment and training.

But there was another side to the story. The government had studied the specific ills of the industry and was moving far to cope with them. Employment was very high, and the backlog of repair and construction suggested it would remain high. Construction of *workers'* houses, the whole point of the state scheme, would obviously be a benefit to labor as a whole; labor, in the broad view, had good reason for making a success of the 1919 Housing Act. Lastly, Whitleyism itself was on trial, for the experiment in joint solution of common problems would be tested by the results in housing. From this standpoint the deadlock in the building trades was far more than an episode in the troubled life of Addison's Ministry of Health; it ranked as a major test of statemanship and good faith, for all the parties concerned. With hindsight one can see that a solution was possible. The failure to attain it casts discredit more on the nation's industrial leadership—in capital and labor—than on Addison and his colleagues within government.

For those with time to think of the past as well as the present, there was irony and a fatal familiarity in the issue. The essential issue was dilution— the very issue, under the name "pledges," that had haunted Addison and bedeviled the cabinet in 1918. Churchill had branded the prewar union practices, forbidding dilution, reactionary anachronisms. Addison—like Smuts and Barnes and Horne—had agreed in principle but had counseled acquiescence. It was the price of industrial peace, they had said; it was the first and greatest step to reconstruction, they had said, and as a palliative they added that unions would prove flexible and cooperative in practice, if their rights were only acknowledged. They faced something worse than a cruel disappointment. Now, when employment was soaring, when the building trade was short 200,000 men, when labor's need for protection seemed least, the unions were undercutting the foremost item on the agenda of reconstruction.

In retrospect, it also seems utterly astonishing that ministers and civil servants had not long ago foreseen the critical shortage of building labor. What had their wartime experiences been, if they were not one long search for manpower? What had plagued the Ministry of Munitions—and that means Lloyd George, Addison, Churchill, and their staffs—so much as the terrible shortage of skilled labor, which had forced them at the very height of battle to call back workers from the lines? What had Prothero found to be the key to farm output, if it was not the increase of labor supply on the land? And yet this blind spot had persisted.

But Addison had no time for retrospect. Seeing the new act through Parliament in December 1919, he pushed ahead on other rescue plans. Housing bonds were accorded the status of "trustee securities," although every chancery judge was opposed; but Chamberlain and Addison saw no other way to finance the housing policy, and the cabinet agreed.[24] It was Addison's last major victory in the cabinet.

Almost all the other work was progressing well, some of it very well. The Ministry of Health took over, on schedule, the Board of Education's powers on child health. It received 218 public works applications and endorsed them all—£3,613,000 for land-settlement and water supply schemes. Loans for land settlement to thirty County Councils were approved—more than £1,000,000 in just one month. Poor Law reform already was being tackled, piecemeal: children were to be removed from Poor Law institutions. Addison made the time to work on a new national health insurance bill; his draft provided for increased benefits and contributions, along with higher fees to doctors. Nor was that all. Without fanfare, the task of the Maclean committee of 1917 was now being resumed: Addison began to work toward that larger dream which had inspired Morant and the Webbs—a complete local health system. Addison turned to his Council on Medical and Administrative Services (just formed within the Ministry of Health); he instructed them to plan "for the systematized provision of such forms of medical and allied services as should . . . be available for the inhabitants of a given area." Here was a stimulus to tackle that other dimension of health reform— *local* integration and amplification of service—which would complement the recent integration at the top. The signal had been given which would result in the comprehensive "Dawson Report," a true landmark, in 1920.

Each of these items represented a success achieved and laid a basis for more.[25] In housing reform, there was another satisfying gain: Addison was granted power to help in the formation of "garden cities."[26]

The Rent Act was a headache, as always; it was too closely related to the housing crisis to be anything else. Worried about the evictions, Addison fought through an uncomfortable session with the Home Affairs Committee and won a new legal requirement that courts must consider alternative housing before they could issue ejectment orders. H. A. L. Fisher, faithful in his fashion to a much different brand of liberalism, spoke up for the owners' grievances and deplored interference with the

24. Cab 12 (10 December 1919), Cab. 23/18; C.P. 158, Cab. 24/93.
25. G.T. 8042 (23 October 1919), Cab. 24/90; Abel-Smith, *The Hospitals*, pp. 289–92.
26. C.H.C. 6 and 7 (25 and 27 November 1919), Cab. 27/66.

freedom of management of property. "There was no doubt that such legislation was wrong from an economic point of view." Claud Schuster countered that it might be necessary to preserve order. Addison was given the task of introducing the bill.[27]

Housing alone was cause for genuine fear. It was no longer the fear that the program would be costly (which had long ago been accepted) and no longer the fear that subsidies would be painfully high; it was the fear that—with the boldest subsidies in history and with unmatched legal powers—the workers' houses might not be built at all.

The Cabinet: Hesitations

The outcome would not be decided on the front lines, where Addison contended with immediate issues. Defeat there could ensure defeat everywhere, of course; but even maximum success by Addison would not guarantee victory. Attitudes and support at the command center might accomplish that. But in turning attention to the cabinet, it is not attitudes and support on housing itself that one looks for. The crucial decisions for housing and all reconstruction might turn on very general factors, might arise from discussions and decisions far afield. An entire context must be viewed.

In viewing this larger scene, however, our knowledge of the outcome is not an unmixed asset. Hindsight dazzles. It assures us that reforms must eventually cease. It tells us that reconstruction must finally be reversed, that its protagonists' strivings will be stilled by decrees from on high. In the sure expectation of fated doom one tends to lie inert. Our present search, however, is for turning points and moments of decision; we seek, at the very least, particular knowledge of how opposing motives contended until the decree was made absolute. In this search the belief that reforms were never seriously meant need not be abandoned; it is sufficient to keep that thought in reserve. But we do better if we begin with the full situation and if we work with things, not as they would become, but as they appeared at the time.

Alternatives

Broadly speaking, government faced three options. Two of these were closely akin, emphasizing reform and welfare; the third, not ostensibly contrary to reform, shifted the emphasis to trade revival. The first alternative was symbolized by the National Industrial Conference. Whitleyism

27. HAC (25 November 1919), Cab. 26/2.

and interclass harmony were the watchwords. Its premises were that only a joint attack by capital and labor on the problems of productivity and output could succeed, that only from a higher material basis could reform and welfare be financed, and that only an interclass partnership could reconcile recovery and reform. Close to this alternative, but less dependent on labor's active help, stood a second option: a policy of reform, welfare, and recovery—minus Whitleyism. But other options, with their powerful defenders inside government, also were strongly attractive; and these alternatives stood far off from the first two. Recovery was their dominant aim, perhaps their only aim; stimuli to profit, tax relief, trade revival, retrenchment, and decontrol were among the means. For reconstruction, it would be the means and methods that counted most; their effect, unintentional or (more dangerous) unsuspected, could be enormous. The cabinet seemed open to all policies, all methods.

But not quite. The pattern of the first six months of 1919 was still visible—or rather the lack of pattern, the welter of conflict and indecision. Thus Chapman's and Hankey's proposals to Lloyd George at Criccieth, on 16 June, differed little from the composite program which Addison had sketched as 1918 closed. In these plans, and in the agenda of the National Industrial Conference, there was continuity with the first days of 1919. But some things were markedly different. The fact of substantial decontrol was now assumed. The sufficiency of the existing list of reform schemes was also assumed. Most important of all, the financial crisis of the state was now apparent, and those most affected pushed their case forward without pause. Remembering the economy drive of 1922, one watches as the case for economy obtrudes itself in 1919. It is clear, even with hindsight fully discounted, that by the end of 1919 economy had established a primary claim on the statesmen.

Much else was different in this last half of 1919. Relations between the government and labor altered, then hardened in a new and foreboding way. As the gulf between Parliament and cabinet widened, the country became more aggressively hostile to bureaucracy and controls. These were changes of degree, and nowise as great as those in 1920, but they blighted the growth of further reform. It is economy, however, the new cry and the coming trend, that calls for first attention.

The Voice of Economy

No one could exceed Austen Chamberlain in this; as Chancellor he had learned the message of thrift and retrenchment by heart. He could fit its words to any occasion. Was milk control proposed? It implied a huge and costly staff. Was the mining of nonferrous metals to be subsidized? Had startling prices been paid for land? Was the state's guarantee proposed for local housing loans? The Chancellor deplored such things. Was Sankey's plan to nationalize coal to be considered? "He would not dare" take on his shoulders a huge purchase of this kind.[28] Must coal-price subsidies go up? Rather let prices go up, and shift the cost from government to consumer. Was the housing campaign to be rescued by state building or new subsidies? The scheme must be recast, to enable the government to meet current liabilities. Was the Water Power Bill to go to Commons? Not until the menace of limitless expenditure was removed.[29]

This highly susceptible Chancellor did not flinch at challenging the proposed army pension increases. "The Cabinet *must* consider the general financial condition of the country."

> Owing to increased expenditure and a decrease in estimated receipts, our deficit for the year would be nearer 400,000,000*l.* than the 250,000,000*l.* upon which he had reckoned. . . . The whole of the new money from the Victory Loan would be swallowed up by this deficit, *i.e.* by the creation of new debt. The proposals now before the Cabinet would cost, for the current year, about 12,000,000*l.*, and for a full year between 20,000,000*l.* and 29,000,000*l.* . . . It looked as though we should be faced in 1920–1921 with a deficit of 200,000,000*l.* . . . The Government was being confronted with the report of one Committee after another, and these reports were being judged separately. The Cabinet were unable to consider the aggregate cost of the proposals.[30]

Elsewhere, that same July day, he said: "The position grows daily more grave."

> No estimates hold good, and the Cabinet sanctions increase after increase without . . . a sufficient appreciation of the aggregate result. Our capital commitments are already enormous. Borrowing is difficult and rates will be exorbitant. If we cannot balance revenue and expenditure next year, our credit—national and international— will be seriously shaken and the results may be disastrous. . . . Will my colleagues consider what this means and how it is to be provided

28. WC 582 (20 June 1919) and 613, Cab. 23/10 and 11; WC 606A (5 August 1919), fols. 162–63, Cab. 23/15; C.H.C. 7 (27 November 1919), Cab. 27/66; WC 607A (7 August 1919), Cab. 23/15.
29. WC 589 (8 July 1919), Cab. 23/11; C.P. 73; G.T. 8345 (16 October 1919), Cab. 24/90.
30. WC 600 (26 July 1919), Cab. 23/11.

for by new taxation in addition to filling the gap left by the repeal of the Excess Profits Duty (£50 millions) and to making good the reliefs which are certain to be recommended for large classes of income-tax payers?[31]

In December, therefore, in protest over present costs and future health insurance increases, he said, "Education estimates will increase £11,000,000 over this year, which is £13,000,000 over last year. Education expenditure can only be met by additional taxation, and affords the strongest argument for refraining from fresh commitments."[32] The Treasury echoed its chief, throwing an accusing spotlight on government staffs. With 8,484 on its staff at armistice time, the Ministry of Labour now had 24,000; since the reintroduction of rationing, the staff of the Ministry of Food was up by 1,500. The Ministry of Munitions had discharged only 1,300 rather than the promised 10,000, keeping costs at £700,000 a month.[33]

With Bank of England pound notes at a 15 per cent discount, surely it was worth the effort "to recover the magnificent credit which the Country has so long enjoyed and which once lost could but slowly if ever be recovered." So pleaded a Bank of England official. With the Treasury holding the money rate to 5 per cent, many persons were finding it more profitable to invest abroad. The Bank, if left free, would long ago have raised the value of money; abandonment of the gold standard was deplorable; the public was living extravagantly and "should be induced to economise."[34] Even Lloyd George at times seconded the cry for the "ruthless" cutting down of expenditure. He wished that the champions of a Churchillian policy in Russia would face facts: "Would they be willing to pay another 6*d.* or 7*d.* on the income tax?" In the secret session of 5 August he came round at last to expenditures. With diminished resources, lost manpower, fewer ships, and falling output, expenditure would be four times what it had been before the war. "We could not afford to go on as we were doing, and it was necessary for us to realise that we could not have the best of everything."[35]

But there were other voices, through those last six months of 1919. In the delusively calm interlude at Criccieth, Hankey and Chapman had drafted policy papers that covered everything, and they had *not* chosen economy as their great theme. Hankey admittedly was concerned about

31. G. 257 (26 July 1919), Cab. 27/72.
32. Cab. 15 (17 December 1919), Cab. 23/18.
33. F.C. (Finance Committee) 8 (8 October 1919), Cab. 27/72.
34. F.C. 5 (25 September 1919), Cab. 27/72.
35. F.C. 30 (20 August 1919), Cab. 27/71; WC 601, 606A.

Britain's reduced position. "Invisible exports" were fewer, debts to America were huge, the exchange position was bad; but he stressed new construction and the building of the nation's health as much as economy in staffs. His and Chapman's message put efficiency before economy. Moreover, economy to them spelled navy and army cuts *first and chiefly*, and lesser foreign commitments. For Hankey, the central issue was diplomacy.[36] "Think boldly" was still the watchword for many—for the Prime Minister on 5 August ("The country must take risks just as the soldier had to take risks," but not with the health and labor of the people. "We had to lay at once the sure foundations of national health and industrial prosperity"); for Winston Churchill, sure that "some big scheme" of capital levy or forced loan eventually must, and would be, adopted; and for Mond, who in December called for a huge national housing loan (the government "must be prepared for a very bold financial policy").[37]

Clearly the cabinet included important spokesmen for reconstruction, energetic champions of costly risk-taking in the interests of efficiency and reform. They guaranteed that Austen Chamberlain and other apostles of retrenchment would not go unchallenged.

Chamberlain's figures spoke louder than his words. Like a great girder collapsing into a rushing stream, they deflected the current and altered all plans. A memorandum, "On National Expenditures," assessed the total for the budgetary year 1919–20 at £1,490,000,000 and found one-third of it irreducible (debt charges, £435,000 in war pensions, £39,000,000 in education grants, £25,000,000 for old age pensions and insurance). The £503,000,000 for munitions and the forces would be met by the sale of surplus stores. Loans and subsidies totaled £326,000,000, and coal, bread, and railway subsidies and out-of-work payments made up more than half of this.

Reduction was advised primarily in the size of the army and in civil aviation, and then in subsidies ("next to the fighting forces, the most obvious field for economy"). Pledges, however, limited the chance for economy; they covered civil liabilities, training for the demobilized, grants for agriculture and health, and aid to new key industries—there, economy was precluded. By abolishing the bread and railway subsidies, £55,000,000 could be saved. *Next* year, the Treasury suggested, £100,000 could be saved by reversing the government's promises and halting the formation of small-holding colonies. "Purely war organisations" must be dissolved. The general conclusion carried weight: "It should be laid down

36. Cab. 21/159.
37. WC 606A; F.C. 11 (22 October 1919), Cab. 27/71; C.P. 107.

as an immutable decision . . . that at whatever cost the national expenditure of 1920–1, including full provision for the Sinking Fund, must be covered by income."[38]

Chamberlain had already reckoned the national debt: £7,685 million (£163 per capita), not counting a possible £65 million more—against £645 million (£14 per capita) in 1914. Worse still, unlike the prewar debt (most of it held in the country, with no fixed date for redemption), the new debt from war included £1,300,000,000 owed overseas, and redemption was pledged for nearly £3 billion in the next five years. Against this, stood assets in national private wealth estimated at £16 billion, up by £4.5 million from prewar, if one made no allowance for decreased purchasing power.

The current *adverse* trade balance was £355,546,000. One billion pounds of foreign securities, exported during the war to America, was gone forever. Future prospects included no likelihood of reaching a "future normal" budget of £766 million; the 1920–21 budget would exceed £1,150 million. Moreover, and outside the budget, unexpected costs were being created by new laws (e.g., £300 million for some 600,000 houses at the optimistic forecast of £500 each, and so on for railways, electricity supply, land settlement, and much else). Even when these burdens fell on local authorities rather than on the Exchequer, the rise in money rates—as localities and businesses competed for loans—would add to state costs. Over and above all this stood inflation, "a danger to the stability of the country."[39]

The recommendations in this 18 July document—cessation of government borrowing, reduction of public debt, immediate retrenchment—were reinforced in October by Chamberlain's "Note on the National Balance Sheet." For a normal year it predicted a gap of £95 million between revenue and expenditure. And this on the most optimistic basis—if all wartime agencies were abolished, all subsidies withdrawn, all training schemes terminated, no more loans to the Allies or the Dominions, out-of-work donations withdrawn, and all grants for health, education, and insurance held at 1919 levels. But already this assumption had been falsified by unemployment insurance costs and by pension bills. And irreducible items made up three-fourths of the £848,800,000 estimated normal outgo. "The document as it stood," said Lloyd George, "was a very terrifying thing."[40]

38. "On National Expenditure," Cab. 27/72.
39. G. 257.
40. F.C. 13 (17 October 1919), Cab. 27/72 and 11 (22 October 1919), Cab. 27/71.

How far would Chamberlain's economy campaign succeed? How many members of the cabinet would substitute retrenchment for reform?

The Measure of Influence

Some men were unmoved. Milner, for example, felt sure the nation would accept the necessity of continued borrowing, perhaps as much as £5 million that year. Expenses could decline only slowly. The situation must be compared with "our expectation of having to go on fighting for two years longer." Churchill pointed out that 11,000 troops had been returning from the army each day; in that context, return to peacetime conditions in a moment was impossible. Bonar Law and Lloyd George concurred.[41]

The outcome nevertheless was that staff cuts were ordered; added coal costs were shifted onto the consumer public; local authority bonds, instead of state loans, were chosen for housing; the government granted itself, almost in panic, an indemnity against war-damage claims; extension of the out-of-work donation beyond November was vetoed; a small profit for the Treasury was built into the electricity supply scheme; and pleas to take on workers at government dockyards were negatived. This last was significant: it was the first clear case, I feel, of explicit refusal to sacrifice economy to employment.[42] Also, the out-of-work donation, as a *lasting* policy, was ruled out (as the Treasury had advised) because it put the entire cost on the state; any permanent unemployment insurance schemes must be contributory. The same logic dictated the level of old age insurance benefits.[43] Economy reached to the right wing of policy, and far to the east: Denikin was allowed £100,000, which Churchill termed "petty cash."[44] Treasury scrutiny was instituted over housing wherever state building and state loans in hardship cases were concerned.[45]

These, however, were half-victories for economy; the basic measures and expenditures went through. In other cases Chamberlain lost. The technical and political arguments for bread subsidy, put forward by Beveridge, prevailed over Chamberlain's cry to "stop all unnecessary waste." Unemployment insurance scales were increased, adding £14 million (and implying an increase in the income tax, Chamberlain

41. F.C. 11, Cab. 27/71.
42. WC 556 and 589; Cab. 3 (6 November 1919), Cab. 23/18; HAC (9 October 1919), Cab. 26/2.
43. Cab. 3 and 7; Cab. 15 (17 December 1919), Cab. 23/18; F.C. 5; Treasury Memorandum (20 September 1919), Cab. 27/72.
44. WC 605 (1 August 1919), Cab. 23/11.
45. *Ibid.*; Cab. 27/66, *passim.*

warned, that the public would not stand). Private builders were subsidized; Public Utility Societies got further aid; freight subsidies for bread imports continued. Nonferrous mines, though unprofitable and inefficient, received subsidy. Chamberlain objected in this case that "there was a universal cry from everyone for the State to help them, although at the same time the greatest objections were put forward by these same people to State Control," but Baldwin had prevailed: unemployment would be unwise.[46]

Other factors and other men modified Chamberlain's economy drive, as did Chamberlain himself. His most sweeping proposals left housing untouched for that year. He dropped economy when it came to coal subsidy reductions, considering the impact on the poor. He did not touch a wide range of heavy costs on the grounds that pledges covered them. He asked no retrenchment by the Ministry of Health, although its staff was up by 50 per cent. He acknowledged that bread, railway, and coal subsidies must stand.[47]

Nor did he try to make headway against inflation, an omission that seems astonishing. He and the Treasury knew that rising prices had made it difficult to borrow; they foresaw, indeed, a time of outright impossibility. "We are now at the parting of the ways," said the Treasury in July. The choice was between a continued policy of cheap money, or a decision to take at least the first tentative steps to prevent inflation. Eventually the bank rate was raised to 6 per cent, but only in November—one of the few clear changes made that year. For the delay and the caution shown, I think there is one perfectly clear explanation: the cabinet relied upon high prices. Chamberlain personally was of two minds. He saw disadvantages in either direction of policy: higher money rates would curb the inflation, but would threaten the still unsure revival of industry; but a lax policy, indulging present inflation, would surely hinder the raising of new capital through loans, notably for housing and for other aspects of reconstruction. His colleagues' thinking was less complicated. The advantages of the current boom, not its disadvantages and future perils, shaped their thoughts. Their simpler views prevailed. Like the misguided reliance on high prices, the failure to cope with wartime profits by drastic taxation ranks as a major miscalculation. In 1921, Churchill would single out this instance of inaction as his major regret; later still, many would face the truth which A. J. P. Taylor has pointed out, that nothing did more

46. WC 582; Cab. 11 (8 December 1919), Cab. 23/18; WC 613; HAC (19 June 1919), Cab. 26/1.
47. F.C. 13 (17 October 1919), Cab. 27/72; F.C. 5 and F.C. 8 (8 October 1919), *ibid.*

than this debt burden to hamper social policy.[48] The chance for real remedies along these lines was missed in 1919 and 1920.

Decontrol: An Uneven Pattern

Economy, as a policy, was growing stronger. What of decontrol, its seeming twin? One force, it appeared, would push decontrol even further than retrenchment had gone: parliamentary opinion.

Parliament's "absolute detestation" for restrictions and for government's bureaucratic legions is attested very often in cabinet records. This feeling—part calculation, part dogma, and part sheer emotion—fed upon the news of departments still double their prewar size; it prompted inquiries into office staffs, sheared acquisition powers from the Ministry of Transport, and removed powers of compulsion from the Electricity Supply Bill; it denied the Ministry of Supply the indispensable power to examine merchants' accounts. It culminated in the famous quote from Lord Inchcape:

> We want to get on with our business, not spend our time arguing with Government clerks, dancing attendance at the Board of Trade, appearing before committees, wheedling Consuls for permission to import what we need, throwing open our books, bills and invoices to inspectors from Whitehall, and going through all the worry and expense to justify every transaction . . . to some official inquisitor.[49]

It was make-believe, of course, this image of arrogant conquerors harrying an industrious Saxondom, or of blanching caitiffs and over-promoted nincompoops quaking before a Community of Virtue about to pronounce deserved doom. Government memoranda overwhelmingly preached decontrol as a premise, and often repeated the rationale in detail. Austen Chamberlain was good for a whole anthology.

> The moment you began control you were inevitably driven to complete control which, if prolonged, led to nationalisation. . . . Control eliminated all the usual motives which induced economic production. . . . All the moral machinery interested in increasing production became moribund.

48. F.C. meeting 1 (24 July 1919), Cab. 27/71; R. H. Tawney, "The Abolition of Economic Controls, 1918–1921," *Economic History Review*, 13 (1943): 15; Beaverbrook, *Men and Power*, pp. 404–7; Taylor, *English History, 1914–1945*, pp. 124–25.

49. WC 569, 597, 610A, and 591; HAC meetings 25 and 28 (March 1919), and HAC 79 (30 November 1920), Cab. 26/1 and 3; G.T. 7007, Cab. 24/77; E. V. Francis, *Britain's Economic Strategy* (London: Jonathan Cape, 1939), pp. 18–19.

To a score of such pieties a technical and pragmatic notion added its force: given the changed circumstances of peace, control would have to be *wider* than in war.[50] But public attitudes ruled this out. It is no surprise, then, that controls were off domestic investments by late July, that the continuance of full milk control was vetoed, that flour mills were decontrolled in June, that trade to Germany was opened, and that Addison dropped the idea of reimposing controls on housing, although he and Horne favored this.[51] Nor is it surprising that the Emergency Legislation (Continuance) Bill, drafted on 8 July to keep many regulations alive, was speedily withdrawn and sliced "to an irreducible minimum." It had met very strong opposition in Parliament. In the redrafting, very many statutes and regulations were therefore termed unessential. Out went thirty-four D.O.R.A. regulations.[52] With some controls blocked, some subsidies also were blocked—the new controls proposed for bread and coal, for instance. "Free competition"—with Addison for once siding with the orthodox H. A. L. Fisher—blocked the control and purchase of hay, against Board of Trade protests.[53]

But all the conventional arguments for decontrol and against subsidy failed to block a new one-year subsidy for the herring industry. Direct Treasury resistance was overridden. So it was for nonferrous mines[54] and such major things as coal and food: basic controls and supports persisted even if fuller controls or further payments were vetoed. New sugar-control orders were authorized. Such cases had their own positive rationale: they were not simple concessions to strike threats or parliamentary outcries. Food controls remained, although deplored, because (in the case of milk) the industry was too disorganized to be left unregulated and (for food generally) because shipping difficulties presaged a shortage. Decontrol of meat, unanimously favored in principle, was postponed when the consequences were thoroughly studied.[55] Where controls were kept, then, their retention was not due simply to inertia; there was often a rational and a circumstantial basis, and the cabinet was open to persuasion by both reason and fact. Even the Treasury—the

50. WC 606A, 582, and 589.
51. F.C. meeting 1; WC 582; E. V. Morgan, *Studies in British Economic Policy, 1914–1925* (London: Macmillan, 1952), p. 64; C.P. 3.
52. HAC (8 July 1919), Cab. 26/1; HAC 42 (15 October 1919), Cab. 26/2; G.T. 8321 (n.d.), Cab. 24/89.
53. HAC (6 August 1919); WC 605.
54. HAC (25 September 1919), Cab. 26/2; WC 613 (13 August 1919), Cab. 23/11.
55. WC 635 (27 October 1919), Cab. 23/12; WC 582; Cab. 11 (8 December 1919), Cab. 23/18.

lofty minaret from which many a faithful sermon was preached in praise of economy and decontrol—had a theory to explain why it kept controls on capital: they would have been useful even before the war![56] Control was not doctrineless. On occasion, *re*control had its advocates, at least on pragmatic immediate grounds. In that case the causation was dual. "An undoubted reaction of public opinion in favour of control," caused and supplemented by the fact of rising prices, led to the continuance of the Food Ministry with full powers.[57]

Decontrol had its critics; control occasionally had positive champions. If Maclay denounced food control, the Food Controller held it indispensable.[58] Geddes, believing hay control and subsidy "absolutely essential," angrily appealed his case to the cabinet after defeat in committee (by a similar maneuver, he and Lord Lee won a subsidy for fishing). The Prime Minister declared it "undesirable to contemplate" the withdrawal of food controls. Bonar Law insisted to his dissenting colleagues that "whether nationalisation [of coal] was decided upon or not, some form of control . . . would be necessary."[59]

The specific merits of particular cases decided these men. Addison, no friend of nationalization at that time and outspokenly against subsidy or full controls in a few cases, championed moderate food control. He joined in paring down basic control regulations on the grounds that drastic cuts would win Parliament's approval for what was absolutely essential.[60] Some men, judging each case by pragmatic need, were decontrollers only for the working day: some for conscience' sake; some for appeasement and appearances. And only a few were ardent for laissez-faire. Maclay, H. A. L. Fisher, and Inverforth upheld the dismal science, but even Austen Chamberlain broke ranks long enough to demand action against profiteering. When Maclay reiterated that "nothing but blight resulted from Government control," Chamberlain countered that private enterprise "was extraordinarily slow to move."[61] Not even Chamberlain was willing to countenance inaction by the state.

Analysis to this point has shown that action, motives, and sentiment on even such kindred topics as retrenchment and decontrol did not take a single unmodified line, let alone a line that pointed to 1914. Perhaps, after

56. F.C. 2 (11 August 1919), Cab. 27/71.
57. WC 582; see also Albert Lauterbach, "Economic demobilization in England," *Political Science Quarterly*, 57, No. 3 (September 1942), 379–80.
58. G.T. 8353 (17 October 1919) and 8410 (25 October 1919), Cab. 24/90.
59. HAC (6 August 1919), Cab. 26/1; WC 587.
60. WC 607A, 562, 582; HAC (6 August and 15 October 1919), Cab. 26/1 and 2.
61. WC 592, 610A.

all, absolute uniformity on these three themes was unlikely, and on closer look they were not synonymous. Decontrol did not necessarily mean economy; subsidy and control, usually close-linked, could be alternatives to each other (a subsidy might be added as a control was *removed*). Even the logical affinity of retrenchment and economy broke down in practice: some short-run savings—above all those that invited inflation—were patently bad economy.

We must still ask why, logic apart, more uniformity was not imposed by sheer outside pressure and by the rising momentum of economy and decontrol. But first we must ask about nationalization; surely we might expect it to be the twin and logical correlate of economy and decontrol! So, at last, overhurdling lesser cases,[62] the Sankey commission reports come before us.

Nationalization of Coal: A Peculiar Debate

On 7 August eighteen divided men, some resolute and some vacillating, met to consider those five reports. Each report had its champion. This fact alone—if we can ignore the cabinet's division on general views and the outside world, where Parliament fretted and Yorkshire was going through a month-long miners' strike—guaranteed that the debate would not be simple. In fact, it was enormous—thirty pages in paraphrase. The debate was prolonged by other causes as well: cabinet members spoke as if they were free to choose, as if they faced an open question that could be decided apart from external pressures. Patently, they were unsure where to take hold of the issue. And, to the last, they were unsure how to phrase their announcement. For the entire session lay under the threat of labor's wrath. The task was not to show labor that the compromise was a good substitute (labor's mind was made up). The problem rather was to devise an announcement that would prevent a strike—or, failing that, would put strikers at a moral disadvantage.[63]

This said—and because the alternative of full quotation is too tedious —it seems needless to cite detailed proofs for the five chief points that were revealed. First, there were voices, none enthusiastic, for *accepting* nationalization. Pledges, implicit at least, weighed with some members, along with their knowledge that labor firmly believed the government was committed to follow Sankey's endorsement of nationalization. Some ministers (Montagu and Sir Auckland Geddes) held that nationalization simply was inevitable; it was promoted by past state measures and would

62. WC 603 (31 July 1919), Cab. 23/11.
63. WC 604, 606A.

prove the ultimate consequence of the compromise that was to be offered. Second, some ministers who drew back from outright nationalization insisted that it not be ruled out: on intrinsic merit, the power to nationalize should be kept in reserve, and labor must not be antagonized by permanently closing the door.

Third, the majority sooner or later spoke against nationalization. Churchill, Addison, and Lloyd George agreed that the miners had not made their case. Churchill declared the public was ready for nationalization of the railways but not for this; public opinion had turned against the miners. "Not opposed to nationalization in principle," he favored the government's adopting "a middle position—which it ought to occupy" anyway. Fourth, nationalization by purchase, others charged, would reward inefficient management and give owners twice the real value. The purchase of mines that were running at a loss made no economic sense; and purchase *now*, at current prices, would be worse.

Finally, cost: "Where is the money to come from?" asked Chamberlain. He would not dare shoulder the burden; it would rule out borrowing for anything else.[64] He and others also were sure the Unionist Party would desert the government; Commons would not pass such a bill, the House of Lords could obstruct, and the whole commercial world would be antagonized. Political factors, Addison conceded, made nationalization impossible.

Any one negative reason, I feel, appeared sufficient to some of the ministers, but considerations of prohibitive cost or political risk closed the issue for most. Major debate subsided. Bonar Law ruled out postponement; there must be an answer—now. But the answer would not be decontrol; all the arguments together did not constitute a case for that. The consensus held no cheer for unfettered enterprise or for a return to nineteenth-century individualism.

Decontrol, if it entered the thoughts of any ministers, arose only to be dismissed. A delicate structure of labor-management agreements, a vital safeguard for consumers and especially the poor, and a guarantee of cheap fuel that was basic for business recovery would all crash to the ground. Prices would skyrocket if the state ceased to hold them far below market levels. Eric Geddes and Bonar Law held that control obviously was necessary. Auckland Geddes and Austen Chamberlain attacked the coal subsidy vainly, in a minority dissent:

> The cost should be borne by the consumer. It was impossible for the
> nation to live by the various sections of the community subsidising

64. WC 607A, 608A, 589, citing G.T. 7405 and 7620.

each other. . . . The solution was . . . to allow the public to realise what the increased costs of production meant to the State. . . . By administering such drastic medicine we might bring the community to a state of sanity.

But thoughts of industrial peace, exports, business outcries, and a tempest against profiteering outweighed such counsels. The most serious question was not between control and decontrol but between control and *control plus an area experiment in cooperative working by miners.*

This point, the rejection of laissez-faire and decontrol, may count most for our purposes; after all, the Sankey commission concerns us chiefly as an index to government thought. But a fifth point also is highly important for reconstruction: the cabinet put its scheme forward *as a reform.* It would be a system of control; it would limit profit, sustain wages, permit reduction of hours, and *it would give the workers a voice* in determining conditions of work. Lloyd George (and perhaps Sir Richard Redmayne) worked hardest to this end.[65]

When the government's final offer came before the cabinet, Milner protested—as did Barnes and Montagu—that nationalization as an ultimate possibility had been too definitely excluded. Charges were made that efficiency and protection of consumers against "tyrannical Trusts" were slighted. Addison had already damned the offer with faint praise: "The one solid thing that the miners got . . . was a promised participation in the management and benefits of the mines." Bonar Law wrangled with Lloyd George over whether the miners or the owners would be most incensed. On this note of discord the announcement went off to Parliament: nationalization of royalties, amalgamation of collieries, limitation on profits, miners' representation, and the seven-hour day.[66] The government held its breath. Against some ministers' forecasts, neither the miners nor the Triple Alliance struck.

The cabinet's decision reflected two factors that had marked the pattern of decontrol, subsidy, retrenchment, and reform as well: anxiety over cost and deference to a conservative Parliament. On the other hand it suggested concern to keep inflation within bounds; resistance to the dogma that damned all control and all subsidy; reliance on public and parliamentary opinion to check labor, where labor was at a momentary

65. WC 589, 598; Richard Redmayne, *Men, Mines and Memories* (London: Eyre & Spottiswoode, 1942), pp. 208 ff.
66. G.T. 7924 (n.d.), Cab. 24/86; Mowat, *Britain between the Wars*, pp. 34–35. For Lloyd George's announcement to Commons on 18 August 1919, see *P.D.* (C.), vol. 119, c. 1981–2022, and comments in London *Times*, 19 August 1919.

disadvantage and was offered a share in control; reliance on divisions within labor; determination to help labor moderates against the "direct actionists"; and the weight of empirical difficulties and complications.

Whatever the cabinet wished, the actual results flowed from its final *action*; and these results are clear enough. Labor—moderate and extremist—felt rebuffed and badly used; whatever chances there had been for positive partnership between government and labor had been dealt a terrible blow. Some of the government leaders, if minutes are any test, felt this reaction was needless and irrational beyond the tolerable point, for the government had put in reforms for labor, rising above its anger over the Yorkshire strike.

I believe that the ministers, well aware that something better than mere industrial peace was the *sine qua non* of recovery and reform, still looked to Whitleyism; they knew that it would not bring nationalization or workers' control, which they held neither sacred nor sensible, but it might sustain prosperity and welfare. Through the spring strikes and threats and the Yorkshire strike they had maintained, if not hope, a door that was open to trust and cooperation. For these and other reasons a patched-up solution of the wretched coal situation might, they felt, be somewhat redeemed by offering mineworkers a voice. The government would have to count on reforms and high wages to do the rest. Instead, labor's angry response suggested that its zeal for nationalization, or its contempt for Whitley moderatism, made the open door valueless. Events that autumn (reviewed below) were judged accordingly.

Forces and Results: Further Thoughts

From the parliamentary views and conservative cabinet pronouncements treated above, the question arises: Why had decontrol, deflation, and retrenchment not triumphed? Or has their impact been underrated? The conclusions I have urged—of an uneven pattern of decisions, testifying to the flexibility and empiricism of a cabinet that thought for itself, reflected many pressures, but capitulated to no single pressure—can now be put more summarily.

1. The trends toward greater decontrol, toward economy, and against subsidy and against nationalization are clear both in deed and utterance. Because of them I feel that July marked a caesura, as January had not.

2. However, these trends were not uniform or unmodified.

Opposite arguments and actions show in the record; the trends were neither complete, in their fields, nor dominant for the whole of policy.

3. Nor—to repeat—were those tendencies, where evident, the proof of dogmatic thinking.

To the above a further thought must be added: New reforms had been stopped; no more would be forthcoming, that year or ever, under the coalition government. The reforms pledged or launched by midsummer of 1919 might be furthered (which included not only old age and health insurance and pensions but also a start on Poor Law reform). But the Finance Committee—a register of the post-July mood—decided one thing at least when faced with Chamberlain's benumbing "balance sheet": The budget would make no allowance for new domestic expenditures.[67] What was not begun was condemned. This, apart from the specifics of decontrol and retrenchment, was the one great landmark of late 1919, marking a significant change.

No doubt there was another result—intangible and very general— of the entire momentum of events. The yearners for decontrol and economy, denied victory but emboldened by partial success, and lustier in their litanies, waxed stronger. They would bring new energies to bear in 1920. Decontrol, like dogmatisms of right and left, fed on itself; economy battened on precedent. But that is a story for 1920 and 1921.

In this atmosphere and in official resolutions that blighted the future were undercurrents not yet reflected in deeds. Nevertheless these coming tendencies were only part of the scene. The other part, still substantial and in some areas dominant, has been neglected thus far. Much more promising for reform were the limitations, still holding, against the impact of orthodoxy. These exceptions to the rising pattern of decontrol and retrenchment were, by every test save hindsight and determinism, signs that reconstruction still had a chance. The "social policy" was very much in effect. The housing program lived; housing law and policy armed campaigners with new weapons. The commitments for land settlement and for many welfare supports, soon to be augmented, held firm. Reform, then, was a great exception to the new, negative forces of economy and decontrol. Trade policy was a second exception. The government's attitude toward labor may have been a third.

67. C.P. 129 (15 November 1919), Cab. 24/93; G.T. 8331 (15 October 1919), Cab. 24/90; HAC (25 November 1919).

Reform: Exception *1*

There were twenty-four trade boards, Horne announced, and by rights there should be one hundred within a year. This, his proposed "campaign for the multiplication of trade boards," attested his ministry's successful action to extend them, once the 1918 act had cleared the way. Both sides, labor and management, wanted them. Horne wisely foresaw that the advent of the bill to set up a Minimum Wages Commission, mistakenly hailed as a solution of problems, might compound them; hence it was all the more imperative to strengthen the tried and more subtle machinery of trade boards. Flat nationwide minima were dangerous; they either encouraged low productivity or fomented endless trouble between skilled and unskilled workers. His campaign was approved in November.

A direct fulfillment of Auckland Geddes' income-stabilization idea, the trade boards were part and parcel of a full attack on the wage, hour, and price problem—with notable Whitley overtones. Another component of the program, establishment of a representative wages commission, also went through (after some difficulties over agriculture were settled)—as did the Industrial Courts Bill. The Maximum Hours Bill had cleared the cabinet on 4 July. Wages were being set to stand, until September 1920, at armistice levels.[68]

All the insurance schemes were bound up with these measures, and there were changes—akin in spirit for health insurance and unemployment insurance. Higher health benefits were speedily ratified: 15 shillings per week for men, as Addison recommended, at a cost of £3,380,000. The proposal, however, had been helped by the fact that it would also bring in money, through added contributions.[69] Economy also tinged unemployment aid, affecting both unemployment insurance and the out-of-work donation. The latter's application to civilians was stopped in November, in a last-minute change of plans, and the scales were decreased.[70] This was meaningful, but the real change was the turn from the out-of-work donation (a noncontributory scheme) to contributory insurance. This change was a setback: it automatically discriminated against the unemployed, the low-paid, and the unskilled; it automatically barred

---

68. WC 588; Cab. 2; C.P. 6 (27 October 1919), Cab. 24/92; conference of 31 October 1919, Cab. 23/37. See also Roberts, *The Trades Union Congress*, pp. 318–19. For the introduction of the "Hours of Employment (No. 2)" bill and the "Minimum Rates of Wages Commission" bill on 18 August 1919, see *P.D. (C.)*, vol. 119, c. 1919.

69. Cab. 15 (17 December 1919) and Cab. 16 (19 December 1919), Cab. 23/18; Cab. 21/181 and 27/54, *passim*.

70. Cab. 3 and 7, 1919.

dependency allowances (in the quasi-contractual theory of *insurance*, the number of one's dependents was irrelevant to one's gainful work). All this flowed from the first premise of insurance: that there was a link between entitlement and wages, indeed a direct relationship to an individual's income, wages, and employment.

This was a change in kind, and a revealing setback. It was due simply to cost, and was against the express and unanimous wish of the National Industrial Conference. The future scale of weekly benefit, 15 shillings for men, was a real drop compared with the out-of-work donation, 29 shillings —and, until the new scales were passed, the insurance benefit was only 7 shillings.[71] Still, insurance as such had its advocates, and the measure continued the prewar and wartime reform trends, lifting the scale impressively over 1911 levels and bringing the total insured to eleven million. The increased cost to the government, according to some alarmed ministers, would be so great (£14 million) as to justify telling Parliament the scheme was impossible. But it was felt by the majority that Commons would accept the increase, and the bill moved on.[72]

After a wordy fracas, the cabinet belatedly voted increases in old age pensions and extended them to an additional 220,000 pensioners. The contributory principle was not included. On the face of it, this was liberal; and the total cost, increased by £17 million, rose to £28 million. Furthermore, some Poor Law disqualifications were dropped, but the weekly benefit was only 10 shillings—quite inadequate for maintenance. A more generous alternative, to make the pensions universal and thus aid another 130,000 aged persons, was backed by all of the investigative committee, except the government members, and the cabinet took the civil servants' side. The whole episode was illustrative—even to the wry Treasury comment that contributory pensions, "at any rate for those over 70," were "not practical politics."[73]

Thus, in these measures, hesitations produced a mixture of economy and reform which was typical for late 1919. There were other measures for trade and development rather than mass welfare: an import-export bill;[74] a "combines bill," which became a vehicle for mild antiprofiteering

71. Horne's memorandum, C.P. 177 (2 December 1919), Cab. 24/93.

72. C.P. 24 (30 October 1919), Cab. 24/92; C.P. 177 (2 December 1919), Cab. 24/93; WC 614; Cab. 11 and 16 (1919); Mowat, *Britain between the Wars*, pp. 45–46; Frank Tillyard, *Unemployment Insurance in Great Britain*, pp. 36–40.

73. Cab. 15; C.P. 299; G. 264 (8 November 1919), Cab. 24/5. See also Gertrude Williams, *The State and the Standard of Living* (London: P. S. King, 1936), pp. 84–85, and Arnold Wilson and G. S. Mackay, *Old Age Pensions: A Historical and Critical Study* (London: Oxford University Press, 1941), pp. 66–73.

74. WC 634; Cab. 6; Cab. 27/67, *passim*; G.T. 8329 (15 October 1919), Cab. 24/90.

measures and a substitute for drastic ones;[75] and a waterpower bill.[76] Submitted on the same day by Sir Auckland Geddes and speeded on to Commons, these three met resistance that was astonishing in view of the prevalent concern for aiding recovery. Three other proposed reforms got nowhere: Addison's drastic and comprehensive system for the compulsory acquisition of land, politely listened to and then dropped; reexamination of land-value duties, the great theme of 1910–11; and extension to other ministries of the powers of immediate land entry as possessed by the Minister of Health. Powers over *cultivation* of the land, it should be noted, were being retained;[77] this was easier to defend, not only because no questions of ownership were raised but because the case for maintaining food supplies at reasonable cost was overwhelming. But questions of title and inheritance were different; even at high tide, reform had never reached here. The larger proposals of the Scott committee did not become law. Addison and Leslie Scott would have to wait for another war.

The statute books and the schedule for 1920 prove that reform disputed the field with economy to the end of 1919.

Trade and General Economic Policy: Exception 2

In their mid-year reviews and proposals, Professor Chapman and Sir Maurice Hankey had devoted most of their policy papers to positive measures aimed at efficiency, development, recapture of overseas markets, and scientific advance—all through *state* action. The need for positive state intervention was still the theme stressed, through December 1919, by the Prime Minister, Milner, Churchill, Mond, Addison, and the Board of Trade; together they resisted successfully the cries for a return to 1914. In the result, policy for recovery and for trade was not dominated by the concepts either of decontrol or of retrenchment.

A full proof of this point would require an unendurable amount of quotation; discussion on trade bulks larger than that on almost any other topic. Summary must suffice; and it may best begin with a list of four primary impressions. I notice (1) a clutching, swift as instinct, for subsidy and protection for domestic manufacturing; (2) acquiescence—but very reluctant and often shamefaced—in protectionism for foreign trade; (3) a marked indifference as to whether the means employed sinned against the true faith of "free" enterprise; (4) a perfect awareness that ministers

75. WC 634; G.T. 8328 (15 October 1919) and 8385, Cab. 24/90.
76. HAC (31 October 1919), Cab. 26/2; WC 634; G.T. 8330 (15 October 1919) and 8345 (16 October 1919), Cab. 24/90.
77. HAC (8 July 1919); Cab. 11; G.T. 7298 (20 May 1919), Cab. 24/79; WC 632 (20 October 1919), Cab. 23/12.

were dealing with an interdependent tangle of infinite delicacy and that skilled surgery, rather than incantation and exorcism, was the need. The cabinet's thought discloses another four assumptions: (5) faith that Britain could—and realization that it must—again triumph overseas, despite present high costs and competitors' wartime gains; (6) acceptance of high prices in view of their stimulus to enterprise and internal prosperity, despite whatever long-term disadvantages they might have; (7) a very strong feeling that Britain, although obligated to think of long-term plans for normal times, was living through a situation so unsettled and novel that improvisation must be relied on. It was perhaps this assumption that sustained another: (8) against the evidence of four prewar decades, Britain's farming—as well as its industry—could flourish and was worth full-blooded support. (To dispose of agriculture more briefly than the records warrant, this meant that farm controls were maintained and that prices were guaranteed, to cover 1920 and 1921, whatever the decontrollers and dissident pressure groups said.)[78]

These, the positive side of attitudes and deeds, were the dominant notes. They betoken an eclectic state of mind, friendly to state action, not strongly swayed by orthodox principle. In a cabinet so diverse and other-wise-minded, there were also contrary impulses. Criticism against the positive policy of state aid was not always in the expectable form of invocations to private enterprise and laissez-faire. Criticism expressed practical misgivings, rooted in fact rather than dogma, as to four likely by-products of state policy: inefficiency, lagging output, profiteering, and encouragement of trusts.

Subsidies, guaranteed prices, licenses, and import bans were criticized, and rightly, as apt to favor giant combines that would be hostile to the public interest. But the problem of profiteers and trusts had triple dimensions: functional, theoretical, and psychological. They angered the public and brought labor to flashpoint. They flouted the assumptions of orthodox economics and they imperiled competition. They threatened to defeat the aims of consumer benefit and rising efficiency, thus endangering both reconstruction and recovery. Then, as ever, this was the evil on which Socialists and Manchester Liberals could close ranks.

All these tendencies of thought were revealed as discussions swirled around three decisions that could not be put off: (1) on imports and exports, which the ministers deemed the most important; (2) on aid to key industries and protection against dumping, decisions that, in practice,

---

78. WC 606A, fol. 155; WC 632.

had to be discussed along with the question of imports; and (3) profiteering, thorniest and most baffling of all.

It is with questions of foreign trade that we must start. Should licenses be required for imports? Should preference, by license or by tariffs, be given to empire goods? Should dumping be prevented? Should home industries receive financial aid? These were Sir Auckland Geddes' specific proposals.[79] But Mond attacked at once. In his view, these proposals would subsidize inefficiency; they would promote inflation as well. Moreover, they would be anathema to Parliament, because they would necessitate a powerful administration and therefore require a new or expanded department. Mond was wholly opposed. Churchill was of two minds. He felt that considerations of wartime utility justified subsidies, but he branded the technique of imperial preference as "protectionism pure and simple"; the warrior and the conventional Liberal fought within him. Lloyd George conceded that protectionism was hard to justify when profits were huge. Barnes feared that Geddes' "protectionism" would thwart the reorganization that industry needed. H. A. L. Fisher criticized on different lines: It was contradictory for the government to draft profiteering bills and then to restrict imports. His was the classic dilemma of the Manchester Liberal: doubtful of tariffs because they nurtured monopoly, doubtful of antitrust measures because they discouraged enterprise and fostered a powerful state. Even Fisher, a most orthodox thinker, nevertheless desired aid to key industries. The Food Controller also yielded: "In theory he was a Free Trader, but theories had to be sacrificed when one was confronted with facts." Lloyd George also built his case on conditions: If restrictions were taken off there would be "a great flood of imports and the American Exchange would go heavily against us." Bonar Law's approach was that this was no time for either free trade or tariff reform; the crucial matter was to "prevent the collapse of our home markets." Imports must not break down the price level. Geddes suggested they "scrap the past and . . . come to some sort of agreement as to the present."

Qualms of principle stilled, there remained the hard questions of means: embargo versus license, license versus tariff, a new department versus a system less likely to enrage Parliament, a broad policy versus a specific and unamendable list of protected items. At this level of techniques, a revealing problem appeared. The ministers favored a flexible system of licenses but felt this was blocked by Commons' "absolute

79. WC 609A, 610A.

detestation" of bureaucracy. Rather helplessly, Bonar Law—weary of business and Parliament that wanted aid but denounced control—said that "it should be made clear to everyone that there was really no alternative course between this licensing system and doing nothing at all." If licensing was unacceptable and total freedom unthinkable, what was left but outright protectionism? But this, Lloyd George predicted, "would rend industry from top to bottom." How could demands for noninterference and protected security be met at the same time? This, nevertheless, was the demand the Government faced. Traders condemned Government control, and in the next breath said they were unable to trade unless Government provided the capital. Lloyd George reported he had been asked by the iron and steel industry (which was "doing exceedingly well" and was "extraordinarily inefficient") for a pledge that "they would be left alone." Did no one think of keeping ready for war, or sheltering key industries at the least? A "craze for profit" gripped those who had been breathing "the larger air of common sacrifice."

For several days the cabinet hesitated, baffled. Ultimately, bills to regulate imports and exports, to afford some imperial preference, and to protect key industries went to Parliament. A limited protectionism, administratively upheld thus far and embodied in the budget, passed into law. The Dye-Stuffs Act of 1920 and the Safeguarding of Industries Act of 1921 were to follow.[80]

That the wavering government again had improvised, resisting the call of dogma, seems obvious; but the debate also proves other and more important things.

Policy and its ramifying consequences were not only complex but mysterious. It was by no means clear what the result of import bans would be: high prices, coddled inefficiency, higher wages, and still more insecurity—or, just possibly, a long-term gain in new industry. Similarly, imperial preference might reassure businessmen and spur trade, or on the contrary might prolong a complacent sloth; it might spark retaliation and shut off markets, or bring a net gain.

The enormous temptation to build plans on the accidental boons of war was glaringly revealed. Half a million Britons slept forever in the fields of France, while benumbed Britannia, unnaturally and unwillingly

80. Mowat, *Britain between the Wars*, pp. 131–32; WC 609A, 610A, 614A; Cab. 27/67, *passim*; G.T. 8329 (15 October 1919), Cab. 24/90; Francis, *Britain's Economic Strategy*, pp. 26–34. For H. A. L. Fisher's opposition to "anti-dumping" legislation, however, see Trevor Wilson, *The Downfall of the Liberal Party*, p. 192.

inheriting from her sons, like a mother turned Saturn, garnered in her grief a harvest of economic gain. Advantage, external and internal, short-lived but immense, had come to her by the accident of victory; so Smuts had grasped, arguing in a brilliant memorandum of October 1918 for a swift and lenient peace before America overtook Britain. Planning in 1919 seemed to rest on a bloodstained but bountiful legacy: continued insulation from competitors, born of wartime isolation from foreign trade and overseas supply; inherited power to keep Britain thus shielded, using the developed technique of protection and control. All these were the results of war, and they proved both convenient and accessible bases for immediate postwar policy. From the moral and humanitarian point of view, such profiteering from the sacrifices of the dead not only was tragic, but seems criminal and perverse; for the fruits of a victory gained in the name of great ideals were being turned to the purposes of self-indulgence. Side by side with this moral judgment, however, there stands a judgment of economics and of statesmanship in amoral but weighty terms. It concerns another major legacy of war: high prices and high costs. Against the warnings of the wiser, the very existence of these conditions became an argument for their continuance; and they were continued. Indeed the maintenance of those high prices is a fundamental aspect of 1919. It is patent that such a foundation of prosperity is insecure. Fully stated, the danger was that this basis of short-term prosperity was both too precarious, and too tempting and valuable to abandon.

Policy and the debate on it present a third revelation: the terrible toll, now being paid at compound interest, for the prevailing unpreparedness at armistice time. The background is familiar to us: as we saw in chapter 14, the cabinet on the eve of armistice was quite lacking in understanding of the full agenda of recovery and reconstruction, and psychologically as well as structurally unequipped to coordinate or implement policy; and chapter 15 showed the resultant habit of forced and frenetic improvisation from October through December 1918. The government from the start of that crisis fell into shallow and hasty (if heroic) makeshifts because it lacked the wit, the ready means, or the time to do anything else. (This is of course a fact, not an indictment; one's feeling grows that war had never permitted anything much better.) Dangerously, the habit had stuck.

Trade policy, patently, amounted to a hodgepodge. Why? Perhaps one basic factor was that the premises and prophecies of planners in wartime had been too extreme—either too pessimistic or too optimistic. Three kinds of prognoses can be identified. The prevalent forecast, typified by statements of Rowntree and Beatrice Webb, predicted immediate, severe, and prolonged mass unemployment, compounded by adverse situations at home and overseas. It was not foreseen that the huge unemployment would be, in part, transitional and would surrender rather swiftly to bold deeds. The exaggerated fears were useful to this extent: they produced bold deeds—as frenzied overcompensation can do.

The other forecasts (to simplify the list drastically) took two forms. One was the optimistic view of men like Addison, that it would take close teamwork to realize progress along the lines of efficiency, reform, and Whitleyism but that national consensus and zeal would be equal to the task, producing recovery and permanent prosperity at a new high level. The other was the optimistic view of orthodox thinkers who felt that retrenchment, falling prices, and a fierce struggle for trade must come anyway; therefore the government should speed the inevitable by decontrolling, cutting costs, reducing wages, and stimulating initiative—again, *ex hypothesi*, to success. Both views presumed that recovery and prosperity could be obtained and sustained on *sound and lasting bases*, but none of the forecasts quite covered what happened: that a very substantial recovery, on *unsound* or *precarious* bases, was attained—and then came to seem too enjoyable, and its false supports too precious, to be boldly transformed. Lloyd George was like a general whose army had occupied a comfortable position so exposed that its destruction was only a matter of time, but whose troops were too tired, unsuspecting, or unruly to shoulder arms and reach safety.

Thus the trade policy is partly explained by the fact that predictions of postwar conditions had been faulty from the start; the cabinet found itself in a position for which it was mentally unprepared. Trade policy, unsystematic and vulnerable to changing circumstance, reflected this legacy of inaccurate forecasts. But if this inheritance from wartime was still present and working its harm, another was fading visibly: the self-sacrificing enthusiasm for whole solutions. Milner alone spoke in wartime tones: "Do not let the country lose valuable industries which it had started for the first time"; protection must ensure "a well-balanced state of industry." For Milner this was the premise for a complete structure that would transcend private interest. His isolation symbolized the ominous decline of a nation's high purpose.[81]

The debate over profiteering suggested that the ministers wavered between mutually exclusive thoughts: nothing could be done, but something *must* be done. News of profits came from every labor news-

81. WC 610A, fols. 225–26.

paper. Statistics to make a minister blush had been fired from the labor side. The sale of Lancashire cotton mills that autumn, with exorbitant profits to owners who had been subsidized all along, kindled fury, as in 1915. Parliament turned a hard face to the profiteers; among ministers, indignation—genuine and feigned—kept the cauldron smoking all year long.

Mond was furious, because of his free-enterprise beliefs or in spite of them. Lloyd George called profiteering "a scandal" and put it at the top of public grievances. Chamberlain, Barnes, Roberts, Horne, and both the Geddes brothers joined the chorus. But what could be done? Sir Auckland shook his head: "it was practically impossible to stop profiteering." And what was the target? Was it "the trusts"—great combinations, however efficient—or was it "profiteering"—in which case the sins of little, hard-pressed men who could do very well through chicane might outreek the misdeeds of the giants? Or was it both?

Few had the hardihood or the vision to say, with Keynes, that profiteers were but a consequence and symptom of rising prices, and that capitalist timidity rather than capitalist arrogance was the fact. Only Churchill heaped scorn: It would be absurd "to treat every business transaction . . . as if it were conducted by an usurious moneylender. . . . Combination itself was essential . . . combination was what was required for the reestablishment of trade in general."[82]

Ministers could not remain aloof. When Billingsgate merchants evaded the price ceilings on fresh fish simply by returning shipments to depot for a day, whereupon they became unregulated "stale fish," even the cabinet got wind of it. But the key problems concerned method: how to avoid scaring or antagonizing the business community; how to strike at major offenses only, and with effect, without deterring recovery.

Sir Auckland, President of the Board of Trade, was endlessly surprising: he stated three alternatives, and had a good word for each.

> 1. The government might compete in a few industries. If this were done in textiles, he forecast a huge financial success. (Bonar Law acknowledged, because promptness was essential, that they "might have to proceed along the lines of control.")
>
> 2. They might allow imports in freely, which "would have a great effect in reducing prices," but it would cut employment. (It would be hard, Bonar Law said, to justify sustaining the present high prices merely to prevent unemployment in some industries. Temporary free import, however, merited thought.)

82. Keynes, *The Economic Consequences of the Peace*, p. 237; minutes (27 October 1919), Cab. 27/67.

3. They might set up local tribunals that would be backed by central price-fixing powers.

Geddes' Board of Trade produced a drastic "Combines Bill," to cope with profiteering by establishing 2,000 tribunals throughout the country. When it reached the cabinet (on Bastille Day, by chance), the bill was suppressed, and supplanted by bland talk of "a more comprehensive measure at a later date"; but its terms reappeared almost intact in the final draft, and eased consciences. A compromise (i.e., a dubious piece of passion and patchwork) thus emerged; the 1919 Profiteering Act, which —typically—had to be amended at once because Parliament's emotions had veered once more. Reconciling the act with the Import–Export Bill's protectionism—let alone with the chronic appeasement of labor combinations—exceeded ministerial skill; but the bill and its amendments[83] remain as small monuments to the thoughts of wartime and the pressures of 1919.

In vain had Horne unearthed the real problem and alerted his colleagues to "a serious legacy of the war."

> The conduct of manufacturing . . . has become more slapdash. . . .
> In times of keen competition . . . sheer necessity compelled forceful and watchful administration. Today in some lines of business the employer seems to be able to get what price he likes.

Worried about the effect on labor, he took comfort that the Profiteering Act would show that profits were being drastically regulated. He was wrong, however; nor had the true problem, efficiency, been tackled. Most measures were simply irrelevant, but this bill was absurdly so.

If all measures are taken together, the whole seemed to have met Chapman's original plan: a mercantilist blend of subsidy, overseas campaigns for new markets, protection for key industries—and a notable try for cooperation with industry. Chapman, however, had seen beyond the overt means—tariff and subsidy—to substantive ends:

> With regard to these . . . industries, tariff protection unsupported by positive action would . . . give no guarantee of reform in methods of production and organisation; and it might even have the effect of stereotyping obsolete methods.[84]

The cabinet's hodgepodge did not justify confidence that efficiency, even if labor's practices had not blocked the way, would be attained.

83. WC 591, 592, 606A, 607, 608; Cab. 11, 18; G.T. 7685, 8385, 8388; Cab. 27/67, *passim*; HAC (6 August 1919).

84. G.T. 8388, Cab. 24/96; Cab. 21/159; Francis, *Britain's Economic Strategy*, p. 30.

Toward Labor, What Attitude?

I have said earlier that government action showed a growing concern for decontrol and retrenchment, but that there were two, and possibly three, exceptions to this trend. One exception was the continuance and extension of reforms. Another exception, just seen, was the policy on trade questions, including profiteering. These showed characteristics impossible to reconcile with the received image of a dogmatically oriented cabinet, or of a cabinet subservient to business opinion. Did the government's attitude toward the unions and the workingman constitute still a third exception? Labor itself, of course, had gained freedom with the armistice, and had gained much power from the war. How did the government face the fact of this independent power within the state?

How much was fated? Was there any chance that either government or labor would show flexibility? Given the legacy of history, was there any latitude for either side? It may be that only hostility or armed truce were possible. Given the pressures on the workingman in 1919—given his need, in *some* way, to assert freedom after four years of restraint, public criticism, and sheer hard toil—the chain of evil may have been unbreakable. Given the well-founded memories of the government's mismanagement in war (which had not grown dim in the telling) and given the deeds and the failures of that government after the armistice, a wave of strikes may have been inevitable—the early outbreaks and tremendous threats, the Yorkshire coal strike in July, the railwaymen's strike from 26 September to 5 October, the police strike of August. The government's retaliation in dismissing all the police strikers, then wielding the machinery of food and supplies to keep the nation fed, also may have been fated—with all its results in labor distrust.

Conflict alone, with every concession or overture interpreted as weakness or ruse—a pure contest of strength—perhaps was all the cards contained. Lloyd George's words in August linger in the mind: "They could not take risks with Labour. . . . We should at once create an enemy within our own borders . . . better provided with dangerous weapons than Germany."[85] And Ernest Bevin spoke a similar language of misunderstanding and distrust: "It is only power they will yield to." If this were the true situation, reconstruction was doomed. If such ideas alone prevailed, then reconstruction was merely pretense, illusion, calculated counter-revolution and a bid for time. But the evidence in government papers,

85. Records of strike committee, Cab. 27/60; WC 606A, fols. 156–57 (5 August 1919), Cab. 23/15.

where ministers had least need to dissemble, abundantly shows that the government ministers often thought along other lines. They sought alternatives less grim; they acted to promote those possibilities; and they strained to avoid the worst.

Nothing said here must imply that the government's good faith is proved beyond the shadow of a doubt, or suggest righteous innocence and an unalloyed effort to please; nothing must suggest that the government's generosity and accommodation were unlimited. On the contrary it is certain that the government did not for a moment favorably contemplate the undermining of capitalism—any more than it desired the replacement of the essential social order by a new one. In this, the government may have been dead wrong; I confess that, although nationalization no longer holds appeal and "workers' control" at the expense of national democracy holds no charms, the essential socialist vision still rings morally true in my ears. To me, therefore, England and England's cabinet had not chosen the better part. Then and there the adoption of substantial parts—industrial and humanitarian—of the socialist program would have been to her credit and advantage. Some of it might have worked, and possibly Britain's later position would have been better. The fact that British democracy did not choose to follow labor then, of course, closes the question.

Moral judgments, however, are beside the point; it is a question of being accurate. Our concern is with the patterns and trend lines of 1919, especially as omens and preconditions for reconstruction. One therefore must begin with the fact that the government prepared for the worst. Whether this attitude was justified or not, it antagonized labor and handicapped all its efforts. The government (most imperfectly, as it found) readied itself with energy worthy of a happier cause. It opposed the Yorkshire and railway strikes with strength, and prepared to use even greater strength against a general strike. Ministers—to give them their day in court—spoke of these strikes as intolerable means, whatever their ends; they declared labor's extreme ends evil and its apologies and theories unreasonable. (But workers' complaints aroused respect: Lloyd George and half a dozen ministers pronounced many labor demands just, and many grievances well founded.) Hence the year-long mixture of concession and resistance. In the words of the Prime Minister, the government must show that

> any disorder would be sternly repressed, and also all impossible and unjust demands. . . . If we were convinced that the demands were unjust, it would be fatal to the Government to settle the dispute on

470

the men's terms. . . . But it must be made clear to the workmen that there was no substance in the views held by the extremists, nor in the view that Parliament would not redress their grievances.

They must make it clear that the government was fighting "because it had come to a point where it was impossible to make any further concessions without irreparable injury to the State."[86]

Thus an undeclared contest for power was always taken for granted; and much time went into anxious appraisals of strength. These estimates could, and did, work either way. Weakness, or a sense of weakness—especially before the bar of public opinion—dictated compromise on railway wages in March; the railwaymen were thought to have made a good case. Then and always, fear of inferiority of powers, or doubts of public support, worked on the side of concession or ingenious postponement. The recurrent spasms of preparation, however, reflected fears that appeasement might fail. A final test might come, precipitated from labor, whether from passion or calculation. (Labor leaders told Lloyd George that some extremists meant "to destroy the present industrial and Parliamentary systems.") Fears of defeat could dictate concessions but not a stacking of arms.

This side of the government's attitudes raises questions and calls for comment. Were such fears sensible? A dispassionate study of the facts would have shown that the railway strike was not disfigured by violence, that other unions did not seek to convert the strike into a melee but wanted to confine it to the railways, and that the extremists were neither representative nor in charge. Keynes declared that England was anything but revolutionary, and perhaps he was right. But the government did not have the facts—at the moment when decision is necessary, governments seldom have. And the government was not dispassionate.

What was their mood? It was not wrath, but a strong, continuous, rising resentment. Ministers resented the lagging output and the crippling inefficiency of the nation's work: Lloyd George put the workers' diminished output even ahead of strikes in listing the nation's grave maladies (strikes were next on his list). Ministers fumed over the toll of strike after strike on vital exports. They saw the bakery unions (as they understood it, *only* the unions, not the masters) press wage demands right through the cost ceilings, thereby wrecking the policy of guaranteed fixed price and forcing higher bread costs onto the public. Long expressed another irritation: "The particular men the Government wished to help were the

86. WC 606A, 599.

working classes . . . and yet it was these very classes who were driving prices up on account of the purchases they made with their higher wages." Long was one of those who felt that the soaring costs were the heart of the problem. Horne was incensed at the collusion that gave private building "a vicious priority." Addison pointed angrily to building workers' obstruction of the national housing campaign.

Their well-founded resentment did not, however, drive the ministers into sympathy with employers and capital. And there were many proofs of this: the hot accusations against profiteers; the denunciation of contractors' "trade selfishness"; Lloyd George's philippic against the national craze for profit; the vocal contempt for subsidized mine owners and steel magnates—who whined for decontrol or denounced nationalization or rushed for tariff shelter, but stolidly refused to turn efficient. Owners, who compounded with unions to get price rises, were blamed as well as workingmen for the Yorkshire strike. Nor, I must emphasize, were labor's just grievances overlooked: in his great policy review of 5 August, Lloyd George drew up an indictment against the government's nonperformance and business profiteering that Smillie or Bevin would gladly have authored. Horne tirelessly and brilliantly expounded to his colleagues the factual basis of workers' unrest.

Nevertheless, resentment persisted and grew. Nothing fed it like the consciousness of governmental reform. The cabinet had cut working hours, extended the war wage, unified the health services, kept food cheap, and kept coal prices down; it tackled a major wage-stabilization scheme; it brought hundreds of thousands under the umbrella of insurance and settled thousands on the land. It had angered mine owners by not decontrolling the mines, pushed Parliament beyond the point of strain, and fought against business pressures time and again. It sold its huge stock of raw materials, under the most orthodox minister in the kingdom, in a way that saved millions of pounds and blocked hundreds of profiteers. It was risking bankruptcy to build houses—for the workingman. And what had it got? Forfeiting vocal and valuable support on the far right, it got denunciation from the extreme left and suspicion from all of labor. Its program went far beyond anything in prewar times, but it was accused of plotting a return to 1914.

Resentment, on all these grounds, figured in the harshness which the government sometimes showed. Not that the combative side of the cabinet's conduct thus becomes excusable (this is irrelevant), but its place in the dismal skein of many causes and many effects becomes clearer. But motive was not everything; there was the question of means. At the level of expediency, capacity, proportion between action and result, the last half of 1918 saw important changes.

A general strike still wore the aspect of calamity, but from July onward, against anything less than this the government did not expect to lose. It had not been as confident in January when the Triple Alliance, the soldiers, and the angry unemployed in hundreds of thousands had threatened it. After June, the subsidence of discontent, the return of the forces, the boom itself, and rumored public revulsion against the Yorkshire and the police strikes marked a real caesura. From revolutionary talk workers turned to attainable goals; or simply returned to work. A new mood within the rank and file, and lesser unity in the whole of labor, altered prospects—or so Lloyd George sensed. His anxiety was so great that he waited three weeks before he announced against nationalization (up to 6 August he feared he might provoke the Triple Alliance to strike); he then took the chance. He gambled on the public reaction to strikes, on public rejection of the miners' case, and on the emergence of a new union mood; and he won. In September the railwaymen faced a cabinet that was surer of its grip.

In a dramatic appeal, Rowntree and Whitley asked the government for one last gesture to contain the railway strike—to guarantee, in short, that no adult full-time worker would get less than 25 shillings per week, or the equivalent reckoned at prewar prices. But the government showed its harder side and turned the two intercessors down; it was a measure of the cabinet's new confidence and its new appraisal of labor. More than ever and more successfully than ever (but there was much ruin in these "successes") the government worked from the assumption that labor's moderates and "direct actionists" were split.[87]

But the ministers preferred *not* to play it this way. Winning a paltry triumph over a bickering enemy was not the goal; treating one's countrymen—those treated the worst and therefore the most embittered of one's countrymen—like witless adolescents would be a contest without laurels; to have to fight that war at all was wrong. The government's policy was not a simple matter of appeasement where this was forced upon it, of aggression wherever feasible. The government wanted something other and better.

Of all the supporting and alternative policies, Whitleyism and joint consultation were the greatest of all. They were tactically sound, functionally promising, and—as long as a ray of hope shone—impossible to

87. WC 604, 607A, 614A, as cited, and WC 625–27 (26 September and 3 October 1919), Cab. 23/12.

neglect. In two great episodes of 1919, hope was put to the test. The first episode was the National Industrial Conference itself. A learned and detached historian has labeled it "a most significant development in industrial relations" for the interwar years; and for 1919, both the promise of its opening sessions, and the manner of that failure, were important beyond words.

The story of that failure is obscure. Into midsummer, cooperation in good faith seemingly prevailed. On hours, wages, and a permanent National Industrial Council, an agreed program was taking shape—the product of compromise on both sides. On 18 August, the last day of that session of Parliament, Horne introduced both the "Minimum Rates of Wages Commission" bill and the "Hours (No. 2)" bill into Commons. On the face of it, this action was a sign of governmental good faith; *The Times* hailed these "first fruits of the National Industrial Conference." There were grounds for misgivings and criticism, however. For one thing, the bills had been introduced so late that enactment must wait until Parliament reconvened on 22 October. More significantly, the hours bill was vulnerable to labor criticism. Farm workers were excluded from its provisions. That exclusion had been seriously debated in the War Cabinet on 4 July. Horne explained to his colleagues on that day that all industries and trades, including agriculture, were covered by his draft bill; he had tried to confine the bill simply to industrial workers, and the Provisional Joint Committee of the Conference had agreed to exclude foremen, seamen, and domestic workers, but "had he persisted" regarding farm workers "the whole of the negotiations would have broken down." Ernle said that agriculture "could not live under this bill"; Horne countered that the bill would give any Minister of Labour power to make exceptions, and that in any case a recent Wages Board decision had settled the matter in favor of a 54-hour week in summer for agriculture. Lloyd George spoke strongly in favor of excluding agriculture from the 48-hour week, and the bill with that exclusion was approved.

If a basis for dissension had thus been provided—justifiably or not— the bill on minimum wages rates looked more like an acceptable compromise. In earlier talks, Horne said he found the committee intent on empowering the proposed commission to fix rates which would have legislative effect. He had however persuaded them to limit the commission to inquiry, with the power remaining in Parliament to give legislative effect to commission proposals. To offset this concession by the Provisional Joint Committee, he had agreed that the bill should cover workers between fifteen and eighteen years of age as well as adults, although he preferred to confine it to adults. Adopting Horne's proposal, the cabinet had to that extent sustained the pattern of compromise.

In early August, Horne went a step further by including the railways in the operation of the 48-hour bill. For their part, the labor leaders on the Provisional Joint Committee began sending messages to trade unions, apparently as a first step toward forming the long-anticipated permanent National Industrial Council. The letter which Arthur Henderson and G. D. H. Cole signed declared:

> The Government having decided to introduce into Parliament Bills for the purpose of establishing a legal maximum working week of 48 hours and for the enactment of legal minimum rates of wages for all employed persons, the Provisional Committee, in pursuance of the decision of the Conference, is now proceeding with the formation of National Industrial Council in accordance with the terms of the report. On behalf of the trade union side of the Provisional Committee, who anxiously hope the trade unions will do everything in their power to insure success for the scheme, we shall be pleased to hear from you that your society desires to be represented upon the National Industrial Council.

At some point thereafter, the issue of these letters was stopped. The trade union members of the Provisional Joint Committee objected to the exclusion of agricultural workers and seamen from the maximum-hours bill. The labor correspondent of the London *Times* hinted at a letter, "tantamount to an ultimatum," which had been sent to the Minister of Labour. Purportedly it declared that, if satisfaction regarding these exclusions was not obtained from the government, all further steps toward establishing the permanent Council would be suspended. On 15 October Horne reported to the War Cabinet that the labor spokesmen had said, on 24 September, that they "could not or would not go ahead to set up the National Industrial Council until the Government agreed to carry the Provisional Joint Committee recommendations fully into effect." In this context, the initiative of February came to a halt. Talks continued, to the end of the year; memoranda within government, and ministerial answers to questions in Commons, implied that the questions of hours was still under discussion. But momentum forward had been lost.

Each side, government and labor, had a case—where maximum hours were concerned—to which it could hold unswervingly. The cabinet could argue that farming conditions, qualitatively different, made a 48-hour limit impractical. It could argue that the true consensus of employers and employed, which alone could give any proposal authority, must come from the broader Council which had not yet been formed, rather than from a committee which was plainly provisional. Labor could insist that justice for the farm laborer, and the security of guarantees for other workers, depended on universalizing the limit. Labor could stress the unanimity of the Provisional Joint Committee for the hours guarantee. But to the independent critic, in view of all that was at stake, it would have been truer statesmanship to accept then a measure deemed faulty, perhaps amending it later but in any case giving the rest of the program a chance; insistence on any single measure, jeopardizing the whole cause, was unwise or worse. Given the perilous context of distrust and the high probability of misunderstanding, there was every justification for extra concessions as an unmistakable proof of good faith. These criticisms seem to apply to both sides. From this standpoint the government's exclusion of agriculture was censurable, and so was labor's view that inclusion was a precondition for setting up the National Industrial Council. Things of great substance, vital to discuss but not yet examined, hung in the balance: shared progress on hours, wages, and unemployment insurance; action on the dilemmas of productivity, export, and finance; creation of a genuine experiment in Whitleyism, at the highest level and with a guaranteed preferential position close to government. But precisely when the will to go the extra mile was most needed, neither side seems to have had the ultimate flexibility and vision.

The historian's task is not of course to assign guilt but to probe the causes and define the context. He must explain what had happened, always with a view to the impact on reconstruction's chances for success. I conclude that the government was influenced by the growing atmosphere of industrial conflict (the Yorkshire strike and the railwaymen's strike, notably); it was also influenced by a sense of increased power to resist strikes, by its specific convictions about the needs of agriculture, and by growing pressures from Parliament and press. Cabinet attitudes were shaped also by the continuing abstention of the Triple Alliance from the Conference. The labor leaders' outlook is explicable on factual grounds, no less: the reservations in the government proposals; the cabinet's apparent tactics of deliberate delay; government behavior in the mining and rail strikes; and the great difficulty, for moderates like Henderson, of maintaining a cooperative stance toward government without losing their leadership within labor, perpetually challenged by the militants. Both sides had "reasons"—reasons which, judging by the outcome, were hardly justifications. Perhaps interpretation must be content with that conclusion.

The cooperative experiment of the National Industrial Conference, launched in February 1919, did not officially end until July 1921. At that point—when Addison resigned, when the housing plans were cut back, when educational programs were shelved—the Provisional Joint Committee resigned formally, amid accusations against government. But the last chance for revival seems to have passed in late 1919. The hopes of wartime had been dealt a bad shock.[88]

Causes beyond reckoning hinged on building a bridge between the classes. Each week's events divided suburb and slum; daily experience, reestablishing the familiar patterns of older days, closed each segment of the nation in a ring of its own illusions and interests. It was vital to break those tightening circles of suspicion and despair, and to span the gulf between hovel and villa, between front office and factory gate. Whitleyism in general, this Conference in particular, seemed made for that purpose. But the remembered frictions of war, the grievances of a century, the cabinet's rejection of Sankey on coal, the hopes of many zealous men for an impossibly great day—and all the causes of all these things—conspired otherwise. Perhaps accident too, or blunder, played their part.

That the cabinet was not to play out its coveted role in building that bridge, putting both human relations and the economy on a high new plane, seemed measurably clearer after Lloyd George met the unions in October, after the bitter railway strike. It was a symbolic and major confrontation. In the deputation from the Miners' Executive and the T.U.C., Lloyd George saw Hodges, Bunning, Smillie, and Brace; nationalization was their great theme. ("It is in their bones," Lloyd George had said, "and you have to win back their confidence.") They put labor's case eloquently. Then Lloyd George put a question: Would Smillie prefer the old system—assuming nationalization was out—to the alternative proposed by the government, "with a voice given to the

88. Francis, *Britain's Economic Strategy*, p. 37; G.T. 8331. Some light is thrown on the July–October negotiations between ministers, cabinet, and the labor side of the Provisional Joint Committee by WC 588, 598, 615 and 625 (4 and 23 July, 14 August and 26 September 1919, respectively) in Cab. 23/11 and 23/12, and by Horne's G.T. 8331 (October 1919) in Cab. 24/90, and his G.T. 8388 (22 October 1919), *ibid*. See also C.P. 61 (6 November 1919) and C.P. 129 (15 November 1919), Cab. 24/92 and 93. For Horne's introduction of the bills on rates of wages and on hours, see *P.D.(C.)*, vol. 119, c. 1919 (18 August 1919); for subsequent discussion and withdrawal on 22 December 1919, see *ibid.*, vol. 122, c. 1319, vol. 123, c. 1234. For a thorough discussion, see Alan Fisher, *Some Problems of Wages*, pp. 70–82. Text of bills, discussion, and reports of obstacles are in the London *Times*, 19, 20, and 21 August, and 16 and 20 October 1919. For the collapse in 1921, see Mary Hamilton, *Arthur Henderson*, p. 215; Mowat, *Britain between the Wars*, p. 37; London *Times*, 20 July 1921.

miners in the executive control of the areas"? The miners' leader replied:

> I believe our people would prefer going on as we are at the present time, or at least as we were prior to the war rather than setting up trusts which might be trusts between the miners and the mine-owners . . . against the general public. We would prefer going on with the old system.

"That," said the Prime Minister, "is a straight answer." Then Brace recaptured the initiative, seeking to brush hypothetical questions aside: "We are here to ask the Government . . . to honor their obligation and their pledge." The government's proposal, he charged, would make the men accomplices in "a movement which is . . . creating power for capital."

But Lloyd George probed at the slogan "workers' control."

> It is not a question of influencing [policy], it is a question of determining it. Who is to determine? Is it those who are engaged in working the industry or is it the general public? That is the point.

"I will make 'effective voice' mean 'effective control,'" Brace answered, because "we mean the same thing." Smillie argued that "effective control"—the words of Sankey's report—did not mean "that the miners are to have the predominant voice in control." Lloyd George turned to the recent strike: Inasmuch as railways were under state control, did the strike not undercut Sankey's argument—that nationalization would promote industrial peace? Sankey had stressed that *private* capital and ownership were the roots of strife, but the fact of government control—which made of any strike "a contest between Labour and the community, not between Labour and Capital"—had not prevented the railway strike. For his last words, however, Lloyd George chose a different tone. Turning from the attack on nationalization, half pleading, he voiced his hopes for the government's plan: "I think Labour is throwing away a great opportunity of having an effective voice . . . in the control of its own industry, and I do not see how it would stand ultimately in the way of nationalization."

One reads the words of these dead men through that invisible film which confers an infinite pathos and shades them with secular meaning. The two final statements—for, with this, Lloyd George had done—still bear all their living force. The Prime Minister's last word stands today as one of the most apt judgments in the whole record of reconstruction.

For the men, Brace spoke the last word—not only for that moment, but for that theme of war and reform which transcended the day and the issue. Past the Prime Minister he spoke straight into the Book of Reconstruction:

> The War has driven us 25 years at least in advance of where we were in thought in 1914.
>
> Our men have come to the conclusion that they are something infinitely more majestic than wage-earners. They have grasped a kind of soul-stirring idea that human life is very sacred, and in the future industrial economy of this Nation they must have their part.[89]

Both men, I feel, were right. One spoke for the hopes that might—one war later—be realized; but his language helped with the present task of compromise not at all. The other spoke for hopes within reach—although his audience's fidelity to dogma, history, and class may have put them out of reach. One cannot condemn a faith that, almost literally from the bowels of the earth, lifted workingmen above their suffering toward a vision of the skies. And one cannot condemn a Prime Minister who asked for something for a world where men did not think alike.

It was a heartbreaker: a session that edged resentment with despair. In the contracting sphere of late 1919 the government would continue its favors: housing, pensions, insurance; but henceforth these would seem, on both sides, handouts to dangerous classes or grudging concessions wrested at the truce line, never the shared benefits of common toil. Those who remembered how Englishmen had performed miracles by comradeship found this infinitely degrading. Those who sought to reconstruct (or was it construct?) life on that honorable and heroic basis felt something more practical: dismay over blighted prospects. The confrontation that day in October was the next thing to a death knell for such hopes.

Sir Robert Horne had most reason, after Addison, to feel dismay. Of the many who championed reform and urged going the extra mile, Horne did the most to state the unpalatable facts of labor opinion; he wasted least time in pointing out that "they" were unreasonable, "they" were undermining the recovery program and threatening the state. His self-appointed functions were to see the government as workers saw it and to spur his colleagues by unpleasant reminders of their own shortcomings. He did this in many memoranda, but his greatest memorandum was that which shortly followed the railway strike. He began where, psychologically, his colleagues were: with the fact of undeniably inadequate production,

89. G.T. 8305 (9 October 1919), Cab. 24/90.

and with the intolerable price rise. He admitted that labor's attitude was irrational; but for him this comprehension was only the beginning, not a self-satisfying end, of statesmanship. Statesmen, his example implied, must identify the key problem calmly, and define it neutrally: for him, this key problem was *prices*. Moral carping and debaters' points aside, how could one keep prices steady now and hope eventually to bring them down? In one of three ways, he said: by curtailing all classes' purchasing power through taxation; by anti-profiteering action, thus reducing business incomes; or by securing "an increased output of socially useful goods and services." His own thinking was devoted to "the third course."

Quickly surveying other causes for the cripplingly low level of production, Horne came to the causes deep-rooted in the mood and temper which led workers to "go easy or hold back rather than to work at top notch." Neither calculation nor command from the top, let alone the influence of doctrinaire intellectuals, could account for this. "Probably not one [worker] in a hundred consciously slacks as a protest against the ill distribution of wealth, or . . . production for profit." Partially the cause was long-standing ca'canny, due to the fear of "standing off" between jobs, but the major cause was "a widespread sourness of mind," caused in turn by "disappointment of hopes raised during the war [and] the very general feeling that all is not well with the world they had hitherto taken for granted."

> The very nobility of the purposes for which men laboured in the war militates against their acceptance of meaner or vaguer purposes for their labour now. They ask—What for?

The government's instinctive recourse to lectures on output therefore was worse than useless. Such appeals were resented; they came from "a suspected source"; they singled out labor for exhortation; they were easily countered "by indignant references to these things, and the indignation they feel is real." *The government must learn.* The appeal for output must be directed to *all* classes. Owners must be required to produce facts about the costs and profits of their businesses. Above all, the dominating ideas of labor must be faced.

> These ideas have been formulated in the doctrines that (1) the more the working class produce, the more the "idle rich" will waste; that (2) a man cannot work his best in a system run for private profit; and that (3) the land-owners and capitalists should loose their stranglehold on land and money before they begin to lecture

labour on restricting production. Such doctrines . . . are not simply "economics," they are the formulae of deep-rooted suspicion and discontent. Not disproof is needed but discussion and drastic action.

There must be strong anti-profiteering measures. The government must not temporize with businessmen's delay, however natural, in taking up orders.

The only effective reply to the belief in capitalist restriction is the demonstration that no class is hanging back while others are being exhorted to work, and that no class will monopolise the surplus gains of increased effort. . . . Exhortations will not do; economic arguments are beside the point.

The Prime Minister was right, Horne summed up, to demand full publicity from *employers* as well as employed; the "frank and free discussion" symbolized by the National Industrial Conference was imperative. Nothing was more urgently needed; nothing would better promote "the spirit upon which alone the increase of output depends."[90] It was wise counsel—and a perfect funeral oration. Given the strikes, the breakup of the Conference, and the miners' outlook, ministers had cause to think that the spirit had fled. Their discouragement was one of many clouds that blackened the skies in late 1919. Among all groups, these and other causes worked to protract a mixture of caution, concession, and cold war.

But some could not live with this. Greenwood the next year campaigned for Labour; Reiss also went over to that side; and varied motives affected other men to other results. Addison, his fame and fate linked to a doomed campaign, soldiered on out of sympathy for labor and devotion to the cause.

And the Prime Minister? Is it unfair to conjecture that Lloyd George acted, maneuvered, and spoke, out of a strong sympathy for Lloyd George? In any case his plight was not simple, whatever his motives. He had to resist Labour, and did so, lest the Tories desert him. He had sometimes to concede to labor, lest defeat at *their* hands drive him from office, and lest he be delivered prisoner into *Tory* hands; he did not wish to be marooned on the Elba of Cheltenham Spa. But speculation on Lloyd George is folly: one will never know. He was the arch-reactionary, to Mrs. Webb; the master of them that do, to Winston Churchill; and in Philip Snowden's discerning eye the man who "never settled anything."

90. G.T. 8388, 22 October 1919, Cab. 24/90.

He was the Welsh wizard—whose final years shake one's faith in the occult; the "left radical" with Addison in friendlier days; the "prism" of Keynes's epitome: "Rooted in nothing . . . void and without content . . . a vampire and a medium at once." Lloyd George would hope to land on his feet.[91]

Keynes sometimes saw things straight on. His words for the Britain of late 1919, as a learned historian has sensed, held truth.

> We are at the dead season of our fortunes. The reaction from the exertions . . . is at its height. Our power of feeling or caring beyond the immediate questions of our own material well-being is temporarily eclipsed . . . we . . . need rest.[92]

Reconstruction Ended?

That reconstruction as a set of enacted and ongoing reforms was moving, heavily handicapped but impressive, into the vast question mark called 1920; that its premises in economic policy were makeshift improvisations of a fearfully precarious kind rather than cunning or consistent contrivances of doctrinaire and conventional minds; that the whole was, barring a miracle, sure to be overtaken by events; that reconstruction therefore, although far from shelved and assuredly not in limbo, faced unfriendly labor and a potentially lethal economic Day of Judgment—all these over-labored interpretations of mine must be left to their fate. On the causes of the situation, its nature, and the prospects for reconstruction in the future, however, further guesswork must be tried.

At the End of 1919

A year had elapsed since Addison warned Lloyd George that his time was not limitless. The view from December 1919 bore him out. Reconstruction and reform labored under heavy handicaps. Prospects for better days had dwindled, although it was true that the reform effort had been sustained for thirteen months past armistice and the attempts at rescue and reinforcement had continued into the last month of the year. The greatest presupposition for success—teamwork that would extend beyond Parliament and the cabinet to a genuine understanding between business, labor, and the politicians—had virtually vanished. Outside Whitehall,

91. Hans Daalder, *Cabinet Reform in Britain, 1914–1963* (Stanford, Calif.: Stanford University Press, 1964), p. 53, citing Keynes's *Essays in Biography*, p. 37.

92. Keynes, *Economic Consequences*, p. 207; S. J. Hurwitz, *State Intervention*, p. 294.

trust in the government and the sense of a high and united purpose had chilled; within Whitehall, the zeal for new things glowed dim.

The Balance of Forces

Labor, Parliament, the government, and the public held attitudes that boded ill. Public opinion, if one can judge by the most vocal opinion, was terribly disaffected. Complaints grew, fed by the rise in prices and the burdens of taxation. By-elections went against the government. Efforts from Downing Street to bring back confidence were treated, more and more, as instances of the Prime Minister's perpetual confidence game. Businessmen who were favorable to control were fewer and less vocal than before. Critics of the government, which had not gone all the way to accommodate owners in the coal question, raised their voices more loudly. Simple demands for decontrol won ever more applause.

Parliament's mood was changing. In 1919—that year of indulgence and generosity, as the Webbs put it—the cabinet could count, even to the end, on Parliament's willingness to vote new taxes for pensions, accept new expenses, enact anti-profiteering measures, and reverse its original opposition to subsidies for private housing contractors. But in 1920 the cabinet ministers would warn each other, and events would show, that the Commons had become much more hostile to expense, to controls, and to the government itself.[93]

The government had hardened—save for men like Addison, Horne, and Churchill, one suspects—because the failure of the National Industrial Conference and the record of strikes dampened hopes for cooperation, and for a variety of other reasons. Success in withstanding a year of strike threats had now produced an inevitable effect. The mood of Parliament barred the cabinet from costly ventures and new reforms. And now at last the message of the Budget had been heard. Labor also, and with factual reasons, would emulate the government in turning from the fading prospect of mutual and honorable gains through common toil; it would reap only the meaner satisfactions of righteous protest and petty battles won, which groups can always rationalize to themselves.

The past year, for all its recriminations, had not been quite like that: Labor, as Professor Roberts contends, had its moderates who recognized the danger of massive strikes, and the ultimate conflict had thus been avoided.[94] In 1920 Labor's distrust would deepen. For all groups,

93. HAC (30 November 1920), Cab. 26/3.
94. In Morris Ginsberg, ed., *Law and Opinion*, pp. 366–68; and in Roberts' *The Trades Union Congress*, e.g. pp. 318, 320.

circumstances and memory would ensure that 1920 would bring reconstruction closer to disgrace.

Briefly, this review of the situation at the end of 1919 and this summary of aspects of 1920 shows the plight in which reconstruction stood. Before looking more thoroughly at the course of 1920, a question long overdue must be faced. Why had this state of affairs come to be?

Handicaps and Their Causes

The whole of 1919 testified that the armistice had taken Britain by surprise. The suddenness with which war had ended goes far to explain how, and why, reconstruction now stood in such danger. In October 1918 the government had envisioned a war that would extend to 1920, which only the wildest optimists expected might end in 1919. At Queen Anne's Gate much was in readiness, but many committee reports and far too many an embryonic structure showed that a margin of time was expected. Elsewhere, even when sketches of postwar policies and drafts of demobilization plans existed, they simply gathered dust. The crushing words of Churchill point to cause and effect:

> What had we to do with Peace while we did not know whether we should not be destroyed? Who could think of Reconstruction while the whole world was being hammered to pieces, or of demobilisation when the sole aim was to hurl every man and every shell into the battle? . . . We had of course a demobilisation plan for the Ministry of Munitions. It had been carefully worked out, but it had played no part in our thoughts.[95]

That the obvious result of unpreparedness, and preoccupation with victory, was a pattern of patchwork and improvisation from the armistice onward, has sufficiently been shown; but the national psychological consequences and implications also need to be identified. The pre-armistice situation militated against an intensive effort to expound in all its details an agreed program and to secure for it a public support grounded in full understanding and acceptance of its difficulties. The unofficial work of the reconstructionists had made the situation far better than it might have been; but still the public level of awareness was short of what was ideal. Swift improvisation behind the scenes did nothing to encourage the growth of such a supportive consensus.

Other handicaps and threats to continued reform, more specific than the above factor, become apparent as one surveys the scene at the end of 1919 and watches the unfolding story of 1920. Some handicaps were

95. Churchill, *World Crisis*, 4: 541–42, and 5: 28–29.

recent in origin, dating from the government's acts of 1919; some became evident in 1920; one was present from the armistice. These handicaps included (*a*) the reliance on high prices, (*b*) the scale of ministers' values and the place of reform within that scale, and (*c*) the disappearance of industrial partnership as a serious hope, and—in great contrast to all these —the positive mood of optimism, perhaps most serious handicap of all.

Prices. The index number of prices, standing at 192 in 1918, had risen to 206 in 1919; it would rise to a peak of 265 in April 1920. The climb prompted serious cabinet comment as early as 5 May 1919, when the index had begun to affect plans for decontrol. The crucial question, however, was not whether it would be observed, but whether it would be seen as a threat and only a threat. Nowadays we can see it as a fateful indicator for that government, and indeed for any British government eager to square happiness at home with success abroad; and contemporaries would see it thus, within a twelvemonth. When first detected, the rising curve of prices was looked on as a danger and a liability: Sir Auckland Geddes was the voice of alarm, louder even than Austen Chamberlain.[96] Soon, however, the price rise was welcomed.

Swiftly, if without candor, the government made a virtue of necessity and an asset of future peril. It was gambling on inflation, as it must. And Bonar Law reminded the ministers that collapse of the domestic markets must be blocked; employment, industrial peace, and business support depended on this. Efficiency and reorganization—even reform in the sense of housing pledges fulfilled—must wait. The "rudderless economy" moved with the tide, without vocal regret. It is not, of course, literally true that "in April 1920 all was right with the world"; there were mutterings from the Treasury and groans from the housing commissioners. But the simple, stimulating effect of rising prices, which ended the condition that had paralyzed trade between the armistice and Whitsunday, seemed best in line with the great goal affirmed by Lloyd George: "The task that lay before the Government today was that of re-constructing the nerves and tissues of the nation, and re-vitalising them for generations to come."[97] That task seemed dependent on inflation.

Scale of preferences. In the government's tacit hierarchy of values, inflation and price maintenance held a dangerous priority. The entire

---

96. WC 562 and 587.

97. Tawney, "Abolition of Economic Controls," p. 15; WC 562, 587, 606A; HAC (1 August 1919); Morgan, *Studies in British Economic Policy*, pp. 375–76; Francis, *Britain's Economic Strategy*, pp. 39–40, 46–48; but see Inverforth's warning of a 300 per cent rise in machinery costs, WC 592.

hierarchy, indeed, was far from favorable to sound long-term prosperity or to fulfillment of reform. One can roughly put the scale this way: avoidance of violent nationwide industrial strife (symbolized by a strike of the Triple Alliance) came first; maintenance of the boom, a close second—including, as noted, a mild inflationary pressure on prices; avoidance of lesser industrial strife, or of pervasive labor unrest, came third; maintenance of the government's general reserve power to control the entire situation ranked fourth; profitable expansion of overseas trade was fifth, along with maintenance of a sure and relatively cheap supply of food. Implicit in what the government had actually done in 1919 was such a set of preferences.

Reform was not absent from the list of high-priority values, but I think that these other values preceded it. Thus, in seventh place so to speak, came reform: not *new* measures, not innovation, but maintenance of the present kind of reform, especially those enacted. Subordinate to these, but also present, were two other motives: economy in government cost, wherever possible; progress toward longer-term financial solvency. I think that this scale of preferences, implying a certain weighting of desirable aims in the ministers' reckoning, has this chief significance: fulfillment of specific pledges that had been made at election time was far from first in priority. Those pledges held seventh place. If the attainment of higher priority goals came to require measures which would make attainment of reform literally impossible, such measures would be followed regardless. Housing, already menaced by the inflationary policy—which served the goal of industrial peace and of trade revival—already illustrated the point. The improvement of Britain's economic efficiency, to improve her competitive strength and thus aid long-term stability and prosperity, had been another goal of reconstruction; it too was menaced by the priority assigned to industrial peace and to price maintenance. These higher priority values perpetuated inefficiency in labor and in corporations and in industrial practice generally; the "world's workshop" was not putting its house in order, although reconstructionists and labor spokesmen and productioneers had stressed that it must.

Whitleyism eclipsed. If reform as an objective ranked low on the list, another goal was simply absent. Industrial partnership had once seemed important and attainable enough to make several overtures to it: in the election speeches, in the establishment of Whitley Councils, in the statements to the National Industrial Conference and to the miners at midyear. For reasons that reveal the tragedy of British labor but not its wisdom, the response had not come swiftly and in time. In wartime this ingredient, industrial cooperation, had been termed indispensable. Its disappearance as a serious hope within a year seems, in retrospect, virtually fatal.

These handicapping factors would not change and would continue to work their harm. It remains to mention one other conditioning element which is distinct from these.

Why Reconstruction Would Fail: Ultimate Factors

The potential menace from inflation, the low place of reform on the cabinet's scale of values, the ominous distrust and strife within industry, were all by nature negative. But the greatest danger, indeed the deepest cause for the peril in which reconstruction now stood, may have been in nature positive: an inherited confident and hopeful state of mind, dating back to the war and ultimately due to the war.

At the end of 1919, one report from Austen Chamberlain ran counter to all the alarmism that he had expressed in that year: revenues would meet expenditures for 1919–20—the prediction was the budget would *not* be unbalanced. This remarkably good omen took its place beside the announcement there was not, and would not be, a shortage of raw materials.[98] Patent encouragements to expensive reform and generous perspectives, *prima facie* evidence of successful reconversion, these facts produced, as they had already produced, a dangerous state of optimism. Britain lived by faith, hope, and charity, and the most dangerous of these was hope.

Keynes had noted a general feeling that "the limits of possibility" could be exceeded in matters of finance with impunity. Among friends and foes of the government, too often such optimism and hope reigned unchecked by the cautious realism of the reconstructionists. These moods doubtless spurred on the miners and railwaymen in their demand for nationalization. Optimism catapulted the nation into the housing campaign and then led most naturally but dangerously to a premature impatience with a slow-starting program of building. The same exaggeratedly swift reaction, the natural concomitant to great expectations, was expressed when there were hesitations over granting a national minimum wage, or when there were delays in business revival.

In great contrast to these short tempers was the mood after World War II. Post-1945 Britain, once again attempting reconstruction, showed a stoic resistance to a train of disappointments and to the delays of a far from speedy legislative reform. Britain's behavior then is a valuable control experiment; the public showed that it had learned to *wait*. It is

98. F.C. 22 (29 October 1919), Cab. 27/72; Tawney *re* coal, "Abolition of Economic Controls," p. 22; Inverforth on abundant materials, WC 592.

also a reminder that almost any reconstruction is doomed if it is expected to produce miracles overnight—or, even worse, if great expectations lead to its dismissal without fair trial. Instant reform and instant recovery were the demands for far too many Britons in that more emotional and less experienced Britain of 1919. One remembers that Churchill dedicated *The Aftermath* "to all who hope": it was a condition that readied men for heroic endeavor, but it made them overcritical of imperfection and delay.

Optimism, of course, was far from the only ingredient of the national psychology from the armistice onward. There was fear, pessimism, and a pent-up passion to rebel. All moods existed side by side; for this is history, where Occam's writ does not run and Aristotle's law of contradiction does not hold good.

In two specific ways, overconfidence left Britain ill equipped to face the troubles of 1920 and 1921; and now this was beginning to be clearer. It had allowed her to shoulder a burden of reform almost too great for the nation's finances, and to shoulder it without full awareness. Optimism accounted also for much of the speed of decontrol. Decontrol got as far as it did not because of simple business pressure alone, or theoretical compulsions, but because it seemed safe. Circumstance reinforced the mood; for the abundance of raw materials, at the moment of armistice, seemed to invalidate the greatest articulate argument for controls. Then the upward movement of the economy, after May 1919, seemed to confirm the initial judgment and reinforced the trend and the hopeful mood.

Keynes traced the mood to the vast expenditures of the war; "what we believed to be the limits of possibility" had been "enormously exceeded," and all sense of magnitude had been lost.[99] How much of all this causation, indeed, comes back simply to "the war"! Optimism about what was obtainable was due to war and its prodigies of production. Abundance of raw materials, which worked to encourage costly ventures and to speed decontrol, was a product of Britain's maritime supremacy in the war and her magnificent inventories at the armistice, which also were due to war. Impatience with controls, on many sides, was a mood that had been fomented and increased by the restraints in wartime.

Labor's suspicions of the government were fed by wartime experiences. Labor's sense of righteousness, grievance, and above all of independent power, were more remarkable legacies of war. Labor's feeling that it no longer need reckon with the Liberal Party was a similar development, as Professor Trevor Wilson well argues, in and because of the war. The costly

99. Keynes, *Economic Consequences*, p. 205.

if admirable commitment to large-scale grain farming plainly was required by war. Shortages of building laborers were intensified by war. An unwise reliance on large-scale organization, on protectionism, and on indiscriminate subsidy—all in place of a genuine attack on problems of efficiency or a real attempt to shift to *new* industries—were understandable in view of wartime recourse to precisely these practices. War also had lifted costs, wages, and prices to new levels, posing a mortal long-term peril to reform and prosperity; by the same token it encouraged a short-term reliance on inflation (which also was perilous). It may also be that the war caused "good times" in a more circumstantial way: it had delayed repairs and construction, thus creating a splendid backlog of work; it had deferred many consumer demands, ensuring a postwar orgy of purchases; it had taxed the shipping facilities of the world so severely that, for many months after the war, the resultant high Atlantic freight rates shielded Britain's manufactures from American competition.

The greatest of all war's harmful effects, which has already been noted, is that it precluded fully comprehensive and thoroughly elaborated planning for reconstruction, by turning attention elsewhere. Mars, mesmerizing all with his bloody game across the Channel, had been the father of delay and inattention, especially concerning the means and structures and advance action needed for reform. The whole history of the reconstruction agencies, struggling for cabinet attention and short of staff (the maximum for Addison's ministry was about 300 in 1918), attests to this. War, which had done so much for reform, also had left a legacy that could undo it.

Can one then conclude, after attempting so often thus far to ponder the relation of war to reform, that war had doomed reconstruction to failure? The list of just cited handicaps deriving from war, especially the legacy of overconfidence, would seem to answer the question. I prefer to say that war created a set of conditions and forces, positive and negative; that, *unless* the negative forces were counteracted in 1919 by events and deeds, over which human beings may have had control, then the persisting negative factors *would* doom the effort; and that actions and omissions on many sides in 1919 had not sufficiently counteracted those negative forces. This is not to say, however, that the doom was sealed by the time of armistice, nor that war was the destroyer. It is rather to say that in 1919 men had failed to profit from such latitude as history afforded them.

Preview of the End

The historian, for these reasons, is entitled to say that by the end of 1919 he knows that, barring a miracle, reconstruction was doomed. Through many, many pages we have sought a turning point, and a straight view to the end. I think that we have found it.

The key to the situation was that reconstruction—as a body of reform measures, founded on a calculation of the possible—had always depended on conditions external to it. It was not self-sustaining. Rather it stood or fell by *policies* and *circumstances* independent of it, and by the *results* that followed from them: *policies* for trade, finance, prices, wages, and the like; *circumstances* such as the national will and capacity for cooperative effort, the nation's readiness to bear exceptional taxes, and its determination to strive for genuine efficiency, forgoing short-term profit and advantage; *results* in the form of solvency, industrial peace, favorable trade balance, and general prosperity. Such were the preconditions essential even for a limited kind of reconstruction that might have left a monument not unworthy of the dead. But preconditions for that—let alone for the kind of reconstruction that would have atoned for the sacrifice of a generation —were gone by the beginning of 1920. If the zeal in enacting welfare and housing measures had been matched by boldness and realism in devising economic policy to give reforms permanent support, the whole might have been a different story. That was not what had happened. Whether or not it could have happened at all is doubtful. Whether at the end of war the psychological and other preconditions were favorable enough so that statesmanship and wiser behavior could have converted opportunity into lasting achievement will forever remain debatable and debated. But from the perspective of January 1920 the historian may say that, for reconstruction to fail, continuation of present trends would suffice. The odds against success had become too high; sooner or later probabilities of failure would turn into certainties. Among all the preconditions, those involving finance and trade would eventually prove most immediately relevant. When reconstruction began in 1919, the economic policy of the moment, however improvised, had seemed sufficient to, and compatible with, reform. But a time of troubles would come—and 1920 would supply many signs thereof, as 1919 already had supplied some—when fiscal, trade, and industrial policy would be changed, having failed to attain the overriding aim of economic survival. The hope would persist at first that such changes might still allow for continued reform; significantly, however, the changes would occur regardless of that. At last, as economic survival became more doubtful, changes in fiscal policy would be made with full awareness that they forbade continuance of reform. Then all pledges would turn to mockeries, and the energy with which action had followed promises would be forgotten. "Homes fit for heroes" would be bitterly redefined as homes that only heroes were fit to live in. Plotting and deception would seem to explain all, and in retrospect the Prime Minister's own statement in August 1919 would take on sinister meaning: "Even if the Government showed that they wanted to do things which it might afterwards be found could not be done, the attempt would create a spirit of confidence which would go far to obtain good results."[100] None would think of Lloyd George, the victor in war, as the most deluded of "All Who Hope."

But this is preview. Reconstruction was still not only pledged but continuing, and would be tackled with anxious energy in 1920. Not until housing expenditures were officially cut in spring of 1921 did the end really come. At the beginning of 1920, even with his foreknowledge that reconstruction was doomed, the historian is not entitled to pronounce it dead.

Commitments without Preconditions: 1920

Signs of the day of reckoning appeared, that year: the revival of agriculture in Europe; the continued excess of imports over exports; the ominous concentration, *within* the empire, of such trade increases as occurred; the stagnation of traditional staple industries, foreshadowing the troubles of the "world's workshop" between the wars.[101] The financial barometers presented storm warnings in public statistics, and in the rising bank rate (to 6 per cent in November 1919 and to 7 per cent in April 1920); there were major policy reviews by the Finance Committee through the year. A July session of the cabinet stressed how much more hostile public opinion had become; an October meeting declared unacceptable the costs of the unemployment donation and of housing; a December memorandum urged cuts in school building; a November discussion introduced, for the first time, the proposal that an absolute limit must be put on the total number of houses to be built.

Beyond these specific items, the cabinet records in 1920 show a marked change of tone. Ministers more and more showed a feeling that in financial terms they were doing too much and reaping no advantage thereby. The concern for economy, one element among many attitudes in 1919, grew disproportionately. Had the cabinet felt itself surrounded and sustained by an understanding public and Parliament, these misgivings about a difficult program might not have grown so strong; signs of popularity and of continued public willingness to accept the burdens of

100. WC 606A, fol. 147.
101. Mowat, *Britain between the Wars*, pp. 259–83.

reform might have encouraged the cabinet to resist the worrisome evidence of rising expense and of worsening trade. But, on left and right, potential supporters fell away; those opposed became more so. As Lord Beaverbrook noted, any appraisal of the years 1919–22 must take account of the enveloping distrust which the nation came to feel for Lloyd George and the Coalition. "The public does not know," one minister characteristically lamented; and though in this instance the cabinet upheld an unpopular and costly measure, the mood of discouragement was bound to affect policy somewhat. An increasingly isolated cabinet inevitably became more self-absorbed. This distrust and self-absorption, translated into the feeling that the inherent difficulty of sustaining costly programs was in fact a thankless task, reinforced the desire for economy and further threatened reform.[102]

Nevertheless there were still signs of the cabinet's will to continue. A new housing loan was authorized, and acknowledged as vital. The cabinet vowed to face the critical public with facts rather than yield to the outcry against expenditures.[103] On the closely related issue of decontrol, although the cabinet held that on its merits the case for meat decontrol was overwhelming, the decision was for continued control. Definitely if reluctantly, rent restriction was kept, against a strong committee report. The Ministry of Food was given another year of life, and plans to wind up the Ministry of Munitions were put off.[104]

Nevertheless, the future trend was suggested in the termination of subsidies to tin mines, reversing the concession of 1919; and Lloyd George, in his meeting with coal-mine owners, found them insistent on decontrol as their price for cooperation in the government's plans for devolution. The owners would accept a consultative structure, and controls on prices and quantities, in exchange for a government announcement that "the goal to be attained was de-control." Even more significant was the cabinet's lowering its sights: in 1919 it had envisioned workers' representation on the national controlling body of directors; now it proposed mine workers' representation merely on a group of local and national advisory committees.[105] Moreover, where the twin themes of coal and labor relations overlapped, there was little to lighten the gloom; the

102. Francis, *Britain's Economic Strategy*, pp. 39–40, 46–48; F.C. meetings (1920), Cab. 27/71; Beaverbrook, *Men and Power*, 326–27.

103. F.C. 40, Cab. 27/72; F.C. meeting 23 (22 July 1920), Cab. 27/71.

104. Tawney, "Abolition of Economic Controls," pp. 20–21; HAC (14 January, 9 March, 22 April, 1 and 25 June 1920), Cab. 26/2.

105. HAC (25 June 1920), *ibid.*; conferences of 27 January and 11 February 1920, Cab. 23/20.

records dwell on preparations for a general strike, and later that year the strikes came.[106]

Reform in 1920: general. Perhaps some ministers knew that hard choices must finally be faced. Britain could have full employment and high prices under the prevailing conditions that year, but to these she could not add an expensive housing program, or even a housing program of more reasonable cost. She could not have full employment and high prices *and* a flourishing export trade, producing a favorable trade balance. Perhaps she could not have a favorable trade balance and the housing program any more than, short of wizardry, she could have both economy and reform. Actually or implicitly, one desideratum ruled out some of the others, and in 1920 the tacit "priorities" of 1919 still obtained: high employment, high wages and costs, inefficient plants, some protectionism, and financial imbalance. Nevertheless there was an official list of reform, although now it was minimal: the 48-hour bill and the Electricity Bill, with the un-employment insurance, minimum-wage, and coal mines bills significantly (if temporarily) held in abeyance.

In the event, some reforms continued and other reforms became law. The Agriculture Act continued the wartime agricultural wages boards. The Unemployment Insurance Act of 1920 was passed, a real landmark, although it lacked the liberal feature of aid to dependents and no longer was need-related. The land-settlement and housing efforts and the establishment of trade boards persisted, as in the reform year 1919. The Standing Committee on Trusts also continued, while Sidney Webb and Arthur Greenwood fretted that so little progress had been made since the Ministry of Reconstruction's Command Paper had come out. But decisions on coal went against the miners' claims, trading miners' control for the owners' cooperation. The Electricity (Supply) Bill met not only strong parliamentary opposition but such criticism in the cabinet on grounds of cost ("The resources of the Government would be taxed to the uttermost to find the money required for its Housing Policy") that the cabinet came near asking Parliament to release it from its pledges. (This is the first case, in the records, in which such an idea came close to acceptance.) Even for veterans, the out-of-work donation came to an end. More fundamentally, the farm program came under fire: a move to expand inquiries into nationalization of the land and a proposal to guarantee security of tenure were quashed, and new acquisitions and starts for land settlement were vetoed in midyear. Still worse, a great effort to rationalize and broaden

106. Mowat, *Britain between the Wars*, pp. 41–42; Cab. S-7, S-10, S-11, and S-18 through S-25, Cab. 23/35; conferences 21 and 47, Cab. 23/37.

the local health services was cut short. In mid-1920 Addison's Council on Medical and Administrative Services, fulfilling the task set in 1919, presented the splendidly comprehensive Dawson Report. This document laid a basis for full medical care, preventive as well as curative; it brought within its scope both communal and individual aspects of health; it urged establishment of health centers. Despite some favorable professional opinion, the report was not carried into operation; only minor implementation was begun. A proposal to create municipal hospitals was defeated on 14 December 1920 in the House of Lords. Here was a decisive defeat.[107] By contrast, some of the other negative decisions on reform in that year seemed to be but straws floating down the wind, however—mere indicators of *future* trouble. The case was indescribably worse for housing: the subject of three full-dress cabinet reviews, it was never out of crisis from first to last.

Reform in 1920: housing. Addison and his campaign lived in 1920 under the shadow of a bleak declaration by Austen Chamberlain: even if the present financial policy was continued (i.e., without the retrenchment or deflation that Chamberlain wished to apply), it was "very doubtful whether the raising of . . . capital" for housing loans would be practicable. This comment was made *in 1919*. It meant that the very laxity of financial policy, which gave other reforms at least a temporary life, *would not work for housing*.

Addison's Ministry of Health had enough special handicaps without this. Anderson left the ministry in 1919; Wallace entered private business; Reiss, after months of waiting for work to do, left for Welwyn Garden City. Influenza and incredible overwork brought the giant Morant to his grave. There was perhaps only one loss that could surpass this, and 1920 brought that too: loss of rapport with Lloyd George. From their first meeting in 1910 the relationship between the two men had been an unresolved compound of dependence and self-assertion, ferocious loyalty and nagging (on Addison's side), and favor and treachery (on the Prime

---

107. See F. 174 (9 February 1920 conference), Cab. 23/20, for the reform list; Mowat, *Britain between the Wars*, pp. 45, 124; 10 and 11 Geo. V, c. 13, for amendment in 1920 to Profiteering Act; reports on trusts, in M. E. Bulkley, *Bibliographical Survey of Contemporary Sources for the Economic and Social History of the War* (Oxford: Clarendon Press, 1922), pp. 123–27, 183–84; Board of Trade Library, Box 55, minutes of meetings 1–71 of Standing Committee on Trusts. For farming, agriculture, coal, and land settlement, see Cab. 23/20, fols. 86–91, 97–102, 174, 224–33, 267–88, Cab. 61 (20) in Cab. 23/38, and Cab. 23/35, and Committee on Land Settlement (1920), Cab. 27/104. For electricity, see HAC (30 November 1920), Cab. 26/3. For unemployment aid see Tillyard, *Unemployment Insurance*, pp. 40–46, 65. See Abel-Smith, *The Hospitals*, pp. 290–92.

Minister's). The strains of 1919 told. Housing, meant to be the flag of honor in the Prime Minister's crusade, lay bespattered in the dust; and Lloyd George, smarting at the discredit, resented his protégé accordingly. And it did not help that Addison had virtues no chieftain likes: stubbornness, quiet but persistent and personalized reproach, a maddening memory for pledges, and an idealist's devotion to causes precisely where subtler courtiers would choose silence or flattery. Only those with unassailable popularity or an inherited position can afford such virtues when policy and place are at stake. Governments as unloved as this one (if not all governments) become cliques cemented together in defense of failure by avoiding the uncomfortable habit of blame and by mutual silence. The community of "peers" depends on equals who reassure the chief that he is indeed first. In the wake of the first policy review of housing failures in 1920, Addison was offered a post as a minister without portfolio—if he would resign as Minister of Health.[108]

Headed straight for failure and disgrace, Addison stayed on—to become a most convenient scapegoat in July of the next year. It is hard, even when one allows for his errors (which no doubt a full study of the Ministry of Health would disclose), to focus blame on him. The preconditions for a successful housing campaign, and indeed for successful long-term reform, were in major part denied. To keep prices up and to keep men at work—these two purposes, rather than the completion of more homes for workers, had been the first premises and political imperatives of government action in 1919; and they still dominated in 1920. The preconditions for continued "prosperity" were in themselves inimical to house building at reasonable cost for low rental: a government, chained to inflation; a government too timid in the face of the building unions' strong position, although fully conscious of the cost and the public harm resulting from restrictionism; a government which put full employment, high wages, and industrial peace at the top of its list. These priorities overbore reconstruction as far as housing was concerned: they doomed it to suffer from the shortage of labor; they guaranteed that costs per house would soar, and thus—because all the surplus cost (by the "penny-rate" limit) fell on the state—they ensured Parliamentary outcry. The unwillingness to control, not a question of money but of guts, made things even worse.

108. Minney, *Viscount Addison*, pp. 172–73; Richard W. Harris, *Not So Humdrum: Autobiography of a Civil Servant* (London: John Lane, 1939), p. 204. Chamberlain's doubts were expressed in the Finance Committee; see minutes, F.C. 1 (24 July 1919), p. 5, Cab. 27/71. See also Violet Markham, "Sir Robert Morant: Some Personal Reminiscences," *Public Administration*, 28 (Winter, 1950): 256, together with Sir Laurence Brock's notes on Morant's plans, *ibid.*, pp. 259–60.

That year, two great attempts at rescue failed again. A housing loan was sanctioned, in the form of local authorities bonds. "We simply cannot afford to risk a failure" (Addison's comment) was echoed by the head of Lloyd's bank:

> In view of the great urgency of housing surely the great thing is to get the money at once.... A $5\frac{1}{2}\%$ rate will spell ignominious failure. Nothing short of 6% will give us the unqualified success the great importance of the Scheme demands.

Even with 6 per cent allowed, the government's decision that spring to raise the bank rate generally to 7 per cent hurt the fund-raising badly.[109] And all this did not aid the negotiations to get building trade unions to relent on dilution and recruitment. Addison had been working on that *since July 1919*. At the height, in 1920, the government offered a guaranteed work week, a Treasury contribution to unions' insurance funds (in return for allowing ex-servicemen to be trained and for a no-strike pledge), referral to the Industrial Court of all disputed cases, and payment of overtime (in return for union acceptance of "payment by results"). The building unions did not consent; the last government offer, in late 1920, was not answered by early 1921. The government had contemplated "going to the country," or defying the unions by training veterans directly on London County Council schemes, but it could not withstand a strike alone, without employers' support; and the employers—unable to face a strike on their own—were complaisantly inclined to accept unions' wishes. Pledges against unemployment, safeguards against overcrowding of the trade, willingness to underwrite increased costs—nothing sufficed. Experience was forcing Addison to the conclusion that he finally voiced in 1922: "Neither the associations of the master builders nor the trade unions concerned, as they exist today, can be relied upon to check extravagant costs."

The situation was studded with ironies and cross-purposes. Workers, holding to their privileges, were in the long run contriving their own unemployment when the slump came (the government's offers would have shielded the building trades against the general decline); meanwhile they were ensuring the unemployment of potential recruits. Labor worked against labor—indeed, against veterans' labor. Hostility to dilution, as in October 1918, menaced full employment, housing, and reconstruction.

109. Memorandum by Addison, F.C. 40 (28 January 1920), Cab. 27/72; conference 30 (30 April 1920), in Cab. 23/37.

Even unemployment policies played an equivocal role: the government toyed with the idea of denying unemployment aid to building trade workers, as a weapon to force open employment and carry housing to success; meanwhile, unemployment payments furnished the unions a retort to the charge that they were leaving fellow workers destitute.

Economy warred against economy. The government would lose additional money if it carried through its offers to the building trades, and it would spend money for the unemployed if it did not carry them through. Industrial peace would be menaced if the housing promises were not made good, and it would break down if the only means to successful building, dilution and/or payment by results, were adopted. This was a capsule version of the problems of reconstruction, which always and before everything depended on teamwork. Decontrol, of labor and capital, also played its baneful part. It was a situation in which everyone was individually right, and where all came out in the wrong.

Through 1920 and into early 1921 Addison fought his colleagues to prevent the imposition of a ceiling on total expenditures; he opposed a top limit on the number of houses (Austen Chamberlain suggested 100,000!). He suggested renewed controls on building, proposed "direct building" by the state, reminded the cabinet of its pledges—and pointed to the future stabilizing effect of a housing campaign; employment had begun to drop badly in late 1920. The 171,000 tenders thus far approved, within which contracts for 141,000 houses had been signed, were a key argument, as was the shameful record of a mere 13,421 houses completed on 25 January 1921 and another 56,000 houses under construction. He sketched a 300,000-house program, to cost £15 million annually by 1923. He also fought for slum demolition. He insisted that steadfast pursuit of a high goal would justify expansion of the building labor force, while cutbacks would be tantamount to surrender.

He failed, all along the line. In a budget statement that assumed that "*all* development of social reforms and schemes will be suspended," Austen Chamberlain insisted on a limit of 160,000 houses. The circle of economy closed tighter. The Finance Committee became the final arena. Addison's aim was cabinet approval of the £15 million figure for annual payments and no cutback in the goal of 300,000 homes. He offered the concession that local authorities be told that costs must be held, and that, until they fell, no new projects would be accepted. Chamberlain opposed even so limited and contingent a promise.

Everyone knew that the Prime Minister no longer felt the cry for economy was mere "newspaper agitation," but Addison still turned to his chief. Bonar Law had resigned in March and was no longer there to give support. Lloyd George offered only a ministership without portfolio, which Addison rejected. Then he accepted on 1 April. The Prime Minister told him "There will be no change in policy." The policy struggle and the personal drama fused: a vote was soon scheduled in the House for the reduction of Addison's salary. Furious, Carson told Addison that "he had done more than all the rest put together to make good the election pledges and was being attacked as part of a disgusting intrigue." Friends in the cabinet and in the medical societies rallied to Addison; ceremonies and testimonial dinners were arranged.

Austen Chamberlain reportedly had warned the Prime Minister not to back Addison; if he did, the Tories would vote against the government. The story wound to a disgraceful finale, as Lloyd George turned at last on the most consistent of his lieutenants. Privately—to Churchill, who had defended Addison straight through—the Prime Minister penned a twisted apology, which put the whole blame on Addison for policies that in fact the entire cabinet had endorsed. Publicly, Lloyd George—after pledging to defend him—ridiculed Addison with insult and innuendo before the Commons. Addison read his resignation to an applauding House, on 14 July 1921.

The cabinet rather than the House of Commons, however, was reserved for the last scene in the drama of housing. Up to the very moment of his resignation, even while merely minister without portfolio, Addison had held on like grim death to his right to speak in cabinet sessions. Throughout June and July—by which time houses were being completed at the creditable rate of 70,000 houses a year—he used that position to reiterate every argument, circumstantial and moral, for the continuance of the campaign. Sites had been cleared; new money must be voted to demolish slums; next year there would be ample labor. "Government would in effect be disregarding its obligations. . . . There would be no confidence in any future Government pledge." But the limit had been voted by the cabinet; the Prime Minister flatly refused to reconsider. Thereupon Addison resigned. It fell to Mond, Addison's successor, to try to find some latitude and to put the case for the housing campaign on its merits. The Finance Committee did not mince words. To Mond—and implicitly to Addison—it replied:

> In view of the difficult financial situation . . . there was no alternative open to the Government but to decide housing questions not on merits, but on financial considerations only. . . . The policy

would never have been changed but for the decision to reduce estimates by twenty per cent. . . . it would be insincere and politically impossible to pretend that the announcement was caused by anything other than financial stringencies.[110]

This was perhaps the best curtain speech for what had happened.

110. Minutes of conference (13 July 1921), Cab. 23/39; see conferences 105 and 107, *ibid.*; F.C. meeting 35 (30 June 1921), and meetings 28, 29, 32, Cab. 27/71; F.C. memoranda 40, 52, 66, 66A, 69, Cab. 27/72; Committee on Housing (1920), Cab. 27/89; conferences 30, 44, 56, 70, 72, 76, 77, Cab. 23/37 and 38; Minney, *Viscount Addison*, pp. 172–82. For the political background, see Lord Beaverbrook, *The Decline and Fall of Lloyd George* (London: Collins, 1963), pp. 31, 61–79, and Appendices. For Addison's resignation and for his comment on housing policy, and for Lloyd George's retort, see *P.D.(C.)* vol. 144, c. 1488–92 and 2455–70; for letters of Lloyd George and Churchill, see Beaverbrook, *Men and Power*, pp. 400–404. For Addison's critique of the building trade, see his *The Betrayal of the Slums*, p. 123.

Marian Bowley tends to corroborate Addison's contentions, by stressing the rising number of buildings completed each month in 1921 by the local authorities, as well as the speed with which they and the Ministry of Health rose to the occasion in 1919–20; see *Housing and the State*, pp. 24–25.

18

Between the Crosses

Of the works of the reconstruction agencies, the interwar years show small trace; of the Ministry of Reconstruction as a form and a precedent, no trace. Addison's mistaken hope that the ministry might be continued by an appreciative government was soon belied; in the event, the very idea of general economic counselors and a broad supervision perished with the resignation of Sir Hubert Llewellyn Smith, who held the honorific but empty title "economic adviser" for his few years at the Board of Trade. The idea, born with Haldane before the war, for a peacetime "general staff" on economic affairs, survived only in the sporadic discussion of a "parliament of industry" (as taken up by Harold Macmillan and Philip Kerr). The Ministry of Agriculture methodically checked off one item after another of the Selborne committee agenda; the Permanent Secretaries of the Lord Chancellor quietly adopted some of Lord Haldane's more specific thoughts; but the Machinery of Government Committee and its greatest recommendations found no echo, even when Haldane himself was Lord Chancellor. The promise to do away with the Poor Law waited till 1928, and then the enactment spelled little change.

The fate of the "Addison Act" in housing was a mixture of repudiation, adherence, and amendment. It was terminated in its financial provisions in 1921, but otherwise was never abandoned even at the worst (as far as the principle of state aid was concerned); Wheatley and Greenwood saw to it that policy was built on that foundation thereafter.[1] The revulsion

1. R. V. Vernon and N. Mansergh, *Advisory Bodies: A Study of Their Uses in Relation to Central Government, 1919–1939* (London: Allen & Unwin, 1940), pp. 262–63; C. L. Mowat, *Britain between the Wars*, pp. 164–65, 365, 508–10. For the "Machinery of Government Committee" report, see R. B. Haldane, *An Autobiography* (London: Hodder & Stoughton, 1929), pp. 323–24; Hans Daalder, *Cabinet Reform in Britain, 1914–63*, especially pp. 274–78; and Vernon and Mansergh, *Advisory Bodies*, pp. 118–19. For Llewellyn Smith's position as Economic Adviser, see Daalder, *Cabinet Reform*, p.

against the act gave way to a sober reassessment that ended with a recommendation for improved administration and slight adjustments in financial terms.[2] These were signs of continuity and of influence. On the new growth of a literature of planning and on the new definitions of goals for housing and urban reform, however, the first reconstruction and its laws served merely as a point of reference and departure, and as a target. There is of course a parallelism between the thought of Addison's crew— and of all reconstructionists for that matter—and the agenda and statements of civic conferences and Liberal Party meetings between the wars. This is no more a testimony to the ministry's influence, however, than a proof of the alchemy of war: the parallelism bespoke the presence of Acland, Rowntree, Wallace, and ultimately Lloyd George. Even more clearly it showed the profoundest truth of all: the three-year reform effort in wartime was part of a recurring pattern in British life.[3]

Such positive and small signs were dwarfed by the prevailing oblivion or ridicule of the times. Against them, too, stood the fact of dispersal, as Addison's group and its supporters found their several ways: many to the Labour Party (Haldane, Addison, Greenwood, Reiss); some to the quieter politics of the civil service (Heseltine, Barter, Gardiner, Anderson, Horace Wilson, Havelock, Nash); some to nonpolitical reform (Rowntree, Wallace, Reiss, Mallon, Hammond, and Comyns Carr); and one to anti-politics (Ernest Benn became author of *The State the Enemy*). Garrod returned to Merton and the classics, but not without a parting shot. He wrote a small set of poems, with an ironic smile for "Hoxton's son" (Addison) and bitterness for the politicians who schemed while young men fell: and he named it "Worms and Epitaphs."[4]

201, and D. N. Chester and M. G. Willson, eds., *The Organisation of the British Central Government, 1914–1956* (London: Allen & Unwin, 1957), pp. 294–96. See also Leonard D. White, *Whitley Councils in the British Civil Service* (Chicago: University of Chicago Press, 1933), pp. 4–6, 24, and Ministry of Labour, *Report on the Establishment and Progress of Joint Industrial Councils* (London: H.M. Stationery Office, 1923), pp. 26–60, 157–61.

2. Marian Bowley, *Housing and the State, 1919–1944* (London: Allen & Unwin, 1945), pp. 19–29.

3. Oxford Liberal Summer School, *Essays in Liberalism* (Oxford, 1922); *Towns and the Land—Urban Report of the Liberal Land Committee, 1923–1925* (London: Hodder & Stoughton, 1925), pp. 3–5, 29–32, 45–48, 104–5; Liberal Summer School, Liberal Industrial Enquiry, *We Can Conquer Unemployment: Mr. Lloyd George's Pledge* (London: Cassell, 1929).

4. Catherine Ann Cline, *Recruits to Labour: The British Labour Party, 1914–1931* (Syracuse, N.Y.: Syracuse University Press, 1963); R. J. Minney, *Viscount Addison: Leader of the Lords*, pp. 200–51; Ernest Benn, *The State the Enemy* (London: Benn, 1952).

The Sincerest Form of Obloquy?

Determination not to follow the path of 1919 gripped the generation that fought World War II, and Whitehall silently vowed to reverse the precedents of 1917–18 as well. There was to be no Ministry of Reconstruction; even when a Minister of Reconstruction was conceded, he was allowed no staff. Churchill, who swore that World War I discredited the independent advisory committee, ruled them out. Mankind is ever the friend of simplification: and the single, simple falsehood that nothing had been attempted—or nothing had been done right—did valiant service in Britain's behalf from Dunkirk on. But that phrase of Abraham Lincoln's, which is surely his cruelest—"We cannot escape History"—held good for a generation bent on making all things new.

"Redeunt Quoque"

The war years, 1939 to 1945, provided many reminders of the earlier conflict and of the reconstruction efforts that accompanied it. Perhaps they also supply an implicit vindication of what was done "the first time."

Men. With surprise and delight one discovers familiar names in the reconstruction of World War II. Arthur Greenwood appears in charge of reconstruction as early as 1942. When Lord Woolton was named Minister of Reconstruction in late 1944, Addison himself was in the House of Lords to give advice. Beveridge, of course, had become a household word. Leslie Scott (now Lord Justice Scott) came back in a familiar role, as chairman of a committee to investigate land use. To make the continuity with earlier times unmistakable as well as to point a moral, he began his committee's report with an exact reprint of recommendations he had made twenty-five years before! Tawney was called back to write numerous reports; and G. D. H. Cole gave the new ministry his unstinting labor, although he withheld his respect from it as fully as he had from Addison's ministry.

Attention to social insurance, to guarantees of employment and minimum wages, to problems of industrial location, and (within reform of the law) to "betterment" are much more evident in World War II than in World War I. Nevertheless the parallelisms and likenesses of the two periods are many.

(1) In 1942 two committees stressed the importance of land; one was Leslie Scott's Committee on Land Utilisation in Rural Areas and the other was the still more renowned Uthwatt Committee on Compensation and Betterment. The latter cited Leslie Scott's recent recommendations,

as did a third report by the Land Transfer Committee. Save for the deliberate reprinting of Leslie Scott's original report of 1917 as a reminder of opportunity lost, these reports do not draw lessons from the earlier experience or rest upon it in any self-evident way. (2) Another familiar topic, forestry, was touched on in two reports and in a law of 1945. Water resources were studied, as in World War I. (3) A white paper on agricultural education likewise struck a familiar note.

(4) Many papers deal with housing policy, and one deals with local government, though without reference to similar work in the first war. (5) Papers on health and on insurance are greater in number and importance, but still they involve a theme that had concerned Addison's staff. (6) Even "domestic help" was made the subject of two reports!

One is not surprised, then, to find some references to the old "gospel of output," against which the *Athenaeum* had inveighed, or to read optimistic accounts of labor-management teamwork. War again opened a vista of forgotten possibilities. Lord Beveridge, recounting the "marvels in the war" wrought by Britons "inspired by the vision of a better Britain in a better world for all," asked his countrymen:

> Why should they contemplate defeat by the social evils of want, disease, squalor, ignorance and unemployment at home? They could not contemplate defeat; they cannot be defeated, if they will go to peace as resolutely as they went to war.[5]

5. Cmd. 6378, "Report of the Committee on Land Utilisation in Rural Areas" (1942); Cmd. 6386, "Final Report of the Expert Committee on Compensation and Betterment" (1942); Cmd. 6467, "Report of the Land Transfer Committee" (1943); Cmd. 6447, "Post-War Forest Policy. Report by H.M. Forestry Commission" (1943); Forestry Bill, cited in *Parliamentary Papers* (1944–45), 1: 477, and 3: 335; Cmd. 6579, "Annual Report of the Ministry of Health for 1943–1944," citing the White Paper on water policy; Cmd. 6433, "Report of the Committee on Post-War Agricultural Education in England and Wales" (1943). For housing, see Cmd. 6621, "Report of the ... Committee on Rent Control" (1945); Cmd. 6609, "Housing" (1945); Cmd. 6759, 6794, 6876, reports of the New Towns Committee of the Ministry of Town and Country Planning (1945–46); Cmd. 6801, "The New Towns Bill and Its Application" (1946). See also Cmd. 6579, "Local Government ... during the Period of Reconstruction," 1945, citing Cmd. 2506 and 3213 of 1925 and 1928, by the Onslow Royal Commission on Local Government. For the impact of Beveridge, see Cmd. 6404, "Social Insurance and Allied Services" (1943); Cmd. 6502, "A National Health Service" (1944); Cmd. 6550, "Social Insurance. Part I" (1944); Cmd. 6527, "Employment Policy," issued by the Ministry of Reconstruction in 1944; Cmd. 6729, "Summary of the National Insurance Scheme" (1945); Cmd. 6861, "Summary of the National Health Service Bill" (1945). See Ministry of Labour and National Service, *Industrial Relations Handbook* (London, 1953), especially p. 13; for Beveridge's statement, cf. Liberal Party, *The Radical Programme of the Liberal Party* (London: Liberal Publication Department, 1945).

Other parallels were less publicized. (1) There developed, unannounced, a "ministry of reconstruction": Sir Norman Brooke, then head of the cabinet secretariat, was convinced that the early effort (which, he said, he had not studied) had erred in setting up a rival ministry in isolation from regular staffs. But he collected a nucleus of civil servants and professors to encourage the departments, and they took on a life of their own. Those who do not study history are condemned to repeat it![6] (2) The net result in economic forecasts by the professionals furnished the acute observer (if he knows the similar pattern of World War I) a foolproof system for predicting postwar world conditions. In World War I experts incessantly warned of a shortage, but there was an abundance of raw materials after the armistice. Sir Norman indicated that his staff predicted huge problems of disposal of surplus; instead, at war's end England entered a time of scarcity. (3) In World War II, as in World War I, each man in retrospect tried to fit his reconstruction service into the broad pattern of his nation's life, and, not altogether astonishingly, each man found that what he had said or done (or "remembered" having said or done) was true prophecy that was vindicated by all that happened afterward.

Improvisation (to turn to major things) had much to do with the first reconstruction efforts in 1942–45, as it had in 1916. The earliest work of Reith and Sir William Holford was a desperate attempt to kindle spirits that were near despair; as a result, the Office of Works became a crucible of wartime planning, as the Ministry of Munitions had been before. The point, however, can be overstressed: long-maturing plans and the slow agitation of interwar reform groups came alive in both wars, as the resurrection of the Poor Law reform and the Barlow report separately show. All this attests that war *invents* nothing. Both reconstruction efforts were thus a reflection of prewar history.

One great contrast stands out: the second reconstruction involved— far more than the first—conscious reflection *on* prewar history. This fact shows in the study of what had gone wrong in interwar urban development, in the history-mindedness of Beveridge's work, and above all in the view that everything must be guided by the (misunderstood) pattern of World War I. As I have stated, a deliberate effort to do the opposite of the past was a great fact of wartime opinion between 1940 and 1946—an illusion that in many respects steeled the will. Those who will not study the past correctly, it seems, are sometimes better off. It was

6. Lord Normanbrooke in a 1953 interview with the author; Daalder, *Cabinet Reform in Britain*, pp. 209–15, 306.

a characteristically human story of the past vindicated, repudiated, and resurgent, both for good and for ill.

Other contrasts also deserve note. A unique feature of World War II, the "blitz," did an immense service to housing reform. The Luftwaffe (as a writer of 1917 had guessed) made large-scale rebuilding possible as well as imperative. Perhaps a greater contrast, however, is the much greater duration of the second reconstruction: this time the reconstructionists would not be cut short before fair trial. The political context was part and parcel of this new situation: reconstruction after July 1945 did not depend on a shaky coalition but on an ideologically unified and massive parliamentary majority of Labour.

Concurrence at Best

How shall we pass judgment on reconstruction? Was it a success, a failure—or a mixture of both? From 1919 to 1945, men unconsciously supplied their answers. Our powers of inference tell us as much: for, in all the above record of deeds and attitudes whether from the interwar years or from World War II, some sort of commentary and judgment on 1916–19 was implicit. But today's verdicts are not implicit; present-day scholarship leaves nothing to be guessed or inferred. Its verdicts on that first reconstruction are flat, outspoken—and various.

Indeed, of explicit scholarly judgments we possess a surfeit today; and it is impossible that this condition will change. Toward our capital concerns—the truth about the timebound reconstruction, and the truth about timeless relationships between war and reform—the historical profession seems to flaunt the boast of an old Girondin, wistful but proud: "La seule idée d'un accord nous révoltait!" There are many reasons why we shall never agree. For one thing, it makes a world of difference *when* one takes the measure of reconstruction: a thing half-planned, in late September 1918; a program buried under the avalanche of the armistice in December; a throbbing and growing thing in July 1919; a heavily (I believe mortally) handicapped program in early 1920; or a repudiated campaign and a failure after mid-1921.

Obviously it makes much difference also whether we sit in judgment on the pre-armistice planning (clearly very extensive, courageous, and farsighted), or the implementation in 1919, or on the continuation. Most of all it matters whether we make reasonable allowances for the difficulties of any such enterprise and for the special difficulties of an effort unprecedented in history—launched six to twelve months earlier than any one had predicted. For some, the delays, faulty predictions, incoordination, incomprehension, blunders, and sheer haste will brand it a *prima facie* failure, even without the evidence of 1920–22. I am no more surprised by such perfectionist judgments than by the failings that prompt them, but I deem such failings normal in any human enterprise. For my part, reconstruction from 1916 through 1919 was a program founded on reasonable hopes and (although this can never be proved or disproved) on far-from-hopeless objective conditions. It was intelligently conceived and was being well prepared, until events overran it—and even then enough of its essentials was preserved, enacted, and vigorously administered to give reconstruction a real chance until late 1919. At that point the decline of its chances for success became more evident; its doom—unless something new and special intervened—was clear; but (to raise questions of inevitability again) its doom was fashioned by protagonists on many sides and by human action and choice rather than by war or any other provable inherited condition. Its doom was the result of many specific decisions and conditions and happenings, not one alone. For completeness it must be added that the reformers themselves, within the government, and their programs, remained strong and purposeful for another year.

Two marginal comments are obligatory. (1) What is said immediately above is an implied dissent from determinist verdicts, whether they are reached through fictions of impersonal forces or through the more satisfying notion of a cast of conspiratorial reactionary characters. Yet a real and gnawing thought remains, I admit, that the nemesis which came in 1921 was implicit and inevitable from the start (determinist hypotheses, like most others, cannot be disproved). If such ideas be entertained, however, they should take one or both of two lines: that (as Keynes and Churchill felt) war was too disruptive and demoralizing to permit a fruitful harvest afterward; and that Britain, for all her goodness and strength, was not a community—but lacked in 1919 either the capacity for the teamwork reconstruction demanded or a bloc that could impose its will. (2) All of my major judgments have been on events and on reconstruction, not on men or reconstructors. To turn to the men, I feel, is to turn to simpler verdicts: they were imperfect and various, but they strove like giants. Their record of courage and labor beggars high praise.

A Treasure of Good Counsel?

Does the reconstruction experiment prove anything about method? Does it simply prove how not to do things? Such was the shallow judgment of the interwar years, and such was the more considered judgment of those who, returning to the same task between 1940 and 1945, strove to follow the opposite path in order to avoid what they considered past failures. Has it any lessons, both in its sound methods and in its mistakes? Leaving aside those skeptics, determinists, or perfectionists who will conclude on the record that the whole effort should not have been made at all, some historians and men of politics will wonder if it could not have been done better; and they will examine the record accordingly for any lessons that it may teach. The cabinet set its secretariat to accumulating data for a new "War Book" and a "Peace Book," from 1919 on. Also in this group of seekers for enlightenment stand the anatomists of wartime controls, the historians and the statesmen who knew they might have to face such tasks again. To them some uncertain observations, hardly qualifying as political science, may be submitted.

(1) Reconstruction benefited from utilizing a combination of civil servants and the best, most representative, amateur or non-governmental counselors. (2) The planning suffered not only from discontinuities (as noted in chapter 2) but from the early abandonment of the best form, which would have combined cabinet authority and compulsion and coordination with a broadly representative council of senior ministers who were backed by the superior resources of the departments. (3) The variety of the forms used—the cabinet committee (including the Prime Minister), leaderless gadflies, a rival ministry—nevertheless shows that each form had its virtues; I conclude, however, that a top-level cabinet power was needed to preserve the gadflies from committing their characteristic sin of assuming the imbecility of predecessors and bureaucrats, and to ensure that the departments did not live unto themselves.

(4) The whole effort tells against the proliferation of new agencies and special advisory committees. (5) From first to last, publicity was overlooked. Whitehall lived too much to itself—as it will ever do unless the powerful are as wise as Clemenceau. (6) Powers within and outside the government should have been yoked. In attempting to do this the Lloyd George committee and the ministry chose well.

(7) A general system for clearance and coordination, despite what has been said about advisory and new groups, was imperative. Addison and Carson—and eventually all their colleagues—were right to set up the Home Affairs and Economic Defence and Development Committees; the fault was that they were simply, but unpredictably, too late. Lloyd George hurt this development by keeping the committees in limbo at armistice time; then he paid them the compliment of similar improvisations in

November and December 1918 and the first half of 1919. The frantic six months after the armistice are a continuous testimony to the search both for the virtues of the Asquith form and of these committees. (8) Improvements in form—for all my stress on them—can succeed only so far, and only up to the eleventh hour. If the experience from 1916 to 1919 is implicitly (in Lord Salter's phrase) "a treasure of good counsel," it is not a book of recipes and charts. There is always an eleventh hour, and in that time only an all-out effort at the top, touching everything and bringing everywhere the light of inquiry and the spark of energy, can accomplish anything.

Valete, fratres . . .

Last of all, the judgment of judgments. It must be a judgment, certainly, on the reconstruction effort itself; it cannot be a judgment on war, for the Red God remains inscrutable; it should be a judgment on reconstruction, and on the men. On Englishmen, indeed, and not only those of that generation. The England of Bevin and Attlee, Bevan and Cripps and Silkin and Reith, faced the same giants; and the England of 1968 is again called by its Prime Minister to solve the dilemma of being "efficient, modern, and internationally competitive," which 1919 did not solve.[7]

Reconstruction, I conclude, *should* be tested by the standards of success and failure—tested all along the line from first planning through enactment to final stabilization, and tested by the objective results. But there is another test: effort and will. The former test brings in the great impersonal world of causation and accident that (a learned Italian reminded us) governs half of human affairs. Such tests and such judgments are not wrong. Yet it is inherent in all such verdicts, dominated by the test of results, that they nevertheless remain judgments as much on the times as on the men. For a judgment on the human actors in a drama, the other test—of effort, purpose, and will—is more appropriate. Indeed for reconstruction from 1916 to 1920, this sort of test is specially fitting. It rests on the view of the gigantic task which contemporaries actually held; and it leads us to discover what, for the Englishmen in the drama, reconstruction was meant to do.

The enterprise attempted was so near impossible as to daunt even the fearless—as awesome as the slopes above Mons, and the mud of Passchendaele. A task next to impossible—but offering a fighting chance: so the reconstructionists, the planners, and the nation behind them saw it.

---

7. Harold Wilson in a speech of 7 May 1967.

They asked no more; indeed, they preferred it so, for only by pitting hope and resolution and daring energy against overwhelming odds might they fulfill the passion of emulation that drove them. So their men had done in France; and such a task they too must have. For, in their civilian reconstruction, Britons at home were attempting to match the example given by the dead. Only by an effort that compared to that of the fallen might the living justify their survival. The results might not come; the essential thing was to try. Only thus might a nation that had strewn its sons from Agincourt to Zeebrugge prove—ultimately, to itself—that it had the right to live. Only after such redemption and atonement might one walk one day to the village war memorial, and face the Hodges and Harcourts, the Llewellyns and Reillys, the Smiths and Mackenzies, the Asquiths, Protheros, Laws, Hendersons, Grants, Gordons, and Vaughans.

In that spirit the work of reconstruction was attempted. The monument of that effort still stands as a tribute to the spirit which engendered it—a monument, indeed, not unworthy of all who hope.

Bibliography

Unpublished Official Records (Great Britain)

Board of Trade. Committee Papers, 1916–1920: Commercial and Industrial Policy, 1916–1917; Safeguarding of Industries Bill, and Key Industries Committee, 1921–1935; Standing Committee on Trusts, 1919–1920.

Forestry Commission. Papers, vol. 1 (1919).

Ministry of Health. Class 1 (1919).

Ministry of Munitions. Council Committee on Demobilisation and Reconstruction, "Interim Report on Post-War Iron and Steel Requirements."

Ministry of Reconstruction. Records, boxes 1–90.

The War Cabinet and Cabinet. Class 21, 23, 24, 26, 27, 32, 33.

Published Records (Great Britain)

Parliamentary Papers

1917–18

> vol. 13, Cd. 9032, "Interim Report by the Committee on Commercial and Industrial Policy on Certain Essential Industries."
>
> vol. 14, Cd. 8760, "Housing in Scotland."
>
> vol. 18, Cd. 8506, Reconstruction Committee, "Agricultural Policy Sub-Committee. Report," pt. 1.
>
> Cd. 8606, "Interim Report on Joint Standing Industrial Councils."
>
> Cd. 8815, "Report to the Board of Trade by the Advisory Committee on Commercial Intelligence."
>
> Cd. 8880, Reconstruction Committee, Coal Conservation Sub-Committee, "Electric Power Supply in Great Britain."
>
> Cd. 8881, Ministry of Reconstruction, Reconstruction Committee, Forestry Sub-Committee, "Final Report."

Cd. 8882, Ministry of Reconstruction, Committee on the Chemical Trade, "Report."

Cd. 8917, Ministry of Reconstruction, Local Government Committee, "Transfer of Functions of Poor Law Authorities in England and Wales."

vol. 38, Cd. 8916, Ministry of Reconstruction, "A List of Commissions and Committees Set Up to Deal with Questions Which Will Arise at the Close of the War."

1918

vol. 3, Parliament, House of Commons, Select Committee on Emergency Legislation, "Report."

Order Papers Nos. 108 and 141, House of Commons, Select Committee on Emergency Legislation, "First and Second Reports . . . with Proceedings . . . and Minutes."

vol. 5, Cd. 9079, "Report on Methods of Effecting an Increase in Home-Grown Food Supplies."

vol. 7, Cd. 9081, Ministry of Reconstruction, Committee on Relations between Employers and Employed [Whitley Committee], "Report on Conciliation and Arbitration."

Cd. 9084, Ministry of Reconstruction, Coal Conservation Committee, "Final Report."

Cd. 9099, Ministry of Reconstruction, Committee on the Relation between Employers and Employed, "Report on Conciliation and Arbitration."

Cd. 9182, "First (Interim) Report of the Committee on Currency and Foreign Exchange."

Cd. 9197, Ministry of Reconstruction, "Report of the Committee to Consider the Position of the Building Industry after the War."

vol. 8, Cd. 9062, Board of Trade, Electric Power Supply Committee, "Report."

Cd. 9153, Ministry of Reconstruction, Committee on Relations between Employers and Employed, "Final Report."

Cd. 9226, Ministry of Reconstruction, "Report of the Engineering Trades (New Industries) Committee."

vol. 9, Cd. 9107, Ministry of Reconstruction, Adult Education Committee, "Industrial and Social Conditions in Relation to Adult Education."

Cd. 9225, Ministry of Reconstruction, Adult Education Committee, "Education in the Army."

Cd. 9237, Ministry of Reconstruction, Adult Education Committee, "Libraries and Museums."

vol. 10, Cd. 9002, "Second Report on Joint Standing Industrial Councils."

Cd. 9166, Ministry of Reconstruction, Women's Housing Sub-Committee, "First Interim Report."

Cd. 9223, Ministry of Reconstruction, Housing (Financial Assistance) Committee, "Public Utility Societies."

Cd. 9227, "Report of Committee on Financial Facilities."

vol. 11, Cd. 8998, "First Report of the Committee Dealing with the Law and Practice Relating to the Acquisition and Valuation of Land for Public Purposes."

Cd. 9157, Local Government Board, "Annual Report."

Cd. 9229, Ministry of Reconstruction, Committee Dealing with the Law and Practice Relating to the Acquisition and Valuation of Land for Public Purposes, "Second Report."

vol. 12, Cd. 8982, "Report of the Acquisition of Powers Sub-Committee of the Reconstruction Committee."

Cd. 9230, Ministry of Reconstruction, Committee on the Machinery of Government [Haldane Committee], "Report."

vol. 13, Cd. 9033, "Interim Report on the Importation of Goods from the Present Enemy Countries after the War."

Cd. 9034, "Interim Report on the Treatment of Exports from the United Kingdom and British Overseas Possessions and the Conservation of the Resources of the Empire during the Transitional Period after the War."

Cd. 9035, Committee on Commercial and Industrial Policy [Balfour of Burleigh Committee], "Final Report."

Cd. 9072, Board of Trade, "Report of the Departmental Committee on the Position of the Electrical Trades after the War."

Cd. 9224, "Report of the Committee of the Ministry of Reconstruction on Financial Risks Attached to the Holding of Trade Stocks."

Cd. 9231, Ministry of Reconstruction, "Report on the Work of the Ministry . . . Ending 31st December, 1918."

Cd. 9235, Ministry of Reconstruction, Committee on the Increase of Rent and Mortgage Interest (War Restrictions) Acts, "Report."

Cd. 9236, Ministry of Reconstruction, Committee on Trusts, "Report."

vol. 14, Cd. 9001, Ministry of Reconstruction, Committee on Relations between Employers and Employed, "Supplementary Report on Works Councils."

Cd. 9005, The War Cabinet, "Report for the Year 1917."

Cd. 9100, Ministry of Reconstruction, "Reports of the Committee Appointed by the Attorney-General to Consider the Legal Interpretation of the Term 'Period of the War.'"

Cd. 9117, Ministry of Reconstruction, Civil War Workers' Committee, "First (Interim) Report."

Cd. 9192, Ministry of Reconstruction, Civil War Workers' Committee, "Second, Third, Fourth, and Fifth Interim Reports."

Cd. 9228, Ministry of Reconstruction, Civil War Workers' Committee, "Final Report."

Cd. 9239, "Report of the Women's Employment Committee of the Ministry of Reconstruction."

vol. 27, Cd. 9087, "Final Report of the Advisory Housing Panel of the Ministry of Reconstruction."

Cd. 9195, "Statement by the Ministry of Reconstruction with Regard to Advisory Bodies (Other than Reporting Committees) Appointed by the Minister of Reconstruction."

1919

vol. 1, Cmd. 156, "Act for Establishing a Forestry Commission."

vol. 10, Cd. 9232, Ministry of Reconstruction, Advisory Council, Women's Housing Sub-Committee, "Final Report."

Cd. 9238, Ministry of Reconstruction, Housing (Financial Assistance) Committee, "Final Report."

Cmd. 321, "Final Report of the Adult Education Committee of the Ministry of Reconstruction."

vol. 24, Cmd. 139, "Report of Provisional Joint Committee Presented to the Meeting of the National Industrial Conference, Central Hall, 4th April, 1919."

Cmd. 413, "Forty-Eighth Annual Report of the Local Government Board, 1918–1919."

Cmd. 501, "Report of Provisional Joint Committee Presented to the Meeting of the National Industrial Conference, Central Hall, 4th April, 1919."

vol. 29, Cmd. 67, "Report of the Women's Advisory Committee of the Ministry of Reconstruction on the Domestic Service Problem."

Cmd. 93, Ministry of Reconstruction, Advisory Council, "Report of the Committee of Chairmen on Electric Power Supply."

Cmd. 136, "Report of the Advisory Council Committee on Local Reconstruction Organisations."

Cmd. 199, "Report on the Position after the War of Women Holding Temporary Appointments in Government Departments."

Cmd. 424, "Fourth Report of the Committee on the Acquisition and Valuation of Land for Public Purposes."

Cmd. 455, Ministry of Reconstruction, Advisory Council (Section II), "Final Report on Anti-Dumping Legislation."

vol. 30, Cmd. 325, The War Cabinet, "Report for the Year 1918."

1920

vol. 17, Cmds. 923, 917, 913, "First Annual Report of the Ministry of Health, 1919–1920."

1941–42

vol. 4, Cmd. 6378, "Report of the Committee on Land Utilisation in Rural Areas."

Cmd. 6386, "Final Report of the Expert Committee on Compensation and Betterment."

1942–43

vol. 4, Cmd. 6433, "Report of the Committee on Post-War Agricultural Education in England and Wales."

Cmd. 6481, "Report of the Committee on Minimum Rates of Wages and Conditions of Employment in Connection with Special Arrangements for Domestic Help."

vol. 5, Cmd. 6447, "Post-War Forest Policy. Report by H.M. Forestry Commission."

Cmd. 6467, "Report of the Land Transfer Committee."

vol. 6, Cmd. 6404, "Social Insurance and Allied Services."

Cmd. 6527, "Employment Policy."

Cmd. 6550, "Social Insurance," pt. 1.

1943–44

vol. 3, Cmd. 6500, "Post-War Forest Policy. Private Woodlands. Supplementary Report of the Forest Commission."

vol. 8, Cmd. 6502, "A National Health Service."

1944–45

vol. 5, Cmd. 6609, "Housing."

Cmd. 6621, "Report of the Interdepartmental Committee on Rent Control."

Cmd. 6650, "Report on Post-War Organisation of Domestic Help."

vol. 10, Cmd. 6579, "Local Government in England and Wales during the Period of Reconstruction."

1945–46

vol. 14, Cmds. 6759, 6794, 6876, "Interim, Second Interim, and Final Report on the New Towns' Committee of the Ministry of Town and Country Planning."

vol. 16, Cmd. 6729, "Summary of the National Insurance Scheme."

vol. 19, Cmd. 6686, "Housing Temporary Programme."

vol. 20, Cmd. 6801, "The New Towns Bill and Its Application."

Cmd. 6861, "Summary of the National Health Service Bill."

Other Official Published Records (Great Britain)

Ministry of Labour. *Gazette, 1918–19.*

Ministry of Labour. *Report on the Establishment and Progress of Joint Industrial Councils.* London: H.M. Stationery Office, 1923.

Ministry of Labour and National Service. *Industrial Relations Handbook.* London: H.M. Stationery Office, 1953.

Ministry of Munitions. *Journal.*

Ministry of Munitions. *Surplus* (1919).

Parliament. *Parliamentary Debates (Official Report).* Fifth series.

The Law Reports. The Public General Statutes, vols. 56–58. London: Eyre and Spottiswoode, 1919–21.

Unofficial Archives (London)

Garden Cities and Town Planning Association (now the Town and Country Planning Association). "Minute Books" for 1900–1947.

National Council for the Social Services. Archives and pamphlets, 1926–56.

National Housing and Town Planning Council. "Minute Books" for 1901–45, and other archives.

War Emergency Workers' National Committee. Papers and Minutes, 1914–18. Library of the Trades Union Congress, London.

Private Papers

Haldane Papers. National Library of Scotland, Edinburgh.

Lothian Papers. Registry Office, Edinburgh.

Personal Diary of Thomas Jones.

Webb Papers. London School of Economics.

Books and Articles

Abel-Smith, Brian. *The Hospitals, 1800–1948: A Study in Social Administration In England and Wales.* Cambridge, Mass.: Harvard University Press, 1964.

Abrams, Philip. "The Failure of Social Reform: 1918–1920," *Past and Present,* no. 24 (April 1963), 43–64.

Addison, Christopher. *The Betrayal of the Slums.* London: Herbert Jenkins, 1922.

————. *British Workshops and the War.* London: T. Fisher Unwin, 1917.

————. *Four and a Half Years.* 2 vols. London: Hutchinson, 1934.

————. *Politics from Within, 1911–1918.* 2 vols. London: Herbert Jenkins, n.d.

————. *Practical Socialism.* 2 vols. London: Labour Publishing Co., 1926.

Alcock, G. W. *Fifty Years of Railway Trade Unionism.* London: Co-operative Printing Society, 1922.

Aldridge, Henry. *The National Housing Manual.* London: National Housing and Town Planning Council, 1923.

Allen, Bernard M. *Sir Robert Morant: A Great Public Servant.* London: Macmillan, 1934.

Anderson, Adelaide M. *Women in the Factory.* New York: E. P. Dutton, 1922.

Andrews, Irene O. *Economic Effects of the War upon Women and Children in Great Britain.* New York: Oxford University Press, 1918.

Anon. *After War: A Future Policy.* London, 1918.

Ashworth, William. *The Genesis of Modern British Town Planning.* London: Routledge & Kegan Paul, 1954.

Askwith, Lord. *Industrial Problems and Disputes.* New York: Harcourt, Brace, 1921.

Bagwell, Philip S. *The Railwaymen: The History of the National Union of Railwaymen.* London: George Allen & Unwin, 1963.

Ballin, H. H. *The Organization of Electrical Supply in Great Britain.* London: Electrical Press, 1946.

Barker, J. Ellis. *Great Problems of British Statesmanship.* London: John Murray, 1917.

———. *Economic Statesmanship.* London: John Murray, 1918.

Barry, E. Eldon. *Nationalisation in British Politics: The Historical Background.* Stanford, Calif.: Stanford University Press, 1965.

Barwise, Sidney. *Never Again.* Derby, 1916.

Beaverbrook, Lord. *The Decline and Fall of Lloyd George.* London: Collins, 1963.

———. *Men and Power, 1917–1918.* London: Hutchinson, 1956.

Beer, M. *A History of British Socialism.* 2 vols. London: Allen & Unwin, 1918.

Benn, Ernest J. P. *The State the Enemy.* London: Benn, 1952.

———. *Trade as a Science.* London: Jarrold & Sons, 1916.

———. *The Trade of Tomorrow.* London: Jarrolds, 1918.

———. *Trade Parliaments and Their Work.* London: Nisbet, 1918.

Beveridge, William. *British Food Control during the War.* Oxford: Clarendon Press, 1928.

———. *Power and Influence.* London: Hodder & Stoughton, 1953.

Blaxland, Gregory. *J. H. Thomas: A Life for Unity.* London: Frederick Muller, 1964.

Bowley, Arthur L. *Some Economic Consequences of the Great War.* London: Thornton Butterworth, 1930.

———. *Studies in the National Income, 1924–1938.* Cambridge: Cambridge University Press, 1942.

Bowley, Marian. *Housing and the State, 1919–1944.* London: Allen & Unwin, 1945.

———. *The British Building Industry: Four Studies in Response and Resistance to Change.* Cambridge: Cambridge University Press, 1966.

Branford, Victor, and Patrick Geddes. *The Coming Polity.* London, 1919.

Bridges, Edward. *Treasury Control.* London: Athlone Press, 1950.

Briggs, Asa. *Social Thought and Social Action: A Study of the Work of Seebohm Rowntree, 1871–1954* (London: Longmans, 1961).

Brown, John. "Ideas concerning Social Policy and Their influence on Legislation in Britain, 1902–1911." Ph.D. thesis, University of London, 1964.

Bruce, Maurice. *The Coming of the Welfare State.* London: B. T. Batsford, 1966.

Bulkley, M. E. *Bibliographical Survey of Contemporary Sources for the Economic and Social History of the War.* Oxford: Humphrey Milford, 1922.

Bullock, Alan. *The Life and Times of Ernest Bevin.* vol. 1. London: Heinemann, 1960.

Burns, Cecil Delisle. *Government and Industry.* New York: Oxford University Press, 1921.

Caldwell, J. A. M. "The Genesis of the Ministry of Labour," *Public Administration*, 37 (1959): 367–92.

Campion, Gilbert, *et al. British Government since 1918*. London: Allen & Unwin, 1950.

Carpenter, Niles. *Guild Socialism*. New York: D. Appleton, 1922.

Carter, Huntly. *Industrial Reconstruction*. London: T. Fisher Unwin, 1917.

———. *The Limits of State Industrial Control*. London: T. Fisher Unwin, 1919.

Cecil, Henry. *Brightest England*. London, 1919.

Cecil, Robert. *The New Outlook*. London, 1919.

Chant, James W. *The Electricity Supply Acts*. London: Stevens & Sons, 1948.

Cherry, Benjamin. *Lectures on the Property Acts*. London: Solicitors' Law Stationery Society, 1921.

Chester, D. N. "Robert Morant and Michael Sadler." *Public Administration* 28 (1950): 109–16.

———, ed. *The Organisation of the British Central Government, 1914–1956*. London: Allen & Unwin, 1957.

Churchill, Winston Spencer. *The World Crisis, 1916–1918*. Vols. 4 and 5. London: Thornton Butterworth, 1927, 1929.

Cline, Catherine Ann. *Recruits to Labour : The British Labour Party, 1914–1931*. Syracuse, N.Y.: Syracuse University Press, 1963.

Cole, G. D. H. *Chaos and Order in Industry*. London: Methuen, 1920.

———. *The Future of Local Government*. London: Cassell, 1921.

———. *Guild Socialism Restated*. London: L. Parsons, 1920.

———. *A History of the Labour Party from 1914*. London: Routledge & Kegan Paul, 1948.

———. *A History of Socialist Thought*. Vols. 3, 4. New York: St. Martin's Press, 1958.

———. *Labour in the Coal-Mining Industry (1914–1921)*. Oxford: Clarendon Press, 1923.

———. *Organised Labour*. London: Allen & Unwin, 1924.

———. *Self-government in Industry*. London: G. Bell, 1918.

———. *Trade Unionism and Munitions*. Oxford: Clarendon Press, 1923.

Cole, G. D. H., and William Mellor. *The Meaning of Industrial Freedom*. London: Allen & Unwin, 1918.

Cole, Margaret. *Beatrice Webb*. New York: Longmans, Green, 1946.

———, ed. *Beatrice Webb's Diaries, 1912–1924*. London: Longmans, Green, 1952.

———. *The Story of Fabian Socialism*. Stanford: Stanford University Press, 1961.

Connell, J. M., ed. *Problems of Reconstruction*. Lewes: Baxter, 1919.

Cranage, D. H. S., ed. *The War and Unity*. Cambridge: University Press, 1919.

Crewe, The Marquess of, ed. *Problems of Reconstruction*. London: T. Fisher Unwin, 1918.

Cullingworth, J. B. *Town and Country Planning in England and Wales*. London: Allen & Unwin, 1964.

Daalder, Hans. *Cabinet Reform in Britain, 1914–1963*. Stanford, Calif.: Stanford University Press, 1964.

Dale, H. E. *The Higher Civil Service*. London: Oxford University Press, 1941.

Dampier-Whetham, W. C. *The War and the Nation*. London, 1917.

Dawson, William H., ed. *After-War Problems*. London: Allen & Unwin, 1917.

Dearle, N. B. *The Labor Cost of the World War to Great Britain, 1914–1922*. New Haven, 1940.

"Demos." *The Meaning of Reconstruction*. London: Athenaeum Literary Department, 1918.

Ehrman, John. *Cabinet Government and War, 1890–1940*. Cambridge: Cambridge University Press, 1958.

Enock, C. R. *Can We Set the World in Order?* London, 1916.

Ernle, Lord [Rowland Edmund Prothero]. *Whippingham to Westminster*. London: John Murray, 1938.

Evans, Thomas C. *Democracy and Reconstruction*. Manchester, 1919.

Fabian Research Department. *How to Pay for the War*. London, 1917.

Fairlie, John A. *British War Administration*. New York: Oxford University Press, 1919.

Falls, Cyril. *The Nature of Modern Warfare*. New York: Oxford University Press, 1941.

Farrow, Thomas, and W. W. Crotch. *The Coming Trade War*. London: Chapman & Hall, 1916.

Fisher, Alan G. B. *Some Problems of Wages and Their Regulation in Great Britain since 1918*. London: P. S. King, 1926.

Fisher, H. A. L. *Political Prophecies*. Oxford: Clarendon Press, 1919.

———. *An Unfinished Autobiography*. London: Oxford University Press, 1940.

Ford, P., and G. Ford. *A Breviate of Parliamentary Papers, 1900–1916*. Oxford: Basil Blackwell, 1957.

Francis. E. V. *Britain's Economic Strategy*. London: Jonathan Cape, 1939.

Gardiner, Gerald. "The Machinery of Law Reform in England." *Law Quarterly Review*, January, 1953, pp. 46–62.

Gardner, Lucy, ed. *The Hope for Society*. London: G. Bell, 1917.

———. *Some Christian Essentials of Reconstruction*. London: G. Bell, 1920.

Garrod, H. W. *Worms and Epitaphs*. Oxford: Clarendon Press, 1920.

Garton Foundation. *The Industrial Council for the Building Trades*. London: Harrison, 1920.

———. *Memorandum on the Industrial Situation after the War*. London: Harrison, 1916, 1919.

Gilbert, Bentley. *The Evolution of National Insurance in Great Britain: The Origins of the Welfare State*. London: Joseph, 1966.

Ginsberg, Morris, ed. *Law and Opinion in England in the Twentieth Century.* London: Stevens, 1959.

Gleason, Arthur. *What the Workers Want.* New York: Harcourt, Brace & Howe, 1920.

Gollin, A. M. *Proconsul in Politics: A Study of Lord Milner in Opposition and in Power.* New York: Macmillan, 1964.

Gosling, Harry. *Up and Down Stream.* London: Methuen, 1927.

Gray, Herbert, and Samuel Turner. *Eclipse or Empire?* London: Nisbet, 1916.

Green, F. E. *The Awakening of England.* London, 1918.

Greenwood, Arthur. *The Education of the Citizen.* London: Workers' Educational Association, 1920.

Griffith-Boscawen, Arthur. *Memories.* London: John Murray, 1925.

Haldane, Richard B. *An Autobiography.* London: Hodder & Stoughton, 1929.

Hall, A. D. *Agriculture after the War.* London: John Murray, 1916.

Hamilton, H. P. "Sir William Fisher and the Public Service." *Public Administration* 29 (1951): 3–8.

Hamilton, Ian. *The Millennium?* London, 1919.

Hamilton, Mary Agnes. *Arthur Henderson: A Biography.* London: Heinemann, 1938.

———. *Mary Macarthur.* London: L. Parsons, 1926.

Harris, Richard W. *Not So Humdrum: The Autobiography of a Civil Servant.* London: John Lane, 1939.

Harrison, Austin. *Before and Now.* London: John Lane, 1919.

Harrod, Roy. *The Life of John Maynard Keynes.* London: Macmillan, 1951.

Heath, H. Frank. *Viscount Haldane of Cloan, O.M.: The Man and His Work.* London: Oxford University Press, 1928.

Henderson, Fred. *The New Faith.* Norwich, 1915.

Hewins, W. A. S. *Apologia of an Imperialist.* 2 vols. London: Constable, 1929.

Hobhouse, Leonard T. *Questions of War and Peace.* London: T. Fisher Unwin, 1916.

Hobson, J. A. *Democracy after the War.* London: Allen & Unwin, 1917.

Hobson, S. G. *Guild Principles.* London: G. Bell, 1917.

———. *Pilgrim to the Left.* New York: Longmans, Green, 1938.

Hopkinson, Alfred. *Rebuilding Britain.* London: Cassell, 1918.

Hurwitz, Samuel J. *State Intervention in Great Britain: A Study of Economic Control and Social Response, 1914–1919.* New York: Columbia University Press, 1949.

Ince, Godfrey. *The Ministry of Labour and National Service.* London: Allen & Unwin, 1960.

"Jason" [J. L. Hammond]. *Past and Future.* London: Chatto & Windus, 1918.

Jennings, H. J. *The Coming Economic Crisis.* London: Hutchinson, 1918.

Jones, Thomas. *A Diary with Letters, 1931–1950*. London: Oxford University Press, 1954.

———. *Lloyd George*. Cambridge, Mass.: Harvard University Press, 1951.

Keeble, Samuel E. *Towards the New Era: A Draft Scheme of Industrial Reconstruction*. London: Charles Kelly, 1919.

Kellogg, Paul, and Arthur Gleason. *British Labor and the War*. New York: Boni & Liveright, 1919.

Keynes, John Maynard. *The Economic Consequences of the Peace*. New York: Harcourt, Brace & Howe, 1920.

Kirkaldy, A. W., ed. *Industry and Finance*. London: Pitman, 1917.

Kirkwood, David. *My Life of Revolt*. London: G. G. Harrap, 1935.

Labour Party. *Labour Manifesto*. London: The Labour Party, 1918.

———. *Nationalisation and state control*. London: Labour Party, 1918.

———. *The Old Age Pensioner*. London: Labour Party, 1918.

———. *Paying for the War*. London: Labour Party, 1918.

———. *Report of the Executive to the November 14, 1918, Emergency Conference*. London: Labour Party, 1918.

———. *Report of the Fifteenth Annual Conference of the Labour Party. January 26–28 1916. Bristol, 1916*. London: Labour Party, 1916.

———. *Report of the Seventeenth Annual Conference of the Labour Party. Nottingham and London, 1918*. London: Labour Party, 1918.

———. *Report of the Eighteenth Annual Conference of the Labour Party. London: June, 1918*. London: Labour Party, 1918.

———. *Report of the Nineteenth Annual Conference of the Labour Party. Southport, 1919*. London: Labour Party, 1918.

———. *The War Aims of the British People*. London: Hodder & Stoughton, 1917.

Leubuscher, Charlotte. *Liberalismus und Protektionismus in der englischen Wirtschaftspolitik seit dem Kriege*. Jena: Gustav Fischer, 1927.

Leverhulme, Lord. *Reconstruction after War*. Port Sunlight, 1919.

———. *The Six-Hour Day*. London: Allen & Unwin, 1918.

Liberal Party Conference at Huddersfield. *Towards Democracy*. Huddersfield, 1917, 1918.

———. Pamphlets for 1917–18.

———. *Liberalism and Industry*. London: Liberal Publication Department, 1918.

Liberal Summer School and Liberal Industrial Inquiry. *We Can Conquer Unemployment: Mr. Lloyd George's Pledge*. London: Cassell, 1929.

Lloyd, E. H. M. *Experiments in State Control at the War Office and the Ministry of Food*. London: Humphrey Milford, 1924.

Lloyd George, and Edward Wood. *The Great Opportunity*. London, 1918.

Lloyd George, David. *The Great Crusade*. New York: George H. Doran, 1918.

Lucas, Arthur. *Industrial Reconstruction and Control of Competition*. London: Longmans, Green, 1937.

Macara, Charles W. *Social and Industrial Reform: Some International Aspects*. 7th ed. Manchester: Sherratt & Hughes, 1919.

McGill, Barry. "Asquith's Predicament, 1914–1918," *Journal of Modern History*, 39, no. 3 (September 1967): 283–303.

McKillop, Norman. *The Lighted Flame: A History of the Associated Society of Locomotive Engineers and Firemen*. London: Thomas Nelson, 1950.

Mackintosh, J. M. *Trends of Opinion about the Public Health, 1901–1951*. London: Oxford University Press, 1953.

Mallet, Bernard, and C. Oswald George. *British Budgets: Third Series, 1921–1922 to 1932–1933*. London: Macmillan, 1933.

Mansbridge, Albert. *The Trodden Road*. London: J. M. Dent, 1940.

Markham, Violet. "Sir Robert Morant: Some Personal Reminiscences." *Public Administration*, Winter, 1950: 249–60.

Marwick, Arthur. *The Deluge: British Society and the First World War*. London: The Bodley Head, 1965.

Mendelsohn, Charlotte. *Wandlungen des liberalen England durch die Kriegswirtschaft*. Tübingen: Mohr, 1921.

Miliband, Ralph. *Parliamentary Socialism*. London: Allen & Unwin, 1961.

Minney, R. J. *Viscount Addison: Leader of the Lords*. London: Odhams Press, 1958.

Morgan, E. V. *Studies in British Financial Policy, 1914–1925*. London: Macmillan, 1952.

Morton, Arthur, and George Tate. *The British Labour Movement, 1770–1920*. London: Lawrence & Wishart, 1956.

Mowat, Charles Loch. *Britain between the Wars, 1918–1940*. London: Methuen, 1955; Chicago: University of Chicago Press, 1955.

Murphy, John T. *New Horizons*. London: John Lane, 1941.

Murray, Gilbert. *The Way Forward*. London: Allen & Unwin, 1917.

National Liberal Federation. *Proceedings in Connection with the Meeting of the General Committee Held at Manchester, September 26–27 1918*. London: Liberal Publication Department, 1918.

———. *Proceedings in Connection with the Thirty-sixth Annual General Meeting of the National Liberal Federation Held at Birmingham, November 27th and 28th, 1919*. London: Liberal Publication Department, 1919.

New Towns after the War: An Argument for Garden Cities. London: J. M. Dent, 1918.

Newman, George. *The Building of a Nation's Health*. London: Macmillan, 1939.

Newsholme, Arthur. *The Ministry of Health*. London: G. P. Putnam's Sons, 1925.

Olson, Mancur, Jr. *The Economics of the Wartime Shortage: A History of British Food Supplies in the Napoleonic War and in World Wars I and II*. Durham, N. C.: Duke University Press, 1963.

Orage, A. R. *Alphabet of Economics*. London: T. F. Unwin, 1917.

Orton, William A. *Labour in Transition*. London: P. Allen, 1921.

Oxford Conference of the Town and Country Planning Association, Spring, 1941. *Replanning Britain*. Edited by F. E. Towndrow. London: Faber & Faber, 1941.

Peddie, J. T. *Economic Reconstruction*. London: Longmans, Green, 1918.

Pigou, A. C. *Aspects of British Economic History, 1918–1925*. London: Macmillan, 1948.

Plaut, Theodor. *Das Enstehen, Wesen und Bedeutung, des Whitleyismus*. Jena: Gustav Fischer, 1921.

Plummer, A. *New British Industries in the Twentieth Century*. London: Isaac Pitman, 1937.

Pollard, R. S. W. *Reconstruction Then—and Now*. Fabian Research Pamphlet 98. London, 1945.

Pollard, Sidney. *The Development of the British Economy, 1914–1950*. London: Edward Arnold, 1962.

Pribicevic, Branko. *The Shop Stewards' Movement and Workers' Control, 1910–1922*. Oxford: Blackwell, 1959.

Radford, George. *Liberalism for Short*. London, 1917.

———. *The State as Farmer*. London, 1916.

Radical Programme of the Liberal Party. London: Liberal Publication Department, 1945.

Reckitt, Maurice B., and C. E. Bechhofer. *The Meaning of National Guilds*. London: C. Palmer & Hayward, 1918.

Redmayne, Richard. *Men, Mines, and Memories*. London: Eyre & Spottiswoode, 1942.

Rees, J. M. *Trusts in British Industry, 1914–1921*. London: P. S. King, 1922.

Reid, Leonard J. *The Great Alternative*. London: Longmans, Green, 1918.

Reiss, Richard L. *British and American Housing*. New York: National Public Housing Conference, 1937.

———. *The Home I Want*. London: Hodder & Stoughton, 1919.

———. *Municipal and Private Enterprise Housing*. London: J. M. Dent, 1925.

———. *New Housing Handbook*. London: P. S. King, 1924.

———. *The Town-Planning Handbook*. London: P. S. King, 1926.

Rhondda, Margaret H. T. *D. A. Thomas, Viscount Rhondda*. London: Longmans, Green, 1921.

Richardson, A. O. *Britain's Awakening*. London: Palmer Newbold, 1916.

Roberts, B. C. *The Trades Union Congress, 1868–1921*. Cambridge, Mass.: Harvard University Press, 1958.

Robertson, J. M. *The Economics of Progress*. London: T. Fisher Unwin, 1918.

Robinson, J. J. *National Reconstruction*. London: Hurst & Blackett, 1918.

Robson, W. A. *Public Enterprise*. London: Allen & Unwin, 1937.

Ruskin College. *Some Problems of Urban and Rural Industry.* Birmingham: Birmingham Printers, 1917.

——. *The State and Industry.* London: Co-operative Printing Society, 1918.

Russell, Bertrand. *Justice in War Time.* Chicago: Open Court, 1916.

——. *Principles of Social Reconstruction.* London: Allen & Unwin, 1916.

Sacks, Benjamin F. "The Independent Labour Party." *University of New Mexico Bulletin,* no. 358, 1 August 1940.

Salter, Arthur. *Personality in Politics.* London: Faber & Faber, 1947.

Sanderson Furniss, H., ed. *The Industrial Outlook.* London: Chatto & Windus, 1917.

Saunders, Edward. *A Self-supporting Empire.* London: Nisbet, 1918.

Schweinitz, Karl de. *England's Road to Social Security.* Philadelphia: University of Pennsylvania Press, 1943.

Scott, Leslie, Lord Justice. *The Parliament of the Village.* London: National Council of Social Service, 1948.

——, and Bertram F. Benas. *The New Law of Property Acts Explained.* London, 1925.

Self, Henry, and Elizabeth M. Watson. *Electricity Supply in Great Britain: Its Development and Organization.* London: Allen & Unwin, 1952.

Seymour, John B. *The Whitley Council Scheme.* London: P. S. King, 1932.

Sharp, Ian G. *Industrial Conciliation and Arbitration in Great Britain.* London: Allen & Unwin, 1950.

Simnett, William E. *Railway Amalgamation in Great Britain.* London: Railway Gazette, 1923.

Smith, Hubert Llewellyn. *The Board of Trade.* London: G. P. Putnam, 1928.

——, and Vaughan Nash. *The Story of the Dockers' Strike.* London: T. Fisher Unwin, 1889.

Somner, Dudley. *Haldane of Cloan.* Vol. 1. London: Allen & Unwin, 1960.

Street, Raymond. "Government Consultation with Industry." *Public Administration* 37 (1959): 1–2.

Tawney, Richard H. "The Abolition of Economic Controls, 1918–1921." *Economic History Review* 13 (1943): 1–30.

Taylor, A. J. P. *English History, 1914–1945.* Oxford: Oxford University Press, 1965.

Tillyard, Frank. *Unemployment Insurance in Great Britain, 1911–1918.* London: Thames Bank Publishing Co., 1949.

Titmuss, Richard M. *Essays on the Welfare State.* London: Allen & Unwin, 1958.

——. "War and social policy." *The Listener,* 3 November 1955, pp. 741–43.

——. *Problems of Social Policy.* London: H.M. Stationery Office, 1950.

Towns and the Land—Urban Report of the Liberal Land Committee, 1923–1925. London: Hodder & Stoughton, 1925.

Bibliography

Trades Union Congress. *Report of Proceedings at the Fifty-first Annual Trades Union Congress*. London: Co-operative Printing Society, 1919.

Tsuzuki, Chushichi. *H. M. Hyndman and British Socialism*. London: Oxford University Press, 1961.

Turner, Samuel. *From War to Work*. London: Nisbet, 1918.

Vago, Alfred. *A Better England*. London: Drane's, 1918.

Verinder, Frederick. *Free Trade and Land Values*. London: English League for the Taxation of Land Values, 1916.

———. *Land, Labour and Taxation*. London: English League for the Taxation of Land Values, 1916.

Vernon, R. V., and N. Mansergh. *Advisory Bodies: A Study of Their Uses in Relation to Central Government, 1919–1939*. London: Allen & Unwin, 1940.

Villiers, Brougham. *England and the New Era*. London: T. Fisher Unwin, 1920.

Walton, Cecil. *The Great Debenture*. Glasgow: Maclure, Macdonald, 1918.

———. *Never Again!* Glasgow: Bissett, n.d.

Webb, Sidney and Beatrice. *English Local Government from the Revolution to the Municipal Corporations Act*. London: Longmans, Green, 1906–22.

———. *English Poor Law History*, part 2: *The Last Hundred Years*. Vol. 2. London: Longmans, Green, 1929.

———. *The History of Trade Unionism*. London: Longmans, Green, 1920.

Wells, H. G. *The War and the Future*. London: Cassell, 1917.

———. *What is Coming?* London: Cassell, 1916.

Wheeler-Bennett, John W. *John Anderson: Viscount Waverley*. London: Macmillan, 1962.

Whetham, H. C. Dampier. *The War and the Nation*. London: John Murray, 1917.

White, Leonard D. *Whitley Councils in the British Civil Service*. Chicago: University of Chicago Press, 1933.

Whitley, John. *Works Committees and Industrial Councils*. London: Longmans, Green, 1920.

Wickwar, W. Hardy. *The Public Services*. London: Cobden-Sanderson, 1938.

Williams, Gertrude. *The State and the Standard of Living*. London: P. S. King, 1936.

Williams, Robert. *The New Labour Outlook*. London: L. Parsons, 1921.

Wilson, Arnold, and G. S. Mackay. *Old Age Pensions: An Historical and Critical Study*. London: Oxford University Press, 1941.

Wilson, Trevor. "The Coupon and the British General Election of 1918," *Journal of Modern History*, 36, no. 1 (March 1964): 28–42.

———. *The Downfall of the Liberal Party, 1914–1935*. London: Collins, 1966.

Wood, Kingsley. *The Law and Practice with Regard to Housing in England and Wales*. London: Hodder & Stoughton, 1921.

Woodward, E. J. *Short Journey*. London: Faber & Faber, 1942.

Workers' Educational Association. *Education Yearbook*. London: Workers' Educational Association, 1918.

Worsfold, W. B. *The War and Social Reform*. London: J. Murray, 1919.

Zimmern, Alfred E. *Nationality and Government*. London, 1918.

Index

Abercrombie, Patrick, 423
Acland, Sir Francis (chairman, Forestry Committee): forestry, 26, 98, 187–89, 289, 338, 483, 501; and land acquisition, 414–15
Acquisition of Land *and* Acquisition of Land (Assessment of Compensation) Act. *See* Land acquisition
Acquisition of Land Committee (Leslie Scott committee): establishment, 41, 60; land legislation of 1919, 413–16; land settlement act, 417; proposals shelved, 461
Acquisition of powers, subcommittee on, 41, 178
Adams, Professor W. G. S., 36
Addison, Dr. Christopher (Minister of Reconstruction, 1917–19), appraises reconstruction progress, 190, 287, 290–92
—, career: establishment of Ministry of Reconstruction, 68–73; estrangement from Lloyd George, 494–95; heads Local Government Board, 340–47; leaves Ministry of Reconstruction, 339; names Reconstruction Committee in Munitions, 103; offered Ministry of Health, 289; offered ministry without portfolio, 495; resigns from cabinet, 477, 498; resigns Ministry of Health, 498
—, deeds and views: coalition victory, 332; committees, campaigns for new, 128–49; controls, 131, 200, 336, 401; dilution, 441; electric power, 357, 428; finance, 76; food control, 453; forestry, 425; government subsidy and orders, 330; health insurance, 459; plans for demobilization, 74; postwar demand, 140
—, and housing: discusses Housing Bill with cabinet, 346; Housing and Town Planning Act (1919), 419; housing controls, 452; housing crisis of 1919, 434, 435–42; housing crisis of 1920–21, 494–99; plans in 1917, 74–77, 87–95; plans, January–June 1918, 107, 110–17; plans defeated, August 1918, 179–81; supports Carmichael committee plan, 322–25
—, and key industries, 192–95; and land acquisition, 353, 416, 437; land reform proposals shelved, 461; land settlement bill, 350–51; land settlement finance, 417; Ministry of Health, 96, 288–89, 353; and Ministry of Munitions in 1917–18, 103–6; nationalization of coal, 455, 456; pledges, 263–66, 276, 281–84; priorities and Standing Council on Post-War Priority, 318; raw materials, 74–76, 118, 123–24, 203–4, 250–57; rent, 443; tariff, 86; trade committees, 165; unemployment, 143, 370; wages and hours, 355–56; Whitleyism, 76, 163
—, viewed by contemporaries: Morant, 354; National Housing and Town Planning Council, 421
—, mentioned, 2, 6, 45–46, 55, 231, 355, 466, 472, 481, 501, 502, 507. *See also* Controls; Housing; Pledges; Priorities
"Addison Act" (Housing and Town Planning Act, 1919): attitudes in 1920's, 500–501
Adult education, 310, 335
Adult Education Committee, 80, 339

527